AUGUSTAN CULTURE

KARL GALINSKY

AUGUSTAN CULTURE

AN INTERPRETIVE

INTRODUCTION

PRINCETON UNIVERSITY PRESS, PRINCETON, NEW JERSEY

Copyright © 1996 by Princeton University Press
Published by Princeton University Press, 41 William Street,
Princeton, New Jersey 08540
In the United Kingdom: Princeton University Press,
Chichester, West Sussex

Library of Congress Cataloging-in-Publication Data

Galinsky, Karl, 1942–
Augustan culture : an interpretive introduction / Karl Galinsky
p.   cm.
Includes bibliographical references (p.) and index.
ISBN 0-691-04435-X
ISBN 0-691-05890-3 (pbk.)
1. Rome—History—Augustus, 30 B.C.–14 A.D.
2. Rome—Civilization.   I. Title.
DG279.G17   1996
937′.07—dc20   95-33469

04297

This book has been composed in Bembo

Princeton University Press books are printed on
acid-free paper and meet the guidelines for permanence
and durability of the Committee on Production
Guidelines for Book Longevity of the
Council on Library Resources

Second printing, and first paperback printing, 1998

http://pup.princeton.edu

Printed in the United States of America

3   5   7   9   10   8   6   4   2

For Harriet

CONTENTS

PREFACE

THIS IS the first synoptic study of the main aspects of Augustan culture by a single author in several decades. The reasons are easy to discern. Not only was the period one of the most creative and crucial for Rome, but it also proved to be one of the most influential and paradigmatic in Western civilization. There has, in this century, been an extraordinary amount of scholarly work on its various parts and on innumerable questions of detail. The result, paralleled by the compartmentalization of the humanities in general, has been an increasing tendency to look at the principal areas of Augustan culture as discrete entities rather than as an interrelated whole. It seemed useful, therefore, to try to bring together once more some major perspectives on Augustan history, ideas, art, literature, architecture, and religion. In their totality, they provide a good overview of the age and its significance.

This book is not a simple synthesis or survey of previous scholarship. One of the reasons, in the words of a recent reviewer, is that "the effort of such a compilation can be as much to suffocate as to inspire new ideas."[1] It would have been much less difficult, in fact, to write a much longer study. The bibliography on matters Augustan is enormous, and I could have increased the size of this book two- or threefold by debating divergent views. In every paragraph, if not in every sentence, I could have argued explicitly for or against the opinions of several scholars. The scholarship on virtually all the subjects treated here is controversial and it would be entirely possible, for someone else, to write another book, on the same subject and with much the same evidence, that would come to different conclusions. The reason is not only scholarly revisionism or contentiousness, but the very richness, variety, and contradictions of Augustan culture.

The footnotes, therefore, are not meant to serve as a staging area for further argumentation or detailed recapitulation, which can be accessed elsewhere, of the state of many questions. Nor have I followed the example of some recent books that have reduced documentation to a bibliographical section. I have, of course, worked my way through far more of the scholarly and ancient sources than can be adduced in this volume. As regards the former in particular, the selection represented here, while up to date, is my own and does not imply the lack of other good discussions of the various problems.

The principal aim, then, is to present a unified and intelligent overview of Augustan culture in its various manifestations. There is no need, at this point, for another historical narrative of the period. Sir Ronald Syme's classic treatment in *The Roman Revolution* will hold its own for quite a while yet and I would urge readers, if they have not done so already, to peruse it in conjunction with my study, which has different aims. There is the proverbial exception: I have deliberately chosen a brief narration of Octavian's vicissitudes from late 44 B.C. to mid-43 B.C. as a reminder of the fact, all too easily ignored in retrospect, that his ascent and the eventual Augustan reign hung in the balance more than once.

There is, of course, more to Augustan culture—a term I am using, without a specific bias, for the sum of creative activities during this period—than the material selected for this study. I have centered this work on some of the major manifestations of literature, art, architecture, political and social processes, and religion for two basic reasons. One is that these are the subjects one would expect in a book whose subtitle includes the word "introduction." The other is intrinsic: these are, in fact, the best-known illustrations of the experimentalism, complexity, dynamics, and sophistication that became the hallmark of the age and, at the same time, contributed to transcending it. There is plenty of room for subsequent books that might take into account other writers, such as Strabo, and material evidence such as Arretine pottery, the art of the freedmen, and more of the epigraphic and provincial culture. My book does not, however, concentrate solely on high culture. The chapter on religion, for instance, deals extensively (and with a considerable number of illustrations) with the religion of the lower classes. Or, to give another example, in my discussion "Tradition and Innovation" in chapter 7 ("Central Characteristics") I deliberately chose, for the sake of balance, "mundane" subjects like the grain supply and road maintenance rather than further examples from the arts and poetry.

This book had its genesis in some summer seminars for college teachers that I offered under the auspices of the National Endowment for the Humanities in the mid-1970s. The participants came from different disciplines and I found this orientation suited to both my own interests and those of the interdisciplinary department in which I have been fortunate to teach for a long time. I pursued the subject in various graduate seminars and in a variety of more specialized publications, and my intention was to write this book in the early 1980s. An administrative commitment, which lasted much longer than I (and, I am sure, others) had anticipated, interfered. As happens so often, however, it all worked out in the end: a number of outstanding studies on various aspects of the Augustan age appeared in the 1980s and I am glad to have been able to take them into account. I was able to give my full attention to preparing this book in the spring of 1991, when I was a visiting scholar at the American Academy in Rome. It was completed during a research leave in 1993–94 that was made possible by awards from the Alexander von Humboldt-Stiftung, the National Endowment for the Humanities, and the University Research Institute at the University of Texas. To all of these, I am profoundly grateful.

It is a pleasure, too, to thank the many friends and colleagues who have been helpful to me in various ways during the writing of this book. Michael von Albrecht, Glen Bowersock, Denis Feeney, Erich Gruen, Christian Habicht, Tonio Hölscher, William Metcalf, and Bernhard Overbeck expertly critiqued drafts of individual chapters or segments thereof. Diana Kleiner and Andrew Wallace-Hadrill read the entire manuscript and I have benefited much from their range of expertise and specific suggestions. The hospitality and assistance I received from Professor Joseph Connors, then director of the American Academy in Rome, and Ms. Lucilla Marino and her staff at the Academy's library were both unobtrusive and outstanding. The same is true of the reception and help accorded to me at the Free University of Berlin by Professor Bernd Seidensticker and his colleagues, in particular W.-D. Heilmeyer. I am also grateful for the discussion of individual issues, on various occasions, with Gian Biagio Conte, Francis Cairns, Diane Conlin, Ann Kuttner, Ruurd Nauta, Barbette Spaeth, and Antonie Wlosok as well as my colleagues David Armstrong, Joseph Carter, Gwyn Morgan, and William Nethercut. Last but not least, several of my ideas were sharpened, modified, or discarded after I tried them out on audiences in North America, Europe, and New Zealand; in particular, I acknowledge with gratitude the invitation by Professor John Barsby and his colleagues to serve as Evans Lecturer at the University of Otago in the summer of 1992. Professor Edward Champlin was kind enough to let me peruse the manuscript of the forthcoming second edition of *CAH* 10, the volume on Augustan history. A term as Visiting Andrew Mellon Professor at Tulane University in New Orleans in 1995 provided a hospitable ambience and additional time for the copyediting.

Garnering the illustrations has been a task that brings to mind the Augustan motto of making haste slowly. I am particularly grateful for the help of D. Arya, A. Barchiesi, M. Bell, K. Bemmann, E. de Bruyn, H.-U. Cain, K. Einaudi, G. Fittschen-Badura, J.-B. Giard, T. Hölscher, S. Hurter, E. La Rocca, J. Larkin, H. N. Loose, S. Mari, B. Overbeck, F. Rutzen, M. Schröder, H. Thomas, and P. Zanker. The color reproductions were made possible through the generosity of Anne Byrd Nalle and George S. Nalle, Jr., Mark and Jo Ann Finley, and Dixie and Marja Smith. I also want to thank the University of Texas Press and the editors of the *American Journal of Archaeology* and *Classical Journal* for permission to reuse a few paragraphs from previous publications. Finally, I wish to thank all my editors for their attentive and expeditious assistance.

mense Iulio
Austin, 1995

AUGUSTAN CULTURE

THE AUGUSTAN
EVOLUTION

ANY ATTEMPT to write on major aspects of the age of Augustus occurs in a context. I should like to delineate that context briefly, both in its own right and in terms of its relation to the emphases of this book.

It is a truism, even if typically overelaborated in contemporary literary theory, that our interpretations of the past are much influenced by our experience with contemporary society, politics, and culture. Syme's *Roman Revolution* is a textbook example, enhanced by the author's emphatic statement of this bias in his preface. The book was to be an Augustan mirror for the political events of the 1920s and 1930s, which witnessed the rise of the dictatorhips of Mussolini, Franco, Hitler, and Stalin, including Stalin's infamous "Constitution" of 1936. "It is not necessary to praise political success or to idealize men who win wealth and honours through civil war," Syme wrote.[1] Since the theme was "of some importance," he decided not to hold the book back "for several years" and rewrite it "in tranquillity," but to publish it in 1939. It was the right decision.

A related factor was, as always, the reaction to previous interpretations. As Syme himself put it: "It is surely time for some reaction from the 'traditional' and conventional view of the period." It is not that views of Augustus had been uniform, not even in "Augustan" England,[2] but the dominant scholarly assessment by the mid-1930s was generally benevolent, as exemplified by the various chapters in the tenth volume of the *Cambridge Ancient History* that appeared in 1934. On the Continent, there was adulation and more as Augustus emerged as the prototypal *Führer* and *duce*. It is a fine irony of historiography that Syme cast him in exactly the same role, though, of course, from a perspective of reprobation rather than admiration. Essentially, Syme's Augustus was a successful party leader who came to power after a ruthless civil war. His "revolution" was to place himself and his followers in control and thus to replace the senatorial ruling class and its interests. His aim was power, and his victory in the power struggle had hardly any redeeming moral foundation or spiritual consequences; the poets, for instance, were simply operatives within the framework of the "organization of opinion."

The impact of all this has been considerable. I am leaving aside any discussion of Syme's preferred method of "prosopography," the study of groups, families, and individuals, because it was followed by much work along similar lines and left few gaps that need to be filled in that area. But it left other voids. As Arnaldo Momigliano remarked in his important review of *The Roman Revolution*, "prosopographical research has the great virtue of reaching individuals and small groups, but it does not explain their material or spiritual needs: it simply presupposes them."[3] It is important, therefore, to look anew at the concepts and ideas that made the Augustan age so remarkable. They are not explained by a mere preoccupation with power; genuine leadership goes beyond the accumulation of power. Nor should renewed interest in them be taken as a return to "the domination of a faction of abstract nouns" from which Syme liberated Roman historiography, as one of his successors has remarked with Oxonian wit.[4] Not only did the political dispensation founded by Augustus last for almost two hundred years, but the Augustan age produced a culture that was remarkable for its creativity and transcended its times. It is useful, therefore, to devote this study to some of its manifestations, which were far from uniform, and to the creative tensions that gave rise to them.

The perspective of the 1930s has had an especially noticeable effect on the interpretation of Augustan literature. Vergilian scholars in particular were left in a quandary. The prevalent, preceding interpretation had been that the major purpose of the *Aeneid* was the praise of Augustus and Rome. Another wisdom, received over centuries, was the Stoic and Christianizing interpretation of *pius* Aeneas. The result was a sort of Saint Aeneas who stood above the emotions of an ordinary mortal. This interpretive straitjacket, of course, did very little justice to the complexities of the *Aeneid*, but the next phase of Vergilian interpretation did not really dissolve it. Theses were simply converted into antitheses. It was necessary to get out of the predicament of cherishing a poet who was the cheerleader for an autocrat. Hence new aspects of the *Aeneid* were discovered at last, such as the poet's assumed "private" voice (as distinct from the official key of the epic), and further voices have been added in the meantime.[5] They were still fitted, however, into the existing framework: if Vergil wrote anything other than the most overt praise of Augustus—and those passages are very rare in the first place—it suggested his tacit and indirect disapproval, and perhaps even his "subversive intent," to use a current catchphrase. When Aeneas acts not like a meek Christian saint, but like a full-blooded and complex human being—as he does at the end of the *Aeneid*, for instance—this was seen as betokening an aversion to "the grandeur for which Augustus seems to stand."[6] Even today, while most Vergilian scholars recognize that the identification of Augustus with the *duce* or the *Führer* may be somewhat simpleminded, anything deviating from the presumed monolithic "ideology" of Augustus or official tenor of the *Aeneid* is styled, in the polite and wonderfully imprecise terminology of contemporary Vergilian criticism, as "disquieting" or "puzzling." This is an improvement, though not by much, over inane dichotomies like "optimism" and "pessimism" and "pro-" and "anti-Augustan"; one of the most telling arguments against the validity of such schematisms is the ease and convenience with which they can be practiced.[7]

Scholarship on Augustan art took a somewhat different direction. After its noisy appropriation by the Fascists, highlighted by the *Mostra Augustea della Romanità* on the occasion of the bimillenary of Augustus' birth in 1937, Roman art historians were understandably reluctant to venture into that area. There is still a marked shortage of Anglo-American specialists on Augustan art today. Without malice, however, it may be observed that an extended period of restrained scholarly publication—almost a moratorium—can result in a remarkable rise in the quality of scholarship. This is exactly what happened in the scholarship on Augustan art when art historians could make an almost fresh start, beginning in the late 1960s, without being caught up in reaction formations. It resulted in a great deal of sophisticated work by scholars like P. Zanker, T. Hölscher, and E. Simon. They were attentive to the complex, nuanced, and multireferential nature of Augustan art. In particular, Zanker's *The Power of Images in the Age of Augustus* posited the substitution of the cliché of Augustan "propaganda" for a system (which is not necessarily systematic) of far more autonomous, complex, and organic interactions. While this model, as well as that of the *Andachtsbild* ("contemplative image") can be fruitfully extended to other aspects of Augustan culture, too, another thesis on which Zanker's book is centered finds limited support even in what survives of Augustan sculpture. That is the assumed dichotomy between *Hellenismus* and *Klassizismus*, categories that have been useful, especially in Germany where they were invented, for organizing the academic discussion into tidy compartments. But even a cursory look at Augustan poetry, for instance, illustrates that no such dichotomy exists there.

As even these preliminary observations indicate, there is no question that we are looking at the Augustan age with different eyes in the 1990s than our forebears did in the 1930s.[8] We have witnessed that "ideology" and "propaganda" are inadequate foundations for lasting political systems. We live in a complex and changing world that defies conceptual straitjackets and facile bipolarities, both in domestic politics and on the international scene. And we also have come to realize the need for true values, guiding ideas, and a sense of direction. We see daily that transformation is not sudden, but often proceeds imperceptibly. Hence the attention in this book to such matters and to the complexity, nuance, and experimentation that are found in Augustan culture.

Some may object that this means too much of a concentration on intellectual history. It is helpful in this connection to review briefly the meaning of *res publica*, because Augustus' central claim was that he restored the *res publica*, and then to state firmly the material basis for the widespread acceptance of the Augustan state.

The first and most obvious aspect of *res publica*, to be translated by "commonwealth" rather than "the Republic," is its various institutions, magistracies, and legal and administrative mechanisms. These do not, however, compose "the Roman Constitution," which was never written down or conceived of as being static.[9] They were considered anything but insignificant by the Romans, but they were only a means to an end. Yet in the scholarship on the Augustan age, emphasis on these "constitutional" and legalistic aspects has received disproportionate attention. The details of Augustus' mode of government were subjected to meticulous scrutiny for any deviations from republican practice with the aim of fixing the shape of "the Augustan constitution." This juridical orientation, exemplified by Mommsen's famous postulate of a dyarchy of the *princeps* and the senate, had its heyday in the decades before Syme, but still exerts a certain influence. There is no question that, after two decades characterized by Tacitus (*Ann.* 3.28) as being destitute of custom (*mos*) and law (*ius*), Augustus strove to present his rule as legitimate. He both observed precedent and extended existing practices and institutions as far as customary allowance for change would permit. His holding the power of tribune of the people (*tribunicia potestas*) without actually being tribune is a good example and may have struck many Romans as a reasonable solution to the ups and downs of that office in the late republic. We can safely assume, however, that most of the populace in Rome, let alone the provinces, was not fixated on constitutional niceties of this sort. One of the truly significant changes under Augustus, which is often ignored and to which I can only advert in this book, was the consolidation of the *imperium Romanum* into a much more unified entity than a collection of provinces. To these contemporaries, the finer constitutional points belabored by so many modern scholars were of little consequence. Strabo, who was well educated, simply said that Rome was governed by the emperor and by the people as he saw both proconsuls and imperial lieutenants (*legati*) operating in the various provinces (17.3.25).

The essence of the republican constitution lay not in its legalistic aspects. Rather, it was a system of values and of "traditional concepts and principles that did not always keep pace with political reality."[10] The failure of the republic was perceived at the time as the failure to adhere to a traditional value system that placed the common good, the *res publica*, ahead of private interests. Without this central attitude, the famous formal checks and balances were ineffectual and could lead to paralysis. As so often, the greatest strength of the republican constitution was also its greatest liability: it depended on the goodwill and cooperation of all those involved in government to function effectively. It placed the spirit above the letter—hence, its lack of codification. The Augustan solution, therefore, was a conscious return to and rearticulation of these basic values and principles. This is a central characteristic of Augustan culture, and it needs to be given due attention. At the same time, the preservation of the republican structure also meant the preservation of its inherent debility, and Augustus realized this well.

This revival of the ideals of the *res publica* was accompanied by the restoration of its third and more material basic function, the protection of private property.[11] The landed gentry that authored the U.S. Constitution recognized this instinctively and hence were attracted to the Roman idea of the state. *Res*, after all, has strong connotations of property, and Cicero, who owned eight villas as compared with Augustus' three, is explicit in defining the protection of private property as one of the chief purposes of the *res publica*. The commitment of the Augustan government to this principle and its effective actions to restore and safeguard private property were root causes for its acceptance and lasting support. The tremendous dislocations caused by the civil wars, which found their poetic expression in the works of Horace, Vergil, and Propertius, are indispensable for understanding the ready embrace of the new stability by the propertied classes of Italy and by the populace at large. This stability did not come overnight, but, like so much else in the reign of Augustus, developed in several steps. His victory over Sextus Pompey in 36 B.C. enabled him to cancel most of the taxes and levies from which Italy had been immune by 60 B.C. Their subsequent reintroduction, compounded by the much larger new burdens and by the triumviral proscriptions, fueled the resentment not only of the senators and equestrians at Rome, but of the nonpolitical, moneyed classes in Italy on whose support the Augustan dispensation came to rest (cf. Dio 47.16.3–4., 17.3). The confiscations of land for returning soldiers were a continuing reminder that private property was still in jeopardy. Setting a precedent which he duly emphasizes in the *Res Gestae* (16.1), Augustus compensated the expropriated landowners from his own funds and by 13 B.C. was able to end the practice entirely. The retirement bonus for soldiers was changed from land to a cash sum. To fund the new pension system, a new military treasury (*aerarium militare*) was established, which Augustus funded for the first two years until its operations were secured by an inheritance tax starting in A.D. 6.

Such actions and others were important both for the material welfare of the citizenry and for the welfare of the Augustan state, the *optimus status*, to use Augustus' own term.[12] In Claude Nicolet's succinct summary: "The protection of property, the safety of the individual, the rejection of the abominable abuses of the time of the civil wars, recourse to taxes as near as possible to the civic fiscal system so well outlined by Agrippa (Dio 52.6.4–5): this was, in the long run, the watchword of the new regime and, it appears, the enduring source both of its popularity and its legitimacy."[13] This, rather than the army or the "power of images" that was of no consequence for remedying food shortages, was the tangible foundation of the Augustan rule and of its acceptance and survival.

In this important respect as in others, the "Augustan program" per se was not anything novel, let alone revolutionary, but simply represented the successful and innovative solution of problems which the senatorial aristocracy had been unable or unwilling to see through. It is not that Augustus had to read Cicero to find out what ailed the Roman state. The problem areas were known to all. The soldiery, the urban plebs, the provinces, and Rome's imperial role were chief among them besides the all-encompassing need for the establishment and continued guarantee of domestic peace and security and for a return to government by laws. "Augustus and his friends and associates tackled these problems, one after the other, with determination, patience, hard work, and, mostly, success."[14] In the process—and this is another paramount aspect of the Augustan reign and its popularity—they strove "to have as many people as possible participate in the life of the state."[15] This is not to be confused with a democratization of politics, which would be an anachronistic expectation. Rather, there were many other outlets, such as the state-related religion, for the active involvement of a far greater number of people from all segments of Roman society. All this contrasted strongly with the cliquish, closed-shop governmental mode of the senatorial nobility that was obsessed with its own privileges. By any standard except that of the senators, no *libertas* was lost; at most, they lost some of theirs because they did not share it.[16]

All this would have sufficed for Augustus' reign not only to gain the gratitude of his contemporaries, as is illustrated by Velleius' catalog of thanks (2.89), but to secure a firm place in Roman history. The distinctive aspect of Augustan culture, however, is precisely that it went beyond purely material aspects and satisfaction and was inspired by ideas, ideals, and values. These found their expression across the wide spectrum of government, social policy, art, literature, and religion. At their core was the revitalization of the mores of the *res publica*; a program of moral legislation, to give but one example, had already been urged by Cicero on Caesar (*Marc.* 23–24). These guiding ideas, which do not amount to an ideology in the modern sense, received further elaboration from all sides and therefore their expression was anything but uniform. It ranged from assent to disagreement, but the ideas themselves stood at the center of much of the discussion and thus contributed greatly to the intellectual and cultural vitality of the period. The shape they were given especially in Augustan poetry and art transcended the times and made such concepts models for subsequent developments in Western culture.

A related point is that many of these Augustan phenomena were in a state of nascence and evolution, a fact that tends to be obscured by their routinization in later times. This applies, most prominently, to the form of government, poetic and artistic conventions, and imperial religion. From the perspective of later ages, including Augustan France and Augustan England, the age of Augustus seemed one of unshakable solidity (that was matched by their own stolidity), reinforced by "classicism," and its achievements in poetry, art, and architecture were considered as static givens. A closer look at the evidence suggests otherwise. It was a time of transition, of continuing experimentation, of "a developing and shifting relationship, without precedents, where all parties involved are feeling their way."[17] The "constitutional settlements" of Augustus were not set in concrete and there was continuing modification of various aspects of government and administration. These continued right to the end of Augustus' reign as did artistic and literary creativity. Another misconception, with which I can again deal only briefly in this book, is that the last part of Augustus' reign was marked by sclerosis. A "classic" like Vergil's *Aeneid* in many ways was a grand experiment while Ovid's *Metamorphoses* recaptures much of the Augustan spirit in its very title. Similar tendencies are obvious in Augustan wall painting and architectural decoration. It is important, then, to look at Augustan culture at the moment of its creation and to appreciate its creativity.

To what extent this change, even in the political realm alone, amounted to a "revolution" is a matter of definition.[18] Even if gradual, it must have been clear to Augustus' contemporaries that important changes were taking place. There was no sudden jump from republic to monarchy, but there was a republican system with a *princeps*, a *novus status* in Suetonius' definition (*Aug.* 28.2), while Tacitus termed it more tendentiously as *versus* ("overturned") *status (Ann.* 1.4.1). The Augustan principate emerged as "the binding link between Republic and Empire."[19] The only writer who speaks of a "revolution" (*metabolē*) in the Augustan context is Dionysius, a contemporary of Caesar and Augustus, who praises the Roman rulers for the return of political order in the Greek cities on the basis of traditional values: revolution equals restoration.[20] Similarly, in his last chapter of *The Roman Revolution*, Syme "provides us with most of the elements needed to balance his [earlier] judgment."[21] Succinctly, he captured much of the essence of the Augustan principate: "By appeal to the old, Augustus justified the new; by emphasizing continuity with the past, he encouraged the hope of development in the future. The New State established as the consolidation of the Revolution was neither exclusive nor immobile."[22] Not only the Augustan state but Augustan culture in general was characterized by a dynamic, evolving process. Instead of a Roman revolution, it is more accurate to speak of an Augustan evolution. This is, therefore, an important theme of this study, which is itself only part of the evolution of Augustan scholarship.

CHAPTER I

A PRINCIPAL CONCEPT:
AUCTORITAS

FEW CULTURAL periods in the history of the world have taken their name from their rulers for intrinsic rather than convenient reasons: political power and cultural creativity are not often related. The age of Augustus was different: when Horace said *tua aetas, Caesar* ("your era, Augustus"), he had more than politics in mind,[1] and the same is true of those who wanted to honor Augustus immediately upon his death by officially designating his lifetime (63 B.C.–A.D. 14) as *saeculum Augustum* (Suet., *Aug.* 100.3); *saeculum* in Rome connoted more than a chronological century. While Augustus' personality remains elusive, the style of his government and the design of his actions were woven inextricably into the fabric of Roman culture during the almost half century of his rule. They are related to many of the characteristics of the art, literature, architecture, and religion of the period and are indispensable for understanding these properly without any lapse on our part into the "biographical fallacy" of interpreting cultural history.

The task is facilitated by Augustus' own definition of the nature of his leadership. A good starting point is his statements at the beginning and conclusion of his own summary of attainments, the *Res Gestae*, which he completed shortly before his death. The exact nature and purpose of this document, which was exhibited in front of his mausoleum in Rome but was meant to be displayed in many other cities around the empire as well, need not concern us here.[2] It suffices to say that the *Res Gestae* is the most important historical document of the period. With extraordinary economy of language—documents chiseled in stone forced our forebears to be lapidary—it presents Augustus' own perspective on his achievements and on what he wanted to be understood as their quintessence.

AUCTORITAS

With deliberate emphasis, Augustus placed the mention of the essential characteristic of his rule near the conclusion of the *Res Gestae* (34.3). After 27 B.C., he maintains, he surpassed all others in *auctoritas*, while possessing no more official power (*potestas*) than those who were colleagues of his in each magistracy. The statement is inseparable from the full context of chapter 34:

1. In consulatu sexto et septimo, postquam bella civilia extinxeram, per consensum universorum potitus rerum omnium, rem publicam ex mea potestate in senatus populique Romani arbitrium transtuli. 2. Quo pro merito meo senatus consulto Augustus appellatus sum et laureis postes aedium mearum vestiti publice coronaque civica super ianuam meam fixa est et clupeus aureus in curia Iulia positus, quem mihi senatum populumque Romanum dare virtutis clementiaeque et iustitiae et pietatis causa testatum est per eius clupei inscriptionem. 3. Post id tempus auctoritate omnibus praestiti, potestatis autem nihilo amplius habui quam ceteri qui mihi quoque in magistratu conlegae fuerunt.

[1. In my sixth and seventh consulships, after I had extinguished civil wars, and at a time when with universal consent I was in control of all affairs, I transferred the commonwealth from my power to the judgment of the senate and people of Rome. 2. For this service of mine I was named Augustus by decree of the senate, and the doorposts of my house were publicly wreathed with laurel leaves and a civic crown was fixed over my door and a golden shield was set up in the Curia Julia, which, as attested by the inscription thereon, was given me by the senate and people of Rome on account of my courage, clemency, justice, and devotion. 3. After this time, I excelled all in *auctoritas*, although I possessed no more official power than others who were my colleagues in the several magistracies.][3]

The historical situation, in brief, was this. In November of 43 B.C., Octavian joined the Second Triumvirate with Antony and Lepidus. For all practical purposes, he retained, while also serving as consul in 33 B.C., his powers as a triumvir past the battle of Actium in 31 B.C. and Antony's suicide in the following year.[4] They amounted to an extraordinary empowerment. From 31 B.C. onward, Octavian also held the actual office of consul on an annual basis. In 28 B.C., however, he passed a decree declaring null and void any nonconstitutional acts of the triumvirs, and in 27 B.C. he returned the operations of the consulship to relative, though not absolute, normalcy. After 23 B.C., he held that office only twice more, in 5 and 2 B.C., nor did he assume any other magistracy in spite of repeated urgings. Such refusals, or *recusationes*, were one of the hallmarks of his reign (*RG* 5–6). During most of it he was, in legal terms, a private citizen, *privatus*, the note on which he begins the *Res Gestae*. He was, to be sure, a *privatus* with very special powers. From 23 B.C. onward, for instance, he held the power, though not the office, of tribune of the people, which provided him with the legal mechanisms for legislative initiatives, including the prerogative to convene the senate. On all this, detailed studies abound.[5] Significantly, Augustus does not emphasize these powers in the *Res Gestae*. They were basically transactional powers (*potestates*) for the operation of the government. They were not negligible and were indeed necessary, but they were secondary to the concept that he, quite rightly, considered to be at the center of his rule—namely, *auctoritas*.

The significance of *auctoritas* lies not only in its being part of a para- or supraconstitutional terminology[6] (other such terms are *princeps*, *pater patriae*, and even *libertas*) by which Augustus bypassed or, on a different view, transcended the letter of the republican constitution. Its qualities also set the tone for the distinctive characteristics that have occasioned so many interpretations of Augustan art and poetry. *Auctoritas* (as well as other such terms) has multiple meanings, connotations, and associations. It is precise without being limiting and it is elastic without being vague. Its power is suggestive and asks for participation, interpretation, and response. These are the very qualities of much of Augustan poetry and art. Syme astutely observed, at the end of *The Roman Revolution*, that "like Augustus, his *Res Gestae* are unique, defying verbal definition and explaining themselves."[7] In a similar vein, another scholar has remarked on this very passage in the *Res Gestae* that Augustus "likes to veil things and leaves it to others to interpret them."[8] Such ambiguity, which corresponds to an essential characteristic of the Latin language,[9] is not indeterminate as interpreters of Augustan poetry in particular sometimes tend to assume, but calls for careful exploration. For *auctoritas* is typical of Augustan culture in that it has strong moral connotations. *Auctoritas*, which as Dio noted (55.3.5) is a quintessentially Roman and therefore untranslatable term, goes beyond material aspects. It is moral in the larger sense of the word and connotes the power of ideas. It expresses "material, intellectual, and moral superiority" and is "the ultimate power of the emperor on the moral level."[10] By emphasizing *auctoritas* as his governing concept Augustus makes it clear that he does not want to be just a functionary or magistrate but that he aims to provide a higher kind of moral leadership. There is a strong center of ideas, then, and a clear authorial intentionality that, far from being confining, encourages creative response and interpretation. The dynamic tension between these two notions—authorial intent and latitude of response—which modern literary theory often treats as irreconcilable, accounts for much of the vitality of Augustan culture.

It is useful, therefore, to outline the range of associations of *auctoritas* in order to illustrate both of these points specifically and to gain a fuller understanding of both the nature of Augustus' leadership and the resulting cultural matrix.[11]

Auctoritas is or denotes a quality that is inherent in and emanates from an individual. One of the early meanings of *auctor*, going back as far as Rome's earliest law, the Twelve Tables, relates to vouchsafing and guaranteeing. A guardian, for instance, is an *auctor* in the sense of guaranteeing any binding action of his ward. Similarly, a seller becomes the *auctor*-guarantor to the buyer that the sold item really belonged to him; should that turn out not to be so, the seller guarantees the appropriate legal remedies. In the political realm, the *auctoritas* of the senate, at which we will look in more detail, is not binding legislation but the sort of approval that precedes it. It involves the actions of others, such as the consuls; it has no legal force but plenty of moral authority. What all these aspects of *auctoritas* have in common is that an *auctor* is a person "who puts his stamp of approval, in a measurable and effective way, on an action which is to be undertaken by another person with the understanding, implicit in 'measurable,' that a certain degree of responsibility is taken on by the approver."[12] An *auctor*, then, as examples from early Roman literature make clear, is more than a simple counselor or persuader.[13] Instead, his *auctoritas* comes from special insight and is so weighty that the person seeking advice will almost certainly accept it.

The relevance of this basic definition alone is instructive for the way Augustus wanted the role of his *auctoritas* to be understood. He can be the initiator but, just as important, he is the guarantor and approver of the initiatives of others. We are not dealing with a political, let alone cultural, model that involves constant top-down commands and Augustus as the sole agent. Instead of a rigidly hierarchical "organization of opinion" in particular,[14] the emphasis is on the initiatives of many, especially in the areas of art and literature. Such initiatives assume special significance when they are carried out under Augustus' *auctoritas*. Reflecting this changing assessment of Augustus' role, the editors of a recent volume on Augustan poetry have captured this spirit of interaction and its nuanced manifestations in the following perceptive formulation:

> We set about this collection in the hope that it would shed some light on an interesting subject which is important both to literary scholars and historians. Our contributors show that easy distinctions such as "Is this poetry or propaganda?" and "Are the poets sincere or are they puppets?" take us nowhere. The matter is complicated by the genuine friendships within the circle of writers and *principes viri*, by the delicacy with which Maecenas treats his poets, by the recognition that Augustus had restored peace, order and idealism to a society which had lost them, by the significance of the form a poem takes and of the time when it was written. There can have been few ages in which poets were so intimately and affectionately connected with the holders of political power, few regimes with a richer iconography, few poets so profoundly moved by a political ideal and so equipped to sing its praises with subtlety, humor, learning, and rapture. The reader of these poems needs a touch of all of these.[15]

Genuine *auctoritas* is based on this kind of mutuality and cannot be mandated. Basic to its reciprocal and social aspect is the recognition that *auctoritas* "presupposes the approbation and voluntary allegiance of those on whom it is exerted."[16] We should take note of this voluntary aspect: *auctoritas* is something that is granted not by statute but by the esteem of one's fellow citizens. It is acquired less by inheritance, although belonging to an influential family or group is accompanied by some degree of *auctoritas*, than by an individual's superior record of judgment and achievement. Again, *auctoritas* is not static but keeps increasing (*augere*, which is derived from the same root) by continued activity of the kind that merits and validates one's *auctoritas*.

In many of our sources, *auctoritas* therefore connotes actual power as contrasted with the transactional power of the governmental machinery and the magistrates. The situation at Augustus' time is most sharply brought into focus by the traditional claim of the senate to *auctoritas*.[17] Clearly, the collective wisdom and experience of members of the senate carried with them an almost axiomatic *auctoritas* that few magistrates, especially consuls, could ignore. We need to keep in mind that while the system of checks and balances of the Roman constitution influenced many a modern constitution, there was no truly bicameral system in Rome in the sense that the senate's concurrence was needed for legislation passed by one of the popular assemblies. The only way the senate could influence such legislation was through its *auctoritas*. A case in point is the situation after the passage of the Hortensian Law in 287 B.C., which gave plebeians full civic status and the assembly of the plebs (*concilium plebis*) full power to legislate. Logically, at that point, the office of tribune of the people should have been abolished because the plebs needed no further legal protection. With the conservatism typical of the Romans, however, the tribunate was retained and it was the tribune who convened the *concilium plebis* and introduced legislation. Since the senate could not block it (except for the veto of another tribune, which could be a messy affair), its recourse time and again was to bring its *auctoritas* to bear *before* any legislation was passed.[18] In other words, the tribunes and the senate reached a consensus prior to the introduction of legislation in the *concilium plebis*; in this way, all legislation, fittingly, occurred "on the authority of the senate" (*ex auctoritate senatus*).

There is another important aspect to all this which is also relevant to Augustus' modus operandi. It is the reliance on consensus, goodwill, and compromise in getting things done rather than on a rigid system of parliamentary rules and cross-checks. Hence Augustus refers pointedly to the *consensus universorum* at the beginning of the chapter of the *Res Gestae* that ends with the mention of his *auctoritas*.

In the republic, such consensus had not been much in evidence since Tiberius Gracchus in 133 B.C. passed his own reform legislation without the *auctoritas* of the senate and was promptly assassinated. For over one hundred years, violence became an accepted means of settling political conflicts in lieu of the reliance on the traditional means of suasion, compromise, and assiduous cooperation. Cicero, in his *Laws* (3.28), would codify the ideal situation that had prevailed, from the senatorial point of view, before then: the *populus* had the *potestas*—the people actually enacted the laws—but the senate had the *auctoritas* that determined their content. It is the same contrast to which Augustus deliberately refers in *RG* 34.3. At the core of the malaise of the late republic, however, is the circumstance that such a system suffers when it is routinized rather than kept vital by the spirit that generated it.[19] It was the self-interest of the senate and its neglect of the larger interests of the *res publica* that gave rise to the Gracchan unrest and undermined the senate's own *auctoritas*: it became an *auctoritas* in form, but not in essence. *Auctoritas* is not simply a given, but needs to be constantly reacquired and validated. In that sense, it is part of the Augustan ethos that emphasized process and ongoing effort rather than fulfillment.[20] On the political level this activity—which is only part of the rededication of the *res publica* to its original spirit—ultimately fell to Augustus. He did not usurp the *auctoritas* of the senate, but came to supersede it because of his ability, and the senate's virtual unwillingness, to solve the various and long-standing problems that were afflicting the Roman state. As always in the Augustan reign, a traditional matrix was used and expanded. The basis of the individual senator's *auctoritas* within the senate was parallel to that of the senate's within the state.[21] Roman political practice was familiar with the role of a *princeps* and *auctor* who could guide the senate and ensure stability and concord in the *res publica*. Augustus came to utilize that role to the fullest.

Auctoritas therefore meant, as before, the kind of substance on which real influence is based. Consequently—and to continue with our overview of the connotations of *auctoritas*—it is related to other basic Roman concepts such as *fides*, *dignitas*, *gravitas*, and even *libertas*. The aspect of *fides* (i.e., trust and protection) is already inherent in the early function of an *auctor* as a guarantor. When *auctoritas* was extended to the political and social realm, so was its connection with *fides*: *auctoritas* is sought to establish *fides* (Cic., *Top.* 73). The statesman-*auctor* is a guarantor of the trust that must be operative at all levels of the *res publica* in order to make it function properly. Speaking from the perspective of the senate, Cicero declares the *auctoritas senatus* to be the foundation for the *otiosa dignitas*, the orderly and dignified condition of the state (*Sest.* 98). Due to its lack of actual implementation, the phrase became one of the major political slogans of the late republic.[22] Similarly, the archetypal Roman quality of *gravitas*, serious comportment stemming from integrity and serious purpose, frequently appears as manifesting itself in those who have *auctoritas*.[23] As for *libertas*, Cicero, again in the senatorial context, stresses the interdependence of the *auctoritas senatus* and the *libertas* of the Roman people.[24] In the *Res Gestae*, in turn, one of the several links between its very beginning and its conclusion is the mention of *libertas* in 1.1, of *auctoritas* in 34.3, and of the senate's proclamation of Augustus as *pater patriae* (father of the country) in 35.1. The point that a Roman *pater* had *auctoritas* needs no elaboration; hence Augustus follows up on his *auctoritas* with his concluding honor as *pater patriae*.[25]

As can be seen, *auctoritas* was a notion with a broad and ever expanding range of applications. They extend from the private realm—we can add here the *auctoritas* of old age (Cic., *Sen.* 60)—and the social sphere (the *auctoritas* of the patron entails the active concern for his clients' welfare) to political decisions that, for all practical purposes, carry the force of law. The boundary, therefore, between the *auctoritas senatus* and a formal decree of the senate (*senatus consultum*) was as fluid [26] as that between an authoritative piece of advice and an order. All this, including the elasticity of the concept, suited Augustus' purposes perfectly: *auctoritas* was indeed the exercise of power fitting for one who had been proclaimed *Augustus*. For good reason, he links *auctoritas* and *Augustus* in *RG* 34 because the two were linked in actuality, including through their etymology.

In both obvious and suggestive ways, *auctoritas* was a different kind of power that was further enhanced by the religious and divine connotations of the very title "Augustus."[27] At the same time, in its transcendence of statutory power it was not without precedent, and Augustus understood the Roman penchant for traditional customs, the *mos maiorum*, all too well. One such precedent was that after certain games had been abolished in 64 B.C. and a tribune ordered the appropriate functionaries (the *magistri vicorum*) to reinstate them three years later, Quintus Metellus Celer, who was consul-elect but did not actually hold an office at the time, prevented them from doing so. "The games," as Cicero puts it (*Piso* 8), "Quintus Metellus as a private citizen [*privatus*] forbade to take place and he achieved by virtue of his *auctoritas* what he could not yet attain by the power of his office [*potestas*]." We have here the same contrast between *auctoritas* and *potestas* as in *RG* 34.3, as well as the connection with *privatus* (cf. *RG* 1.1). Similarly, the link between *auctoritas* and the *principes viri*, the eminent citizens of the state, is attested frequently[28] and was easily transferable to the *princeps* Augustus. The aspect of moral authority again is of major significance: once before, on the counsel of the Delphic oracle, the Romans had designated a leader for a special task because he was the best (*optimus*) in this regard. In 204 B.C., Publius Cornelius Scipio Nasica was chosen to receive the statue of the Great Mother Goddess from Troy on Rome's behalf. This distinction ranked above any conveyed by the magistracies and triumphs and could aptly be called *principatus morum* (Val. Max. 8.15.3), a phrase that captures much of Augustus' rule, too.

When the young Octavian appeared on the scene in 44 B.C. after Caesar's assassination, he had all too little *auctoritas*. That, at least, was Cicero's assessment in one of his letters to Atticus (16.14.2). By the end of the year, Rome's elder statesman sang a different tune. Octavian had taken command of two of Caesar's legions that had defected from Antony and followed, as Cicero put it, the senate's *auctoritas* (*Phil.* 3.8) due to Octavian's "admirable initiative" (*admirabili virtute*). With the legions' help, it could be claimed, he had prevented Antony from marching on Rome. Since he was commanding them as a *privatus* and not with an official command (*imperium*), Cicero now asked the senate to remedy that deficiency by blessing Octavian with its own *auctoritas* (*Phil.* 3.39; 11.20), an *auctoritas* Octavian had earned by delivering the commonwealth as a *privatus* from the scourge of Antony (*Phil.* 3.5; cf. 11.20).

Two additional factors soon contributed to augmenting the *auctoritas* of Octavian. One was the deification of Caesar. When Octavian, overriding some republican opposition, celebrated the games in honor of Caesar's Victory (*ludi Victoriae Caesaris*) in late July of 44 B.C., a fortuitous comet appeared. It was interpreted promptly, and with the help of a proper seer, as a symbol of Caesar's deification and as an omen of good times to come.[29] To be the son of a slain dictator was a mixed blessing; to be the son of a god, an unmitigated one. Cicero's initial comment shows that being heir to Caesar was not sufficient in and of itself for *auctoritas*, but this can only have changed in the course of Octavian's vigorous assumption of the role of *divi filius* and the official recognition of Caesar's deification in Roman sacred law in 42 B.C. Henceforth, *divus Iulius* and Octavian, *Caesar divi filius*, appeared on coins along with an image of the temple of the Divine Julius Caesar (Fig. 1) which

1. Denarius of Octavian, 36 B.C. Obverse: Octavian, Caesar Divi Filius.
Reverse: Temple of Divus Iulius with Caesar and his comet.

was being built in the Roman Forum and on which the emblem of the *sidus Iulium*, the comet, was prominently displayed. So was it, by Octavian's command, on all of Caesar's statues. Extraordinary as such a cult was in Rome, it was based on the idea that men could become divine because of their great deeds. Caesar's had been primarily military, and to the poets, therefore, his deification could connote Rome's supremacy in the world.[30]

A ramification of Octavian's Caesarean *auctoritas* was its connection with the traditional *auctoritas* that accrued to victorious generals. Octavian, even if with the substantial help of Agrippa, had built up his own string of military successes, culminating in the battle of Actium. An arch commemorating that victory was built in the Roman Forum (Dio 51.19.1).[31] That kind of *auctoritas* also assimilated Octavian to the republic's other great general, Pompey, to whom Augustus alludes, among others, in the very first sentence of the *Res Gestae*. For good reason, Augustus, in the *Res Gestae*, dwells on his many victories and conquests. They are integral to *auctoritas* which, in its various dimensions, is the organizing principle of the *Res Gestae*.[32]

By 29 B.C., then, Octavian was without equal in *auctoritas* in Rome. It had been further enhanced by his tenure of two major priesthoods, including the augurate,[33] from 41 B.C. and from 37 B.C. onward: *augur*, too, is connected with *auctoritas*. It was increased yet further, as part of the settlement and compromise of 28–27 B.C., by the title Augustus (cf. Dio 53.16.8) and by the unique honors and the golden shield with the four virtues, all of which the senate voted him.[34] That alone, however, is not enough to explain his return to constitutional government instead of his self-perpetuation as a military strongman. This return—and I will discuss its precise aspects in the next chapter—was no sham but rested on his confidence that his *auctoritas* could effectively be the primary guarantee of the ensuing order. It is another illustration that he viewed *auctoritas* not as static but as a process, a notion that again informs the spirit of Augustan culture in general. *Auctoritas* was a concept with many dimensions, but ultimately it was directed at the commonweal, the *salus rei publicae*. Most important, it connoted the kind of moral and transcending leadership on which true power is ultimately based. Augustus did not want to relinquish his powerful position in the state but wanted to continue it on an even more effective basis. Hence his preference of *auctoritas* to *potestas*.

It is useful at this point to expand on the distinction between leadership by *auctoritas* and the transactional kind. While "leadership" in contemporary politics has become a buzzword that tends to be invoked in inverse proportion to its actual manifestations, it has also been discussed perceptively in the past two decades by political scientists. The preeminent study, distinguished for its documentation from modern, though not ancient, history and for its insightful definitions, is that by James MacGregor Burns,[35] a well-known American historian and biographer of Franklin Roosevelt and John Kennedy. He criticizes earlier students of leadership for their preoccupation with power and argues that this emphasis has led them to ignore the far more important task of a leader to inculcate purpose. The two basic types of leadership he identifies coincide easily with the views of historians, both modern and ancient, of Augustus. One is the category of transactional leadership. Leaders approach followers with an eye to exchanging one thing for another; this involves rewards for political support or, to give a specific example, favors such as the remission, after Augustus' consolidation of power in 31 B.C., of certain sums that the tax farmers, the publicans, owed the treasury.[36] In addition, the normal everyday activities of simply carrying out the government's business comprise transactional leadership. They are well documented in Syme's book and in Fergus Millar's comprehensive study on *The Emperor in the Roman World*.

More important is what Burns defines as "transforming leadership," which seeks to inculcate values and to satisfy needs that are more than material, and may convert leaders into moral agents. Transforming leadership

> occurs when one or more persons *engage* with others in such a way that leaders and followers raise one another to higher levels of motivation and morality. . . . Various names are used for such leadership. . . : elevating, mobilizing, inspiring, exalting, uplifting, preaching, exhorting, evangelizing. The relationship can be moralistic, of course. But transforming leadership ultimately becomes *moral* in the sense that it raises the level of human conduct and ethical aspiration of both leader and led, and thus it has a transforming effect on both. . . . The fundamental process is an elusive one; it is, in large part, to make conscious what lies unconscious among followers.[37]

Condensing some of Burns' illustrative discussion, T. Peters and R. Waterman list a set of concrete characteristics of transforming leaders and their agenda:

> The transforming leader is concerned with minutiae, as well. But he is concerned with a different kind of minutiae; he is concerned with the tricks of the pedagogue, the mentor, the linguist—the more successfully to become the value shaper, the exemplar, the maker of meanings. His job is much tougher than that of the transactional leader, for he is the true artist, the true pathfinder. After all, he is both calling forth and exemplifying the urge for transcendence that unites us all. At the same time, he exhibits almost boorish consistency over long periods of time in support of his one or two transcending values. No opportunity is too small, no forum too insignificant, no audience too junior.[38]

All these characteristics, and the basic distinction, are singularly applicable to Augustus. To turn to the most important, the outstanding quality of the reign of Augustus was precisely his concern for moral transformation. He was not content with merely restabilizing the mechanics of government. After one hundred years of civil war, the last and bloodiest chapter coming in Octavian's struggle against Mark Antony and Cleopatra, the Romans proba-

bly would have been satisfied with a good transactional leader. Far from
being simply the victorious head of a political party, however, Augustus had
his true base of support in the nonpolitical classes of Italy who had no higher
ambitions than to get on with their lives and businesses without seeing them
disrupted by selfish Roman politicos in the name of liberty in which they did
not share. But Augustus went beyond this. He sounded the note of moral
revitalization and followed through on it; it was a time for rededicating the
state to values, virtues, ideas, and ideals. Especially in the arts and literature,
the phenomenon is more complex than mere "propaganda";[39] it is a reciprocal and dynamic process in which the emperor's role is hard to pin down.[40]

The importance of the nature and practice of Augustan *auctoritas* was well
understood. It found resonance not only in the kindred multi-facetedness of
Augustan culture and in its pursuit of certain values and ideals; *auctoritas* was
also directly reflected in literature and the arts, including the coinage. I will
limit myself to three examples here before returning, in the next chapter, to
a discussion of the opening of the *Res Gestae* and the themes of the liberation
and restoration of the *res publica*.

AUCTORITAS IN THE AENEID: THE SIMILE OF THE STATESMAN

Roman epic before Vergil had been mostly of the historical kind, either
dealing with Roman history in a diachronic fashion, as in Ennius' *Annales*, or
focusing on a specific event or an individual's *res gestae* with perhaps a flash-
back to "mythological" times for resonance. One of Vergil's many innovations was a more sophisticated interaction between the past and the present.
He shifted the emphasis to endeavor and process rather than achievement
and therefore wrote an epic about the beginnings of Rome and the journey
ahead rather than looking back at the formation of the Roman people from
the pinnacle of his own time. In short, he wrote an *Aeneid* rather than an
Augusteid. Accordingly, Vergil begins his epic with the "mythological" journey of Aeneas to Italy. More precisely, he begins *in medias res* with the sea
storm caused by a vengeful Juno. Neptune restores calm to the sea and, as he
does so, the poet uses a simile. It is of special significance because it is the first
simile of the *Aeneid*.[41] The realm to which Neptune's action is compared is
that of Roman history and politics, which are thereby introduced into the
epic:

> ac veluti magno in populo cum saepe coorta est
> seditio saevitque animis ignobile vulgus;
> iamque faces et saxa volant, furor arma ministrat;
> tum, pietate gravem ac meritis si forte virum quem
> conspexere, silent arrectisque auribus astant;
> ille regit dictis animos et pectora mulcet:

sic cunctus pelagi cecidit fragor, aequora postquam
prospiciens genitor caeloque invectus aperto
flectit equos curruque volans dat lora secundo.

(1.148–56)

[Just as often happens when in a great nation turmoil breaks out and the
base masses go on a rampage; firebrands and stones fly, and madness
supplies the weapons: then, if they have caught sight of some man who
carries weight because of his public devotion and service, they stand
silent, their ears ready to listen. Then he prevails in speech over their
fury by his authority, and placates them.[42] Just so, the whole uproar of
the sea died down, when the father of the seas looked upon the waters.
The sky cleared, Neptune turned his horses around, and flying onward,
gave free rein to his compliant chariot.]

At the center of the simile is the statesman who prevails over a serious civil
disturbance by means of his *auctoritas*. Servius acutely explained the phrase
pietate gravem: "Because of his devotion he has *auctoritas* that carries
weight."[43] The man's *auctoritas* rests on his *gravitas*, on his devotion to country and gods (*pietas*), his ability as a speaker,[44] and his actions and achievements (*meritis*). Furthermore, the simile is a paradigm of the multiple dimensions typical of Augustan poetry and culture, and of the nexus between
Augustan ideas, literature, and art. It is worthwhile pursuing a few of these
aspects.

First, the simile's applicability is broader than an identification with any
specific Roman leader. Plutarch refers to such an incident involving Cato the
Younger, but so does Cicero (*Brut.* 56) concerning Popilius Laena (mid-
fourth century B.C.): as a flamen, he was engaged in a religious rite when he
had to rush off, still in his priestly garb (the very one [*laena*] that gave him his
surname), to calm the crowd; his characterization as *pietate gravem* in that case
has a particular appropriateness. Both Cato and Popilius settle the tumult
with a speech and with their *auctoritas*.[45] The association of the Vergilian
passage with Augustus readily suggests itself both in the general terms of
Augustus' settling down the civil wars[46] and the specific representation of
Octavian as Neptune on a cameo from the 30s B.C. (Fig. 2).[47] Holding a
trident and riding on a quadriga drawn by sea horses, he surges atop the
waves over an opponent who disappears into them. The unfortunate enemy
seems to be either Sextus Pompey or, more likely, Mark Antony. Vollenweider's apt characterization of the image on the cameo is quite appropriate
for the simile: "In the hippocamps who are rearing up, in the staggering of
their wildly gesturing heads with their raised crests, in the restless jumble of
their legs, in their jagged and coiled tails there manifests itself a vehemence
and turbulence which corresponds to the spirit of the 30s B.C. In contrast to
it arises, like the principle of order and law, the figure of the charioteer who

2. Intaglio with Octavian as Neptune, late 30s B.C.

stands upright and drives over the floods of the sea. He may be understood as the symbol of a young hero who is constraining the chaos of his times, when he holds the unruly horses in his reins."[48]

This may explain, at least in part, Neptune's untraditional intervention in Aeneas' behalf. For the god had been anything but kindly disposed toward the Trojans in the *Iliad* and, for that matter, toward another Homeric model for the Vergilian Aeneas, namely, Odysseus in the *Odyssey*. [49] Moreover, Neptune was appropriated by the Caesar murderers Brutus and Casca and appears on one of their denarii, with the goddess of Victory on the reverse (Fig. 3). Sextus Pompey, who exerted his power over the seas until his defeat in 36 B.C., extensively identified himself with Neptune. Nor is that dimension missing from Antony's image: the reverse of a sestertius minted in 36–35 B.C. shows him and Octavia riding in a chariot like that of Neptune and Amphitrite (Fig. 4).[50] Octavian evidently inverted that situation and was "reconciled" with Neptune as is indicated by various coins (cf. Fig. 147) and the dedication of a statue to the sea-god at the site of Nicopolis, his camp at

3. Denarius of Brutus and Casca, 43–42 B.C.
Obverse: Head of Neptune. Reverse: Victory.

4. Sestertius of Mark Antony, 36–35 B.C. Reverse: Neptune-like Mark Antony and Amphitrite-like Octavia.

the battle of Actium,[51] but the passage in the *Aeneid* should not be read as a simple reflection of this contest of images. Vergil, as so often, transcends such realities. Here he does so by changing the process of inversion to an aesthetic one: instead of the conventional comparison of an agitated crowd to the sea, the tempestuous sea is now compared to a crowd. The traditional simile is revitalized. The procedure is paralleled, on a larger scale, by Vergil's revitalization of traditional epic and, on a larger scale yet, by Augustus' revitalization of the traditional *res publica*.

Second, the simile shares a deliberate multiplicity of meanings with the concept of *auctoritas* that it expresses. *Auctoritas*, as we have seen, could mean different things to different people; its prevailing connotation depended on the recipient and the context. To a member of the Roman plebs, Augustus' sounding of *auctoritas* as the keynote of *RG* 34 and the *Res Gestae* in general might mean primarily his unprecedented munificence as a veritable *patronus* of the city's population. A soldier would associate with it mainly Augustus' conquests whereas to members of the senatorial class it evoked the role of *auctoritas* in government. In a like fashion, Vergil's simile is easily applicable to various Roman leaders, including Augustus and, for that matter, Aeneas: the programmatic characterization of Aeneas as *insignem pietate virum* (1.10) is echoed by that of the statesman as *pietate gravem virum* (1.151). The simile does not express one simple equation, but is generic and paradigmatic, and it calls for the reader's involvement. In this respect, it can also be viewed usefully in the light of the evolution of historical representation in Roman art from the late second century B.C. to the first where increasing conceptualization takes the place of reliance on the realistic representation of specific events. The change is observable especially in the coinage.[52]

Again, this is a phenomenon I will discuss in more detail in the next chapter, because it also created a problem of intelligibility. It included the attempt to find an appropriate symbolic language for values that were prominent in the political and public life, such as *libertas, pietas, virtus,* and *pax*. The result was not one-sided allegorical identifications, but the creation of an almost emblematic pictorial language that was capable of various combinations and could be associated with various individuals. The same is true of the simile and of the *auctoritas* it illustrates: it does not simply represent one particular historical event, such as Cato's taming of a frenzied crowd, but stresses an exemplary quality in a generic way, making it applicable to many different individuals and situations. This is an example in microcosm of the multilayered nature of the characters of the *Aeneid*[53] and of the epic itself; the search for the proper equilibrium between the exemplary and the individual is one of the principal creative tensions in the *Aeneid*.

AUCTORITAS IN ART: THE AUGUSTUS STATUE FROM PRIMA PORTA

The Augustus statue from Prima Porta (Fig. 5), which is perhaps the most famous representation of Augustus in art,[54] is closely connected with the Vergilian passage I have just discussed. It shows Augustus in an authoritative pose after the return of the Roman standards by the Parthians in 20 B.C., an event that the pictorial program of the cuirass elaborates. The fact that the statue conveys *auctoritas* is clear from precedents and comparable works. A forerunner of the commanding gesture of laterally projecting the upper right arm, with an upward thrust of the forearm and hand, is the so-called Orator (or Arringatore) from the second century B.C., the first such statue of a public figure in Etruscan art (Fig. 6).[55] It derives from several traditions, including one of statues of deities; we might recall that in the Vergilian simile a god is compared to a man. In addition to conveying his *auctoritas*, the Prima Porta statue envelops Augustus, the "Revered One," in a fitting aura of divinity, alluding to his ancestry from Venus by means of the Cupid at his side and by the presence on the armor of his patron god Apollo along with Diana, Venus, and Mars. The general pose, the spear, and the dress are found on denarii of the *divi filius* that were issued between 31 B.C. and 28 B.C. (Fig. 7); after both Actium and the Parthian settlement Augustus erected a triumphal arch in the Forum—the latter seems to have stood next to the Deified Caesar's temple (cf. Fig. 172). The gesture is that of a rhetorical address, an *adlocutio*. Being devoid of a specific audience and not limited to a specific occasion, it assumes, like the Vergilian simile, a symbolic and exemplary value "demonstrative of the power which makes possible such a gesture and the circumstances of its making."[56]

Even if the fingers of the right hand, except for the ring finger, had to be restored, there are good reasons for their restoration in accordance with the *adlocutio* type. To these can be added the joint resonance that both the Doryphoros (Fig. 8), the classical Greek model for the Prima Porta Augustus, and the Vergilian simile found in Quintilian's *Institutio Oratoria*. Quintilian's discussion also recognizes the *auctoritas* of the simile and the statue. In contrast to Homeric similes, the Vergilian simile is more than an aesthetic device. It expresses an ethos, and for that reason Quintilian cites it as a paradigm for his tenet that the good orator also is a good man—the ideal of the *vir bonus atque dicendi peritus* (12.1.27–28). In an earlier, but related passage in book 5 (12.20–21), Quintilian contrasts the insipid spectacle of the effete rhetoric of his own day with the rhetoric that serves a purpose—namely, moral rectitude—and is therefore virile. The image that comes to his mind is that of Polykleitos' Doryphoros whom he characterizes as *vir gravis et sanctus*.[57] Similarly, the Vergilian speaker is *vir gravis et pius*. The two come together in the Augustus statue, which was modeled on the Doryphoros. *Pius* in the Vergilian passage is paraphrased by Servius as *venerabilis*, the Latin equivalent of the Greek *sebastos*. That, in turn, was also the Greek translation of the name of Augustus (Dio 53.16.8) whose *sanctitas* is caught up in a statue for which the Doryphoros served as a model.

Some implications emerge. By using this particular characterization, Quintilian indicates that he considers the Doryphoros an exception from the norm of Polykleitos' works. In his famous juxtaposition of orators and sculptors in book 12 he characterizes Polykleitos' statues as surpassing in *diligentia* and *decor*, but not in *pondus* ("weightiness") and *auctoritas* because he made statues of young men only and not of those who had *aetatem graviorem*, a more advanced age that called for a graver representation. The Doryphoros, by contrast, is *gravis* and even *sanctus*, a characterization without precedent for a Polykleitan statue of a Greek athlete. Nor is *sanctus* part of the standard terminology, which was often inspired by rhetoric, for Greek and Roman art.[58]

An explanation for this exception would be Quintilian's acquaintance with copies of the Prima Porta statue and with its aura. As for the Prima Porta statue itself, the Doryphoros was a model it imitated very closely as is evidenced even by such details as the stylization of the hair on both statues (Figs. 9a and b). It is obvious, however, that the Augustus statue elevated and sublimated the spirit of the Greek model. The feet, for instance, are planted on the ground more firmly (Figs. 10a and b), reflecting the statue's greater *pondus*, to use Quintilian's term. Moreover, the iconography of the cuirass, which is another example of the Augustan wealth of allusive references, the limitation of the onlooker to the frontal view, and the projection of the arm of the Augustan statue provide it with more *auctoritas*. This aura reflects back on the Doryphoros, who thereby transcends even his Achillean idealization and becomes *gravis et sanctus*.[59] While Quintilian's characterization involves the entire statue, we do not know how many copies of the Prima Porta statue were in existence at his time, although copies of the head of the Prima Porta type have been estimated to have numbered in the thousands.

The affinity of the Prima Porta statue to the passages in Quintilian and Vergil suggests that an *adlocutio* is by no means inappropriate. More important, this particular representation of Augustus, as is clear from the precedent of the "Orator" (Fig. 6), conveys *auctoritas* while other iconographic details elevate the statue yet further to the level of *sanctitas*. The connection between the two is underscored by the next to the final chapter of the *Res Gestae*, which was the starting point of our discussion: *auctoritas* (34.2) follows upon the mention of the divine aura implied in the title *Augustus* (34.1).

5. Statue of Augustus from Prima Porta. Based on an original dating from after 20 B.C.

6. Statue of the "Arringatore,"
second century B.C.

8. Doryphoros by Polykleitos, fifth
century B.C. Roman marble copy.

7. Denarius of Octavian, ca. 31–28 B.C.
Reverse: Octavian addressing the troops.

9a. Head of the Augustus
from Prima Porta.

9b. Head of the Doryphoros.
Bronze copy from the Villa dei Papiri,
Herculaneum.

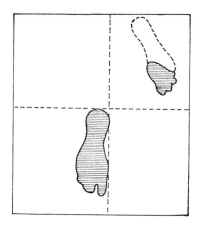

10a. Diagram of footprints
of Doryphoros.

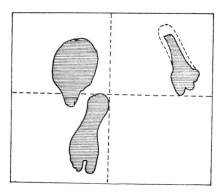

10b. Diagram of footprints of Augustus
from Prima Porta.

AUCTORITAS AND THE COINS: THE MUTUALITY OF LEADER AND FOLLOWERS

We saw earlier that the transforming kind of leadership represented by *auctoritas*, as opposed to a regimented system of obeisance to commands from the top, requires the initiative of people other than the *princeps*; in the end, he, with his *auctoritas*, is only the guarantor and approver, though not in a legalistic sense. Besides, *auctoritas* is not a static or self-contained attribute but exists for an individual only to the degree that society recognizes it or renews it. Some aspects of Augustus' coinage are a good example of this reciprocity in addition to helping redefine the notion of "propaganda," a label which, as so many others that have gained currency for Augustan phenomena, is convenient rather than precise.[60]

One source of monetary issues at Augustus' time was the mint at Rome which since 23 B.C. was administered, as it had been before the triumviral period, by a board of three moneyers (*tresviri monetales*), usually young men at the beginning of their magisterial careers.[61] In addition there were major imperial mints in the east and west. These issues are faithfully recorded in the standard catalogs. In addition, however, there were over two hundred cities in all areas of the Augustan empire that issued coins independently, usually in bronze.[62] Many of these autonomous local authorities, which, with few exceptions, had no precedent for placing the portraits of living Romans on their coins, chose to represent Augustus' in ever greater numbers; witness the coins of Cnossus with the labyrinth on the reverse (Fig. 11). They were

11. Bronze coin from Cnossus, Crete. Obverse: Augustus. Reverse: labyrinth.

under no legal obligation to do so nor did the head of Augustus signify that the coins bearing his likeness had been issued on his authority or been authorized by him. Another novelty is that the issuing authority, whether cities or individuals, is indicated on the reverse rather than the obverse, contrary to prior convention. The decision to put the head of Augustus on the obverse was the result of two considerations. One evidently was to honor the emperor. He was not only *pater patriae*, but the father of the world, *pater orbis* (Ovid, *Fasti* 2.130). The other, even more important, was to have his *auctoritas* translate into the economic efficiency of the coin—to encourage its circulation and unquestioned acceptance. Such issues, in turn, reinforced the *auctoritas* of the *princeps*.

The intertwining of legal and supralegal aspects in this domain is but a reflection of the larger interconnection between *auctoritas* and *potestas* that we already have noted. "In an atmosphere," as Andrew Wallace-Hadrill summarized it, "in which the ruler was seen not simply as the embodiment of the 'official' and 'legal,' but as a charismatic force on the veneration of whose majesty depended the survival of the Roman world, the head is not an emblem of legality which we see in the sovereign's head, but an appeal to a potentially powerful emotive response."[63] For, as he points out on the basis of detailed evidence, coins quite literally have two sides to them: one is official, legal, or legalistic, whereas the other constitutes an appeal to values shared by the user. Thus the philosopher Epictetus (first/second century A.D.) counsels to retain a coin with the image of Hadrian, an *optimus princeps*, and to get rid of a coin with Nero because of his unsavory character. In terms of their official function, both coins were legal tender.[64]

We should note again the importance attached to values, a characteristic that is true of the macrocosm of the *res publica* and of the Augustan rule, which maintained this attachment in the spirit, if not the letter. From the second half of the second century B.C., an appeal to such values increasingly appears on Roman coins. Iconographies proliferate, and their variety mirrors the increasingly fragmented values of the *res publica*.[65] That, in turn, reflects only the general malaise of "the lost *res publica*."[66] As we will see shortly, the real meaning of the Augustan "restoration" of the *res publica* was precisely to revitalize central Roman values and to use them as a unifying ethos. Hence, if coins indeed had served primarily propagandistic purposes and had been "used to insinuate into every home in the empire each changing nuance of imperial achievement and policy,"[67] they would present themselves as a rather uncomplicated vehicle for Augustan "propaganda."

In actuality, matters were a great deal more nuanced. Even when we turn to the imperial mints, a careful study of the evidence indicates no pattern of control by the *princeps* himself. Augustus' concern was, quite properly, with the economic priority—with the money supply, rather than with the coins' imagery. Accordingly, Barbara Levick has proposed a model of initiative from below. On her view, the symbols on the coinage do not produce a message from the emperor to his subjects, but rather are offerings of respect by the subjects to the emperor: "Types were intended to appeal, not to the public, but to the man whose portrait as a rule occupied the obverse of the coins: they were a tribute to a great individual."[68]

Some refinements need to be made to this general concept. One concerns the relationship between the emperor's role in suggesting broad themes and their specific elaboration by artists, writers, and moneyers. In keeping with the encouragement of individual initiatives there was no simple overall matrix. In the arts, for instance, there is ample evidence for the autonomous development of many "official" themes and their appropriation, with varying degrees of creativity, for private purposes.[69] As for literature, some poets not only seem to have been active discussants, in their own terms, of the central issues of the age but may actually have suggested some of them. Although apt for the post-Augustan principate, Levick's concluding characterization undervalues the greater degree of experimentation and development that prevailed under Augustus in the realm of coin types and their issue just as it did in his management of the government at large.[70] While the designers of the coins (and we do not know to what extent they interacted with the moneyers), like everyone else, operated in the context of Augustan ideas—Augustan in the sense, though not exclusively, that they were suggested and emphasized by the emperor himself—they retained considerable latitude in deciding whether and how they wanted to express them, if they wanted to express them at all. Another relevant distinction is the one between the coins' referring or alluding to contemporary events and their urging a program.[71] Since Augustus' policies and ideas concerned the public, the coins do address that public and, at times, specific audiences or segments (such as the legionaries) as well as the emperor. It is one of the characteristic phenomena of the age that such interactions remain dynamic and defy rigid demarcation. The important consideration is that the flow was not merely in one direction.

Reflecting this fluidity, the images on the coins run the whole gamut from recalling republican traditions to innovations such as the appearance of the emperor's head on *both* sides of the coin. Until Caesar, there had hardly been any Roman coins with the likeness of a living individual. The Augustan coinage overwhelmingly features the *princeps'* image on the obverse. Again, however, that should not mislead us to consider the situation, especially early in his reign, as irreversible, let alone mandated. The same reasons apply here as in the coinage of the local mints at which we looked earlier.

An additional factor is that Augustus' *auctoritas* after his accession was a challenge that evoked creative responses instead of degenerating into routinized flattery. Some of the most inventive issues come from the mint at Rome which issued gold and silver coins between 19 and 12 B.C. One of the moneyer's names was Aquillius Florus; hence an open, six-petaled flower playfully dominates the reverse (with the moneyer's name written in the margin) even more than Augustus' head does the obverse (Fig. 12). On a more serious note, the same moneyer reproduced other types taken from coins struck by his republican ancestors, such as the reverse with a warrior and the personification of Sicily (Fig. 13a) that reproduces a type struck by Mn. Aquillius in 71 B.C. (Fig. 13b), whose purpose was to commemorate the suppression of a slave war in Sicily by the consul Mn. Aquillius in 101 B.C.[72]

An interesting case is presented by an aureus struck in the same year, 19 B.C., by Marcus Durmius: on the reverse appears a crab holding a butterfly in its claws (Fig. 14b).[73] It recalls a denarius struck by one of Caesar's assassins (ca. 43–42 B.C.), which showed the more martial symbol of a ship's

12. Denarius of Aquillius Florus, 19 B.C. Obverse: Augustus. Reverse: Flower.

13a. Denarius of Aquillius
Florus, 19 B.C. Reverse:
Warrior raising up Sicily.

13b. Denarius of Mn. Aquillius,
71 B.C. Reverse: Warrior
raising up Sicily.

14. Aureus of Marcus Durmius, 19 B.C.
(a) Obverse: head of Augustus. (b) Reverse: crab holding butterfly.

15. Denarius of M. Servilius, 43–42 B.C.
(a) Obverse: head of Libertas. (b) Reverse: crab holding aplustre.

beak, an aplustre, in the crab's fangs (Fig. 15b). It had the head of Libertas on the obverse (Fig. 15a); on Durmius' coin, its place is taken by that of Caesar Augustus (Fig. 14a). The resulting imagery can be viewed both as an expression of independence or as fitting in with Octavian/Augustus' appropriation and inversion of the political mottoes of his former opponents.

Similar considerations apply to the general mix of reverse types chosen by the moneyers until the Roman mint ceased issuing gold and silver after 12 B.C. when the minting of silver coins was centralized in Lugdunum (modern-day Lyon). Some of the designs are unrelated to Augustus, whereas others are celebratory to the point where his image appears on both sides. On an aureus of Lentulus (12 B.C.), for instance, Augustus extends a helping hand to a kneeling *Res publica* (Fig. 16). In 17 and 16 B.C., there are appropriate allusions to the Secular Games, including the appearance of a rejuvenated Julius Caesar with his comet (Fig. 17lb). It is another example of the frequent Augustan combination of dynastic legitimization and the revival of a republican tradition. The issues of the final two years are characterized by a strong emphasis on Agrippa's role, and on members of the Augustan family.[74]

16. Aureus of Cossus Lentulus, 12 B.C. Reverse: Augustus extending his hand to the *Res publica*.

How are we to interpret this development, small as it may seem? The proper balance between individual, if not "republican," initiatives on the coinage and the Augustan *auctoritas* as a guarantee or approval was, like so many other reactions to his *auctoritas*, a matter of experiment and gradual exploration. The year 23 B.C. marked another stage in this evolution. As part of the "Second Settlement," Augustus abdicated his consulship, returned two additional provinces to the senate's administration, and let two censors be appointed while receiving the *tribunicia potestas* (it is beginning with this event that he dated his principate) and his first five-year term of the *imperium proconsulare*. The reappearance of the republican office of the *tresviri monetales* belongs in this context.[75] It had been superseded by the direct issuing of coins on the part of Julius Caesar and the triumvirs, and the mint of Rome had been closed since approximately 40 B.C. After it reopened in 23 B.C., it started a new bronze coinage according to the currency reform of Augustus that was approved by the senate. It is possible that the mover of the pertinent senate decree was the republican loyalist Calpurnius Piso, whom Augustus persuaded to return to the consulship "after a protracted interval of retirement or recalcitrance."[76] Augustus solicited the participation of such independent minds and actively sought to convey the *auctoritas* of the senate through the new coinage. That is done primarily by the letters SC on the reverse of the bronze coinage (Fig. 17). They were complemented on the obverse by

17. Sestertius of Gallius Lupercus, 16 B.C.

emblematic references to Augustus: the oaken crown and the laurel trees (cf. *RG* 34.2), and the legend OB CIVIS SERVATOS ("because of the citizens he saved"). The coins conveyed to all that his role and the senate's were complementary. Before they gained currency, however, Calpurnius' son Cn. Calpurnius Piso, who was one of the *tresviri* in 23 B.C., took the initiative to issue a special series of bronzes. They showed Numa, Rome's second king, on the reverse instead of the senatorial SC, while the portrait of Augustus was on the obverse (Fig. 18).[77]

In true Augustan style, the framework of references is more than one-dimensional. There is an allusion, in the tradition of republican coinage, to a specific contemporary event, the closing of the Temple of Janus. The action recalled that of Numa, the priest-king who oversaw Rome's internal consolidation after the warrior king Romulus. His representation thus can be

18. *As* of Cn. Calpurnius Piso, Naevius Surdinus, and Plotius Rufus, 23 B.C.
Obverse: Augustus. Reverse: Head of Numa Pompilius.

seen more broadly, and befitting the context of the "Second Settlement," as a compliment on the stage that Augustus' rule had reached.[78] Cicero, in fact, had praised Numa in the book on the ideal ruler in his *Republic* (5.3) for the long-lasting peace he had given the city and his establishment of law and religion; *pax Augusta* and *pax Numana* were easily assimilable. But Numa was also claimed as an ancestor by the Calpurnian family, and Roman aristocratic families (*gentes*) liked to glorify themselves in this fashion.

Moreover, Numa had appeared on three coin issues of the late republic. They included a coin from the years 49–48 B.C. by the elder Piso (the consul in 23 B.C.) in honor of Pompey, whereas the other two issues associated Numa and Apollo.[79] All this evokes even more associations. Are we dealing with residual Pompeian sympathies on the part of the Pisones or with a recognition of the Augustan supersession of Pompey, whom Augustus himself used for comparison?[80] The situation is made even more complex by the fact that the father of the elder Piso was as ardent an enemy of Pompey as his son was his defender. Within one generation, the allegiances of the Calpurnii Pisones had changed once again: the young moneyer of 23 B.C. would be one of the staunchest friends of Tiberius. Fierce independence was a family trait, and the acceptance by such men of Augustus' *auctoritas* could only enhance that *auctoritas*. Finally, the association of Numa with Apollo fits in easily with Augustus[81] while the notion, conveyed by the other republican Numa coins, of the simple and pristine religion personified by Numa also was esteemed by Augustus. Hence the Numa bronzes can also be connected with his plans to hold the Secular Games in 23 B.C., even if these were eventually postponed until six years later.

The meaningful nature of the Numa issue is enhanced by some additional characteristics. The balance of homage to both the *princeps* and the republi-

19. Togate Augustus as priest. Probably after 12 B.C.

can family of one of the moneyers was not only appropriate at this juncture but also recalled the precedent, which again includes Pompey, of republican coins on which moneyers had honored the consul.[82] At the same time, the Numa bronzes look forward to two abiding qualities of the imagery of Augustan coinage.[83] One was a deemphasis of rank military subjects in favor of the theme of peaceful consolidation by a *civilis princeps*. This does not mean, as we will see, the projection of a blissful "Golden Age" or a renunciation of world conquest because *pax* and *victoria* remained closely linked. It was simply that the former now received as much expression as the latter, often with the help of the emblems of a religion that had originated with Numa. A parallel phenomenon was the increasing, and increasingly popular, representation of Augustus in his priestly capacity as exemplified in the famous statue from the Via Labicana (Fig. 19).[84] The other fundamental characteristic the Numa issue shares with much of Augustan coinage and art is an intentional multiplicity of associations and their determination by the beholder who thereby becomes an active participant. This applies even to a standardized image, devoid of much actual information, like the laurel trees (Fig. 17).[85] They evoked the historical compromise of 27 B.C. and the "restitution" of the republic, while the modesty of this emblem called for a comparison with Caesar's honors. Other observers, for equally good reasons, would place more emphasis on the connection of these images with the cults of Vesta and Apollo, and on Augustus' own connection with these cults. In addition, as a symbol of Apollo, the laurel trees signified victory as well as peace.

In its complexity, this example, which is not unique,[86] is instructive of the workings of Augustus' *auctoritas*. It could solicit and accommodate the participation even of those who "did not know to obey," as Tacitus characterizes the youngest of the Pisones (*Ann.* 2.46). Augustus' direct control over this highly unusual and much debated series of Numa bronzes can be safely ruled out. His actions suggested the broad themes, in this case the revival of the old religion, the reestablishment of peace and republican traditions, and the importance of a new *saeculum*. These themes were expressed, elaborated, and extended by individuals in their own way. By connecting them with other themes of their own choice, these participants extended the range of references even further. The same process, with some variations, applies to literature and the arts.

Dio's testimony on the period during which the silver and gold coinage was issued at Rome—the next to the last decade B.C.—provides some valuable background. It illustrates a great deal of give and take between Augustus and the senatorial nobility over an issue that cut close to home, the size of the senate. Attempts to reduce it met with the kind of resistance one would expect. In addition to its swollen numbers, writes Dio (54.13.1), Augustus disliked "not only those who were notorious for some baseness, but also those who were conspicuous for their flattery"; we saw that the coins issued by the moneyers never degenerated into simple adulation. As for concern for values and morals, it became the touchstone of senatorial selection just as it was the hallmark of much of the culture in general: Augustus charged a core of the thirty "best"—in the sense of morally best—men with the selection of the senators (Dio 54.13.2). Finally, the number of members in the senate was brought down to six hundred, with quite a few eligible candidates waiting in the wings. They could work their way up through the magistracies and make up for the natural attrition of the senate's membership.

Those magistracies included the vigintivirate (which included the three moneyers), the quaestorship, and the tribunate of the people. The pattern that developed especially between 16 and 11 B.C. is that of a virtual strike:[87] while there were many qualified candidates, a great number refused to run

for these offices, thus creating a shortage of candidates. Objections to the
new property qualification of 1 million sesterces for a senator were one
factor.[88] Another sore point was the weakening of the traditional role of the
tribunate. Interestingly enough, the opposition came precisely from those
who had the easiest access to senatorial membership, the sons of patrician
senators. Formerly, holding one of the various offices included in the vigintivirate, such as that of *tresvir monetalis*, was enough for a senator's son to join
the senate; now that equestrians were admitted to the vigintivirate, the
quaestorship—by a decree of the senate passed in Augustus' absence—
became the necessary precondition.[89]

The result was that the office of moneyer in the later part of the decade
was not crucial to anyone's ambitions. It was neither a stepping-stone nor a
reward for loyalists, though it continued to be held mostly by young patricians, a large percentage of whom went on to higher offices, including the
consulate.[90] It could even be argued that the self-induced shortage of and
the premium placed on such candidates at the time gave those who held the
office a freer hand and put less pressure on them to curry favor.[91] Whatever
changes took place in the thematics of the coins of the period cannot be
attributed to conformity. Even later at the imperial mint in Lugdunum, Augustus, "by giving no orders at all . . . left the choice of types to an official . . .
whose ideas diverged from those of the other provincial officials."[92] Whereas
Augustus' direct involvement in matters affecting the money supply is evident,[93] the choice of coin types did not merit similar vigilance.

The mint at Rome produced bronze (*aes*) coinage until the year 4 B.C.
When it resumed production after a hiatus in A.D. 10, the place of the
moneyers' names on the reverse is taken by Augustus' titles next to the senatorial SC (Fig. 20). There is no evidence that this development, as well as the
"trend" of types on the precious metal issues from 19 to 12 B.C., was due to
imperial fiat. The decision on what to put on the coins, we may assume, was
still that of the same officials, possibly the individual moneyers. The changed

20. *As* issued in A.D. 11–12. On the reverse, the legend
PONTIF MAXIM TRIBUN POT XXXIIII.

situation with which they—and the poets and artists—had to deal is not that Augustus became more authoritarian, but more authoritative (cf. chapter 8). Increase is endemic to the proper pursuit of *auctoritas*; for good reason, *auctoritas* is related to *augere*. Similarly, as we already have seen, it is also related to *augur* and other priestly offices that Augustus highly prized, culminating in his assumption of the office of *pontifex maximus* after Lepidus' death in 12 B.C. His titulature on the new *aes* coinage of A.D. 10 begins with these priestly titles. Tacitus would sweepingly characterize the phenomenon as the Roman nobility's headlong rush into servility (*Ann.* 1.7). More correctly, the motivation came from a recognition of the *princeps'* increasing *auctoritas*, which was, in turn, enhanced by the increased tribute to him on the coins. A concomitant result was the yet greater authority of such coins, we may assume, in comparison to those with butterflies and flowers.

Finally, increased *auctoritas* denoted increased spiritual and material obligations of the ruler toward those in his care (*cura*). The increasing number of coins with themes and titles related to Augustus can also be understood as an appeal to, and reminder of, his increased role in that sense.[94] Like *auctoritas* and *pater*, *cura* was a concept that was based in the personal realm and could denote official functions of the *princeps* without being legalistic. In contrast to the standardization of such themes under his successors, the process of finding a proper equilibrium between individual initiative and the *princeps' auctoritas* was characterized by dynamic experimentation in Augustus' time. In sum, we are dealing with a subtle system of mutualities, which, due to the elastic and suggestive nature of *auctoritas*, is resistant to simplification.

Certainly, the conventional label of "propaganda" is inadequate to do justice to such a complex and often inscrutable phenomenon. In recent years, there has been a commendable reaction against this traditional perspective, shaped largely in the historical environment of the 1930s, on the function of Roman coinage and imperial coinage in particular.[95] On that view, coinage at best can reaffirm "propaganda" though not create it. At most, coin types can serve as a reflection on, and as a record and affirmation of, something that is already known through other sources. Conversely, some of Augustus' major programs, such as the legislation on morals and marriage (see chapter 3), found no expression in his coinage. Nor do concepts like propaganda or even publicity explain why coins struck in honor of the elevation of Augustus' grandsons to *principes iuventutis* continued to be issued for several years after their premature deaths.[96] Their "publicity" value would be irrelevant. Other suggestions, ranging from inertia to a response to Augustus' abiding attachment to Gaius and Lucius, are therefore more appropriate.

The discussion of Augustus and his coinage—and, for that matter, Augustan literature and art—in terms of propaganda has been characterized by the almost total absence of references to scholarship on propaganda and related topics.[97] It is easy to see why. Propaganda is a complex phenomenon, sus-

ceptible to many different definitions: one survey in 1958 listed twenty-six
such definitions,[98] and there are others. Lindley Fraser, for example, defines
propaganda "as the activity, or the art, of inducing others to behave in a way
in which they would not behave in its absence."[99] Few would ascribe such
stupendous powers even to an *aureus* with Augustus' image on both sides;
further, many "speaking" coins in precious metal had extremely limited
issues while the bronze coins, which had a much larger circulation, were
relatively uninformative. There is agreement, as one modern scholar puts it,
"about one thing only: that propaganda attempts to influence the thinking
of people."[100] Yet, propaganda hardly produces major changes in people's
mental and emotional outlook. Its function is ancillary compared with
deeper values, such as spiritual and religious convictions, and it is not as
important as is often assumed.[101]

Consequently, more recent explanations of propaganda have become
more careful and nuanced and, at the same time, make propaganda less
distinguishable from other kinds of discourse especially in semiotic terms.[102]
As a result, the real power of propaganda now is considered to lie in "its
capacity to conceal itself"—the very criterion Ovid used for the efficacy of
art (*ars adeo latet arte sua; Met.* 10.252)—"to appear natural, to coalesce completely and invisibly with the values and accepted power symbols of a given
society."[103]

We can usefully combine this definition with Michael Crawford's study of
the relation between Roman imperial coin types and the formation of public
opinion. Such a relation is slight, if it exists at all: "There is little evidence,"
he concludes, "for official interest in coin types and even less evidence that
in the Graeco-Roman world coin types which may be called programmatic
had much impact, although other aspects of coins and coin types were noticed."[104] Paramount among these was the identification of authority, which
was the main reason, as we have seen, for the adoption of the obverse with
Augustus by dozens of local mints around the Mediterranean. In his pro-
monarchic advice to Augustus, Maecenas had counseled him that "none of
the cities should be allowed to have their own separate coinage . . . they
should all be required to use ours" (Dio 52.30.9). Augustus neither did so nor
did he need to; *auctoritas* once more triumphed over *potestas*. In addition,
Crawford stresses the importance of experimentation and an independent
artistic tradition.

Propaganda, therefore, is a notion that, like so many others, needs to be
seriously rethought before continuing to be routinely applied to the coinage
and other aspects of Augustan culture. Instead of making sweeping generalizations, we need to proceed on a case-by-case basis. The considerations that
apply to coins from the triumviral period issued at the direct behest of Octavian and Antony, for instance, are not the same as those applicable to the
Augustan principate in the context of the claim that the *res publica* had been

restored. The former are an example of what Ellul and others call propaganda of agitation, especially as used in times of crisis and war. It cannot be sustained for too long and, once the crisis is over, cedes to propaganda of integration, a long-term, "self-reproducing propaganda that seeks to obtain stable behavior in terms of the permanent social setting."[105] While this definition is more applicable to the Augustan principate, the inherited view of the coins as a principal medium of that message needs to be modified considerably.[106] Certainly, many of the extraordinarily varied subjects on Augustan coins do not serve as mere ornamentation. They have a declarative, topical intent, but they are not "propaganda" aimed at winning the hearts and minds of a populace whom we, deprived as we are of so much evidence pertaining to their lives, imagine to be grasping at any tangibles from their times as anxiously as we are.

CHAPTER II

THE RESTORATION OF THE
RES PUBLICA

THE PHRASE "making a statement" has lost a great deal of its meaning today due to overuse, but it applies with full force to the beginning of the *Res Gestae*. The starting point is not Augustus' birth, which, according to traditions current at his time, was accompanied by miraculous premonitions (Suet., *Aug.* 94), or his early years at Velitrae, or his first public appearance in Rome (at the age of twelve, he gave a funeral speech for his grandmother in the Forum), or his adoption by Caesar, or Caesar's assassination, to mention only a few obvious alternatives.[1] Instead, this is how the emperor, when he was seventy-five years old and looking back over his career and accomplishments, presented himself as entering on the stage of Roman history:

> Annos undeviginti natus exercitum privato consilio et privata impensa comparavi, per quem rem publicam a dominatione factionis oppressam in libertatem vindicavi.

> [At the age of nineteen on my private initiative and at my private expense I raised an army, with which I redeemed into liberty the *res publica* when it was oppressed by the tyranny of a faction.]

Every word here is chosen with utmost deliberation because the sentence is designed to open up the principal and manifold dimensions of Augustus' reign. True to what we saw in our discussion of *auctoritas*, the range of associations evoked here is considerable. They are combined with the typical focus on essential concepts for which Augustus provides detailed documentation in the subsequent chapters of the *Res Gestae* before he summarizes them once more in chapter 34. Beginning and conclusion, as several scholars have seen, are intrinsically linked with one another. The young Octavian who comes to the aid of the Roman state as a *privatus* becomes Augustus whose private *auctoritas* is the ultimate guarantee for the state's continuing welfare.

We need to keep in mind that the *Res Gestae*, and especially its momentous beginning and conclusion, was written by an Augustus who had ruled Rome for an unprecedented four decades and who was interpreting events more than describing them.[2] The document is important for what it says as well as for what it omits. This is an essential perspective especially on the historical events that Augustus telescopes and encapsulates in *RG* 1.1: they are shorn of any actual detail so as not to obscure their significance. That significance is developed in ever widening thematic circles, and my analysis of them will follow the same progression. What Augustus implies, evokes, and states programmatically at the beginning of the *Res Gestae* relates to the central values, ideas, and themes that we find in every aspect of Augustan culture. Again, they were not simply the product of his will; the phenomenon is more nuanced, but he was undoubtedly the catalyst.

THE EVENTS FROM LATE 44 B.C.
TO AUGUST 43 B.C.

We saw earlier that as late as October 44 B.C., Cicero regarded Octavian to be without sufficient *auctoritas* although he was Caesar's heir. As Augustus himself put it, he was able to rule by *auctoritas* after he had "extinguished civil wars and was with universal consent in complete control [*potitus*] of all affairs" (*RG* 34.1), but that moment had not arrived in the months following Caesar's assassination. There are different kinds of power, and the sort Octavian needed first and foremost was military muscle, which in turn was based on the availability of ample financial resources and the willingness to expend them.

Having secured the necessary resources, Octavian went to Campania in October of that year and recruited about three thousand of Caesar's veterans.[3] The resulting contingent was more in the nature of a bodyguard (Appian 3.166) than a regular army. It was no match for the legions whose arrival from Macedonia the consul Mark Antony was expecting. With this band, and after trying to solicit the support of Cicero who was absent from Rome, Octavian marched on Rome in early November. He gave a speech to the people on November 10 in which he characterized his action as that of "a servant of the state who harkened to its needs" (Appian 3.169), and he offered the use of his troops against the machinations of Antony. This display of political immaturity led to a fiasco: upon hearing this message, his Caesarian veterans largely defected, keeping their generous pay, while Octavian's impolitic oath that he aspired to the honors of Caesar provoked Cicero's caustic reaction, no doubt shared by others, that he'd rather not be saved by such a fellow (*Att.* 16.15.3). In sum, Octavian had clumsily managed to alienate both the supporters and the enemies of Caesar. The episode ended with his having to leave Rome to the north for Arezzo so as not to encounter Antony, who arrived in the city by the second half of November. Antony did so without his legions, but the reasons for the absence of a coup, if Antony had indeed planned one, had nothing to do with Octavian's actions. Quite the contrary: the discontent that spread among Antony's troops was due to Antony's own dilatory behavior. Loyal Caesarians that they were, they expected to march on Rome and against the senate in order to take revenge for their slain leader. Instead, Antony negotiated with the senate. Had he wanted to stage a takeover and impose his regime on Rome, he could have done so successfully with the enthusiastic backing of his army. Octavian was in no position to stop him.[4]

Another cause of the restiveness among Antony's troops was the disappointingly small monetary incentive he had paid them. Two of his legions proceeded to mutiny, perhaps encouraged by Octavian's emissaries. Deviating from the marching route along the Adriatic coast, they took up positions in Alba Fucens not too far from Rome in order to keep an eye on Antony and his remaining troops who were stationed at Tibur (today's Tivoli) outside the capital. Once more they asked for higher donatives but refused Antony entry into Alba Fucens for direct negotiations. Antony considered the military situation in the north of Italy, where Decimus Brutus held out with several legions loyal to the senate, a greater threat and headed north by the end of November. He left the two mutinous legions to themselves and, for that matter, to Octavian who brought—and bought—them over to his side. Octavian himself turned up in Alba Fucens in the first half of December to take command of them.

He now had a viable army, which he had acquired on his private initiative and at his private expense. Because he was lacking an official power of command (*imperium*), the soldiers, who wanted to lead him to Rome, "furnished him with lictors provided with fasces and urged him to assume the title of propraetor, carrying on war and acting as their leader, since they were always under the command of magistrates. He thanked them for the honor, but referred the matter to the senate" (Appian 3.194).

The decision turned out to be one of the most crucial Octavian was to make. He correctly realized that without the official sanction of the senate, he would remain an illegitimate warlord. The senate, that acknowledged repository of *auctoritas*, could bestow the same on him and he would emerge with *auctoritas* in addition to naked military power. The *quid* of this *ex post facto* sanction of Octavian's military command would be traded off with the *quo* of his renewed offer to put his troops at the disposal of the senate, with no immediate military objective, though in cooperation with the consuls-elect Hirtius and Pansa (both Caesarians from Italy), who were readying their army in support of Decimus Brutus against Mark Antony. The senate, Octavian told his troops, was not likely to refuse his offer this time. Its majority, after all, was still composed of Caesarians; why settle for an extralegal position if he could obtain it legally? Any remaining misgivings of the soldiers were calmed by another round of donatives.

Did Octavian thus rid the *res publica* of the tyranny, such as there was, of the Antonian faction?[5] The answer is: only in Cicero's exquisite rhetoric. Octavian proved a quick learner from his misadventure of the previous month. He now maintained contact with both sides in the struggle and adroitly appealed to Cicero's elephantine ego, seeking him out as a mentor and leading him promptly into the mentorial fallacy of assuming that all of his protégé's plans flowed from Cicero's wise counsel.[6] Whether this was the episode that made Octavian see the light of the *res publica* is a question that deserves more intense consideration later.[7]

The civics lesson (as propounded especially in Cicero's *Third Philippic*) that was about to unfold was certainly most peculiar, though by no means untypical of the late republic. Antony still was the legal consul, soon to be proconsul, and entitled to an appropriate command. If anyone, it was Octavian who had raised arms against all legal authority and could be legitimately defined as an enemy of the state. Cicero's rhetorical pirouettes made it seem exactly the other way around.[8] Octavian's action was to be legitimized; *publica auctoritas* was to be bestowed on *privatum consilium*. Appropriately enough, the argumentation was introduced with the same rhetorical question as the speech against Catiline two decades earlier, which also had led to the approval of illegal procedures: "Up to what point—*quo usque tantum*—will this dreadful war against a nefarious enemy be beaten back by private initiatives [*privatis consiliis*]?" (*Phil.* 3.3). It was high time that it should be joined by *publica auctoritas* because

> the young Gaius Caesar, just about a boy still, with an incredible, nay divine[9] mind and courage [*virtus*], when the rage of Antony was burning at its most intense and when his cruel return from Brundisium was feared like the plague, he [i.e., Octavian], while we were neither urging, nor making plans, nor indeed wishing for it, put together [*comparavit*] a very strong army from that undefeated kind of veteran soldiers, and he spent his patrimony on it . . . no, he used it for the welfare of the state. . . . Had it not been for this, that monster and butcher by the name of Mark Antony surely would have marched on Rome, and that would have been the end of us all and the *res publica.* . . . Of this plague on his private initiative Caesar [i.e., Octavian] delivered the *res publica* [*qua peste privato consilio rem publicam Caesar liberavit*] and if he had not been born in this *res publica*, we would, through the wickedness of Antony, not have a *res publica.* (*Phil.* 3.3–5)

Several things stand out here. First, the obvious parallels with *RG* 1.1:[10] the private initiative, the private army, the deliverance from Antony's oppression, the clause endings *comparavi/comparavit* and *in libertatem vindicavi/liberavit*, and the repeated emphasis on the *res publica* (three times in *RG* 1, five times in one paragraph in the more expansive *Philippic* [3.5]). There is no question, therefore, that Augustus considered the event so important a juncture as to recall Cicero's memorable rendition of it at the very beginning of his *Res Gestae*. When he was Octavian, their import was not immediately clear to him. As late as April 43 B.C., Cicero had to keep convincing him that "we owe our salvation to his initiative" and that he had kept Antony from taking over the city (*ad Brut.* 9.1). After two more *Philippics*, the senate, on January 2, 43 B.C., granted Octavian the *imperium pro praetore*. It also made him a member of the senate with the voting privileges of a former consul (*consularis*). In addition, it reduced Octavian's age qualification for a consulship by ten years, making him eligible for that office in 30 B.C. And he was voted an equestrian statue in his honor.[11]

21. Aureus of Octavian, ca. 29 B.C. Reverse: his equestrian statue.

Augustus' fond memories of this signal event are also indicated by the retention of the statue on Roman coins until ca. 29 B.C. (Fig. 21)—it may not have been completed until then—not long before he discouraged the proliferation of silver statues, including equestrian ones, in his honor in Rome.[12] The aura, however, of saving the *res publica* in Ciceronian terms was not uppermost in the young Octavian's mind: by August of 43 B.C. he had marched on Rome, shortened the senate's generous reduction of his waiting period for the consulate by yet another twelve years by having the people duly elect him consul after the deaths of Hirtius and Pansa in battle, and begun his rapprochement with Antony. By the year's end, Cicero's restless tongue had been pinned to the cave of his mouth when his severed head was displayed on the Rostra. Even while this was the doing of Antony's vengeful wife Fulvia, Cicero while alive was far from trusting Octavian to be the savior of the *res publica*. He appealed to Marcus Brutus to bring his army to Italy (*ad Brut.* 18.1) and vigorously resisted Octavian's contention for the consulship. He was also instrumental in securing a vote in the senate that provided for not filling the consular vacancies until the following year as well as for a consolation prize for Octavian, namely, granting him eligibility to run for praetor at that time. Octavian, quite cognizant in the meantime of Cicero's ambiguous statement that "the young man should be praised, adorned and uplifted" (either to the next rank or to the great beyond),[13] once more appealed to his "mentor's" vanity and ambition by proposing both Cicero and himself for a joint consulate, a proposal the senate rejected.[14]

With that, whatever pretense may have been made about Octavian's regard for the *res publica* vanished. Instead, he appealed to his more than willing soldiers (eight legions by now) on the grounds of "coming to the help of his father" (Appian 3.359). With their eager acclaim, he sent a delegation of four hundred centurions to "negotiate" with the senate. The battle-hardened officers turned out to be remarkably conversant with the eloquent argument Cicero had made in favor of Octavian in December and January, including the irrelevance of age barriers to high office in his meritorious case. The senate still did not accede to their demands and in a show of residual *auctoritas*, some of its members harrumphed a great deal about their interlocutors' lack of "military discipline." The final vignette of the encounter is the leader of the centurions pointing to his sword and announcing that "this will do it, if you don't" and Cicero's sarcastic answer: "If that is the way you ask, he [Octavian] will surely get his consulate."[15] Dio adds that this riposte sealed Cicero's doom. Perhaps not: when Octavian, after the return of the ambassadors, moved with his army against Rome, the senate at the last minute decided to agree to his demands in Cicero's absence. Then Cicero reappeared with the report that new legions had arrived from Africa that supported the senate. The senate promptly reversed itself and enjoined Octavian within a radius of fifteen kilometers around the city. Octavian and his troops entered Rome anyway, amid a generally friendly welcome. Many senators came to pay a visit, including Cicero who reminded Octavian that he had proposed him for the consulate earlier. Octavian poignantly remarked that Cicero seemed to be the last of his friends to greet him (Appian 3.382).

The implied declaration that he was withdrawing his friendship (*renuntiatio amicitiae*) was amply justified: the next night, a rumor spread that the very two legions that had defected from Antony to Octavian in December of 44 B.C. now had gone over to the republic. Cicero promptly tried to organize a night session of the senate and just as promptly disappeared in his litter into the dark when the rumor turned out to be false. His political career was finished; Octavian granted his petition to be released from his duties as senator and, in his reply, Cicero expressed his illusory hope that Octavian would let the past be the past and that there might be a better future. On August 19, Octavian was elected consul and before long became, with Antony and Lepidus, one of the triumvirs "for putting the state back in order" (*rei publicae constituendae*). All this and more lies behind the calm facade of the final sentence of the first paragraph of the *Res Gestae*: "In the same year, when both consuls had fallen in battle, the people appointed me consul and triumvir for the organization of the republic" (*populus autem eodem anno me consulem, cum cos. uterque in bello cecidisset, et triumvirum rei publicae constituendae creavit*).

It is clear that the opening statement of the *Res Gestae*, and its first sentence in particular, were not intended as a precise historical representation but

were meant to be understood in terms of the larger meaning and significance
that Augustus wanted to convey by referring to these events. The process
again is the same as in the case of historical representation in Roman art from
the late second century B.C. on: events are not presented *qua* events, but are
conceptualized and transformed into a paradigm that can be interpreted in
various ways.[16] It is beside the point to label this representational mode as
deception; even the all too copious current practitioners—most of them a
great deal less successful than Augustus—of the contemporary genre of *res
gestae* will not begin their work with outright lies and distortions, but usually
wait for at least two or three chapters.

Augustus' claim was to have liberated the *res publica* on his own initiative
and at his own expense. That is the keynote of the *Res Gestae*, fittingly
amplified by the emphasis on his *auctoritas*, which he ultimately mentions
explicitly in the concluding section. That larger frame of reference, which is
also important for understanding what he means by *res publica*, is evident from
the way he uses the historical events. The real liberation from the oppression
of the Antonian faction came not in 44 B.C. or 43 B.C. when Octavian and
Antony in fact became allies, but in the process of the civil war that concluded with Actium. Augustus' self-representation at the beginning of the
Res Gestae is meant to be suggestive and true in the larger sense rather than
in the documentary sense. As in art, such events take on a fuller and emblematic dimension as time goes on.[17]

Hence, to give but one example here, there is the programmatic emphasis
on his age. Nineteen years—that was younger than Alexander's age when he
set out to leave his imprint on the world. Alexander and his world reign, the
oikumenē, became the inspirational model for Roman leaders in the late republic and the *imperium Romanum*.[18] Coin types and early portraits of Octavian assimilated him to Alexander (Fig. 22)[19] and the typical partition of his
front locks, even in his subsequent and never aging portraits (cf. Fig. 9a),
preserved Alexander's unruly hair in stylized form, expressive of his dynamism. Augustus' use of the Alexander head as his seal can be dated to the
same time as his Alexander-like image;[20] later, two paintings with Alexander
by the great painter Apelles were prominently displayed in Augustus' forum
(Pliny, *HN* 35.93–94); and the poets hint at Augustus' surpassing the feats of
Alexander.[21] Nineteen also put Augustus a few years ahead of Scipio and
Pompey whose early accomplishments had come at an incomparably young
age. Augustus from the very start belonged in the company of these great
men[22] and the younger age at which he joined their ranks was one area of
many in which he aimed to surpass them. There is also an echo of the arguments made at the time on both sides about the issue of Octavian's age. It was
a matter of pride even then for the young Octavian: Velleius reports that his
age was prominently inscribed at the base of the equestrian statue which the

22. Marble head of Octavian, early 30s B.C.

senate had voted him in January of 43 B.C. and notes that except for Sulla, Pompey, and Caesar no Roman had been honored in this way, with an equestrian statue on the Rostra in the Roman Forum, for some three hundred years.[23]

PRECEDENTS

Another important aspect of the opening sentence of the *Res Gestae*, which it shares with the entire document and, indeed, the age itself, is the conscious appeal to an earlier tradition and precedents. It is a typically Roman phenomenon, and the loyal Velleius' phrase is a good example of Augustus' supreme skill at having it both ways: his eminence was extraordinary and yet by no means unprecedented. This abiding respect for Roman sensibilities on Augustus' part stood in strong contrast to Julius Caesar's overt disdain of them and is one of the reasons why Augustus died in his bed after a long life whereas Caesar's was cut short at the base of Pompey's statue.

Thus Augustus' claim to have acted responsibly as a *privatus* for the deliverance of the commonwealth had the firm footing of many antecedents.[24]

The very foundation of the republic had been due to such an initiative, that of Lucius Brutus, who, although he

> was only a private citizen, he sustained the whole *res publica* and was the first in our state to demonstrate that no one is a mere private citizen when the liberty of the citizens needs protection.

> [qui cum privatus esset, totam rem publicam sustinuit primusque in hac civitate docuit in conservanda civium libertate esse privatum neminem. (Cic., *Rep.* 2.46)].

The citizens had been saved: that is exactly the most frequent motto on Augustan bronze coins (Fig. 17).[25] It was all right for a private citizen to take matters in his own hands and rid the state of a public menace. Such had been the case, on Cicero's interpretation, with Scipio Nasica's killing of Tiberius Gracchus because the latter had undermined the state of the *res publica* (*Cat.* 1.3; cf. *Off.* 1.76). More objectively, Scipio Nasica's resort to violence in this instance ushered in one hundred years of civil strife, a situation that was finally exorcised by Augustus. Augustan culture cannot be understood without this background.

For better or for worse, the examples of such appeals increase in the late republic. Pompey, that paradigm of republican virtue, organized a private army drawn from his father's veterans and clients in 83 B.C. and fought on Sulla's behalf. Cicero cites this with approbation as well as Pompey's mission, six years later, to Spain as a *privatus* with proconsular *imperium* where he superseded the regular magistrates. "So much hope was placed in him that the task of two consuls was entrusted to the *virtus* of one young man."[26] A moral quality, *virtus*, took precedence over ordinary legalities, a phenomenon that we already observed as being central to the general operation of *auctoritas*, and Augustus' *auctoritas* in particular. The line is extended to Pompey's son: in the war against Julius Caesar in Africa, Cato tries to stir up the junior Pompey by evoking the memory of his father as a private defender of the *res publica* against oppression (Ps.-Caes., *BA* 22.2):

> Tuus pater istuc aetatis cum esset et animadvertisset rem publicam ab nefariis sceleratisque civibus oppressam bonosque aut interfectos aut exilio multatos patria civitateque carere, gloria et animi magnitudine elatus privatus atque adulescentulus paterni excercitus reliquiis collectis paene oppressam Italiam urbemque Romanam funditus deletam in libertatem vindicavit.

> [When your father was your age, he recognized that the state was oppressed by wicked and vicious citizens, and that good men had either been put to death or else, punished by exile, were deprived of their country and civic rights. Whereupon, impelled by his ambition and the

nobility of his nature, though a mere private citizen and a mere youth, he mustered the remnants of his father's army and delivered Italy and the city of Rome into freedom when they were all but utterly overwhelmed and destroyed. (Loeb trans.)]

The recurrence of the key phrases in the first sentence of the *Res Gestae* is remarkable.[27] Pompey was a respectable predecessor—his image even was carried in Augustus' funeral procession—and so were the elder Brutus and Scipio; this last one, too, had acted decisively as a *privatus* in the public interest. There was nothing revolutionary about Cicero's making the same argument on Octavian's behalf repeatedly in the *Philippics*.[28] The difference was that it was Octavian and his troops, and not the state, that did the prompting (cf. *Phil.* 11.20).

Even that circumstance, however, fades into the background, given the contemporary context of the fluidity between private and public spheres[29] and the rationalization, both genuine and specious, in the name of a higher principle. One of the recognized malaises of the late republic—one that has had a tendency to recur in history in general—was that public officials acted in their private interests. Why, then, not reverse the equation and resort to a *privatus* who was acting *pro re publica*? Nowhere is the extent to which this argument could be pushed more patent than in Cicero's approval of Decimus Brutus' actions in Cisalpine Gaul against Mark Antony. Antony, who was consul, tried to take the province away from Brutus who, in Cicero's words, had undertaken the war on his own initiative (*privato consilio: Phil.* 5.3, 28) even if, as in Octavian's case, the senate subsequently sanctioned it. But that is not all. By the very fact that Brutus had proceeded *privato consilio*, "he judged, and judged most correctly, that [Antony] was not consul" (*Phil.* 3.12)—though, in fact, there could not be the slightest doubt about the legality of Antony's consulate. It was a triumph of deconstructionist politics: one could simply deny the legitimacy of an elected official with whose views one did not agree. It all hinged on one's definition of "the public interest."

The resolution of this issue, which is anything but unfamiliar to us moderns, lies in the realm of moral rather than legal attitudes. It is a good example of the precedence of the former (*mores*) over the latter (*leges*) and is a central aspect of the Augustan "ideology,"[30] parallel to the distinction between transforming and transactional leadership. If the intentions of a *privatus* were indeed to aid the *res publica* in the sense of the *res populi* (cf. Cic., *Rep.* 1.39)—that is, the public interest or commonwealth—then his actions were salutary, appropriate, and justified; it is in those terms that Cicero makes the case for Octavian in *Fam.* 11.7.2. But the Romans also knew of other *privati* who did not act in this exemplary fashion and therefore served as cautionary examples.[31] Moreover, the Roman tradition is unanimous about the individual who tries to rule with strong-arm tactics and does not care about the welfare of the state: that is a *dominus*, a tyrant.[32] Augustus, therefore, contrasts the good *privatus* with the *dominatio* of a faction.

What mattered was the dedication or, at Augustus' time, rededication to the spirit of such ideas, including that of the *res publica*, rather than to the letter. The opening sentence of the *Res Gestae* is meant to capture this theme that informed Augustus' reign and actions and, with it, the entire culture. He did not, at the age of seventy-five, have to defend to his contemporaries, let alone to modern scholars, the constitutional legitimacy of his rule. Instead, as we already saw in his reference to *auctoritas*, he was concerned with present-ing the larger dimensions that pertained to his ideas and shaped the character of the age, including its cultural achievements. Once again, the figure of the *privatus* as a deliverer shares with other Augustan concepts both their multi-faceted, evocative character and their emphasis on a moral core.

Similar considerations emerge from the phrase "I delivered the *res publica*, which was oppressed by the tyranny of a faction, into freedom." Like *privatus* and *auctoritas*, it had a traditional ring to it. *Vindicare*, in fact, occurs in Rome's earliest law, the Twelve Tables. At the same time, *libertas*, just like liberty today, meant different things to different people. The issues raised by Augus-tus' programmatic employment of such words reveal additional aspects of the themes and ideas that guided his principate. Not only were the phrases traditional, they were so well worn as to be hackneyed. Despite all the attri-tion of evidence from antiquity, there are abundant examples of the trope *rem publicam* (or *populum*) *in libertatem vindicare* or its equivalents.[33] Unsurpris-ingly, their temporal range extends from the elder Brutus to Cicero's charac-terization of Octavian's actions. Such slogans are subjective and mirror the absence of *libertas* as a consistent political program in the republic. They can be applied in a totally contradictory fashion, depending on political point of view. For instance, both Tiberius Gracchus and his assassin, Scipio Nasica, are praised, respectively, by Sallust (*Iug.* 42.1) and Cicero (*Brut.* 212) for *vindicare in libertatem* the plebs and the *res publica*. Caesar, whose *vindex* Octa-vian became in fact (*RG* 2), justified the crossing of the Rubicon with the need to right the senate's unconstitutional expulsion of the tribune of the people in order to "deliver into freedom himself and the Roman people who were oppressed by the faction of a few [i.e., the senate]." The phrase is virtually replicated by Augustus, although with the deliberate omission of "himself."[34]

What was good for Caesar had been good, as we saw earlier, for Pom-pey.[35] And for Marius: chiseled in stone, the phrase recurs on the basis of his honorary statue in the Forum of Augustus (*ILS* 59). It was, in the words of an astute observer, "a blank check to be filled in according to the politi-cal persuasions of the user."[36] That, however, did not mean that it could not become strikingly meaningful and effective again at certain times, as is shown by Caesar's example.[37] It depended on who wrote the check—and especially on his credibility and *auctoritas*—for what purpose, and under what circumstances.

We should not assume that Augustus chose this phrase for the beginning of his mature political testament if he, with all due regard for its elasticity and range of associations, had wanted to exhaust its meaning in a mere platitude or in its connotation of cynical manipulation. Rather, the phrase serves several purposes. By deliberately appropriating ideas and a slogan that had been used across the political spectrum in the republic by friends and foes, Augustus signaled that these enmities were a matter of the past and that a new synthesis, drawing on republican precedents, was taking their place. He was the heir not only to Caesar, but to Pompey, Brutus, the Gracchi, Marius, and others; as in the case of *auctoritas* and the coin images, it was left to the beholder to determine the exact association. Another dimension is that the Ciceronian echoes place the sentence in the context of its immediate historical starting point, the years 44 and 43 B.C. This context enlarges the perspective to both the republican tradition of the mottoes and their decline into meaninglessness, which was pithily summed up by Sallust (*Cat.* 38.3): "For, to tell the truth in a few words, all who after those times took part in the government used slogans that had a good ring to them, some in order to defend the rights of the people, others in order to make the *auctoritas* of the senate the greatest. They all pretended to care for the public good, but in reality strove to increase their own power." Against this backdrop, Augustus intends to restore substance to the catchphrase in terms of both its original meaning and its transformation during his reign. Related to the distinction between moral and transactional leadership, *res publica* in essence denotes, as we have seen, a set of principles and values rather than the operation of institutional mechanisms. Hence Cicero could write in the *Republic* that "a state which is in the total control of a faction cannot be truly called *res publica*."[38] These aspects were essential to the *aetas Augusta*, and the beginning of the *Res Gestae* is a carefully planned introduction to it.

It is instructive to note again the parallel between Augustus' technique at the beginning of the *Res Gestae* and that which underlies the most sophisticated examples of Augustan art, such as the Ara Pacis, the Prima Porta statue, and even the Gemma Augustea.[39] They use a concrete historical event as a starting point for illustrating, in an associative manner that is never imprecise, some wider dimensions and meanings of Augustus' rule. The opening of the *Res Gestae* goes yet one step further by referring even to the historical events on two levels: the reference, as we have seen, is not just to Octavian's initiative in 44 B.C. and its immediate aftermath, but to his struggle against Antony in general which was not concluded until 30 B.C. Two years later, the

23. Silver cistophorus, minted in Ephesus 28 B.C.
Obverse: Octavian as *Libertatis Vindex*. Reverse: the goddess Pax.

mint in Ephesus issued the famous silver coin with Octavian's head and the title *Libertatis Vindex* on the obverse, and the goddess Pax on the reverse (Fig. 23).[40] Imperator Caesar had freed Rome and the east from Antony and established security and peace.

LIBERTAS

The conjoining of the particular themes that we find on this coin is not untypical of the meaning of *libertas* in the Augustan principate. While it is a truism that *libertas*, both in concept and practice, "meant different things to different people" even in the republic,[41] its principal meanings can be classified into active and passive. We are dealing either with the freedom *of* doing something actively or with the freedom *from* some kind of prohibition and interference. The long-standing debate about *libertas* under Augustus arises from these different viewpoints. The senatorial aristocracy—and most writers, including Tacitus and Cicero, reflect its bias—very much espoused the former, even if they defined it selfishly in terms of their own freedom of action and not the people's. On the other hand, even the very beginning of the *libera res publica*, to which Augustus alludes by reference to the elder Brutus' actions as a *privatus*, is defined in the "negative" terms of liberation from arbitrary rule by force.[42] The same meaning is, of course, present in the first sentence of the *Res Gestae*. It properly reflects the Augustan inclination to this second definition of *libertas*, which characterized his reign. After one hundred years of civil war, the concern of the populace understandably was to live in tranquillity and peace and to be free from the machinations and disorders that political factions had inflicted on the *res publica*. The excess of *libertas* had degenerated into license (*licentia*); the reaction to it is the redefinition of *libertas* in terms of *securitas*. The concept was pervasive; its attestations include Dio's summary of Augustus' reign (56.43.4), the Alexandrian sailors who cheered him on the eve of his death (Suet., *Aug.* 98.2), and the obverse

24. Denarius of Mescinius Rufus, 16 B.C. Obverse: first letters of a prayer (*vota*) of the Roman senate and people for Augustus.

of a denarius (Fig. 24) with the most comprehensive of Roman numismatic legends, ending with *quod per eum res publica in ampliore atque tranquilliore statu est* ("because through him the commonwealth is in a greater and more tranquil condition").

The basic change under Augustus affected only the senatorial oligarchy adversely. Cicero's writings on the subject of *libertas* are instructive for the prevailing self-perception. He is not a champion of popular *libertas* because it is a threat to senatorial *auctoritas*.[43] He can accept the tribunate, that "bastion of Roman *libertas*,"[44] only so long as it operates within the authoritative consent of the senate. On several occasions he stresses the importance of preserving the appearance (*species*) of popular freedom while keeping all power in the hands of the leading citizens.[45] Livy agrees, noting the timocratic structure of the electoral assemblies (*comitia*), and the absence of the equality of each vote (1.43.10). Given the lack of a truly representative system, there is the realization, expressed by Cicero's spokesman Scipio in the *Republic* (1.47–48) that "the people hardly possess freedom under an aristocracy any more than under a monarchy, however beneficent."[46]

In essence, therefore, the vast majority of citizens in Rome and Italy, who were excluded from significant participation in political decision making, became double losers in the last decades of the republic. *Libertas* in its affirmative sense had traditionally been greatly circumscribed for them, even in regard to freedom of speech (as differentiated from merely expressing an opinion),[47] nor did they enjoy any longer the blessings of freedom from the oppressive misery—economic, social, or political—caused by incessant party strife. Hence they would gladly settle for the welcome return of domestic tranquillity. The fact that it was a monarch who guaranteed it rather than an aristocracy was, for all practical purposes, irrelevant to them. "The monarch was, inevitably"—and at least—"the monarch of everybody"[48] instead of looking only after the interests of a small clique as the senatorial regime had done in the name of its *libertas*. "The Romans," as Arnaldo Momigliano well summed it up, "lost their freedom because they had not shared it." The victory of Augustus, as we noted earlier, was in essence that of the nonpolitical classes of Italy. To them, freedom was linked with benefits, economic and otherwise: "Peace, tolerable justice, an increasing amount of political equality, and fair prospects of a career."[49] At the most basic and tangible level, it was, in the words of the grateful Velleius, "the assurance of each citizen's property rights" (2.89.4), a concept basic to the Roman idea of the state. Such citizens had suffered enough of the abuse of aristocratic power, which led to "an ebullition of protest and hatred,"[50] most of it portrayed unsympathetically by our sources, which, in the characteristic fashion of antiquity, present only the side of the aristocracy and thus condemn such protests as excess of liberty, *licentia*.

Augustus became the ultimate champion of that vast majority. It was for good reason that the only constitutional power, in addition to the *imperium proconsulare*, by which he chose to rule for most of his reign was the *tribunicia potestas*, the power of the tribune, that "bastion of liberty." Augustus chose it aptly: it was the enabling vehicle for carrying out the transactional aspects of his leadership while its legacy of transforming leadership complemented that more important aspect of his rule. For the *res publica* comprised more than aristocratic self-interest: *res publica*, as Cicero says in the vein of a different tradition, is *res populi* (*Rep.* 1.39; 3.43–44). And, in yet another example of the same phrase that Augustus uses in *Res Gestae* 1.1, he affirms that the *res publica*, as *res populi*, is customarily "delivered into freedom from the domination of both kings and senators" (1.48). Like all the words in the overture of the *Res Gestae*, *factio* is not limited to one meaning. As an immediate historical reference it applies to the unnamed Antony. In a larger sense—and again no names needed to be named—it connoted the old-style senatorial clique that had failed in its stewardship of the *res publica*. In fact, as we saw earlier, Cicero says in a similar context (*Rep.* 3.44) that there properly is no *res publica* when it is in the control (*potestas*) of a *factio*.

The senators, we may assume, understood the Augustan writ only too well. It appropriated the traditional vocabulary and syntax, which they had employed for so long, for a new kind of political grammar. As Brunt has noted, in Cicero's conception of the Roman state—and he was the senatorial spokesman par excellence—"the liberty of the people and the authority of the senate are countervailing forces, which must be balanced in such a way as to content the people but permit the senate to preponderate."[51] The system was now moving to another plane where the relationship between the senate and the *princeps* took on the form of the earlier one between *populus* and senate; hence, the passionate proclamations of *libertas*—senatorial *libertas*, to be sure—and its reverberations in the aristocratic tradition, exemplified by Tacitus, which is hostile to Augustus and has been a strong factor in shaping his image over the centuries.[52] In all the ramifications of *auctoritas* we surveyed earlier no mention is made of its encroachment on *libertas*. Preeminent *auctoritas*, however, such as that enjoyed by the senate during the republic and now by Augustus, could have a limiting effect on truly independent initiatives; we have observed some of the resulting nuances, which recur in literature and the arts, in connection with some of the coin issues.

There is an instructive literary parallel that provides a valuable perspective on this question of interdependence and autonomy. Octavian initially was hailed by Cicero as *vindex libertatis* from the menace of Antony. For obvious reasons, he ceased asserting this claim while he cooperated with Antony as a triumvir, only to take it up again in his final showdown with Antony and Cleopatra. At the time of their triumviral entente, it is Horace who uses this claim as a counterchallenge to the Pompeians in behalf of the triumvirs.[53]

He began to write his *Satires* in the late 40s B.C. and presented himself as a new Lucilius. It was de rigueur for a Roman author to define his place in the existing literary tradition, and Lucilius (second century B.C.) had been Rome's most prominent and independent-minded satirist. But when his use of Lucilius as a role model is set against the contemporary political context, Horace's claim gains yet another dimension. Gaius Trebonius, one of the liberators or assassins, celebrated his first taste of that *libertas*, which he evidently hoped the murder of Caesar had restored, by composing an invective explicitly in the manner of Lucilius as a concrete demonstration of this newly found *libertas* (Cic., *Fam.* 12.16.3). His invective was probably aimed at Mark Antony, his former friend and the future triumvir.

It is clear from Sallust and others that to many the Second Triumvirate was a tyranny and incompatible with *libertas*, however one chose to define it. In this context, Horace's choice of Lucilius as a model was not politically naive. When he, the supporter of the triumvirs, is setting himself up in the *Satires* as the new Lucilius, he is inviting us to see the triumvirs as friends rather than enemies of *libertas*. "His own redefinition of Lucilian *libertas* as something morally responsible" suggests "that the triumvirs are opposed not to true *libertas*, which is traditional and responsible, but rather to license, the irresponsible, malicious, and divisive exercise of freedom with which true *libertas* is wrongly confused by those who oppose them."[54] The Pompeians had made capital out of their association with Lucilius as the poet of republican *libertas*. Horace simply inverted their claim. So did Augustus, with reference to several previous claims of the sort, at the beginning of the *Res Gestae* and throughout his political career.

It would be futile to fall back on the schematic explanation that one man "influenced" the other or, worse yet, to relapse into the hierarchical model according to which Horace takes orders from Octavian. Rather, what we see here at an early stage, long before Augustus' expanding *auctoritas*, is a sense of shared direction. Its elaboration is left to the inclination and creativity of the individuals. This accounts for another characteristic that the implementations of both Horace and Augustus have in common: neither is content with simply replicating, respectively, Lucilius' poetry and the catchwords of liberating the *res publica*. Rather, both turn their creative energies to surpassing the model and giving it a meaning of their own.[55] It is a process that is profoundly characteristic of Augustan culture.

RESTORING MEANING TO THE *RES PUBLICA*

Augustus brackets the *Res Gestae* by stating that he set the *res publica* free from oppression and then, in 27 B.C., transferred it to the power of "discernment" (*arbitrium*) of the Roman senate and people, while staying on as its guarantor by means of his *auctoritas*. The immediate meaning of *res publica*, with reference to the events of 44–43 B.C., may well be "the city of Rome" (including the senate),[56] but that is only a starting point. Regardless of whether "republic" is spelled with capital or small *r*, phrases like "the restoration of the republic" (*res publica restituta*) or "the return of the republic" (*res publica reddita*) defy attempts to define them in precise legal and constitutional terms[57] and call for a wider perspective.

That perspective is one peculiar to the Romans' view of their state and history.[58] The Augustan manifestation is but one example of it. Principally, the *res publica* was defined in moral terms. Brutus was wrong, Seneca says, in thinking that "the state could be recalled into its previous form after the former *mores* had been lost."[59] Cicero expands on this subject at greater length at the beginning of the fifth book of the *Republic* in which he discusses the qualifications of the ideal statesman, the *rector rei publicae*. He starts off with a famous quote from Ennius—*moribus antiquis res stat Romana virisque*—and then goes on to employ a metaphor that is consonant with other parallels between artistic and political developments. Like Seneca, he emphasizes that the substance of the *res publica* is lost to the point where it affects even its *forma*:

The commonwealth of Rome is founded firm on ancient customs and on men of the old kind.

This verse, in its brevity and its truth, our poet seems to have spoken in an almost oracular fashion. For neither men alone, unless the state is one of *mores*, nor *mores*, unless men of that kind are in charge of the state, could ever have been sufficient to found or to preserve so long a commonwealth [*rem publicam*] whose dominion extends so far and wide. Thus, before our own time, the moral ways of our forefathers produced excellent men, and eminent men preserved those ways and the institutions of our ancestors. But our age, although it had received the *res publica* like an exquisite painting whose colors, however, were already fading with age, not only has neglected to freshen it by renewing the original colors, but has not even taken the trouble to preserve its configuration [*formam*] and, so to speak, its general outlines. For what is now left of the "ancient customs" on which he said "the commonwealth of Rome was founded firm"? They have been, as we see, so completely buried in oblivion that they are not only no longer practiced, but are already unknown. And what shall I say of the men? For the loss of our *mores* is due to our lack of men, and for this great evil we must not only give an account, but must even defend ourselves in every way possible, as if we were accused of a capital crime. For it is through our own faults, and not by just some accident, that we retain only the letter of the *res publica*, but have long since lost its substance. (5.1–2)

Cicero's comment is representative of a host of others during the period of the late republic.[60] Caesar's was most brusque: "The *res publica* is nothing except a mere name without substance or form" (Suet., *Caes.* 77). Most of these plaints, however, clearly link the ineffectiveness of republican government to a lack of adherence to the old principles and *mores*. The theme is central to the work of the foremost historian of Augustus' times, Livy, whose goal is to demonstrate "what the *mores* were and by what kind of men and by what practices [*artibus*] both in domestic politics and war Rome's *imperium* was brought forth and increased . . . until the dark dawning of our modern day when we can suffer neither our vices nor their remedies."[61]

Lack of *mores* in this context should not be confused with the popular modern conception of Roman "decadence." The Ciceronian passage again is typical in this regard. It defines *mores* positively. Instead of viewing the decline of *mores* simply as a decay of individual morals in the sense of corruption (though corruption certainly existed),[62] it describes the phenomenon in terms of "the disappearance of the substance of shared moral, cultural, and human efforts"[63] and of the lack of public-spiritedness. The *res publica*, as summed up by Ennius' verse, was indeed built on such attitudes. Its formal structures, as I noted earlier, could be totally paralyzed without these. The underlying premise of the *res publica* was the continuing moral challenge to those involved in it to put the commonweal above their personal interests. There was, in fact, no structural safeguard against the selfish manipulation of the government: the famous checks and balances were no protection because they, too, could be used, and were used, for purposes unrelated to the common good. The very structural debility of the constitution mandated constant unselfish cooperation and striving for consensus for the sake of the *res publica*. The cessation of that spirit, and not the technical dysfunction of one or the other magistracy or political entity, was the underlying cause of the problems of the late republic. Even Tacitus, who was no friend of the principate, severely criticizes that period, and especially its final twenty years, for its absence of *ius* and *mos* (*Ann.* 3.28).

It is in moral terms of this order that virtually all our sources describe the decline of the political vitality of the republic. Some attendant dramatization[64] does not detract from the reality of this decline nor does the Roman tendency, from the second century on, to consider any change as a change for the worse. Historians of decline may have a field day with this aspect of the Roman mentality, but it is too generic to be probative of actual decline.[65] The strictures on the inefficacy of the republic, however, go beyond such

25. Fragment from the Esquiline Tomb painting: treaty scene, third century B.C.

traditional jeremiads. "With the disappearance of the old moral attitude . . . the surprisingly primitive [Roman] constitution lost its foundation of functioning meaningfully."[66] If the *res publica* was to be restored meaningfully, a revival of these morals was the precondition.

Before we consider the Augustan dispensation under that aspect, it is useful to look at the diminishing notion of a shared *res publica* in Roman representational art of the late republic. Because of its relative abundance, we have to rely mostly on the coinage. The degree to which it reflects artistic monuments that have not been preserved may vary, although it is reasonable to assume that some kind of overall similarity of conceptualizing tendencies exists.[67]

An instructive backdrop is a painting from the Esquiline tomb of the Fabian family who appeared as another exemplar of assuming, in a private capacity, a military responsibility for the *res publica*.[68] The painting (Fig. 25) refers to a later involvement of the family in the Samnite Wars and combines the aspect of private glorification with the demonstration of public values.

Special importance is given to the making of treaties as expressed by the handshake of the Fabian (on the right) and his defeated opponent. The Roman general, who carries the spear—the sign of *imperium*, which is also one of the connotations of the staff or spear carried by Prima Porta Augustus—guarantees the *fides* of the Roman state. *Fides*—and this again is typical of Roman thinking—is not so much the faithfulness of the conquered subjects to their masters, but the fiduciary obligation of the powerful to all those entrusted to them. It was a cardinal, shared Roman value and an essential concept for Rome's *imperium*.[69] It found its public recognition, among other ways, in the building of temples to Fides and to the personifications of similar values, such as Concordia and Libertas, in the fourth and third centuries.

Beginning with the late second century, there is an increase of self-advertising on the coins as formerly shared public concepts are fragmented into an unrestrained proliferation of private respresentations and values. There are disparate efforts to urge the acceptance of such individual values or "programs" as public ones, but all this expresses only the excessive relativization

of the *res publica* into a multiplicity of *res privatae*.[70] Traditionally communal values are privatized: the Roma Victrix of the entire Roman people on a denarius of 119 B.C. (Fig. 26) changes into the personal goddess of victorious generals from Marius to Caesar, especially the Venus Victrix of Sulla, Pompey, and Caesar.[71] A good example is one of Caesar's denarii (Fig. 27), struck in 44 B.C., which shows his crowned head, with the legend "Imperator" on the obverse, and his ancestress Venus, holding a statuette of Victory in her right hand and a scepter in the left, on the reverse.

26. Denarius of Furius Philus, 119 B.C. Reverse: Roma Victrix crowning a trophy.

27. Denarius of Caesar, 44 B.C.
Obverse: Caesar as Imperator with wreath. Reverse: Venus Victrix.

A related development, which also provides one of the backgrounds for the polysemy of Augustan art, is the plethora of personifications into which the representation of formerly communal concepts and abstractions, such as *libertas, pietas, pax,* and *fides* is dissolved by moneyers who use them for the projection of personal interests.[72] Their representation, which originated from the cult statues of these deities in their temples, now is freed from such a referential context and develops into a multiplicity of personifications, allegories, symbols, and emblems that can be combined and recombined in ever new associative constellations. The range of personifications exceeds the

availability of clearly differentiated iconographies: the same female head, for instance, can represent Pietas, Libertas, and Venus, whereas the same male head can serve for Vulcan, Saturn, Jupiter, and Neptune.[73] The interchangeability continues on Octavian's coinage: the female head (Fig. 28) on the obverse of one of the "triumphal" denarii he issued as *divi filius* ca. 29 B.C. (Fig. 7) has been interpreted variously as Venus, Pax, or Concordia.[74]

28. Denarius of Octavian, ca. 31–28 B.C. Obverse: head of Pax. For reverse, see Fig. 7.

To distinguish between such generic types and others for the purpose of greater intelligibility, a semiotic system arises exemplified by the *pileus,* the cap of the free Roman citizen, which was presented to slaves upon their manumission. The *pileus* becomes the symbol of Libertas and therefore helps to identify her as such (Fig. 29). The symbol makes its reappearance, in a totally abstract fashion, on the coins of Brutus celebrating Caesar's assassination (Fig. 30). An instance of an infinitely more complex combination of various symbols and signifiers of this kind to illustrate a wide-ranging program is a denarius of Caesar from the same series as his Venus/Victory type. The reverse (Fig. 31) is now taken up by the crossed rods or *fasces* (power of *imperium;* the absence of the ax signifies *libertas*) and *caduceus* (staff denoting *felicitas*), while the various sectors are used for a globe (world rule), an ax connected with religious ceremonies (Caesar's priestly offices; *religio* and *pietas*), and a pair of clasped hands (*fides* and concord), besides the moneyer's name. We will consider the complexity and, for that matter, intelligibility of such pictorial programs more properly in connection with Augustan art. For our present purposes, it is enough to note the chorus, though not the symphony, of many different speakers and voices in the late republic, and the discordant din of their proclamations, aspirations, achievements, and designs. This is not to be confused with healthy diversity. It was a far cry from the concord of all citizens (*concordia ordinum*) and the universal agreement (*consensus universorum*) which were essential for the viability of

29. Denarius of Farsuleius
Mensor, 75 B.C. Obverse:
Libertas with *pileus*.

30. Denarius of Brutus, 43–42 B.C.
Reverse: The Ides of March:
pileus between daggers.

31. Denarius by Aemilius Buca
for Caesar, 44 B.C.
Reverse: programmatic emblems.

the *res publica* and were ultimately based on the bonds of the old *mores* about whose loss our sources complain so insistently.

Any true restoration of the *res publica*, therefore, had to begin with the substantive renewal of these values and ideals. Although the much discussed Augustan "program" was a product of many minds, it was single-mindedly intent on reviving the old *mores*. "By new laws," Augustus emphatically says in *RG* 8.5, "passed on my proposal (*me auctore*), I brought back into use many exemplary practices of our ancestors which were disappearing in our time, and in many ways I myself transmitted exemplary practices to posterity for their imitation." Even Ovid, whose attitude to the old *mores* was mixed at best, would agree: "By his own example he [i.e., Augustus] will govern the *mores*" (*exemploque suo mores reget*) a knowledgeable Jupiter prophesies in the *Metamorphoses* (15.834). In the preceding lines, he calls Augustus the *iustissimus auctor* of laws and the bringer of *pax*. "It is as if we were reading words from the *Res Gestae*," one scholar has remarked in amazement.[75]

The essence, then, of Augustus' restoration of the *res publica* was not "the Augustan constitution" but a summons to the old spirit and values of the *res publica* that made it a commonwealth.[76] The republic needed to be rescued not only because Antony's legions threatened it, but because its soul had been lost. Such renewal cannot be mandated by monarchical fiat in a static fashion. Rather, it involved, as it did during the good old days of the republic, a reciprocal process and dynamics of negotiation and renegotiation between ruler and subjects.[77] It called for the activity and initiative of all involved on a broad scale, and not just for those of the emperor. Such initiative and activity are, as we saw earlier, a vital part of the concept of *auctoritas*. Augustus was the ultimate guarantor instead of simply handing down orders. This necessary, wider definition of *res publica* accounts for several aspects of Augustus' "transfer" of government in 28–27 B.C. that are left unexplained by a narrow focus on the governmental or constitutional mechanics of that particular "settlement." It is useful to remind ourselves once more, in this context, that even the republican constitution was only "a system of traditional concepts and principles that did not always keep pace with political reality."[78]

For there are considerable difficulties with construing *res publica* in *RG* 34 as "the Republic."[79] Livy, for instance, in a passage written shortly after 27 B.C., uses the phrase *res publica restituta* to characterize the actions of Cincinnatus (3.20.1) and his phrase refers to "the commonwealth" or "the condition of public affairs." Other contemporary sources, including inscriptions, vary in terminology but point in the same direction. In the epitome of his *History* (134), Livy refers to the events of 27 B.C. simply by saying *rebus compositis*, that is, "when the state's affairs had been put back in order" or "when things had been put back together again." Nor do later writers, such as Tacitus, employ a terminology that denotes "Republic." Others, like Appian (*BC* 5.152), Dio (53.1.1), and Suetonius (*Aug.* 28.1) speak in terms of Augustus' giving back power, which is perfectly consonant with the tenor of *RG* 34, although it does not reflect its wider dimensions. Vitruvius matter-of-factly states that Augustus "freed the Roman senate and people from fear, guides them with his counsels, is taking care of 'the order of the state' [*constitutionem rei publicae*], and is the heir of Caesar's power" (1.1–2). There is not a word in this testimony, which dates to the 20s B.C., of a momentous reassertion of the republic.

Nor do the contemporary poets speak of Augustus in such terms. To Horace, he is *custos rerum* or *custos gentis* (*C.* 4.15.17; 4.5.2), an appellation similar to that found in official inscriptions[80] and which Horace uses in a context of revived traditions (4.15.29: *more patrum*) and freedom from civil wars (17–20). In a similar vein, he addresses Augustus as one who guards the *res Italas* with his arms and adorns them with his *mores* (*Epist.* 2.1.2). That is the endeavor, an ongoing one as we will see, which left an impression on his contemporaries. The evidence does not permit us to speak of the restoration of the republic (or Republic) unless it is in these terms of attempted moral restoration.

Augustus himself does not use a phrase like *res publica restituta* or *reddita*. He stresses that he was in a position of strength, that he was master "of all things" (*rerum omnium*). Of these, he transferred the "public thing," *res publica*, to the *arbitrium* of the senate and the Roman people. *Arbitrium* is a term to which little attention has been paid, perhaps because it is not as much a part of the standard political vocabulary as are other terms. Obviously, Augustus did not rely solely on established political catchwords. The original meaning of *arbitrium* is the "discernment or discussion of what is good and just."[81] *Arbitrium* connotes a participatory, evaluative process. It is the attribute of persons who excercise *potestas*, but it connotes not simply power (*imperium*), but also *ius* and *cura*. Livy, reflecting by his choice of words the legislative power of the people as opposed to the advisory one of the senate, differentiates between *potestas populi* and *arbitrium senatus* (10.24.7). In that light, Augustus' linguistic balancing act is exquisite: he transfers the *res publica* from his sole *potestas* not to the *potestas* of the senate and the Roman people, but to their *arbitrium*. The force of that *arbitrium*, given the meaning of *res publica* as commonwealth, will be proportionate to their commitment to the high-minded principles and values that are essential for maintaining *ius* and *cura* and thus assure the continued existence of such a commonwealth. Augustus is inviting the senate and people to participate with him in taking care of the commonwealth on the basis of law (*ius*) and concern (*cura*) for the common good.

Equally deliberate is the choice of *transferre*. In a passage written not long after these events, Livy has the dictator Camillus return a matter in his *arbitrium* to the senate (5.22.1) in the vain hope that the senate would stand up for an unpopular measure. The term used there, however, is *reicere* ("passing the buck"), whereas *transferre* is a positive summons to accept some responsibility. Even more positively, the moral challenge that complemented the return to legal government can be discerned in Dio's account. This is all the more significant because that account is basically unsympathetic to Augustus (53.2–10). Augustus' speech on that occasion is vague on constitutional details. Instead, it is more important for Dio to have Augustus end it (53.10) with a ringing exhortation to return to the *leges* and *mores* of old and to subordinate private interests to the common good (53.10.4). Preparatory to this is the definition of the state, which he puts at the disposal of the senate and the people, as "the commonwealth."[82]

On the constitutional or transactional level, Octavian's primary aim in allowing his consular colleague to carry *fasces* and in abolishing the illegal and unjust provisions of the triumvirate was, as we saw earlier, to put behind himself the extraordinary powers he had held during the civil war period. But there is yet another aspect to it, appropriate for the nature of the *Res Gestae* as a paradigm of the multireferential nature of Augustan culture. No one else but the late dictator Caesar himself had agreed to such a divestiture in 49 B.C., on the reasonable condition that Pompey do the same.[83] He was ready to rid the state from fear and from his and Pompey's armies, and to turn over free assemblies and the entire *res publica* to the senate and the Roman people. The vast majority of senators accepted the proposal, except for a faction of a few.

The echoes of that event are part of the total texture of the beginning and the conclusion of the *Res Gestae*. Caesar's heir, though he was "in complete control of all affairs," was now reiterating a similar offer. The senate accepted and in turn bestowed on him the honors he mentions in *RG* 34.2, including the name Augustus. He returned all provinces to the senate, and the senate promptly granted him back for ten years a huge chunk of the *imperium Romanum*, consisting of the provinces of Spain, Gaul, Cyprus, Cilicia, Syria, and Egypt. The entire arrangement—and I will return to it shortly for some additional considerations—was, of course, anything but unpremeditated. It is a good illustration of the incipient dynamics of give-and-take and of the experimentation that characterized both Augustan government and the culture at large.

Another perspective on the *Res Gestae* and the interpretation of its momentous beginning and conclusion is provided by some aspects of historical representation in Augustan art. The figural decoration of a set of two silver cups from Boscoreale constitutes a thematic synthesis of many of the guiding ideas of Augustus' reign. The cups date to the very last years of his rule, precisely the time when he composed the *Res Gestae*.[84]

The sides of the first cup show two representations of Augustus. On one side (Fig. 32a), he is seated on a curule chair, the emblem of Roman magisterial power, holding a globe in his hand and turning toward Venus. Venus holds a statuette of Victoria out to him and is followed by the goddess Roma and the Genius Populi Romani, the personification of the entire Roman people. To his left, Mars leads a procession of the personifications of seven provinces. On the cup's other face (Fig. 32b) we see a seated Augustus as the successful imperator, sitting on the Roman commander's chair and receiving, with the gesture of *clementia*, barbarians who are surrendering themselves and their children. The image combines specific and generic aspects. The dress of the subjects points to imperial campaigns in the north or, possibly, the west, and therefore the scene can fit several events. The reliefs on the other cup represent an imperator's sacrifice, prior to a military expedition, in front of the temple of Capitoline Jupiter (Fig. 33a) and, on the other side, his return in triumph (Fig. 33b); his physiognomy there marks him as Tiberius. We see here somewhat of a reversal, which kept Augustan art from becoming schematic, of the progression from the specific to the general: there is the same interplay between latitude and precision of reference that we have observed repeatedly, beginning with the concept of *auctoritas*, but the frame of reference is limited because Tiberius celebrated only two triumphs.

The salient point is that the pictorial program aims at more than presenting a history of events. The panel with Augustus as a world ruler is the most general with its range of intentional associations and symbols that speak to essential aspects of his rule. The triumph with Tiberius is the most specific, although being applicable to more than one occasion, and the scene with the peaceful surrender of the barbarians lies between these two poles. The overall conception has been summed up well as follows: "The scenes in their ensemble are arranged not so as to constitute a biography, but to represent a concept of exemplary attitudes. They are arranged according to perspectives not of chronology, but of guiding ideas."[85]

The characterization is just as apt for the *Res Gestae*. Like the artistic representations, it is remarkable also for what it chooses not to include. It is not a chronological list of achievements and honors but is guided by the concepts that made the age specifically Augustan, such as *auctoritas*. If the referential dimensions were limited to specific events and no more, Augustus' choice of commencing the document with recalling the vicissitudes of the years 44 and 43 B.C. would project him as no more than a political adventurer who, aided by luck and tenacity—though mostly by luck in the early stages—ultimately prevailed in the struggle for power.[86] The referentiality of the *Res Gestae*, however, is far more opalescent. Behind the mention of the *res publica* especially in *RG* 34.1 and the transfer of involvement in it, stands the commitment to a transforming, moral program of values and ideals.

In that sense, the evocation of the *res publica* was not a pretense. The new regime was serious about restoring the morality and dignity of the old senatorial and equestrian orders.[87] Nor did Augustus treat the transactional aspect of the *res publica* as a sham. A great deal of respect was paid to republican formalities, quite in contrast to Caesar's modus operandi. Even if we accept their characterization as ritualistic and ceremonial to some extent, the connotations are not pejorative: ritual and ceremony are vehicles of meaning and even power.[88] Just as important, as several recent studies have documented, true substance in terms of real negotiations and compromise was not lacking from the settlement of 27 B.C. and subsequent arrangements.[89] The role of the senate changed, but it was anything but insignificant. The same is true of senatorial self-representation: traditional means of self-enhancement, such as buildings in the capital, gave way to others like buildings in cities and towns other than Rome—the Augustan vision involved more than the *urbs Roma*—

32. Silver cup from Boscoreale. (a) Augustus the world ruler.
(b) Augustus receiving the surrender of barbarians.

and to much longer lists of honors in their honorific inscriptions. These
could now be displayed during an individual's lifetime rather than be commemorative as had been the practice earlier.[90] As the *Res Gestae* itself illustrates, accumulations of honors were a strong basis of *auctoritas*.

Nor was membership in the senate an empty honor: "It is beyond question that the new system involved continual reference of all sorts of measures
to the senate for its approval in accordance with Republican practice."[91]
Hence the fierce resistance, as we have seen, of the senators to Augustus'
attempts to trim their number to three hundred, which, paradoxically, had
been the senate's traditional size under the republic.[92] There were genuine

33. Silver cup from Boscoreale. (a) Sacrifice at Tiberius' departure.
(b) Tiberius triumphant.

debates on proposals such as new taxation for military expenses and the marriage legislation.[93] Augustus punctiliously attended senate meetings, though
with armor under his toga (Suet., *Aug.* 35.1; Dio 54.12.3); the debate could
become heated and laced with personal invective to the point where Augustus sometimes left the house, defending all the while the senators' right to
speak freely about the *res publica* (Suet., *Aug.* 54.1; cf. 55–56. and Dio
54.27.4). There was the mix of tradition and innovation that is typical of
Augustan culture, but the changes made by Augustus were consistent with
the senate's purpose: (1) Augustus himself, instead of the republican censor,
performed the review of the senatorial roll (*lectio senatus*) three times. Even

on the first such occasion in 29 B.C., the purpose was not simply to eliminate political opponents (several of Antony's supporters, such as C. Furnius and C. Silius, stayed on), but men who were morally and socially disreputable.[94] (2) A smaller advisory committee, the *consilium principis*, which began functioning some time between 27 and 18 B.C., consisted primarily of fifteen senators who were chosen by lot and thus constituted an additional, less formal way to solicit opinions from a cross section of the senate.[95] (3) The *Lex Julia de senatu habendo*, put forward by Augustus in 9 B.C., seems to have been a comprehensive codification of existing rules, which had never been written down, such as attendance and the requirements for a quorum.[96] There had been neglect, and Augustus wanted the senate to function properly.

Two considerations emerge that illustrate once more the nuanced character of the Augustan dispensation and its underlying dynamic tensions. One is the connection between expediency and high-minded purpose. No one wanted a return to the civil wars, which had been brought about by a republic out of control. The immense yearning for peace and order was genuine. It found eloquent expression in the poetry of Vergil and Horace; both also were greatly worried about Octavian's permanence.[97] Augustus, the republican monarch, was the only guarantee against the relapse into the bad old days of that very republic. The Romans were unpleasantly reminded of these days when, in the wake of the revival of republican practices encouraged by Augustus, the two censors of 22 B.C. started infighting (Vell. 2.95.3; Dio 54.2.2) and one Egnatius Rufus, who was popular with the plebs and had tried to get himself elected consul before he was eligible, caused violent unrest in 19 B.C. when the consul of that year tried to block his efforts.[98] The matter was settled with an iron fist after Egnatius was found guilty of conspiring, with several accomplices, against the *princeps*, who was absent from Rome at the time: Egnatius was imprisoned and put to death.

Occurrences like these testified to the inherent weakness of the republican institutions. That weakness was compounded by the successful revival of the traditional way of conducting politics in the senate: there returned "competition, rivalry, disagreement on issues and principles."[99] It was not disadvantageous to Augustus, therefore, to maintain these institutions "for they generated a perpetual state of emergency and crisis; civil war was a permanent threat; and that created a perpetual need for and reliance on an Augustus, as savior of the *res publica*."[100] This is definitely one aspect of the continual maintenance of the republican system on Augustus' part. A similar convergence of self-interest and a higher idealism applies to the relationship between one of his institutional powers, the *imperium proconsulare*, and his legislation on morals and marriage: that power called for new conquests, which had to be justified by the superior moral standards of Rome's ruling classes.[101] Much to the chagrin, perhaps, of modern historians, there is no quantifiable way to determine the exact extent to which Augustus' commitment to republican traditions was based on calculations of self-interest. I would argue, however, that it was secondary rather than primary in nature. He demonstrated a real commitment to the spirit rather than the letter of republican *mores*, which, at the same time, necessitated that republican forms not be treated cavalierly. That commitment, in turn, may have stemmed from the realization that there were no desirable alternatives. Augustus, then, attempted to revive the *moral* foundations and traditions of the *res publica* without restoring the republic in all its *transactional* workings. The result is the peculiar mix of the principate as part monarchy and part republic.

Before we return to the question of the genesis and formation of these convictions on Augustus' part, a few comments are in order on another, basic issue that is central to an assessment of Augustus' relationship with the senate and to the culture of his age at large. It is the problem of the relation between a de facto monarch, who has preeminent *auctoritas* and definite intentions, and the possibility of genuine *libertas*, and especially freedom of creativity, on the part of other individuals. There is no easy answer precisely because we are looking at a process (and not a state) of mutuality and reciprocity, which, at Augustus' time, was far from rigid; the ramifications of the Numa coins issued by Calpurnius Piso in 23 B.C. are, as we saw earlier, a good illustration of the pertinent complexities.[102] The Augustan mode of government was new and experimental and required continuing adaptation on the part of all those involved. Any fixity, if there ever was such, materialized only in the reign of later *principes*. As a result, the culture—political, literary, artistic, and other—that developed under Augustus called for a creative response. For the most part, it could be shaped, and was shaped, as much by individuals besides Augustus as it was by him: the Augustan culture is Vergil's and Ovid's as much as Augustus'.

True enough, the degree to which this was achieved was different in the arts and letters than in politics. Even there, however, the parameters for creative adaptation were extensive, being delimited only by the accepted impossibility, short of assassination, of removing Augustus from power. But then it was he, aided by men like Agrippa and others, who tackled with "determination, patience, hard work, and, mostly, success"[103] the real problems that the senate had been unwilling to solve, such as the needs of the urban plebs and the professional soldiers, the provinces, and the neglected municipal aristocracies of Italy. That framework left a great deal of room for initiative and even invited it. The real reason for the lack of outstanding individual achievement in this area, in contrast to its presence in other areas of the culture,[104] may have been the relative lack of talent rather than the uncertainty of how to behave vis-à-vis the princeps with his *auctoritas*; that mildly paralytic attitude itself can be considered an inadequate response to the challenge that was posed. The response is understandable in view of the equivocal appearance of Augustus as the center of real power and, simultaneously, his emphasis on being an accountable servant of the state: "How could men be sure when he was seeking advice for form's sake, or sincerely wished for counsel and was prepared to act in accordance with the general wish? Moreover, his patronage in the conferment of offices and privileges was vast, and those whose careers depended on his favor might naturally think it best to say what they supposed, not always correctly, to be in his mind rather than their own."[105] It was for reasons like these that Tiberius expressed the wish he could be called "counselor" (*suasor*) rather than *auctor* (Suet., *Tib.* 27).

The mutual responsibility for the creation of a suitable political atmosphere was well recognized by Tacitus. To him, *libertas* and its opposite, *servitus*, are the result not so much of external constraints as of inner will.[106] In his opinion, one of the worst aspects of the principate is that it can lead to abject servility on the part of those who were essential to the governance of the state: consuls, senate, and equestrians (*Ann.* 1.7.1). But, as he makes clear on several occasions, that condition stems primarily from self-inflicted attitudes. They were exemplified by the senators' large-scale refusal to assist in needed activities, such as a more efficient system for the grain supply and the sponsorship of rebuilding roads.[107] Activities of this kind, however good for the commonwealth and in spite of the Via Appia, were not considered prestigious enough by Roman aristocrats for gaining honors and distinction. New initiatives, therefore, fell to Augustus almost by default, and the senate passed on its responsibility, and opportunity, "to reformulate the relationship between the *res publica* and the man who had formerly possessed total power."[108]

By contrast, such attitudes did not prevail among the foremost Augustan writers who were perfectly aware of Augustus' status. It is typical of Horace that he brings up the matter playfully. Poets have a mind of their own, he says in one of his earliest Satires (1.3). They do not want to recite (or write, for that matter) even when you want them to, but when they are not ordered (*iniussi*) you can't get them to stop. Tigellinus was a notorious case in point; Caesar Octavian, who could have compelled him, begged him in the name of his own friendship and Julius Caesar's, but to no avail whatever (1.3.1–6). The vignette can be viewed against the backdrop of Julius Caesar's prevailing, with the promise of a huge fee, on the aged mime-writer Laberius to perform as an actor in one of his own creations, despite his equestrian status (Macrob. 2.7.1–3). Laberius, an exemplar of fierce independence (*libertatis*) as Macrobius calls him, did so but prefaced his performance with a lengthy complaint, which elicited Macrobius' comment that "power does compel, not only when it invites, but also when it beseeches." "Power" here is rendered as *potestas*. Augustus' *auctoritas* made matters more nuanced. It is possible to argue that it was perhaps easier to practice a greater degree of *libertas* in the arts than in the realm of government and politics under Augustus, which might explain the fruition of some outstanding talents in the former. That, however, does not amount to a complete explanation. In literature, at any rate, men emerged who had similar talents as Augustus, whose creative works were similarly complex, and who, whether they agreed with him or not, used the moral direction he provided as a point of departure for their own reactions and reflections. It is these qualities, and not any ideological concurrence, that make them "Augustan." They were not afraid to innovate and thus become pioneers.[109] The same is true of art and architecture where the impetus given by Augustus leads to autonomous developments and a pinnacle of creativity rather than "propaganda."

The history and culture of the Augustan age, therefore, cannot be understood simply as the product of one man's will, a biographical fallacy that haunts many studies of the period.[110] The phenomenon, as we already saw in connection with *auctoritas*, is more variegated, and the cultural dynamics of the age were not simply a manifestation of his "program." The developments could not have taken place without his providing a vision that could be shared, resisted, and individually interpreted by many, therefore calling forth the kind of creativity, vitality, originality, and transcendence of its own time which made his age one of the most vibrant and influential in history. Much of this was due to a conscious rethinking and reviving of essential Roman values and *mores*. If they had not been convictions that were deeply held by Augustus, their inspirational value would soon have dissipated or lapsed into the frozen forms we know from neoclassicism. To what can we attribute Augustus' commitment to them?

We can—quite easily, in my opinion—dismiss the naive picture that has been drawn of the young Octavian learning about the value of republican principles at Cicero's knees in 44–43 B.C.[111] The events, and that is one reason I set them out in some detail earlier, clearly reveal Cicero's duplicity and opportunism no less than Octavian's. A major difference, perhaps, was that Cicero, who earned his living by rhetoric, talked out of both corners of his mouth infinitely faster.[112] He had praised Caesar as a god, then helped stab him in the back; he advocated a special command for Octavian, but pleaded exactly the opposite argument in the case of Publius Servilius a few months later, even while being uncomfortably reminded of the precedent (*Phil.* 11.19–20); he boasted of being the source of all of Octavian's plans only to hint at Octavian's demise with a not so subtle double entendre. The list need not be prolonged. In his behavior, Cicero exhibited all the speciousness of the late republic. Vain weathervane that he was, he is an unlikely candidate for impressing on "that very young man, almost a boy still" the true spirit of Rome's *mores* of old.

Though Cicero was no role model, Augustus did enact, for all practical purposes, Cicero's transactional program such as reestablishing the rule of law, dealing effectively with military affairs and the grain supply, and enhancing the *dignitas* of the Roman empire both by military and diplomatic successes and by a building program in the capital.[113] It is not that the senatorial aristocracy of the late republic did not know what needed to be done; it is simply that they failed to do it. Yet another matter is Augustus' ostensible exemplification of traits of the ideal ruler whom Cicero depicts in the *Republic*. Phraseological and conceptual parallels abound. In Cicero's own words, the *res publica* is about the *optimus status civitatis* (*ad Q. Fr.* 3.5.1). To be called *auctor optimi status rei publicae* was also Augustus' cherished goal (Suet., *Aug.* 28.2). He aimed to lay a foundation of the *res publica* that would last. For achieving such an optimal condition of the state it is essential that *mores* be sown, as Cicero put it (*Leg.* 1.20). A close relation exists between the character of the *res publica* and that of its ruler or rulers: *talis est res publica, qualis aut eius natura aut voluntas qui illam regit* (*Rep.* 1.47; cf. *Leg.* 3.31). The leader of the state—defined as *gubernator*, *rector*, or *moderator*—governs by his *auctoritas* and only incidentally by his *potestas*.[114] That, in essence, is the nature of the *principes rei publicae*.

The "ideology of the *princeps*" in the *Republic*, as it is sometimes called, however, was not a blueprint for Augustus because, first, Cicero referred to several such *principes* or leaders in the Roman past[115] and, second, Cicero was not advocating a de facto monarchy for even the wisest and most just ruler because "*libertas* does not consist of serving a just master, but no master at all" (*Rep.* 2.43). In addition, and in accordance with Cicero's vanity, several passages indicate that the characterizations he chose for the *princeps rei publicae* are applicable to none other than Marcus Tullius Cicero himself.[116] Furthermore, the excessive extent to which we have to rely on the few written sources from antiquity too often blinds us to the obvious fact that so much of what went on was a matter of oral discussion. Clearly, the disarray of the late republic occasioned all kinds of exchanges among thoughtful people about the nature of the government, the role of the citizens, the duties of the rulers, and related topics. That is the source of many phraseological echoes and recurrences we constantly observe, whether they be slogans or coincidences between passages in the *Res Gestae* and in Ovid and Propertius.[117] The extended though fictional debate in Dio between Agrippa and Maecenas is a splendid reflection of the vivid discussions that must have taken place in Augustan and other circles about the kind of rule he should adopt and its goals (52.1–40). Augustus did not need to study Cicero's *Republic* to chart his course.

Instead, his commitment to the *res publica* and its traditional values was more likely a gradual and evolutionary process.[118] The one constant of which we can be sure is that from his beginnings as Caesar's young heir, his aim was to seize power, to remain master of the state, and never surrender his ultimate control of it. The senate's sanction of his propraetorian *imperium* in January 43 B.C. was a marriage of convenience at swordpoint which left few illusions at the time (cf. Cic., *Phil.* 11.20) and should not give rise to any now about his early conversion to republican ideals. The decade of the 30s was marked increasingly by Octavian's assuming the mantle of the true protector of Italian and Roman traditions against Antony's presumed orientalizing. The tenor of this campaign against Antony was so strong[119] that it appears even in the *Aeneid*, which overwhelmingly transcends such purely nationalistic aspects otherwise.

> On one side Augustus Caesar, high on the stern, is leading
> The Italians into battle, the Senate and the People with him,
> His home-gods and the great gods: two flames shoot up from
>   his helmet
> In jubilant light, and his father's star dawns over its crest.
> Elsewhere in the scene is Agrippa—the gods and the winds
>   fight for him—
> Prominent, leading his column: a proud decoration of war,
> The naval crown with miniature ships' beaks, shines on his head.
> On the other side, with barbaric wealth and motley equipment,
> Is Antony, fresh from his triumphs in the East, by the shores of
>   the Indian
> Ocean; Egypt, the powers of the Orient and uttermost Bactra
> Sail with him; also—a shameful thing—his Egyptian wife
>
> . . . .
>
> Barking Anubis, a whole progeny of grotesque
> Deities are embattled against Neptune and Minerva
> And Venus.
>
>   (8.678–88, 698–700, trans. C. Day Lewis)

We have no way of determining, however, to what extent such exploitation of nationalistic themes and the proclamation of the traditional virtues of Italy were transformed into genuine convictions at the time. There is certainly much of the latter in Vergil's *Georgics*, written in the 30s, despite fashionable attempts to deconstruct the poem, and Vergil's emphasis on unremitting effort can be considered a significant contribution to the formation of the Augustan ethos.[120] As for Octavian, his primary goal was the elimination of Antony, and any attempt to revive national feeling was subordinated to that purpose.

Then came the juncture that has puzzled so many modern historians. Despite their premise that history is about change,[121] that recognition is privileged for interpreting events and designating "transitional periods" rather than for understanding human character. In retrospect, which is another privilege of the historian, we can see that, after Actium, Octavian had basically two choices. One was simply to continue as a military strongman. It was no obstacle that the dictatorship had been abolished, at Antony's request, soon after Caesar's death. Other extraordinary commands and powers were available and would have sufficed. But regardless of formulaic niceties, that would have looked like the rule of a king, and *affectatio regni*, the striving after kingship, was one of the strongest negatives in Roman government and thinking. So were the kindred *dominatus* or *dominatio* ("rule by force" or "strongmanship") that verge dangerously on tyranny.[122] That is precisely the kind of rule which Augustus abjures in the first sentence of the *Res Gestae* and which he instead imputes to others.

As for other options, the traditionalism of the Romans and their fixation on the *mores maiorum* left little alternative except for the seemingly paradoxical one of revitalizing that very traditionalism.[123] It was more than a superficial appeal to national feelings. Rather, it invited intense reflection—which was by no means uncritical—on the special character of the Romans, their *Romanitas*, and the resultant obligations and responsibilities. It did not mean a facile return to the pre-Rubicon republic, something nobody expected to happen anyway. Continuing modification was well recognized as a principle for the maintenance of tradition, and the governmental adaptations made by Augustus fell within the boundaries of continuity through inoffensive change. Radical new departures were neither feasible nor palatable.[124] Hence, for instance, we cannot expect the creation of a representative or more democratic form of government. It would have been too startling an innovation without promising the immediate existence of a leadership ready to take on the accumulated unsolved problems. At the same time, it was unsatisfactory to return the traditional forms of doing things to a state of normalcy without a meaningful attempt to revitalize men's consciousness of the concepts and the spirit to which these forms owed their existence.

All this is more easily conceptualized than realized, and in the actualization lies the special character of Augustus' rule. It was a process that called, as we have seen repeatedly, for participation; one recent scholar has well observed that "his striving to have as many citizens as possible participate in the life of the state represents a common characteristic of Augustus' religious policy, his building program, and his support of the arts."[125] At the same time, the particular course that Augustus chose is again thoroughly rooted in the many-sided Roman concept of *auctoritas*. As Richard Heinze noted in his fundamental discussion, *auctoritas* for the Romans was a way to compensate for the limitation placed on officially recognized power in both the private and public realms. In their private life, this affected mostly the power of the *pater familias*—and we should not exclude these connotations from the title *pater patriae*, which Augustus received in 2 B.C.—while in public life, the traditions of the republic limited most office holders to terms of one year, though exceptions burgeoned in its last century. But, as Heinze points out, the Romans were *Machtmenschen*, men who had a strong urge for power, "and this urge for power finds a substitute for these deprivations [caused by the restrictions] in the possession of a power which is not legally guaranteed or in a legal position to command, but [in a power] which is actually brought to bear."[126] It can be exercised, Heinze continues, both for the good and the bad; at its best, it merges with the Roman concept of social responsibility and is put in the service of the commonweal.

It is clear from the preceding discussion merely of the political aspects of Augustus' reign how complex, dynamic, and even contradictory a creation it was. It was a mix of political calculation, pragmatism, a sure sense of the true nature of power and its use, and a genuine understanding and appreciation of Roman traditions and sensibilities—perhaps due in part to Augustus' upbringing in the small Italian town of Velletri—in addition to some deeply held convictions and a resulting vision and sense of direction. It provided a broad spectrum of possible meanings, a characteristic it shares with other aspects of Augustan culture. Tacitus, in two famous chapters at the beginning of his *Annals* (1.9 and 10), furnishes a prominent example of two different ways of looking at the Augustan phenomenon. It has been recognized less fully, however, to what extent several of his references in the preceding chapters can also be read as a pointed commentary on some of Augustus' major claims.[127] With as much doggedness as perception, Tacitus controverts or quietly contradicts them, thereby laying the basis for his indictment of the principate. The Tacitean mirror, therefore, is useful both as a contrapuntal epilogue and as negative proof of the accuracy of our identification of some of Augustus' distinctive attainments.

A TACITEAN CODA

In the beginning sentences of the *Annals*, Tacitus boldly moves from Rome's beginnings to the time of Augustus. He juxtaposes the rule of the kings with the establishment of *libertas* by Brutus, stresses the absence of protracted office holding and the relatively brief time even of the *dominatio* of Sulla, and before we know it we have arrived at the reign of Augustus, who took everything under his own *imperium* because of the general exhaustion from the wars. In their immediacy, sweep, omissions, and lack of preliminaries, the sentences are a match for their counterpart in the *Res Gestae*, in contrast to which not a word is said here or later of Augustus' liberating the *res publica*. Quite the opposite: his rule is marked by everyone's readiness for servility (2.1; cf. 7.1); he held offices several times over (9.2)—the precedents are not mentioned— and his *dominatio* as *dux*[128] outlasted anything Rome had previously seen. As for the sources of his power, there is no mention of *auctoritas*. Instead it rested on (1) the elimination of all competitors (2.1; 10.1–4); (2) "his seducing one and all with the sweetness of leisure" (*otium*; 2.1)—not only is the reference to *otium* ironic, implying the perversion of a political ideal of the late republic ("peace from civil strife, and order"), but the specifics of the Augustan solution (which, as we have seen, amounted to a successful implementation of the program of Cicero and others) to the problems of the soldiery, the grain supply, and the end of civil unrest, are presented as a bribe that effectively reduced the populace to political indolence; and (3) the troops, who even had to come out to guard his funeral (8.6).

In that vein, the nuanced interplay between Augustus' *auctoritas* and the latitude of everyone's participation is wiped away with reductionist terms such as Augustus' "commands" (*iussa*; 4.1) and everyone's *servitium* (7.1). Instead of being, in his own words, *auctor optimi status* (Suet., *Aug.* 28.2), Augustus perverted it (*verso civitatis statu*, 4.1).[129] Quite in contrast to the revival of the old *mores*, nothing was to be found of them anywhere (*nihil usquam prisci et integri moris*; 4.1). In fact, opportunistic nobles disclaimed the old ways and preferred the security of the present, "increased as they were" (2.1: *aucti*, from the verb etymologically related to *Augustus* and *auctor*) by the new "state of affairs" (*novis rebus*); the phrase *res novae* in Latin is almost always pejorative and usually means something like "overthrow." So far from being morally reformed they were bought off by wealth (precisely a major source of evil in the various denunciations of the collapse of traditional morals) and by honors; the latter may well refer to the quantitative reorganization by Augustus of senatorial honors.[130] The foil for the Tacitean phrases is Augustus' nuanced statement in *RG* 8.5: legibus novis *me auctore latis multa exempla maiorum exolescentia iam ex nostro saeculo reduxi*—"by new laws passed on my proposal I brought back into use many exemplary practices of our ancestors which were disappearing in our time."

The beat goes on: Octavian's unsavory ascent was that of a *privatus* (10.1), guided only by lust for power; even his revenge on Brutus and Cassius, who commanded the last army that was *publica* (2.1), was an act of private vengeance (10.3); and the legitimation of all these actions by the senate or the people is totally omitted because it was phony by implication. There was a *consensus universorum* of sorts, indicated by the phrase *consules, patres, eques* (cf. *RG* 35.1): they all rushed into servility (7.1). Instead of heralding the advent of the *pater patriae*, Augustus' reign became notorious for inflicting the machinations of Livia, who was a harsh mother (*gravis mater*), on the *res publica* (10.5). There is a possible slur here: she was pregnant, that is, *gravis*, when Octavian married her and then became *gravis* toward her family and the citizenry. Its level is matched only by that of Tacitus' snobbery toward Agrippa, who was "ignoble by descent" (3.1). It was a well-aimed hit: Agrippa never used his family name, Vipsanius, in any of his numerous inscriptions. Other qualifications, and Agrippa's record and achievements, did not matter to our aristocratic writer. After all, Tacitus' peers had snubbed Agrippa even upon his death (Dio 54.29.6).

Tacitus was not unaware of the severe shortcomings of the republic (*Ann.* 3.28; *Dial.* 40–41). His perspective on Augustus, however, is thoroughly jaundiced and proceeds from the narrowest of biases. The problem, to which I adverted before, is the paucity of our sources from antiquity and their frequent limitation to an aristocratic perspective. Both these considerations make it abundantly clear that Tacitus' influence on later historiography, which often served as a comment on its own times as much as on those of Augustus, has been disproportionate.[131]

CHAPTER III

IDEAS, IDEALS, AND VALUES

SEVERAL guiding ideas and values were part both of an ongoing discussion in Augustus' time and of Augustus' style of transforming leadership. They do not, however, amount to an "ideology" in the modern sense of the word.[1] It is useful to examine four examples in some detail.

THE *CLUPEUS VIRTUTIS*[2]

At the senate session of January 13, 27 B.C., when Octavian returned the *res publica* from his *potestas* to the *arbitrium* of the Roman senate and people, the first action of the senate was to honor him with the title "Augustus" and to set up a golden shield in the new senate house, named Curia Iulia after Julius Caesar. The inscription on the shield lists four virtues: *virtus, clementia, iustitia,* and *pietas*. The mention of all this, as we saw earlier, is part of the finale of the *Res Gestae* and leads up to Augustus' statement that he ruled by his *auctoritas*.[3]

As always, there are multiple dimensions. In accordance with the meaning of *auctoritas*, the shield is an example of the reciprocity between the *princeps* and the senate and people: he called for their judgment (*arbitrium*) and participation, and they reciprocated by acknowledging the basis of his uniquely moral leadership. That leadership was not simply "charismatic" but was defined in terms of traditional virtues. They speak to the merits Augustus has already demonstrated and to his obligation to continue such in the future. They are also the virtues of the *res publica* and as such shared by all. Augustus thus confirms a tradition and restores it to its original purpose.

We saw earlier that in the late republic the concept of the *res publica* was fragmented into several *res privatae*. A concomitant development, again traceable in both the numismatic and the literary evidence, is that traditional and communal Roman virtues, especially *virtus* and *pietas*, were used by individuals such as Sulla and Pompey in an increasingly self-referential way.[4] Under Augustus, their application is broadened out again: they refer to his exceptional qualities, but they also belong to the *res publica*, which he repre-

34. Victoria and *clupeus virtutis*, Belvedere Altar. Compare Figs. 149–51.

sents and which he restored not in a legalistic sense, but on the basis of its values. Hence several of these virtues were also those attributed to Romulus and Numa, although Octavian, apparently after some consideration, es-chewed being styled a second Romulus—one tradition had it that Romulus was cut into slivers by the senators—and wisely opted for the unique appella-tion "Augustus" instead. A similar uniqueness is reflected by the choice of the virtues: despite many previous catalogs of virtues, such as Plato's and Cato's (four in each case),[5] the Augustan list is not canonical, nor did it become so. It represents the usual Augustan combination of tradition and individual innovation.

There are other "typically" Augustan aspects here that we have seen in operation before. The virtues and the shield itself speak to both an immediate and a larger context. The immediate context is the victory at Actium and its aftermath. It is Victoria, therefore, who holds the shield on a plethora of representations in art and coinage, including an altar in the Vatican (Fig. 34)

35. Denarius from Spain,
19–18 B.C. Reverse: Victoria
with *clupeus virtutis*.

and a denarius from Spain (Fig. 35).[6] In their inclusiveness, all virtues refer to the events preceding 27 B.C.: *virtus* in that context is the traditional *militaris virtus*;[7] *clementia* refers to Augustus' treatment of some, though not all, of his opponents, such as Messalla Corvinus (Vell. 2.71.1); *iustitia* and *pietas* refer to the fact that the war against Cleopatra—and Octavian was careful to present it largely as such and not as a civil war against Antony—was a pious and just war (*bellum pium et iustum*). But mainly the virtues point to the future and to the tasks ahead, in accordance with Augustus' endeavor to put the past behind everybody and to rule with the *auctoritas* of an Augustus *princeps* rather than the force of an Octavianus *vindex*. *Virtus* then implies the labors and travails that will be necessary; *clementia*, the operative principle after ongoing conquests and submission of other peoples (cf. *RG* 3.1–2); *iustitia*, the return to a government of *leges* and *mores*; and *pietas*, the kind of social responsibility and respect for divine powers, including the restoration of religious shrines and priesthoods, which gave true cohesiveness to the *res publica*.

Three further purposeful evocations may be singled out. One is the usual Augustan appropriation of the claims to these virtues made by political opponents or predecessors. *Pietas* had been claimed by Pompey (it was the watchword of the Pompeians at the battle of Munda in 45 B.C.), Sextus Pompey, Antony, and his brother Lucius.[8] Similarly, Cicero could not say enough about Pompey's *virtus* (*Manil.* 45); it was the basis for his *auctoritas* and his proposed empowerment for the war against the pirates (*Manil.* 49). Two, even after his rise to power in the wake of Caesar's comet, Augustus did not simply divest himself of Julius Caesar. The placement of the shield in the Curia Julia was an almost dynastic tribute and an act of *pietas* toward his adoptive father. One of Caesar's last actions had been to undertake the rebuilding of the Curia, which had been destroyed by fire in early 44 B.C. The task was continued by Octavian and the rededication took place in 29 B.C. On that occasion, the Curia Julia appears on coins as a virtual temple of Victoria whose statue is shown on its roof (Fig. 36).[9] She commemorates Octavian's, and the Roman senate's and people's, victory at Actium. As for the virtues, *clementia*, while echoing an old concept, was associated almost exclusively with Julius Caesar, and a temple to Clementia Caesaris was decreed in 45 B.C.[10] Three, while the virtues are fundamentally Roman the custom of honoring rulers and benefactors with golden crowns or shields, and with an accompanying inscription recording two or three virtues, is well

36. Denarius of Octavian, ca. 30–29 B.C.
Reverse: Curia Julia with Victoria.

attested in Hellenistic Greece where it was also used for Roman governors
and Julius Caesar.[11] This is only one example of the synthesis of Greek and
Roman culture that became a hallmark of the Augustan age especially in
literature, art, and architecture.[12] At its best, the process is always the same:
Greek forms and traditions could be adapted for and revitalized by Roman
traditions and meaning. Such is certainly the case with the *clupeus virtutis*.
Another element in this synthesis was the previous Roman custom of honoring great individuals with shields on which their portrait was represented
(*imago clipeata*). They were "a source full of virtue" (*origo plena virtutis*), as the
Elder Pliny put it (*HN* 35.12–13). This was all the more true of the Augustan
clupeus virtutis, which listed four cardinal virtues specifically.

The Virtues

Roman virtues may be easily categorized, but they were anything but com-
partmentalized. While it is instructive to highlight the main aspects of each
of the four virtues, we should be aware that their import does not end there.
The four virtues on the shield are associated with several others and the
resonance of these associations is almost endless. A quality such as *virtus* is
only the principal theme in a symphony composed of themes such as *forti-
tudo, labor, vigilantia, diligentia, cura, industria*, and *prudentia*,[13] quite apart from
the principal meanings of *virtus* itself. And yet, in a typically Augustan way,
as we saw in our discussion of *auctoritas*, the multiplicity of these meanings is
meant to strike many chords without being diffuse and is subordinated to
clear tendencies that leave no doubt about the general significance of the
virtue.

Virtus was the quintessential "competitive" virtue from early on. "The principal Roman virtues are two," states one Roman writer, "military *virtus* and *pietas*."[14] One of the principal connotations of *virtus*, therefore, was manly (*virtus* is derived from *vir*) valor on the battlefield. *Virtus* thus is connected with *victoria*, and with distinction and recognition, *honos*. Virtus and Honos had a joint cult and temple in Rome since 205 B.C. The Scipios were so proud of their *virtus* that they put it on their tombstones; one of them, significantly, declares that "I accumulated the virtue of my race by my *mores*" (*CIL* I² no. 15). *Virtus*, then, is a result of moral effort, too. It is omnipresent in the characterization of the great statesmen of the late republic, in particular Marius, Caesar, and Pompey. In sum, "*virtus*, for the Republican noble, consisted in the winning of personal preeminence and glory by the commission of great deeds in the service to the Roman state."[15] Its occurrence on the shield is a reaffirmation of that concept in its fullness: individual distinction, but in the service to the *res publica*. The award of the *corona civica*, the wreath of oak leaves, fittingly accompanies it: it was the traditional award for saving the life of a citizen. As we have seen, the wreath with the legend OB CIVIS SERVATOS is one of the most common themes in Augustan coinage (Fig. 17).

The mention of *virtus* on the shield looks both backward and forward. Octavian achieved military *virtus*, which he will continue to exercise against foreign peoples as the *imperator* of the Roman state. In connection with the much heralded *pax Augusta*, it is important to distinguish between the end of the civil wars[16] and the resulting internal consolidation on the one hand, and continuing foreign conquests on the other. Augustus was both Numa and Romulus. He added more territory to Rome's domain than anyone before him: Egypt, Pannonia, Moesia, Noricum, and Raetia. Even in the last decade of his reign, he sought to incorporate Bohemia and Germany. There is, as we will see, a significant moral corollary to this mission and its underlying military *virtus*.[17] Applied to the internal task of rebuilding the *res publica*, however, the connotations of *virtus* are those of struggles and perils that need to be faced. Finally, *virtus* is not something that is simply inherited by a noble bloodline, a notion that was strongly contested by the nonpatrician new men who made their way into the senate in the first century B.C. and on whom Augustus drew extensively. Instead, they viewed it as being achieved by ongoing effort.[18] That is also the ethos of Vergil's *Aeneid* and *Georgics*.

Clementia, as noted earlier, is the one of the four virtues most specifically connected with Julius Caesar.[19] The concept, of course, had been in existence long before then, covered by terms such as *moderatio* or *lenitas*, but its specific elaboration was Cicero's on behalf of Caesar, following Caesar's impulse to leniency after the capitulation of the Pompeians at Corfinium in 49 B.C. Caesar's actions contrasted with those of Pompey, who was demanding more proscriptions on the model of Sulla (Cic., *Att.* 10.7.1; 8.11.2). With his usual hyperbole, Cicero likens the man who practices clemency to the gods (*Marc.* 8). Imitators materialized quickly: Brutus promised clemency to his adversaries after Caesar's assassination—over Cicero's objections (*ad Brut.* 5.5; 8.2). And Octavian wrote the senate after Philippi that he "would do everything in a mild and humane way, after the manner of his father" (Dio 48.3.6). That, however, was not quite the way things turned out to be until Antony had been overcome.

For Augustus' contemporaries in the 20s, therefore, clemency had two main aspects. The first relates, as in the case of *virtus*, to the conduct of military affairs by the Roman state and its generals—that is, to practice moderation toward a defeated enemy, provided the latter was not recalcitrant or heinous (cf. Cic., *Off.* 1.35), but submissive to the *pax Romana*. Augustus stresses explicitly in the *Res Gestae* that he acted in accordance with this principle (3.1–2). It also forms the conclusion of Vergil's famous summary of the Roman national character (*Aen.* 6.853): "To spare the conquered and war down the proud" (*parcere subiectis et debellare superbos*). With Caesar, however, it had also become the virtue of an individual, directed at his fellow citizens; *clementia* is appropriate for the *patronus* of a *clientela*. It is typical of the Augustan ambience again that this is not a one-sided relationship but a reciprocal one: *clementia* obligates both the holder of power and those in his care.[20] This characteristic of reciprocity was operative not only in the "settlement" of 27 B.C. but was integral, due to the very nature of *auctoritas*, to the Augustan age in all its aspects.

IUSTITIA

It goes without saying that any good ruler needs to be just. Justice, therefore, is the cardinal virtue from Plato to Cicero and could not possibly be left out. Besides the appeal to that tradition, however, there are some specific Roman and Augustan implications. First and foremost, Augustus' agreement with the senate signaled the return to a government based on justice and just laws rather than the continuation of his rule in the manner of a triumvir. Legality had not been absent from Octavian's actions and rise to power; it is well to observe that, in the *Res Gestae*, he scrupulously points out that legality at the appropriate junctures.[21] But just as Augustus transcended Octavian, justice transcended mere legality. It is a much fuller concept than self-justification, which is too narrow a perspective on the *Res Gestae* anyway. *Iustitia* includes, as do the other virtues, a reference to war and foreign policy: it was a traditional Roman concept that war could be waged only if it was "pious and just" (*bellum pium et iustum*; cf. *RG* 26.3). As for domestic policy, justice was expected to be the basis of the laws of which Augustus was *auctor* and it was expected to moderate his power; both formulations come from

Ovid (*Met.* 15.833; *Trist.* 4.4.12). Caesar, too, had invoked *iustitia* in that sense (*BC* 1.32.9). *Iustitia* also involves the fight against injustice: the "just man is not shaken from his resolve by the face of the threatening tyrant or by the frenzy of his fellow citizens clamoring for what is wrong," as Horace puts it in his third "Roman Ode" (*C.* 3.3.1–4). This is reminiscent of Antony, the *dominus* and *tyrannus*, and of Augustus' liberation of the *res publica* from the tyranny of such a band to return it to its old values, including justice. Such pursuit of justice does not go unrewarded:

> hac arte Pollux et vagus Hercules
> enisus arces attigit igneas,
>   quos inter Augustus recumbens
>   purpureo bibet ore nectar.

(C. 3.3.9–12)

[By such merits Pollux and the wandering Hercules exerted themselves and reached the starry citadels. Augustus will recline among them and drink nectar with his red lips.]

Similarly, Scipio the Younger had been exhorted by the Elder Scipio to pursue *iustitia* and *pietas* especially for the sake of his country because "that kind of life is the way to heaven" (Cic., *Rep.* 6.16). *Iustitia*, then, befits an Augustus and enhances his divine aura. For good reason, Augustus himself established a cult of Iustitia Augusta[22] at the end of his reign when, fulfilling the prayer Horace had uttered decades earlier (*C.* 1.2.45: *serus in caelum redeas*), he was ready to return to heaven at the end of a long life.

PIETAS

Pietas is the culminating and most quintessentially Roman virtue of the four virtues on the shield.[23] If *virtus* is a "competitive" virtue, including the notion of self-aggrandizement, *pietas* is its "cooperative" counterweight, representing the time-honored Roman ideal of social responsibility, which includes a broad spectrum of obligations to family, country, and gods. The inscription preserved on a copy of the shield at Arles (Fig. 37) specifically mentions *pietas* toward gods (*deos*) and country (*patriam*); the *patria* was Augustus' family and he was designated its *pater* in 2 B.C. Pietas had a temple in Rome since 181 B.C., and the range of the connotations of *pietas* was extensive. To be sure, it represented the sense of duty that animated the actions of moral exemplars in Livy's account of early Rome, such as Horatius at the bridge. But there is also a coldness that accrues from simply doing one's duty. *Pietas*, since it involves caring for people in the manner of a father, therefore also has an affective and sentimental quality. It is inherent, for example, in the depiction of Aeneas carrying his old father and leading his young son (Fig. 38). Finally, *pietas* again is a quality or a bond that cannot function

37. *Clupeus virtutis.* Marble copy from Arles.

38. Altar of Gens Augusta, Carthage, ca. A.D. 60.
Aeneas fleeing with Anchises and Ascanius.

without reciprocity. It requires the unselfish effort of all for the common good.

The relevance of all this to the incipient reign of Augustus with the senate and the people in 27 B.C. is clear. There is no evocation here of a mythical Golden Age, let alone a utopia. Instead, the *res publica* will be refounded and administered on the basis of traditional, proven virtues. Such virtues are not abstract but need to be exemplified by individuals. That demonstration was the avowed purpose of Livy's monumental history: to show "what the life and what the *mores* were, and by what men and practices in domestic politics and in war Rome's *imperium* was brought forth and increased" (pref. 9). The revived *pietas* toward the gods found its expression in Augustus' extensive rebuilding of over eighty temples and shrines that had fallen into disrepair, as had the *res publica* in general, not least because of neglect on the part of the nobles.[24] That this activity also enhanced his *auctoritas* is evident, and so did the four virtues and their implementation by him. *Pietas* was retrospective, too: Octavian had exercised it in avenging the murder of his adoptive father, in being his devout son, and in fighting a pious and just war against Cleopatra under Caesar's star (cf. Vergil, *Aen.* 8.678–81, cited in chapter 2). That war, and its climactic battle, also represented the struggle of the Roman gods against the mongrel gods of Egypt (*Aen.* 8. 698–700). The pious ruler fights on the side of the Roman gods and subordinates himself to them: *dis te minorem quod geris, imperas* (Hor., *C.* 3.6.5)

Like other traditional concepts, *pietas* under Augustus was not simply called forth from the past but developed some new aspects that related especially to him. In the context of political patronage, *pietas* came to denote the special bond of loyalty between the ruler and his followers. Messalla Corvinus, formerly an ally of Brutus and Cassius, went over to the side of the triumvirs and then Octavian, becoming consul in 31 B.C., the year of Actium. Velleius praises him as an exemplar of *pietas* toward Augustus,[25] and the bond of *pietas* "toward the entire Julian name" was transferred to his son Messallinus, the consul of 3 B.C. (Ovid, *Pont.* 2.2.21). The attitude extended beyond mere individuals and in the following decades denotes that of entire populations, such as the islands of Cyprus and Cos, toward the *domus Augusta*. The development had begun with Julius Caesar[26] and was continued vigorously by Augustus and his successors.

Resonance

The four Augustan virtues did not freeze into a "canon." Such routinization is more typical of the later Roman empire; the Augustan period was more dynamic and less conformist. The virtues were, in a way, the famous "Augustan constitution." Exemplifying his transforming leadership, they were a statement of principles that the senate and people attributed to him and on

which he and they were to act as part of a new *consensus universorum*. He was
the guarantor of these principles; their implementation was not his alone, but
needed to be shared by all. Therefore the resonance they found, especially in
literature, is far removed from the rigid schematization of an ideology.

In the *Aeneid*, Vergil singles Aeneas out for his *virtus, iustitia*, and *pietas*.
Aeneas is not only preeminent for his *pietas* (1.10: *insignem pietate virum*)
but distinguished by his *pietas* and arms (6.403: *pietate insignis et armis*). The
epic begins on the note of arms and the man (1.1: *arma virumque*) and Aeneas' *virtus* is as conspicuous as his *pietas*. When Ilioneus characterizes Aeneas
for Dido, he introduces him as the epitome of these two virtues and of
iustitia:

> rex erat Aeneas nobis, quo iustior alter
> nec pietate fuit, nec bello maior et armis.
>
> (*Aen.* 1.544–45)

> [Aeneas was our king; none other was more just in
> *pietas*, nor more outstanding in war and arms.]

His *pietas*, much misunderstood because of centuries of Christianizing interpretation and romantic prejudice, manifests itself in such diverse ways as his
constant attentiveness to the deities, the subordination of his individual desire
to the needs of those entrusted to him, the loyalty to his allies (especially
Evander and Pallas), and his just punishment of the impious treaty-breaker
Turnus. This last instance shows that there were limits to *clementia*,[27] which
was true of Caesar and Augustus also.

As for Horace, the old virtues that return to usher in the new *saeculum* are
Fides, Pax, Honos, Pudor, and Virtus (*CS* 57–58); the traditional festival of
Honos and Virtus was transferred by Augustus to May 29 so as to lead up to
the first day of the Secular Games (Dio 54.18.2). Given the overlapping
nature of many Roman virtues and the absence of any ideology, the omission
of the strict Augustan "canon" is anything but surprising. For the same reason, there is no need to force Horace's "Roman Odes" (*C.* 3.1–6) into such
a scheme. There he celebrates, in his own elaboration, *virtus* and *religio* in
C. 3.2 and, as we have seen, the "just and steadfast man" in *C.* 3.3, where he
places Augustus in the company of the gods because of his *iustitia*. The six
odes deal with Augustus' moral leadership at large, but do so, characteristically, in a dynamic rather than static way: "Against the backdrop of virtue,
Horace plays out the melancholic counterpoint between the godhead of
Augustus and the godlessness of his people."[28]

The perspective was Horace's own. Transforming, moral leadership is an
ongoing process, which is never quite complete. The wide dissemination of
the shield betokens the recognition of the virtues though not their swift
acceptance to guide everyone's deeds. The *clupeus* appears extensively on

39. Terracotta lamp from Carthage.
Victoria holding the *clupeus virtutis.*

coins, on altars of the Lares Augusti (Fig. 143b) and the Gens Augusta
throughout Rome, and copies of it were also shown in cities of the empire;
Arles is hardly an isolated example.[29] This commemoration of the virtues
obviated their individual personifications on coins, a solution that also remedied the problem of iconographic ambiguity. On lamps and coins the inscription on the shield was not copied literally, but was summarized with the
legend OB CIVIS SERVATOS either on the shield itself (Fig. 39) or surrounding
it while the abbreviations CL. V. and SPQR appeared on the shield; the virtues
were those of the savior of the citizens. When Pietas reappeared on the coins,
she evolved, over the next two centuries, into the personification of the
specific piety practiced in connection with the cult of the deified Augustus.[30]
This is a final testimony to the strong association of the shield's virtues with
him.

THE GOLDEN AGE

The Augustan age is often called the Golden Age, *aurea aetas* or *saeculum
aureum.* Its virtually interchangeable use, within a few generations after Augustus,[31] with *felix saeculum* and the sweeping manner in which it is applied
even today to explain some of the imagery of Augustan art, ranging from the
Yellow Frieze in the "House of Livia" to the vegetation on the Ara Pacis
Augustae, should not blind us to the fact that it was a highly differentiated

concept at Augustus' own time. We are dealing, once more, with a notion that was evolving during this period. It was based, as always, on previous traditions that led to new adaptations and departures.

Vergil's Fourth *Eclogue*

Few literary works from antiquity took hold on the imagination of later ages as much as Vergil's "Messianic" *Eclogue*, written in 40 B.C.[32] This popularity has had its drawbacks. Besides the poem's extensive interpretation in a Christian key, it came to be considered as the quintessential formulation of the aspirations of the age. A resulting misconception is that it was a seminal text of the Augustan era proper and on everybody's lips at the time. Other important texts and developments have been ignored in the process. The poem is, no doubt, an evocative expression of the yearning for peace and tranquillity after decades of civil wars (with no complete assurance as yet that they will come to an end), all of which explains why Augustus' rule was accepted so widely. Yet while the Augustan era fulfilled some of the hopes voiced in the poem, we need to be careful not to view the eclogue as a kind of poetic blueprint even of the incipient Augustan dispensation.

One of the main obstacles is the eclogue's patently utopian nature, which it shares, albeit in a different way, with its Horatian pendant, *Epode* 16. It evokes the return to a paradise where no human toil will be required. The images are vivid: animals will bring milk home by themselves (21–22) and the earth will sprout flowers (18–20, 23–25) and vegetation (28–30) without needing to be cultivated. Human effort will go out of fashion while rams and sheep will sport multicolored fleeces:

> omnis feret omnia tellus.
> non rastros patietur humus, non vinea falcem;
> robustus quoque iam tauris iuga solvet arator;
> nec varios discet mentiri lana colores,
> ipse sed in pratis aries iam suave rubenti
> murice, iam croceo mutabit vellera luto;
> sponte sua sandyx pascentis vestiet agnos.
>
> (*Ecl.* 4.39–45)

[Every land will bear forth all things. The soil will not suffer the hoe, nor the vine the pruning hook; then the sturdy plowman, too, will release the oxen from the yoke. Nor will the wool learn to counterfeit various hues, but in the fields the ram will himself change his fleece, now to sweetly blushing purple, now to saffron yellow; of its own accord will scarlet clothe the grazing lambs.]

All this is far removed from the realities and the ethos of the Augustan age and calls for considerable suspension of disbelief.

The poem's central and greatest innovation lies in the notion of a return of "the age of Saturn" and the casting of that return in the present tense. In addition, Vergil draws on a variety of traditions in the fourth *Eclogue*, some eastern and some western,[33] a fact that underlines both the universality of the poem and the necessity not to ignore the specific historical context amid all the universality.

While Vergil combines Sibylline oracles speaking of the Return with the Hesiodic system of the ages, which can be considered both sequential and cyclical, and with some Etruscan ideas of the *saecula*, the sum total cannot be interpreted as a millennial event. The Etruscan *saecula*, for instance, generally correspond to no more than a generation,[34] and the Hesiodic myth works in terms of races, a concept that is clearly echoed by Vergil (*gens aurea*, line 9). There is the hope that with Pollio's consulship—the event that the fourth *Eclogue* celebrates—a time of prosperity and happiness will return after the long, dark days of turmoil and misery, but this does not mean placing faith in a charismatic leader. The miraculous child ultimately is no more than a symbol or personification of the new age. The occasion for the poem was a political, republican act, namely Pollio's accession to the consulate, but nowhere is it suggested that he shall be the sole ruler or that Rome's salvation will depend on one. After the mention of this historical dedicatee, the poem quickly moves into the mythical sphere, though this should not be interpreted as an antithesis to republican institutions. Their actual workings were hardly the literal stuff for great poetry; Cicero's poem on his consulate is a salutary example. The closest poetic model on which Vergil drew belongs to a different realm:[35] Catullus 64, with its prophecy centering on Achilles, the baneful heroic warrior par excellence, who also makes his overt appearance in *Eclogue* 4 (35–36).

Similar tensions underlie the myth of the ages. Hesiod's scheme has been traditionally interpreted as sequential, but it may well be that Vergil recognized its "positive and negative capabilities on different planes of reality,"[36] which implied a cyclical chronology. The alternation of positive and negative aspects, which has bothered careful readers of the fourth *Eclogue*, finds a convincing explanation against this background. In the eclogue proper, the advent of the Golden Age is retarded by that of the age of the heroes, such as the Argonauts and Achilles, and of the concomitant human engagement in city building, seafaring, and agriculture. This is an inversion of the role of the heroic age in Hesiod's *Works and Days*, where it interrupts the process of decline. More important, Vergil follows Hesiod in taking a dialectical perspective on the succession of the ages and in allowing for an alternation. That, in the end, enables him to speak of a *return* of the Golden Age.

Of the Greek and Roman authors up to his time, Vergil goes furthest in stating the return of the Golden Age most directly. As we have already observed, the tense he uses at the beginning of the fourth *Eclogue* certainly is unique: the return is described as actually taking place. This perspective changes to the future tense from line 11 on and in the two references to the Golden Age under Augustus in the *Aeneid* (1.291–96, 6.792–94). The reason, to anticipate some of the conclusions in the next section, is not chronological perspective or grammatical convention, but the poet's moral attitude, which reflects that of the age in general. The *Aeneid* does not celebrate fruition— it does not end, for example, with the foundation of Rome or even Lavinium—but stresses the ongoing process that ultimately will lead to the accomplishment of a lasting, civilized order. In the words of Cervantes, the emphasis is on the journey, and not on the destination. It is a view that, as we shall see, is foreshadowed by Vergil's treatment of the Golden Age at the beginning of the *Georgics* (1.121ff.).

In sum, the fourth *Eclogue* cannot be considered as a programmatic matrix of things to come and as being so influential, at Augustus' own time (as opposed to later ages), that it would allow us to use it as a frame of reference for aspects ranging from imagery in art to the ideology of the ruler. In a most evocative, associative, and even vague manner, the poem contains many themes that were worked out in a more precise fashion over the next three decades, including by Vergil himself. This applies in particular to the interconnected themes of the Golden Age and Saturn. The modifications were substantial.

The *aurea aetas* and Saturn

One of the most significant changes in the Golden Age concept at Augustus' time is that the Golden Age comes to connote a social order rather than a paradisiac state of indolence.[37] In a programmatic passage at the beginning of Vergil's *Georgics* (1.121ff.),[38] the Golden Age that existed before Jupiter is shown not to be a desirable ideal because it represented slothful existence that required no mental or physical exertion:

> pater ipse colendi
> haud facilem esse viam voluit, primusque per artem
> movit agros curis acuens mortalia corda,
> nec torpere gravi passus sua regna veterno.
> ante Iovem nulli subigebant arva coloni;
> ne signare quidem aut partiri limite campum
> fas erat: in medium quaerebant, ipsaque tellus
> omnia liberius nullo poscente ferebat.
>
> (*Geo.* 1.121–28)

[The Father himself has willed that the way of cultivation should not be easy, and he was the first to cause the land to be cultivated by men's skill, sharpening men's minds with cares, nor letting his realm be sluggish in heavy lethargy. Before Jupiter no tillers subdued the land. Even to mark the field or divide it with boundaries was unlawful. Men strove for the common property of all, and the earth herself used to bring forth all things more freely when no one begged for her gifts.]

Jupiter, therefore, sends blights and pains into this world. His intent (contrary to prior versions) is not malicious; rather he wants to provide a stimulus for human activity and efforts:

> ille malum virus serpentibus addidit atris,
> praedarique lupos iussit pontumque moveri,
> mellaque decussit foliis ignemque removit,
> et passim rivis currentia vina repressit,
> ut varias usus meditando extunderet artis
> paulatim, et sulcis frumenti quaereret herbam,
> ut silicis venis abstrusum excuderet ignem.
> tunc alnos primum fluvii sensere cavatas;
> navita tum stellis numeros et nomina fecit
> Pleiadas, Hyadas, claramque Lycaonis Arcton;
> tum laqueis captare feras et fallere visco
> inventum et magnos canibus circumdare saltus;
> atque alius latum funda iam verberat amnem
> alta petens, pelagoque alius trahit umida lina;
> tum ferri rigor atque arguta lammina serrae
> (nam primi cuneis scindebant fissile lignum),
> tum variae venere artes. labor omnia vicit
> improbus et duris urgens in rebus egestas.
>
> (*Geo.* 1.129–46)

[He added hurtful venom to the black snakes; he commanded wolves to be predators and the sea to swell; he shook honey from the leaves and hid the fire away; he held back the wine that was running everywhere in streams, so that experience by taking thought might gradually hammer out the various arts, might seek to produce corn by plowing, and might strike forth fire hidden in the veins of flint. Then did the rivers first feel hollowed-out alder trees; then did the sailor number the stars and name them—the Pleiades, the Hyades, and Lycaon's offspring, the gleaming Great Bear. Then men found out how to snare game in traps and birds with lime, and to surround vast mountain glades with hounds. And now one lashes a wide stream with a casting net, seeking the depths, and another drags his dripping net through the sea. Then came iron's stiffness and the blade of the shrill saw (for early man cleft the splitting wood with wedges); then came the remaining arts. Unrelenting toil has come to occupy all areas of existence and want that is pressing when life is hard.]

Not only is this catalog of human efforts an almost complete inversion of those condemned in *Eclogue* 4, but neither is there any mention of a savior hero, whether a wondrous child or Prometheus. In Hesiod's *Works and Days*, Jupiter's termination of human sloth and infliction of labors on men is explained as his punishment of mankind for Prometheus' benevolent deed. In the passage in the *Georgics*, by contrast, men depend on their own efforts, though under the aegis of helpful gods like Ceres (1.147). These efforts are unceasing (1.145–46), driven as they are by want and need, two stimuli for civilization that were singled out by numerous writers before and after Vergil, starting with the Sophists. *Labor improbus*, a phrase that has received many different interpretations, can be a force for the good, but can turn negative when men go to excess in satisfying more than legitimate needs, a concern that had been voiced a generation earlier by Lucretius.

In the context of the *Georgics*—and I will turn to the wider implications of the passage for the Augustan ethos in the next section—the passage does not stand alone, but is complemented by the description of the farmer's existence in book 2 (458–540). There Golden Age notions and human labor coalesce: the Golden Age is the result of *labor*. The farmer is removed from the strife of the city and from the incessant quest for materialism exemplified, among other things, by the hankering for exotic dyes (2.465)—a clear allusion to *Eclogue* 4.42–45. The earth brings forth willingly (2.500–501); there will be enough acorn and arbute trees for animals to feed on (2.520, recalling 1.148–49), but the farmer's blessed existence is the result of year-round *labor* (2.514) without respite (*nec requies*: 2.516). It is a Golden Age which, in contrast to that of *Eclogue* 4, is based on agriculture and includes the fortification of cities (2.535). In other words, it is a Golden Age based on blood, sweat, and tears.[39] It is not a paradisiac state, but implies both a social order and an ongoing effort.

In this context, the myth of Saturn underwent a typically Roman and Augustan redefinition.[40] In Hesiod's version, Cronus is a cruel father figure who is overthrown by Jupiter and banished below Tartarus (*Theog.* 851; cf. Homer, *Il.* 14.274). Euhemerus (third century) seems to have been the first to make him into an exile in Italy, but Euhemerus' Cronus also is a coward and moral weakling. Diodorus, who wrote his universal history at the time of Caesar and Augustus, lessened the negative aspects of Cronus/ Saturn. Nothing is said of his coming to Italy, but in his "sincerity of soul" (5.66.4) he is a bringer of civilization and justice to many lands, and Jupiter succeeds him peacefully. At the same time, there was the usual etymologizing epitomized by Varro: Saturn's Italian existence was anchored in the derivation from *sator*, the sower (from *serere*, "to sow"), and further etymologies connected him with saturation and plenty.

It is in this incarnation of the Italian farmer king that we encounter Saturn at the end of the second *Georgic* where he is the tutelary deity of a Golden Age of peace based on agricultural labor (536–40). At the same time, Vergil proceeds in the true Augustan mode by using concepts, myths, and phrases that have multiple associations and traditions. In the "Praises of Italy" earlier in the same book of the *Georgics*, therefore, it is not surprising that the concept of the *Saturnia tellus*, the land of Saturn, includes warfare, war harbors, and warriors from the Sabines to Octavian (2.161–76). The Hesiodic dialectic—and Vergil significantly ends the passage with a reference to Hesiod (2.176)—of complementary and contrasting aspects is transferred to Rome and Italy, which are both pacific and warlike. Just as the farmer's peace is based on *labor*, so the *pax Romana* is based on conquest and war. The concept of the "Saturnian land" is extended in the process.

Similarly, Vergil does not present one reductive version of Saturn in the *Aeneid*.[41] King Latinus paints an idealized picture of the Latins, whom he calls "the race of Saturn, being righteous not because of laws or the threat of prison, but living a disciplined life of their own accord in the manner [*more*] of the ancient god" (7.203–4). Good *mores* make *leges* superfluous, a notion of the Golden Age that we find also in other authors.[42] But such were neither the realities in Augustus' "Golden Age," nor in early Latium according to the more objective Greek king Evander. Saturn, he says, was first in a line of refugees to Italy, who include Evander himself and Aeneas:

> primus ab aetherio venit Saturnus Olympo
> arma Iovis fugiens et regnis exsul ademptis.
> is genus indocile et dispersum montibus altis
> composuit legesque dedit, Latiumque vocari
> maluit, his quoniam latuisset tutus in oris.
> aurea quae perhibent illo sub rege fuere
> saecula: sic placida populos in pace regebat,
> deterior donec paulatim ac decolor aetas
> et belli rabies et amor successit habendi.
>
> (*Aen.* 8.319–27)

[First from heavenly Olympus came Saturn, fleeing the arms of Jove and exiled from his lost kingdom. He brought together this untaught race, scattered as it was over the mountain heights, gave laws to them, and preferred that the land be called Latium, from his latency of safe concealment in this countryside.[43] Under this king were the golden centuries men tell of: in such quiet peace did he keep ruling the nations until gradually a baser and tarnished age came in and madness for war and lust for gain].

Peace prevailed under Saturn, but it was a peace born of *labor*.[44]

The connection with Augustus is evident. The one passage in the *Aeneid* that casts him explicitly as Saturn's successor does so in the context of both Augustus' legislation on morals and marriage and the ever expanding Roman *imperium*. The two concepts are linked, as we shall see shortly. "This, this is the man," Anchises prophesies excitedly,

> of whom you so often have heard the promise,
> Caesar Augustus, son of the deified,
> who shall bring once again an Age of Gold
> to Latium, to the land where Saturn reigned
> in early times. He will extend his power
> beyond the Garamants and Indians,
> over far territories north and south
> of the zodiacal stars, the solar way,
> where Atlas, heaven-bearing, on his shoulder
> turns the night-sphere, studded with burning stars.
>
> (Aen. 6.791–97, trans. Fitzgerald)

> [hic vir, hic est, tibi quem promitti saepius audis,
> Augustus Caesar, divi genus, aurea condet
> saecula qui rursus Latio regnata per arva
> Saturno quondam, super et Garamantas et Indos
> proferet imperium; iacet extra sidera tellus,
> extra anni solisque vias, ubi caelifer Atlas
> axem umero torquet stellis ardentibus aptum.]

As R. G. Austin, in his standard commentary on book 6, has well noted, Vergil's words here "have a special social significance; the Golden Age of Saturn symbolized the purity and simplicity of early Italian life, the ways that had made Rome great (cf. *Geo.* 2.538). It is highly probable that in *aurea condet saecula* there is an allusion to Augustus' social and moral reforms, attempted unsuccessfully in 28 B.C., but given fresh impetus in 22 B.C., then postponed until 18 B.C. when his legislative program was finally carried through and celebrated by the revival of the *ludi saeculares* in the next year."[45]

This raises another central issue. In the Augustan context, the "Golden Age"—and in many accounts of the various ages, gold and the lust for gold are associated with deterioration rather than the state of pristine existence[46]—denotes the spiritual *mores* of early Italy, though not a retrenchment of the material standard of life. While living unostentatiously and wearing homespun clothes (Suet., *Aug.* 73), Augustus rebuilt Rome as a city of unprecedented material splendor. Many of the decayed shrines were rebuilt all right in wood as in the olden days, but the showplaces were the new buildings in gleaming marble that transformed the city.[47] The princeps' *dictum* to have found Rome a city of bricks and made it into one of marble was more than a mere metaphor. Ostentatious palatial domains, like that of the shady entrepreneur Vedius Pollio—Ovid remarks, probably with some exaggera-

tion, that it occupied more space than many a small town (*Fasti* 6.641–42)—
were torn down (after Vedius had left his estate to Augustus) to make room
for more public buildings financed by the emperor.

The material splendor did not end here. Jasper Griffin has well documented the life of material luxury at Augustus' time.[48] Most of the references
we find to it in the Augustan writers are based on this actuality rather than on
mere literary conventions. Similarly, some of the games sponsored by
Agrippa clearly conveyed the message to the urban plebs that a return to the
life-style of early Italy was anything but imminent:

> Furthermore, he distributed olive oil and salt to all, and furnished the
> baths free of charge throughout the year for both men and women; and
> in connection with the festivals of all kinds which he gave—on such a
> scale, in fact, that the children of senators also performed the equestrian
> game called "Troy"—he hired the barbers, so that no one should be at
> any expense for their services. Finally, he rained upon the heads of the
> people in the theater tickets that were good for money in one case, for
> clothes in another, and again for something else, and he also set out
> immense quantities of various wares for all comers and allowed the
> people to scramble for these things. (Dio 49.43.2–4, Loeb trans.)

To be sure, this was in 33 B.C., when an all-out effort was made to win the
hearts, minds, and stomachs of the populace against Antony. But it shows
that actual practice could be quite elastic in transcending the propagandistic
dichotomy between Antony, the Dionysiac bon vivant, and Octavian, the
summoner of Italy's pristine virtues. Furthermore, the *Res Gestae* gives
eloquent testimony to Augustus' unabated sponsorship of lavish spectacles:
eight gladiatorial games with up to 10,000 participants; three international
athletic contests; twenty-seven other games; twenty-six beast hunts with
3,500 animals provided from all over the world; and a mock sea battle, with
thirty biremes and triremes in a newly constructed basin measuring 1,200 by
1,800 feet. In addition, there were the horse and chariot races in the Circus
Maximus and a plethora of theatrical shows and other professional entertainment.[49] Augustus' rule was not marked by an unconditional return to austerity. This was well noted by Tacitus (*Ann.* 3.55), who comments that luxury
of the table and the profuse expenditures associated with it had been on the
increase since Actium and came to an end only at the accession of Galba after
Vespasian had set a good example.

Yet Augustus emphasized a commitment to the values of the Roman past.
The resulting dilemma is one of the many creative tensions of the Augustan
culture: the difficulty of a return to a pristine Golden Age ethos, for which
there was a sincere longing, amid the material splendor and standard of living
of the modern Golden Age, which were appreciated just as much. None of
the Augustan writers, for example, tries to revive *simplicitas* as a contempo-

rary virtue; it is simply relegated to the mythical past. Ovid's poetry provides an articulate illustration of the basic tension.[50]

Ovid revels in the sophisticated ambience of Augustan Rome and in the milieu of leisure created by theaters, porticoes, basilicas, and baths. Earlier ways of life were crude by comparison, and Ovid clearly discerns the nexus between the *aurea Roma* of his day and the conquests she has made:

> simplicitas rudis ante fuit; nunc aurea Roma est
> et domiti magnas possidet orbis opes.
>
> (*AA* 3.112–13)

[Crude simplicity is a thing of the past. Now Rome is golden and possesses the vast wealth of the conquered world.]

He goes on to praise the Augustan building program, including the Temple of Apollo on the Palatine—those buildings are a vast improvement over the early huts and pastures. Worship of the past is for others; Ovid is glad to be part of the present generation, though he is selective in the praise of his own civilization. The buildings are fine, but technological progress, poignantly identified with the mining of gold (3.123), is not what matters. Rather, it is *cultus et ars*, the refinement and culture of his own time, that are vastly preferable to the simplicity and primitivism of the time of Saturn:

> sed quia cultus adest nec nostros mansit in annos
> rusticitas priscis illa superstes avis.
>
> (*AA* 3.127–28)

[But because there is cultured refinement now, and there didn't linger on into our days that rusticity, a survival from our hoary forebears.]

That does not mean the old values are passé. In *Amores* 3.8, a poem admittedly written out of frustration over a girlfriend's leaving him for a richer man, Ovid denounces his age's preference for gold rather than poetic talent (*ingenium*; line 3), the contempt in which the rich hold the poor (a clear contrast with the Saturnian age depicted in *Georgics* 2.498–99), and the crass materialism that is the opposite of the Golden Age (lines 57–60). The last stage in this degeneration is the plutocracy of his own time: money and wealth, and nothing besides, qualify one for rank and office in Rome. Personally motivated as they may be, Ovid's strictures (cf. Prop. 3.13, especially 47ff.) intersect with Augustus' concern for both the moral and the material qualifications of his ruling class.

From this perspective, then, the Golden Age is the antithesis of the actual present. Ovid's account of the Golden Age in the first book of the *Metamorphoses* (1.89–112) presents a combination of elements drawn from the paradise myths and the myth of the four metal ages proper.[51] What is significant for our purposes is that the poet, through the use of no fewer than sixteen

negations, takes the present as his point of departure and views the past as its
antithetical counterpart. The Golden Age is characterized not by positive
aspects of its own, but by the absence of contemporary practices, greed and
war in particular. We find out at the beginning of the subsequent description
of the Silver Age (1.113–14) that the Golden Age was the time of Saturn;
Ovid does not emphasize his role in any way nor does he ever speak of a
return of the *Saturnia regna* to Rome. Ovid stops short of the Vergilian synthesis of the Golden Age and *labor*, though in *Fasti* 2.289–302 he follows
Vergil in considering the Golden Age as a primeval state that is not admirable, but needs to be improved upon. Ovid combines Vergil's criticism of
a life without any exertions (*vita nullos agitata per usus*; *Fasti* 2.291) with his
own criteria: the *vulgus* was crude (*rudis*) and without skill or refinement (*artis
expers*). The phrase both echoes the Vergilian notion of the invention of skills
caused by the expulsion from slothful paradise (*Geo*. 1.133) and adds to it the
dimension of taste and culture.

As can be seen—and additional passages in Ovid and the elegists could be
adduced—the definition of the Golden Age and the attitudes to it were
anything but uniform. These differences are reflected by later authors also. A
remark by Tacitus (*Dial*. 12.3), cited earlier, illustrates that "golden" could
become a byword for any subsequent age, in conjunction with the connotation of felicity, whereas Seneca would look upon such a Golden Age in terms
of its materialistic preoccupation with gold and wealth (*Ep*. 115.3). In sum,
especially when we look at the Augustan evidence, we are dealing, not surprisingly, with a highly differentiated notion rather than a convenient label.
Moreover, because the Augustan concept of the Golden Age was anything
but definitive, a plethora of later writers down to Corippus (sixth century)
could claim the final return of the *saeculum aureum* for their emperor. The
"saeculum" of Nero, for instance, was characterized by Seneca as "purer"
and "happier" (*felicior*) than that of Augustus.[52]

The *ludi saeculares* and the *saeculum*

Similarly, the Secular Games of 17 B.C. should not be taken out of the context into which they were carefully integrated.[53] They did not celebrate the
advent of millennial, passive bliss but took place only after one of the corner-
stones of the Augustan program, the legislation on marriage and morals, had
been passed in 18 B.C. The health of the new *saeculum* was not merely an
automatic, god-given blessing but was to depend on the moral effort of the
Romans, the ruling classes in particular.

There were diverse definitions of the exact duration of a *saeculum* and we
find similarly multiple meanings of the word in the *Georgics* and the *Aeneid*.[54]
Frequently it is considered the equivalent of a lifespan, defined flexibly from

thirty (like "a generation") to one hundred years. The idea, naturally enough, coalesced with that of an era or dynasty: even Nero, as we have just observed, was hailed as the bringer of a Golden Age. Additional connotations were operative by the time of the late republic.[55] The lifetime of a nation, such as the Etruscan one, was considered to last ten *saecula*. Sometimes the number four occurs due to the conflation with the Hesiodic tradition of the ages, and there were beliefs in cycles and in the "Great Year" (again of varying duration), which comprised them all. Further, there were various eschatological and palingenetic speculations and announcements of the coming of an exceptional man. These had all the flexibility of modern-day horoscopes and could crystallize easily enough around various events and leaders, such as Pompey and Sulla.

The multiplicity of associations that had accrued to the concept of the *saeculum* was congenial to Augustan culture. Just as important and typically Augustan, however, was the combination of the concept with a definite intention and a sense of direction. The specific tradition adapted by Augustus was the reported celebration of the games from the sixth century onward in intervals of 100 or 110 years. The only games that are historically attested, though not without problems, are those of 249 B.C. amid the First Punic War, and of 146 B.C., the year of Scipio's victory and destruction of Carthage in the Third Punic War. The games were a combination of the Etruscan idea of the *saecula* and the traditional practice of Greek religion to institute cultic performances at the threshold of particularly portentous and serious occasions in the life of the state. As can be seen by the 103-year interval, this last consideration was more important than a regularized chronology.

To make the festival truly meaningful, Augustus chose to wait until external stability had been achieved and internal regeneration was well under way. The settlement with the Parthians betokened a secure *pax Romana* in the east and Agrippa's conquest of the Cantabrians in Spain in 19 B.C. heralded the same for the west. Augustus returned to Rome in the same year and devoted his efforts to domestic legislation. Probably as a result of these priorities, the senate and the people, both in 19 and 18 B.C., offered Augustus the sole curatorship of laws and morals (*cura morum et legum*) "without a colleague and with supreme power." Augustus, however, recused himself. He saw the contradiction of formally assuming an unprecedented office for the purpose of legislating a return to the old ways: "I could not accept," he declares in the *Res Gestae* (6.1), "any office contrary to the custom [*morem*] of our ancestors."[56]

Instead, Augustus used his powers as a tribune to carry out the requisite legislation. It included a new law against electoral bribery. This shows, with reference to the important decade (20–10 B.C.) we have already scrutinized, "that he did not control all elections; no one would waste money on corrupting voters, if the result was a foregone conclusion."[57] In addition, he passed some sumptuary measures that recalled earlier such efforts by the elder Cato, among others, like restricting the cost of meals being served at dinner parties (Gell., *NA* 2.24.14–15). Augustus also used his censorial powers for another review of the senatorial roll in 18 B.C. in which he aimed, as we have seen, to restore the senate to its original number of three hundred members, and for which he used moral criteria such as baseness and excessive flattery (Dio 54.13.1).

Leges were needed, but *mores* were even more important. "What good are empty laws if we lack *mores*?" as Horace put it.[58] A further vignette, provided by Dio (54.10.6–7) and probably authentic, exemplifies this thinking. When the senate and people urged Augustus to pass any legislation of his liking, they coupled it with a further stipulation of everyone's taking an oath to abide by it. That Augustus rejected "for he well knew that, if any measure they decreed should represent their judgment, they would observe it even without taking an oath, but if it should not, they would pay no attention to it, even if they should offer ten thousand guarantees." A proper moral attitude was more fundamental than laws and oaths to abide by them.

This, then, was the highly specific context of the Secular Games of 17 B.C. They amounted to more than a general evocation of bliss, *felicitas saeculi*, of which we find little in the sources from the Augustan period proper.[59] The tenor of the festival, reflecting that of the age in general, expressed more of a striving for peace and plenitude than a celebration of their fulfillment. The Sibylline books, which were recopied in 18 B.C., were now found to contain an oracle specifically providing for the celebration of the games with an emphasis on sacrifices for the "all-creating Fates" and the "childbearing goddesses of childbirth." The reference to the marriage legislation is clear. These deities, and Mother Earth, Jupiter, Juno, Apollo and Diana, replaced the underworld couple of Pluto and Proserpina of the previous games. Rituals during the day were added to those at night. Apollo, of course, was one of Augustus' favorite gods, but his associations do not simply exhaust themselves in that function only: he, too, had a tradition as a chthonic god, even in Italy.[60] Augustus had himself elected as head of the Fifteenmen (*XVviri*) in charge of the games and was their chief functionary along with Agrippa. At the end of the three-day ritual, which was staged elaborately and performed impressively, a chorus of twenty-seven boys and twenty-seven girls, representing the result of marital fecundity and the future hope of Rome, chanted Horace's *Secular Hymn* (*Carmen Saeculare*) on both the Palatine and the Capitol.

The hymn suggestively voices some of the grand Augustan themes but, like the oracle and the acts of the games, stops short of proclaiming a Golden Age, and especially a Golden Age of automatic bliss or felicity. It begins with an invocation to Apollo and Diana and continues with one to the "nourish-ing Sun-god":

> alme Sol, curru nitido diem qui
> promis et celas aliusque et idem
> nasceris, possis nihil urbe Roma
>   visere maius.

$$(9-12)$$

[Nourishing Sun-god, who in your gleaming chariot bring forth the day and hide it, and are reborn another and yet the same, may you be able to behold nothing greater than the city of Rome.]

The references again are multiple: besides being a cosmic god in his own right and one dear to Hellenistic rulers, Sol was closely associated and even identified with Apollo—his chariot appeared on both the Palatine Apollo temple and the cuirass of the Prima Porta statue (Fig. 73)—and he was also the legendary ancestor of the Latins.[61] In whatever capacity he would behold Rome, it was a city that, due to Augustus' building program, had indeed become unrivaled in its splendor. Its moral restoration, however, was just as important as its physical one. Hence two of the stanzas that follow clearly address themselves to the marriage legislation:

> diva, producas subolem, patrumque
> prosperes decreta super iugandis
> feminis prolisque novae feraci
>   lege marita,
>
> certus undenos decies per annos
> orbis ut cantus referatque ludos
> ter die claro totiensque grata
>   nocte frequentis.

$$(17-24)$$

[Goddess, bring forth offspring and make prosper the decrees of the fathers about wedlock and the marriage law that is to be fruitful in new offspring, so that the sure cycle of ten times eleven years may bring back chants and games repeated on three bright days and as many welcome nights.]

Prayers for general prosperity follow. Then the poem proceeds to the mention of the Trojan and Julian ancestor, Aeneas, whose moral integrity is stressed (41–42) and leads to a prayer for upright *mores* for Rome's youth (deliberately placed first), some well-deserved rest and quiet for her (civil-) war weary elders, more good things in general, offspring for the race of

Romulus and, finally, *virtus*, honor, valiant accomplishment, and moral dignity (all summed up by *decus*)[62] in all things:

> di, probos mores docili iuventae,
> di, senectuti placidae quietem,
> Romulae genti date remque prolemque,
>   et decus omne.
>
> (45–48)

The illustration of *res* and *decus* follows: it is the warlike extension of the *imperium Romanum* by Augustus and the return of old-fashioned *virtus* to a morally reconstituted Rome:

> iam Fides et Pax et Honos Pudorque
> priscus et neglecta redire Virtus
> audet.
>
> (57–59)

[Now Faith, Peace, Honor, old-fashioned Shame, and Valor, which had been neglected, dare to return.]

These are the true basis for any prosperity, the icon of which is the cornucopia (59–60): *apparetque beata pleno / Copia cornu* ("and Abundance appears, blessed with her full horn").

Finally, trust is expressed in Apollo that he will preserve the *res Romana* and Latium for another happy *lustrum* and for a better age (*melius aevum*) always (66–68). The terms are traditional: a *lustrum* was the five-year period, commencing with the appointment of the censors, though in the course of time *lustrum* could also connote a longer period.[63] Similarly, *felix* is a traditional epithet of *lustrum*, going back, significantly, to the time of Cato, the archetypal preserver of Roman *mores*.[64]

The best summation of the expectations at the time is the phrase *melius aevum*. Typically, it is not overblown, but it is simple and sober, nor does it have overtones of a millennium or Golden Age. It is enough that it contrasts with the pessimistic conclusion of the "Roman Odes":

> damnosa quid non imminuit dies?
> aetas parentum, peior avis, tulit
>   nos nequiores, mox daturos
>   progeniem vitiosiorem.
>
> (C. 3.6.45–48)

[What do the ravages of time not injure! Our parents' age, worse than their parents', has brought forth us who are yet more worthless and will soon produce a more depraved offspring yet.]

The reason for Horace's perspective here is the moral degeneration of the Romans. Similarly, Livy wrote, in the preface to his history of Rome, "we have reached the point where we can tolerate neither our vices nor their remedies." Moral decline had to be remedied before there could be any hope for better times. The first three books of *Odes* were published in 23 B.C., the moral laws were passed in 18 B.C., and the Secular Games took place one year later. There could be cautious hope for amelioration. *Aevum* can be an age, a lifetime, or a generation.[65] Its etymology also included the notion of eternity, although Horace uses a more explicit phrase (*in aevum . . . aeternet*) when he speaks of eternalizing Augustus' *virtutes* (*C.* 4.14.3–5). *Aevum* in *Carmen Saeculare* 68 may be a tacit allusion to the concept of *Roma aeterna*, which Horace elsewhere affirms (*C.* 3.30.8–9) and which Ovid implicitly rejects in his epilogue to the *Metamorphoses* (15.871ff.). Intentional, too, are the affinities, in both diction[66] and sentiment, with the prediction of Vergil's Jupiter that a Trojan Caesar, after his conquest of the east, will usher in a gentler age that will set an end to the civil wars and be characterized by a return of law and the ancient virtues (*Aen.* 1.283–94).

In sum, the literary evidence suggests a sober and finely balanced perception of the new *saeculum*. While the notion occurs that it was to be coextensive with Augustus' lifetime,[67] it more generally expressed a hope for better times ahead especially as the preceding decades had been singularly ruinous. And the new era was not one of automatic blessings but was grounded in moral and even military effort.

A final aspect is, once again, the continuing connection with Julius Caesar. As the *ludi saeculares* approached, the moneyer Marcus Sanquinius issued gold pieces and denarii with Julius Caesar and his comet on the reverse and, on the obverse, a messenger for the games with his winged herald's staff (*caduceus*), a shield embossed with a star, and a helmet with two feathers, all encircled by the legend *August[us] Divi F[ilius] ludos sae[culares]* (Fig. 40).[68] We are

40. Denarius of M. Sanquinius, 17 B.C.
Obverse: Herald for the Secular Games. Reverse: Julius Caesar and his comet.

looking at a rejuvenated Caesar whose image is assimilated to the youthful image of Augustus to such an extent that one numismatic expert proposed a different identity such as the Genius of the new *saeculum*.[69] The implication, however, is quite clear: when Caesar's comet appeared in 44 B.C., one of the omnipresent seers interpreted it as an omen of the end of the ninth *saeculum* and the arrival of the tenth (in the Etruscan scheme).[70] Caesar's star was hailed as the bringer of fruitfulness by Vergil (*Ecl.* 9.47–49). Its connection with the *ludi saeculares* was certainly not out of place, given, among other things, the association of the festival with Rome's *imperium* and the program of moral reform Cicero had urged on Caesar (*Marc.* 23–24). We have no other evidence for the actual appearance of a comet in 17 B.C. nor, as we saw earlier, must we assume that the coin was designed at Augustus' request. Its suggestiveness, however, was by no means inappropriate: in Jupiter's prophecy in the *Aeneid*, too, "Caesar Iulius" (1.286–88) can refer to both Caesar and Augustus.[71]

The Representation of the Golden Age in Art

As we have seen, the notion of the Golden Age or *saeculum* at Augustus' time was distinctive and specific in the sense that it involved ongoing labor and moral effort rather than being a celebration of easy fulfillment. Since Augustan art is quite different from socialist realism, we cannot expect a palpable translation of this concept into artistic representations, such as a scene of Saturnian bliss awaiting a sweating plowman and his oxen, with Caesar's comet discreetly illuminating the horizon. In addition, there is the usual limitation to a small number of iconographic types. In this instance as in others, including the catchphrases about *libertas* and the like, Augustan culture uses traditional chiffers, such as the cornucopia, and invests them with contemporary meanings. What is remarkable, however, and thoroughly in accordance with the emphasis on the happiness of the times as a goal and process rather than a millennial guarantee, is the restraint in conveying the message and, more generally, the paucity of representations. This very fact has often been overcompensated for by a certain effusiveness of interpretation, but the suggestive intent even of major icons of *felicitas*, such as the female figure on the Ara Pacis, needs to be considered within the balanced perspective of the entire monument or artifact.

There is no question that of all the relief panels of the Ara Pacis Augustae, this is the one most emblematic of peace and tranquillity.[72] A goddess, whose iconography is characterized by multiple associations, sits at ease in the center of the composition (Fig. 41). In her lap are fruits, and two small children, whom she is holding, are reaching out to her. Reeds, poppies, and ears of grain are sprouting up next to her. A cow (or an ox; the head is a modern restoration) lies peacefully at her feet together with a sheep that is drinking from the water which flows from her rocky throne. Two female companion figures with billowing veils, one sitting on a swan, the other on a sea animal, flank her on both sides.

It is a simple and suggestive idyll indeed, despite all the complexity of the underlying iconography, but not an idyll that stands in a vacuum. For the complementary panel on the northeast side showed the goddess Roma, in a similarly seated pose, on a pile of arms and, probably, with spear and shield (Fig. 42). Likewise, the scene of Aeneas' sacrifice on the west side (Fig. 43) was complemented by the presence of Mars on the other relief on that side. Tranquillity is made possible only through war, victory, and dominance. "Peace was achieved through victories" (*parta victoriis pax*) was Augustus' own explicit comment on the Ara Pacis (*RG* 13). Ovid articulates the same notion in his hymnic description of the Ara Pacis: the whole world, near and far, shall live in terror of the sons of Aeneas (*Fasti* 1.717–18). The Ara Pacis, on the Field of Mars, was part of an architectural ensemble (Fig. 64) that glorified conquest, especially the conquest of Egypt. The tip of the monumental sundial contained a small globe, symbolizing world domination. In Augustan poetry, including the *Carmen Saeculare*, the nexus between conquest and *pax* is a constant refrain. For the same good reasons, therefore, does Vergil's praise of Italy in *Georgics* 2.136ff. include her warlike aspects; here as elsewhere, they are complementary to the blessings of peace rather than merely "ambiguous."

Likewise, the imagery on the cuirass of the Prima Porta Augustus is permeated by Rome's newly found dominance of the Parthians in 20 B.C. The center of the composition is held by the Parthian surrender of the Roman standards to the god Mars (Fig. 73). The scene is flanked by the dejected personifications of lands under Rome's domination in both east and west. The rear of the breastplate, which is often ignored because of the frontal orientation of the statue, depicts a helmeted trophy, a *tropaeum* (Fig. 44), and a winged Victoria was probably represented, too. As a pendant to the sky-god, who is shown at the top of the armor, a representation of Mother Earth lies at the bottom. She has a crown of grain ears, as do goddesses like Ceres and Pax, and she holds a cornucopia. Fruitfulness and prosperity are not simply handed down by the gods. Instead, they are the result of Rome's dominance, which is based on efforts in war and takes place under the tutelage of supporting deities such as Venus, Apollo, and Diana, all of whom appear on the cuirass.

The same nexus is found on the armor of an imperial statue from Caesarea in North Africa (Fig. 45).[73] Mars has taken the place held by the sky-god Caelus on the breastplate of the Prima Porta statue. The middle scene shows Victoria crowning a member of the Julian family, either Julius Caesar or the young Gaius Caesar. The bearded faces on the (simulated) leather flaps of the armor allude to the conquered Parthians. Such martial efforts result in the

41. Ara Pacis Augustae. Female deity with symbols of fruitfulness.

42. Ara Pacis Augustae. Panel with Roma, restored.

43. Ara Pacis Augustae. Aeneas' arrival in Italy.

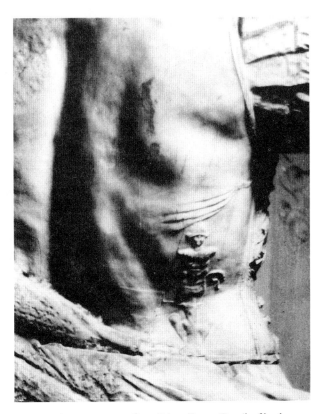

44. Augustus statue from Prima Porta. Detail of back.

45. Cuirassed statue from Cherchel, Algeria, with images of victory and prosperity.

blessings on land and sea, symbolized by a land centaur and a sea centaur in
the lower tier of the cuirass. The sea centaur (on the left) holds up a part of
an enemy ship's prow. The land centaur carries a cornucopia. His body, in
the same fantastic fashion as in wall paintings in contemporary Augustan
villas, ends in a vegetal scroll. It is an acanthus scroll, which was associated
with the Venus Victrix of Caesar and elaborated in great detail on the Ara
Pacis.

Even more concisely, the same connection between war and peace is
expressed by the cornucopiae on the shoulder flaps of the cult statue of Mars
Ultor in the Forum of Augustus (Fig. 46).[74] The Temple of Mars was built
to preserve the memory of both the revenge on Caesar's assassins and the
Parthian conquest. In its pediment, therefore, Fortuna with her cornucopia
and rudder is flanked by the central figure of Mars and a victorious Roma
similar to that on the Ara Pacis (Fig. 47). Another example is the representation of Mars on an Augustan relief with a cornucopia out of which spring the
twins Romulus and Remus, who reach out for a *tropaeum* commemorating
the subjection of the Parthians (Fig. 48).[75] Similarly, when Horace speaks
about "the golden goddess of Plenty pouring out fruits for Italy from her full
horn" (*Epist.* 1.12.28–29) he does so very specifically in the context of the
interventions that illustrated Rome's military might in the year 20 B.C.: Tiberius' march into Armenia; Augustus' reduction of the Parthians (their king
"Phraates accepted the Roman law and rule [*imperium*] on his knees"; *Epist.*
1.12.27–28), and the conquests in Spain of Agrippa, who shared an estate
with Iccius, the addressee of Horace's *Epistle*. Moreover, "golden Plenty"
(*aurea Copia*) is no more than a relative and wishful invocation coming
against the backdrop of poor harvests and a terrible famine in 22 B.C.[76] Likewise, the nexus between agricultural prosperity and the subjugation of the
Parthians recurs in Horace's final ode (*C.* 4.15.4–8), his poetic *summa* of the
Augustan age, which he calls simply *tua, Caesar, aetas* instead of *aurea aetas* or
aureum saeculum.

In general, the cornucopiae we encounter on Augustan coins and gems
cannot be interpreted indiscriminately as betokening a Golden Age suggestive of the fourth *Eclogue*. The emblem itself denoted prosperity and happier
days. It had a long tradition on coins of the republic, beginning in 207 B.C.[77]
amid the Hannibalic war and the damage it inflicted on Roman agriculture.
It occurs, in characteristic association with the globe (symbolizing world
dominion) and Victoria, in contexts such as the war against Sertorius in
74 B.C. or celebrating with similar imagery, including Honos and Virtus on
the obverse, the reconciliation between Rome and Italy.[78] Cornucopiae appear as the emblem of a composite deity who is mostly Isis, but has attributes
of Minerva, Apollo, and Victoria, and in the ambience of Sulla's Fortuna.[79]
And, as could be expected, we find cornucopiae on the coins of Caesar, again

46. Statue of Mars, modeled on Mars Ultor in the Forum Augustum, ca. A.D. 90.

47. Pediment of the Mars Ultor temple. From the Ara Pietatis Augustae, time of Claudius. To the right of Mars (center): Fortuna and Roma.

48. Fragment of Augustan relief. Mars with cornucopia and the twins.

49. Aureus of Mark Antony, 41 B.C. Obverse: Antony.
Reverse: Fortuna with rudder and cornucopiae; legend: PIETAS COS.

50. Aureus of Octavian, ca. 40 B.C. Obverse: Octavian, Divi Iuli Filius.
Reverse: Fortuna with rudder and cornucopiae.

in conjunction with imperial symbols such as globe, scepter, and rudder, and of Antony, who was profiling the *pietas* of his brother Lucius in 41 B.C. (Fig. 49).[80] Shortly thereafter, Octavian issued his own coins with his image as *divi filius* on the obverse and Fortuna (possibly the Fortuna Caesaris), a rudder, and cornucopiae on the reverse (Fig. 50),[81] perhaps in the wake of a resettlement of veterans after the Perusine War in which he starved out Lucius Antonius and his followers.

The other strand of inspiration may have been Ptolemaic Egypt. There the cornucopia was a standard symbol on the reverse of coins depicting Ptolemaic queens on the obverse.[82] A cameo (Fig. 51), probably made shortly after Octavian's conquest of Alexandria in 30 B.C., shows him as the heir of the Ptolemaic god-kings.[83] He is seated on a throne decorated with a sphinx, and holds a scepter and a double cornucopia. Seated next to him is Roma, holding her shield and pointing to heaven. The double cornucopia, symbol of the blessings dispensed by the royal pair of brother and sister, appears also on coins of Cleopatra in conjunction with two other emblems found on Augus-

51. Ptolemaic cameo with Octavian and Roma, ca. 30–28 B.C.

tan representations, the globe and the *caduceus* of Mercury. The type was promptly appropriated by Antony.[84] To this iconography, Augustus added his birth sign, the capricorn, and the development of the type at times evidences the same playful fantasy that characterizes Egyptian motifs in Augustan wall painting: a cornucopia almost grows out of the capricorn, and the final stage is the representation of cornucopiae ending in goat's heads (Fig. 52).[85] On coins, the association with world rule is steadily maintained by the inclusion of globe and rudder in the depiction of the cornucopia-bearing capricorn (Fig. 53).[86] Struck in Spain, these gold coins and denarii date from the time of the Secular Games.

Even if after Actium a more sedentary type of Victoria complements the images of her impetuous, globe-storming predecessor,[87] the conjunction of cornucopiae with the Victory icon remains true to the original concept of "prosperity through victory and conquests." The more "peaceful" type of Victoria does not simply replace the other, which survived handsomely.

52. Augustan altar: cornucopia with goats' heads.

53. Denarius, minted in Spain ca. 17–15 B.C.
Reverse: Capricorn with cornucopia and globe.

54. Terracotta lamp with Victoria and the Lares.

55. Dupondius (?) issued 7 B.C. Obverse: Augustus with Victory and cornucopia.
Reverse: SC with moneyer's name (M. Salvius Otho).

On a lamp in London with the *clupeus virtutis*, a swirling Victoria carries both
the legionary standard and a cornucopia (Fig. 54) while the two flanking
Lares allude to the cult of the Genius Augusti.[88] On the splendid bronze
coinage of 7 B.C. (Fig. 55), the space next to Augustus' head is filled by a
Victoria who holds both a cornucopia and a laurel crown,[89] the traditional
sign of the triumphator; the Prima Porta Augustus stood at Livia's villa where
the laurel grew with which the Julio-Claudian *triumphatores* were crowned.
A final image, on a gem, is Livia contemplating the radiate bust of Augustus
that rests on a globe on top of a cornucopia (Fig. 56).[90]

56. Gem: Livia with bust of Augustus.

In sum, no specific iconography exists that would point to a "Golden Age" of easy bliss. The reason is simple enough: there was no intention to convey such an impression. To be sure, these were to be *felicia saecula* (Ovid, *Trist.* 1.2.103–4), a phrase that, like so many other Augustan tropes, became routinized in the reign of his successors. But there was no attempt to obscure, through a plethora of blissful images, the realities of the age. Besides the imagery we have surveyed, there is rather little that can be adduced:[91] the fountain reliefs from Praeneste, showing various she-animals nursing their young, are probably of a later date; birds feeding their young turn up on a relief from Falerii, but then we see a snake attacking a bird's nest on the very Ara Pacis Augustae (Fig. 69); and, as for agricultural scenes, it would be unreasonable to expect representations of emaciated cows rather than well-fed ones. Few as they are, such representations in Augustan art were the equivalent to the literary commonplace of agriculture as a symbol of peace under an ideal ruler. It was a concept as old as Homer and was restated persuasively by Philodemus in his treatise *On the Good King according to Homer*. Philodemus, who attracted some of the brightest and most influential Romans while he taught near Naples from 75 B.C. to around 40–35 B.C., stressed that the good ruler had to be warlike without being a warmonger; Homer hates both the lover of war and of civil strife. "The result of such unity is material prosperity. . . . Homer really believes that good harvests go with a benevolent and just ruler."[92] If Cicero could claim that Rome's fields lay barren during his exile (*Red. in Sen.* 34; *Red. Quir.* 18), Horace's praise of the *aetas Augusta* in terms of the return of fertile fruits to the fields (*C.* 4.15.4–5) was anything but extravagant.

Besides the ethos of an ongoing effort rather than easy fulfillment, the economic realities of the Italian countryside were another restraint on too celebratory a rendition of the *aurea aetas*. There is no evidence of sudden prosperity during Augustus' reign. The civil wars had been a destabilizing factor, but so was Octavian/Augustus' resettlement of veterans by means of land confiscations. The process did not cease until 13 B.C. or, more precisely, until the very return of Augustus in 13 B.C. which prompted the vow for the Ara Pacis: Augustus' principal action after his return, as Dio relates in the same chapter in which he discusses the genesis of the Ara Pacis, was to settle the long-standing problem of the compensation of the soldiery, a measure that "in the rest of the population . . . aroused confident hopes that they would not in the future be robbed of their possessions" (54.25.6). That was one aspect of *pax*, too, as a lingering relic of the civil wars was finally laid to rest. It is realistic concerns like these, rather than the fourth *Eclogue*, that were on people's minds when the pictorial program of the altar was designed. The reestablishment of security, however, by this measure and others did not amount to a favoring of rural property and an immediate upswing of agriculture.[93]

This picture is confirmed by the studies of the increasing, though still regrettably small, number of scholars who have ventured beyond the allure of urban edifices to look at the economy of the countryside. The very region near Rome, as Timothy Potter has observed, does not present a picture of uniform prosperity. In the Sabine area, for example, "no less than 67% of Republican sites appear to have gone out of use at the end of the first century B.C., while an even greater proportion, 76% of the early imperial farms, represent new foundations."[94] A few prospered; many failed. Similarly, the area of southern Italy or Magna Graecia, as evidenced especially by the excavations in the countryside of Metaponto, reveals a real decline of the physical environment and the agricultural economy during the Augustan period. It is only decades after the *aetas Augusta* that relative stability was established in the area in terms of both the environment and human settlement.[95] We can add to these economic straits the well-documented shortage of the money supply in the second half of Augustus' reign.[96]

In the light of all this, it is understandable that the presentation of the arrival of a new age did not amount to a steady irrigation of the populace

57. Gemma Augustea, ca. A.D. 10.

with literary tropes and artistic images that conjured up a utopia devoid of
any credibility. The actual realities of Roman life also explain the modification of the original Golden Age concept in literature into one where ongoing *labor* is the prevailing virtue. They further explain the frequent iconographic emphasis on the relation of warlike effort to prosperity. This is
exemplified, to use a final illustration, by the so-called Gemma Augustea, a
large cameo that dates from the last years of Augustus (Fig. 57).[97] More than
three-quarters of the decoration is taken up by references to war. In the
lower part, there is a generic scene of Roman soldiers erecting a trophy amid
defeated barbarians. In the upper portion, Augustus and Roma are seated
on a throne and hold the spear and scepter of imperial power. In addition,
Roma rests her left hand on the handle of her sword and Augustus is
crowned by Oecumenē, the personification of global empire since Alexander, with the *corona civica* of oak leaves. To the left is a young prince, most

probably Germanicus, in military dress while the triumphing Tiberius descends from a chariot driven by the goddess Victoria. But the emphasis is not on celebration: she is impatiently urging on her horses to take him to his next campaign, a realistic reflection of his and Germanicus' almost constant campaigning in the last decade of Augustus' reign. Corresponding to Tiberius and Victoria is the pair, on the right, of Neptune and Italia, who is distinguished from Mother Earth by the *bulla* she wears around her neck, and who is accompanied by two children that probably represent the seasons of summer and fall. It may not be accidental that the corncucopia held by Italia is now empty as famines and poor harvests were not infrequent.

A fundamental point, made for the visual arts by Paul Zanker, remains unchanged: both the literary and the artistic expressions of the Golden Age were the product not of a central authority but of the participatory creativity of many, and these expressions had their own, autonomous development. That development, however, was grounded in the realities we have observed.

VERGIL AND THE CREATION OF THE AUGUSTAN ETHOS

The poets in particular contributed significantly to the creation of the Augustan ethos. An outstanding example is the passage in Vergil's *Georgics* which I cited earlier (1.121–46; see pp. 93–94). It has been well observed that this passage and others in the poem signal a complete agreement with the "restorative tendencies of the new Augustan order of state and society."[98] The poem, however, was written mostly in the 30s when those tendencies where hardly in evidence. They became Augustan tendencies in the following decade and we may assume that they had been under discussion for some time. Vergil's contribution was an early, fundamental formulation and poetic creation of a vision that proved to be one of the lasting and most basic aspects of Augustan culture.

The placement of the passage early in the first book of the *Georgics* leaves little doubt that Vergil intended it as a programmatic statement. He emphasizes several distinctive characteristics of the ethos of human existence. One, as we have seen, is that of incessant human effort and toil. The traditional Golden Age is rejected because it is one of torpor and inertia; the chain of civilizational attainments begins only with man's expulsion from paradise. The new Golden Age, identified with the existence of the farmer, is full of stress and depends on ongoing effort; it is not finite and god-given, but needs to be worked for every day anew. Fulfillment comes in large part from the incessant effort to reach that goal rather than from actually arriving at it.

Related to this aspect is the impossibility and even undesirability of a nostalgic return to a stagnant past. That past is exemplified by the sloth of paradise. A different past, which needs to be revitalized, is the existence of the independent Roman farmer. Vergil's presentation of it deliberately does not correspond to the contemporary realities of the *latifundia*, large estates owned by nonresident investors, that were managed for profit and mostly with slave labor. The basic Roman values and mores, which were in need of restoration, had been traditionally associated with those of the small, independent landholder. Along these lines, Vergil rejects the ideal of communal property instead of private property (1.127). The same conjunction of larger moral issues and concern for private property was to characterize the Augustan legislation on marriage and morals. The point in all this, as in similar endeavors in Augustan culture, was not to turn the clock back to the actual social conditions of fourth-century Rome, but to retain and revivify the old concepts and values amid changed political, economic, and social circumstances.

Another, and related, important aspect of Vergil's ethical vision is the meaning of *labor improbus*, which conquers all (1.145). *Improbus* is used here primarily in the sense of "immense."[99] Labor is a positive value and it needs to be immense to make human existence fulfilling. But by saying *improbus* rather than *immensus* and by alluding to at least some of the other connotations inherent in *improbus*—such as "wicked" and "accursed"—Vergil also sounds a meaningful cautionary note. *Labor improbus* connotes not only the avoidance of paradisiac inertia, but also the avoidance of materialistic excess caused by a *labor* that is more than the means to the end of fulfilling the simple and self-sustaining needs arising from want (*egestas*; 1.146). The parallels with book 5 of Lucretius cannot be ignored here.[100] This quest to observe the fine line between the comfortable and justifiable fulfillment of basic needs, and greed and excess, adds to the challenge of human existence as defined by Vergil. It is clearly relevant to the tendencies that comprise the so-called Augustan moral program.

A final aspect of the Vergilian ethos in the *Georgics* is that man's effort is not autonomous, but takes place under the aegis of providential gods like Jupiter and Ceres. Instead of the Promethean ethic of Hesiod, who has Zeus create inordinate labors for man out of revenge, and instead of the ethic of the Sophists who made abstract principles such as *penia* ("lack" or "need") the prime impulses for the development of human civilization, Vergil regards man's efforts and troubles as divinely providential. Man is not the measure of all things: "Above all, worship the gods" says Vergil (*Geo.* 1.338; cf. *Aen.* 6.620). Unremitting human struggle, as exemplified by the existence of the farmer, is an essential part of the divine world order. Nor are the gods aloof, but, like Ceres, they assist mankind. The emphatic renewal of Roman religion in the Augustan age was ultimately based on these very concepts.

We have isolated in the *Georgics*, then, the following principal aspects of Vergil's definition of the ethos of human existence: the infeasibility of a simple return to the past; the emphasis on unceasing human effort, which, more often than not, is *not* rewarded by immediate fulfillment; the avoidance of materialistic excess; and the sanctioned place of human effort within a providential, divine world order. All these elements, which formulate and express fundamental Augustan ideas, are also constituents of the ethos of the *Aeneid*. It may suffice to concentrate on the first two of these aspects.

Besides adverting to *labores* as a major theme of the epic in the proem (1.10), Vergil deliberately presents Aeneas initially as someone who, like many a good Roman, is trying to seek recourse in the past, only to wean him away from it—Aeneas literally cannot go home again—and have him develop an existential ideal, which, like the revised Golden Age ideal in the *Georgics*, is far more trying, far more challenging, and ultimately far more meaningful. The first actual appearance of Aeneas in the epic sets the tone. The circumstances of this entrance are quite untraditional and unheroic—the hero is about to drown pitifully—but there is a great deal of conventional attitude left in him. He wishes he were back at Troy:

> extemplo Aeneae solvuntur frigore membra;
> ingemit et duplicis tendens ad sidera palmas
> talia voce refert: 'o terque quaterque beati,
> quis ante ora patrum Troiae sub moenibus altis
> contigit oppetere! O Danaum fortissime gentis
> Tydide! mene Iliacis occumbere campis
> non potuisse tuaque animam hanc effundere dextra,
> saevus ubi Aeacidae telo iacet Hector, ubi ingens
> Sarpedon, ubi tot Simois correpta sub undis
> scuta virum galeasque et fortia corpora volvit.'
>
> (1.92–101)

[At once Aeneas' limbs weaken with the chill of death.
He groans and stretching out both hands to heaven
says this: "Oh three and four times blessed you
who met death before their father's eyes
beneath Troy's lofty walls! Bravest of the Greeks,
Diomedes! Why could I not go down on Ilium's
battlefield and breathe out my soul at your hand,
at Troy where fierce Hector lies struck by Achilles' spear,
where huge Sarpedon lies, and where the river Simois
seizes and sweeps beneath his waves so many shields
and helmets and bodies of the brave!"]

The prayer is based on Odysseus' in *Odyssey* 5.306ff., and the changes Vergil makes are significant, as always. Odysseus refers to his homecoming in Ithaca. For Aeneas, Troy is still home, and the nostalgic references to Troy are expanded; the phrase "before their fathers' eyes" (*ante ora patrum*), for instance, has no equivalent in the Homeric model. Aeneas' plea goes beyond

the warrior's wish to have died nobly in battle; it appeals to the typically
Roman inclination to turn to the past, including heroic death, especially in
times of duress, and to prefer the safety of the past to the uncertainties of the
present, let alone the future. This attitude is shown to be inadequate, in the
subsequent part of the poem, by the prophecy of Jupiter (1.257ff.) in which
he dismisses Venus' *Biedermeier* ideal of a placid recreation of the Trojan
existence, as exemplified by Antenor (1.242–49) and instead places the emphasis on the ongoing *labores* of Aeneas:

> bellum ingens geret Italia populosque ferocis
> contundet moresque viris et moenia ponet.
>
> (1.263–64)

> [A huge war he will wage in Italy. Warlike peoples he will crush
> and then for the people there establish *mores* and city walls.]

Aeneas will not complete this process in his lifetime. His travails will be only
the beginning and they will reach their culmination centuries later, at the
time of Augustus (1.291–96).[101]

In book 3, Aeneas' wish to return to the past is actually fulfilled when he
encounters Hector's widow, Andromache, now married to Helenus, another Trojan. They have transformed their habitat in western Greece into a
replica of Troy, a sort of Disneyland Troy, complete with the Scaean Gate
and even the river Simois, the very river mentioned by Aeneas in his first
speech. The architecture is only the most palpable manifestation of the inhabitants' attitude: they have retreated into the past and live there. Andromache has resolutely recreated her life before the fall of Troy. Her values,
beliefs, and thinking are at home there and everything has to conform to
them. To her, Aeneas' son Ascanius is not a future ruler, but a surrogate for
her own dead son, Astyanax. She gives him a gift, a Phrygian cloak, that ties
him to his past, and she expresses the hope that the martial virtue of Hector
will live on in Ascanius. Aeneas is strongly affected by this pull toward the
past, but he recognizes its limitations and realizes that such a return is not for
him although the past, to any good Roman (and even some modern politicians), is a solid symbol of felicity. His poignant farewell epitomizes the
difference between their outlook and his:

> vivite felices, quibus est fortuna peracta
> iam sua; nos alia ex aliis in fata vocamur.
> vobis parta quies.
>
> (3.493–95)

> [Live happily; your fortune is already achieved.
> We, however, are called from one vicissitude to the other.
> For you there is quiet rest.]

It is a summary full of poignant echoes. When she first saw Aeneas, Andromache had pronounced Cassandra to be *felix* because she died "beneath the high walls of Troy" (*Troiae sub moenibus altis*; 3.322), just like the heroes whom Aeneas evoked in his first utterance (1.95). *Quies* is precisely the ideal Venus had envisaged for Aeneas and it is also the term that Lucretius associates with the Epicurean gods.[102] As for Aeneas, he merely repeats what he said at the outset of his encounter with Andromache and Helenus, which sets his particular situation a world apart from theirs (3.315): "I'm alive, to be sure—living through every kind of adversity" (*vivo equidem vitamque extrema per omnia duco*). In other words, Vergil's emphasis is on the timeless moment of the *labores* of his hero. If Vergil does not depict Aeneas in the posture of success, glory, triumph, or attainment, it is not because he takes a skeptical view of that success or the Augustan achievement, but because a depiction of Aeneas' honestly trying to work out his destiny and being caught up in the complexities and vagaries of life enables the poet to say far more about the human condition.

The next way stations of Aeneas' progressive separation from the past are his leave-taking from Dido, who restored him to his status as an oriental prince, his encounter with the insubstantial shades of the Trojan war heroes in the underworld, and his introduction to Roman austerity by King Evander in book 8. The culmination comes with the pact between Jupiter and Juno near the end of the epic: the Trojan nation will lose its separate identity and merge with the Latins into the Italian and Roman race. Vitality comes not from withdrawing into the past, but from using it as a basis for transformation.

Related to this perspective is the reorientation of the time frame of the *Aeneid*. In line with the earlier Roman epic tradition and contemporary expectations, Vergil could have written—and this is suggested by the proem to the third *Georgic*—an epic centering on Augustus and incorporating the story of Aeneas by flashbacks. The essential difference would have been the vantage point: Roman history as seen from the pinnacle, that is, the reign of Augustus. In other words, there would have been the notion that the goal had been attained and the high point had been reached, with the rest of the story appearing as mere preliminaries to that final achievement. Instead, Vergil turned the perspective inside out. Chronologically, we are at the beginning of the journey. The dynamics of getting there give a vivid sense of the effort required. Life is a process, characterized by steady toil and struggle, rather than restful repose at a fixed point. It is more meaningful to work toward a goal than to enjoy the fruits of reaching it. Renewal is more important than fruition which leads to stagnation. The reorientation of the time perspective in the *Aeneid*—it is an *Aeneid* rather than an *Augusteid*—reflects an ethos that Vergil outlined in the *Georgics* and which permeates much of the Augustan age.

We encounter the same attitude in other Augustan poets, including Ovid's *Art of Love*. It is characteristic of Ovid that he understood only too well the intentions of Vergil, Horace, and Augustus. The late Brooks Otis once aptly characterized the *Art of Love* as a glorification, however peculiar, of the Augustan way of life.[103] Refracted in the Ovidian mirror, the Augustan ethos we have just delineated emerges with its own kind of distorted brilliance. For in the *Art of Love*, quite in contrast to modern manuals on the subject, the emphasis again is not on fulfillment or gratification, but on incessant effort and pursuit and on the journey ("the hunt"; 1.253) rather than the arrival. "In the beginning," proclaims Ovid, "exert yourself [*labora*] to find the object of your love" (1.35). The next step—to win over the lady and to keep her love—is explicitly characterized as *labor* (1.37). Purposefully, Ovid presents the pursuit of love as analogous to the principal arts of human society that Vergil enumerated in his seminal passage at the beginning of the *Georgics*: navigation, hunting, and farming. Georgic imagery, in fact, colors much of the poem.[104]

A more imposing literary reflection of this particular Augustan ethos, which leads us back to the emperor, is Horace's *Letter to Augustus*. It is one of Horace's last works and a summation of many of the concerns he voiced throughout his earlier poetry. Rather than being a forced eulogy of Augustus, as Suetonius would have it,[105] or a political and social document in the eighteenth-century view, it is a thoughtful if discursive statement about the state of literary and intellectual life at the time. Quite purposefully, therefore, the emphasis from the very beginning is not on achievement, but on struggle, and especially on the difficulty with which the new and modern Augustan poetry has to contend. Horace begins the poem by asserting that while Augustus, though following in the footsteps of the toiling Hercules, is receiving due recognition, the same cannot be said of the contemporary poets, Horace, of course, in particular. They are victimized by the Romans' inordinate craving for the literary tradition of the past and by the axiomatic equation of the good with the old. The tension to which Horace is pointing, between outward traditionalism and actual, experimental innovation was, as we have already seen, another hallmark of the Augustan age.

While Augustus was by no means a staunch antiquarian,[106] the Roman populace, Horace continues, is so inured to looking backward and extolling tradition that its lacks any understanding of the creative innovation that makes a tradition possible in the first place. Witness the Greeks—if they had been inhibited by popular taste, as Horace and his contemporaries are, no literary tradition would have arisen in the first place (line 91). The final thrust is directed at the *Carmen Saliare*, the hymn of the Salian priests, which continued to be performed under Augustus and was piously celebrated in *Aeneid* 8. To Horace, it is yet another symbol of the deadweight of excessive traditionalism. He points out that even the admirers of the poem cannot figure out what it means. Therefore such people do not really favor and applaud the buried geniuses; they simply attack the modern temper. They hate us moderns, says Horace, and anything of ours:

> ingeniis non ille favet plauditque sepultis,
> nostra sed impugnat, nos nostraque lividus odit.
>
> (88–89)

[He does not favor or applaud buried talents,
but he attacks ours, and he spitefully hates us and our works.]

Horace concludes his discussion of the contrast between traditionalism and modernism in Augustan Rome with the extensive example of the state of the Roman theater (161ff.). It is backward, it has not progressed past Plautus (second century B.C.); if anything, it has regressed in sophistication and artistry. The only progress that has been made is in the area of material opulence. The shows now are replete with chariots, bears, camels, and even the proverbial white elephant. Peacetime prosperity has resulted in both this new lavishness and the concomitant loss of literary taste. The double tide of materialism and traditionalism makes further attainment in the theater impossible. And although Horace does not say so, Augustus seemed to be quite content with the situation. While his criterion for literature was moral salubriousness (Suet., *Aug.* 89.2), theatrical spectacles that had pure entertainment value were among the things that delighted him most (Suet., *Aug.* 43–45).

Horace realizes it would be unfair to the literary achievements of the Augustan age to end on the note of the failure of the theater. He therefore turns to the example of Vergil and Varius, whose literary merits found due recognition and encouragement. But once more, Horace is careful not to end on the note of completeness. Whereas the poetry of Vergil and Varius belongs in the epic tradition and therefore finds ready acceptance, we are left with Horace's efforts that were not nearly so successful: the final vignette is that of Horace's poetic sheets being used as wrapping paper in the neighborhood grocery store (267–70). It is not as abrasive a picture as that presented earlier, but it recalls the earlier argument on the plight of the modern innovator amid traditional and misguided antiquarian preferences.

The *Letter to Augustus*, then, is not an exercise in self-satisfaction, but a call to continued effort. It is typical of Horace that he, like Vergil—and we need only to think of all the straits into which Aeneas is constantly placed—calls attention to the dilemmas and the incomplete state of affairs that require ongoing effort rather than to finite solutions and contentment even with the Augustan cultural milieu. The *Letter* was one of the last works, if not the last work, of Horace and its spiritual affinity with the tenor of the *Georgics* and the *Aeneid* confirms the continuity of this Augustan ethos in literature for at least three decades.

What emerges from all this is that the Augustan age did not view itself as a period of complete fulfillment, attainment, and, especially, contentment and self-satisfaction—quite in contrast to Augustanism in England and France or, to give a more current example, the perspective that informs the strictures of a Robert Graves on the "Virgil Cult."[107] A twentieth-century observer has defined the phenomenon of the fullness of time, the *felicitas saeculi*, by saying that "there have been various periods in history which have felt themselves as having attained a full, definitive height, periods in which it was thought that the end of the journey had been reached, a long-felt desire obtained, a hope completely filled."[108] But he goes on to conclude, quite rightly, that this famous plenitude is in fact an illusion, and that genuine vital integrity does not consist in satisfaction, attainment, or arrival. In that vein, Pliny the Elder's famous characterization of Augustus (*HN* 7.149–50) does not dwell on the *felicitas* of the man, but on the numerous setbacks and travails in his life.

THE LEGISLATION ON MORALS AND MARRIAGE

While the concept of an "Augustan program" has often been overstated, it fully applies to the legislation on morals and marriage: Augustus was the prime mover behind this unmistakable legislative program. It was central to his reign.[109] One indication of this, as we saw earlier, was the postponement of the Secular Games until the principal laws had been passed. Another, concomitant testimony was the role Horace accorded them in the *Carmen Saeculare* and, as we shall see, in some of his other poems, too. Similarly, when we look forward in time, we find that the Augustan marriage laws, which remained in effect for over two hundred years, attracted more comment from the Roman jurists than did any other laws. They were also the basis for a famous excursus by Tacitus (*Ann.* 3.25–28) who regarded them as the height of state's interference with personal freedom and as "the end of fair law" (*finis aequi iuris*).

The reason for all these reverberations, including the vigorous protest in Augustus' own time of those that stood to be affected (Suet., *Aug.* 34.1), is that the laws were far-reaching indeed, though not with reference to externals such as a stimulation of the birthrate; this traditional explanation has rightly come to be considered as extraneous and been largely discounted. Rather, the significance of the legislation, even though its special thrust aimed at the nobility, was that the private life of virtually every Roman now became a matter of the state's concern and regulations. The state massively intruded on matters of private conduct such as marriage—the question was no more whether to marry, but how soon and whom or whom not—and divorce and adultery; the latter was taken out of the jurisdiction of the family and transferred to a public court. Other palpable effects on people's everyday lives included the prohibition for unmarried men and women to attend the spectacles.

It was, in short, the most pronounced attempt at moral and even moralistic leadership, which in this case forcefully transcended the mere exercise of *auctoritas*. The resort to laws about morality is another counterindication to the assumption that the Augustan age viewed itself unreservedly in terms of Golden Age fulfillment; Greek and Roman writers were quite specific that in a true Golden Age good moral conduct happened of its own accord and needed no legislative remedy.[110] Another typically Augustan aspect of this extraordinary endeavor lies in the combination of an ostensible evocation of the past with a new departure. Augustus suggests this much in his own summary of the legislation:

> Legibus novis me auctore latis multa exempla maiorum exolescentia iam ex nostro saeculo reduxi et ipse multarum rerum exempla imitanda posteris tradidi. (*RG* 8.5)

> [By new laws passed on my initiative I brought back into use many exemplary practices of our ancestors that were disappearing in our time, and in many ways I myself transmitted exemplary practices to posterity for their imitation.]

It is also a paradigm of what Burns has aptly defined as "the cardinal responsibility of leadership," that is, "to identify the dominant contradiction at each point of the historical process."[111] The very phrase "new laws" (*leges novae*) would indicate to the Roman ruling class that something almost revolutionary was afoot;[112] the Roman term for "upheaval" was simply *res novae*. And yet it was all done in the name of restoring the traditional values, whose neglect was said to have caused the decline of the *res publica*, and in the name of changing public and private attitudes with the force of law. As I have noted on several occasions, Horace, anticipating the dictum of twentieth-century American politicians that "you cannot legislate morality into the hearts of men," asked the proper rhetorical question: "What do empty laws avail without *mores*? (*C.* 3.24.35–36) and there is considerable evidence, as we saw earlier, that this was also Augustus' view. Still, it was left to him to emphasize the converse: *mores* cannot flourish unless they are backed up by laws. Laws were the means to the end of producing good *mores*. The spirit allowed exceptions to the letter: Horace, Vergil, and others, though unmarried and childless, could be given the same privileges as a citizen with three children because they were serious about the social and moral responsibility that the laws sought to inculcate.

The motivation behind the marriage laws was typically multiple and goes well beyond mere moral zealotry. Before we return to these aspects, a brief word is in order about some of their specific provisions and their chronology.

The marriage laws were part of a cluster of moral legislation which, as we have seen, was passed prior to the celebration of the Secular Games in 17 B.C. The *Lex Julia de maritandis ordinibus* made marriage and remarriage mandatory for men from the ages of twenty-five to sixty and women between twenty and fifty. Divorced women and widows were required to find a new husband within six months and a year, respectively. Prohibitions were levied against fathers who obstructed their children's marriage. The childless or unmarried could not inherit nor could they leave an inheritance to anyone except for blood relatives to the sixth degree, otherwise the state became the sole beneficiary. While the law liberalized marriages between Romans and freed men and women, it prohibited members of the senatorial class from entering into such unions. There were some incentives as well, especially the *ius trium liberorum*, which gave tax relief to women with three or more (surviving) children and rewarded the male heads of such families with favored status for magistracies and the like.

The concomitant *Lex Julia de adulteriis coercendis* aimed to rein in a wide range of extramarital liaisons. The traditional jurisdiction of the family in these matters was superseded by a permanent court (*quaestio perpetua*) with well-defined procedures. A wife's adultery, if discovered by the husband, could not be condoned by him unless he wanted to make himself a punishable accessory to the crime. The penalties for all principals were stiff and ranged up to banishment. At the same time, easy divorce on the pretext of adultery was made more difficult and, for married men, the distinction between engaging in *adulterium* and *stuprum* (such as consorting with a prostitute) was effaced. Similarly, married women now were protected against forcible *stuprum*, including rape, by not being considered guilty of adultery, in apparent contrast to their previous treatment when jurisdiction belonged to the *pater familias*. The state now safeguarded the family against any involvements that might subvert it.

These laws, as so much else in Augustan culture, were experiments. The outcry they produced was considerable. In Suetonius' vivid words (*Aug.* 34.1): "When he had framed his marriage law more stringently than the others, he was unable to enact it because of an open revolt against some of its provisions. He therefore had to soften those dealing with penalties and allow three years' grace before compulsory remarriage in addition to increasing the rewards. Even so the equestrians were clamoring for its abolition." There followed, then, as several scholars have plausibly argued,[113] a typical period of further experimentation, evolution, and modification, which culminated in the *Lex Papia Poppaea* of A.D. 9. That law lightened some of the financial penalties on those who were married but childless; it extended the compulsory remarriage period to eighteen months and two years after divorce and death (the three-year period mentioned by Suetonius is not supported by our other sources); and it increased the rights especially of women with three or more children.

Given this evolutionary aspect of the laws, it stands to reason that Augustus unleashed the Julian laws of 18 B.C. only after considerable deliberation and some tentative steps in their direction. Such an attempt may have taken place at the very beginning of his reign, in 27 B.C. Propertius speaks of Cynthia's joy that "a law has been abolished which made both us cry for a long time once it was promulgated, for fear that it would divide us" (2.7.1–3). This suggests a law that forced men and women to marry and to have children; "no one from my blood shall be a soldier," Propertius adds defiantly (line 14). Whether there was in fact such a law has been a matter of heated controversy.[114] There are no references to it in other writers, though Dio mentions that in the same year Augustus granted special privileges to any senator who had a large number of children or was married (53.13.3). This indicates that such matters were certainly on his mind from early on.

It is obvious that the laws were singularly important to Augustus. In their pursuit he risked not only the profound disaffection of the very nobility, senatorial and equestrian, with whose consensus he wanted to govern, but he ran roughshod over some hallowed traditional ideals, such as the *univira*, the woman who had only one husband and remained faithful to him after his death (witness Vergil's and Propertius' poetic monuments to such women), and the *patria potestas*. His behavior was paradigmatic of the transforming leader, the "value shaper . . . who exhibits almost boorish consistency over long periods of time in support of his one or two transcending values. No opportunity is too small, no forum too insignificant, no audience too junior."[115]

Thus he harangued the senate by reading to them a speech by Metellus Macedonicus, censor in 131 B.C., on leading women in marriage.[116] The fragments of the speech are redolent with homespun moralizing. Echoing a long misogynistic tradition, Metellus says that women are a bother and that the Romans would be better off without them. He concedes, however, as Saint Paul did in 1 Corinthians, that for most this is impossible: "But since nature has passed it on to us that we can neither live with them pleasantly nor live without them in any way, it is better for us to look out for the long-term welfare than for short-term pleasure." It is doubtful that most Romans looked upon women that way, but the moral message transcended Metellus' idiosyncracy: *salus perpetua* was more important in all things than *brevis voluptas*. This is reinforced by another highly moral notion: Metellus' insistence that virtue should come from within, that the "immortal gods ought to support, but not supply, *virtus*."

With a more specific application, Augustus' speech to the equestrians in A.D. 9 centered on the theme of *extra familiam nulla salus* (Dio 56.1–9). First he highly praised the married minority. Then he laced into the others, offering his own variation of "friends, Romans, countrymen": "A strange experience has been mine, O—what shall I call you? Men? But you are not performing any of the tasks of men. Citizens? But for all that you are doing, the city is perishing. Romans? But you are undertaking to blot out this name altogether." After the usual evocations of Rome's past, Augustus strikes the dominant note: the practice of social responsibility is impossible without responsibility for a family. Freedom from that is not *libertas*, but *licentia* (56.7.1). Yes, there are disagreeable and painful things that come with marriage and raising children (56.8.2). That leads to the true Augustan ethos, whose articulation we traced back to the *Georgics* and which also is the keynote of the *Aeneid*: no good exists without some accompanying burden. In fact, with our greatest and most abundant blessings come our greatest and most abundant aggravations. "Therefore, if you decline to accept the latter, do not seek to obtain the former, either, since for practically everything that has genuine excellence or enjoyment one must strive beforehand, strive at the time, and strive afterward" (56.8.3). Caring for a family exemplifies this highest, moral form of existence and makes a man a true citizen of the *res publica* (56.6.6.). By contrast, refusal to have offspring is *impietas* (56.5.2).

There are several important aspects to Augustus' laws. One is that, while broadly applicable, the legislation aimed particularly at the governing classes—hence the Julian Law *relating to the marriages of the (senatorial and equestrian) orders* and Augustus' singling out the senators and the *equites* in his speeches on the subject. The laws provided both special restrictions and special rewards for them. Augustus considered it important that they should abide by higher moral standards. This was, of course, desirable simply in general terms, but there were also some specific rationales.

Chief among them is that the Roman ruling class was also ruling an empire. That empire was anything but static; imperial expansion was one of the hallmarks of the Augustan reign. Aside from establishing domestic tranquillity at home, he was the prince of *pax* in foreign affairs, but it was *pax* in the Roman sense: making a pact after conquest. As we saw earlier, no one in previous Roman history added more territory to Rome's domain than did Augustus: Egypt beyond the First Cataract; the eastern and central European regions of Pannonia, Moesia, Noricum, and Raetia; and northwestern Spain. Judaea was converted into a province; Armenia came under Rome's indirect hegemony; and campaigns were carried out against tribes in North Africa. Bohemia and Germany became the targets of Augustus' attention in his final decade. Detailed examination of the archaeological evidence from the Roman military bases in Germany clearly indicates an offensive rather than a defensive strategy. There is no indication that either the Elbe or the

Danube were meant to be permanent frontiers. Diplomacy went a long way in the Parthian dispute; when additional manpower became available, the expedition against southern Arabia was undertaken, an expedition that aimed at conquest (Strabo 16.4.22).

Augustus' biographer, Nicolaus of Damascus, summed it up when he observed that Augustus enormously enlarged the empire and subdued peoples whose names were formerly unknown.[117] The *princeps* himself, in the *Res Gestae*, assigned a prominent place to conquest and expansion. The preamble could not be clearer: "The deeds of the divine Augustus by which he subdued the earth for the rule of the Roman people" (*rerum gestarum divi Augusti, quibus orbem terrarum imperio populi Romani subiecit*). This is "how Augustus wished to be remembered, as the world conqueror, the greatest and most successful of Rome's generals."[118] That was also the programmatic purpose of the statues in his forum, to honor those who "raised the rule of the Roman people from the smallest beginnings to its greatest extent" (Suet., *Aug.* 31.5). His own statue, probably as triumphator on a quadriga, was the most conspicuous among them. Below the titulatory inscription as *pater patriae* there presumably followed a list of his martial conquests.[119] How important this event was to Augustus can be seen from the fact that he chose to end the *Res Gestae* with a reference to that statue.[120]

It was only after the revolts in Illyricum in A.D. 6 and Germany in A.D. 9 that second thoughts developed about the feasibility of further conquests.[121] For thirty-five out of forty years, however, Augustus' policy had been one of conquest, one of "warring down" and "subduing," to use Vergil's words (*Aen.* 6.853). It was reflected in art and architecture and ennobled, in the well-known Vergilian and Horatian passages, into a vision, which was Augustus' own, of the Roman people as the imperial civilizers of the world.

That it was a noble vision is also clear from the grounds on which the Roman expansion and conquests could be justified. These justifications, in turn, are connected with Augustus' assiduous attempts, through moral legislation, to make the ruling classes of Rome and Italy into a morally superior people.[122]

The debate about the justification for Rome's imperialism had begun by the middle of the second century B.C. when the the Greek philosopher Carneades, on an embassy to Rome, singled it out as an example of injustice and urged the Romans, even if facetiously, to restore the conquered territories to the natives and to go back to their fabled simplicity of life in ancient Latium. Before his audience could ponder the implications further, Carneades found himself enjoined by Cato to commence his own journey back home without delay. There followed, in turn, a steady tradition, developed especially by Stoic philosophers friendly to Rome, such as Posidonius, of equating the justifiable conquest of other peoples not with the right of the stronger, but the duty of the better, "better" entailing, among other things, higher moral and ethical standards. In terms of actual practice, Livy (22.13.11) thus attributes the loyalty of some of the Campanian cities in the Second Punic War to their realization that they were ruled by the Romans with justice and restraint and therefore chose to obey those who were "better." Similarly, Tacitus has the governor of Lower Germany, Avitus, respond to a spokesman of a German tribe in A.D. 58 that "the rule of the better must be tolerated" (*Ann.* 13.56.11). The Roman tradition cites further examples of the benefit of Roman rule.[123]

While part of this was undoubtedly self-serving, the philosophical basis for such arguments was not restricted to utilitarianism, but consisted of the postulate of the moral and spiritual superiority of the conqueror over the conquered. Hence authors like Sallust single out the mistreatment of Rome's subjects as the epitome of moral decline (*Cat.* 12.4–5). Similarly, Posidonius, who justified Rome's imperial mission on the basis of the natural authority of the most worthy, bitterly attacked provincial maladministration brought on by the rapaciousness of the equestrians. If the behavior of the Romans, and the ruling class in particular, did not exhibit superior morals and ethics, the justification of continued conquest was untenable. Consequently, if Augustus wanted to engage in further expansion of Rome's rule he had to be solicitous of the morals of the Romans who would exert that rule.

That meant those of senatorial and equestrian rank. The senate at Augustus' time was composed, at least after 19 B.C., of a minority of old-style *nobiles* and a majority of ascending "new men" (*novi homines*) who came mostly from the municipalities of Italy. The contrast between the two groups was not only political but ideological, and the relevant ideology had developed definite moral overtones already in the late republic.[124] The basic antithesis was between the energetic newcomer challenging the degenerate nobles by his *virtus* and *industria*. The new men rejected the assumption of inherited ability and experience on the part of the *nobiles*. Instead, they considered themselves superior on moral grounds: they had *virtus* instead of *genus*, and they had *labor* and *industria* instead of the *nobilitas* of a bloodline. As time went on, they went even further: they claimed they had *nobilitas* also. That *nobilitas*, however, was not an inherited characteristic, but was a spiritual and and moral quality—a superiority by means of *virtus* and *industria*. Consequently, as Velleius (2.34.3) put it with rare poignancy, Cicero was a *vir novitatis nobilissimae*.

The new man challenged the old noble not with his own ancestors, but with his spiritual and moral predecessors. *Virtus*, then, was the *prisca virtus* on which the greatness of Rome was founded and which the degenerate and luxury-prone nobility had discarded. Only subsequently was this *virtus* of the *novus homo* identified with all the ancient virtues of the central Italian peoples' most famous father figures, the Sabines and Cato, for instance.

There was, of course, the usual disjunction between such claims and actuality. Evidence is scant that Augustus' new aristocracy especially lived up to their claims of pristine virtue and devoted self-denial. Quite on the contrary, it is astounding that with all the attrition that afflicts evidence from ancient times, the tradition has preserved case after case of Augustan Sabines chasing married women, raping mime actresses, and practicing assorted other immoralities and moral delinquencies. These involved even the mistreatment of conquered subjects, which had been so strongly condemned by Sallust and Posidonius and gave the lie to the Roman justification of conquest by virtue of ethical superiority. In Peter Wiseman's words: "Although it may have been true—before Caesar and the triumvirs, at any rate—that only an energetic *novus* could reach the highest offices of the state, the vast majority of *municipales* in the lower reaches of the senate were no more or less corrupt and inefficient than their contemporaries of senatorial families, many no doubt meriting Cicero's happy description of one of them as *levis, libidinosus, tagax*"[125] ("light-minded, libidinous, and light-fingered").

It was not entirely Machiavellian of Augustus, therefore, to hold the feet of his new governing aristocracy to the fire of their own rhetoric. Their vaunted moral superiority was hollow, and steps had to be taken to implement it by the force of law. The aim was not to oppress the nobility, but to remind it of its obligations. A similar program had been urged by Cicero on Caesar (*Marc.* 23); it included the restraining of wantonness (*comprimendae libidines*) and ended with the injunction that "everything that had gone to ruin and been abandoned must be recaptured and bound with severe laws." Tacitus, too, stresses that the third time Pompey was chosen to be consul it was "so that *mores* might be corrected" (*corrigendis moribus*; *Ann.* 3.28). What was new was the highly specific elaboration of using nuptial conduct as the major standard for higher morality. Conversely, the decline of marital morality was now viewed as the major symptom of moral decline, the very moral decline that was the root cause for Rome's ruinous civil wars.

This is particularly evident from some of Horace's odes that were written in the early 20s B.C.,[126] such as 3.24, which starts out and ends with the conventional castigation of material greed as the source of evils. As a counterexample, antiquity's noble savages, the Scythians, are introduced, but the main point Horace makes about them—somewhat incongruously because they had communal wives and children—is their virtuous family life: stepmothers are kind to their children; wives do not give themselves over to adulterers; and parental virtue and chastity prevail. The real sin, which cries out for punishment, is not desire for wealth but immorality that destroys the respect for marriage. In 3.6, the last "Roman Ode," the peculiar nexus between between sexual immorality and the civil wars and threats to the empire is elaborated even more clearly. Both the onslaughts of foreign nations and Rome's own internal strife came about because of the decline of Roman marital morality:

> fecunda culpae saecula nuptias
> primum inquinavere et genus et domos;
>   hoc fonte derivata clades
>   in patriam populumque fluxit.

(3.6.17–20)

[Teeming with sin, our times (Horace significantly uses the word *saecula* here) have defiled first our marriages, our race, and homes; sprung from this source, disaster's stream has overflowed our fatherland and our people.]

The merits of these arguments may strike us, as they perhaps did some of the Romans, too, as somewhat simplistic. What is more relevant is that such passages clearly indicate that Augustus' legislation was thoroughly grounded in moral concerns and principles. Horace goes on to illustrate marital misbehavior by concentrating on adultery by the wife and on the husband's connivance at it, precisely a situation made punishable by the *Lex Julia de adulteriis coercendis*. On a more positive note, after these laws were enacted, Horace links, as we have seen, Rome's imperial mission with Rome's moral strength and superiority in the *Carmen Saeculare* (51–59); even the Scythians now become Rome's suppliants (55–56).

Similarly, the interdependence between Rome's morals and her *imperium* is one of the leitmotifs of Livy's history as he immediately makes clear in the preface (9–10). His exemplars of the old *mores* frame his *History* as conspicuously as Augustus' did the Forum of Augustus.[127] Moreover, Livy used the Romans' superior *mores* to differentiate them from Alexander (9.17–18). The Greek king could not have conquered Rome if he had tried, asserts Livy, because he had become too degenerate by that time. A further implication is that the Romans were entitled to follow in Alexander's footsteps—we have noted the force of the Alexander model on various occasions—and to conquer the *oikumenē* because they were morally better than Alexander. Or so they thought, until Augustus, whose rule extended to more than appearances, enacted his moral legislation to remind the new and the old Roman nobility of their obligations.

The intent, therefore, was anything but the weakening of that nobility. The inheritance provisions, in particular, of the Julian laws make it clear that Augustus was strongly interested in keeping the families intact by stabilizing the transmission of property.[128] The Augustan system, as so often, involved both moral and practical considerations. The practice of legacy hunting, which had reached its heyday during the late republic when many members of the propertied classes chose to remain childless, certainly had no morality to recommend it, but the concomitant dissolution of family property was just as much of a threat. Hence Augustus made specific provisions about eligible heirs. It is important to view this aspect of the laws in conjunction with Augustus' raising the property qualifications for senators, which provoked a great deal of ire at the time. Underlying all this is the strong Roman conviction that an essential function of the state is the protection of private property. Once more, we are not dealing with a Roman revolution under Augustus, but with the solidification of a received system.

It is in this general context also that the Augustan laws about manumission take on their full significance.[129] Three laws were passed: the earliest (*Lex Junia*) perhaps in 17 B.C.; the *Lex Fufia Caninia* in 2 B.C., and the *Lex Aelia Sentia* in A.D. 4. They imposed considerable restrictions on the number of slaves who could be admitted to Roman citizenship. One of the many ways in which the Romans became a multicultural people was the frequent emancipation of slaves, especially the urban slaves, at the end of their useful life or before. Usually, the right to intermarry, if not outright citizenship, would result within two generations. As a consequence, the Roman citizen body was constantly enlarged by the inclusion of non-Romans. An underlying principle, reinforced by Augustus, was that such citizenship was not simply an entitlement but obligated the new citizen to a higher moral standard. The contemporary account of Dionysius of Halicarnassus (*AR* 4.24.4ff.) about the earlier practices of emancipation makes it clear that concern about the lack of moral fitness was instrumental in bringing about the legislation:

> The noble traditions of the Roman commonwealth have become so debased and sullied that some who have made a fortune by robbery, housebreaking, prostitution, and every other base means, purchase their freedom with the money so acquired and straightaway are Romans. Others, who have been confidants and accomplices of their masters in poisonings, murders, and in crimes against the the gods or the state, receive from them this favor as their reward. Some are freed in order that, when they have received the monthly allowance of corn given by the public or some largesse distributed by men in power to the poor among the citizens, they may bring it to those who granted them their freedom. . . . Most people are grieved and condemn the custom, looking upon it as unseemly that a dominant city which aspires to rule the world should make such men citizens. (Loeb trans.)

"A dominant city which aspires to rule the world"—once more, the nexus is emphasized between imperial rule and high moral standards.

The moral legislation, therefore, was central to the Augustan era both in its own right and in its typical combination of a moral center with a complex of multiple inspirations, associations, and aspects. The moral core was the time-honored ideal of social responsibility, which permeates the *Aeneid* and was resolutely identified with responsibility for a family. There was the usual call to a moral awakening and to a return to the past, though it was combined, as always, with considerable innovation. The conceptualization of the laws drew on a sophisticated tradition of justifying Roman conquest; in that sense, the legislation was a necessary corollary to Augustus' imperialistic ambition. And there was the mix between transcendent higher idealism and practical needs, such as the protection and stabilization of private property, which was one of the fundamental purposes of the Roman *res publica*. If we need a visual example of this multiplicity, we need to look only at the Ara Pacis. It was, as we have seen, a monument to "peace won through victories" and, as part of the design for the sundial, it commemorated the Roman world rule. The senate convened on the day of Augustus' return in 13 B.C. from an extended tour of pacification in the west and voted him an altar; the next day he convened the senate and promulgated several decrees, chief among them the provision that henceforth retiring soldiers would be paid a certain sum of money rather than given expropriated land. In other words, private property was finally secure again, a development, as we have seen, that was greeted with "good hopes" by property owners (Dio 54.25.3–6). As for the sculptural decorations of the monument itself, the processional friezes represented not only the men of the imperial house, but their wives and children, too: "The emperor and his retinue were thus depicted as the embodiment of the Augustan social program; they set a standard for the rest of the population to emulate."[130] The richness of the altar's associations, which have often been commented upon, was not merely an aesthetic phenomenon, but was reflective of the fabric of the entire Augustan culture. Before we turn to this monument and others in the next chapter, one final perspective can help to illuminate the complex of issues we have surveyed so far.

The idea that underlies the Augustan ethos is that peace and bliss (*felicitas*) are a threat to energetic human endeavor, the quest for excellence, and the maintenance of high morality. We find the expression of this concern in various Greek and Roman writers from the second century B.C. onward.[131] It is encapsulated, in the second century A.D.—the period that Gibbon pronounced to be the most happy and prosperous in the history of mankind—in Juvenal's pithy denunciation (6.292–93) that "we now suffer the ills of a long peace; luxury presses on us more fiercely than arms and avenges the world we conquered" (*nunc patimur longae pacis mala, saevior armis / luxuria incubuit victumque ulciscitur orbem*). It is clear from the writings of Dionysius of Halicarnassus that the idea was debated in Augustan times also.[132] Tacitus' variant of it is well known from his *Dialogus de Oratoribus*: the rise of the principate led to a stifling atmosphere in which gifted individuals could not flourish because of the loss of liberty; hence rhetoric, the benchmark for intellectual activity, went into decline.

That conclusion, however, was not universally shared. Cato already warned, after the Roman defeat of Macedonia, that success (*res secundae*) and general happiness (*laetitia*) tended to steer people away from "the right resolve and the right insight."[133] One of the principal merits that Polybius (6.18.5) saw in the Roman "constitution" was the ability of the Romans to keep the people from deteriorating in times of peace because there was always some fear to prod them. Similarly, both the elder and the younger Scipio worried that with the demise of Carthage, the Romans would be adversely affected by "freedom from care."[134] Taking the destruction of Carthage as his starting point, Sallust works out an entire sequence of cause and effect.[135] When Rome was faced with *labores* and dangers, he reasons, all was well, including *iustitia* (*Cat.* 10.1). After Carthage had been overcome, those *stimuli* ceased and the *res secundae* resulted in a corruption of *mores*, a dulling of *virtus*, and an indulgence in *otium* and *luxuria*. To afford this *luxuria*, the Romans undertook new wars. The desire for empire (*cupido imperii*), therefore, stemmed from morally flawed impulses. Under the emperors, when peace was a general subject of discussion, the emphasis shifted somewhat. There is less concern that *res secundae* may lead to hubris; rather, they produce a decline into sloth and inertia. Thus even the second Einsiedeln *Eclogue*, which is addressed to Nero and depicts the virtual fulfillment of the state of affairs that was hoped for in the fourth *Eclogue* of Vergil, voices the note of worry and anxiety precisely because of the dangers of so much bliss. Similarly, it is not lack of *libertas*, but too much ease and tranquillity that concern the elder Seneca and Pliny. This, according to them and others,[136] is the real reason for cultural decline. Accordingly, Tacitus did not miss the opportunity of blaming Augustus for "seducing one and all with the sweetness of peace" (*cunctos dulcedine otii pellexit; Ann.* 1.2).

The Augustan ethos stands out yet more clearly against this background. It was a balancing act and its vitality was due to its negotiation of several conflicting tensions. Domestic tranquillity was to be restored without resulting in intellectual and cultural torpor and in a loss of moral fiber. At its best, the resuscitation of traditional values could lead to their renewed vitality. At their worst, such efforts could produce the sort of somnolent antiquarianism about which Horace complains in his *Letter to Augustus*. On the foreign front, wars and conquests continued and were justified by values higher than sheer profiteering. The seemingly contradictory images of peace and war coalesced in the expression of the new Golden Age, whether in poetry or in art. The *res publica*, through its spokesman Valerius Messalla, gratefully acknowledged *perpetua felicitas* when it named Augustus *pater patriae* (Suet., *Aug.* 58.2). True Augustan *felicitas*, however, was not a state of repose and fulfillment but was based on the ideal of unceasing effort—moral, political, and intellectual. Accordingly, far from being static, the culture both viewed itself as, and was, a continuing process marked by creativity and initiatives from many quarters. It is for reasons like these that it became one of the high points of Western civilization.

CHAPTER IV

ART AND ARCHITECTURE

INSTEAD OF prefacing this chapter with a general characterization of Augustan art and architecture, I have chosen to discuss some of the major monuments individually. We will see that some of the basic characteristics of Augustan architecture and art are not dissimilar from those of Augustan poetry, which are summarized at the beginning of the next chapter.

THE ALTAR OF AUGUSTAN PEACE
(ARA PACIS AUGUSTAE)

The Ara Pacis is the most representative work of Augustan art. Only that judgment is conventional; the monument itself is not, nor has its discussion been frozen in the tracks of traditionalism.[1] In its combination of experimentation, deliberate multiplicity of associations and inspirations, and a clear overall meaning, it is both a splendid example of the culture in general and an illustration of many of the aspects I have already discussed, including Augustus' *auctoritas*. For the sake of an orderly overview, it will be necessary at times to discuss some of these characteristics separately, but we should not lose sight of the fact that they form a closely integrated totality.

As before, it is best to start with Augustus' own words. The Altar was of such importance that he mentioned it in the *Res Gestae*:

> On my return from Spain and Gaul in the consulship of Tiberius Nero and Publius Quintilius, after I had successfully arranged affairs in those provinces, the senate decreed that an altar of the Augustan Peace should be consecrated next to the Campus Martius in honor of my return, and ordered that the magistrates and priests and the Vestal Virgins perform an annual sacrifice there. (*RG* 12.2)

Significantly, this mention leads up to that of the closing of the gates of the Temple of Janus (*RG* 13). The Ara Pacis thus is linked with the concept that peace is the result of military victories which secure the *imperium Romanum* on land and sea: *cum per totum imperium populi Romani terra marique esset* parta victoriis pax.[2]

As always, we are dependent on other writers not for the meaning of the Ara Pacis—because Augustus always provides the meaning—but for more detail about the actual circumstances relating to its genesis. The occasion was Augustus' return from Gaul and Spain where he had been on a military expedition for more than three years. His return was characterized by several understated actions:[3] he avoided a large public outpouring by entering the city quietly the night of July 3, 13 B.C., and he refused a triumph and the senate's offer to build an altar in the senate chamber itself in honor of his return. Instead, he approved the building of an altar to Pax Augusta one mile from the sacred boundary of the city, its *pomerium*, on the Field of Mars. The altar, therefore, was built on the demarcation line between the military and the domestic *imperium* of chief Roman magistrates.

This is only the first of the altar's multiple dimensions. The exact ceremony in which Augustus, his family, and Roman senators and priests are engaged on the reliefs of the altar (Figs. 58, 59, 63) cannot be limited to one specific, "historical" occasion. It is neither the actual "constitution" of the altar on July 4, 13 B.C., nor its dedication on January 30, 9 B.C. It includes, along with the stone garlands hung up on the inside walls of its enclosure (Fig. 60), elements that fit both events, but it goes beyond both in the manner of the Boscoreale cups (Figs. 32 and 33). The principal intent is to present the idea of the return of Augustus, the guarantor (*auctor*) of peace; formally, it presents "the meeting that could have taken place."[4] We saw the subordination of actual "reality" to the guiding ideas behind it in the *Res Gestae*, too. This was a typically Roman conception whose antecedents are found, in different ways, in republican art and in the very concept of the *res publica* as a system of normative concepts. The implementation of these concepts is not so much an individual action as a reflection of the underlying idea; the implementing actions, therefore, are thought of as repetitive and generic or general rather than individual and specific.[5] Hence it is also left open whether Augustus and his entourage of family and senators form two processions or one, or whether they should be envisaged as standing in a circle (Fig. 61). But there is no ambiguity about the central intent: the attention is focused on Augustus (Fig. 62), and he, his arrival (*adventus*), and the rite he is performing are enhanced by the representation of Aeneas on the panel next to his. The ancestor of Augustus and the Roman people, accompanied by his son Julus from whom the Julian family took its name, sacrifices to the gods upon his arrival in Italy (Fig. 43). The ritual reality of the annual sacrifice on the altar itself is represented by a procession of sacrificers and animals on the small frieze that runs along the top of the altar itself (Fig. 63).

The structure and function of the building itself exhibit the same qualities of dynamic tension between formal variety and unified conceptualization, and of the resolution of opposites that is at the heart of the classical mode. The concept is unmistakable: a sacred monument to Pax under her Augustan aspect. As such it is a *templum*, a precinct carved out of the Field of Mars, and several of its details, especially the lower, inside wall of the precinct with its

58. Ara Pacis Augustae, south frieze. Augustus, priests, and lictors.

59. Ara Pacis Augustae, south frieze. Imperial family.

60. Ara Pacis Augustae. Inside of the enclosure wall.

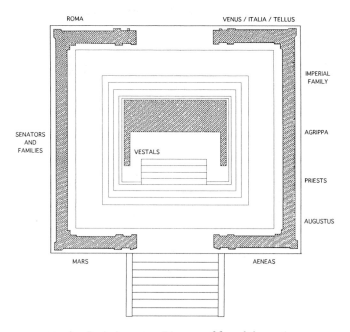

61. Ara Pacis Augustae. Diagram of figural decoration.

62. Ara Pacis Augustae, south frieze.
Augustus (on right) sacrificing.

63. Ara Pacis Augustae, upper section of altar. Sacrificial procession.

simulation of wooden boards or slats (Fig. 60), closely follow the augural tradition and precepts for the establishment of such *templa minora*. With its two accesses and location at the exact point of transition from military to domestic *imperium*, the structure also recalls the shrines to Janus.[6] In addition, this is the building Augustus wanted in lieu of a triumph; despite its understatement, the triumphal dimension is not absent. It is understated on the relief decoration of the altar, but the larger building context into which it was inserted made it, if anything, into something far more significant and imposing.

The procedure is similar to that involving Augustus' house on the Palatine, which was modest by comparison with the houses of the well-to-do at the time, but extraordinary due to its architectural integration with the Temple of Apollo. The Ara Pacis was part of a gigantic sundial whose hand was an obelisk imported from Egypt. Its height, including the base, was some one hundred feet.[7] It was, as its dedicatory inscription announces, a monument to the conquest of Egypt and dedicated sometime between June 10 B.C. and June 9 B.C. The actual dedication date probably coincided with that of the Ara Pacis, January 30, 9 B.C., which was also the birthday of Livia (as well as the last day of the month dedicated to Janus). The dynastic dimensions were palpable: both monuments were begun in 13 B.C., when Augustus turned fifty, and Augustus' mausoleum, which was built some fifteen years earlier, became part of the overall design (Fig. 64). More speculative is the assumption that the Ara Pacis and the obelisk were constructed on the basis of a precise mathematical relationship so that on the day of the fall equinox, September 23, the obelisk's shadow pointed directly to the center of the altar. It would make perfect sense: that day was Augustus' birthday and he was born to peace, *natus ad pacem*. It was a peace based on world domination, which was symbolized by a globe, with a diameter of more than two feet, directly below the point of the obelisk. It cast its shadow on an elaborate system of lines, marked in bronze on the travertine surface, which indicated the days, months, and seasons. The sundial was centered on the winter solstice (in Capricorn), the day of the conception of Augustus who used the Capricorn as one of his emblems.[8] Several denarii minted in Spain a few years before Augustus' return from there to Rome are a microcosm of the pictorial program of the complex on the Campus Martius: horn of plenty, capricorn, and globe are linked with Augustus' name (Fig. 53). The whole piazza, double the size of Saint Peter's Square and probably connected with a system of parks built by Agrippa, was undoubtedly one of the most remarkable public spaces in Rome.

To return to the Ara Pacis proper: it is an example of remarkable multiplicity also in terms of artistic styles and traditions. The processions, for instance, "cite" those of the Parthenon, but they also draw on traditions of Etruscan painting which in turn may be indebted to Greek monumental

64. Mausoleum of Augustus, obelisk of sundial, and Ara Pacis. Reconstruction.

65. Ara Pacis Augustae, north frieze. Floral scroll and procession of senators.

painting.[9] The artistic style of the figural reliefs cannot be reduced simply to neoclassicism, but combines classical, Hellenistic, and Roman elements.[10] The head of Augustus (Fig. 62), for instance, does not follow the prevailing, classicizing Prima Porta type, but a different one.[11] Similarly, the floral friezes (Fig. 65), which occupy more space than the figural ones on the outside of the enclosure walls, can be related to Etruscan, Pompeian, and Pergamene traditions, among others.[12] All this amounts to more than the schematic source hunting so dear to classical scholars: Augustan culture, and especially the arts, architecture, and poetry, were a sophisticated and cosmopolitan blend of many traditions. Rome was now the head of the world, *caput mundi*, in a more significant sense than mere power.[13] Augustan Rome drew on many traditions and revitalized them in the process.

The same deliberate pluralism of meanings and traditions applies to the mythological reliefs on the east and west sides of the altar's exterior walls. The challenge undertaken by the artists was to convey the many dimensions and associations of the Augustan peace. A simple statue of Pax was inadequate for the purpose. Its absence once occasioned the argument that the monument therefore could not be the Ara Pacis,[14] but this line of reasoning ignores that the pictorial program as a whole and in all its richness is the expression of the concept of *Pax Augusta* in all its ramifications. A relevant numismatic precedent is the evolving representation of peace on Octavian's coins ca. 32–29 B.C. At first there is simply the goddess Pax who is holding an olive branch in her right hand and a cornucopia in her left (Fig. 66). This

66. Denarius of Octavian, ca. 32–29 B.C. Reverse: the goddess Pax.

straightforward representation yields to the multiplicity of historicizing and mythologizing images on the "triumphal series" that can be combined and recombined in a variety of ways. Besides Pax (Fig. 28), they involve Venus, Victoria, and Octavian both Neptune-like (Fig. 147) and addressing the troops (Fig. 7), in an attempt to capture the complexity and range of the concept of *pax*.[15]

The relief in which this iconographic polysemy is most evident is that of the so-called Tellus on the southeast side (Fig. 41). As we saw in chapter 3, a female figure is seated in the center amid abundant vegetation. She holds two children who look up to her and she is flanked by two companion figures on the right and left who, with billowing veils, are seated on a sea creature and a swan or goose. A sheep and cow are at the feet of the central figure. To varying degrees, the iconography draws on that of Mother Earth, Venus, Ceres, and possibly even Pax herself, but we cannot limit the figures to any one type. The various images of the altar's decoration are meant to be viewed in conjunction with one another, just as the full meaning of individual wall paintings in Pompeian villas becomes clear only in relation to the other paintings in the same room.[16] Peace alone, for example, is too unspecific; this is a monument to Pax Augusta, and hence the aspect of Venus relates best to the dynastic dimension illustrated also by Augustus and his family, and by the presence of Aeneas, Venus' son and the Julian ancestor, on the east side (Fig. 43). The figure also complements that of the goddess Roma, sitting on a pile of arms accumulated in the process of war (Fig. 42). War and victory, as we have seen, are the precondition for peace—the *pax Augusta*, in Augustus' own words, was *parta* victoriis *pax*—and Venus also was the goddess of Victory, Venus Victrix. Venus Victrix and Venus Genetrix were both combined by Julius Caesar into Victoria Caesaris.[17] Mars on the west side is connected with all of this: he is the god of war but also, through Romulus and Remus who were shown with the wolf-nurse in the same relief as Mars, the ancestor of the Romans just as Venus, through Aeneas and his son Julus, was the ancestress not only of the Julian family but of the Roman people in general. Members both of that family and the Roman nobility populate the north and south sides of the frieze (Fig. 61).

These are only some of the connections that can be usefully pursued and which the artistic program of the altar is asking us to make. It is, in the best sense of the Augustan program, a monument which solicits the viewers' participation rather than suffocates it with the massive onslaught of frozen neoclassical forms that we know from public buildings of the nineteenth century. Three important and related considerations bear on the involvement of the viewer:

1. The intentional multiplicity of meanings can be experienced on several levels, depending on the sophistication of the viewer. To some, the pictorial program would be understandable in relatively simple terms: prosperity; the linking of the Augustan present to the Roman past in the basic manner of Vergil's *Aeneid*; references to peace and relaxed tranquillity, as is indicated, too, by the demeanor of some of the participants in the procession. Cognoscenti would appreciate the complex allusiveness of the imagery far more. For them, the function and appeal of individual reliefs and their entirety would be that of a "contemplative image":[18] one goes back time and again, looks at the icons, and discovers new meanings and associations. The reliefs are rooted in rich artistic, literary, religious, and mythological traditions. It is like reading the *Aeneid*. At the same time, it is not a matter of purely subjective and impressionistic understandings, which lead to misinterpretation. Instead, the variety of evocations operates within the framework of a clearly established overall meaning.

2. That, in turn, constitutes a deliberate turning back from the fragmentation of the pictorial program especially on late republican coins, which we analyzed earlier (see chapter 2). Their iconographic fragmentation only reflected the political one—that is, the disappearance of generally shared values in favor of a multiplicity of individual ones. The Venus Genetrix, for instance, of the entire Roman people yielded to the Venus Victrix of individual generals. A concomitant phenomenon was the inadequacy of the

available iconography to express the new multiplicity of meanings: the same female or male heads came to stand for diverse deities and concepts.

We can see the change that comes about in the pictorial program of the Ara Pacis. It is underpinned by the Augustan program of a return to a central value system: "Peace as prosperity now depends on Roman mores."[19] With the Augustan restoration of genuine meaning to concepts such as the *res publica* in the political and moral realms comes the establishment of genuine polysemy to the images and symbols in art: the female personification on the Ara Pacis is not simply a blank check that can be filled in as one wishes but has a variety of significances that complement one another. This is accompanied by another reciprocal process: compared with the confusing multiplicity of republican representations (and individual "programs") there is now a reduction, in Augustan public art in general, to a few repeated motifs.[20] This quantitative reduction, however, is more than compensated for by the multiplicity of associations and evoked meanings.

3. The full understanding of every last facet of such a work of art presupposed an exceptionally high level of education and sophistication. It did exist as is shown by an honorary monument set up in Rome in 91 B.C. by the Mauretanian king Bocchus for Sulla.[21] Its pictorial decoration was distinguished by a high degree of conceptualization suggestive of the various qualities of the honoree. The Ara Pacis is far more successful in its integration of the suggestive power of such concepts by means of a more vital imagery, but in that sense it was also an experiment that was not repeated. On a relief from Carthage (Fig. 67),[22] therefore, the complex iconography of the "Tellus" relief is simplified: the accompanying figures are transformed into an astral goddess on the left and a male sea deity on the right. The resulting program of land, air, and sea is made more intelligible while it is given a cosmic interpretation.

Yet the appreciation of the Ara Pacis was not limited to an intellectual elite. Motifs from it could be easily transferred to private art. For example, funerary reliefs commissioned by middle-class people adopt the grouping of adults and a child tugging at the mother's dress (Fig. 68).[23] It is a motif not found in art before the Ara Pacis, where it occurs several times (cf. Fig. 59). It is the kind of privatization of themes from public art that has nothing to do with "propaganda." A monument like the Ara Pacis was successful because it appealed to a variety of people and sensibilities.

Part of the reason is that it is one of the most humane monuments ever built by a powerful ruler. In contrast to the Parthenon frieze, let alone its imperial predecessors, the reliefs of the Persian kings at Persepolis, mothers and children are represented. It is a pity that many of the original faces of the Romans on the Ara Pacis were lost and replaced with eighteenth-century restorations, but, as we can tell from those that have been preserved and from the posture of the figures, there was an exquisite balance between stylization

67. Relief from Carthage, first century A.D.
Female deity and companion figures. Compare with Fig. 41.

68. Funerary relief from Augustan times. Parents with child.

and informality. The variation of the postures, gestures, and demeanor of the human participants in the "procession" goes beyond the aesthetic endeavor to avoid monotony. These are real people. They chat, even to the point of having to be admonished to be quiet (Fig. 59, center), and the children wiggle and squirm all over the frieze as we know them to do at any official ceremony or church service. This is not the pompous and grim monument of a party leader whose subjects are bullied into conformist submission.[24] The relaxed attitude of the participants, though *gravitas* is certainly not missing, is in fact another manifestation of the blessings of *pax*.

The contrast between the Ara Pacis and other rulers' monuments could not be clearer: at Persepolis, there is the relentless monotony of imperialism, while the Parthenon friezes bespeak more cosmic grandeur, which in Rome was shifted to the Augustan sundial. Nor are any such humane touches recaptured in later classical adaptations, whether the monument of Victor Emanuel with all the tribes of Italy on its typewriter-like configuration, or Albert Speer's and Adolf Hitler's designs for the new *caput mundi*, Berlin, or on the standard neoclassical government edifices of nineteenth- and twentieth-century America with their panoply of frozen symbols.

It is typical of the multivalence of Augustan art and the Ara Pacis in particular that the representation of the Romans as families has the additional dimension of a serious moral purpose. It reflects Augustus' social policy and especially his legislation on morals and marriage.[25] *Pax* and *imperium*, as we saw earlier, cannot be sustained without maintenance of *mores*, as exemplified first and foremost by a commitment to and responsibility for families.

The abundant floral frieze, which is larger than the figural ones, sets the tone for much of the monument and enhances its many aspects. It expresses the abundance and fertility of nature without assuming the dimensions of "paradisiac" Golden Age. Augustus' return to Rome was marked not by exuberant fantasies of the sort, but by the more realistic assurance that the returning soldiers would no longer be compensated with land taken from private citizens (Dio 54.25.6). Amid the leafage, there are reminders that peace and growth are never unthreatened: a snake attacks a bird's nest (Fig. 69) and there are scorpions (Fig. 70). The basic floral motif is an acanthus, developed in an orderly fashion especially in the form of candelabras, and including some shoots of laurel and ivy. Nature is ordered, but not excessively so: there are some asymmetries, though they are barely perceptible to the eye—the distance, for instance, between the swans and the floral stalks varies on the north and south friezes.[26] The swans are symbols of both Apollo and Venus and thus underscore the dynastic aspects of the monument. Not by accident, therefore, the most immediate predecessor at Rome of that kind of decoration happens to be the frieze from the Temple of the Divine Julius Caesar. There figures of Victories, rising from acanthus flowers

69. Ara Pacis Augustae, floral frieze. Snake attacking bird's nest.

70. Ara Pacis Augustae, floral frieze. Scorpion.

71. Victoria Caesaris. Frieze fragment from Temple of Divus Julius, Rome.

and being surrounded by floral scrolls, recall both Venus Genetrix and Venus Victrix and Venus' vegetal associations (Fig. 71)[27] besides attesting Augustus' lifelong emphasis on Victoria.

Finally, the Ara Pacis is a good example, in several ways, of Augustus' *auctoritas*. It was established at the initiative of the senate, an initiative sanctioned by him as *auctor* and involving some negotiation. No doubt he was involved in the consultations about the design and pictorial program. No doubt he was not simply their sole author: "The leitmotifs of the imagery come from the close circle of Augustus' advisers."[28] They include the poets; numerous passages can be adduced especially from Vergil's and Horace's poetry that read like a commentary on the Ara Pacis.[29] Already in the *Georgics*, for example, Octavian, associated with Venus, is the *auctor frugum* (1.28), a notion on which Horace expands in his last ode:

> tua, Caesar, aetas
> fruges et agros rettulit uberes.
>
> (C. 4.15.4–5)

> [Your era, Caesar,
> brought back fruits and fertile fields.]

The representation of the resulting plenitude especially on the floral frieze again illustrates the intended process of interaction between viewer participation and the guiding *auctoritas* of an overall meaning. The two elements of the abundance of vegetation and ordered composition call for a synthesis by the viewer. They take on their full significance with reference to the general theme of the creation of order under Augustus' rule.[30] The same theme recurs with several variations at the beginning of Vergil's *Aeneid*.

It seems likely that the altar's artists were Greeks from the east, in particular from Aphrodisias with whose sculpture several connections can be demonstrated in terms of style and iconography. They obviously thrived on the challenge of both the unparalleled sophistication of the monument and its thorough adaptation to the Roman ethos. That ethos includes the representation of the *auctoritas* of Augustus. Augustus himself is part of the Roman populace and not elevated above them like a Hellenistic potentate. He is *princeps* and *Augustus*, sublimated by the presence of all the priestly colleges to which he belonged and by reference to Aeneas and Romulus, who were founders as he was.

THE CUIRASS OF THE AUGUSTUS STATUE FROM PRIMA PORTA

The pictorial program on the cuirass of the statue of Augustus from Prima Porta precedes that of the Ara Pacis by about a decade. While being similarly associative, it is more directly intelligible not in the least because it is visible almost at once in its totality.[31]

Again, as we noted in chapter 3, its center and starting point is a specific historical occasion, the return by the Parthians of the standards that Rome's army under Crassus had relinquished in 53 B.C. in one of the most shameful Roman defeats ever. The chorus of those urging revenge never stopped.[32] Caesar's departure for a military expedition against the Parthians was cut short by his assassination. Antony fought them only to incur further losses, and the Augustan poets kept announcing ongoing plans to defeat that archenemy. Then, in 20 B.C., the matter was settled by diplomacy. Armenia became a client kingdom, "brought back into the power of the Roman people."[33] For all practical purposes, it became part of the Roman empire. Augustus could freely interfere in its internal affairs and impose rulers of his choice (*RG* 27.2). Armenia served as a valuable offensive base which was a constant threat to the Parthians. While no Roman army had beaten them on the battlefield, the Augustan settlement was presented as anything but an agreement between equals. The terminology used by Augustus himself is unequivocal: "I *forced* the Parthians to restore to me the spoils and standards of three Roman armies and to ask as *suppliants* for the friendship of the Roman people" (*RG* 29.2). The Parthians had been brought to their knees:

72a. Denarius of 19 B.C.   72b. Denarius of 19 B.C.
Reverse: kneeling Parthian returns   Reverse: Armenian in robe and tiara,
          Roman standard.   kneeling and supplicating.

their king Phraates is shown on Augustan coins as kneeling (Fig. 72a) just like
his Armenian counterpart (Fig. 72b).[34] That is how Horace depicts him, too:
"On humbled knees Phraates accepted the law and rule of Caesar" (*Epist.*
1.12.27–28). His children were kept, like those of client kings, as security in
Rome. As Augustus himself put it, Phraates did so "not because he had been
overcome in war, but because he sought our friendship by pledging his children" (*RG* 32.2).

The whole settlement, then, was portrayed as a tremendous triumph. Augustus duly celebrated it by building a commemorative arch in the Roman
Forum. All this was a welcome turnabout from the famine and disease that
had plagued Rome and Italy only two years earlier (Dio 54.1). The populace
interpreted those afflictions as the gods' retribution for Augustus' not being
appointed (little did it matter that it was he who had refused) as consul for
the first time in ten years. Riots ensued. The plebs clamored for Augustus to
become dictator or at least censor. He refused both, but he assumed some of
the censorial functions and took charge of the grain supply. The situation,
which, in Dio's words, had bordered on anarchy, forced Augustus to post-
pone his plans to leave Rome for Sicily, Greece, and the east until Agrippa
was put firmly in charge as his viceroy (Dio 54.6.4–6).

It is important to keep these historical circumstances firmly in mind even,
or especially, when we consider the more transcending aspects of the images
on the cuirass. Some of them were assimilable to themes suggested by the
subsequent Secular Games, which is not surprising in view of the nexus
between the latter and the Parthian triumph. But it is in terms of the significance of the Parthian settlement that the pictorial program must be understood primarily. Its center (Fig. 73) recalls the specific historical event: a

73. Statue of Augustus from Prima Porta. Cuirass.

representative of Rome receives the standards, topped by Jupiter's eagle, from a Parthian. The Roman most probably is the god Mars: "These standards," wrote Augustus (*RG* 29.2), "I deposited in the innermost shrine of the Temple of Mars the Avenger" which was still being built at the time in the Forum of Augustus.[35] In his long account of the feast day of Mars Ultor (*Fasti* 5.545ff.), Ovid says that the temple came to commemorate two events: the defeat of Caesar's assassins at Philippi (5.569–78) and, at greater length (5.579–96), the return of the Roman standards by the Parthians. He explicitly mentions the legionary eagles:

> signa, decus belli, Parthus Romana tenebat,
>   Romanaeque aquilae signifer hostis erat!
>
> (*Fasti* 5.585–86)

[Roman standards, the emblems of martial honor, the Parthian kept, and an enemy was the standardbearer of the Roman legionary eagle!]

And he uses the same motif again for his finale:

> Parthe, refers aquilas, victos quoque porrigis arcus:
> pignora iam nostri nulla pudoris habes!

(5.593–94)

[Parthian, you return the eagles, and you surrender your bows that have been overcome: now you do not possess any more tokens of our disgrace!]

The most visually oriented of the Augustan poets was well aware of this expressive image in the arts of his day.

On the cuirass, Mars is accompanied by the Roman she-wolf, the *lupa*, whose head we also see peering forth from the prows of Augustus' ships on monuments commemorating his naval victories (cf. Fig. 164).[36] On the two sides of the central scene are the personifications of regions that have experienced, in different ways, the *pax Romana*. The figure on the right (from the perspective of the viewer) is not armed: she holds an empty scabbard, a military standard with a boar, and a dragon trumpet (Fig. 74). These are emblems of Celtic tribes. The figure on the left still has her sword (Fig. 75). She thus stands for nations who are nominally not subjected, like the client states of Armenia and Judea. Or she may be a symbol of the tenacity of others, such as Spain, and the Romans' even greater tenacity in overcoming them: Spain was finally brought under control by Agrippa in 19 B.C. Both Gauls and Spaniards are mentioned by Horace in the same context as the capitulation of the Parthians (*Epist.* 1.12.26–27). Overall, the representations on the armor's central panel proclaim the Roman domination over east and west. It is, of course, an *Augustan* domination, too: he himself fought the principal campaign against the Cantabrians in Spain in the 20s; he was in Syria when Phraates surrendered the standards; and the key provinces in the east and west were under his direct control.

As on the Ara Pacis, mythological figures accompany the historical event and enlarge its dimensions. Now that the long-standing disgrace of Rome in the east has been remedied and inveterate enemies have been brought to heel in both east and west, the sun-god can joyously traverse the sky. Caelus, the sky-god, therefore forms the top of the composition (Fig. 73). His billowing mantle recalls the vault of the firmament.[37] In a syncretism that was well established at the time, the sun-god was also identified with Apollo, with whom Augustus gradually cultivated a special association.[38] Apollo is represented in a different mythological configuration somewhat below the sun-god's chariot and the surrender of the trophies: the two are deliberately associated while their primary identity is kept separate, in contrast to the

74. Augustus statue from Prima Porta. Detail: personification of conquered nation (Gaul).

75. Augustus statue from Prima Porta. Detail: personification of unconquered nation.

more polysemous Venus figure on the Ara Pacis. Preceding Sol's quadriga is Aurora, the winged goddess of Dawn. She sprinkles dew from a vessel in her left hand and is carrying a female deity, again characterized by her billowing mantle, and her torch. While it is true that Horace speaks of Diana, who was identified with the moon-goddess Luna, as *Noctiluca*, Dawn,[39] ushering in the new day of Sol, would in that case be carrying a goddess who illuminates the night. The most likely identification, therefore, is that with Venus, who in turn was identified with the Morning Star. She carries the torch of "light-bearing" Aurora. Again we are dealing with the deliberate Augustan endeavor to establish as many references as possible: Venus is the ancestress of Augustus; her star preceded Aeneas until he reached Italy;[40] and Vergil connected the comet of the deified Caesar with the star of Venus, which heralded the fruitfulness of the earth:

> ecce Dionaei processit Caesaris astrum,
> astrum quo segetes gauderent frugibus et quo
> duceret apricis in collibus uva colorem.
>
> (*Ecl.* 9.47–49)

[Behold, the star of Caesar, offspring of Dione, has gone forth so that under this star the crops might rejoice and the grape might absorb its color on the sunny hillsides].

Vergil refers not only to the newly named month of July, when fruits and harvests ripen, but to the specific agricultural prosperity that would hopefully occur under the star of the Julian house. After Augustus had helped the Romans overcome the poor harvests and famines of 22 B.C., such a hopeful evocation was more than fitting.[41]

The representation of Venus is complemented by two others, developing further associations. Cupid, Venus' son, is riding on the dolphin that functions as a support for the statue (Fig. 5). The dolphin is an allusion to the sea victories of Augustus. After his victory over Sextus Pompey 36 B.C. at Naulochus, for instance, the lap markers in the Circus Maximus were changed by Agrippa into dolphins and the motif rapidly found its way into popular art.[42] Cupid reinforces the association of Augustus with divinity by means of his divine ancestress and the deified Julius Caesar. They contribute to the *sanctitas* of the statue.

In view of such special divine relationships and of the confirmation of Roman power in east and west, prosperity cannot be far away: it is expressed, at the bottom of the cuirass, by the reclining figure of the Bountiful Earth, Tellus, with her cornucopia. Her crown of grain ears is the same as that worn by goddesses such as Ceres and Pax; Venus, too, has grain ears as symbols. Within the ensemble of the pictorial program, the earth-goddess also corresponds to the sky-god and thus rounds out the cosmic dimensions of the imagery. And, predictably, there is more: at her feet, there is a tympanon, the emblem of the Trojan Mother Goddess who was brought to Rome in 204 B.C. and had her temple on the Palatine next to Augustus' house. She, too, was the protectress of Aeneas and appears prominently in the *Aeneid*. In the parade of heroes in *Aeneid* 6, she and Augustus are joined together:

> qualis Berecynthia mater
> .   .   .   .
> laeta deum partu, centum complexa nepotes,
> omnis caelicolas, omnis super alta tenentis.
> huc geminas nunc flecte acies, hanc aspice gentem
> Romanosque tuos. hic Caesar et omnis Iuli
> progenies magnum caeli ventura sub axem.
> hic vir, hic est, tibi quem promitti saepius audis,
> Augustus Caesar, divi genus, aurea condet
> saecula qui rursus . . .
>
> (*Aen.* 6.784, 786–93)

[Just like the Phrygian Mother . . . joyful in her offspring of gods and embracing a hundred of her children's children, all heaven dwellers, all tenants of the heights above. Turn your eyes here now and behold this people, your own Romans. Here is Caesar and the entire offspring of Julus, destined to pass under the great dome of the sky. This, this is the man whom so often you hear promised to you: Augustus Caesar, son of the deified, who shall once again establish an age of gold . . .]

With this we come to the frequent interpretation of the figural program of the armor in terms of the Golden Age. It is, as we saw earlier, a notion that needs to be used with care. The representations of the cuirass first and foremost come from the context of the Parthian success, especially as contrasted with the dismal domestic crisis of the immediately preceding years. Commensurate with the bearer of the armor, the imagery also stressed clearly the quasi divinity of "Augustus," a title that moved him above the mortal sphere. That aura, however, is not the main reason for the statue's lack of footwear. The statue is a copy, and the footgear of the original may well have been removed to have the posthumous copy represent him more fully as *divus* at Livia's villa in Prima Porta, where the statue was found. It thus enhanced the already quite evident notion of Augustus' sanctity, which may have led Quintilian to characterize the Polykleitan model as *sanctus*.[43] These associations are enhanced by Augustus' dress in addition to the cuirass, in particular the mantle he wears around his hip. By that time, the *Hüftmantel* had become an emblem specifically associated with Caesar, *divus Iulius*. It is another reflection of the fact that there was no attempt on Augustus' part to dissociate himself in all ways from his adoptive father. Instead he used him, as is clear from Augustan poetry, too, as a model for his own divinity.[44]

A more relevant question is to what extent the program of images was also influenced by the Secular Games for which planning was proceeding at the time. The festival, as we saw earlier, was restructured by Augustus to give prominence to Apollo and Diana, as is evident also from Horace's *Secular Hymn*. Both deities appear on the armor: Apollo riding on a swan with his lyre (Fig. 73, lower left), and Diana on her hind (Fig. 73, lower right). The new *saeculum*, as we have seen, was characterized by a return not to a utopian paradise but to specific Roman virtues that Horace highlights in the *Carmen Saeculare* (57–60; see chapter 3). Those conditions, in turn, were made possible by the pacification of the east in particular (*CS* 53–56). All this will result not in a Golden Age—Horace never mentions the term in his hymn—but, as we have seen, in a "better age" (*melius aevum;* 67–68), characterized by upright mores and tranquillity (45–46: *probos mores . . . quietem*).[45] Within this framework, the Caelus figure can also be interpreted as Saturn, the guardian god of the "Saturnian land" (*Saturnia tellus*), Italy, which is another suggestive dimension of the reclining Tellus figure. As has been noted, though not by interpreters of the Prima Porta statue, the "Golden Age of Saturn symbolized the purity and simplicity of early Italian life, which had made Rome great."[46] And, as we saw earlier, part of Vergil's intention in his hymning of Augustus' *aurea aetas* in *Aeneid* 6 by reference to Saturn's was to allude to Augustus' moral and social reforms in the years before the revival of the *ludi saeculares*.

The pictorial program of the Prima Porta Augustus was shaped precisely during those years and reflects these ideas in its own way. It is an even more compressed program than that of the Ara Pacis, which it anticipates with its recourse to multiple meanings. These meanings emerge in full only when the various images are connected with one another. It is, in that sense, another "contemplative image." Its final element, the sphinxes on the shoulder flaps, share in this wealth of suggested meanings. Augustus used the emblem of the sphinx as his seal for some years; they stand for Egypt, a province that was his and the direct source of his wealth, and they allude to the prophesies in the Sibylline Books, which were edited at Augustus' behest and predicted the impending peaceful reign of Apollo. All this solemnity and sophistication is accompanied, as it was to be more extensively on the Ara Pacis, by the presence of a light touch, in this case the visage of the dolphin crumpling under the weight of an oblivious and not altogether lean Cupid (Fig. 5).

One further aspect in which the Ara Pacis and the Prima Porta statue are characteristic of Augustan art is that there are few representations of war and battle. Instead, there is a preference for still lifes and we see a world at peace, which is expressed by various allegories, divinities, and symbols. Again, more is involved than mere aesthetics. *Pax*, for one, is the more inclusive concept, which, as we have already observed, presupposes conquest. *Pax* comes from *pangere*, "to make firm," and *pacisci*, "to make a pact"; it is the "pact" one imposes on a conquered enemy. The *Res Gestae*, with its enumeration of conquests and victories, is an eloquent reflection of this concept. So while Augustus never forswore further conquest, he considered it, unlike Alexander, a greater challenge to rule the resulting *imperium* on the basis of order and laws (Plut., *Mor.* 207D). This attitude, which is traditionally Roman, finds its own artistic expression. One reason for the emphasis on classical art at Augustus' time is simply that representations of battle scenes, which had been a cynosure of Hellenistic art—we need to think only of the Alexander Sarcophagus and Pergamon Altar—now become even less frequent than under the republic.[47] This should not be confused with a rejection of Hellenistic pathos and "excesses" and a return to classical forms because they supposedly implied a claim to higher morality. The primary cause is that the Romans, as we saw earlier, were thinking in terms of normative concepts rather than ephemeral military events; this is clear even from early representations like the Fabian tomb from the third century B.C. (Fig. 25). For representations of abiding concepts and of ceremony and ritual, which were similarly timeless, a quieter, classicizing style suggested itself: form follows function. Yet even on the Ara Pacis, we find examples of the Hellenistic style, which suggests caution in identifying style completely with ethos; the relation between the two is complex and variable.[48] Similarly, the Prima Porta statue itself is a good example of the deliberate synthesis of several traditions, as one further example may illustrate.

76. Hellenistic ruler, second century B.C.

In his left hand, Augustus originally held a spear; the scepter is a modern restoration.[49] The spear derives from three traditions: classical, Hellenistic, and Roman, a derivation that has its counterpart in Augustan poetry, where it has been named the mixing of genres.[50] Classical: it is obviously the spear of the Doryphoros, Polykleitos' fifth-century statue (Fig. 8). Hellenistic: after Alexander, who commenced his conquest of Asia by ritually throwing his spear on that continent's shores, the spear becomes a staple in the statuary of Hellenistic rulers (Fig. 76).[51] The model was the famous Alexander statue of Lysippus, which was itself modeled on the Doryphoros.[52] While statues of Romans in the Augustan age tend to eschew the Hellenistic mode of bulging muscles and nudity, which are still much in evidence on the cameo with Octavian/Neptune (Fig. 2), the spear does not disappear and retains its symbolic value: Augustus is the world conqueror, the heir to Alexander. As such he projected himself especially in his endeavors to subdue the Parthians, the successors of the Persians.[53] Not surprisingly, the representation of Augustus himself and the pictorial programs on the cuirass form a finely balanced entity. While the portrait, for instance, minimizes any association with the portraits of Hellenistic dynasts, the representation of the sun-god on the armor has the additional dimension of echoing of Alexander's association with Helios. In the Rome of the *res publica*, Augustus would not have himself represented with the crown of solar rays as did Alexander.[54] Typically, he prefers to be allusive and indirect, and the result is a great deal richer. Yet another dimension of Sol, relevant to the context of the Secular Games, was that he was the legendary ancestor of the Latin people.[55]

To return to the spear: its third aspect is Roman. In Roman thinking, the spear represented the essence of arms and power: *hasta summa armorum et imperii est* (Festus, p. 55.3 L.). It means that the most important weapon in early Rome became the expression of the ruling power, as is attested by detailed numismatic and artistic documentation.[56] On the Ara Pacis, too, Aeneas (Fig. 43), juxtaposed as he was with Augustus, held a *hasta* in his left hand, as the extant traces indicate. He is a man of peace, but like the peace of Augustus, Aeneas' will result from victories in war. Such, as we have seen, is Aeneas' mission, according to Vergil's Jupiter:

> bellum ingens geret Italia populosque ferocis
> contundet moresque viris et moenia ponet.
>
> (*Aen.* 1.263–64)

> [In Italy he will fight a massive war
> Beat down fierce armies, then for people there
> Establish city walls and a way of life.]
>
> (trans. Fitzgerald)

THE PORTRAITS OF AUGUSTUS

As the Augustan rule often did in retrospect, especially to the Augustans of the eighteenth century, the dominant, "Prima Porta" portrait of Augustus (Figs. 9a, 19) effectively conveys the appearance of calm and composure. It came about, however, only after a great deal of experimentation with different portrait styles and traditions. Typically, the result was due not merely to Octavian's or Augustus' early volition, but to a gradual, autonomous process characterized by a variety of initiatives. Nor was there a monolithic end product, just as there was none in Augustan culture at large. Rather, the portraiture in the Augustan era follows the larger pattern of the times: continuity, change, adaptation, experimentation, and nuance.[57]

The study of the Augustan portraits has been a paradigm of the methodological tendencies to present the age as more one-dimensional than it actually was. There are four primary or distinctive portrait types of Octavian/Augustus.[58] One tendency has been to relate these types closely to political events—hence, for instance, the misnomer "Actium" type for a portrait style whose beginnings can actually be traced to the mid-30s. Similarly, the "main" type was long considered to be a reflection of the title "Augustus," awarded in 27 B.C., but a recent study has shown convincingly that its genesis goes back several years before then.[59] Proper self-representation was obviously a matter of the greatest concern to Augustus, as it was for anyone in Rome or, for that matter, today. Shrouded as the exact details are from our sight, we can assume that he took an active part in shaping his representation in portraits. But even in this instance of singular import, art had its own autonomy[60] and in the end was the result of Augustus' *auctoritas* rather than of a simple restyling at the ruler's command after major historical events, which appear as convenient junctures only in retrospect. We can deduce from this that the autonomy of Augustan literature, whose "organization" has been discussed in similarly reductive terms, was even greater.

Along with this tendency toward organizing the portraiture into types goes another: to create tidy taxonomies and impose a linear progression on a dynamic phenomenon. We observed an analogous situation in connection with the attempts to construe the Augustan settlement in purely constitutional and legal terms. Concerning the portraits—and other aspects of Augustan art—much has been made of the antinomy between the Hellenistic and the classical. Not all of Hellenistic art, however, stood for extravagance. Its relationship to classical art was complex and nuanced—it incorporated a classicizing trend, for instance—and so was the Roman reception and assimilation of both classical and Hellenistic art, and of classical and Hellenistic culture in general. These larger topics, therefore, merit special discussion (see chapter 7). Realism, to give but one example, was a component of both Hellenistic and Roman portraiture, and influences went in both directions: members of the philo-Roman ruling classes in the Greek east adopted veristic Roman self-representations while cultivated Italians adopted Hellenistic traditions of realism. If it is not always easy for art historians to differentiate such influences and traditions from one other, it was even less so for the citizens of the ancient world.

Another aspect that tends to be overlooked is that the transition from republic to principate was not marked by the kind of éclat that is posited by such antinomies. Much of Augustus' success was due precisely to his ability to effect transition quite subtly, to avoid sharp breaks, to present his rule as a continuation of the republic, and to draw on inspirations that already existed in republican times. We need to think only of Vergil, Horace, and Livy, who were not born-again Augustans but brought their own experiences, shaped under the republic, to bear on "Augustan" literature.[61] With regard to the Augustan portraits, the uniqueness of Augustus and of his role produced a corresponding subtlety of image. It partook in many different traditions[62] without being a slave to them and, in one of the many paradoxes characteristic of Augustus and his culture, its most "de-individualized" type became the one that was most recognizable and distinctive.

The function of the Roman portrait was more than the mere reflection of

a likeness. Rather, its aim was to convey an ethos.[63] In that regard, portrait
art is a part of the general moral context and of the concern for values we
have encountered time and again. A major trend in Roman portrait art for
the last century and a half of the republic was verism, but in more than an
aesthetic sense. Heightened realistic emphasis was meant to convey the

77. Roman denarius, ca. 47 B.C.
Obverse: Antius Restio.

Roman ethos of *severitas, gravitas, virtus,*
and *simplicitas*; witness that formidable
tribune of the people in 68 B.C., Antius
Restio (Fig. 77).[64]

One problem that immediately presented itself for Octavian was the matter
of his age. Roman virtues, as expressed
by physiognomy, were a corollary of advanced age. *Gravitas* and *auctoritas* accrued
to a man in representative dimensions not
before his forties; the minimum age for the
consulship, after all, had been traditionally
fixed at forty-two. Hence, "portraits of
later Republican Romans usually look be-
tween forty and sixty,"[65] whereas Hellenistic kings look a great deal younger,
between twenty and twenty-five. Quintilian's comments, cited earlier
(p. 25), reflect the continuity of the Roman value judgment into the second
century A.D.: he does not think much of Polykleitos, because Polykleitos
represents only young men who do not exhibit the *gravitas* and *auctoritas* that
come with a more advanced age; the only exception, because of its Roman
adaptation in the form of the Augustus statue, is the Doryphoros. How was
the young Octavian, consul at the age of twenty, to be represented and what
connotations would his image have?

A prematurely wizened image was neither feasible nor desired. He craved,
as we have seen, an equestrian statue on which his incomparably young age
was as prominently inscribed as he flaunts it in the opening words of the *Res
Gestae.* He wanted to be known and remembered as one who outdid Alexander and Pompey at an earlier stage of his life. Portraits of both Pompey and
Alexander, therefore, were appropriated as models. The coin portraits of
Octavian from 43 to 30 B.C. bear witness to considerable experimentation.[66]
On one of the earliest (Fig. 78), his bearded image (cf. Figs. 79–81) is on the
obverse and his equestrian statue, showing him with raised right hand, on the
reverse.

Octavian's early portrait in sculpture in the round, the so-called type B,
has been contested to the point of denying its representation of Octavian
altogether and assigning it to later Julio-Claudian princes such as Augustus'
grandsons Gaius and Lucius.[67] As always, discussion of the various detailed
arguments would require separate treatment. A central point, as Erika Simon

78. Denarius of Octavian, 41 B.C.
Obverse: the young Octavian. Reverse: his equestrian statue.

79. Portrait of young Octavian. Florence.

has shown, is that such typological arguments are controvertible.[68] Type B, therefore, can validly be considered the earliest portrait and may well stem from his coveted equestrian statue. It exists in eighteen copies, such as the heads in Florence (Fig. 79), Verona (Fig. 80), and Arles (Fig. 81). As the scholarly controversy indicates, it is not easy to categorize—a fitting reflection of its subject. There is a "citation" of Alexander by means of the parted hair over the right forehead. It is reminiscent of the youthful world

80. Portrait of young Octavian. Verona.

81. Portrait of young Octavian. Arles.

82. Alexander the Great. Detail from a
mosaic in the Casa del Fauno, Pompeii.

83. Pompey the Great. Claudian copy of a
portrait of ca. 50 B.C.

conqueror's tossed-back hair (Fig. 82), which Pompey deliberately affected in imitation of Alexander (Plut., *Pomp.* 2) and which appears in Pompey's portraits in combination with his placid, kindly mien (Fig. 83).[69]

Pompey's highly dichotomous image influenced Octavian's in another important aspect also. There was a conscious effort on the part of both Julius Caesar and Pompey to project calm and moderation in their portraits.[70] The times were turbulent enough, and a statesman should not appear agitated but able to spread balm over troubled waters, just as the poignant first simile of the *Aeneid* suggests. That endeavor, in turn, had another corollary: there was a downside to presenting a Roman leader with the kind of rugged realism we observed in the portrait of Antius Restio (Fig. 77). In his speech for Sestius (56 B.C.), in which he pragmatically sets forth the qualities of a *princeps*, Cicero pointedly distances himself from such an old-style appearance. The butt of his derision is a member of one of Rome's oldest families, the distinguished former consul Lucius Calpurnius Piso Caesoninus: "Great gods! How loathsome he was as he went about his way, how truculent, how terrifying to look at! You might think you were beholding one of those bearded men of old, an example of the old kind of power, the very image of the past, a true pillar of the *res publica*!" (*Sest.* 19). Further physiognomic details follow, such as the rough hair and, for that matter, the *gravitas* in the man's eyes. Even with all due allowance for Cicero's rhetoric—he conversely describes Piso's partner Gabinius as a milquetoast, who is coiffed effeminately and reeks of perfume—there were limits on self-representation in the old style because it might border on caricature. It was fine to preserve the essence of the old *mores*, but their incarnation needed some updating. Nobody realized this as well as Augustus, and that attitude informed much more than his portraits.

Overly realistic features, therefore, are relativized in the portraits of Octavian. He sprouts a beard on his cheeks, which is a typically multiple allusion to his youth, to his mourning for Caesar, and to Alexander. The hair is wavy, but not unruly; the face is somewhat bony, but even; and the movement of the head is controlled as is the facial expression. It reflects firmness and *auctoritas*. It also suggests the limits to framing the discussion exclusively in terms of "Hellenistic" and "classicizing." The portrait incorporates both influences, but its significance cannot be understood fully in just those terms. In that regard, too, it is a fitting reflection of Roman culture both in the late republic and under Augustus.

The same considerations apply to the subsequent principal portrait types of Octavian/Augustus. For a considerable time, the so-called Actium or Octavian type, which came to the fore in the 30s and early 20s B.C., was explained, with an overemphasis on some formal details, as reflecting the image of a Hellenistic dynast.[71] That is precisely one association Octavian wished to avoid, embroiled as he was in his propaganda battle against Antony that pitted the *virtus* of Italy against Antony's demeanor as an eastern potentate.

84. Portrait of Augustus, Actium type. Florence.

Instead, the real issue was again the artful representation of a young ruler, for which Hellenistic art furnished many a precedent, with a Roman aura. When we look at the earliest specimens of the new type, a head from a private collection on Mallorca (Fig. 22) and one from the Uffizi Gallery in Florence (Fig. 84), some formal aspects of Hellenistic royal portraiture are present, though carefully modified, such as the turn and tilt of the head and the tossing of the locks in front. Later Augustan copies of the type, such as that in the Capitoline Museum in Rome (Fig. 85), tone down even more whatever "pathos" this implied. More important is the absence of features typical of Hellenistic rulers like the dynamic long curls that are replaced by short Roman hair lying flat against the head. Add to this the veristic portrayal in the Roman tradition: small and almost protruding eyes; the pointed chin and prominent cheekbones; brows that are knitted closely together (according to Suetonius [*Aug.* 79.2], Augustus' eyebrows actually merged, but there were well-considered limits to such realism); the thin lips are pressed together especially on the late Augustan copy in Rome (Fig. 85); and the ears standing away from the head. More details yet: the wrinkles on the forehead reflect seriousness and concern (*cura*) for the *res publica*, and the two "rings" around the neck are those found on statues of Venus, his and Julius Caesar's divine ancestress. Finally, the Octavian head often appears with a veiled head

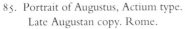

85. Portrait of Augustus, Actium type. Late Augustan copy. Rome.

86. Portrait of Octavian, Actium type. Venice.

(*capite velato*) even from early on, as is shown by the example from Mallorca (Fig. 22) and a posthumous copy from Venice (Fig. 86). Due to this simple fact, and to Hellenistic traditions, the hair that looks out from under the veil tended to be treated more dramatically. Such representations refer to Octavian's holding two major priesthoods (one since 41 B.C. and the other since 37 B.C.), a factor that contributed, as we saw earlier, to his *auctoritas* along with his descent from the deified Julius Caesar.

Typically enough, then, the image conveys multiple meanings. We have hints of an Alexander: after Actium and even the settlement of 27 B.C., that association served Octavian/Augustus to appear not as an oriental monarch, but as the conqueror of the east.[72] It is misplaced to construe his representation in these terms merely as being directed against Mark Antony. It continues, as we have seen, to the time of the Parthian settlement, as exemplified by the Prima Porta statue and its pictorial program, and even beyond that event. The youthful portrait of a Hellenistic king is transmuted into that of a young savior figure,[73] reminiscent of the saving youth (*iuvenis*) in Vergil's first *Eclogue* (especially lines 6–10, 40–45). Hence he again bears the marks of Venus. The simultaneously appearing more youthful portrait of Julius Caesar (Fig. 87) shows that Caesar now is assimilated to his young heir rather than the other way around.[74] In 38 B.C., both appear on the same side of a

87. Dupondius (?) of Octavian, ca. 38 B.C.
Obverse: Octavian, Caesar Divi Filius. Reverse: Divus Iulius.

88. Denarius of Octavian,
38 B.C. Obverse: Caesar
and Octavian.

denarius (Fig. 88)[75] and, from then on, Octavian is called *Imperator* on his coinage. That, too, is one of the aspects of his portrait. It presents him as thoroughly Roman in the main details of his appearance and, again, as a member of the two priesthoods. This was the emerging savior of the citizens (cf. Fig. 17) and of an oppressed *res publica*.

Given this inherent adaptability and this multiplicity of associations, it is understandable that one portrait series did not simply replace the other, but even as new types emerged, the copying of previous types continued: to each their own Augustus. The imperial image, as we know from a vivid passage in Fronto addressed to Marcus Aurelius, was produced en masse due to untrammeled demand.[76] It defied, in this regard alone, rigid control from the top over each aspect of production. The total panorama, therefore, is one of adaptations and variations rather than the state-sponsored production of mere replicas. In addition, types are modified under the influence of one another. The Octavian type, for instance, recurs in a quite naturalistic fashion on a bronze equestrian statue that was recovered from the Aegean sea not long ago and can be dated to the last decade B.C. (Fig. 89).[77] The elongation of the neck recalls the very young Octavian; the face is almost gaunt and the brows are nearly knitted together, as Suetonius says they were. All this creates special problems for the art historian bent on establishing rigid classifications. More important, it reflects the largely autonomous nature of the entire portraiture process,

89. Bronze equestrian statue of Augustus from
the Aegean Sea.

90. Portrait of Augustus, Prima Porta
type. From Meroë, Egypt.

which has ample parallels, even though with special nuances, in the literary
and political culture. Certainly, the ruler is an active participant in determining his self-representation. An image is designed that can be adapted and
interpreted in various ways by both public and ruler as historical circumstances progress. The "Actium" type, as we noted earlier, began several years
before Actium, but the portrait was inherently elastic enough to serve in due
course as a reflection of that great triumph. The next portrait type continued
the attempt at transcendence even more successfully.

That was the Prima Porta type, so called because it was used for the head
of that statue (Fig. 9a). It is "a deliberate and thoughtful adaptation of the
Actium type."[78] Both the continuities and the changes are significant. Any
allusions to the royal Hellenistic portrait disappear, but the youthfulness remains, although this was the "official" portrait until Augustus' death at the
age of seventy-five. It outnumbers all the other portraits by far and has been
found in all parts of the Roman empire, including Egypt (Fig. 90).[79] Far from
being at odds with *dignitas* and *auctoritas*, his youthfulness, which Augustus
stressed so prominently in the *Res Gestae*, is transformed into a timeless char-

acteristic and enhanced by the imitation of the Doryphoros, including his hairstyle (Figs. 9a and b).[80] The hair of both is ordered carefully in the manner of movement and countermovement, a resolution of opposites that is at the heart of the classical aesthetic. Symmetry is suggested by the parted, forklike locks of hair in the center of the forehead. At the same time, the individual Augustan "pincer" of locks over the right eyebrow is retained. The face is fuller and smoothed out with a resulting loss of wrinkles and boniness, while the protruding ears (relative to those of the Doryphoros) add a touch of realism. There is a complex blend of generalized physiognomy with a minimum of individualistic traits.

"Deindividualization" is a fitting characterization of the portrait,[81] and yet the portrait reflects the very essence of Augustus. Instead of being a "personality" in an individualistic, let alone idiosyncratic sense, he exemplified certain general norms and values: *exemploque suo mores reget* (Ovid, *Met.* 15.834). We saw already from the *Res Gestae* that he used generalized mottoes only to fill them with new meanings of his own. The values for which he stands are generally valid. His representation, therefore, is supraindividual: "The individuality of Augustus recedes behind a recognized principle of value concepts, which are set above it and determine in equal fashion the structure of the principate and the actions of the *princeps* Augustus."[82] The portrait of Aeneas was conceived by Vergil along similar lines, which explains some of the problems romantic and modern critics have had with it.

The references to a classical model complement this aspect. There was no human predecessor who could serve as a model. The portrait is removed from the human sphere without amounting to outright deification: "To the princeps is granted surpassing stature, which has accrued to him due to his personal, incomparable abilities and virtues, and especially due to his *auctoritas*."[83] Moreover, ideal and reality intermingled. According to Suetonius (*Aug.* 79.1–2), "he always wore a serene expression, whether he was talking or was at rest . . . Augustus' eyes were clear and bright, and he liked to believe that they shone with a divine kind of radiance." Both these qualities, Suetonius relates, had an almost supernatural impact on others. Augustus no doubt cultivated them and the portrait was effective in perpetuating this aura.

The connotations do not end there. The evocation of the youthful savior persists; the genesis of the portrait places it in the context not of his declaration as Augustus in 27 B.C., but of his emphasis in the 30s on being *imperator Caesar divi filius*.[84] Because of its inherent richness of content, the portrait was adaptable in various ways. It could, with a strong emphasis on its transcendent and transpersonal aspects, become indeed a fitting emblem of the aura of Augustus, the Sublime One, after 27 B.C. A contrasting trend, however, was in the direction of somewhat greater individualization[85]—to some, the deindividualization of the portrait had progressed too far and they wanted

91. Augustus as togate priest. Detail of Fig. 19.

to see more of a flesh-and-blood Augustus. This trend cannot be limited to the preferences of a "private" clientele, as one of the best examples is the famous "public" statue of the togaed, priestly Augustus from the Via Labicana (Fig. 91): the face is more elongated and pointed, the eyes are smaller, the cheekbones are more visible, the jug ears are more pronounced, and the line of the mouth is much more intense. Conversely, the greater stylization of the Prima Porta type affected subsequent copies of the "Actium" and "B" types. The variety of and latitude for these "interpretations" parallel those of the *Res Gestae*, the meanings of *res publica* in Augustan Rome, and of Augustan poetry, but they did not come, in all these cases, at the expense of a clearly established overall significance.

The final portrait type, called the Forbes type after the original owner of one of the busts, is a further adaptation of the less abstract and more lifelike variant of the main type (Fig. 92).[86] The stylization of the hair on the forehead now yields to an even, "normal" cut, brushed into three unobtrusive locks. The proportions of the face are changed slightly in order to appear more natural. That impression is intensified by the somewhat bonier looks and the stronger suggestion of wrinkles at the corners of the mouth and at the base of the nose. This indeed is the consummate *civilis princeps*,[87] and the

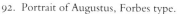

92. Portrait of Augustus, Forbes type.   93. Augustan portrait of Julius Caesar, 20s B.C.

portrait was fittingly chosen for Augustus' representation on the Ara Pacis amid Roman men, women, and children (Fig. 62). It is a carefully understated image of one who does not have to accentuate his sublime aura because he is securely in possession of it. The Prima Porta type and the Forbes type parallel the sequence of *Res Gestae* 34 and 35 from *auctoritas* to *pater patriae*, though neither these terms nor these two portrait types are mutually exclusive: it is simply a matter of a somewhat different emphasis. While copies of the Forbes type are not as numerous as those of the main type (approximately 30 vs. more than 170), there was considerable crossover between the two. A comparison of the new Caesar portrait, which was designed in the 20s (Fig. 93),[88] and the Forbes type is instructive also. Caesar is neither a god, nor an abstraction, nor the scourge of the civil wars. Instead his portrait is more bourgeois and suggests accessibility and *clementia*. The more muted features of the Forbes Augustus convey the same aspects even more strongly.

Two final comments on the portraits of Augustus are in order. One is Paul Zanker's splendid illustration of the assimilation of the portraits of private citizens to the imperial style.[89] It is an intriguing mixture of the impact of Augustus' charisma, of aesthetic trends, of a recognition of and participation in the underlying moral aspects, and of a sharing of ideas. The phenomenon is not limited to portrait art. It debunks the notion of propaganda, and its

94. Augustan portrait of a young man.

reductive characterization as a fawning, "claqueur mentality"[90] ignores the
same range of reactions and nuances vis-à-vis Augustus' *auctoritas* that is operative throughout Augustan culture. It is doubtful, for instance, that mere
sycophancy impelled a young nobleman to imitate the youthful Octavian in
his own portrait (Fig. 94).[91] It is a spontaneous, fresh image that echoes, but
does not replicate, the early portraits of Octavian in its hairstyle, beard, and
wrinkles on the forehead. These are commingled with strictly individual
features: mouth, chin, eyes. An admirer of Octavian's dynamism, obviously,
but one who retained his own personality.

Second, the same independence is illustrated by the fact that the "Hellenistic" type of representation did not simply cease to exist in Augustan Rome
but appears prominently, for example, in the statues and portraits of Augustus' principal associate and son-in-law, Agrippa. This is another salutary reminder that the discussion of Augustan art, and of the culture in general,
cannot be reduced to a simple opposition between Hellenistic and classicizing aspects. For example, in a colossal statue which can be dated to the
decade before his death in 12 B.C., Agrippa appears like a Hellenistic paragon with swelling muscles and energetic movement (Fig. 95).[92] Some of
Agrippa's portraits are so "Hellenistic" that they have been identified with
those of Mark Antony.[93] This again should caution us against reducing of the
intent of Octavian/Augustus' portraits to a "classical" antithesis to the "New

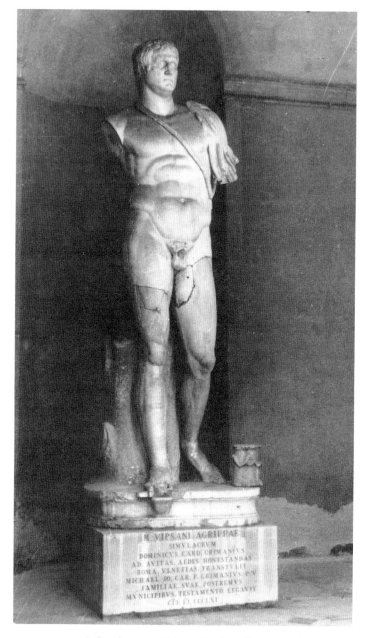

95. Colossal statue of Marcus Agrippa, late 20s B.C.

Dionysus" Mark Antony. The process that is at work in the portraits of Octavian and Augustus is similar to that which we saw in the *Res Gestae* where the implied reference to Antony (*RG* 1.1) is only a starting point, superseded by additional meanings which keep accruing.

WALL PAINTING

While the Roman house had a public as well as a private function[94] and while some of the best preserved houses from the Augustan period belong to the imperial family, wall painting is a more private domain of art than the public art we have surveyed so far. The interaction between this private art and political and social circumstances is complex and difficult to assess.[95] One solution is to claim that any evolution is simply the inherent product of artistic styles and tastes and that external factors do not impinge on it. Conversely, the remarkable development which Roman wall decoration undergoes at the time of Augustus has led to the assertion that the resulting styles and motifs are but another manifestation, in private art, of the same morally oriented classicism considered to be the main characteristic of Augustan public art. The true nature of the phenomenon lies between these two poles; what is Augustan in general is, once again, its evolution, experimentation, variety, creativity, and considerable nuance. The changes wall painting undergoes in Augustan times are conspicuous. Even though it has been astutely observed that fashions in Roman painting occur in an almost regular chronological cycle[96]—artists and patrons simply want something new—the Augustan changes are related in a general way to the new mood of peace, order, and stability. But the paintings also reflect many individual impulses and solicit similar responses. That aspect and the limitations of the actual evidence stand in the way of reductive and facile generalizations. Augustan private art illustrates that characterizations of it need to be more inclusive precisely in order to be more exact.

The characteristics of innovation and tradition again apply as they did to the Augustan transformation of the *res publica*. From the very beginning, Roman wall painting included an element of make believe. The first or so-called incrustation style simply gave the impression that the wall was made of precious stone materials as it mimicked blocks of multicolored marble through the medium of stucco relief and painting. It gradually yielded to the second or architectural style (all paint), which opened up the wall to views on make-believe buildings. The upper part of the wall now becomes a window on fantastic architectural vistas (Fig. 96). As the painted blocks in the first style, these buildings, illusionist as they clearly are, are at the same time rarely so fanciful as to be completely unrealistic.[97] They did offer the houses' owners an expanded opportunity for competition in ostentation.

96. Architectural vista, Second Style. Villa of Fannius Sinistor, Boscoreale.
Bedroom M, northwest corner, ca. 50–40 B.C.

Again, however, we cannot simply reduce the contrast between this late republican style and the Augustan one to that between unrestrained materialism versus spiritually ennobled simplicity: the perspective in these rooms onto vistas beyond a crosswall (*Scherwand*) has been meaningfully related to that of Lucretius' Epicureanism, which aims to transcend our everyday existence by a wise contemplation of the world beyond the dimension of its walls.[98] The age of Augustus coincides with the transition to the third style and its development: the wall now afforded not only views of architecture, but became an expanse for a variety of paintings whose meaning varied with their patrons and beholders. Nor was there any lack of fantasy and display. It is useful to follow some of these developments though it should not be implied that they took place in an absolutely linear progression.

A room in the Casa del Labirinto in Pompeii (ca. 40 B.C.) is an example of the successful integration in the second style of painted and real architecture (Fig. 97). The columns in the house and those in the painting complement one another. The painted architecture is illusionistic: the structure composed

97. Representational room, Second Style.
Casa del Labirinto, Pompeii, ca. 40 B.C.

of columns, architrave, and pediment is cut in two by a small round building (tholos) placed in its center. The painted crosswall reaches up to about half the height of the real wall. There is concern in this instance, which is not always found in the second style, for symmetry and centering. Less than two decades later, we see both the remnants of and the differences from this scheme in the "House of Livia," which was part of the Augustan complex on the Palatine (Fig. 98).[99] The architectural views now are relegated to the far sides of the wall and the crosswall has been reduced to a low podium broken up by socles. The painted columns have attenuated and serve a decorative rather than a structural function; the calyx-shaped bases, for instance, could not in reality support even the slender columns placed on top of them. The painting with Mercury, Io, and Argus in the center can be considered either as being painted on the wall or as a scene taking place in the landscape setting behind it. But fantasy takes over: witness the two winged creatures beside the upper part of the picture, the vegetal candelabra placed on the crossbeams, and the general abandonment of realistic standards for the painted structure with which the viewer is faced.

98. Painted wall from the "House of Livia" on the Palatine, ca. 30–25 B.C.

99. Painted wall from the "Aula Isiaca" on the Palatine, ca. 20 B.C.
Watercolor by F. Bartoli (1724).

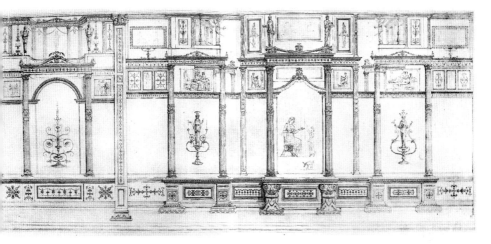

100. Augustan villa beneath the Villa Farnesina. Cubiculum B,
drawing of the side wall, between 20 and 10 B.C.

Even more striking in its exuberant variety is the wall decoration from the
approximately contemporary "Isiac Hall," or Aula Isiaca (named after some
of the decorative motifs related to the goddess Isis) on the Palatine (Fig. 99).
Architectural views now are reduced to no more than fanciful suggestions in
the upper panel: two receding beams are supported by female herms that
grow out of the middle frieze, which is composed of a series of small painted
panels and has the overall effect of a *pinacotheca*, a picture gallery. The place
of the crosswall is now taken up by landscapes, such as the one on the left
with a shrine of Apollo. Eclecticism prevails: there is an abundance of fili-
gree, Cupids hover in the two panels next to the central shrine (aedicula),
and there are Egyptianizing motifs. The slender columns, such as they are,
grow out of flower petals and are richly decorated, mimicking inlay of various sorts. The residual symmetry and axiality are anything but oppressive.

The wall paintings in the Villa under the Farnesina, which date from the
next to the last decade B.C. and may have been commissioned by Agrippa
and Julia, exhibit further refinement.[100] The only large figural representation
on the side wall (Fig. 100) of Cubiculum B is that of Venus in an aedicula that
is placed off-center in an arrangement that does not insist on complete symmetry. Other wall panels, between the ever more reedlike columns, are
treated in monochrome and alternate with representations of candelabra,
two of which incorporate a figure of Isis. The opposite wall in the same room
exhibits the character of a *pinacotheca* yet more (Fig. 101). The central painting, depicting nymphs caring for the infant Dionysus, is flanked by two
white-ground panels, which are held up by Sirens whose feet end in those of

101. Augustan villa beneath the Villa Farnesina. Picture wall of Cubiculum B.
In the center: nymphs and baby Dionysus.

birds of prey. In the anteroom, surrounded by small panels with erotic and
theatrical scenes and set against a red background, a candelabra-like Egyptian
deity, with the crown of Isis, holds two slender cornucopiae (Fig. 102). They
harmonize with the vegetal scrolls out of which two griffins grow who support her. Egyptian, classical, and Hellenistic motifs are combined for a striking overall pictorial effect. The place of the former architectural vistas in the
upper tier is now taken by a plethora of framed pictures (all painted on the
wall, of course) separated by slender caryatid-like figures.

This decorative profusion yields in other rooms to a more subdued mono-

102. Augustan villa beneath the Villa Farnesina.
Detail: Egyptianizing figures.

chromatic treatment of the walls: black in the Farnesina and red in the villa
at Boscotrecase (ca. 10 B.C.), which may have been built by Agrippa and
been bequeathed to his son, and Augustus' grandson, Agrippa Postumus.[101]
In the Boscotrecase villa, the red walls are used effectively to set off the lone
and central picture, painted on light background, of a bucolic landscape with
a seated statue of Cybele (Pl. 1). So far from vanishing, the decorative wealth
has been transferred to the stalklike columns and small bands that separate the
colored panels (Fig. 103). The columns look almost bejeweled—far more
intricately than those of the Casa del Labirinto (Fig. 97)—while miniaturized
vegetal motifs are prominent in the vertical decorative bands on which plant-
like candelabra are resting. Instead of establishing a connection with an
imaginary world outside the walls of the house, both gems and candelabra
relate to the interior decoration of such houses.

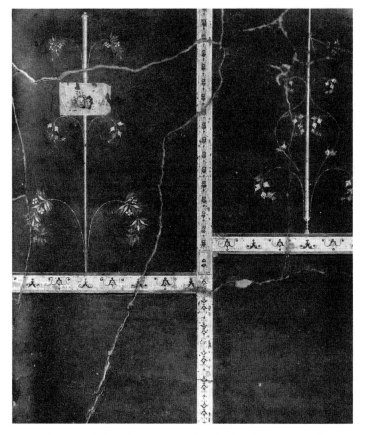

103. Augustan Villa at Boscotrecase. Detail of wall decoration (Pl. 1).

Gems, as we know from Pliny's culminating disquisition in his *Natural History* (37.54ff.), were among the most highly prized luxury articles in Rome. No business was more lucrative than the production of imitation gems (*HN* 37.197ff.). Luxury was alive and well among the upper classes in the Augustan age and Augustan poetry is full of references to it.[102] The point of Vitruvius' famous strictures, which I will take up shortly, of contemporary wall decoration (7.5.3ff.) is not the denunciation of materialistic excess. On the contrary, Vitruvius is quite specific about building suitably for different social classes. For persons of high rank, he says (6.5.2), we must build kingly (*regalia*) vestibules; the Roman animus against kings and their trappings did not apply here. On the grounds of such mansions, he continues, there are to be "plantations of trees and promenades completed for the enhancement of grandeur" (*ad decorem maiestatis perfectae*), a notion that is parallel, in the realm of private houses, to his programmatic statement addressed to Augustus, that

104. Attendants decorating a baetyl. Terracotta plaque
from the Apollo sanctuary on the Palatine, ca. 30 B.C.

mances was not exactly highbrow—Horace, for good reason, lamented the
state of the Roman theater both in the *Art of Poetry* and the *Letter to Augustus*—and that, in the very hour of his death, he assumed the role of a
mimeplayer:[107] "He called for a mirror, and had his hair combed and his
lower jaw, which had fallen from weakness, propped up. Presently he summoned a group of friends and asked: 'Have I played my part in the mime of
life creditably enough?' adding this theatrical tag:

> If I have pleased you, kindly signify
> Appreciation with a warm good-bye."

The inspiration for the central prospect on this wall of the Room of the
Masks comes from religion and again is relevant to Augustus. It refers to his
divine alter ego, Apollo. A baetyl, that is, a cone-shaped cult monument
sacred to the god, is placed into a light and spacious landscape. The same
motif recurs on one of the Campana plates (Fig. 104) from the Temple of
Apollo that was part of the Augustan compound on the Palatine: two attendants are shown adorning a baetyl with garlands. The artifacts date to the

Plate 1. Bucolic landscape with statue of a goddess. Augustan Villa at Boscotrecase, north wall of red cubiculum, last decade B.C.

Plate 2. House of Augustus on the Palatine. "Room of the Masks." South and west walls, ca. 40–30 B.C.

Plate 3a. House of Augustus on the Palatine, "Room of the Masks."
Detail of west wall: fantasy creatures.

Plate 3b. Forum of Augustus. Pattern of marble pavements: Portico floors (left);
exedra (lower center); Room of the Colossus (upper center);
cella of Mars Ultor Temple (right).

Plate 4. House of Augustus, Augustus' study, ca. 30–20 B.C. Various details of the south and north wall decoration.

Plate 4, cont.

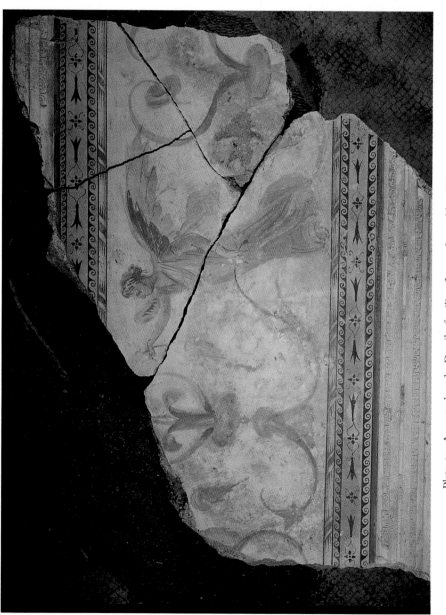

Plate 5a. Augustus' study. Detail of ceiling fresco: the goddess Victory.

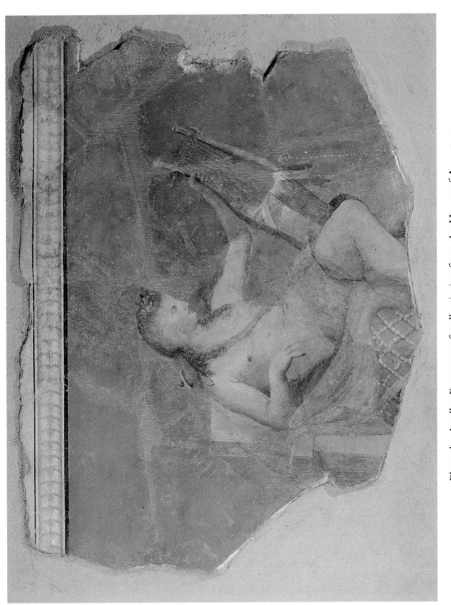

Plate 5b. Apollo. Fragment of wall painting from the House of Augustus.

Plate 6. Wall painting with Lares and Genius. House of the Vettii, Pompeii, ca. A.D. 65.

time when Octavian began to develop his association with Apollo, an association that continued throughout his reign.

A third characteristic element in the Room of the Masks is the fantastic miniature creatures that populate the top of the painted timberwork. They include winged females whose legs and feet end in vegetal scrolls, animals whose lower body ends similarly, and a profusion of similar shapes especially on the "frieze"—and beyond it—of the edifices of the right and left sides of the west wall (Pl. 3a). Such "grotesques" recur in the adjacent House of Livia (Fig. 110) and in other houses of the period and obviously were a favorite of the imperial family.

Still, the wall decoration in these rooms and others on the ground floor, which had at least a semipublic function, is conservative in comparison to that in Augustus' private retreat in the upper story, his "Syracuse" or *technophyon* (which most translators render with "workshop") according to his unauthorized biographer (Suet., *Aug.* 72.2). Here we enter into a totally different dimension. "Everything on these walls is free, full of fantasy, animated by a joyous mood, and by a sophisticated play of contrasts between form and color."[108] There is a precious balance between the discernible precision of the architectural organization—black podium, red orthostates, and an aedicula with mostly yellow tones—and the extraordinary fantasy of the decorated upper friezes, which spills over into the vegetal forms of the pediment of the aedicula and the column bases below: spiraling candelabra, griffins with tendril-like tails next to stylized obelisks that arise from calyxes, swans that hold up strings of pearls and garlands of flowers, herons amid lotus blossoms (Pl. 4). Everywhere we look there is polychromy and a profusion of detail, which effectively contrasts with the monochromatic reds of the orthostates. The abundance of architectural vistas that used to occupy the upper part of the wall in the second style now is taken up by an equal abundance of exquisite and minute decorations. We are dealing not with a movement from lavishness to simplicity, but with a shift in decorative preferences, which is also found in the House of Livia—witness the vegetal griffins on the upper part of the some of its walls (Fig. 105)—the Villa under the Farnesina, and others.

The inspiration for many of the motifs is Egyptian and, more specifically, the cult of Isis. They include the *urceus*, a metal can with an elongated spout, and the *situla*, a metal urn covered with pointed metal leaves (Pl. 4, center), along with Egypt's sacred snake, the *uraeus*, which recurs in a variety of configurations such as the handles of some *urcei*. The Egyptomania resulting from the conquest of that country in 30 B.C. was, to be sure, mostly an aesthetic phenomenon,[109] comparable with fashions like the chinoiserie of the seventeenth and eighteenth centuries. Such decorations became quite popular and are found in the Aula Isiaca on the Palatine, the Villa under the

105. Room I of the "House of Livia." Reconstruction after Rizzo.

Farnesina, and Pompeian villas. It is interesting to note nonetheless that Augustus had his inner sanctum, a "jewel" as the excavator has rightly called it, painted in this manner by an outstanding Alexandrian artist not long before he and Agrippa tried to limit the cult of Isis in Rome around 20–18 B.C. This indicates, at the very least, that Augustus could keep aesthetics separate from ideology and that not everything he touched was laden with moral meaning. If that is true of his own four walls, we may safely assume that it is just as true of other private houses. Further dimensions are more speculative: the Egyptianizing decoration may have been a reminder of Actium and his appropriation of Egypt; it was not untypical of Augustus, as we have seen on several occasions, to appropriate the watchwords and emblems (including obelisks) of former enemies.

The effect of the room was enhanced by the intricate decoration of the ceiling, a mix between stucco work and painting. While the areas of decora-

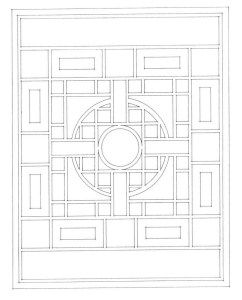

106. Augustus' study. Diagram of ceiling (E. Paparatti).

tion were carefully laid out (Fig. 106), the variety of the decoration itself almost concealed the underlying symmetrical scheme: art was hidden by its own art, as Ovid would say (*Met.* 10.252). The subtle interplay between the various decorative elements complements the interplay between the architectural elements on the walls. "Scheme-generating" would be a fitting characterization, and it happens to be the literal meaning of *technophyon*,[110] a unique word for a unique creation. The ceiling decoration displays the same kind of elegant fantasy and polychromy as the wall decorations and abounds in vegetal and Egyptian motifs. Victories in pastel colors float through the air like butterflies (Pl. 5a)—a charming transformation of the portentous *Victoria Augusta* into the private domain. Similarly, on the central rondo appeared a duo of winged female figures, one carrying the other in flight, a schema that occurs in a more "serious" context on the armor of the Prima Porta statue which is dated only slightly later (Fig. 73). Likewise, the archetype of the figures ending in shoots or growing from plants is the winged Victoria Caesaris from the relief decoration of the Temple of Julius Caesar (Fig. 71) whose construction was finished in 29 B.C., which coincides with the time of the paintings in the houses of Augustus and Livia and slightly predates the decorations of the Farnesina Villa.

Such perspectives on the decorativeness of Augustus' rooms have tended to be neglected amid the attention paid to the strictures of Vitruvius [111] who denounces, in his *De Architectura* dedicated to Augustus, this widespread fantasy style as an aberrration because it is not imitative of reality:

> Imitations based upon reality are now disdained by the improper mores of the present. On the stucco are monsters rather than definite representations taken from definite things. Instead of columns there rise up stalks; instead of gables, gablets with curled leaves and volutes. Likewise, candelabra which hold up the images of aediculae; on their summits, clusters of thin stalks rise from their roots in tendrils with little figures seated upon them at random. In the same fashion, slender stalks with heads of men and of animals attached to half the body. Such things neither are, nor can be, nor have been. On these lines the new mores have brought it about that bad judges condemn good craftsmanship as lack of art. (7.5.3–4)

This echoes the language of Augustan morality, except that Augustus is among the innovators. It shows—and the point would not need to be made if the portrayal of Augustus as the godfather of the despots of the 1930s had not been so influential—that spirited disagreement with the *princeps* was not uncommon, and without further repercussions for the dissenter; we have seen another example in Horace's *Letter to Augustus*.[112] There was no dogmatic consistency: the beginning of Horace's *Ars Poetica* (1–5) takes Augustus' side of the issue as it almost parodies Vitruvius' fulminations against "avant-garde" painting.[113] The gradual disappearance of these decorations in the continuing evolution of wall painting under Augustus is best viewed as an aesthetic development rather than as the vindication of a higher, "classical" morality.

That evolution was toward a more marked character of the wall as a picture gallery, a *pinacotheca*, with an emphasis on mythological and landscape painting. "The reason for the dominance of the *pinacotheca*," as Eleanor Leach has well noted, was "quite simply the equality of its appeal to painters and patrons."[114] The opportunities this style offered to both were infinitely greater than the display of yet another set of imaginary architecture. It is in this important sense that the Augustan fantasy style prepares the way for the third style. It gave much greater latitude to inventiveness and creativity, leading to a style that was yet stronger in intellectual and suggestive content.[115]

The same qualities, in accordance with the reciprocal and dialogic nature of Augustan *auctoritas*, carry over to the response of the viewer. Mythology and landscape are inherently evocative. The artist may make certain suggestions, but unless he is overtly didactic much will remain in the eye of the beholder. The procedure has its consummate literary counterpart in Ovid's *Metamorphoses*, a product of the same taste and environment. In terms of

107. Polyphemus and Galatea. Wall painting from
Room II of the "House of Livia," ca. 30–25 B.C.
Copy and reconstruction by A. Sikkard and G. Gatti.

Greco-Roman myth in general, a moral can be applied to most myths. Whether this is really the guiding intention of their pictorial representations is not so easily discernible; the story of Daedalus and Icarus, to take just one frequent subject, may have the same variety of functions or meanings in wall painting as it has in both Ovid's *Art of Love* (2.23–98)[116] and the *Metamorphoses* (8.182–259). It is impossible to fit Augustan painting into a simple moral scheme: the hallmark of the rendition of the story of Polyphemus and Galatea in the House of Livia, for instance, is not only the amused and almost taunting manner in which Galatea and her companions move in nimble circles around a hugely static Polyphemus, but the poor fellow's fright of the water into which they have lured him (Fig. 107);[117] even Ovid left him safely on land (*Met.* 13.778ff.). It is a humorous, lighthearted depiction—entertainment, just like Ovid's *Metamorphoses*, removed from preoccupation with moral problems and values. At the same time, the very introduction of mythology and landscape—a combination we find on the Ara Pacis, too— shares the impulse to reflection with such works of public art. The important difference is that most often no specific message is intended.[118] The painting in the Farnesina Villa with the nymphs and the infant Dionysus (Fig. 101) is a good example. It is yet another reminder that Dionysiac motifs even in the early Augustan period extended beyond references to Mark Antony.

What is Augustan, then, about Augustan painting is, as in the case of Augustan literature, its impulse to variety, its multiplicity of subjects (which contrasts with their deliberately limited number in public art) and their associations, its creativity, innovation, and experimentation, its eclecticism of styles and themes, and its ongoing development. The new atmosphere of peace and tranquillity did find some artistic reflection, though not in a progression from republican "excess" to Augustan "classicism." A pertinent example is the manner of painting whose beginnings Pliny (*HN* 35.116) attributes to the Augustan painter Studius.[119]

Pliny characterizes this style as "the most pleasant kind of wall painting" (*amoenissimam parietum picturam*), integrating into the landscapes not only all kinds of places and buildings, but the representation of everyday people pursuing everyday activities: strolling about, sailing, traveling overland (sometimes in donkey carts), fishing, hunting, gathering the vintage. The subjects tend to be portrayed with a gentle kind of humor and with whimsy, "producing a charming effect with minimal expense" (*HN* 35.117). While we have no further clues as to the identity of Studius, the genre, which coexists with the others we have surveyed, is a common one during the entire Augustan period. We find excellent examples in the usual, best-known houses: that of Livia, the Farnesina Villa, and the Villa of Agrippa Postumus at Boscotrecase. The foot-high Yellow Frieze in the House of Livia exemplifies the almost miniaturist application of this style: the landscape, diversified with many different buildings and settings, is populated with men and women who stroll, fish, sail, travel on donkey- or camel-back or drive donkeys, shake hands with other travelers, and repair buildings. We are witnessing no momentous or mythological events, but domestic scenes depicted with an undemanding humor: a dog chases a man who fends it off with a stick (Fig. 108) while in a picture from the Villa at Boscotrecase a shepherd talks to his dog who obediently raises a forepaw in response (Fig. 109). Such a detail does not diminish the sacredness of the surrounding landscape but helps to humanize it. We saw a similar concern, albeit without recourse to man's best friend, in the presentation especially of the children on the Ara Pacis (cf. Fig. 59).

It was a congenial style for enjoyment by Augustus' main constituency, the nonpolitical classes of Italy. Accordingly, and not as a result of moral or

108. Scene of everyday life. Yellow Frieze, "House of Livia."

109. Detail of rural scene. Augustan Villa at Boscotrecase,
east wall of Red Room. Last decade B.C.

110. Wall from Room III in the "House of Livia."
The Yellow Frieze is above the white panels
while fantasy creatures occupy the upper register.

sumptuary legislation, there is a lack of ostentatiousness in both subject and treatment. This does not result in absence of sophistication or refinement: the Yellow Frieze, for instance, is the effective highlight of Room III where it contrasts with the large white orthostates and the largely nonfigural decoration (Fig. 110). But, as noted before, people are shown here engaged in ordinary activities and not in actions of great moment or drama. An obvious literary counterpart, which shares the same qualities and the same gentle humor, is Ovid's tale of Philemon and Baucis (*Met.* 8.616-724).[120]

One of the most appealing aspects of the age of Augustus is precisely its emphasis on humanity amid the power of empire and the might of the ruler and the governmental machinery. The emperor, while not "setting the tone" in all things, found this humane atmosphere congenial. Suetonius' *Life of Augustus* is impressive for its numerous references to Augustus' sense of

humor—"there was no form of good humor in which he did not indulge"(98.3)—and to his jesting, literary humor, and the irony he directed at
himself.[121] Fragmentary as it is, the correspondence between Vergil and Augustus and, especially, between Horace and Augustus suggests a relaxed inti-
macy and familiarity that transcends the formal requirements of *amicitia*. He
made fun of the contrast between Horace's slim books of verse and his somewhat globular physique, called him *purissimum penem* and "a most charming
manikin" (*lepidissimum homuncionem*) and demanded, in mock-threatening
tones, that Vergil should send him a first draft of the *Aeneid* or at least a *kolon*
of it. It prompted a recent scholar to remark "that Augustus could be informal, even charming—but only in private. We perhaps spare a sigh for the
informal and human poems which his poets might, had his public persona
been less rigorously exigent, have composed for him."[122] Most of Horace's
poems, however, are occasional rather than manifestos, nor was the boundary between public and private art inflexible.

In fact, the existence of humaneness amid great power and complexity is
natural, although it is not often realized. As Wolfgang Schadewaldt outlined
many years ago,[123] the need for the expression of humanity becomes especially acute when our daily lives, the economy, the government, and domestic and foreign affairs become overstructured, unwieldy and bewildering in
their complexity, and unresponsive to our simple instincts. Western history
has been full of such reactions—from the *Bacchae* to *Walden*, and from the
Saint Vitus' dance to the Hare Krishnas—whenever life tends to become
overstructured and dehumanized. The Augustan reaction stands out among
the others by being quintessentially humane: the relaxed humor, the light
touch, the bantering, the easy communication (devoid of its modern
buzzword overtones), and, most of all, by incorporating this humaneness
both informally and formally into the literary and artistic milieu of the time.

THE FORUM OF AUGUSTUS

While providing meaningful civic spaces, public architecture did not admit
of such informality. In the prefatory dedication of his work to Augustus,
Vitruvius succinctly defined the purpose of public buildings as enhancing,
through their *auctoritas*, the grandeur of the empire (*maiestas imperii*). The
Augustan culmination of this idea was his forum (Fig. 111).[124] It was dedicated in 2 B.C. and was truly stupendous; Pliny counted it both among
the architectural miracles and the most beautiful edifices of the world he
knew (*HN* 36.101–2). The reason lies in its combination of material splendor
with a wealth of inspirations—architectural, spiritual, and historical. We
again find tremendous multiplicity operating within the *auctoritas* of guiding
ideas.

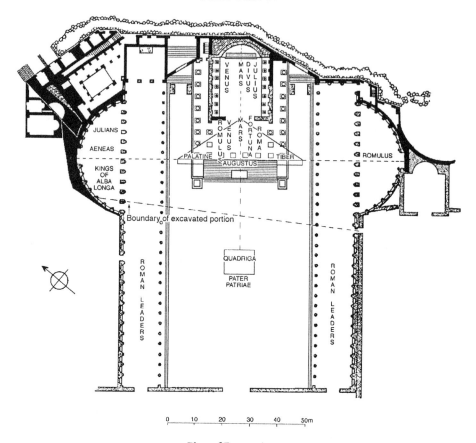

III. Plan of Forum Augustum.

Most of the latter are clear from Augustus' own statements and from the topographical and visual aspects of the forum itself. Consonant with the nature of his rule, it was to be a monument where his personal intentions and the public purpose coalesced. Returning to the concept of the *privatus* with which he began the *Res Gestae*, Augustus emphatically states that he built the Forum Augustum and its Temple of Mars Ultor "on private ground" and "from the proceeds of booty" (*RG* 21.1). And he meant it: the land needed for the complex was in one of the most heavily built-up areas of Rome, but Augustus did not invoke public domain and expropriate any of the owners. The protection of private property was, after all, one of the main rationales for the *res publica* whose restabilizing marked the Augustan reign. The process of land acquisition must have been an extended one and some owners apparently never sold. The asymmetry at the east corner of the precinct (Fig. 111), emphasized by the irregular course of the massive enclosure wall, most probably was due to such reasons: Suetonius remarks, in the context of his description of the behavior of this *civilis princeps* (*Aug.* 56.2), that Augustus made the forum smaller because "he did not dare to take away by force some nearby houses from the owners." Another personal imprint on the forum was Octavian's original vow, in 42 B.C., to build the Temple of Mars Ultor to commemorate his act of revenge on Caesar's assassins at Philippi. First, however, he completed the Forum of Julius Caesar, and there are several intentional connections, as we shall see, between the two.

Another aspect, again reminiscent of that singularly multireferential opening of the *Res Gestae*, is the evocation of Alexander, the world conqueror. Two large canvases by the painter Apelles occupied a highly frequented spot in the Augustan forum (Pliny, *HN* 35.27 and 93–94). One depicted him with the goddess Victoria and the Dioscuri while the other showed him riding triumphantly in his chariot, accompanied by the deity of war whose hands had been tied behind his back. The less subtle Claudius had the face of Alexander cut out from both works and replaced with Augustus'. One of the chief purposes of the forum was to convey the idea of the *imperium Romanum*, if not *Augustum*, its conquests, and might. After the "victory" over the Parthians, therefore, the building of the Temple of Mars Ultor acquired a second intention (Ovid, *Fasti* 5.579ff.), the commemoration of the revenge on the Parthians for the earlier Roman defeats. The standards that were returned to the Romans in 20 B.C. (cf. the cuirass of the Prima Porta statue [Fig. 73]) were displayed, along with Julius Caesar's sword, in the inner shrine of the temple after its long-awaited completion. In addition, the stated functions (Dio 55.10.1–5; Suet., *Aug.* 29.1–2) of the forum signified its relation to foreign policy and conquest: (1) victorious generals were to make dedications to Mars Ultor after their return from war; (2) governors, who were setting out for a military command in their provinces, were to take their leave publicly from the forum; (3) senate meetings concerning wars were to be held in the Temple of Mars Ultor. A further purpose was the accommodation of the ever increasing legal business. The salient point is that the forum was meant to be more than a museum. Instead, it was a constituent setting of Roman public life, being large enough to be used, on at least one occasion (Dio 56.27.4), even for games normally held in the Circus, such as horse races and beast hunts.

Peace and war, as we have observed on several occasions, were intrinsically linked in Augustan thinking: *parta victoriis pax* (*RG* 13). Both also needed to have a moral foundation. The two aspects were brought together in the forum in what we might call the Hall of Fame of distinguished Roman ancestors and statesmen, beginning with Aeneas and Romulus. The criteria for selection were their contributions to "making the Roman *imperium* the greatest from the smallest beginnings," and their civic and moral qualities. As we saw earlier, the same nexus of ideas[125] informed the moral legislation and is reflected on the reliefs of the Ara Pacis. The culminating example, fittingly placed in the center of his forum, was the statue of the victorious Augustus in his quadriga. It paralleled the painting with the triumphant Alexander and was accompanied by an inscription of both Augustus' military conquests and his new title, bestowed on him by the senate in the year of the forum's dedication, of *pater patriae*. This culminating appellation (*RG* 35.1), given to him a quarter century after he had received the name Augustus, was inclusive of all his civic virtues and of his transcendent status; the latter, too, was reflected by the forum.

It is instructive to survey how these themes and others interacted to shape the architectural and sculptural components of the forum. The forum was, as Augustan culture in general, an innovative synthesis of Greek and Roman elements. Strict axiality and striving for symmetry were traditional characteristics of Roman architecture, but late Hellenistic temple squares that were organized along similar lines furnish an even more complete precedent for the forum's layout.[126] The same combination is reflected by the architecture of the Mars Ultor temple. It was a massive Italic podium temple, but the lower pitch of the pediment, for instance, is closer to that of Greek temples, and the bases of the outer columns are modeled on those of the Propylaea, the entrance gate to the Acropolis in Athens. The same pervasive synthesis applies to architectural details. The Corinthian capitals (Fig. 112), for example, recall late classical and fourth-century models, but achieve an even more balanced relation between tectonic and ornamental elements.[127] The vegetal ornamentation is both abundant and ordered, though not on the basis of strict symmetry. The result is an organic whole. Acanthus leaves were indigenous to the Corinthian capital (Vitruvius tells a charming story about its genesis [4.9–10]), but assume a further dimension here in view of their use on dynastic monuments such as the Ara Pacis and the Temple of Divus Julius (cf. Figs. 65 and 71). Nor, as could be expected, was experimentation absent from the overall design of the forum or its small details. A typical example of the latter is the shaping of the corners of the Corinthian capitals inside the temple in the form of Pegasus heads (Fig. 113). Their wings go on to end in floral scrolls. This distinctive element of the "fantasy style" of contemporary wall paintings here is used as an organic transition to the traditional vegetal elements of the capital.

As is clear from these examples and others, the forum was not a static, classicistic structure. Rather, its aim was to be a comprehensive and creative citation of Greek architectural and artistic styles from all periods—archaic, high classical, late classical, and Hellenistic—in combination with Roman, Etruscan, and Italic traditions. It was meant to illustrate the entire sweep of the *imperium Augustum*, the more perfect heir to Alexander's *oikumenē*. The most stunning means of visual communication used to that end was the

112. Corinthian capital from the Temple of Mars Ultor.

113. Column capital from the Temple of Mars Ultor.

114. Forum Augustum, upper portico: caryatids framing
a shield with the head of Jupiter Ammon.

multicolored variety of marbles for pavements, columns, and statues and for
the interiors and exteriors of the various buildings.[128]

The visual impact on the observers must have been extraordinary. The
forum was not a traditional forum or agora that could be entered from anywhere. A huge precinct wall cordoned it off at the back of the temple from
one of Rome's most densely populated quarters, the Subura. Users were
channeled into the forum through a limited number of carefully chosen entrance points, especially the main entrance in the southwest. They would
find themselves looking immediately at the dominating facade of the Mars
Ultor temple, gleaming with white Carrara marble. The open plaza of the
forum, with Augustus' quadriga in the center, also was paved with white
marble to contrast all the more effectively with the yellow and reddish colonnades on the right and left that were made of *giallo antico*, marble quarried
in Numidia. The second story of the colonnades, with its architectural decoration of caryatids and shields (Fig. 114), again was kept in white marble. The
marbles used for the pavement of the temple itself were, besides *giallo*, *africano*
(reddish purple from Ionia) and *pavonazzetto* (purplish white from Phrygia)
in a variety of patterns (Pl. 3b). The columns of the interior shrine were also
made of *pavonazzetto*, thus continuing vertically the predominant material of
the pavement of the anteroom. The pavements of the other buildings were

equally as colorful and differentiated from one another by their composition. The marble floors of the porticoes were laid out in large cross-hatched designs of bluish gray *bardiglio* (from Carrara), enclosing a square center of *africano* with a rectangular border of *giallo* (Pl. 3b). Where the porticoes curved out into two semicircular exedrae (see Fig. 111), the pavement changed to a checkerboard pattern of *africano* and *giallo* (Pl. 3b). At the rear of the north exedra was the almost square "Room of the Colossus," housing a monumental statue possibly of Alexander and, after Augustus' death, of Augustus himself. Its checkerboard pavement was made of *pavonazzetto* and *giallo* (Pl. 3b), materials that were also used for its pilasters and columns. Some other building elements in the forum were made of *cipollino*, a marble with a greenish hue from Euboea in Greece.

In so many words: the visitor to the forum walked on and was surrounded by a colorful array of materials from all parts of the Roman empire. Native stone figured predominantly, too: the imposing precinct wall was made of tufa from nearby Gabii, with harder materials, such as peperino and travertine, being used at points of stress. Italy literally enclosed and held together its own empire; the names of the Roman provinces, too, were prominently displayed in the forum (Vell. 2.39.2). The ensemble was lavish and so were the games on the occasion of its dedication, including a mock sea-battle recreating the battle of Salamis (Dio 55.10.7). We observed earlier that it would be quite wrong to equate Augustus' reign, despite all its emphasis on values, with the end of luxury. There was plenty of latitude, however, between austerity and extravagance. In the Forum Augustum, this is exemplified by the use of marble sheathing, not solid marble blocks, for buildings such as the temple. Rational planning and utilization of progressive technology were eminently compatible with expressing the majesty of empire.[129]

So were the "citations" from the considered acme of Greek culture, fifth-century Athens. Some basic similarities could be easily accommodated. Both the Athenian and the Augustan high points had come after a threat from the east was decisively turned back. Actium thus could be viewed as another Salamis. The sumptuous staging of the sea battle in 2 B.C. was a public suggestion of this equation and there are references to it in Augustan private art.[130] The Augustan forum was the equivalent of the Acropolis to express, through architecture and its decoration, the grandeur and the meaning of empire. The most palpable allusion to the Acropolis was the long row of caryatids in the upper stories of the porticoes (Fig. 114). They were virtual replicas of those of the Erechtheum, except that they were not freestanding. The Erechtheum had been associated with a number of ancestral cults, and the tomb of Cecrops, Athens' legendary first king, was at one of its corners. Similarly, the caryatids of the Augustan forum accompanied, in the upper story, the statues of the Roman ancestors, beginning with Rome's mythical first king, who were displayed at the ground level of the colonnades and the exedrae. Augustus could unproblematically invoke the Periclean tradition; as Thucydides had well observed, Athens under Pericles was a democracy in name, but in reality was ruled by one man (2.65.9). More was involved, however, than mere power politics. In his funeral oration on the Athenians who died in the war against Sparta, Pericles stressed the spiritual and moral values of Athenian culture (Thuc. 2.34ff.). As we have seen time and again, this emphasis also was an integral aspect of Augustan culture and found its principal expression in the forum in the gallery of exemplary Roman leaders and statesmen.

They were, as Augustus himself put it, to be viewed by the citizens as exemplars both for himself and for the *principes* of future generations (Suet., *Aug.* 31.5). Hence they were chosen in order to personify both civic and military virtues. This complementary duality originated with the representation of the two founders, Aeneas and Romulus, whose statue groups occupied the center niches of the two exedrae. Their juxtaposition has been well preserved from the paintings on the outside of a shop on one of the main streets of Pompeii (Figs. 115, 116).[131] Aeneas, ever the incarnation of *pietas* especially since Vergil's *Aeneid*, here was shaped into the abiding icon that was widely copied for the fora of many Italian and provincial towns and for private artifacts ranging from lamps to tombstones. Modernized as he is—he wears the boots of a Roman patrician—he leads his son Julus, distinguished by his Phrygian cap, by the hand while carrying his lame father Anchises, who is holding the box with the Penates, the household gods, "until he could found a city and bring his gods to Latium" (Vergil, *Aen.* 1.5–6). He is also the traditional and Vergilian man of arms and wears a Roman cuirass, but the emphasis is on his exemplary virtue of social responsibility. This is all the clearer from the deliberate contrast with Romulus. Romulus, also cuirassed, carries the *spolia opima*, the trophy taken from the slain leader of early Rome's enemies, and a spear. We can see the corresponding schema of the two representations: where Romulus bears the military trophy, Aeneas carries his father who, compared with the other human figures, appears somewhat diminutive because he is adapted to the dimensions of the trophy, while the line of Romulus' spear finds its pendant in that of the arms and hands of Aeneas and Julus. Both *virtus* and *pietas* had been written on Augustus' golden shield. The inscription with his name, therefore, on the front of the Mars Ultor temple was directly in the middle of the axis between the statues of the two ancestors. The same constellation appeared once more in the form of the three sculptural ornaments on the roof above the temple pediment, as we know from coins (Fig. 117) and other sources: Romulus on the left, the Trojan group on the right, and Augustus in his quadriga in the center. Here, as in their representations in the exedrae, Romulus and the Trojans—and this is yet another element of correspondence between their representations—are shown as moving toward Augustus. He was their

115. Aeneas, Anchises, and Ascanius/Julus.
Pompeian mural, first century A.D.

116. Romulus with *spolia opima*. Pompeian
mural, first century A.D.

117. Sestertius of Antoninus Pius.
Reverse: Temple of Mars Ultor with sculptural decoration.

worthy descendant who brought to fruition what they had begun. At the same time, living up to such exemplars was an ongoing effort and obligation.

It is not surprising, therefore, that even after the completion of the forum, statues of worthy statesmen were added by both Augustus and later emperors.[132] Besides Aeneas and Romulus, we have evidence for twenty-seven of the original honorees. This amounts to perhaps one-quarter of the total number and gives us a good idea about the variety of these honored men and the reasons they were chosen. They comprised plebeians and patricians, friends and foes. Pompey was included, which is not surprising in view of the allusion to him in the first sentence of the *Res Gestae*. Some men were chosen on the basis of the military accomplishments while others were extolled for their virtues in civilian life, including the holding of priesthoods. Their representation seems to have followed these respective merits as the extant marble fragments come from statues in both military dress and togas, corresponding to Augustus' own representation and to a line he is known to have quoted from the *Aeneid*: "The Romans, the lords of the world, the togaed people" (*Romanos, rerum dominos gentemque togatam*; 1.282).[133] Nor is it accidental that the majority of the known republican honorees "had held positions of extraordinary and exceptional powers during their careers, positions that could be cited by Augustus as precedents when he claimed to have held only magistracies consonant with Republican custom (*RG* 6.1)."[134] The style of the surviving heads, few as they are, suggests the usual Augustan variety of inspirations from Hellenistic art, Roman realism, and idealizing classicism.

The *titulus* of the person, consisting of his names and offices held, was inscribed on the statue base. The larger and more descriptive *elogium* was written on a larger plaque underneath (Fig. 118).[135] These *elogia* are, as we might expect, original creations, written for this specific purpose, rather than updated copies of earlier honorific inscriptions or adaptations of the accounts of their lives and deeds in Livy, for instance. Pliny's notice (*HN* 32.13) that Augustus wrote them is exaggerated, but it is more than probable that he had some say about their composition just as he was involved in the selection of these exemplars. As usual, it is not that the inspiration came only from him. The relation of this architectural and sculptural "Hall of Fame" to Augustan poetry, especially the catalogs of distinguished Romans in books 6 and 8 of the *Aeneid*, has often been pointed out[136] and is another example of the prevailing reciprocity of ideas and impulses. Vergil is likely to have been one of the inspirations behind the Augustan idea for an equivalent in his forum; since we are dealing with independent and original minds, and with different media, there are differences as well as commonalities. As the instructions for his funeral cortege show, Augustus had made the idea thoroughly his own by the end of his life (Dio 56.34.2–3). As in his forum, his image was shown riding on a triumphal chariot. "Behind these," Dio continues, "came the

118. Forum Augustum, honorific statue.
Reconstruction by A. Degrassi.

images of his ancestors and of his deceased relatives (except that of Caesar, because he had been deified) and those of other Romans who had been prominent in any way, beginning with Romulus himself. An image of Pompey the Great was also seen, and all the nations that Augustus had acquired appeared in the procession, each represented by a likeness that bore some local characteristic."

In the forum itself, the complementary martial and civic virtues of the Roman exemplars and ancestors were enhanced by the contrapuntal sculptural decoration in the story above them. There caryatids framed squares in the centers of which were shields with the heads of Jupiter Ammon (Fig. 114) and other male heads. The caryatids, as we have seen, signify the devotion to ancestral customs and cults. The shields comprise several references. They recall the Roman tradition of ancestral heads on shields (*imagines clipeatae*). This tradition also played a role in presentation of the *clupeus virtutis* to Augustus; the virtues inscribed on it also were commemorated by the virtuous exemplars in the lower level of the porticoes. While the unidentified male heads probably allude to various conquered lands, the heads of Ammon serve as another association with Alexander and also point to Augustus' transcendent state: it was at the shrine of Jupiter Ammon that Alexander was told of his divinity. For good reason, therefore, the head of the colossal statue of Alexander in the forum was replaced with that of the deified Augustus at the time of Claudius.[137] In addition to that colossus and the paintings by Apelles, two statues from Alexander's tent in Alexandria had also been placed in the forum (Pliny, *HN* 34.48). According to Dio (60.5.3), the day of the dedication of the Forum Augustum was August 1.[138] That was the anniversary of Augustus' conquest of Alexandria, fittingly beginning the month that was named after him in 8 B.C. Here, then, was the new Alexander, but an Alexander who, as Augustus himself defined the difference between himself and his model (Plut., *Mor.* 207D), was good not only at conquering lands but also at holding them stably together.

Just as deliberately, the association with Julius Caesar was pursued in both the architecture and the sculptural decoration of the forum. The Forum Augustum was closely linked with the Forum of Caesar (Fig. 119), which Augustus finished building before serious work began on his own. The deities of the two forum temples complemented one another: Venus Genetrix was the ancestress of the Romans and Julians whose illustrious scions populated the "Hall of Fame," while Mars was the Roman ancestor. The temple in Caesar's forum was the first Roman temple with an apse, an innovation that was used for the Temple of Mars Ultor also. For good reason: in that apse stood the cult images of Mars, Venus, and the Divine Julius as we know from a derivative statue group in Algiers (Fig. 120). Caesar wears his typical *Hüftmantel*, emblematic of his deification. So does the Mars figure in the center of the pediment (Fig. 47) and Augustus was to follow; we have already observed that he wears the same kind of cloak on the Prima Porta statue, even if in combination with the cuirass (Fig. 5).[139] The Mars statue in the temple was cuirassed also, but its distinctive mark, which strengthened the connection of the entire group with Augustus once more, was the representation of the crown of oak leaves, the *corona civica*, on his shield. Since 27 B.C., when it was presented to him along with the *clupeus virtutis* and when he affixed it to the doors of his house (*RG* 34.2), it had been the emblem of Augustus, the savior of the people (Fig. 17).

We are looking at another example, then, of a network of associations that relate in various ways to Augustus himself. Julius Caesar once more appears as a model for the deification of Augustus, who began his career as *divi filius* and took Caesar's name. The remaining pedimental figures (Fig. 47) comprise various icons with similarly wide resonances. To the right and left of Mars are Fortuna, holding a cornucopia and a rudder and Venus with a Cupid and a scepter. They are followed, respectively, by the seated figures of Roma (on a pile of arms, as on the Ara Pacis) and Romulus, in the short

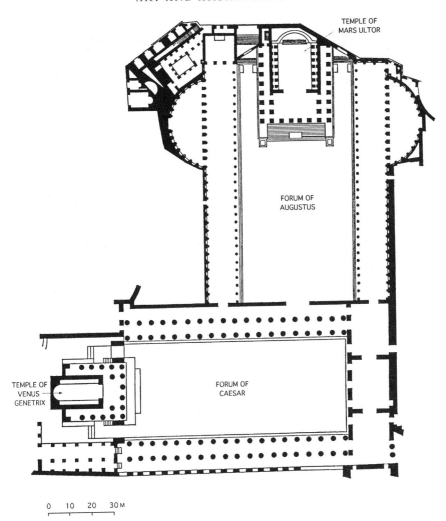

119. Fora of Caesar and Augustus. Reconstruction of ground plan by G. Gatti.

garment of a shepherd. He is holding the staff, or *lituus*, of an augur and taking the auguries that led to the foundation of Rome. Since Ennius (fr. 155 Skutsch), that *augurium* had been hailed as *augurium augustum*, providing for an easy connection between the first and the second founder of Rome. The customarily reclining figures in the corners of the pediments are representations of the Palatine (where Romulus performed his *augurium* and where Augustus had his house) and the Tiber. Mars, Romulus, Roma, and Venus also were represented on the Ara Pacis, where the multivalent Venus image subsumed the aspect of bounteousness that is expressed here by Fortuna.

120. Statue group of Mars, Venus, and the Deified Caesar,
first century A.D. From Algiers.

Given this sophisticated richness of allusions, it is not surprising that many connections have been noted between the design of the forum and the poetry especially of Horace and Vergil. Michael Putnam has given an excellent demonstration of such a nexus between Horace's concluding ode, 4.15, and many major aspects of the Forum Augustum; other Horatian passages from book 4 can be adduced also.[140] Similar relationships, as we have noted, have been discerned between the catalogs of Roman exemplars in the *Aeneid* and in the forum. The connections can be extended: at the beginning, the center, and the end of the *Aeneid* we find significant themes that recur in the program of the forum. The extended proem, which is a brilliant anticipation of the major themes of the epic, concludes (1.263–96) with Jupiter's prophecy of the arrival of Aeneas and Iulus in Latium; Mars' fatherhood of Romulus; the *imperium* without end of the Romans, "the togaed people"; the coming of both Julius Caesar and Augustus who are deliberately identified with one another; the return of the old values under Augustus' reign; and the depiction, which according to Servius (*ad Aen.* 1.294), was traditionally linked to Apelles' painting in the Forum Augustum, of the war fury with his hands tied behind his back. At the end of book 6, at the *Aeneid's* center, is the review of future Roman leaders by Anchises (6.756–846). It begins, as on the forum, with the offspring of Aeneas and the Alban kings (they were in the left exedra, flanking their ancestor Aeneas), and with Romulus in his martial attire (in the right exedra) whose augury was the starting point for the Roman *imperium* (6.777–82). From there we proceed immediately to the mention of Augustus, the world conqueror (6.795) and bringer of *pax*, followed by a throng of Roman exemplars who, as on the forum, include friends and foes, such as Caesar and Pompey. The intent is the same as on the forum: all these are part of Roman history and any discord now is overcome. This leads, fittingly, into the famous definition of the Roman national character that concludes:

> tu regere imperio populos, Romane, memento
> (hae tibi erunt artes), pacique imponere morem,
> parcere subiectis et debellare superbos.
>
> (6.851–53)

[Remember, Roman, to rule the earth's people with your *imperium*. Your arts are to be these: to mark peace with civilized custom, to spare the conquered, and war down the proud.]

This is a fitting motto for the Augustan forum, too. Vergil follows this up with an extended, sorrowful description of Augustus' nephew Marcellus and his premature death (6.860–86). Marcellus, too, was honored with a statue in the forum.

The *Aeneid* ends with Aeneas' killing of Turnus, a justified act of vengeance that has both a personal and a public dimension. As for the latter, it suffices to quote Servius again, who clearly saw (*ad Aen.* 12.949) that it was *ultio foederis rupti*—revenge for the breaking of the treaty, a violation of divine and human law for which there was no clemency in Rome. This public aspect is complemented by Aeneas' private obligation (an act of *pietas*, as Servius noted) to avenge the death of Evander's son Pallas who had been entrusted to him. "Pallas," Aeneas cries out, "Pallas sacrifices you with this wound and exacts due punishment from the criminal blood of his murderer!" (*Pallas te hoc vulnere, Pallas / immolat et poenam scelerato ex sanguine sumit!* 12.948–49). Similarly, the Temple of Mars Ultor was a monument to both Augustus' private and public revenge, respectively, on the murderers of his adoptive father and on the Parthians. As for the avenging of Julius Caesar, it is no accident that Ovid, Vergil's most astute reader ever, writes in his account of Octavian's vow to build the Temple of Mars Ultor that he did so with "pious arms" (*pia . . . arma*; *Fasti* 5.569), "with soldiers of a just cause" (*milite iusto*; 5.571), and called on Mars to help him satiate his sword "with the criminal blood" of Caesar's assassins (*scelerato sanguine*; 5.575)—precisely the same phrase as in the *Aeneid*. That Ovid had the *Aeneid* in mind is further suggested by his characterization, immediately preceding the passages we have quoted, of the temple as Augustus' "grander work" (*maius opus*; 5.568).

It is the famous phrase that Vergil had used to characterize the second half of the *Aeneid* (7.45).[141]

These parallels are another good illustration of the dynamic of mutual inspirations and participatory processes that shaped Augustan culture so profoundly. We cannot simply say that Augustus got the principal ideas for his forum from Vergil. Rather, we can assume that these were ideas and themes that, like so many others, were discussed over time by many thoughtful and creative individuals who went on to give them their own expression. As W. Eder has observed, "his striving to have as many citizens as possible participate in the life of the state represents a common characteristic of Augustus' religious policy, his building program, and his support of the arts. None of these areas can be neatly separated from the others."[142] Certainly, Augustus was keenly interested in the *Aeneid* and in Vergil's formulation of some of the guiding ideas of the age. While the forum goes beyond being a mere reflection of the *Aeneid* in stone and marble, one of its undeniable dimensions, illustrating one side of the relations between poets and holders of political power at the time, is that in many ways it is a monument to Vergil as well as Augustus.

Two final characteristics relate to the forum being an exemplar of the Augustan spirit. One is that the forum at large took its cue from the Italic podium temple, which, in contrast to Greek temples, was not open on all sides and instead, and because of its elevated position, immediately exerted its authority in defining its relationship, both spatial and spiritual, with any human observers and participants. Unlike the old Roman Forum or the Athenian Agora, the Forum of Augustus was not, as we have seen, open on all sides. This Augustan *auctoritas*, however, had another aspect, as always: the width of the porticoes is considerably larger than that of any Greek counterparts, allowing for more latitude and open circulation. A second and related characteristic is the remarkable convergence between overall meanings of the forum and small architectural details. Donald Strong's and John Ward Perkins' summary is quite apropos:

> It is true that from one point of view Augustan architecture in general, and architectural ornament in particular, may seem to be remarkably conservative harking back as it so often did to earlier classical models. But such a view is apt to disregard another hardly less important aspect, namely its very great variety and the extraordinary amount of detailed experiment that took place within the broad framework of conventional classical practice. Some of the new ideas never really caught on; others, such as the composite capital, had to wait half a century or more before passing into general use. But the seeds of so much of the later development are to be found already present in the architecture of the Augustan age that it may without exaggeration be claimed as the great-

est moment of original experiment in the field of Roman architectural ornament.[143]

Or, to cite the conclusion by another scholar of his study of the Temple of Mars Ultor: "What is typical of the Augustan age seems to be that it was not the end of a fixed line of development, but that it comprises several of these and produces appropriate new formulations."[144]

THE TEMPLE OF APOLLO ON THE PALATINE

In a conventional historical survey, chronology would dictate that our discussion of the Temple of Apollo, dedicated in 28 B.C., precede that of the Forum of Augustus. By turning to it as the final example in this chapter, however, we can see it in its own right as an incipient paradigm rather than as a teleologically complete example of "the Augustan program," which is all too easily supposed to have been marvelously finished, exactly defined, and almost preordained even at that early time. In its magnificence, which ancient writers duly emphasized,[145] the Palatine complex was a worthy companion to the Augustan forum. Furthermore, it exhibits many of the same Augustan aspects, such as complexity, evolution, and the mingling of dynastic and public objectives. The Apolline area on the Palatine did not turn into a static museum after its dedication, but was given several additional functions over time. It is doubtful that these were preplanned at the time of its construction. The Palatine complex, therefore, exemplifies the spirit not of the pinnacle of Augustus' reign, as his forum does, but of its beginning: it provided, as do his definitions in the *Res Gestae*, an elastic framework that could accommodate various modifications and additions. We are looking, again, at the deliberate evocation of many associations within a clear overall meaning, though the Palatine complex does not exhibit the same conceptual unity, completeness of thought, and fullness of details that characterize the Forum Augustum.

The very genesis of the Temple of Apollo illustrates these perspectives. Octavian vowed the temple after defeating his most stubborn opponent in the western Mediterranean, Sextus Pompey, in the sea battle of Naulochus in September of 36 B.C. (Vell. 2.81.3). The victory was as welcome as it was significant. It had come only after considerable reverses for Octavian and marked the beginning of his ascendancy in the triumvirate.[146] The occasion called for a prominent architectural association with Victory, and the Palatine Hill was a good choice for that reason alone.

The Palatine was Rome's most venerable hill. It was here that the Arcadian exile Evander had founded the first settlement at the site of Rome, naming it Pallanteum after his son Pallas. The Lupercal, the grotto in which the legendary wolf-nurse had nourished Romulus and Remus, was at the

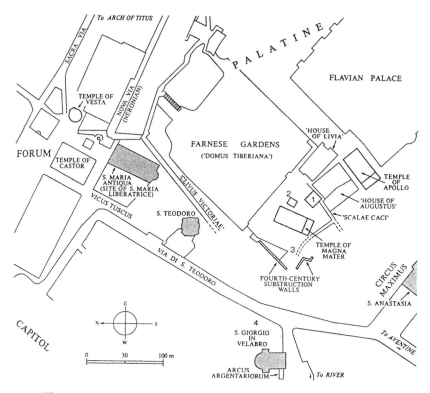

121. The northwestern Palatine. (1) Temple of Victory. (2) Shrine of Victoria Virgo.
(3) Upper course of *Clivus Victoriae*. (4) Approximate location of the Porta Roman(ul)a
at the bottom of the *Clivus Victoriae* (close to the Lupercal).

bottom of its western slope, and the hut of Romulus, which was preserved
and renovated throughout Rome's history, was at its top. So was the precinct
of Victory.[147] Tradition attributed its origin to the time of Evander, and
Dionysius further relates that sacrifices were brought to her throughout
the year, including at his own time (*AR* 1.32.5; cf. Livy 29.14.13). A temple
was dedicated to the goddess in 294 B.C. (Livy 10.33.9), complemented in
193 B.C. by Cato the Elder's dedication of a small shrine to Victoria Virgo
(Livy 35.9.6). Both were standing in Octavian's time in the precinct of Victory to which the *Clivus Victoriae* ascended from the Lupercal (Fig. 121). The
day of the dedication of the Apollo temple, October 9, coincided not with
the dates of Naulochus or Actium, but with the anniversary of a religious
triad associated with victory, including Venus Victrix on the Capitoline. The
anniversary of the goddess of Victory on the Palatine, however, as one of
the official calendars informs us,[148] was celebrated in Augustan times on August 1, the date of his conquest of Alexandria, "because on that day Impera-

tor Caesar freed the republic from the most grievous danger." By select-
ing this particular site for his temple, therefore, Octavian associated himself
both with Victory—a general theme he pursued at the time[149]—and with
some of the most hallowed traditions of the founding of Rome. We can add
to the latter the so-called Roma Quadrata, Romulus' original settlement,
which thus came to be located "in front of the Temple of Apollo" (Festus,
p. 310 L.). And, as Dio (53.16.5) observes in connection with the emperor's
house, named "palace" after the Palatine, it "gained a certain degree of fame
from the mount as a whole also, because Romulus had once lived there."

A practical advantage enhanced these conceptual considerations. The
Palatine Hill was largely residential and properties could still be acquired,
quite in contrast to the official citadel of the Capitoline and the third histori-
cal site par excellence, the Roman Forum, on which most buildings, how-
ever deteriorated, dated from republican times. On the Palatine, therefore,
Octavian was able systematically to buy out well-to-do residents, such as
Hortensius, and ultimately create a compound consisting of the "House of
Livia" (a misnomer), his own house, and the closely connected Temple of
Apollo with its porticoes and library. The acquisitions were financed by his
own resources as a *privatus*, but no temple could be built on private land.
When a timely thunderbolt, therefore, struck the site soon after the vow in
36 B.C., the future precinct of Apollo was declared public land.[150] The close
connection between Augustus' house and the temple by means of a ramp is
a manifestation in architecture of the confluence between private and public
aspects typical of both Augustus' style of government and Augustan culture.

Why was Apollo chosen as the dedicatory deity? As so often in the Augustan milieu, the likely reason was the latitude of possible associations and the
concomitant opportunity for further development. By comparison with
other Olympians, the cult of Apollo had held a respectable, though by no
means major place in Roman religion.[151] He had only one temple in Rome,
which was restored by the former Antonian admiral Gaius Sosius in the
20s B.C. This temple was not even inside Rome's sacred boundary, the *pomerium*. There had been some connection between Apollo and the Julian
family and Octavian, but it was neither limiting nor fully developed.
Cn. Caesar, consul of 431 B.C., had dedicated the earlier Apollo temple.
Although Caesar's birthday, July 13, coincided with the last day of the *ludi
Apollinares*, an important theatrical festival in Rome since 212 B.C., his emphasis on Apollo was next to minimal. As for Octavian, he learned of Caesar's death while he was in Apollonia in Illyria, and he came dressed as Apollo
to a dinner party where other members of the *jeunesse dorée* also masqueraded
as Olympian gods. This earned him a great deal of bad publicity (Suet., *Aug.*
70.1) as ordinary Roman citizens suffered from a famine at the time. The
legend, inspired by those of Alexander's birth, that he was the son of his
mother Atia and Apollo may or may not have been current in the 30s B.C.

Another element, which we have observed earlier in other contexts, is the Augustan appropriation of the slogans of his adversaries: Brutus and Cassius, as evidenced by their coins and their watchword at Philippi, had associated themselves with Apollo, and Octavian deftly proceeded to claim that association for himself just as he did with Neptune after defeating Sextus Pompey.[152] Apollo, who had an existing temple on the Actian promontory, also became the god who helped Octavian win at Actium, though the city built in Greece in commemoration of that event was Nicopolis, Victory City.[153] In sum, we might say that Octavian chose Apollo, just as Vergil chose Aeneas, because Apollo was relatively unencumbered by the constraints of a previous tradition, which left him with much creative latitude for shaping the image of Apollo in Rome and, especially, his association with the god. It was a meaningful association: the starting point for Roman triumphal processions was the earlier Temple of Apollo and the *ludi Apollinares* were instituted, as Livy says explicitly (25.12.15), to secure powers not of health, but of victory.

In the first place, then, Apollo was received by Victory on the Palatine. The event may be be alluded to in one of the Villa Albani reliefs (Fig. 122): Apollo and Diana, and their mother Latona, approach a typically winged Victoria from the left, which also happens to be the direction of the *Clivus Victoriae*.[154] The timelessness conveyed by the archaizing style is combined with contemporary actuality: Diana was also associated with the victory at Naulochus (Appian, *BC* 5.484). Behind a precinct wall appears the Temple of Victory, distinguished by its pedimental decoration with a Gorgoneion on a shield, flanked by two Tritons. All are figures associated with Victory. The divine triad and their symbols are the same on a late Augustan statue base from Sorrento (Fig. 123): Apollo on the left, Diana in the center, and Latona on the right. At Latona's feet is a Sibyl who is leaning on an urn filled with oracles. For good reasons, this representation can be considered as reproducing the cult statues in the Palatine temple. They were, as Pliny (*HN* 36.24–25, 32) points out, Greek originals: the Apollo was made by Scopas (fourth century); the statue of Artemis/Diana by Timotheos (fourth century); and the Latona by Cephisodotus (third century). The reuse of Greek statuary, which was to become a common phenomenon in Augustan Rome, added another dimension of dignity and tradition to the temple. As usual, this was accompanied by innovation: in 12 B.C., upon becoming *pontifex maximus* after Lepidus' death, Augustus transferred the Sibylline Books from the Temple of Jupiter on the Capitoline and deposited them in two gilded bookcases in the base of the cult statue of Apollo (Suet., *Aug.* 31.1). The Sibyl on the Sorrento base alludes to that event.

A few months after the dedication of the temple, the senate, in the famous session that laid the groundwork for his future rule, named Octavian Augustus and voted him, besides the honor of the golden shield, the distinction of

122. Apollo received by Victoria on the Palatine. Augustan marble relief.

123. Diana, Apollo, and Latona. Augustan statue base.

having the two doorposts of his house on the Palatine adorned with laurel trees while the civic crown of oak leaves was permanently affixed over its door (RG 34.2). Both these emblems were originally associated with victory and war. The oaken wreath, as we have seen, came to signify more generally his salvation of the citizenry (Fig. 17), and the symbolism of the laurel, Apollo's sacred tree, was marked by a similar extension.[155] The laurel crown stood for victory and, in Rome, was worn specifically by the triumphator; the members of Augustus' family would later garner their triumphal laurels from the trees at Livia's Villa at Prima Porta. The triumphator was above ordinary mortals—hence, the permanence of this emblem for Augustus expressed the sacral overtones of his very name. Moreover, Apollo was also the patron god of those victorious in nonmilitary pursuits and their pacific activities: "Victorious Apollo," as Propertius puts it (4.6.69–70), "now asks for the lyre and lays down his arms for peaceful choruses" (*citharam iam poscit Apollo / victor et ad placidos exuit arma choros*; cf. Ovid, *Trist.* 3.1.39–44). Propertius' description was inspired by the two statues of Apollo on the Palatine: the cult image in the cella of the temple and his colossal statue in the precinct in front of it (cf. Prop. 2.31.5–6 and 15–16). Both times, Apollo was shown as a lyre player. As such he also appears on an evocative fragment from a fresco that belonged to Augustus' house on the Palatine (Pl. 5b). Important as Actium was, the overall evidence clearly suggests that Augustus was anxious to get beyond the memories of the civil wars and to move forward with the construction of the ensuing peace and its activities, a factor that also explains the tremendous popularity of the motif of the two laurels in Augustan private art and on the coinage.

The immediate architectural manifestation of the blessings of Apolline peace was the Palatine Library of Greek and Roman writers.[156] It housed their works and even the images of some of the poets. In his later years Augustus used it for convening the senate and for holding the meeting where he brought the lists of senatorial and equestrian jurors up to date; the library is also mentioned as a repository for writings on civil law. Prominently displayed in the library was a statue of Augustus as Apollo with all his insignia. And in the festival that marked the attainments and aspirations of the Augustan peace, that is, the Secular Games of 17 B.C., the Palatine assumed a prominence equal to the traditional one of the Capitoline. The precinct of Apollo was one of the sites where fruits and incense for expiation were distributed to the populace before the ritual. On the third day of the games, Augustus and Agrippa sacrificed to Apollo and Diana in the Apolline sanctuary, and Horace's *Carmen Saeculare* was performed there before it was repeated on the Capitoline.

The Corinthian Temple of Apollo was built of white Luni (Carrara) marble and on a high podium: *claro surgebat marmore templum* (Prop. 2.31.9). Propertius also informs us about some details of its decoration. Its roof was crowned by the four-horse chariot of the sun-god, who was identified with Apollo since Hellenistic times. We are again looking at multiple suggestions: the sun's rule of the universe, again from the Hellenistic period onward, was a potent symbol of dynasts and their aspirations. But Sol was also the ancestor of the Latins (cf. Vergil, *Aen.* 12.164), and Horace's invocation in the *Secular Hymn* of "nourishing [*alme*] Sol" includes that notion, while his ensuing description of Sol in his chariot looking out over the city of Rome ("may you be able to behold nothing grander than the city of Rome") is a topical allusion to the Palatine, where the hymn was sung (*CS* 9–12). An additional element is the personal connection between Augustus and Apollo, which recurs on an arch that was a part of the Palatine complex.[157] The arch, according to Pliny (*HN* 36.36), was built by Augustus in honor of his father Gaius Octavius. By the end of the republic, such arches were adorned with images of the honoree or the dedicator, but the Augustan arch on the Palatine was conspicuous because an already existing quadriga, by the Greek sculptor Lysias (second century), of Apollo and Diana was placed on its top. The combination of traditions is exquisite: while honoring his father and, at the same time, underscoring his association with these deities and the temple, Augustus also returned to the earlier republican practice where arches, often associated with victory and triumph, were crowned by statues of divinities— "I brought back into use many exemplary practices of our ancestors that were disappearing in our time" (*RG* 8.5). As in Augustan culture in general, previous traditions served as a vehicle for innovation.

The doors of the Apollo temple were made of ivory. The carvings on them depicted a historical and a mythological scene (Prop. 2.31.12–14). The former was the failed attack of the Gauls on Delphi in 278 B.C., who were turned away by a miraculous snowfall and a thunderbolt that killed their leader; both occurrences were ascribed to Apollo. The myth was Apollo's (and Diana's) punishment of Niobe (repeated in a statuary group in Sosius' Apollo temple; Pliny, *HN* 36.28) who had bragged that she was superior to their mother Latona because she had borne more children. Apollo thus appeared as savior and avenger, two characteristics that resonated in the Augustan context far beyond a mere reference to the battle of Actium. Delphi was the symbol of civilization, saved by Apollo. Similarly, Augustus became the general "savior of the citizens." The arrogant example of Niobe contrasted with the Augustan tenet, articulated by Horace (*C.* 3.6.5), that "by holding yourself lesser than the gods, you rule, Roman."

In addition to the Greek and Roman library or libraries, the temple precinct comprised porticoes; it has not been possible to establish the exact configuration of either on the basis of the available archaeological evidence. But we might note even at this point that the ensemble was a striking blend of Roman and Hellenistic traditions. In the midst of some of Rome's most hallowed ground arose a complex whose components are familiar to us from

Hellenistic royal citadels such as Pergamum.[158] The votive gifts in the Apollo temple included an elaborate lampholder given to the same god by Alexander the Great from war booty (Pliny, *HN* 34.14), thus underscoring Augustus' continuing association with Alexander. Augustus' house, however, was not a royal palace. Suetonius, who wrote at a time when Augustus' successors had constructed far more ostentatious residences on the Palatine, pointedly remarks on the relative modesty of Augustus' abode: the columns of its court were made of peperino, and marble and richly decorated floors were lacking from its private quarters (*Aug.* 72.1–2). The emperor practiced what he preached. It was not by its luxury, but by its connection with the temple and precinct of Apollo (in addition to the permanent laurel and oak insignia) that the house of Augustus was marked as more than the residence of a mere mortal. The same message was conveyed by its proximity to the hut of Romulus; for that reason alone, an extravagant edifice would have been unseemly. All these dimensions were further enhanced when part of his residence was converted to public use as a shrine of Vesta upon his becoming *pontifex maximus* in 12 B.C. (Dio 54.27.3) and when many people from various walks of life contributed to a fund to have his house rebuilt after a fire in A.D. 2; unlike modern rulers, Augustus accepted only a token contribution.

The most imposing part of the pictorial program was the portico of the Danaids that was completed in 25 B.C. It must have been highly effective visually: its red and yellow marble from Africa contrasted strikingly with the white marble of the temple, and the statues of Danaus and his daughters were set between the columns (Prop. 2.31.3–4; Ovid, *Trist.* 3.1.61). In its form alone, the choice was another typical mixture of tradition and innovation. The alternative of a Roman historical frieze was eschewed. Instead, in the Greek tradition of programmatic monuments,[159] a mythological subject was chosen because it added a timeless aspect to the intended topical reference. At the same time, the particular representation of the daughters of Danaus in the act of fighting off and killing their Egyptian suitors had hardly any Greek precedent; the far more common subject in art was their doing penance in the underworld by carrying leaky water jars.

The reference to Egypt could not be missed. Danaus and Aegyptus, both eponymous representatives of the Danaids (or Greeks) and the Egyptians, quarreled. Danaus and his fifty daughters then went to Argos. Aegyptus' sons pursued them; by most accounts, the Danaids then pretended to consent to marriage but proceeded to kill their cousins, with one exception, on their wedding night. The statuary in the portico may have shown a somewhat different presentation of the murder of the Egyptians. While the version according to which the Egyptians were represented on horseback cannot be verified, at least they seem to have been shown attacking the Danaids and suffering their just fate. On the one hand, then, there was the unmistakable

124. Denarius of Antistius Vetus, 16 B.C.
Reverse: Apollo.

reminder that Egypt's attack on the west—Greece in the myth, Rome in
recent history—had been beaten back. But there was another important dimension to the choice of this myth. Danaus and Aegyptus were brothers.
The war against Antony and Cleopatra, though nominally declared as a
foreign war against Cleopatra, was really directed against Antony (Dio
50.4.3–5) and therefore was a civil and fraternal war, the last of a whole series
since the times of Marius and Sulla. It was an episode that had to be termi-
nated by victory as well as purification. All these elements were inherent in
the Danaid myth while the aspect of expiatory purification figured prominently in the myth of Apollo and its artistic representations, including his
sacrifice to Nike/Victoria. Apollo had taken possession of Delphi after killing the monstrous dragon Python. Rightful as that victory was, there was
blood on his hands that had to be expiated. The image of Apollo on the coins
by the moneyer Antistius Vetus of 16 B.C. may recall that of his statue on the
Palatine, whether the cult image in the temple itself or, more probably, the
statue in the precinct bounded by the portico (Fig. 124).[160] Holding his lyre,
he is shown as pouring a libation on an altar, an act of purification.

    The evidence suggests that from the beginning of his reign, Augustus and
the artists working with him were intent on developing an imagery that
involved experimentation and multiple meanings. This involved risks: the
traditional condemnation the Danaids had incurred in literature and art
hardly would make them a fitting emblem, for instance, during the heyday
of the marriage legislation.[161] But such considerations should bother us as
little as the makers of these images. Augustan culture was characterized not
by frigid homogeneity, but by the existence of plentiful tensions and contradictions, the monarchic republic or republican monarchy being the prime

example. As for the Danaids, the multiplicity of their associations was adapted in his own way by Vergil. He put the bloody scene of the killing of their young suitors on the baldric of Pallas:

> impressumque nefas: una sub nocte iugali
> caesa manus iuvenum foede thalamique cruenti.
>
> (*Aen.* 10.497–98)

[Engraved with a legendary crime—that band of young men foully slain (or: slain for their foul crime) on their wedding night, the bedchambers swimming in blood.]

Turnus takes the baldric from Pallas and wears it, and the sight of this "monument of savage sorrow" (*saevi monimenta doloris*) leads to Aeneas' furious killing of Turnus at the end of the epic (12.941–52). There are several references here. Turnus was from Argos, the site of the slaying; he, too, is a suitor whose claim to a marriage that was resisted brings about his death. The bloody death of the young men also "reflects the untimely death of the young Pallas and suggests that Turnus' deed is equally nefarious."[162] Also, following Aeschylus, Vergil viewed the Danaids "not as lusty mankillers, but in their Aeschylean persona of pious creatures, moved to violence only by utter despair. . . . The 'savage sorrow' of the Danaids is also that of gentle Aeneas, dragged by an inexorable chain of events into the brutality of war."[163] The example further illustrates that the relationship between Augustan art and literature consists of many multilayered inspirations and ideas that lead to various creative adaptations.[164] Instead of simple and obvious "messages," Augustan art (and poetry) asks for the intellectual participation of the viewer or reader and for their scrutiny of alternative interpretations in order that the intentions of the creators may be understood all the more thoroughly.

Similar considerations apply to other parts of the pictorial program, such as the terracotta or Campana plates with the representation of Hercules, Apollo, and the tripod (Fig. 125).[165] Measuring about two by two and a half feet, they were brightly painted. Fragments of at least five plates have been found, which suggests that they served as a kind of thematic decoration (cf. Fig. 104). The style is archaizing, though not consistently so, as indicated by the billowing drapery of Apollo; the entire architectural and artistic program on the Palatine prefigures the typically Augustan combination of various Greek and Roman styles, constituting a composite that has a parallel in the combination of various genres in major poetic works of the age, such as Vergil's *Aeneid* and Ovid's *Metamorphoses*.[166] Equally as important is the return to a composition of the scene that is markedly different from most of the earlier representations of Hercules' struggle with Apollo over the tripod. Previously, Hercules has wrested the tripod away from the Delphic god,

125. Apollo, Hercules, and the tripod. Terracotta plaque
from the Apollo sanctuary on the Palatine.

who pursues him to retrieve it. Here we have a stylized, symmetrical design
with the tripod in the center while both Hercules and Apollo are laying
hands on it. There is no sign of a struggle, and the suggestion that the scene,
therefore, represents the reconciliation of the two after their struggle is per-
suasive, given the context. It is true that Antony prided himself on his descent from Hercules, but the hero also had a much longer and entirely positive place in the tradition of the Palatine. One tradition had him, and not
Evander, be the father of its eponymous hero Pallas (Dion. Hal., *AR* 1.43.1);
the mother was Evander's daughter Lavinia. According to Diodorus (4.21.4),
Hercules had been received hospitably on the Palatine by one of Evander's
nobles, Cacius. The *Scalae Caci* or Steps of Cacus, which ran by Augustus'
house to the precinct of Victory (Fig. 121), were named either after him or
after a local menace, Cacus, of whom Hercules rid the settlers of Evander's
Rome. It was an act of "saving the citizens," and Hercules' fierce struggle
against Cacus in the *Aeneid* (8.185ff.) prefigures that of Octavian against
Antony and his victory, culminating with the triumphal procession that Augustus views from the threshold of the Temple of Palatine Apollo (8.720).

Augustus again "appropriated" Hercules from one of his enemies; the representation of Hercules on the Campana plates is not simply a one-dimensional emblem for Antony. Similarly, Dionysiac motifs were successfully incorporated into Augustan imagery and combined with the Apolline laurel[167] without being redolent of Antony, the "new Dionysus." It was time to leave Actium and the preceding propaganda wars behind; the Apolline complex of the Palatine was a memorial as well as a new beginning.

CHAPTER V

AUGUSTAN LITERATURE

POETRY:
GENERAL CHARACTERISTICS

The main aspects of Augustan culture that we have observed in the arts and the political system apply to Augustan poetry also. It was anything but monolithic and evolved even in purely chronological terms. It represented new heights in creativity and sophistication. It was a product of its time not by simply echoing a party line or dissenting from it, but by reflecting in various ways, including the sophisticated manipulation of poetic conventions, on the complexity of the times and on the many dimensions of the Romans' view of themselves both as individuals and collectively. The corollary was not only the usual multifaceted richness of meanings and intentional multiplicity of associations, but a transcendence of the times as well: the *Aeneid*, for instance, has "succeeded in doing something that no epic has done before and since, and helped many generations . . . to formulate their views on the chief problems of existence,"[1] while Augustan love elegy can be usefully viewed in a wider than contemporary context.[2] At the same time, as in the case of *auctoritas* or the reliefs of the Ara Pacis, the polysemy of the *Aeneid*, for instance, is not a mere presentation of diffuse purposes, but is combined with a strong moral center. The poets, then, were creative participants in the ongoing discussion about ideals and values, and they had their own minds about them; this could range from contributing to the articulation of the Augustan ethos, as we saw in connection with Vergil's *Georgics*, to Horace's critique of the state of Augustan letters in his *Letter to Augustus*, and the rejection of *arma* for *amor* by the elegists. Finally, as was true of the Augustan dispensation in general, Augustan poetry is characterized by a great deal of experimentation and by the melding of new departures with inherited traditions. And, like the political system and Augustan art, Augustan poetry often defies easy categorization.

It is in all these respects that Augustan poetry is "Augustan" rather than in the narrow sense of political agreement with the *princeps*.[3] The latter again presupposes a static model, which is contradicted by the many dynamic interactions and autonomous processes that characterized the culture of the period and, in fact, made it so unique and influential. It is useful, therefore, to comment briefly on these principal aspects of Augustan poetry before we turn to the individual protagonists.

Evolution

The forty-five years of Augustus' rule were not one undifferentiated period. Simply in political terms, there were several "settlements" and discernible stages within his reign.[4] As for the poets, it comes down to a matter of generations.[5] Vergil (70 B.C.), Horace (65 B.C.), and Augustus (63 B.C.) were born within eight years of one another; the same is true of Maecenas and of the versatile Varius (both ca. 70 B.C.). This was a generation that had lived through the turmoil of the late republic and the civil wars, and that experience profoundly shaped its outlook. It yearned for peace, stability, and a restoration of basic Roman values. Bucolic poetry for Vergil is not escapism as dire historical realities, represented by the expropriations of landholders under the triumvirs, intrude into the programmatic first *Eclogue*. While Tityrus is saved by the intercession of the *divus iuvenis*, who is suggestive of Octavian, it is with the powerful evocation of Meliboeus' uncertain fate that the poem ends, and the ninth *Eclogue* takes up the same theme in an even more negative key. While the typically autobiographical interpretation of the poem ("Vergil lost his farm") cannot be validated, there is no question that he and his contemporaries had seen the fullness of human suffering, helplessness, and displacement: Aeneas' existence as a refugee and exile is one of the many responsive chords this character would strike at the time. Or, to give another example: as for moral reform, Horace needed no Augustan legislation to remind him that concern with morality was one of the purposes of poetry. Song and poetry, he says in his *Ars Poetica* (396–98), first taught men "the wisdom to distinguish public from private property, to forbid random sexual intercourse and give laws to those who are married." Contrary as it may be to modern sensibility, the moral purpose of poetry was perfectly legitimate in Greece and Rome, although the result did not have to be overt moralizing. "The Augustan poets," especially the first generation, "found a source of inspiration in reflection on moral ideals, and some of their greatest poetry takes its origin from it."[6] That did not guarantee the poets immediate acclaim; Horace's unique blend of occasional with moral poetry in *Odes* 1–3 may have caused the disappointing popular reception of that collection.

The elegiac poets Propertius and Tibullus were born ca. 50 B.C. They had been mere children at the time of Caesar's death, and they grew up in the years dominated by the confrontation of Antony and Octavian. They mirror the Augustan culture at large by their exquisite artistry and allusiveness, by their elegant transformation of Hellenistic inspirations, and, especially in

Propertius' case, by a high degree of experimentation and receptivity to the sculptural and pictorial arts of the period. But they evince little concern for the *res publica* and *mores* in the public realm. Their frame of reference does not extend back into the republic and, without this backdrop, their poetry is devoid of the mood of a national reawakening. Instead, it is the chaotic civil war between Antony and Octavian that produces some bitter reminiscences. A good example is the programmatic conclusion (*sphragis*) of Propertius' first book of elegies, the *Monobiblos*. Instead of giving precise answers to the questions of his friend Tullus, let alone commenting on his art or artistic aims, Propertius describes his descent from Assisi by reference to the loss of a relative (also the topic of the preceding poem) during the dreadful siege and destruction of Perugia in 40 B.C.:[7]

> Qualis et unde genus, qui sint mihi, Tulle, Penates,
>   quaeris pro nostra semper amicitia.
> si Perusina tibi patriae sunt nota sepulcra,
>   Italiae duris funera temporibus,
> cum Romana suos egit discordia civis,
>   (sic mihi praecipue, pulvis Etrusca, dolor,
> tu proiecta mei perpessa es membra propinqui,
>   tu nullo miseri contegis ossa solo),
> proxima supposito contingens Umbria campo
>   me genuit terris fertilis uberibus.
>
> (1.22)

[Tullus, in the name of our eternal friendship you ask me what kind of man I am, where my family is from, and who my household gods are: if our country's graves at Perusia are known to you, Italy's burial places in harsh times, when Rome's discord drove her citizens against one another (thus you, dust of Etruria, bring pain to me especially: you have allowed my relative's limbs to lie in the open, you are not covering the poor man's bones with any soil); there I was born in fertile Umbria, where it borders on Perusia and lies below it in its plain.]

Hence the constant aversion to war in his poetry and Tibullus', who in the final elegy of his first book excoriates the inventor of the sword and warfare in general, and proceeds to extol an idyllic *pax* without any reference to the concept of "peace won through victories." The ideal life for Tibullus is a *vita iners* (1.1.5), a life without the kind of *artes* or accomplishments that, as we saw earlier, Vergil described as following upon mankind's demise from the inertia of paradise (*Geo.* 1.133ff.). Similarly, Propertius in his introductory elegy (1.1.6) announces that he was taught by Amor *improbus*, who takes the place of Vergil's *labor improbus* (*Geo.* 1.145–46), to live without any plan or purpose (*nullo vivere consilio*). To him, then, "love is a transcendental power, and all accepted values—nobility, power, wealth—are revalued by love,"[8] although he is also preoccupied with death, which again is not inconsistent with the historical milieu. Tibullus actually served in the military, but his poetry is even more escapist than Propertius'; the two poets construct a world of their own that is both aloof from the Augustan state and yet, as we will see, permeated by Augustan themes.

The final representative of Augustan poetry is Ovid. It makes no sense to call him anti-Augustan or un-Augustan; in a way, he is the truest product of the Augustan age. Being only thirteen years old by the time of Actium, he belonged to the generation that knew only the *pax Augusta* and its *otium* "with whose sweetness," as Tacitus put it, Augustus "enticed one and all" (*Ann.* 1.2). He had no recollection of the travail that produced the Augustan principate or of its precarious genesis. The generation of Augustus, Vergil, and Horace appreciated the restoration of peace and domestic tranquillity against the background of the preceding turmoil; Ovid appreciated these conditions for their own sake. They made possible a time of refinement, elegance, and sophistication, all expressed by Ovid's ideal of *cultus*. Any hankering for the past is not for him:

> prisca iuvent alios, ego me nunc denique natum
>   gratulor: haec aetas moribus apta meis.
>
> (*AA* 3.121–22)

[The old times may please others; I count myself lucky to have been born now: this time is suited to my manners.]

So far from being an escape from the Augustan milieu into love or the countryside, erotic poetry is a mere game for him and takes place in a context that lives and breathes the ambience of the city of Rome with its splendid theaters, porticoes, and other public spaces. They, and public events such as triumphs, are the setting from which the activities of a *jeunesse dorée* are inseparable. The Augustan milieu goes beyond such material aspects: Ovid, as we have seen before,[9] acutely articulates the tension inherent in many Augustan ideals, such as the Golden Age, and he was and has remained Vergil's most perceptive reader. The *Metamorphoses* was his counterpoise to the *Aeneid*, with an entirely different perspective on myth and narrative. At the same time, Ovid's work has many affinities with phenomena in Augustan art, such as the avoidance of large narrative friezes in favor of individual images and scenes and their arrangement. To a much greater degree than Vergil, Ovid emphasizes individual episodes and vignettes.[10] And, as in Augustan art, the *Metamorphoses* calls for the constant participation of the beholder. There is an authorial center as the poet is very much in evidence, ultimately tying together the heterogeneity and flux of the material: the parallel with Augustus' similar role in the public realm is suggestive. The difference, which is also that between the *Metamorphoses* and the *Aeneid*, is the virtual absence of a moral center. Instead, that place is held by the *poeta ludens*, the poet at play.

Complexity and Multiplicity of Meanings

Augustan poetry was not simple "propaganda" or "organization of opinion" that drummed home straightforward messages. Like Augustan art, it delighted in being a complex mixture of different traditions, many of them Greek, which provided an unprecedented range of allusiveness and resonance. As the most immediate and available predecessor, Hellenistic poetry with its elegance, learning, and sophistication was more than congenial. Accordingly, the ideal audience for the Augustan poets possessed similar qualities[11] and such an audience would be able to appreciate the full extent of the poetry's associative wealth. Like Augustan art, however, much of the poetry was accessible to other audiences as well; as in the case of the Ara Pacis, the intentional multiplicity of resonances of the *Aeneid* and the *Metamorphoses*, for instance, can be experienced on several levels, depending on the intellectual and social horizon of the reader.

The main characters in the *Aeneid* are a good example; let us focus on Dido. The emotion and force of her personality can be felt immediately and without any detailed knowledge of literary models or contemporary references, an appeal that is enhanced by Vergil's presentation of her not "objectively," but with typical empathy and sympathy.[12] Even at this level or stage of "aesthetic reading,"[13] the character speaks for herself and can be readily appreciated as one of Vergil's most compelling creations. But a full understanding of the character's complexity comes with the reader's awareness of the literary models of Dido.[14] Their identification amounts to more than mere scholarly source hunting; the *Aeneid* was the result of meticulous labor—Vergil averaged about two and a half lines a day—and Seneca (*Suas.* 3.7) states explicitly that Vergil wanted his allusions to and borrowings from earlier writers to be recognized. In *Aeneid* 4, the Homeric presence is less conspicuous than it is in the other books of the *Aeneid*, but the Homeric matrices include Nausicaa, Circe, and Calypso. The allusion to Nausicaa perhaps seems most surprising, but Vergil deliberately adapts the first simile employed by Homer for Nausicaa, which compares her with Artemis (*Od.* 6.102–9), to mark the first actual appearance of Dido in the *Aeneid* (1.498–502). There are important differences between Nausicaa and Dido, and already in the first century A.D. was Vergil criticized for the supposed inappropriateness of this borrowing,[15] which brings us to two important points. First, Vergil uses such literary resonances for the purpose of both similarity and contrast. Certainly there are analogies between Dido and the Phaeacian princess: both help a shipwrecked sailor; both are attracted to him; marriage becomes a topic; both have other suitors; both know how to take charge, and so on. But there is never any total, let alone exclusive identification (again, reminiscent of the multivalent imagery in Augustan art): the reader is invited to reflect on both the similarities and dissimilarities, to respond to them emotionally and intellectually, and to sort them out. Second, the Homeric model is a springboard not merely for such reflections and responses, but for further development by the poet. This is borne out by the function of the simile itself: the comparison with Diana, while having a Homeric antecedent, now complements Aeneas' comparison to Apollo (4.143–50), thus underlining the affinity between Dido and Aeneas and, at the same time, the impossibility of a marriage: Apollo and Diana were brother and sister. The poet also makes us view all this against the background of the story of Jason and Medea: Apollonius had reused the same Homeric simile for Medea (3.876–86) and compared Jason at various points to Apollo.[16]

With this we arrive at a second prototype for the Aeneas-Dido story that was recognized as such from early on. Servius simply says about *Aeneid* 4 that "Apollonius wrote the *Argonautica* and in the third book introduced Medea in love: from here this whole book has been taken over." This summary judgment is analogous to Suetonius' and Dio's ascribing many actions to Augustus when, in fact, the process was a great deal more nuanced. For again, Dido both is and is not another Medea. She is similar to her in her all-encompassing passion, which turns into rage after her desertion by the hero; for the latter, Greek tragedy rather than Apollonius furnished the precedent, and extensive echoes of Greek tragedy, and not just Euripides' *Medea*, were incorporated by Vergil into the Dido episode.[17] Dido is further assimilated to Medea (and Circe) by her resort to magic. On the other hand, she is not a young maiden but the resourceful leader of her people who depend on her; she has lost her spouse (and has made a vow not to marry again); she is an exile trying to reestablish a new existence. In these respects she is the perfect match for Aeneas, who is as different from and similar to Jason as Dido is different from and similar to Medea. Again, the poet is asking the reader to determine the exact extent of such resonances. And there are more: Ariadne and Theseus, especially as rendered in Catullus 64 (the helpful bride is abandoned by the "hero"); Jason and Hypsipyle in *Argonautica* 1 (the hero interrupts his mission to stay with a strong woman); Hercules, both for Dido and Aeneas (too many associations to list, most of them positive);[18] affinities of Dido with the lover in Roman elegy "with all the associations of excessiveness, antisocial behavior, and general *nequitia* [indolence and self-indulgence] attaching to that *persona*";[19] and Dido's portrayal in the earlier Roman epic tradition, especially in Naevius' *Punic War*, with an apparent emphasis on violence, greed, duplicity, and hatred.[20] Along these lines, there is a faint echo of Cleopatra (especially in view of the Fama episode);[21] conversely, the epitaph Dido pronounces for herself (4.655–56) "recalls, in

its starkness and simplicity, the *elogia* or sepulchral inscriptic
worthies"[22] and thus is a fitting capstone of the many Roman q
as *virtus*, *pietas*, and *industria*—she displays.

This web of associations and contradictions is more than eno
a deconstructionist's heart, but such an approach would be as
the urge, in this instance and others relating to Augustan art aɪˌu poɪɪucs, to
impose a tidy homogeneity on a complex characterization that is appropriate
to the complexity of the age. Although Vergil's portrait of Dido is an example with few parallels in intensity, it is by no means untypical of the creative
tensions of Augustan culture in general; in contrast to Apollonius' Medea, for
instance, the moral situation alone of Dido is more intricate.[23] At the same
time, an authorial center exists along with the intended polysemy. We are
meant to view Dido without reducing her to one matrix or the other: she is
both great and flawed, strong and weak, Carthaginian and Roman, victim
and agent. The reader's response is to be commensurate to the multilayered
nature of the characters and issues presented by Vergil. The reaction may
vary from reader to reader, but we are asked to work our way through all the
nuances as carefully and honestly as the poet does, and an escape into indeterminacy is to be only a last and rare resort. All this is an essential aspect
of the greatness of Vergil's poem and of his Augustan sensibilities.[24]

Another example of the complexity of Augustan poetry is one of Ovid's
most popular tales, that of Philemon and Baucis (*Met.* 8.616–724).[25] Again
this story can be appreciated at the first reading: it deals with two singularly
decent people and thus offers a deliberate relief from the obsessive carryings-
on of the protagonists of many other episodes in the *Metamorphoses*. Ovid's
gentle humor is not missing from the narration and creates a distancing effect,
which, however, can be easily ignored by the serious-minded. Hence the
reception of the tale in later literature has been marked by its rendition as a
moralistic idyll on the one hand and as a satirical burlesque on the other.
Such schematizations reduce the many facets of Ovid's narrative. In contrast
to Vergil's Dido, we are dealing not with complex characters, but with a
complex handling of the story in addition to its creation from multiple religious, mythological, and literary traditions.

There are several backgrounds in cult and myth to the tale whose locale
is Phrygia. One is the tradition of the flood and, in particular, the flood as
punishment for human impiety. The tradition is found not only in Greek
literature but, of course, in the Near Eastern and Hebrew traditions also.
There was a local variant in Phrygia that may have been the result of interaction with a large-scale Jewish settlement there in the third century B.C.[26]
With the flood story comes the motif of the appearance of the gods on earth
so they can exempt those who treat them well from the punishment inflicted
on their wicked peers. The Sodom and Gomorrah story is relevant in this
context, which includes the themes of the hospitality extended by good

humans to gods (theoxeny) and the gods' eventual epiphany (theophany). Another principal religious element is the tree cult, involving a sacred tree with votive garlands hung on it and a wall around it. Its existence has been attested in Asia Minor both in Greco-Roman times and later, and its roots may extend to an early stratum of Greek religion.

The literary component of Ovid's tale goes as far back as Homer and consists primarily of the motif of a humble person hosting someone of superior status, though not a god. The examples include Odysseus in the hut of the swineherd Eumaios (*Od.* 14); Theseus stopping at the humble abode of the poor woman Hecale, as we know from Callimachus' elegant version; and, also by Callimachus, the similar tale of Hercules and the peasant Molorchus. That Ovid wanted the reader to recall these stories is clear from his remark that of all the listeners to the story of Philemon and Baucis, Theseus in particular was moved by it (8.726); after all, he had enjoyed similar hospitality in a similar setting. The Hellenistic tradition, however, diminished the religious content of the theme by not involving divine guests.[27] Ovid's use of such Hellenistic versions, therefore, to describe a theoxeny is an example of his general effort to make the *Metamorphoses* as multivalent as possible.

That applies to his presentation of the narrative, too. It defies straightforward categorizations. Not one, but three narrators are involved. The ostensible principal is Lelex, a participant in the Calydonian hunt, "mature in mind and age" (8.617), who tells the story to others, including Theseus, at a banquet given by the river-god Achelous; the backgrounds of the participants are aristocratic. Lelex presents the tale in response to the provocative remark of Peirithous who dismisses as fiction the gods' power to effect transformations. But while Lelex saw the oak and the linden tree into which Philemon and Baucis were transformed (620–22), it later turns out that he got the story from some locals: "These things old men, who were not conceited, narrated to me" (721–22). And then there is Ovid. While he is not telling the story directly, we do not lose sight of him. At various points, he alludes to the similar Orion story he tells in the *Fasti* (5.493–544).[28] In addition, the many touches Ovid borrowed from Nicander, one of his major Hellenistic sources, for Lelex's speech constantly suggest Ovid's own strong role in shaping the narrative as does Ovid's sense of subtle humor.[29]

These various narratorial stances are fluid throughout *Philemon and Baucis;* they intersect, diverge, or coincide. Lelex's stances alone are similarly diverse. To use some definitions from Genette's narratological system:[30] Lelex wants to tell more than a story from which the narrator is absent (*heterodiegesis*). After all, he has been to the place and can report what happened (*homodiegesis*). He wasn't exactly present at the transformation, but he knows those events from others who were there (*extradiegesis*) or who at least claim to be reliable sources. He did, however, see tangible evidence of it all so in a way he has some direct knowledge, too (*[intra]diegesis*). The shifting nature of Lelex's perspectives illustrates the lack of total comfort on his part with this tale of humble bliss. Thus he can stand outside his narrative as, for example, when we see the old couple's abode for the first time during the search of the gods (629–30): "A thousand homes locked them out, but one received them, a small one, though" (*mille domos clausere serae: tamen una recepit, parva quidem*). Modifiers such as *quidem* "allow the narrator to say hypothetically what he could not assert without stepping outside internal focalization."[31] Readers, of course, can adjust their own perspectives just as flexibly. Not only is what we are seeing subject to change, but even our very way of seeing it.

The relevance of this to the basic theme of metamorphosis is clear. The deliberate phrasing of Peirithous' remark, which occasions the Philemon and Baucis story, recalls Ovid's thematic statement at the very beginning of the *Metamorphoses*:

> "ficta refers nimiumque putas, Acheloe, potentes
> esse deos," dixit, "si dant adimentque figuras."
>
> (8.614–15)

["You are talking about fictions," he said, "and you consider the gods as far too powerful if they give and take away shapes."]

> in nova fert animus mutatas dicere formas
> corpora, di coeptis (nam vos mutastis et illas)
> adspirate meis . . .
>
> (1.1–3)

[My intention is to tell of bodies changed to different forms; you gods, who also made these changes, inspire my undertaking.]

How much credence did Ovid give to such transformation stories? None in their literal sense. He says this much in his long letter to Augustus from his way into exile, *Tristia* 2, where he refers to the *Metamorphoses* as his "major work" (*maius opus*), the very phrase Vergil had used for the second half of the *Aeneid* (7.45):

> inspice maius opus, quod adhuc sine fine tenetur,
> in non credendos corpora versa modos.
>
> (*Trist.* 2.63–64)

[Look at my major work, which is not quite finished yet, look at the bodies that were changed into shapes that are not to be believed.]

Accordingly, metamorphosis is important for Ovid not as a literal subject, but for its resonances and imaginative qualities, in particular the ever changing variety of narrative forms, styles, moods, and subjects.[32] The Philemon and Baucis story, placed near the center of the *Metamorphoses*, needs to be viewed in this context. Fittingly, the story illustrates narratological metamorphosis.

Once more, as in Vergil's characterization of Dido, there is the dynamic relationship between the poet's *auctoritas*, which is not moral in this case, and an intended latitude of reader response. For the pious, *Philemon and Baucis* is an inspiring parable; its touches of a simple life-style, even if set in the hills of Phrygia, fit in well with Augustan morality (though there is no need to interpret them as a concession to Augustus). Similarly, the total equality of the sexes in this story is appealing. As in the "contemplative images" of Augustan art, however, there are further dimensions. Their exploration, in the words of a recent writer, "does not invite the reader to abandon the desire to find ethical, religious and political meaning in narrative, but to seek for it in new ways."[33] That, too, is a typically Augustan endeavor.

Experimentation

From its very beginnings in the third century B.C. Roman poetry was characterized by experimentation. The Latin language was adapted to Greek meters, and existing Greek genres were developed and changed. The whole process reached a new stage with the so-called neoteric (or, modern) poets in the late republic of whom the Augustan poets were keenly aware.[34] Like Augustan art and statecraft, Augustan poetry drew on republican traditions and took them in new directions. The tradition of experimentation did not merely continue but reached new heights.

This characterization applies to all the Augustan poets. Horace's *Epodes*, published in 29 B.C., is a collection, diverse in style, meter, and content, of seventeen sophisticated literary experiments. Besides drawing on Callimachus, they ambitiously introduce into Roman poetry the manner and prosody of the great archaic Greek poets Archilochus (seventh century) and Hipponax (sixth century).[35] Similarly, his *Odes* represent an achievement unprecedented in Roman lyric poetry purely in the diversity of their forms and meters. As for Vergil, even his earliest work, the *Eclogues*, is a testimony to ongoing experimentation. The bucolic genre, such as it was,[36] is constantly expanded, transgressed, and combined with other generic features and subjects; *Eclogues* 4, 6, and 10 are only the most conspicuous examples.[37] The *Aeneid* represents a major experiment in combining Greek "mythological" and Roman "historical" epic, and its literary, aesthetic, and psychological novelty is related to that basic point of departure. Wherever we look in Ovid's oeuvre, we find experimentation: nobody had ventured to put the Roman religious calendar into elegiac verse, as he did in the *Fasti*; while his playful manipulation of elegiac conventions betokens the final stage of that genre in his amatory poetry, he revitalizes elegy in the *Heroides*, which have been aptly called "the declension of the elegiac paradigm in the feminine gender";[38] and the *Metamorphoses*, because it defies any categorization, is inimitable. On all these aspects, copious scholarship exists, though the discussion of a specific example will be helpful. The overriding perspective, however, should not be lost: the urge to experiment was congenial to the Augustan age and the Augustan poets were a constituent part of that milieu.

Of all of them, Propertius is often considered the most "difficult." The reason is his unique style and thought: he freely associates both verbally and visually and he juxtaposes verses without elaboration, leaving it to the reader to grasp the connecting train of thought. He compresses and reworks conventional expressions, coins new words and phrases, innovates grammatical constructions, and creates new verbal connections that result in the changed meaning or significance of a word.[39] One result is the messiest manuscript tradition of any Augustan poet, as scribes and commentators have attempted time and again to reduce the Propertian density to more manageable norms.

One example may stand for many. Poem 3.20 is addressed to a woman who has just been left by her husband or lover. Propertius starts out by denouncing him for his harshness and implies that he was more interested in lucre than in the woman. Promising her faithfulness (*fidus . . . fidus* in lines 9 and 10), Propertius urges her to hasten into his bed. For once, wish fulfillment is unproblematic (although some scholars have posited the beginning of a new poem here): from line 11 on, Propertius imagines her to be with him and prays that the day will be short before Venus rouses both lovers to arms; *arma* are fine in the service of *amor*, a conventional elegiac conceit. But, in accordance with his earlier emphasis on fidelity, Propertius makes it clear that this love is meant to be more than a one-night stand or temporary affair:

> foedera sunt ponenda prius signandaque iura
> et scribenda mihi lex in amore novo.
>
> (15–16)

[Agreements need first to be drawn and legal clauses must be signed, and a contract for this new love needs to be written by me.]

The language, if not from marriage contracts, borrows some weighty terms from conventional and public ethics. *Foedus* is a sacred agreement, ratified at the altar as it is, for instance, in *Aeneid* 12. There as here, its breach leads to divine revenge:

> namque ubi non certo vincitur foedere lectus,
> non habet ultores nox vigilanda deos.
>
> (21–22)

[For where the bed is not bound by a firm agreement a lover's sleepless night finds no gods to avenge it.]

To reinforce the point, the next couplet contrasts *libido* with *fides*. Then comes the creation of the new expression with which we are concerned, introducing the following sentence:

> ergo, qui pactas in foedera ruperit aras
>   pollueritque novo sacra marita toro,
>   illi sint quicumque solent in amore dolores . . .
>
> (25–27)

[Therefore he who broke the altars that had been made firm for our treaties and who defiled the sacred rites of marriage on a new bed of love, for him let there be as many tribulations as love usually brings.]

The phrase *pactas in foedera ruperit aras* is a verbal experiment that is full of associations and powerfully compresses and heightens the themes of the poem. The normal phrase would be *foedera rumpere*, to break treaties, that is, treaties that were *pacta*, "concluded." Instead of settling for such an abstraction, however, Propertius is taken with the visual image of the altar at which solemn agreements were sworn. He develops that image further—it is the altar that is actually broken—and makes it more graphic yet by drawing on the etymology of *pacisci* and *pangere*. *Pactas* can be the participle of both; *pacisci*, "to make a pact," is derived from *pangere*, "to make firm." Again, the usual phrase for "making a treaty" would be *foedus pangere* or simply *pacisci*; in order to say "at the altar," *ara* would then added with a preposition. Here, however, *pactas* modifies *aras* and the resulting purpose, *foedera*, is connected by means of the preposition *in*. The resulting expression is at once hard and easy to understand, and the violent transfer of "breaking" (*rumpere*) from treaties to altars is commensurate to the violence of the transgression condemned by Propertius.

Ultimately, such trial expressions result only from the larger attempt, evident throughout this poem and elsewhere, to invest the nonmarital relationship with the same aura as an actual marriage.[40] That attempt, in turn, is reflective of the larger experiment, the creation of love elegy, which is a specifically Augustan phenomenon. We encounter experimentation at each stage, involving both the larger concepts and specific stylistic details.[41] The seriousness and dignity with which Augustus sought to reendow Roman marriages is adopted by Propertius for his love affair: it is an eternal agreement, it is based on fidelity, it involves the signing of a solemn pledge, and so on. Far from being ironic, the procedure is a good example of the interaction of the elegist's own world with that of the state, and I will return to that aspect.[42] More generally, the very genre of love elegy was a tentative one and encouraged continuing experimentation.

This explains, to use a final example, the peculiarities of the poem with which Propertius introduces his fourth book. Its first part (4.1.1–70) is a survey of subjects and scenes from early Rome and her history. This prepares for several of the elegies in book 4, but the change from Propertius' earlier elegies to the "Augustan" book 4 is not as fundamental as has often been posited and is anticipated by some of the elegies in book 3.[43] By writing etiological poems on Roman customs (4.1.69), of course, Propertius becomes the Roman Callimachus (64); at the same time, the comparison Propertius makes between his own poetry as an act of founding and the building of the city (57ff.) is deliberately un-Callimachean.[44] In the first part alone of 4.1, therefore, he experiments with two kinds of poetic concepts.

His interlocutor in the second part (71–150), the seer Horus, will have none of this. When all is said and done, he tells Propertius to stop attempting any of this new poetry and simply to write elegies: *at tu finge elegos* (4.1.135). Conservative and antiexperimentalist that he is, Horus means the kind of love elegy written by Propertius earlier: his next verses reiterate some of its standard conceits, such as the military metaphor for love. This is not a programmatic announcement of the quite different love elegies that actually appear in book 4; similarly, Propertius suggested, as we have just seen, that he was not going to write the etiological poems in a strictly Callimachean key. In sum, in the introduction to book 4 Propertius indicates that he will strike out in some new directions and combine several generic conventions, such as they were. He will experiment with some new topics and with themes he has treated previously. It is in that sense again that book 4 is "Augustan" rather than a mere concession to "Augustan pressures." This characterization also applies, as we saw earlier,[45] to Horace's *Letter to Augustus* (*Epist.* 2.1): both works also mark a moment of poetic reflection.

Transcendence

It is a truism that literary classics are classics precisely because their appeal does not vanish with the period during which they were written. They speak to important issues that transcend time and they are inherently rich enough to allow for ever new perspectives that keep their appeal vital. It is important to distinguish here between the ongoing reception of such works through the constant creation of new interpretations and the breadth of meanings inherent in a classic as it raises substantive questions about the human condition, whether spiritual, social, or intellectual. We are not talking about timelessness in the sense of the modern maxim that "no text is resistant to interpretation," thus assuring endless topicality. Rather, we mean a classic's ability to define, in exemplary artistic form, some abiding characteristics of human existence and endeavor that each generation needs to evaluate anew.

Some ages may be more conducive to the creation of such classics than others. Greek tragedy was pushed to its highest point in the culture of fifth-century Athens, which owed much of its energy to the impetus of the Persian

Wars and the subsequent reflection on and affirmation of its specific values. The threat of ruin created a defining moment that led to a burst of unprecedented vitality in politics and the arts. Not surprisingly, Athenian culture was an inspirational model for Augustan culture, though by no means exclusively so.[46] In addition, the complexity of Augustan times provided a congenial stimulus for the thoughtful exploration of the Roman experience. It was a time of genuine transition, which was felt by all to varying degrees and called for an appropriate articulation. The merit of the poets is to have framed the resulting reflections in universally human rather than narrowly Roman terms.

The *Aeneid*, of course, is a stellar example. Instead of writing a historical epic in the tradition of his Roman predecessors, Vergil aimed for greater universality by writing a Roman *Odyssey/Iliad* that was both "mythological" and "historical." Aeneas, therefore, is much more than just the Roman and Julian ancestor. While he is inextricably woven into the fabric of the Roman and Augustan experience, the range of resonances he is given is even more comprehensive than Dido's. The result is a character full of vital human tensions. One essential aspect that contributes to his timelessness is the increased emphasis in his characterization, and in the *Aeneid* in general, on internal rather than external dimensions.[47] This is to minimize neither the role of Aeneas as a traditional warrior nor the psychological aspects of Achilles and Odysseus. Instead of the outward exploits of Aeneas, however, it is his inner qualities, his dilemmas, and his complex moral choices that are at the heart of the *Aeneid*. The transcendent aspect of his heroism is internal. This requires self-control and self-discipline; the tone is set early in the epic when, after the disastrous shipwreck off the coast of Africa, Aeneas tries to raise the spirits of his companions with a speech that includes, as an example of the *Aeneid's* permanent appeal, the oft quoted phrase that "some day, perhaps, it will be a pleasure to remember even this" (*forsan et haec olim meminisse iuvabit*; 1.203). Outwardly, he is the confident leader, building up the morale of those entrusted to him. Immediately after Aeneas has finished speaking, however, Vergil makes us look into the hero's soul:

> talia voce refert curisque ingentibus aeger
> spem vultu simulat, premit altum corde dolorem.
>
> (1.208–9)

[He said such things; though sick inside with huge cares, he feigned hope on his face and kept his grief hidden deep in his heart.]

The passage exemplifies three aspects of the inward shift in the *Aeneid*. One is that Vergil often comments on the inner state of his characters. Sometimes he editorializes and, while remaining the narrator himself, presents the narrative from their point of view. Brooks Otis aptly characterized all these

qualities as Vergil's "subjective style."[48] Second, the inner struggles and dilemmas of the main characters are just as important, if not more so, than their
external exploits. The basic choice of Achilles was between a short and glorious life and a long and uneventful one. He chose the former, and great heroic
deeds constitute it. The choices Aeneas has to make are more complex, and
less outwardly heroic. That is why he is stripped of any of the external trappings of heroism in the poet's first direct presentation of him—as he is about
to drown—and that is precisely why Aeneas on that occasion begs for a
return to the grand heroism of the old days.[49] And this actual appearance of
Aeneas, in contrast to that of Achilles in the *Iliad*, is delayed so that the poet
can define him first and programmatically in terms of the new heroism, that
of *pietas* and *labores*, in the very proem. Similarly, while ever present dangers
confront both Odysseus and Aeneas, Aeneas' *Odyssey* to an even larger degree becomes an inner one with significant tests and trials of his character,
such as the Dido episode.[50] Third, the passage we are discussing reiterates, at
the level of human affairs, the leitmotif of the extended proem of the epic
(1.1–296), which anticipates one of the basic themes of the *Aeneid*[51]—the
restoration of order out of disorder. By saving the human example for last,
Vergil reinforces the meaning of the simile of the statesman (pp. 20–21):
such order cannot be established merely in an external way, as by the use of
force, but has to come about by the practice of virtues such as self-control for
the sake of the common good. That kind of *pietas* (1.151) is the basis for the
auctoritas of the statesman.

It is obvious that the complex of these ideas is "Augustan." They are
indeed some of the fundamental and underlying ideas of the Augustan restoration. Vergil uses them, however, not as "propaganda" or "ideology," but
as a springboard for meditations on humanity and heroism. The Augustan
ideas are extended to the point where the scope of these meditations becomes universal. Augustanism and universality become complementary.
The writing of universal histories at Augustus' time is another manifestation,
even if less sublimated, of the same phenomenon.[52]

A further brief example may illustrate another aspect of the *Aeneid*'s permanence, its reflection on basic questions of human existence. The relation
between fate, free will, and the role of the gods was raised in the *Iliad* and
became the essence of much of Greek tragedy in the fifth century. Vergil
offers one of the most concise formulations of such a theodicy:

> sua cuique exorsa laborem
> fortunamque ferent. rex Iuppiter omnibus idem.
> fata viam invenient.

(10.111–13)

[To each one his own undertakings will bring toil and fortune. King
Jupiter is the same to all. The fates will find their way.]

The central idea is that "destiny is not independent of human will or effort."[53] It is an affirmation of the concept of human freedom and responsibility. Yet Jupiter, as a representative of the gods, is present, professing to be evenhanded. Moreover, there is not chaos in the universe, but the order of fate. Fate is not an external force, however, but incorporates the freedom of human action. With unparalleled concision, Vergil restates the theodicy he formulated at the beginning of the *Georgics* and sets some new accents. We have seen how central his formulation was to the ethos of Augustan culture, and the moral law expressed here animates much of the *Aeneid*. At the same time, these "Augustan" concepts and meditations have a timeless quality.

No Augustan poet was like the other. When Horace called Vergil "half of my soul" (*animae dimidium meae*; *C*. 1.3.8) he did not refer to unanimity or uniformity of mind but to the recognition that in all their differences the two poets complemented one another—an outlook that we find time and again in Augustan culture. Horace does not share the intensity of existential preoccupation that characterizes Vergil's *Georgics* and *Aeneid*. Value judgments, such as that Horace is shallow by comparison and is not possessed of the same largeness of soul, tend to miss the point. A major reason for the transcendence of his poetry is his ability to make the reader reflect, with each new reading, on abiding issues of the human existence, but he does so genially. In the *Odes*, this reflective impulse is combined with an unsurpassed mastery of the forms of lyric poetry. Horace was fully aware of that achievement and in *Ode* 3.30, proclaimed it in terms that take their inspiration from the Augustan milieu.[54] His claim, for instance, to have "built a memorial more lasting through the years than bronze" (*exegi monumentum aere perennius*) can be usefully connected with the pervasive Augustan practice to affix monumental inscriptions, made of bronze letters that were gilded, to the multitude of new marble buildings especially in Rome; Horace goes on to relate the permanence of Rome to the immortality of his poetry later in the same poem (lines 6–9). That, in turn, leads to the mention of his poetic achievement: he was *potens* and *princeps*—the resonance with Augustan terminology is fully intentional—"to adapt Aeolian song to Italian verse" (11–13).

Horace was quite correct to view his formal achievement as an essential aspect of his poetic transcendence. His lyric poetry in particular is another example of the Augustan ethos of unremitting *labor*: it is characterized by incessant striving for perfection in language, style, and verse. He averaged one line a day for the first three books of *Odes*, published in 23 B.C. His craftsmanship became a model for generations of poets and was aptly summarized by Nietzsche: "This mosaic of words, in which every word, by sound, by place, and by meaning, spreads its force to the right, to the left, over the whole; this minimum in extent and number of symbols, this maximum thereby achieved in effectiveness of symbols—all this is Roman and, believe me, elegant par excellence."[55] We might note how appropriate this characterization is, *mutatis mutandis*, for artistic monuments such as the Ara Pacis and the cuirass of the Prima Porta Augustus.

Horace attains all this with a diction that is anything but recherché or overemphatic; he rarely uses superlatives, for instance. The diction is commensurate to thought and content: his achievement lies both in expressing commonplaces in new ways and, especially, in engaging the reader in humane reflection on them. This is different from Vergil's intense probing or Lucretius' anxious proselytizing, and we rarely catch a glimpse of metaphysics. "Thoughtfulness" is a good characteristic, defined as "an appreciative, sympathetic vision into men and their affairs."[56] At the same time, and reflecting the spirit of the Augustan culture, a Horatian ode is not static. Instead, it is an ongoing process of reflection in which the reader is asked to participate, with ever new associations. This dynamic underlies the transcendence both of Horatian lyric and the Augustan age, as we can see in one of Horace's lesser known poems.[57]

> Otium divos rogat in patenti
> prensus Aegeo, simul atra nubes
> condidit lunam neque certa fulgent
>   sidera nautis;
> otium bello furiosa Thrace,
> otium Medi pharetra decori,
> Grosphe, non gemmis neque purpura ve-
>   nale neque auro.
> non enim gazae neque consularis
> summovet lictor miseros tumultus   10
> mentis et curas laqueata circum
>   tecta volantis.
> vivitur parvo bene, cui paternum
> splendet in mensa tenui salinum
> nec levis somnos timor aut cupido
>   sordidus aufert.
> quid brevi fortes iaculamur aevo
> multa? quid terras alio calentis
> sole mutamus? patriae quis exsul
>   se quoque fugit?   20
> scandit aeratas vitiosa navis
> Cura nec turmas equitum relinquit,
> ocior cervis et agente nimbos
>   ocior Euro.
> laetus in praesens animus quod ultra est
> oderit curare et amara lento

temperet risu; nihil est ab omni
    parte beatum.
abstulit clarum cita mors Achillem,
longa Tithonum minuit senectus,   30
et mihi forsan, tibi quod negarit,
    porriget hora.
te greges centum Siculaeque circum
mugiunt vaccae, tibi tollit hinnitum
apta quadrigis equa, te bis Afro
    murice tinctae
vestiunt lanae: mihi parva rura et
spiritum Graiae tenuem Camenae
Parca non mendax dedit et malignum
    spernere vulgus.   40

                            (C. 2.16)

[Ease is the prayer of the man caught in the open Aegean, as soon as a black cloud has hidden the moon and the stars fail to shine as certain guides to sailors, ease the prayer in war of raging Thrace, of the Medes whose ornament is the quiver, ease, Grosphus, that jewels and purple cannot buy, nor gold. For it is not eastern treasures nor the consul's lictor that clears away the wretched tumults of the mind and the cares that flutter around coffered ceilings. One lives well on little, if the father's salt-cellar gleams on a frugal table and fear and base desire for gain do not steal easy sleeps. Why in our short life do we strongly hurl our javelin at many marks? Why change, for our own, lands hot with another sun? Who in exile from his country has escaped himself as well? Flawed Care climbs aboard armored ships and does not abandon the squads of horsemen, swifter she than deer, swifter than the east wind as it drives the storm clouds. A mind cheerful for the present should reject caring about what is further on and temper bitterness with a mild smile; nothing is blessed in all respects. Swift-footed death stole glorious Achilles, long old age made Tithonus shrink, and to me perhaps, what she has denied you, an hour will freely hand over. Round you a hundred flocks and Sicilian cows low, for you the mare fit for racing teams whinnies, you are dressed in wool twice dyed in African purple; for me a small estate and the delicate breath of the Greek Muse is the gift of truthful Fate, and contempt for the crowd's malice.][58]

The themes of the ode are universally human: the threat of death, freedom from difficulties, material security, inner peace, the fleeting nature of our existence, coming to terms with ourselves, the impossibility of perfect bliss, wealth, contentment with less than wealth or because of less than wealth, and the active choice of the kind of life that can minimize anxiety. All this would be enough for a lengthy philosophical disquisition, but, in deliberate contrast to Lucretius and Epicurus, this is not how the poem works. The topics are suggested in sparse, almost prosaic language but are vividly exemplified by a succession of vibrant images: the sailor; the foreign soldiers; the Sicilian land-owner to whom the poem is addressed with his flocks, race horses, and purple dress; the palaces of the rich and their coffered ceilings; the salt-cellar in a more modest abode; the onslaught of Anxiety personified amid armies and navies; death depriving Achilles of his swift feet; the shrinkage of overage Tithonus; and Horace's small estate. *Otium* is the key word, emphasized at the beginning of three of the first six lines, reminding the reader of a famous stanza of Catullus 51. In true Augustan style, *otium* has multiple connotations, both positive and negative,[59] and the reader is invited to explore their range. And, again in true Augustan style, Horace provides a guiding framework and imparts a new meaning to a traditional notion: *otium* now comes to mean inner tranquillity. *Otium* was an important slogan in the late republic; cou-pled with *dignitas* (Cic., *Sest.* 98–100; cf. *Phil.* 8.11–12), it connoted the domestic tranquillity necessary for the stability of good government. Such was provided by the *pax Augusta*, as Horace himself says in the final poem of his last book of *Odes* (4.15.18). Tacitus, by contrast, capitalized on the other aspect of *otium*, which is related to the complex of ideas I explored earlier (pp. 138–40): prolonged tranquillity leads to lack of political initiative and to decline; Augustus "seduced one and all by the sweetness of *otium*" (*Ann.* 1.2). Horace, in the manner of many Augustan artists and poets, takes a concept current at the time, internalizes it, and universalizes it in the process. *Otium* now is the inner peace we all are trying to attain. The Roman official, the consul surrounded by his lictors, becomes the foil: he may have *otium cum dignitate*, but that is an external situation which does nothing about the real upheavals, those of the mind. The shift from external to internal aspects is the same as in Vergil.

Consonant with all this and with the Augustan milieu is the poetic stance Horace adopts. The flow of admonition is not simply from the top down. Lucretius, the proud apostle of Epicurean enlightenment, had surveyed hu-manity's woes from the superior vantage point of the "serene precincts of the wise." Horace, by contrast, is at the same level as the other seekers. His attitude, therefore, is more empathetic and humane.[60] He genially urges constant reflection, a process that he consummates for himself by the coales-cence of his life-style and his poetic outlook.[61] "One can live well on little" (*vivitur parvo bene*); hence Horace combines his small estate (*parva rura*) with his predilection for "the slender spirit of the Greek Muse" (*spiritum Graiae tenuem Camenae*). Along the way he asks the kind of simple questions that do not aim at high metaphysics but are of timeless importance for anyone seek-ing to lead a good life: why do we scatter our efforts over so many things in the short life we have? Why do we hope in vain to change our real condition when we move from one place to another? In a mere six words (*patriae quis exsul / se quoque fugit*; 19–20), Horace uses the topic of displacement, with all the resonances it had at the time as we have seen from Vergil's use of it for Aeneas, and turns to its permanence: we cannot escape ourselves even if we change external settings. The notion is found in Lucretius (3.1068–69) and recurs in Horace's *Epistles* (1.11.25–27), but the phrase *patriae exsul* gives the idea special poignancy in *Ode* 2.16.

In various ways, then, Horace elevates themes suggested by the historical and cultural situation of his time by imparting to them perspectives that are more enduring. The endeavor is representative of Augustan culture in general. In the political realm, we can cite the foundation of the Augustan rule on abiding values and ideals rather than on an enforced ideology or mere propaganda, which, as our experience with such regimes has shown, can be quite evanescent. By contrast, the political solution alone of Augustus proved to be anything but ephemeral. The achievement of the poets turned out to be longer lasting yet.

And they were aware of that transcendence, as Ovid's epilogue to the *Metamorphoses* shows (15.871–79). It echoes Horace's *Ode* 3.30. Horace, as we have seen, had phrased his own permanence in terms of that of Rome. Ovid politely follows him in saying that his poem will be read through all lands ruled by Rome, but he proceeds to predict for himself an even greater permanence:[62] "Through all ages I shall live in fame" (15.878–79). The ultimate reason, besides Ovid's yet more developed ego, is that whereas the *Aeneid* and many of Horace's *Odes* were a universalization of the Roman experience, such a Roman dimension is largely absent from many myths and stories of the *Metamorphoses*. Rather, Ovid's stories are a kaleidoscope of human (and divine) behavior, emotions, and vicissitudes. The guiding *auctoritas* of the poet is narrative and not moral. We are dealing not with the eternal nature of Rome but with eternal human experiences to which a Roman reader, among others, may respond in various ways. The result, as a recent writer has well put it, is *homo Ovidianus*, "unburdened of nationality, liberated from the past, unoppressed by the future, delivered from responsibility and morality."[63] Ovid's outlook in the *Metamorphoses* is the timeless celebration of the *otium* afforded by the *pax Augusta*.

INDIVIDUAL POETS

Augustan poetry has often been interpreted in terms of the relation of the poets to Augustus and his supposed wishes and requests. It is not an unimportant perspective, but the overemphasis on it reflects the inadequate top-down conception of the Augustan reign. Few scholars today would still maintain that the poets were simply mouthpieces of the government, which patronized them, after all. Patronage itself does not produce superior poetry, as Augustus well knew from Choirilus' proverbially wretched epics on Alexander,[64] nor did it have to lead to poetic submissiveness. The equation, in fact, can be reversed: "It is not the poets who are the clients, but the patrons."[65] Nor does the available evidence suggest that Maecenas was simply the minister of propaganda vis-à-vis the poets.[66]

The interaction, including patronage, between Augustus, Maecenas, and the poets cannot be confined to the simplistic matrix that we find in the ancient grammarians and which shaped subsequent views and the reaction against them. For instance, Donatus, Tiberius Claudius Donatus, and Servius all assert that the *Aeneid* was written primarily for the glorification of Augustus. This view was elaborated from the seventeenth century on, though there was no lack over time of interpretations of the *Aeneid sub specie aeternitatis*. Yet that aspect of reception was largely ignored when the imperial "Augustan" purpose was reemphasized in the context of the depiction of Augustus' rule as a forerunner of the authoritarian regimes in the 1930s and 1940s. The inevitable antithesis, starting with the 1960s though occasionally anticipated before then,[67] was that Vergil, Horace, the elegists, and certainly Ovid, if their texts were read with the proper attention to subtexts, could be shown to harbor darkly subversive or "disquieting" views of the Augustan system. More recently, the pendulum has swung back a bit: the poets are seen neither as ideological supporters nor cryptocritics, but as purveyors of ambivalences, ambiguities, and ironies on a rather massive scale. Such qualities, of course, as Gerald Graff has aptly pointed out, can be found in any poetic text "under the right kind of close inspection."[68]

All this raises important questions of methodology with which I have dealt elsewhere in detail.[69] The very fact that Augustan poetry transcends its own times and is intent on reader participation means that each generation interprets such classical works differently. At the same time, it is important not to project modern sensibilities blithely back into antiquity. We must differentiate between our personal response, conditioned as it is by our culture, and the determination of the meaning of the literary work in the milieu—social, political, and cultural—in which it was written. In that sense, my approach to the Augustan poets is "historical." We are dealing not with exclusive categories but with a typical mutuality; as we have seen, the transcendence of their poetry is directly related to the specific historical moment at which they wrote their works.

Their Augustanism, then, is not simply a matter of their relations with Augustus. There is not much to be gained by measuring Augustan poems by the standard of his wishes, whatever they may have been. Suffice it to say that if Augustus had written an epic it would, of course, have been different from Vergil's. The poets had their own minds, a fact fully recognized by him and Maecenas. They are Augustan because they lived during his reign, and their poetry in many ways is a response to their times. They had their own perspectives on them, which often are not uniform even within the same poet's oeuvre and which range, as we noted earlier, from the articulation of shared ideals to frank criticisms. Moreover, the poets were anything but merely reactive; they helped to shape Augustan culture as much as he did.

Vergil's *Aeneid*

Since the *Aeneid* is thoroughly woven into the Augustan context, I have discussed several of its aspects already, such as its emphasis on the creation of order from disorder. It is the leitmotif in the extended proem (1.1–296) and has been rightly recognized as setting the tone for the entire epic. Yet it is only a consequence of the epic's basic theme which Vergil, who could be as plain and unambiguous as he could be complex and allusive, states at the end of the proem proper:

> tantae molis erat Romanae condere gentem.
>
> (1.33)

[A matter of so much toil was it to found the Roman nation.]

The emphatic nature of this line, in purely rhetorical terms, was well recognized by Quintilian (8.5.11); in addition, the fact that word accent and verse accent clash in it only once underscores the realistic quality of the message. The essence is toil; "great things," as Donatus commented on this line, "cannot be accomplished without great *labor*." *Condere* is another example of the polysemy on which Servius remarked in connection with the very first verb in the *Aeneid*. It conveys the sense of "joining together" (the Latins and the Trojans) and it implies the founding of the city (*urbem condere*). That event, however, will not be told in the epic; it is the toil necessary for the achievement, and not the achievement itself, that is the stuff of the *Aeneid*.

It is from this central idea that most characteristics of the *Aeneid* originate. The epic is a spiritual and poetic reflection of the Roman national experience, and it is an honest one at that. Worthwhile achievement comes at a price. From the start, Jupiter pointedly rejects the tranquil vision Venus has in mind for Aeneas on the model of Antenor who

> was allowed to found Padua, make a home for
> Trojans there—could give his people a name, and nail up
> His arms, could settle down to enjoy peace and quiet.
>   (1.247–49; trans. C. Day Lewis)

> [hic tamen ille urbem Patavi sedesque locavit
> Teucrorum et genti nomen dedit armaque fixit
> Troia, nunc placida compostus pace quiescit.]

For her son, by contrast, there will be no such *finis laborum* (1.241). Nor will such toil and efforts end with Aeneas. The reign of Augustus is the natural culmination of Rome's existence from Vergil's perspective, but it will not be one of ease. Augustus is mentioned only three times in the *Aeneid*, though at important junctures. At the end of Jupiter's prophecy, he is hailed as ending "harsh generations" (*aspera saecula*) and their wars (1.291), thus preparing for the return of justice and other traditional virtues. Despite the imagery of the closing of the doors of the Janus temple, the reference is mostly to the civil wars that were characterized by the bloodthirst of *furor impius* (1.294–96). The next two times we see Augustus, he will extend the empire beyond the Garamants (in Africa) and Indians (6.794–95) and fight valiantly against Mark Antony and Cleopatra (8.675–728), a depiction that ends with his great triple triumph.

Besides the lack of repose, which is characteristic of the Augustan concept of the Golden Age,[70] Vergil continually emphasizes the cost of the Roman effort. Few other heroic epics show so consistently the grief of the non-combatants and the pathos of the premature death of the young. The end of book 6 is a prime example. We have seen, through Anchises' prophecy, the inexorable march of the Romans through history, culminating in a formulation of the Roman national character that remains unexcelled in its conciseness and substance (6.847–53). The poet could have splendidly ended the first half of the *Aeneid* on this high note. Instead, he balances it with an extended description of extraordinary sadness. Its subject is the young Marcellus, Augustus' nephew and heir apparent, who died at the age of eighteen in 23 B.C. His death was not due to battle. Vergil, therefore, here does not even evoke the notion of the sacrifice of such young people in the service of their country but simply reminds us that both glory and sorrow are part of the Roman experience, as they are of the human experience in general and of the Augustan experience in particular: "Catastrophe following hard on the heels of triumph is an obstinate motif in the story of the age."[71]

Related to this is a realization of greater complexity. The choice Achilles had to make was fundamentally simple: a short and glorious life or a long life that was less distinguished—hence his rank individualism and his constant preoccupation with himself and with his standing in his warrior society. Odysseus is another individualist; he loses all his men and, despite all adventures, he is able to return safely to his status quo. Another foil is Apollonius' Jason. He is not superman, but more like an ordinary Hellenistic citizen who incongruously is put in charge of a major mythical exploit where he stumbles from one dilemma of his making to the next. While Vergil purposely borrowed from all these characters in his creation of Aeneas, two major changes stand out that clearly derive from the Roman and Augustan context. One is that along with martial valor, social responsibility is Aeneas' hallmark. The egotism and megalomania of ambitious leaders had brought the *res publica* close to disintegration. By contrast, the revitalization of the moral ideal of the *res publica* as the common good, with all its supporting virtues such as *pietas*, was the real meaning of Augustus' "restored republic." The new leader or hero had to have the appropriate moral and intellectual qualities; Aeneas exemplifies them. The choices he has to make are at once wider-reaching and subtly complex, and the dilemmas he is facing are more profound. The second and related change is that the exertions of the proto-Roman Aeneas have a purpose that is more than individualistic and ephemeral. Odysseus has one miraculous escape after the other; so, in a different way, does Jason. Aeneas, by contrast, is not an individual adventurer, but the founder of a fated new society and nation.

As a result, one perceived drawback is that Aeneas seems to be less of an individual and more of a normative type. He talks a great deal less, for instance, than his Homeric predecessors: 18 percent of the lines in the *Odyssey* are spoken by Odysseus; 13 percent of those in the *Iliad* by Achilles; whereas only 6 percent of those in the *Aeneid* belong to Aeneas. The general issue has been defined most succinctly by C. M. Bowra:[72]

> It is wrong to treat them [the characters of the *Aeneid*] as if they were dramatic characters like Homer's. They are more, and they are less. They are more, because they stand for something outside themselves, for something typically and essentially Roman; they are types, examples, symbols. And they are less, because any typical character will lack the lineaments and idiosyncracies, the personal appeal and the intimate claims, of a character who is created for his own sake and for the poet's pleasure in him.

The phenomenon is the same as the one we have observed in Augustan art. What mattered on the Boscoreale cups (Figs. 32 and 33), for instance, was the representation not of a biography, but of a concept of exemplary attitudes, and the same is true of the "processions" on the Ara Pacis friezes. "Reality" is subordinated to the guiding ideas behind it; this also applies, as we saw earlier, to the *Res Gestae*.

Each medium is different, however. The hero of the literary epic is not merely an icon, but a flesh-and-blood human being who is capable of great emotions. Often he controls them, even though they run deep. After Aeneas breaks off his futile argument with Dido, for instance—and mistrust of powerful language was a very Roman trait, too[73]—Vergil uses a striking simile that makes palpable the inner dimension of Aeneas and the depth of his emotion and self-control:

> ac velut annoso validam cum robore quercum
> Alpini Boreae nunc hinc nunc flatibus illinc
> eruere inter se certant; it stridor, et altae

consternunt terram concusso stipite frondes;
ipsa haeret scopulis et quantum vertice ad auras
aetherias, tantum radice in Tartara tendit:
haud secus adsiduis hinc atque hinc vocibus heros
tunditur, et magno persentit pectore curas;
mens immota manet, lacrimae volvuntur inanes.

(4.441–49)

[As when some stalwart oak-tree, veteran of the Alps,
Is assailed by a wintry wind whose veering gusts tear at it,
Trying to root it up; wildly whistle the branches,
The leaves come flocking down from aloft as the bole is battered;
But the tree stands firm on its crag, for high as its head is carried
Into the sky, so deep do its roots go down towards Hades:
Even thus was the hero buffeted for long with every kind of
Pleading, and in his great heart he felt cares through and through;
His mind remained unchanged; the tears fall in vain.][74]

The psychological state of the hero is exquisitely rendered by the corresponding details in the world of the simile. The tears are those of Aeneas, but may be those of others, too.

On the battlefield, however, there is no such restraint. Martial fury was a traditional aspect of warfare,[75] and especially after the brutal death of Pallas at Turnus' hands, Aeneas turns into a veritable archangel of death. His behavior is evocative of Achilles' rage after the death of Patroclus. He mows down enemies, including two suppliants and a priest, and he cruelly disparages their supplications. Yet his war is still a *bellum pium et iustum*. The *Aeneid* ends with Aeneas, "inflamed with fury and terrible in his wrath" (*furiis accensus et ira terribilis*, 12.946–47), dispatching the soul of Turnus to the shades below. Since the second half of the *Aeneid* used to be greatly neglected, despite the poet's emphatic announcement that it was his *maius opus* (7.45), and since there had been centuries of Christianizing interpretation that portrayed Aeneas as a good proto-Christian or at least Stoic, his outbursts were quickly converted into implying his failure, Vergil's dark view of Augustus and Rome, and so on. That is simply turning one cliché into another. When we return to the text, we see that Vergil is presenting us not merely with the personified abstraction of Roman virtues and a sophisticated construct of allusions to literary predecessors, but also with a believable human character whose range of expressions—at times Aeneas also shows pity for his opponents to an extent unprecedented in heroic epic—greatly exceeds that of the stylized sculptural portraits of Augustus. The result again is the kind of dynamic, typical of Augustan culture in general, between the general and the individual.

Like the art of the Ara Pacis and like the Augustan political system, the *Aeneid* continually asks for response and involvement, all, to be sure, within the framework of a guiding *auctoritas*. The epic's final scene, much debated over the past three decades, is a good example. Realistic as it is, the *Aeneid* ends with a dilemma; as R. D. Williams noted in his general characterization of the *Aeneid*, "the Roman way of life was one involving constant problems," and that is one of the realizations that animates Vergil's epic.[76] Significantly, the dilemma Aeneas confronts in the end is a human dilemma rather than one rooted in Roman customs or practice. As a breaker of treaties, Turnus has forfeited his life before gods and men and we know of no instance where the Romans extended *clementia* to such an individual. In those terms, the situation is clear. Yet as Turnus begs for his life—an action that, typically, belies his earlier words and vows—Aeneas reacts with humane sensibility: "Touched in his inmost being, Aeneas hesitates . . . an extraordinary moment of humanity; for the epic warrior never hesitates."[77] When Aeneas sees the baldric of Pallas, however, which is now worn by Turnus, his reaction changes to full-blown anger and fury; the objective causation for Turnus' death and Aeneas' human emotions converge. Anger was one of the most debated topics in ethics at Vergil's time and the reader certainly is challenged to reflect on the validity of Aeneas' behavior, including a comparison with Achilles' behavior at the killing of Hector and with the more peaceful, but less real ending of the *Iliad*. As usual, the range of resonances is extraordinarily rich and also extends to the role of anger in the administration of justice. The invitation to the reader is to work through all these aspects carefully, to explore their pertinence, and to assess Aeneas' action in their light. Our active judgment is constantly involved and given considerable latitude within the authorial parameters that Aeneas' action is just and a fitting conclusion to the *Aeneid*, the Roman *Odyssey/Iliad*; in all three epics, anger plays an important role.

It is in this sense that the *Aeneid* is Augustan;[78] indeed, it is hard to imagine that it could have been written at any other time except Augustus'. The interaction between its historicity and its transcendence is an important part of the *Aeneid's* special dynamic. It is not simply an *Augusteid*, the expected alternative that Vergil still seems to have been contemplating in his preface to the third *Georgic* (3.12–48), but much more. Aeneas was the ancestor not only of the Julian family, but of the Romans in general. Moreover, so far as we can tell, his character had been developed relatively little in the previous literary tradition. That is particularly true in comparison to heroes such as Odysseus and Hercules who were tremendously popular in Italy. The choice of Aeneas, therefore, was attractive because of the almost unprecedented creative opportunity that he afforded Vergil. The many innovations of the *Aeneid* in terms of epic style, narrative, and characterization go hand in hand with its mythopoeic innovations. Some of the latter were necessary consequences of the Augustan milieu. Anything eastern had been vilified by Octavian's propaganda campaign against Mark Antony. The eastern prince Aeneas, therefore, is divested by Vergil not only of his riches, *Troia gaza* (1.119)—the same word used by Horace in his *otium* Ode (2.16.9)—in the shipwreck and inured to the simplicity of Italian life by King Evander, but he is actually cast as a native son returning to Italy because Dardanus, one of his ancestors, originally went from there to Troy (7.240; 8.134). The *Aeneid* is the epitome of Augustan culture in its combination of tradition with new departures.

Attentiveness to this context does not demonstrate Augustan "ideology" in the *Aeneid*—that Vergil shared in the basic values of the Augustan reform is self-evident—but allows us to appreciate the poet's own attentiveness to the Augustan ambience. Again, one example of many must suffice. At the end of his prediction to Venus, to which I briefly referred earlier, Jupiter says this about the coming of someone named Caesar Iulius:

> nascetur pulchra Troianus origine Caesar,
> imperium Oceano, famam qui terminet astris,
> Iulius, a magno demissum nomen Iulo.
> hunc tu olim caelo spoliis Orientis onustum
> accipies secura; vocabitur hic quoque votis.
> aspera tum positis mitescent saecula bellis . . .
>
> (1.286–91)

[There will be born a Trojan Caesar from that splendid line, whose reign will end at the Ocean, whose fame at the stars, Julius, a name derived from great Iulus. Him one day you will receive, without cares, in heaven, loaded with the spoils of the east; he, too, will be called in prayers. Then harsh ages will put aside wars and grow gentle. . .]

There follow unmistakable references to the Augustan age, such as the return of the primeval virtues, the closing of the Gates of War, and the subduing of civil unrest.

The question of the identity of Caesar Iulius has vexed many scholars—is he Julius Caesar or Augustus?[79] The answer is that Vergil is deliberately blurring the line between the two, which is quite consistent with Caesar's role elsewhere in Augustan poetry and, especially, with the use Augustus made of his association with Julius Caesar. It is, as always, a matter of prudently delimiting such resonances: Augustus was as little identified with Caesar in toto as Aeneas is with Achilles, Odysseus, Hercules or, for that matter, Augustus. The poets emphasize Caesar's installation as a god in heaven as a sign of Roman supremacy in the world.[80] In that sense, Augustus was Caesar's heir; hence also the purposeful applicability of the phrase "loaded with the spoils of the east" to both. Augustus certainly was not intent to identify himself

with Caesar the man, though he did not shy away from recalling the precedent of Caesar's actions in the *Res Gestae*. He finished the rebuilding of the
Curia as the Curia Julia and linked his forum to Julius Caesar's (Fig. 119).
Above all, however, he took "Caesar" as his family name, clung assiduously
to Caesar the god, and took a personal interest in his cult, regarding it, quite
possibly, "as a maquette which he had the liberty and time to shape in prep-
aration for his own apotheosis."[81] The Vergilian passage, besides reflecting
the name "Caesar Augustus," is an insightful reflection of this tendency. Its
most palpable visual representation, as we have seen, is the mantle of the
Augustus statue from Prima Porta (Fig. 5), whose particular type, the *Hüftmantel*, is a clear reference to Julius Caesar. The oscillation between the
human and the divine overtones of that statue and the allusion to the
conquest of the east on its armor have their counterpart in the Vergilian
description.

As in all these comparisons, it is not a simple matter of poetry being like
painting, *ut pictura poesis* (Hor., *AP* 361). The general legitimacy, however,
of drawing such parallels in the Augustan context is suggested by an important passage in the *Aeneid*. In book 1, Aeneas, after the encounter with his
mother Venus, proceeds to the city of Carthage. He does not know what to
expect and he has, as yet, no inkling of what kind of people live there. Are
they barbarians or are they civilized? Then he comes upon the temple that
the reader knows was built by Dido for Juno. "Here in this grove," Vergil
writes (1.450–51), "a new thing put in his path allayed his fears" (*hoc primum
in luco nova res oblata timorem / leniit*); "here first did Aeneas dare to hope for
safety and put surer trust in his shattered fortunes": *hic primum Aeneas sperare
salutem / ausus et adflictis melius confidere rebus* (1.451–52). What brings this
change about? The sight of the sculptures on the temple.

Friedrich Klingner has well observed that art here serves as the true touchstone of humanity and as the means by which humanity is recognized.[82] In
the Ciceronian precedent (*Rep.* 1.28–29), a philosopher, possibly Plato, is
shipwrecked on an unknown coast, but assuages the worries of his companions by pointing to the evidence of humans, for he has discovered geo-
metric figures drawn in the sand. It is not the sight of tilled fields that con-
vinces him, but the testimonies of science (*doctrinae indicia*). Vitruvius tells a
similar story about Aristippus (preface to book 6). The point of Cicero's story
is that only those are men in the fullest sense of the word who have the
particular qualities of humanity (*politi propriis humanitatis artibus*). If they
know mathematics, they can be expected to to act like humans toward the
shipwrecked crew.

In the Vergilian passage, there is yet more emphasis, even if through the
eyes of Aeneas, on the empathetic nature of this humanity; hence the famous
line *sunt lacrimae rerum et mentem mortalia tangunt* ("even here tears fall for
human happenings, and things mortal touch the heart"; 1.462). More sig-

nificant, the quintessence of humanity is identified not with science, but with art. That is, of course, entirely commensurate with the important role of art in Augustan Rome. It is in terms of such cultural sensibilities that the *Aeneid* is Augustan without sacrificing any of its timelessness.

Horace

The characterization that has been applied to Horace's *Odes* applies to his work in general: it is "a wonderfully varied collection of poetry."[83] There is no way to reduce that variety to a simple matrix, let alone "ideology": in that sense, Horace's poetry is full of contradictions. While I will concentrate mostly on the *Odes*, his first book of *Epistles*, some of which were written contemporaneously with the *Odes*, is an illustrative backdrop for his independence of mind.[84] Many of the *Epistles* center on philosophy, especially philosophy of human conduct rather than ethics in the strict sense of the word; that in itself is a prime example of Horace's penchant for redefining traditional concepts in his own terms. Not only does he not adhere to any particular sect—*nullius addictus iurare in verba magistri* (*Epist.* 1.1.14)—but he cuts free from the terminology that governed both the questions and the answers of the sects. He is not a seeker who looks for a permanent home in any of the philosophical habitats. Rather, he is a perpetual wanderer or, at most, a guest who does not stay long (*hospes*; *Epist.* 1.1.15; cf. 1.11.11–12). Once more, we see the Augustan theme that the journey is more important than the arrival. Horace uses it to stress that independence is central to him.

His independent thinking is exemplified by the facts of his life, such as we know them. He fought in the army of Brutus and Cassius at Philippi without disavowing supporters of the republic later.[85] His joining with the circle of Maecenas in the 30s was not due to economic exigency because Horace had a good income and comfortable life as an *eques* even before then. More has been preserved of his interchanges and correspondence with Augustus than of those of the other poets. They indicate a bantering tone on both sides. Among other things, Augustus referred to Horace's rotund physique and called him the purest penis, and he tried to entice him to become his private secretary, an offer Horace refused. On both sides, the whole tone suggests a genial informality but also, to put it in modern parlance, a protectiveness of personal space.

Certainly, the conventional dichotomy between public and private poetry is too blunt an instrument for doing justice to the variety and complexity of Horace's poetry. In several poems, the two spheres coalesce, and any attempt to overemphasize one aspect at the expense of the other distorts the intended balance. A famous example is *Ode* 3.14, celebrating the return of Augustus from Spain in 24 B.C. In the first three stanzas, we see the preparations that are made in Rome to celebrate his arrival; they are also a typically Augustan blend between the stylization of a Greek literary motif—the poet, as *vates*, prescribing and describing a ritual[86]—and the infusion of Roman content. Like Hercules, Augustus is coming from Spain to Rome; Horace reuses the Herculean comparison at the beginning of the *Letter to Augustus* (*Epist.* 2.1.10–12). Augustus' wife and the young people of Rome in particular will be leading his welcome. Then the poem turns to the meaning the event holds for the poet:

> hic dies vere mihi festus atras
> eximet curas; ego nec tumultum
> nec mori per vim metuam tenente
>   Caesare terras.
>
>   (13–16)

[This day, truly festive to me, will drive away black cares. I shall fear neither the uproar of civil strife nor death by violence so long as Caesar is holding the earth.]

We saw in *Ode* 2.16 that *cura* and *tumultus* appeared as the opposites of *otium*. Here the context is more specifically related to Augustus: violence has been abolished and order has been restored, producing a security in which Horace can devote himself to his *otium*. It consists of his private celebration with his girlfriend Neaera, who is as real as she is inspired by Greek poetry. This private celebration, in turn, is linked with the theme of the public one by reminiscences about various upheavals in Italy in the past decades: the Social War, the insurrection of Spartacus, and the civil war ending with Philippi. As the times have mellowed, so has Horace: he tells his messenger not to brawl with the girl's doorkeeper. Augustus has rid Rome of *vis*, and Horace will not use it either. The political theme becomes a private one and in poems such as *Ode* 2.16, the human dimension is generalized even further.

The grand ode to Maecenas (3.29) exhibits this interdependence at greater length. This remarkable poem is part of the thematic conclusion to the first three books of *Odes*, which were published as a collection in 23 B.C. Even structurally, there is an almost constant interplay between the world of Maecenas, that of Horace, and that of humanity in general. We begin with the physical setting of Horace's, in the Sabine ambience, where Horace invites Maecenas to join him. That world stands in marked contrast to the conditions in Rome:

> omitte mirari beatae
>   fumum et opes strepitumque Romae.
>
>   (11–12)

[Stop wondering at the smoke, the riches, and the din of blessed Rome.]

The word order mimics what Rome contains: *beatae . . . Romae* enwraps the "riches" of city life with its constant smoke and noise. It is time, then, for Maecenas to enjoy the simplicity of the country and to smooth his furrowed brow (13–16). The country is described in the idyllic images of the reposing shepherd, the grove of Silvanus, silent river banks, and midday breezes (21–24). By contrast, Maecenas is the man of *cura*:

> tu civitatem quis deceat status
> curas et urbi sollicitus times
>   quid Seres et regnata Cyro
>   Bactra parent Tanaisque discors.
>
> (25–28)

[You worry about the proper condition for the state and you, anxious for the city, fear what the Seres may be plotting, and Bactria once ruled by Cyrus and the quarrelsome tribes on the Tanais' banks.]

In Horace's typical fashion, the private and the public world are not played off against one another. Instead, they merge into that of general human conduct. We cannot see the future and therefore, placed in the very center of the poem (lines 32–33), stands the maxim: *quod adest memento / componere aequus* ("remember with an even mind to put in order what is at hand"). True control of affairs comes from within and from the realization of our limitations:

> ille potens sui
> laetusque deget, cui licet in diem
>   dixisse: "vixi."
>
> (41–43)

[That man will live happily as master of himself who can say each day: "I have lived."]

With this, there is no more direct mention of Maecenas, and the final four stanzas deal with Horace's acceptance of vicissitude and with his divine protection amid the storms of life. While expressing an unchanging affection for Maecenas, the overall movement in the *Odes* that Horace addressed to him is in the direction of independence.[87] This is done for aesthetic effect and does not reflect a biographic development: Horace maintained his personal and artistic freedom from the start.

Hence, the eighty-eight poems in *Odes* 1–3 are as variegated in attitude and topic as they are in meter: there is never any "aesthetic indigestion."[88] Most of them are what we would call occasional poetry, and subjects such as love and drinking keep recurring. The wellspring for others is moral concern. Even the so-called Roman Odes (3.1–6), however, which often have been used to cast too one-sided a perspective on Horace, are not panegyrics on the *princeps*—if such had been Horace's aim, he passed up many an opportunity in this collection.[89] Rather, they emphasize the need to reach a goal, and the process involved in that effort. This intellectual and moral attitude also affects the poetic aesthetic.

Ode 3.2 provides a good illustration.[90] Horace starts out with an exhortation to young Romans to observe the virtue of "poverty that constrains" (*angustam pauperiem*), in other words, a life-style not characterized by hankering after wealth but emphasizing unselfishness and hard work. Such conditioning will benefit the soldier fighting against the Parthians. The next sequence is not quite what we would expect: the young Augustan soldier is seen through the eyes of a Parthian princess who fears that her lover will be mangled by the lionlike Roman. Both her perspective and the reference to Homeric single combat contribute to the movement of the poem in anything but a simply straightforward fashion. Then comes the famous maxim, quoted by many different men for many different purposes over the centuries, that "it is sweet and glorious to die for one's country" (*dulce et decorum est pro patria mori*; line 13), but the rationale again is unexpectedly unconventional: death catches up even to the coward who runs from battle. Therefore, by implication, it is better to confront it bravely.

This leads, in the next two stanzas (17–24), to the definition of *virtus*. It was, as we have seen, an essential Augustan concept, and Horace does well not to present it in a standardized way. First, he gives an example of what it is and what it is not:

> Virtus repulsae nescia sordidae
> intaminatis fulget honoribus,
> nec sumit aut ponit securis
>   arbitrio popularis aurae.
>
> (17–20)

[Courage, knowing no disgrace in defeat (at elections), shines with untarnished honors, nor does it take up or put down the axes (of office) at the whim of popular favor.]

Horace captures an essential quality of Augustan *virtus*: it comes from within. We might note, too, that the example would be pointless if elections had been unimportant at Augustus' time.

Another fundamental aspect of Augustan *virtus* was that it connoted ongoing effort. That concept also is articulated by Horace, albeit in his own way:

> Virtus, recludens immeritis mori
> caelum, negata temptat iter via,

>   coetusque vulgaris et udam
>   spernit humum fugiente penna.
>
>   (21–24)

[Courage that opens up heaven to those who do not deserve to die attempts a journey along a path (usually) denied, and disdains the vulgar crowds and damp earth with escaping wing.]

We have moved from the notion that death is inevitable in some circumstances, especially on the battlefield, and therefore should be faced courageously, to the more positive articulation of the immortalizing power of *virtus*. Significantly, and reflecting the Augustan ethos, Horace emphasizes concepts like journey and trial. They proceed along uncommon routes—the road less traveled by, indeed. It is the same courage displayed by the statesman of the *Aeneid*'s first simile in front of the *ignobile vulgus* (1.149). The image of soaring to the heavens (thus leaving behind the earth) on wings recalls Horace's prediction of his own immortality in *Ode* 2.20.

The final two stanzas deal with silence and especially the punishment for breaking it. Again, the connection with what precedes is not routine. Horace starts out by paraphrasing a line from Simonides that was one of Augustus' favorite quotes ("a gift without harm is that of silence") and significantly adds the Roman notion of *fides* (*fideli silentio*; 25). His example of a breaker of silence is someone who violates the mysteries at Eleusis; if Horace harbored such a transgressor, he would risk being destroyed himself because "the sky-father, when ignored, punishes the innocent along with the guilty," and punishment always catches up with the guilty. Now *virtus* is a broad concept and the private virtue of being discreet can be accommodated within it in a general way, though it is not exactly the point we might expect Horace to make at the conclusion of the ode. More specific links have been suggested, ranging from a reference to Cornelius Gallus' hubris to the emphasis, throughout the poem, on human initiative. Moreover, the poem is connected with several others where *virtus* is a personal concern of Horace's.[91]

The central characteristic, illustrated on the aesthetic level by the scholars' concern about confused imagery, gaps, and unpredictable connections, is that Horace does not pontificate or pretend to greater certainty than his audience. He holds to a moral core, but he illustrates the process of trying to reach it by exploring its various aspects and contradictions. Just as basic is the fact that Horace, instead of being a mere imperial versifier, carries on a creative dialogue with the Augustan milieu. He reacts to some of its ideas and reshapes them in his own way. Above all, he is never passive.

We can illustrate some of these aspects further. In the prologue to his *Aitia*, the Hellenistic poet Callimachus rejected the writing of longer and more weighty poems about kings and heroes in preference for his own kind of

"slender" poetry.[92] The contrast has been reduced unnecessarily to that between epic versus elegy; what is important is that the Augustan poets took
their lead from Callimachus and wrote *recusationes*—that is, poems in which
they expressed their refusal to write on such grand themes, citing various
reasons for their unwillingness. A Horatian example is *Ode* 1.6, addressed to
Agrippa, where Horace suggests that his colleague Varius Rufus is really far
better suited for this kind of poetic endeavor than Horace. The precise mix
of real pressures, if any, and the choice of the topic for art's sake varies from
recusatio to *recusatio* and remains elusive. Ovid, who marks the end of the
development, seems to have played with this kind of theme as he did with
others. But another inspiration suggests itself. It was part of Augustus' *auctoritas* to recuse himself from honors and offices he was offered (*RG* 5–6.1). Just
about every year he was in Rome, Augustus received a donation, usually of
silver, from the senate and the people to have a statue made of himself. Just
as habitually, Augustus would refuse and instead use the material more suitably, as, for instance, for a statue of the goddess Pax in 11 B.C. (Dio 54.35.2).
Or, as we saw earlier, he refused consulships and the office of *curator legum et
morum*. He was independent and secure enough in his *auctoritas* to do so. So
were the poets. Such requests added to his *auctoritas* and theirs, and the refusals augmented it even more.

Another aspect in which Horace is representative of a general Augustan
trend is his predilection for multireferentiality. This is an awkward term, but
"ambiguity" in English does not quite denote what the Romans meant by
ambiguitas. "Ambiguity," like "ambivalence," has strong overtones of uncertainty and the inability to make a decision; this quality, not surprisingly, has
enhanced its appeal among academics as a favorite *modus interpretandi*. *Ambiguitas*, by contrast, was oriented more positively toward the exploration of
multiple meanings.[93] This was a characteristic of the Latin language: since
there is a basic and limited vocabulary, words take on multiple meanings
(rather than new words being created for each new meaning). From there
the phenomenon is carried over to syntactical constructions. This allows for
suggestive latitude within the framework of a clear overall concept, which is
not at all ambiguous in the English sense of the word. The phenomenon is
pervasive: it applies to Roman law, to the *Res Gestae*, and essential Augustan
concepts such as *auctoritas*. The same multireferentiality characterizes Augustan art and Augustan poems like the *Aeneid*. In Horace, another reason for its
appeal to the Romans is more readily discernible than in the larger and more
complex works of Augustan literature, namely, the liking the Latins had for
riddles and conundrums. This entire background explains, too, why Augustus could aptly be called "chameleon."[94]

A few examples must suffice. One of the vignettes of seekers of *otium* in
Ode 2.16 involves the Thracians: *otium (rogat) bello furiosa Thrace* (line 5). They
were a proverbially warlike people; hence *bello* can be taken as modifying

furiosa: even war-mad Thrace is asking for *otium*. Alternatively the phrase can mean that "(even) wild Thrace, in war, asks for *otium*." The second reading is more topical as Rome subdued the Thracians after heavy fighting in 27 B.C., but it does not exclude the first. In *Ode* 3.9, placed not far from the "Roman Odes," a love duet between Horace and one of his former girlfriends occurs. Both contemplate ridding themselves of their current lovers and reuniting. "What if the old love returns," asks Horace, "if fair-haired Chloe is shaken off and the door is open *reiectae Lydiae*?" (17–20). *Reiectae Lydiae* can be genitive or dative; either Horace returns to the open door of his rejected former love or his door stands open to her. The popular motif of the poem is a congenial context for the riddle and the double meaning. By contrast, the *ambiguitas* of the first stanza of *Ode* 3.5 captures the elusiveness and elasticity of Augustus' divinity. He was, as we will see in chapter 6, not honored as an actual god during his lifetime in Rome, though he was extensively assimilated to deities, including his deified adoptive father, in Rome and Italy. Outside of Rome, he was worshiped as a god in both east and west. Here is Horace's phrasing:

> caelo tonantem credidimus Iovem
> regnare: praesens divus habebitur
> Augustus adiectis Britannis
> imperio gravibusque Persis.
>
> (*C.* 3.5.1–4)

[We have always believed that the thundering Jupiter reigns in heaven; Augustus will be held as god present (*either:*) when the Britons and the dangerous Persians have been added to the empire (*or:*) even for the Britons and the dangerous Persians once they have been added to the empire].

Several of the expressions used by Horace have more than one meaning. *Caelo* can go with both *tonantem* and *regnare*, and *praesens* can mean "immediately at hand and discernible" (cf. *Epist.* 2.1.15) or someone who reveals his power. Most important, there are three possibilities for the phrase *adiectis . . . Persis*: (1) "now that Augustus has added the Britons and Persians to the empire." That would be extravagant flattery since the poem was written probably in 27 or 26 B.C. when such a conquest was far from a reality. (2) "When he will have added the Britons and Persians to the empire." This sounds like an unbecoming condition: only if Augustus conquers these outlying peoples will he become a god. (3) "One day, he will be a god even to the conquered Britons and Persians" (cf. *C.* 4.14.41–48). The statement is matter-of-fact and is coupled with the actuality of the continuing expansion of the empire. The problematic immediacy of the *praesens divus* in Rome is deftly transposed to the realistic future. Even if that is the major meaning of the phrase, however, the reader is at least asked to reflect on the others. In all this, there is the typically Augustan attempt to assimilate multiple and contradictory aspects.

The fourth book of *Odes*, published after 13 B.C., represents the height of the fusion between the poet Horace and the Augustan milieu.[95] The relationship, as always, is far more subtle than Horace's being a mere apostle of the regime. In these fifteen poems, Horace sets a monument to himself as well as to Augustan Rome. Even more specifically, he emphasizes again and again the importance of poetry to assure a truly lasting achievement for worldly deeds, leaders, and civilizations that are otherwise subject to the ineluctability of time. With this comes a yet greater intensity of the lyric form concentrating on festivity and ritual, and resulting in a new "poetic dynamism."[96] For the poet, the celebration of the Augustan present under the *species* of poetic eternity is completely integrated with his own creative past: there is a constant recurrence and original reworking of many of the themes from *Odes* 1–3. In 4.15, particularly, the parallelism between the courses of Roman history and Roman poetry from their origins to the present is pervasive. Along with the celebration of Romans past and present go the allusions to Lucretius, Propertius, Vergil, and Horace himself. The two final stanzas become the true summation:

> nosque et profestis lucibus et sacris
> inter iocosi munera Liberi
>   cum prole matronisque nostris,
>   rite deos prius adprecati,
> virtute functos more patrum duces
> Lydis remixto carmine tibiis
>   Troiamque et Anchisen et almae
>   progeniem Veneris canemus.
>
> (25–32)

[And we, on common and sacred days, amid the gifts of merry Bacchus, with our children and wives will first duly pray to the gods; then, in the manner of our fathers, in song accompanied by Lydian flutes, we will sing of those who have shown courage, and of Troy, and Anchises, and and the offspring of fostering Venus.]

Here are the ritual and the celebration (in honor of Bacchus, which shows once more that ideological Antonian interpretations of the god are not warranted after the triumviral period); as on the Ara Pacis, we see the Romans with their families, reflecting the importance of the marital legislation; the significance of *virtus* is clear; the flawed progeny in the pessimistic coda to the "Roman Odes" (*C.* 3.6.45–48) yields to that of the nourishing Venus, especially the Julians; the "I" of the proud *sphragis* of the first collection, *Ode* 3.30, cedes to the communal "we"; Troy, Anchises, and Venus' offspring recall the *Aeneid*, as *canemus*, the last word in Horace's lyric poetry, recalls *cano*, the first verb in the *Aeneid*. *Cano*, as Servius observed,[97] is polysemous: it can mean "praise," "prophesy," and "sing." Schoolmaster that he was, he decided that Vergil used it in that last sense. That does not exclude the presence of the other connotations, and the polysemy is even more marked in Horace: he sings, he praises, and he is a seer. It is a fitting note, not in the least because of the intentionally polysemous nature of so much of Augustan culture, on which Horace ends his greatest and most innovative achievement, his lyric poetry.

Two final aspects of Horace's work need to be mentioned briefly. One is that there are considerable thematic affinities between *Odes* 4, in particular *Ode* 4.15, and Augustan monuments such as the Ara Pacis and the Augustan forum.[98] Besides exemplifying the need to study Augustan culture wholly, the common themes suggest a reciprocity of inspiration that is very much in accordance with the workings of Augustan *auctoritas*. Second, while we may deprecate the conventional portrait of Horace as an amiable, cheerful, and comfortable exemplar of golden-mean contentment in favor of greater complexities, we would be wrong to minimize the geniality, good humor, and humane attitudes that characterize so much of his poetry, especially the *Satires* and *Epistles*. The age was not lacking in such characteristics as we saw earlier in connection with what Pliny called "the most pleasant kind of wall painting," and Augustus himself was noted for his sense of humor. It is for good reason, therefore, that the setting of the conclusion of Horace's *Odes* is "amid the gifts of jocose Bacchus" (*C.* 4.15.26). *Virtus* (line 29) and this kind of joyful *humanitas* were complementary. Already in the first ode to Augustus (*C.* 1.2) his ancestress Venus, who is mentioned again at the end of 4.15, appeared in the company of Iocus (1.2.34) and was appropriately smiling (*ridens;* 1.2.33).

Ovid's *Metamorphoses*

The *Metamorphoses*[99] is the most representative work of late Augustan literature. It is the product of the security and sophisticated ambience of the *pax Augusta*. Its raconteurial geniality should not mislead us: it was a highly ambitious undertaking, one, in fact, that was without precedent, as Ovid rightly emphasizes in the very first line of the poem (*in nova fert animus*). We took note earlier of the Augustan concern that an extended period of prosperity and tranquillity should not lead to cultural inertia. The brilliant, creative achievement of Ovid's poem suggests that such was far from being the case.

In its own way, therefore, the *Metamorphoses* is as Augustan as any literary work of that long and changing period. The fundamental characteristics we isolated at the beginning of this chapter—evolution, experimentation, complexity, and transcendence of the times—could easily be shown to apply in detail to Ovid's unique poem. But within their framework we can be even more specific and examine some of the poem's special aspects that relate to both the Augustan milieu and the remarkable reception of the *Metamorphoses* in later times.

Formally, the *Metamorphoses* mimics the tendency toward universal history in Augustan times. It achieves its true universality, however, because it comprises a truly comprehensive range both of literary traditions and genres and of depicting human emotions.

The first of these aspects reaches back to Homer, and the choice of that literary model tells us a great deal about the universality Ovid wanted to achieve. The ancient view was that all the literary forms took their origin with Homer. He was the "Ocean" from which all literary streams flowed.[100] Vergil's *Aeneid*, "greater than the *Iliad*" in Propertius' famous phrase (2.34.66), also represented an attempt to "reabsorb into . . . epic all the diverse forms of literature which had originated from the Homeric epics,"[101] but its fundamental seriousness kept it from including genres such as comedy and burlesque. By contrast, there were no such limitations for Ovid. The *Metamorphoses* is a kaleidoscope of literary forms and moods—drama both comic and tragic, mime, hymn, catalog poetry, epic, epigram, epyllion, and elegy, to name only the most important. Compared with the work of Vergil, there is a definite change of perspective; whereas the *Aeneid* started out with the Roman experience, as embodied principally in one myth, and proceeded to view it under the *species* of human eternity, the scope of the *Metamorphoses* and its 250 myths is the variety of human experience in general. It can be applied to the Romans and their experience, though by no means exclusively so, if that is what the reader wishes to do.

The mixture of styles and genres in Ovid's work was a thoroughly Augustan phenomenon not only in literature but as we have seen, also in art and architecture.[102] The sculptural decoration of the Ara Pacis exemplifies this comprehensive fusion, including Hellenistic elements. So does the Forum of Augustus where the architectural ornamentation draws on all Greek styles.[103] The *Metamorphoses*, written mostly in the decade after the completion of the Augustan forum in 2 B.C., is a perfect analogue in poetry of the Augustan mixture of styles. Another architectural contemporary, which exhibits the same tendencies and was completed two year's before Ovid's exile in A.D. 6, was the rebuilding of the Temple of the Dioscuri in the Roman Forum.[104]

A second, important aspect of the *Metamorphoses* is that it was conceived as an alternative to the *Aeneid*. For all we can tell, Ovid did not suffer greatly from the anxiety of influence. He understood the meaning of Vergil's epic probably better than any reader has since; merely in terms of verbal reminiscences, the *Metamorphoses* is an almost constant dialogue with the *Aeneid*.[105]

Vergil reendowed myth with the sort of serious, metaphysical dimensions it had possessed in Hesiod and Aeschylean drama or, to follow the categories of G. S. Kirk,[106] its speculative, explanatory, and validatory functions. Myth, in that sense, serves to explain or offer a solution for a problem, often a complex problem, that defies ultimate rational analysis. By contrast, Ovid, while not depriving myth of these qualities, does not emphasize them. Instead he brings out, in an unequaled fashion, myth's narrative and entertaining qualities. He chose the metamorphosis theme for that very reason. Whereas its importance as a subject often is quite tangential, it is the imaginative qualities of metamorphosis that shape the spirit of the poem. Foremost among them is that metamorphosis provides an untragic and noncommittal solution to any problems, especially moral problems. Daphne is pursued by Apollo; the problem disappears when she is changed into a tree. In the Erysichthon story (8.738–878) the untragic way out is effected not even by a metamorphosis, but by the protagonist's devouring himself in the end. People may suffer, experience the most unusual passions, and reach an impasse that begs for some profound discussion, but neither does such an exploration materialize nor do they die: they just are metamorphosed into animals, plants, or stones.

The result is an extraordinarily creative tension between the moral dimension of the myths and its narrative effacement by Ovid. The story of Actaeon (3.131–252), for instance, raises serious questions about divine justice. In contrast to earlier versions that had emphasized Actaeon's just punishment by Jupiter because he had wooed Semele (Apollod. 3.4.4), Ovid maintains Actaeon's innocence:

> per nemus ignotum non certis passibus errans
> pervenit in lucum: sic illum fata ferebant.
>
> (3.175–76)

[He comes wandering through the unfamiliar woods with unsure footsteps, and enters Diana's grove; for so his fate would have it.]

Ovid deliberately injects the notion of *fata*, which is full of possible meanings, but just as deliberately refuses to elaborate on it. It is really the pique of Diana that is Actaeon's downfall. There is no great outburst of moral outrage on her part, because the offense would not warrant it. Instead, she tersely sums up her resentment:

> nunc tibi me posito visam velamine narres,
> si poteris narrare, licet!
>
> (3.192–93)

[Now you are free to tell that you have seen me all unrobed—if you can tell!]

The Vergilian reader would be familiar with such behavior: at the very beginning of the *Aeneid*, Juno's motivation for persecuting Aeneas was presented in terms of similarly petty vindictiveness. The result in the *Aeneid* is one of the great theodicies in Western literature, whereas the result in the *Metamorphoses* is one of the great tours de force of epic style: a catalog of Actaeon's thirty-four dogs (3.206–24), all mangling their master (by now turned into a stag) to the tune of impeccable dactylic hexameters. Bravura narration of this sort tends to distract even the most metaphysically oriented reader, though Ovid typically raises the underlying issue once more at the end of the story, albeit in a most general and inconclusive way. Some people, he says, talked about the matter this way, and others, the other way, and both had their reasons:

> Rumor in ambiguo est: aliis violentior aequo
> visa dea est, alii laudant dignamque severa
> virginitate vocant; pars invenit utraque causas.

> (3.253–55)

> [As the tale spread, views varied; some believed
> Diana's violence unjust; some praised it,
> As proper to her chaste virginity.
> Both sides found reason for their point of view.]

> (trans. Melville)

When we try to locate the author's point of view, we are faced with considerable elusiveness. From the perspective of reader participation, however, which in typical Augustan fashion is strongly invited, the effect is to open up the narration of the myths to various reader responses. But in contrast to Vergil, Ovid does not force the reader to become embroiled in conflicting arguments. The serious-minded may do so, while Ovid's narration helps most readers glide pleasantly over deeper undercurrents. The enjoyment is intellectual rather than moral: the more familiar the audience is with the many-layered traditions of each myth, the more it will be able to understand Ovid's sophisticated allusions and reworkings.

It has often been argued that because of Ovid's emphases (or deemphases), he is not "Augustan" in the sense of not sharing Augustus' own literary preferences. As Suetonius informs us,

> in reading Greek and Roman writers there was nothing for which he looked so carefully as precepts and examples that were salutary for the public or for individuals; these he would often copy word for word and send to members of his household, or to his generals and provincial governors, whenever any of them required admonition. (*Aug.* 89.2)

This is the time-honored, didactic or utilitarian view of literature, the Horatian *prodesse* (*AP* 333). But there was another side even to Augustus himself without which Horace's long plaints about the state of Roman drama would be pointless. Augustus fully shared the populace's enthusiasm for nonliterary spectacles such as the mime and the pantomime. After the bad times of the civil wars, it was not surprising that the public should have been tired of tragic subjects and unwilling to experience pity and fear through the deep involvement and shared spiritual experience that tragedy demanded. Full-blown tragic performances still had flourished during the final decades of the republic when the tragic horror corresponded to contemporary realities. By contrast, the public of the *pax Augusta* was bored with the endlessly repeated subjects of tragedy, but it did not want to part with them either.

The new dramatic form that made allowance for the changed taste of the public was the pantomime. The tragic pantomime, which survived to the end of antiquity, took the place of tragedy. The subjects were taken from Greek mythology or else the pantomime consisted of single scenes taken from tragedies. The scenes were taken out of their context and the tragic impact of the total drama thus disappeared. The tendency was reinforced by an emphasis on the most sensational and visually gripping episodes; Oedipus' blinding, for instance, relegated like other such acts of violence to a messenger speech in Greek drama, now was shown in performance. What mattered was not the tragic content or the "message," but the actor's versatility. Even the element of change was involved: "One actor performed the most diverse roles with changing masks while either a chorus or one interpreter sang or declaimed the content of the story."[107] It amounted, like the writing of the *Metamorphoses*, to a cultivated solo performance that required, on the actor's part, a good knowledge of mythology and a superior education. Shortly after its introduction in 22 B.C., the tragic pantomime became the rage and its stars, the darlings of the higher classes. This is precisely the public for which Ovid wrote.

For the leisured generation, therefore, that knew only the *pax Augusta*, the presentation of mythology in a tragic, profoundly moral vein was out of fashion. The emphasis on single scenes in the *Metamorphoses*, the narrator's bravura performance, his sophistication, the constant shifts and changes, and the graphic, visual appeal of many scenes all have their counterpart in the pantomime. Conversely, the pantomimic qualities of episodes like that of Narcissus (3.339–510) are striking. Besides, in the most comprehensive ancient discussion of the nature of the pantomime, Lucian's *On Dance*, the scope of the pantomimic artist's undertaking is defined in terms that are very similar to Ovid's *primaque ab origine mundi ad mea . . . tempora* (*Met.* 1.3–4): "Beginning with chaos and the primal origin of the world, he must know everything down to the story of Cleopatra the Egyptian" (Lucian, *Salt.* 37).

Lucian's speaker follows this up with a catalog of myths, which has been supplemented with the titles of pantomimes found in other authors, and only a very few are not among the myths that Ovid tells in the *Metamorphoses*.

Even with all these affinities, however, it is important not to confuse terms: avoidance of moral problems is not the same as being unserious. At bottom, Ovid's undertaking was most serious: to present a lasting alternative to Vergil's interpretation of myth. Nor does the narrative of the *Metamorphoses* proceed in one key; rather, it ranges widely from the deeply moving to the hilariously grotesque with every imaginable shading and tone in between.

Still, it is appropriate to give special attention to the humor of the work because humor is part of Augustan *humanitas*.[108] The emperor himself, as we have seen, was no exception. Humor was a constituent part, too, of Horace's oeuvre, but its pervasiveness in the *Metamorphoses* is something special. More is involved than comedy. Rather, it is the kind of *perpetua festivitas* Cicero described in *De Oratore* (2.219). As such it is very appropriate for Ovid's *perpetuum carmen* (*Met.* 1.4). It subsumes the other category of humor defined by Cicero as *dicacitas*, that is, the verbal, manipulative, and artistic kind; this includes conceits, word plays, clever interjections, some of the literary parodies and allusions, double and even triple entendres, the incongruous use of epic devices such as similes, the *bon mot*, and others. Much of this Dryden would classify as "wit," but *perpetua festivitas* is the sum instead of the parts. It is an ongoing attitude that is integral to the spirit of the *Metamorphoses* not in the least because play and humor are essential qualities of myth. It also keeps the right equilibrium between detached amusement and sympathy and contributes to the narrative exuberance of the poem.

Ovid's version of the underworld (4.432–80) is an extensive example.[109] It had been a set piece in epic and other poetry since Homer and certainly had its pitfalls by Vergil's time: few sophisticated readers would believe in the literal truth of details such as the ferryman Charon, Cerberus, frogs, and subterranean swamps and firmaments. Vergil overcame this handicap by hinting at the end of *Aeneid* 6 that not all of it should be taken literally, and, far more so, by endowing the descent to the underworld with unprecedented metaphysical and spiritual dimensions. Significantly, Ovid did not choose the easy alternative of presenting the anachronistic mythological details as high camp. Instead, with a delightful sense of the incongruous, he almost completely demythologizes Hades and its horrors by humanizing them. For instance: the underworld is a city, and the main problem the new shades have is that they don't know their way around it and have trouble finding Hades' kingly abode (*regia*; 437–38).[110] Further, Ovid continues, it is really quite remarkable that with all the influx of newcomers the place somehow never becomes too small; implicitly, no extension of the *pomerium* is needed. Most of the crowd, as could be expected, throngs the forum. In their professions, too, they simply mimic their old behavior (445); it is telling that the next line, mentioning punishment as the reason for the activities of others, almost certainly is not Ovidian, but a later addition by pious hands.

When we encounter Cerberus, Ovid calls attention to the remarkable fact that his three heads barked in consonance (451). Nor are the Furies hell's loathsome monsters. Rather, they are occupied with combing the snakes out of their hairs (454), and they rise politely when Juno approaches. Sure enough, since by now we have reached the deepest pit of hell, we get a glimpse of famous penitents such as Tantalus, Sisyphus, and Ixion. Instead of the Vergilian admonition, however, to "learn justice by such warnings and not to scorn the gods" (*Aen*. 6.620), we are left with the paradox of Ixion who is racked on the wheel (461): "Ixion is turned around and around; he both flees from and follows himself" (*volvitur Ixion et se sequiturque fugitque*). It is all a matter of perspective. The humanization of Tisiphone continues against the backdrop of Vergil's Allecto: once more she shakes her snake-hair out of her face before she addresses Juno (474–75) and Ovid presents her onslaught, with snakes and all, on Athamas and Ino (481–511) as a circus act rather than the external manifestation of an inner process, as was the case with Turnus' succumbing to Allecto's madness (*Aen*. 7.412–74). When she has done her job, she goes back to Pluto's realm and "unbuckles the snake she had strapped around her waist" (*sumptumque recingitur anguem;* 511), just like a police officer taking off her belt at the end of the day.[111]

Ovid's humor is not mordant or destructive. E. J. Kenney has well observed that "there is *gravitas* enough and to spare elsewhere in Roman literature."[112] Nor would it make any sense to posit false dichotomies. *Humanitas* comprised both seriousness and humorous charm, and ancient literary critics, who looked at more than rhetorical utility, had only warm praise for writers who had the ability to treat somber subjects with charm and wit (Demetrius, *On Style* 134–35). Humor has a liberating quality as well, contributing to no small degree to the creation of *homo Ovidianus*, freed from the past. Besides painting—and the connections between the *Metamorphoses* and the visual arts have rightly received much emphasis—the spirit behind the depictions on a late Augustan silver bowl is akin to Ovid's (Fig. 126). It is different from the mentality that led to the conversion of the randy god Priapus (Figs. 127a and b) into a figure of *dignitas*: fully dressed, with archaic features, and adorned with little boys who are testimony to his reproductive powers harnessed by the Augustan legislation on marriage and morals. On the silver crater, the floral ornamentation and its basic symmetry are indebted to the public monuments. Along with the flowers, however, the stems sprout pudgy babies who animatedly move along the thinnest of branches, catch fish, and even hunt crayfish. Zanker has well observed that Augustan artists

126. Augustan silver bowl. Playful adaptation of floral scroll and Cupids.

could engage in this kind of playful inventiveness when they were not obligated to convey serious meanings,[113] and the characterization is quite apropos for the *Metamorphoses* and the genius behind it. Like the artifact, however, Ovid's poem gains its deliberate resonance only when compared with
Vergil's and others. In the Augustan context, the *Aeneid* and the *Metamorphoses* are complements rather than opposites.

   It is misguided, therefore, to overinterpret the reasons for Ovid's banishment. For someone who enjoyed life in Augustan Rome to the fullest, it was
punishment that reached to the core and reveals the uncompromisingly harsh
side of Augustus that coexisted with his appreciation of humor and charm. In

127a. Archaizing statue of draped
Priapus with small children.

127b. Archaizing head of Priapus.

his prolix apologia (*Trist.* 2), Ovid says there were two reasons: a poem (*carmen*) and a serious transgression of some sort (*error*). The poem, most probably the *Art of Love*, had been published years earlier and was no more than a pretext. And despite Ovid's frequent references to the *error*, the rest is silence, an attitude we must respect precisely because it is so uncharacteristic of Ovid.[114]

Elegy: Propertius and Tibullus

Roman love elegy is a specifically Augustan phenomenon.[115] Its founder, Cornelius Gallus, born approximately in the same year as Horace, had a brilliant military and administrative career as a friend of Octavian/Augustus. He became the first prefect of the *princeps*' private province of Egypt but was recalled to Rome for malfeasance, including an excessive personality cult.

Threatened with prosecution, he committed suicide in 27 or 26 B.C. Only a few lines of his poetry have survived. The end point of elegy's development comes with Ovid.

This particular literary form, therefore, is a paradigm of the larger question of whether there would have been an Augustan culture without Augustus. The answer is: perhaps, but certainly not in the same way. Roman elegy is a product of its cultural ambience.[116] It is in large part—and I will focus especially on Tibullus and Propertius—a constant dialogue with Augustan themes that is anything but one-dimensional. As I noted earlier, Propertius and Tibullus belong to the "middle" generation whose formative experience had been the civil war between Antony and Octavian. They construct their own world, a poetic one which should not be pressed for biographic details. Nor should it be simplified into an antiworld (*Gegenwelt*) of constant provocation and inversion of Augustan society and its values. Instead, it includes a wide variety of reactions to that "real" world and, especially, a wide and complex range of appropriations from that world for the world of their poetry. The first poem of Tibullus' collection is a good example.

Its themes are easily recognizable as Augustan: the rejection of wealth and of greed for gold and huge possessions (lines 1–2); by contrast, *paupertas* (5), which, as always in the Augustan context, "is not 'poverty' in the modern sense but 'simple sufficiency without surplus'";[117] further, assiduous *labor* (3); a commitment to the life of the *rusticus* (9) with an extended listing of various deities—such as Spes (9), Ceres (15), the Lares (20), and Pales (36)—that underscores the *pietas* of Tibullus the country dweller. Less is more: Tibullus is *contentus vivere parvo* (25) and he conjures up the sort of details typical of the existence of a Philemon and Baucis, such as a modest table and earthen vessels (37–38). The application of these themes, however, is Tibullus' own. In the first part of the poem (1–53), he contrasts the man who has an active and perilous existence with the (relatively) inert life (5) of the *rusticus*. In contrast to the *Georgics*, where the ethic of unceasing effort was exemplified by the farmer's existence, *labor adsiduus* now characterizes the farmer's foil, the man who is acquisitive. This does not result in a condemnation: Tibullus' farm once was better off and now has fallen into more modest circumstances that were not of his will (19); it is hard not to relate this to the confiscations of 42 B.C. Certainly, the man who takes risks is entitled to their fruits (49–50). But such is not Tibullus' way of life. We hear little of hard work on his farm—again, it is irrelevant to speculate whether that farm really existed—and its description merges into the fantasy that his urban lover, the elegiac *domina*, will join him in the country (45–48).

This leads to the second part of the poem (53–78) that juxtaposes the existence of the lover with the one of the warrior, personified by Tibullus' patron Messalla. The latter wages war on land and sea (*terra marique*), which echoes the Augustan motto *terra marique pax*; war, of course, was the precondition for *pax*. By contrast, the lover once more is indolent (*iners*, 58). That inactivity leads to thoughts about death; the analogue in the public realm was the concern that extended periods of peace and tranquillity tended to produce inertia and decline. Tibullus, therefore, ends the poem by shifting the notion of inertia to old age (71) and depicting his vigor as a youthful lover: he breaks down doors and starts a fight. And he proceeds to contrast this kind of "warfare" with the real thing:

> hic ego dux milesque bonus: vos, signa tubaeque,
>   ite procul, cupidis volnera ferte viris,
> ferte et opes: ego conposito securus acervo
>   despiciam dites despiciamque famem.

(75–78)

[In this respect I am a good leader and warrior: away with you, standards and trumpets. Bring wounds to greedy men, bring riches also: free from cares and from the heap I have piled up, I'll look down on both riches and hunger.]

The last line typefies the balance that prevails throughout the poem. Tibullus does not use his foils in order to denigrate them—he once was a real soldier and wants his epitaph to read that he followed Messalla *terra marique* (1.3.56)—nor does he consider his current pursuits inferior to theirs. *Desidia*, *inertia*, and *nequitia*—all meaning "worthlessness"—are standard elegiac terms for the love poets' alternative life-style. In this introductory poem, Tibullus suggests that the difference between the *vita activa* and his is limited to material aspects. In moral terms, they are equivalent: his "indolence" is justified by his attachment to the rustic life and its piety. He knows of the Vergilian farmer's ethic of incessant effort, but transfers it to the life-style of his foils in order to incorporate into his poem the longings Vergil expressed in the grand finale of *Georgics* 2.[118] There Vergil stresses the peace of the country, the rejection of fame (*Geo.* 2.496; cf. Tib. 1.1.57), and the bliss of the man "who knows the rural gods" (*Geo.* 2.493), and he contrasts the farmer's existence with the ambition of others. There is also a reminiscence of the themes of Horace's *Ode* 2.16 on *cura*;[119] significantly, Tibullus is *securus* and echoes the Horatian principle of the golden mean in the final line. The fact that his first book appeared before Horace published his first collection of *Odes* is another testimony to the commonality and evolution of some basic Augustan themes.

A further illustration is the phenomenon that Tibullus does not reject Augustan values,[120] but adapts them for himself and in his own way. For instance, after the introduction of Messalla as a military man, Tibullus appropriates military pursuits as a metaphor to characterize his own amatory activities. It expresses, all at once, recognition of the normal societal standard,

128. Marble table leg with sphinxes and vine scrolls.

dissociation from it, and a striving for equivalence: what I am doing in my realm, Messalla, is equally as privileged as what you are doing in yours; your actions are a model for mine. This sort of transference began with Catullus; when he totaled up the kisses exchanged between him and his mistress (5.7–10), he mimicked the serious bookkeepers of the business world. The military metaphor became a popular one in Augustan elegy[121] and was accompanied by an efflorescence of similar appropriations. They include the characterization of the relationship between the two unmarried lovers in terms of the values governing marriage, such as *fides*;[122] the use of the triumph as a figure for the poets' own achievement;[123] the utilization of the stuff of epic, especially the Troy myth, for the portrayal of the lovers and their affairs; and the espousal of *pax* as the operative principle of love (Prop. 3.5; Tib. 1.10). Similar adaptations involve themes such as the Parthian Wars and the condemnation of vices like *luxuria* and *avaritia*.

The poets' stance in all of these is characterized by a great deal of fluidity. Before we return to some representative examples, it is useful to enlarge our perspective by looking at a related phenomenon in the arts. That is the adaptation of official and public motifs for private purposes.[124] Augustan emblems such as Victoria, the *corona civica*, the sphinx, the two laurel trees of his house, and representations of Aeneas now turn up as decorative elements in private art and monuments, from furniture to funerary reliefs. The decoration of a marble table support, for instance, consists of the type of floral scroll familiar from the Ara Pacis and of sphinxes in the early classical style (Fig. 128). Another table implement (Fig. 129), made of bronze, is styled as Victoria, standing on the globe and holding a memorial of victory (*tropaeum*); similarly,

129. Bronze table support: Victoria standing
on globe and holding a war trophy.

Victoria with the *clupeus virtutis* was a popular motif on lamps (Figs. 39, 54).
So were symbols and images from official art on the armor of gladiators and
we already noted the transference of family groups from the Ara Pacis to
private funerary reliefs (Fig. 68).

Various interpretations of this process are possible. One is purely aesthetic,
analogous to the Egyptianizing style in wall painting. The novelty of the
subjects was attractive, offering an alternative, on lamps for instance, to traditional motifs such as chariot races or erotic scenes. At the other end of the
spectrum, the preference for such themes can signify the acceptance and

130. Gladiator's helmet. On the front of the crest: Mars Ultor.

support of concepts and values like world domination and principled government, as conveyed by the iconography of Victoria with the shield. At the same time, this very emblem illustrates a further variation: it occurs on lamps that are New Year's gifts (the inscription on the shield is changed accordingly) and thus becomes an expression of private and personal hopes and wishes. The same is true of the gladiators' appropriation of representations like that of the Mars Ultor statue from the Forum of Augustus on their gear (Fig. 130). The identification with the ethos of struggle and victory provides for an easy connection. Yet another variant is the playful adaptation of Cupids and acanthus scrolls on the Hildesheim silverware (Fig. 126). The meaning such subjects had in state art is now depoliticized and becomes a starting point for personal creativity in the private realm. Juxtaposition with the original may be implicit, though it is difficult to ascertain how pointed it was.

The same range of suggestiveness applies to the appropriations by the elegists although, due to the verbal medium, they can be more explicit at times. Propertius begins elegy 3.5 with

> pacis Amor deus est, pacem veneramur amantes:
> stant mihi cum domina proelia dura mea.
>
> (3.5.1–2)

[Amor is a god of peace; we lovers revere peace;
hard battles persist between me and my mistress.]

The contrast with the preceding poem, where the divine Augustus (*deus Caesar*) is planning warfare (*arma*) against India (3.4.1), is intentional. But, as in the real Augustan world, Propertius' *pax* is linked with *proelia*: poem 3.4 goes on to celebrate the anticipated triumph over the Parthians. Propertius does not wish to participate in that kind of warfare but prefers to enjoy this spectacle at the bosom of his loved one (15). The booty goes to those who toiled for it, whereas he is content with being a bystander:

> praeda sit haec illis, quorum meruere labores:
> me sat erit Sacra plaudere posse Via.
>
> (21–22)

[Let the booty belong to those who earned it by their toils:
for me it is enough to cheer them on the Sacred Way.]

The ethic of *labor*, as in Tibullus, characterizes the life of the soldier, not his. At the same time, Propertius is a soldier and triumphator in love (cf. 2.14.21–24). He does not reject the notions of war, conquest, and triumph, but he uses them for the construction of his private world.[125] That private world is both an antithesis to the public world and is linked to it by the same, if differently adapted, concepts.

This does not ipso facto amount to a polemical debasement of such "public" values, however. Vergil, for example, used the extensive metaphors of the triumph and the construction of a temple at the beginning of *Georgics* 3 to characterize his own poetic endeavors. The passage is likely to have been written under the impression of Octavian's memorable triple triumph in 29 B.C. and the completion of the Temple of Palatine Apollo in the following year.[126] The Vergilian appropriation does not take away from these events. Instead, the poet uses them to ennoble his own undertaking: he will be as accomplished in his realm as Octavian is in his. Octavian provides a positive model of attainment that can be transferred to other areas of human endeavor. At the same time, there is the implication of parity, reflecting the self-confidence of the poet.

The same is true of similar appropriations by the elegists, though there are additional nuances. In one of his poetic manifestos, Propertius views his Muse as triumphant:

> A valeat, Phoebum quicumque moratur in armis!
>   exactus tenui pumice versus eat,
> quo me Fama levat terra sublimis, et a me
>   nata coronatis Musa triumphat equis,
> et mecum in curru parvi vectantur Amores,
>   scriptorumque meas turba secuta rotas.
> quid frustra missis in me certatis habenis?
>   non datur ad Musas currere lata via.
>
>   (3.1.7–14)

[Begone the man who detains Phoebus with themes of war! Let my verse run smoothly, perfected with fine pumice, whereby soaring Fame uplifts me from the earth, and the Muse that is born of me triumphs with garlanded steeds; with me in the chariot ride little Loves, and a throng of writers follows behind my wheels. Why do you loosen rein and vainly compete with me? No broad way is appointed for the race to the Muses. (trans. G. P. Goold)]

His poetic triumph is not based on the epic poetry Vergil was predicting in *Georgics* 3. Instead, it is a triumph of slender (*tenuis*) verse, which nonetheless will make Propertius equal in fame to any poet. He is superior to most because he does not take the wide road, but the one less traveled. Besides, it celebrates *pax* rather than further conquests:

> multi, Roma, tuas laudes annalibus addent,
>   qui finem imperii Bactra futura canent:
> sed quod pace legas, opus hoc de monte Sororum
>   detulit intacta pagina nostra via.
> mollia, Pegasides, date vestro serta poetae:
>   non faciet capiti dura corona meo.
>
>   (3.1.15–20)

[Many, O Rome, shall add praises to your annals, singing of Bactra as the future limit of empire. But this work, which you may read in time of peace, this work my book has brought down by an untrodden path from the Sisters' mountain. Muses of Pegasus, grant delicate garlands to your poet: a hard crown will not suit my head.]

Instead of the harsh crown of the triumphator, which also stands for the roughness of epic, he will wear the soft garlands that are appropriate to his private world of love and peace and to the poetic style describing that world. On the other hand, but again appropriate for a different context, Propertius styles the funeral of Cornelia as a well-deserved triumphal procession (4.11.71–72).

Another instance of personal appropriation is Propertius' use of the Troy myth. This is not un-Augustan: a significant aspect of Vergil's achievement was his rescue of Rome's Trojan legend from the political manipulation by the state and some noble families, and his creation of Aeneas as a meaningful exemplar of personal conduct. When Propertius overcomes Cynthia's rejection of him, he compares the event to the joy of Atreus' sons at the conquest of Troy (2.14.1–2). Cynthia's beauty can be measured only in terms of that of Helen: Troy should have fallen for Cynthia's beauty, not Helen's (2.3.34), and Cynthia once more brought beauty back to earth after Helen (2.3.32); the implicit parallel is the return of the goddess of Justice after centuries of desolation (cf. Vergil, *Ecl.* 4.6). Similarly, his inspiration is not the Muse, but his lover, and their (nude) wrestling bouts are the stuff of the *Iliad* (2.1.13–14). Poem 2.1 is programmatic, and the nexus of ideas later in the same poem is a typical example of Propertius' constantly having reference to Augustan ideas and Roman values. He defines himself by them, even if he does not accept them the way they are. He cannot bring himself, he says, to write on (Augustus) Caesar's Trojan ancestors in the "harsh meter" of epic (2.1.41–42); his subject is the battles (*proelia*) on a small bed (41–45). Glory (*laus*), however, exists for him just as it does for those in public and military life. It is the glory to die in love or even to enjoy just one love (47–48). This leads to the concern about relationships that are not monogamous: his lover, whom he calls harsh (*dura*, 78) in the same way as epic verse (*duro versu*, 41), condemns the entire *Iliad* just on the basis of Helen's behavior (49–50).

Propertius 3.8 is an example of a similar association of ideas and illustrates that Augustan ideas are an integral part of the elegiac world. As Lyne has well pointed out,[127] the elegiac poets strove for "whole love." They wanted all the values of a real marriage—such as fidelity, commitment, and supportiveness—combined with the true passion that they found wanting in such marriages. The values of the real world, therefore, are not rejected per se but are made part of their private world. This applies, as we saw earlier, even to war and peace. As in actuality, they can coexist or one can be rejected for the other. "With you," Propertius proclaims to his lover, "or with my rivals for you there will always be warfare. When you are concerned, no peace suits me":

> at tecum aut pro te mihi cum rivalibus arma
> semper erunt: in te pax mihi nulla placet.
>
> (3.8.33–34)

This only three poems after the assertion that "Amor is a god of peace" (3.5.1)! We encounter the same fluidity as in the real world, though the contrast is illustrated once more by reference to the *Iliad*: there are the battles of Hector with the Greeks, and those of Paris with Helen (29–32; cf. 2.22.29–34). In fact, the whole first part of the poem is the description of an all-out fight between the lovers. But that is all to the good: it indicates real passion (*amor gravis*; 10) and true love without which there is no true *fides* (19). *Fides*, a constant theme (cf. 2.24B), is introduced by way of Iliadic references in 2.20.1–2.

The "other world" of the elegiac poets was as little uniform as the real world in which they lived. Contradictions abound,[128] or more precisely, as in Augustan culture in general, we find reelaborations of the same themes from different perspectives. Such is the case with Tibullus 1.10 and 2.3.

At the end of the book, elegy 1.10 returns to the major subjects of 1.1, its introductory poem. The poet's main concern is the contrast between war and peace. The present age is not a Golden Age; in fact, desire for gold caused this Iron Age with its incessant warfare (1–14). The antithesis is the humble life in the country with its old-fashioned virtues of *pietas*, *fides*, and *paupertas* (15–29). War only brings death (29–38); greater glory accrues to the man (*potius laudandus*; 39) who spends his life with wife and family to a ripe old age on the farm (39–44). *Pax* is hymned as the true creator of agriculture and viticulture (45–50). Nothing is said about love up to this point while Tibullus presents his own adaptation of Augustan themes: war, peace, old times versus new, and the importance of family. As in 1.1, there are again some similarities with another passage at the end of *Georgics* 2 (523ff.), Vergil's depiction of the bliss of the farmer's family. It is these ideas that really matter to the poet. The connection with the amatory element is effected quite awkwardly: the countryman returns home, "not quite sober" (51) with his wife and children and before we know it, "the wars of Venus are kindled" (53); the "wife" (*uxor*, 52) becomes a "woman" (*femina*, 54) and then simply a *puella* (58) or "girl," the standard term for the loved one in elegy. Some violence is all right in love, but too much makes a man into a piece of iron (59). Such wild men are better off being soldiers, away from "soft Venus," and the poet concludes with an invocation of Pax and her imagery of agricultural fruitfulness (65–68). In sum, Tibullus' private world in this emphatically placed poem consists of his version of various Augustan themes. His attempt to relate them in some way—and this can include contrast and inversion—to the theme of love elegy is not the most successful. There was no instant formula and, as always, further experimentation ensued.

A different, if paradoxical, attempt at integration occurs in 2.3. Now the power of love, illustrated by Tibullus' attachment to his new beloved, Nemesis, is so complete that he sacrifices for her the very values we have seen him claim earlier. Tibullus is in the city, where he prefers to be. Nemesis, however, is in the country—with a rich landowner. There is nothing ideal about country life and Tibullus needs to accept its backbreaking work, almost that of a slave, if he wants to be near her. So he curses the country and viticulture because they belong to his rival who uses them to spirit beauties like Nemesis out of the city (61–66). There is no doubt about the poet's priorities, hyperbolic as they may be (67): "Away with the fruits of the field, if only there be no girls in the country!" (*O valeant fruges, ne sint modo rure puellae!*). As before, he condemns the vices of *avaritia* and *luxuria*, summed up by various manifestations of *praeda* ("loot" or "profit") that he catalogs in the center of the poem (35–40). Lust for *praeda* makes this an Iron Age. *Praeda*, and not *pax* as in 1.10, now is the the driving force, and it causes civil discord (37). Tibullus abjectly has to compromise with acquisitiveness and luxury if he wants to remain a credible suitor of Nemesis:

> iam veniant praedae, si Venus optat opes,
>   ut mea luxuria Nemesis fluat utque per urbem
>   incedat donis conspicienda meis.
>
> (50–52)

[If Venus wishes for rich possessions, then let loot come so that my Nemesis may glide in luxury and strut through the city, conspicuous for my gifts.]

Another reflection, which again is typical of Augustan culture and woven into the poem, is on the progression of the ages.[129] In the preagricultural Golden Age, men subsisted on acorns and water and their love was unhindered and unending (68–74). In the time of shepherds, exemplified by the myth of Apollo and Admetus, some civilizational skills flourished, but no one had to be ashamed to be a lover even if it led to ridicule (11–32). Finally, "the Iron Age gives glory not to Venus, but to *praeda*" (35). The result is an inverse relation between "progress" and love.

More generally, in book 2, Tibullus recasts and inverts some of his central ideas of Book 1.[130] The fact that this is an inversion rather than a conversion serves as a reminder that we are dealing with poets, and not with ideologues. Their treatment of "Augustan" themes in general needs to be viewed in this light. Like the other Augustan poets, the elegists had minds of their own and their independence has larger perspectives than a narrow focus on Augustus. It is true, for instance, that Tibullus makes no mention of Caesar and Augustus, but then, "unlike his contemporaries and neoteric predecessors, he never mentions the name of any poet, living or dead. He almost never says anything about the craft of poetry or his own place in it"—two standard themes—and, again in contrast to other practitioners, "his elegies are singularly devoid of explicit mythological allusion."[131] Ovid, finally, treated Augustan and other motifs of love elegy mostly as literary gestures and thus brought its formal development to an end while adapting many of its elements for his *Heroides* and *Metamorphoses*.

PROSE: LIVY

Livy[132] and his historical work provide another good example of how we need to define, or perhaps redefine, Augustanism. He was not a political partisan of Augustus, but he shared many of his moral ideas and values. Characteristically, he expressed them in his own way. He was on good terms with the *princeps*, but, like Horace, he kept his own counsel and prized his independence. He lived at the time of the creation of the principate with its fluid contours and its evolving coexistence of republic and monarchy; later historians, such as Tacitus and Dio, claimed the benefit of hindsight while projecting the shape the principate had taken by then back into the age of Augustus. Livy also shared in the fundamental ethos of Augustan culture by opting for ongoing effort rather than easy fulfillment: his restless mind (*inquies animus*), and not the pursuit of further fame or an obligation to Rome, was the main cause for his continued writing of history, as he said in the preface to one of his lost books (Pliny, *HN* preface 16). Like Vergil—and especially the early books of Livy's history have often been called a prose epic—he viewed the Roman experience in terms of the human experience. And like other Augustans, he was an innovator—he was the rare nonpolitician to compose history in Rome—and the mixture of styles he employed has its counterpart in Augustan poetry, art, and architecture. It is also typical that he depicted Roman virtues as evolving, a concept that is paralleled by his narrative style.

The Augustan dispensation was, in essence, the victory of the nonpolitical classes of Italy.[133] Livy was their consummate representative. He was born into the *haute bourgeoisie* of Patavium (modern Padua), a town known for both its commercial interests and its traditional morals (Pliny, *Epist.* 1.14.6). To thousands of Italians like him, who were cut off and yet suffered from the political machinations in Rome, the last decades of the republic epitomized the greatest decay the Roman state had yet experienced. That decay was moral in nature. One of the stated aims of his history, therefore, was to provide both positive and warning examples of moral conduct. Livy made all this plain in the preface he wrote to book 1 or, perhaps, to the first pentad of books, the kind of larger compositional unit he employed for several components of his 142-book history. "I am aware," he says,

> that most readers will take less pleasure in my account of how Rome began and in her early history; they will wish to hurry on to more modern times and to read of the period, already a long one, in which the might of an imperial people is beginning to work its own ruin. My own feeling is different: I shall find antiquity a rewarding study. . . . I invite the reader's attention to the much more serious consideration of the kind of lives our ancestors lived, what their *mores* were, and by what

kind of men and by what abilities both in domestic politics and war Rome's power [*imperium*] was first acquired and subsequently expanded; I would then have him trace the process of moral decline, to watch, first, the sinking of the foundations of morality as the old teaching was allowed to lapse, then the rapidly increasing disintegration, then the final collapse of the whole edifice, and the dark dawning of our modern day when we can suffer neither our vices nor the remedies needed to cure them. The study of history is fruitful medicine; for in history you have a record of the infinite variety of human experience plainly set out for all to see; and in that record you can find for yourself and your country both examples and warnings. . . . I hope my passion for Rome's past has not impaired my judgment; for I honestly believe that no country has ever been greater or purer than ours or richer in good citizens and noble deeds. (pref. 4–5, 9–11)

The guiding ideas, as can be seen, are the definition of *res Romana* in moral terms, the concern about its decline, the need for regeneration and the realization that it will be anything but easy, and an immense patriotism, including pride in foreign conquests. Livy needed no Augustus to imbue him with such sentiments. Rather, as we observed earlier, these convictions were shared by many in the late republic and explain why the rule of Augustus found such ready acceptance, with the exception of some senatorial opposition, once he started implementing these ideas. They were not only his; they were those of the generation to which he and Livy belonged.

Attempts to narrow down this convergence between Livy's concerns and Augustus' to questions of political adherence are unduly limiting.[134] Such definitions of Livy's exact political stance have run the entire gamut from joyous cheerleading for Augustus to subversive criticism. The larger issue that matters is again Augustus' transforming leadership. It was, as we have seen, moral in nature: transforming leadership occurs, in Burns' words, "when one or more persons engage with others in such a way that leaders and followers raise one another to higher levels of motivation and morality."[135] Furthermore, we noted that mutuality was essential to this process.

A good illustration is the question of the exact meaning of Livy's reference to the remedies (*remedia*) the Romans are not yet ready to use for their moral sickness. The established interpretation, following the traditional view of Augustan "influence" from the top, was that Livy's phrase reflects an early, and unsuccessful, attempt by the *princeps* in 28 B.C. to enact some laws affecting marital morality. It is very likely, however, that the preface and the first decade were actually written several years earlier and even before Actium.[136] In that case, it is clear that Livy's moral ideas had already taken shape by that time, as we may surmise anyway; like Vergil in the *Georgics*, he articulated an ethos that was shared widely. Nor do we have to reverse the equation by arguing that Livy, in turn, "influenced" Augustus in this respect—there was simply a mutuality of inspirations about such topics that weighed on the minds of thoughtful people at the time. Hence *remedia*, against the backdrop of the political chaos of the late republic, may well refer to some kind of constitutional autocracy, a reading that is supported by Tacitus' use of the same metaphor in his succinct summary of Augustus' rule (*Ann.* 1.9.4). The tone that Livy strikes is deliberative and guarded rather than boldly encouraging. Any such solution had its dangers. The cure in this case could be hardly worse than the disease, but who could know for sure?

This is not the only possible interpretation following from an early dating of the preface. Not surprisingly, the passage also exemplifies Augustan polysemy and leads to a consideration of the tendency, which Livy shared with the Augustan poets, to look at a given phenomenon from several perspectives. The "vices" (*vitia*) Livy deplores, referring to contemporary history, may be moral in nature but manifested themselves in the form of ruinous civil wars; we may recall the similar connection in Horace's poetry (pp. 135–36). One remedy for civil discord was the continuing pursuit of foreign wars or at least the existence of foreign rivals: *externus timor, maximum concordiae vinculum* (2.39.7).[137] This also relates to the Augustan distinction between domestic *pax* and the continuance of foreign conquests; extended periods of tranquillity and *otium* were seen as leading to inefficacy. Livy expresses himself similarly in connection with the reign of Numa (1.19.4). Since any concern about attacks by foreign enemies had been put aside, he writes, "in order that their minds, which had been held in check by fear of enemies and by military discipline, might not luxuriate in leisure, Numa decided . . . to inspire them with the fear of the gods." Though much praised by Polybius, this means of discipline was again complemented soon after Numa's kingship by persistent Roman engagements in foreign wars and challenges. Still, our Roman sources also cite the lack of respect for the gods and religion as characterizing the period of the civil wars. Augustus, who was both Numa and Romulus, brought back the *remedia* of both religious restoration and expansion of the empire by foreign conquests.

A proper balance was needed, as in all things; one reason for the Roman decline, according to Sallust and others, was precisely the all too successful completion of foreign campaigns especially in the east.[138] In connection with Numa, Livy offers a variant (1.19.1): force and arms (*vi et armis*) needed to be complemented by justice, laws, and mores (*iure . . . legibusque ac moribus*) because military service alone made men savage. Again, this is applicable to the time of the civil wars and the proscriptions; Tacitus, as we have already noted, pithily described the period as one in which there was *non ius, non mos* (*Ann.* 3.28). The convergence of Augustan ideals and Livy's again is evident. The sharpness of his formulation about the effect of military service is due to the context of contrasting Romulus and Numa. After thus laying the ground for a synthesis, Livy proceeded with extolling the military *virtus* of the Romans in the most traditional way.[139]

What makes Livy an Augustan author, therefore, is not a fixed ideology, but his constant formulation and reformulation of some of the central ideas of the age, a discussion to which the poets contributed also. Nor is it surprising that, being witness to a period characterized by evolution and change, he looked not only on Roman institutions but also on Roman values as unfolding. The Roman character to him was the product of a historical process.[140] Concomitantly, he perceived that "the virtues required of Romans changed with the years."[141] Qualities such as *iustitia* and *prudentia*, therefore, are given more emphasis in the last extant pentad, books 41–45, which deal with the increasing Roman power in Greece and the Greek east.

This, in turn, is related to the recognition—and few Augustans, except for Ovid, express it with similar openness—that the past, however laudable, was different from the present. It did not provide a matrix for simple replication. Instead, the values of the past had to be actualized amid the changed circumstances of contemporary Rome, a realization we encountered in connection with the reworking of the concept of the Golden Age in Augustan culture. The mind of the past could be something alien, too (nowadays we use the fashionable term "alterity").[142] A case in point is the religious practices whose revival by Augustus entailed the constant risk of anachronism. The mention of the various prodigies of the year 169 B.C., which included a talking cow and a rain of blood, leads Livy to the following reflection (43.13.1–2): "I am not unaware that the same disregard of religion, which has many nowadays believe that the gods portend nothing, is also the reason why prodigies are no longer publicly announced and no longer recorded by historians. And yet as I write of bygone days my mind in some inexplicable way becomes old-fashioned [*antiquus*], and religious scruples [*religio*] prevent me from considering things, which those sensible men judged to be matters of public concern, as unworthy to be recorded in my history." Livy's attitude to the ancient religion was complex, as was Vergil's and Cicero's. The problem was to use the old traditions despite their often outdated meaning. Vergil's use of the underworld is a splendid example. Few of his educated contemporaries believed in a literal Hades; it was an old wives' tale according to Cicero (*Tusc.* 1.48)[143]—hence Aeneas' exit through the gate of false dreams, which does not affect the updated spiritual message that is conveyed. Similarly, and on an even larger scale, it was the moral and spiritual dimensions of the *res publica* that Augustus revitalized in preference to a mere maintenance of its forms. If the past was to be meaningful, it required the kind of empathy that Livy expresses with the phrase *antiquus animus*. More generally, a recent commentator has put it well by saying that Livy not only renarrated Roman history, but also felt and experienced it.[144] This saved him, despite his constant avowal that the past was morally superior to the present, from the kind of unthinking worship of the past that Horace decried in his *Letter to Augustus*.

Form followed content. Livy's narrative style evolved and was a mixture of many styles. Befitting Augustan times, we are dealing with a gradual and subtle evolution.[145] Although the case has often been overstated, the first books have more of an archaic and poetic coloration than the later books, where there is also a development toward a more uniform syntax. To some extent, this is due to the Greco-Roman notion of appropriateness, whether in architecture, rhetoric, or literature. By using this particular form of Latinity, Livy's description was appropriate to the subject of archaic Rome, which, as he states in the preface (6), was more suited for poetical than historical treatment. While there is a progression toward a more classicizing style in the manner of Cicero, whose historiographical precepts Livy largely followed, this notion of appropriateness, combined with Livy's use of heterogeneous sources, accounts for the tremendous variety of the work merely in stylistic terms. Parallel to similar tendencies in Augustan art, architecture, and poetry, it is a conscious mixture of many previous traditions and genres. Quintilian (10.1.101) likened him to Herodotus and Sallust to Thucydides, but Livy can be quite Sallustian—and even Thucydidean[146]—at times besides being expansive in the Herodotean manner. He is also indebted to Hellenistic historiography with its emphasis on dramatization and "tragic" portrayals, while the sources he most commonly uses were the Roman annalists. Quintilian lauds him for evincing, more than any other historian, "a very pleasing disposition" (*adfectus dulciores*), and yet Livy is obviously capable of some very pessimistic sentiments. To this we can add Livy's admiration for Cicero (cf. Quint. 10.1.39). The speeches, for instance, reflect a great deal of Ciceronian texture, but there are also considerable differences between Livy's syntax and Cicero's. The vocabulary of the speeches, a favorite means of ancient historians since Thucydides to bring out character, is unusually wide-ranging; "no other Roman historian was so inventive."[147] An underlying reason for all this variety—as is true of Ovid, Vergil, and Horace—was the deliberate pursuit of variety itself. It was indispensable for sustaining the breadth and movement of the work.

In a superlative essay, Ronald Syme once remarked that "Livy, the pride and glory of Augustan letters, should perhaps be claimed as the last of the Republican writers."[148] The statement is another illustration of the often indistinguishable confluence of republican and Augustan ideas; the values that Augustus sought to restore were, after all, traditional ones. Livy, in his own way, was just as zealous in this regard as the *princeps* (cf. Suet., *Aug.* 89.2). He tended to look at every character, issue, or event from a moralistic perspective. There is no Thucydidean analysis in terms of surface appearance and deeper causation nor is much attention given, even in the portraits of leading generals like Scipio and Hannibal, to more abstract qualities such as their mastery of strategy. Instead, Livy presents us with human *exempla* of virtues and vices and with actors in a morality play. They are given appropriate lines: "Trust least of all the greatest fortune" (*maximae cuique fortunae minime credendum est*) Hannibal tells Scipio at their meeting before Zama (30.30.1). The concomitant and almost obsessive emphasis on Roman virtues can lead Livy, as P. G. Walsh has well demonstrated,[149] to suppress any mention of unseemly Roman behavior. This includes atrocities, such as those committed by the Roman army on their fleeing opponents after the battle of Cynoscephalae (33.10.3) or the gory despoliation of the Gaul by Manlius Torquatus (7.10.10–11); we can usefully contrast Vergil's far greater frankness in the portrayal of the raging Aeneas in *Aeneid* 10. Livy pushes these tendencies almost to the point of caricature when he eliminates, in his concern for *gravitas*, any instance of laughter, however benevolent, by Roman officials. This was certainly not "Augustan": "There was," to quote Suetonius, "no form of good humor [*hilaritas*] in which he did not indulge" (*Aug.*, 98.3).

On a grander scale Livy was, of course, anything but blind to the shortcomings of the Romans, and the chronicling of warning examples and the fall from virtue is a major theme of his work. At the same time, there are strong indications that he believed regeneration was possible.[150] In the preface, the mention of the *vitia* and *remedia* is followed by the assertion that no *res publica* "has ever been greater or purer than ours or richer in good examples" (11: *nulla umquam res publica nec maior nec sanctior nec bonis exemplis ditior fuit*), and he introduces the Romans programmatically as "the leading people of the world" (3: *principis terrarum populi*). Livy ascribes the early Roman defeats in the Second Punic War, besides the shortcomings of individual leaders, to the general moral and religious laxity of the Roman senate and people, a situation that is rectified as the war goes on. And even as Rome's subsequent expansion has the unwelcome by-product of moral and ethical slippage (see especially books 39–40 and 43–44), this does not mean that the culprits go unpunished nor is there any lack of examples of probity. Besides, decline was not finite but could always be viewed from the cyclical perspective of history as a phase that would be followed by a return to better things.[151] It may well be that Livy viewed the Augustan restoration—and his history ends with one of the high points of Augustus' reign, the year 9 B.C. (the conclusion of the successful campaigns of Tiberius and Drusus)—as Rome's coming back full circle to a period that was characterized, like the early one, by sound emphasis on morals and glorious expansion under strong leadership; we observed the same nexus of ideas in connection with the legislation on morals and marriage. Like so many other Italians and Romans, Livy saw his own program take shape under Augustus: Augustus, the transforming leader, actualized in the public aspirations that had been dormant.

This convergence between Livy and Augustus was accompanied, and this again is typical of leading personalities during Augustus' reign, by distance and independence of mind. Livy was not a member of any of the fashionable patronage circles in Rome, such as Maecenas' (Vergil, Horace, Propertius) or Messalla's (Tibullus). He was Augustus' friend, and Tacitus (*Ann.* 4.34) explicitly relates that Livy's high admiration for Pompey did not get in the way of that friendship. This is not altogether surprising in view of Augustus' inclusion of Pompey among his models, but Livy went quite a bit further by wondering aloud whether the world would not have been better off if Julius Caesar had not been born (Sen., *QN* 5.18.4). As regards the Julian ancestry, Livy submits that Ascanius may have been the son of Aeneas and Lavinia rather than Aeneas' Trojan son Julus—"no one can pretend to certainty on a matter this remote in time" (1.3.1–3). Resorting to unusually detailed antiquarian research, Livy rejects the authenticity of an inscription, brought to his attention by Augustus himself, on a linen corslet that designated Cornelius Cossus as consul at the time (437 B.C.) he fought the Etruscan commander Tolumnius in single combat and dedicated the spoils to Jupiter (4.20.5–11). Instead, Livy insists that Cossus then was only an army tribune, regardless of any political repercussions for Octavian/Augustus who had denied a triumph to M. Licinius Crassus, who was a proconsul, on the grounds that no triumph had ever been granted to someone unless he was consul at the time. Livy softens the disagreement by complimenting Augustus, in the same breath, as the "founder and restorer of many temples," a matter of great pride to the *princeps* (cf. *RG* 19–20). Nor did Augustus follow Livy's script: the *elogia* of the famous Romans in the Augustan forum stress qualities and achievements that are often markedly different from those recorded by Livy for the same men.[152] As so often in the Augustan milieu, however, we can also look upon such instances as complementary rather than oppositional.

Since the Augustan books of Livy's history have not been preserved, speculations about his attitude to the properly political and constitutional aspects of Augustus' principate must remain inconclusive. It is interesting that none of the later historians, such as Dio, uses Livy as a source for the period after 29 B.C. Perhaps they found him unhelpful in shedding light on the problematic issues in which they saw the seeds for abuses by later emperors. The underlying reason for this perceived defect may have been Livy's emphasis, in which his Augustan books did not differ from the rest of the work, on the primacy of the moral purpose of the *res publica* over its other functions. This primacy was one of the essential coincidences of Livy's work and the call to an awakening of national consciousness in the Augustan principate.[153] Another such convergence is Livy's faith in the eternity of Rome, *Roma aeterna*,[154] in conjunction with the realization that such permanence incorporates evolution and change. In the words of the most prescient tribune Canuleius (445 B.C.): "Who would doubt that in a city that is built for eternity and will grow without end, there will be instituted new powers, new priesthoods, and new rights for families and individuals?" (4.4.4: *quis dubitat quin in aeternum urbe condita, in immensum crescente nova imperia, sacerdotia, iura gentium hominumque instituantur?*).

Alongside all these shared concepts and ideas, however, are some fundamental divergences. Livy's history has little in common with the sophistication we find in the best Augustan poetry, art, architecture, and government. Livy was for boys, Quintilian would say, whereas Sallust was *historiae maior auctor* (2.5.19). Livy's outlook remained parochial; perhaps this is what his contemporary Pollio meant by criticizing Livy for his *Patavinitas* or "Paduanism" (Quint. 1.5.56; cf. 8.1.3). Augustus was the conscious heir to Alexander's *oikumenē*, and Augustan culture was cosmopolitan: "The Roman world was opened up both physically and mentally."[155] Against this stands Livy's lack of interest in foreign cultures, his constant stereotyping of foreigners, his admonition to keep free of foreign ideas and practices because they lead to contamination and subversion (cf. 37.54.1ff.), his old-fashioned belief in the influence of geography on character, and so on.[156] Like Vergil, Livy viewed Roman history as an instructive example of human conduct and behavior. Unlike Vergil, however, he did not do so under the aspect of humanity at large; for good reason, the hero of Vergil's national epic was not someone who had lived all his life only in Italy.

CHAPTER VI

RELIGION

IN ITS multiple dimensions, Roman religion during Augustus' reign exemplifies Augustan culture in general. There is the same combination of restoration and innovation that characterizes Augustan government. Like other aspects of Augustan culture, Augustan religion was evolutionary and adaptive, providing an elastic framework for many different purposes and needs. Once more we are dealing with a process that, far from being rigidly controlled from the top, left ample room for initiatives from all levels of a diverse populace. The result is a web of interactions, mutualities, and reciprocities that often had Augustus at its center. In many ways, Augustan religion, with its manifold individual endeavors in the presence of guidance from the *princeps*, is a textbook illustration of his *auctoritas* at work. In this area as in others, we are looking not at a simplistic return to tradition but at a constant process of experimentation and negotiation that, all at the same time, increasingly converged on the emperor's ultimate transcendence as *divus Augustus*.[1]

THE RESTORATION AND ITS BACKGROUND

Religion can be defined in various ways. In the Roman context, we have to be especially careful not to transpose later and Christian notions of what constitutes belief and faith to a system that was *sui generis*. But even when we use the most general definitions, it is clear that religion had to be an integral aspect of the restabilization of the Roman state and empire at the time. Fundamentally, religion is a response and alternative to chaos;[2] it is an attempt to provide structure, order, and meaning, the very efforts that lay at the heart of the Augustan reconstitution of the *res publica*. The *res publica* had been lost (*amissa*),[3] and there were many similar sentiments in the late republic about the state of Roman religion. Religion and the Roman state had been intricately linked. As A. D. Nock aptly remarked: "Something like the Augustan restoration would probably have been undertaken by any responsible Roman" ruler; "it would have seemed to him an integral part of any bringing back of public order."[4] It is useful to expand on some of these points.

The religiosity of the Romans and its importance for their success were connected by Dionysius, Caesar's and Augustus' contemporary, and by others with Rome's very beginnings. Romulus, he writes (*AR* 2.18.1), "understood that the good government of cities was due . . . in the first instance to the favor of the gods, because its presence makes everything that pertains to humans turn out greater." One specific manifestation was his appointment, aside from the priests for family cults, of sixty priests for the public cults: "No one could name any other newly founded city in which so many priests and ministers of the gods were appointed from the very beginning" (2.21.2). Concern with religion began not with Numa, but with Rome's founder. And for good reason: "There is really no human activity," Cicero writes at the beginning of the *Republic* (1.12), "in which human *virtus* approaches more closely the divine power [*numen*] of the gods than the founding of new states [*civitatis*] or the preservation [*conservare*] of those already founded." The relevance to Augustus is quite immediate. The state had been restored by his *virtus*, which was commemorated on the golden shield, and he had saved the citizens—*ob cives servatos*, as the coins proclaimed (Fig. 17). Hence he came closer to the gods than any living Roman.[5]

The fraying of the *res publica* in the fifty years preceding Augustus' accession affected the public religion tangibly. Priesthoods—a public service—were filled intermittently or not at all; the most notorious example is that of the priest of Jupiter, the *flamen Dialis*, which stood vacant for seventy-six years, from 87 to 11 B.C., the year after Augustus became *pontifex maximus*. This occurrence, while being complicated by the many taboos to which this particular priestly office was subjected, is another useful reminder that, after decades of republican disarray, the Augustan restabilization took time, and not only in the area of religion. Cicero, who served on the augural college, repeatedly complains about the woeful state of the national religion and the decay of the augural discipline in particular.[6]

It was matched by the yet more overt decay of sacred buildings, temples, and shrines. Their continuing ruination was depressing to witness, and more was involved than a sense of architectural aesthetics. Roman religion was not an actively moral religion like Christianity; however, it was not unconnected with morality, either.[7] When Cicero gives an actual listing of the various laws that should govern a state, they turn out to be almost exclusively religious laws (*Leg.* 2.18–25). These, as Atticus well remarks (2.23), are no different from "our *mores*."[8] Hence, an appropriate moral disposition is mandatory for those who approach the gods; Marcus Cicero states outright that the purity required needs to be not simply ritual but should pertain to the person's spirit (*animus*) even more (2.24). Conversely, the sight of sacred buildings and rituals could function as an inducement to moral behavior. The nexus was something like this: the gods protect the Roman community.

The survival of that community depends on proper moral behavior. Cults, rites, and buildings devoted to the gods can only enhance that behavior. Their delapidation has the opposite effect.

That these were the concerns not just of the naive and the unsophisticated is evident from the extensive discussion of such matters by many intellectuals and leaders of the late republic.[9] Besides Cicero and others, such as Nigidius Figulus, the most resonant voice is that of the polymath Varro. His compilation, in sixteen books, of Rome's "Divine Matters" (*Res Divinae*) was an extensive listing and, in many cases, a reconstruction of the details concerning Roman priesthoods, cult places, festival times, rites, and deities. Its particulars do not concern us here, but some of its major characteristics do.

Varro is part of the chorus of voices in the late republic that attributes the decay of the public religion to the neglect or indifference of the citizens (*neglegentia civium*). His work, therefore was a salvage operation, comparable with Aeneas' rescue of the household gods from the destruction of Troy:

> [Varro] was afraid the gods were perishing not because of incursions by Rome's enemies, but because of neglect on the part of the citizens; in a manner of speaking, they were being rescued by him from this ruin and put back again in the memory of good citizens by means of books of this kind. The gods were being preserved, therefore, by a concern on his part that was more useful than Metellus' saving the sacred relics in the Vesta Temple from the flames and Aeneas' rescue of the Penates from the fall of Troy. (fr. 1.2a Card.)

Many of the *nobiles* did not share this concern. Some undertook a few ostentatious rebuilding projects during the triumviral period,[10] but the efforts were scattered and many of the shrines were left in disrepair. In 28 B.C. alone, Augustus writes in the *Res Gestae* (20.4), "I restored"—or perhaps more accurately, began to restore (cf. Tac., *Ann.* 2.49.1)—"eighty-two temples of the gods in the city on the authority of the senate, neglecting none that required restoration at that time." The main issue, as is clear from Varro, was not the physical aspect of the shrines, but the underlying attitude of neglect. The ruination of the temples was simply a stark symptom of the latter, of the concomitant inattentiveness to general morality, and of the grievous consequences for Rome. A vivid summary of these sentiments is the beginning of the last of Horace's "Roman Odes":

> delicta maiorum immeritus lues,
> Romane, donec templa refeceris,
>   aedesque labentes deorum et
>   foeda nigro simulacra fumo.
> dis te minorem quod geris, imperas;

> hinc omne principium; huc refer exitum,
>   di multa neglecti dederunt
>   Hesperiae mala luctuosae.
>
> (3.6.1–8)

[You will continue to atone for the sins of your ancestors undeservedly, Roman, until you have rebuilt the temples and crumbling houses of the gods and the images fouled with black smoke. You rule because you keep yourself lesser than the gods: with them all things begin, to them refer each outcome. Neglected, the gods have brought many woes on sorrowing Italy.]

Horace then goes on to develop the themes of the decay of general morality and marital morality in particular.

The prevailing attitude of neglect provoked a positive reaction of serious concern from intellectuals and other leaders in the late republic. Julius Caesar was *pontifex maximus*, and it is no coincidence that Varro's *Antiquitates Rerum Divinarum* was dedicated to him. Caesar's interest in Roman religion has sometimes been overstated,[11] but there is undeniable evidence that he and his circle did care a great deal about the religious affairs of the state. The justification is plain from Varro, who followed the commonly held division of theology into the mythical or poetic type, the philosophical type, and the *genus civile*, which pertained to the state. Roman religion, then, was not a matter of faith, but the Roman state was unthinkable without it. Its cohesion depended on it. Concern with religion was mandatory for any statesman who wanted to keep the *res publica* together. Absolute truth could sometimes take a backseat to the utilitarian role of religion in the life of the state. It is useful, for instance, writes Varro (fr. 1.24), that the crowd believe great men to be of divine origin. Ovid, as ever the true Augustan, put it just as forthrightly (*AA* 1.637): *expedit esse deos et, ut expedit, esse putemus* ("it's expedient that there be gods and, as it is expedient, let us believe so").[12]

Before we proceed with further details, therefore, two essential aspects of the Augustan restoration of religion need to be clearly recognized. First, as in so many other respects, there was considerable continuity between the concerns and "programs" of the late republic and those enacted under Augustus. Parallel to the political restoration, the restoration of religion proceeded on the basis of needs, both general and specific, that had been articulated in the late republic. The difference, as always, is that they were addressed successfully in the Augustan period. And again, it was not a matter of mandates flowing only from the top: "The prince was led in great part as much as he led."[13] Second, it would be wrong to confuse this "restoration" with a rote return to previous traditions; again the parallel holds with the Augustan management of the political traditions of the Roman republic. There was hardly anything that amounted to a restoration of Roman religion on the basis of Varro's learned and archaizing reconstructions. Tiberius pointedly gave Augustus credit for "accommodating certain relics of rude antiquity to the modern spirit" (Tac., *Ann.* 4.16: *sicut Augustus quaedam ex horrida illa antiquitate ad praesentem usum flexisset*). There was, as always, the admixture of innovations.

Significantly, the point of departure for many of these innovations was practices of Roman private religion. As in everything pertaining to the private lives of the ancients, our evidence is woefully limited. But the neglect and decline of the public religion should not be equated with that of Roman private religion in the late republic: people still paid decent respect to their household gods and engaged in their private rituals. One of the first instances of Augustus' restoration is a useful example.

It involved the Fratres Arvales, the "Brothers of the Cultivated Fields."[14] This was a group of twelve men that, before Augustus, had had anything but a high profile. During the republican period, they are mentioned only once, by Varro. Characteristically, the reference occurs not even in his work on Roman religion, but in his treatise on the Latin language (1.1.5). Their task, according to him, is "to make public sacrifices so that the fields bear fruit." While the brotherhood had a public function, it had the character of a group of private individuals, chosen by co-optation, who performed once a year at the public level the kind of ritual the Roman farmer would conduct privately with his *familia*. That was the Ambarvalia, a procession around the boundaries of the field (cf. Tib. 2.1). For the imperial period, we have plenty of evidence about the Arvales and their practices, including their meeting complex on the right bank of the Tiber five miles outside of Rome on today's Via della Magliana. It included a shrine to a goddess called Dea Dia, altars, and a small circus. The fundamental event was the reorganization by Augustus, datable to the early 20s B.C.

Under Augustus, the brotherhood assumed elite status. He himself became a member; for that matter, as he unfailingly points out in his *Res Gestae* (7.3), he was a member of all such sodalities (fellowships) and priesthoods. This was a constituent part of his *auctoritas*—even the most distinguished Romans of the republic had rarely belonged to more than one such group. Augustus' brethren were the scions of Rome's most illustrious families, some of whom had fought each other during the civil wars, and they included individuals who had been Augustus' enemies. A good example is Valerius Messalla Corvinus, an erstwhile supporter of Cassius, Brutus, and Antony who, even after transferring his allegiance to Augustus, resigned with eclat from the special position of prefect of Rome (*praefectus urbi*) in 26 B.C., protesting the "uncivil power" of that office.[15] Yet he remained Augustus' Arval brother. The group, then, is another example of Augustus' effort to lay the civil wars to rest, to foster the process of reconciliation in the spirit of *clementia*, and to reach out to his former opponents. It was time for fraternization,

literally. The Arval brotherhood was an ideal vehicle: the public functions of
Arvals alternated with private rituals and meals in the house of the *magister* of
the group.

Another typically Augustan aspect was the attempt to impart some substantive ideas and meaning to the existence of this fellowship. The natural
starting point was its association with agriculture. As we have seen repeatedly, one of the central Augustan preoccupations, which again had ample
republican precedent, was the maintenance of the traditional values of an
agricultural society in the midst of a time of intellectual and material sophistication. Here, then, was an emblematic commitment of the *princeps* and the
leaders of Roman society to the agricultural heritage of Rome and its values,
a process not unlike the one we found in Vergil's *Georgics*. The cult of the
Dea Dia is not attested outside the Arval brotherhood. She was their special
agricultural deity. The main celebration, a three-day affair, took place in
May, even if on different days from year to year. It was a time that could be
easily connected with the ripening of the grain. For all we can tell, much of
the ritual was largely left intact, including the recitation of the Arval hymn
whose archaic Latin is a good analogue to some of the archaizing tendencies
in Augustan art, albeit with the resulting quality, from which the visual medium was exempt, of being virtually incomprehensible. Perhaps that made it
all the more awe-inspiring; we may recall Horace's railing against the worship of archaic poetry in his *Letter to Augustus*.

The cult was not so much restored, therefore, as given a more elevated
profile that accorded with Augustus' political and spiritual goals. Not only
did the membership become thoroughly aristocratic, but the Arvales also
became highly visible as they participated, throughout the year, in public
functions related to the welfare of the emperor. Accordingly, modifications
took place that illustrate another component common to many of the religious developments under Augustus—the dynastic one. In the case of the
Arval brotherhood, the dates for the *indictio*, the announcement of the (mov-
able) feast of the Dea Dia, are likely to have begun to be so chosen as to
coincide with significant anniversaries of the imperial family. Upon Augustus' death, special commemorative days in honor of the *divus Augustus* were
added to the Arval calendar.[16]

Augustus' "restoration" of this particular cult and fellowship exhibits some
major directions the religious developments at his time were to take. He did
not make a demonstrative example of an important republican cult. It was
just as well not to return to some republican practices, including auguries and
prodigies that had been shamelessly abused for political ends in the late republic.[17] Hence the almost total deemphasis of prodigies in the Augustan
reign (cf. Livy 43.13) and his outright destruction of some two thousand
prophecies when he became *pontifex maximus* in 12 B.C. (Suet., *Aug.* 31.1);[18]
the same ends could be accomplished much more elegantly by the reedition

of the Sibylline books. The quite obscure Arval cult carried no such baggage and its elevation signaled a commitment to traditional piety while also providing the opportunity for ongoing adaptation. That, in the end, is what the Augustan restoration of Roman religion was about.

AUGUSTUS' POLICIES

In one scholar's concise formulation, Augustus' religious policies served two principal goals: the propagation of the new order and the elevation of his own position.[19] Since the evidence about the former is well established, it will suffice to survey it briefly before we deal at greater length with the extensive and complex manifestations of the second phenomenon, which also relates to the ruler cult. Both purposes, of course, were grounded in the view of Roman religion as *theologia civilis*.

After Actium, Augustus lost little time in reestablishing lapsed priesthoods, temples, and religious customs. In 29 B.C., the Temple of Janus was closed for the first time since the First Punic War to signify that "throughout the entire empire of the Roman people on land and sea peace had been achieved through victories" (*RG* 13; cf. Dio 51.20.4) and the augury for the welfare of the nation (*augurium salutis*) was taken concomitantly. It was a solemn imprecation of the gods for the welfare of the state that could not be carried out while the army was in the field. There was another closing of the Janus temple in 25 B.C. and one more at some later time. Reconstituted priesthoods included the Luperci and the Sodales Titii as well as the individual priestly offices of the *fetialis* and, as mentioned earlier, the *flamen Dialis* in 11 B.C. Festivals like the Lupercalia were restored to dignity, and others were simply revived. One of the high points was the celebration of the Secular Games in 17 B.C. which, as we have seen, was typical in its combination of a past practice with contemporary innovations.

The next milestone was Augustus' election as *pontifex maximus* in 12 B.C.[20] It was an office, once held by his adoptive father, that he had coveted for many years. As he pointedly remarks (*RG* 10.2), his former triumviral colleague Lepidus had taken advantage of "civil disturbance" to seize it for himself after Caesar's death. Though scornful of Lepidus as a person, Augustus characteristically obeyed strict legality by not stripping him of the priesthood. The people offered it to him, he says, but he recused himself. While displaying his usual sensitivity to overt tampering, Augustus de facto emerged as the true *princeps* in the area of religion as he did in other affairs of state. Lepidus lived in virtual seclusion in Circeii in southern Latium. He was not around for the Secular Games, for instance, and as early as in 29 and 28 B.C., Augustus received the authority that enabled him to carry out his program of religious reconstruction, such as the appointment of priests, including the permission to exceed their statutory number (Dio 51.20.3), and the rebuilding of the temples (*RG* 20.4). This last event merits some further comment before we return to Augustus' pontificate which ushered in yet another series of developments.

In the capital alone, twelve new temples were built and eighty-three were restored.[21] The nobility was asked to participate in the latter effort and did: L. Marcius Philippus, Augustus' stepfather, rebuilt the Temple of Hercules Musarum in 29 B.C. (cf. Fig. 173); Sosius, the original Temple of Apollo (ca. 30–28 B.C.); and Lucius Cornificius, the Temple of Diana on the Aventine. Restoration in most cases did mean restoration.[22] Most of the older temples, such as the eighty-two mentioned for the year 28 B.C., were not part of the ambitious makeover of Rome from a city of brick into one of marble. That included even the Temple on the Palatine of the Magna Mater, who figures so prominently in the *Aeneid*. It was rebuilt only in the original peperino stone after it burned down in A.D. 3. On the one hand, such restorations to the original appearance could easily be taken as demonstrating Augustus' sense of *religio*. The pious maintenance, just in terms of their location, of the jumble of antique shrines, altars, and sanctuaries was a constant impediment to rational city planning. The dedicatee of Varro's *Res Divinae* had simply solved the problem by burning down such obstacles (Dio 43.49.3). Augustus took no such measures; he cleared up the forest of honorary statues in the Capitoline area by transferring them to the Campus Martius (Suet., *Calig.* 34.1) and there were some pragmatic compromises in some of the restorations.[23] The other side of these religious scruples redounded to Augustus' advantage, too: there was a noticeable difference between such restorations and the new habitats of the gods that were built by him and his family. The new temples were a splendid visual manifestation of his *auctoritas*.[24] The discovery of the marble quarries at Luni (Carrara) around the middle of the first century B.C. enabled the Augustan builders to rival Greek temples in magnificence, expenditure, and wealth of detail. The result was the usual synthesis: the Italic heritage of the podium temple was maintained and combined with the most elaborate of the Greek architectural orders, the Corinthian style (cf. Fig. 112). I have already quoted the apt summary of Strong and Ward Perkins on the resultant mixture of classicism and experimentation (pp. 212–13) and remarked on the tension between the attempt to maintain the values of the past and the desire for sumptuous architecture.[25] For private architecture, conspicuous extravagance was largely taboo. For public buildings, it was entirely appropriate as Vitruvius eagerly points out in the dedication of his *De Architectura* to Augustus; few Augustan architects would spurn the unprecedented opportunities coming their way by invoking the modern Miesian motto that "less is more."

Such *magnificentia* certainly was the hallmark of the new temples that had a close connection with Augustus, his family, and major events in his life. The obvious examples are the Temple of the Deified Julius, the Temple of

131. Augustan denarius, ca. 19–18 B.C.
Reverse: Temple of Jupiter Tonans with cult statue.

Apollo on the Palatine, the Temple of Venus Genetrix in Caesar's forum, and the Temple of Mars Ultor in Augustus'. And there were more. The Temple of Jupiter Tonans (Jove the Thunderer) was not imposing in size but distinguished by the splendor of its materials, the wealth of its decoration, and the significance of its location. It commemorated Augustus' narrow escape from lightning in Spain in 26 B.C.[26] and was dedicated on September 1, 22 B.C. It was built of solid marble; its cult statue was an original by the Greek sculptor Leochares (fourth century) (Fig. 131); and another Greek sculpture group, of Castor and Pollux, stood in front of it. This architectural gem was erected near the entrance to the Capitoline Hill, where it effectively competed with the hallowed shrine of Capitoline Jupiter at least in Augustus' attentions. The ensuing rivalry is the point of one of Suetonius' anecdotes (*Aug.*, 91.2; cf. Dio 54.4.2–4): Jupiter Capitolinus appeared in a dream to Augustus and complained that the newcomer was taking away his worshipers. Augustus replied that the Jupiter Tonans was only the Capitoline Jupiter's gatekeeper and, upon awakening, had bells hung from the gable of the new temple to make it look like an entrance door. He also adorned the older temple with a colossal statue of Zeus by Myron (Strabo 14.637b). But he who giveth also taketh away: the Temple of Capitoline Jupiter no longer served as the repository of the Sibylline Books which, as we noted earlier (chapter 4), were transferred to the Palatine Apollo temple. And for Horace, the association with Jupiter Tonans is the starting point for his meditation on Augustus' godlike rule on earth:

> caelo tonantem credidimus Iovem
> regnare: praesens divus habebitur
>   Augustus . . .
>
> (C. 3.5.1–3)

[We have always believed that the thundering Jupiter reigns in heaven; Augustus will be held as god present.]

The resonance of the Thunderer was heard beyond Rome. In Pompeii, the statue of a standing Jupiter Tonans replaced the seated Jupiter in the group of the Capitoline triad in the Jupiter temple in the early first century A.D.[27] Cults and cult images were not only restored, but they also changed.

Of no cult was this truer than that of Apollo. Octavian had capitalized on the god's associations with victory when he established him on the Palatine. This was followed by a steady enlargement of references to Apollo's peaceful and cultural activities. As we have seen, Apollonian symbols, especially the laurel, soon became one of the hallmarks of Augustan decorative art in both the private and public domain.[28] On the occasion of the dedication of the Palatine Apollo temple in 28 B.C., Augustus took significant action: "Some eighty silver statues of me," he writes in the *Res Gestae* (24.2), "on foot, on horse, and in chariots, had been set up in Rome; I myself removed them, and with the money that they realized I set golden offerings in the temple of Apollo, in my own name and in the name of those who had honored me with statues." The new offerings included tripods, which promptly appeared both on utilitarian pottery (Fig. 132) and in Pompeian painting, where they were incorporated, somewhat incongruously, into the prevailing style of architectural fantasy (Fig. 133).

In addition, several statues of Apollo, including Greek originals, were set up in Rome (Pliny, *HN* 36.34–35) and Apollonian imagery was integrated extensively into the sculptural and pictorial program of the Temple of Concord, which was redesigned as the Temple of Concordia Augusta and dedicated by Tiberius in A.D. 10 or 12.[29] Both the literary sources and the surviving architectural fragments (Fig. 134) attest its lavishness. The rebuilt temple was a veritable showplace, full of sculptures especially from the late classical period, and it housed some splendid paintings. An Apollo and a Juno by the Greek sculptor Baton (Pliny, *HN* 34.73) were paired and the union between the two old enemies, whose opposition was legendary in the Trojan myth right up to the *Aeneid*, was a palpable expression of concord. The famous paintings exhibited in the temple all referred to Apollo, including his

132. Arretine cup with tripod, ca. 25 B.C.

133. Wall painting with tripod in center.
From the Villa of Oplontis at Torre Annunziata, ca. 25 B.C.

134. Fragment of the entablature from the Temple of Concord, A.D. 10.

reconciliation and even identification with Dionysus. Augustan concord had replaced once and for all the antinomy of Antony/Dionysus and Octavian/Apollo. There had been a long tradition in Rome of honoring virtues or abstractions, such as Fides and Pietas, with shrines. As always, Augustus continued and amplified that tradition. Concordia Augusta also included the implicit admonition to his family, now that Tiberius had been chosen as heir, to practice that virtue. Besides Concordia, Augustan Rome contained

135. Augustan denarius, 19 B.C.
Reverse: Altar of Fortuna
Redux with two cushions
and inscription: FORT RED
CAES AUG SPQR.

statues, altars, or temples for Iustitia Augusta, Victoria Augusta, Pax Augusta, Ops ("Might") Augusta, and Fortuna Redux (Fig. 135), Good Fortune that had brought him back safely to Rome in 19 B.C. to settle down a difficult situation.[30]

Many of these phenomena already relate to the second purpose of the Augustan religious program, the elevation of his own position. They illustrate the simple fact that the two purposes we have observed were inherently linked: the new order was that of the Augustan principate, and its firming up, by means of the revived religion, inevitably enhanced the status of the *princeps*. Another obvious example of this process was the rescheduling of the anniversary dates of many of the restored temples so they would coincide with significant Augustan anniversaries.[31] Prominent among them were September 23, his birthday; September 2, the battle of Actium; August 1, his conquest of Alexandria; August 13, the first day of his triple triumph; and January 16, his assumption of the title Augustus.

This was not merely a one-way process, however, imposed on an unwilling populace. Augustus celebrated his election as *pontifex maximus* on March 6, 12 B.C., amid an unprecedented popular outpouring. It was a signal manifestation of his appeal to all of Italy, *tota Italia*, and not just Rome alone. Augustus' own recollection of the event rings true, his fondness of it no doubt enhanced by the terrible contrast with the memory of Agrippa's sudden death later that month: "I received this priesthood, in the consulship of Publius Sulpicius and Gaius Valgius, and such a multitude poured in from the whole of Italy to my election as has never been recorded at Rome before that time" (*RG* 10.2: *quod sacerdotium . . . cuncta ex Italia ad comitia mea confluente multitudine, quanta Romae nunquam fertur ante id tempus fuisse, recepi, P. Sulpicio C. Valgio consulibus*). An almost immediate result was the reorganization of the cult of the Lares at the crossroads in Rome, which exemplifies the mutuality that prevailed.[32]

Augustus' first step was to rebuild the main Temple of the Lares on the Sacra Via near the future arch of Titus (*RG* 19.2). At the same time, he reorganized the administrative division of Rome into 14 *regiones* and 265 smaller *vici* (wards), a process that was concluded in 7 B.C. Each of these *vici* and its leaders in particular were in charge of the cult of the Lares at the crossroads or *compita*. The populace to whom all this applied was mostly the urban plebs, freedmen, and slaves. The cult of the Lares Compitales, which included festivals and games, had for decades been a popular and politically volatile center of associations (*collegia*) that were formed by these lower members of society. They often were an important nucleus of any threats against the established order. The senate outlawed the *collegia* in 64 B.C. only to see them reinstated, in even greater numbers, by a Clodian law in 58 B.C. Caesar reduced them to their original number and Augustus outlawed them once more in 22 B.C. after severe disturbances in the city due to electoral riots and famine. In short, the *collegia* for the cult of the Lares Compitales had been outlets for social unrest. Augustus changed them into outlets for social stability.

The cult traditions, therefore, were not abolished but refocused. Moreover, the participation that was now offered to the *collegia* had to be truly meaningful. Instead of continuing their role as fomenters of discontent, the leaders of these *collegia* now were invited to be visible participants in the new order. Four *magistri* from the ranks of the freedmen were the chief officials of each *vicus*, assisted by *ministri* from the slave population. For all we can tell, they accepted the new opportunity with alacrity.

Tradition again blended with innovation. In Roman private religion, the combination of the household Lares with the *genius* of the *pater familias* had been quite common.[33] The Genius of Augustus, who not by accident became *pater patriae* in 2 B.C., was now added to the Lares Compitales. The guardian deities were joined by a special protector. An inscription from the 50s B.C. had referred to them as Lares *augusti*, the revered Lares.[34] *Augusti* now came to be spelled with a capital *A*, and more was involved than semantics. The Lares Compitales became the Lares of Augustus and they were also melded with the remaining major aspect of the cult of the Lares, that of the so-called Lares Praestites. At least this is what Ovid perceived when he described their celebration on May 1 (*Fasti* 5.129–48). His concluding comment is:

> bina gemellorum quaerebam signa deorum:
>   viribus annosae facta caduca morae.
> mille Lares Geniumque ducis, qui tradidit illos,
>   urbs habet, et vici numina trina colunt.
>
> (5.143–46)

[I kept looking for the images of the twin gods: they had fallen into decay by the might of the years that dragged on. The city (now) has a thousand Lares and the Genius of the leader who delivered them, and the city wards worship a threesome of divine powers.]

The statement is colored by the notion that Augustus was, in Ovid's words, *templorum positor, templorum sancte repostor* ("the builder and holy restorer of temples"; *Fasti* 2.63). Close as it was to the populace, the cult of the Lares Compitales had been ongoing; what mattered was its transformation into an Augustan cult with official pomp and circumstance. It was a transformation for which, as always, haste had been made slowly.

After Augustus became *pontifex maximus*, he did not move to that priest's official residence near the Temple of Vesta in the Roman Forum. Instead, in a characteristic blurring of private and public domains, part of his house on the Palatine was made *domus publica* and dedicated to the worship of Vesta. The Lararium of his household thus became "almost *ipso facto* a shrine of the state as well as of Augustus' family."[35] The Romans, as we have seen, were used to associating and representing the Genius of the *pater familias* with the twin Lares, as is clear, for instance, from the pictorial evidence in Pompeii (Pl. 6). The customary offering to the Genius was flowers and incense and, especially, unmixed wine. In 30 B.C. Octavian had received the honor that henceforth a libation to his Genius should be poured at banquets, both public and private (Dio 51.19.7). The practice was followed widely, as we know from literary and artistic sources. A particularly illustrative example is the addition, in the lararium of a private house in Pompeii, of a second Genius figure to that of the *pater familias*.[36] It is the Genius of Augustus, as is clear from the accompanying inscription EX S.C. that refers to the senate's decree to honor him with the libation. This libation is integral to Horace's encomium on Augustus (*C.* 4.5.29ff.), where he is associated with Castor and Hercules who, along with some other gods, had been worshiped together with the Lares Compitales. In the new cult of the Lares Augusti at the *compita*, Augustus was honored not with a mere libation or flowers, but with the sacrifice of a bull (Figs. 137, 140), an animal reserved for major gods of the state such as Hercules, Apollo, and Mars Ultor. The choice of a bull rather than a steer (the sacrifical animal of Jupiter and other great gods) is related to the generative powers of the Genius, a word connected with *gignere*, "to beget." Hence the Genius was always represented as a young figure and his chief insignia was the cornucopia, symbolizing fertility and prosperity.[37] We may note the obvious parallel with the ageless Augustus portrait and the emblematic use of cornucopiae in Augustan iconography.

With the increased prominence of Augustus came that of the *vicomagistri*, or ward magistrates. From late republican times, they had had the privilege of wearing the special toga of the magistrates and of having two attending lictors during the games over which they presided. Augustus added to their official status by giving them supervisory police and firefighting duties in their districts and by recording their names, beginning in 7 B.C., in the special *fasti* of the *vicomagistri*. This annual list literally took its place next to the prestigious *fasti* of the consuls: both were inscribed on the two sides of the same marble panels.[38] There was further reciprocity: the *vicomagistri* began their term of office on the first day of the month that in 8 B.C. was officially named after Augustus. After his death, the commencement of their term was changed to January 1.

The major artistic evidence pertaining to the cult and its sponsors has, therefore, more than aesthetic significance. Some fourteen altars of the Lares Augusti in Rome have survived, slightly more than 5 percent of the total.[39] Their sponsorship by the *vicomagistri* and the sudden and large demand for them after the reorganization of the cult precluded the level of craftsmanship that was attained in the public monuments. Nor, however, were they simply copies of a mandated prototype. In accordance with the workings of Augustus' *auctoritas*, their basic themes suggested themselves instead of being regimented in every aspect. The shaping of these themes depended on the imagination and quality of the workshops and on the sponsors' initiative. It is understandable that they increasingly tended to emphasize the desire for visible self-representation.

The decoration of one of the earliest altars (Figs. 136a–c),[40] securely dated by its inscription to 7 B.C., is simple, straightforward, even repetitive, and

136. Altar of the Lares. (a) Genius of Augustus on the left; the two Lares and the two Augustan laurel trees. (b) Sacrifice of two *vicomagistri*. (c) Sacrifice of the two other *vicomagistri*.

centers on the divine figures. The two Lares and Augustus' Genius occupy
its front. They are juxtaposed rather than forming a fluid ensemble. The
Genius, who originally held a cornucopia, is turned slightly away from the
Lares who animatedly move to pour a libation from their drinking horns into
a bowl (patera). Between them are the two laurel trees from Augustus' house.
They are complemented by the other emblem from there, the crown of oak,
which is prominently displayed on the back of the altar. The images on the
other two sides of the altar show the sacrifice to the Lares by two magistri each
to the accompaniment of a flute player. The reason for the repetition of the
scene may be that all four magistri wanted to be shown. They are, at this
initial stage, clearly subordinate to the divine center.

On the altar of the vicus Aesculeti from A.D. 2 the four vicomagistri have
moved to the front (Fig. 137).[41] Their harmonious sacrifice dominates the
composition. One consequence is that the size of their attendants and the
sacrificial animals—a bull for the Genius and a pig for the Lares—has been
reduced disproportionately. A lictor flanks the scene and the flute player fills
the vacuum between the sacrificers. One Lar each now appears on the right
and left sides of the altar (Fig. 138). Their compositional schema, including
their square bases, is taken from statuettes, and they hold large laurel
branches. The oaken wreath again appears on the back of the altar, but there
is an additional element of correspondence as acorns form the decorative
band that runs along the altar's top. This is also an allusion to the name of the
vicus after an oak grove, aesculetum, which is misspelled Aescleti in the inscription on the altar's base. On the compitum Acili, however, the sumptuous
inscriptions are used to convey a sense of grandeur (Fig. 139) as the dedication is made directly to Augustus. As G. Alföldy has well documented, the
explosive growth of inscriptions under Augustus was no less effective a
means for demonstrating his auctoritas than was the power of images: inscriptions like that of the compitum Acili are part of both visual and written
communication.[42]

The execution of other altars is modest rather than grandiose. The front
panel at times is reduced to one toga-clad sacrificant who stands for the
others (Fig. 140).[43] The size of the attendant figures, including the flute
player, is dramatically shrunk to make the lone togatus loom large. The
number of sacrificial animals has been diminished, too; only the bull for the
Genius Augusti is left. The Lares once more are relegated to the left and right
sides of the altar, while on the back additional symbols besides the corona civica
enhance the stature of Augustus (Fig. 141). They include his augural staff, the
lituus, and the simpulum (ladle) of the pontifex maximus. The tribute to the
imperial family is even more obvious on the reliefs of an altar that was dedicated in 2 B.C.,[44] the year Augustus became pater patriae, dedicated his forum,
and highlighted the role of his grandsons and designated heirs Gaius and
Lucius. The front represents an imperial group (Fig. 142a). The figure in the

137. Altar of the Lares from the *vicus Aesculeti*. Sacrifice of the *vicomagistri*.

138. Altar of the Lares from the *vicus Aesculeti*. Laurel-bearing Lar.

139. *Compitum* of Acilius. Inscription on the architrave.

140. Altar of the Lares, front. Sacrifice to the Lares and the Genius Augusti.

141. Altar of the Lares, back. Symbols associated with Augustus: oaken crown (*corona civica*), augural staff, and priestly ladle.

center most likely is Augustus. He holds the augur's *lituus* while a sacred chicken is feeding busily by his side; this may be the good omen for the departure of Gaius Caesar, on the left, on his military campaign to the east. Since she wears a torque, the female figure on the right probably is a priestess of Cybele, although others have interpreted the group as comprising Livia, Julia, or the goddess Iuventas and Gaius and Lucius Caesar. On the back (Fig. 142b), as we might expect, appears the *corona civica*, flanked by the two laurel trees and with the addition of priestly utensils (*patera* and *urqueus*) to enhance Augustus' representation as a priest in front. The Lares appear on just one of the small sides to make room on the other for the representation of Victoria with the *clupeus virtutis* and a trophy (Figs. 143a and b).

In a typically Augustan paradox, such dynastic emphasis was accompanied by the increased participation of segments of the populace who had not been afforded much involvement of this kind before. In the *vicus* of Stata Mater on the Caelian Hill stood an altar whose sponsors were the slave *ministri* of the cult.[45] It was not made of inferior material—like all the other altars, it consists of Luni marble—but since it belonged to an additional dedication for the cult and not to the main shrine built by the freedmen *magistri*, its decoration

142. Altar of the Lares from the *vicus Sandaliarius*. (a) Front: Gaius Caesar, Augustus, and priestess of Cybele. (b) Back: *corona civica* and priestly symbols.

143. Altar of the Lares from the *vicus Sandaliarius*. Sides. (a) Lares. (b) Victory with shield of virtue and trophy.

144. Altar of the Lares Augusti dedicated by slaves. (a) Side: Laurel.
(b) Front: Names of dedicants enclosed by *corona civica*.

is far simpler so as not to compete with the latter. There is no representation
of the Lares, let alone the *ministri*. Instead, the reliefs are limited to the basic
Augustan symbols (Fig. 144a): large branches of laurel occupy the small
sides, and the oak wreath in front surrounds the names of the four *ministri*
that are proudly inscribed once again in back: Felix, Florus, Eudoxsus, and
Polyclitus (Fig. 144b). Women, too, participated in the cult. They were
members of the *collegia* and were not inhibited about representing themselves. It is on one of their altars—obviously not the official altar of the
vicus—that the Lares return to the front while the sacrificing women are
shown on the sides (Figs. 145a–c).[46] For both slaves and lower-class women,
there were few opportunities to gain social prestige. The cult of the Lares
Augusti filled that need.

It was, therefore, a triumph of *theologia civilis* in both concept and practice.
Religion was the conduct of social policy by other means. It afforded participation in the life of the state, and particularly, in the new order, to those
who were not enfranchised or were second-class citizens while no new polit-

145. Altar of the Lares Augusti dedicated by women. (a) Woman sacrificing.
(b) Lares. (c) Woman sacrificing.

ical rights needed to be given to them. By way of religion and cult, they were
granted more of an involvement in Augustus' new order than they had ever
had in any other. It is no surprise that they kept supporting it, though it
should not be inferred that all remained tranquil among this volatile part of
the populace. There were severe disorders, for instance, in A.D. 6 (Dio
55.27.1), which manifested the continuing need to keep the plebs under
control.

For good reason, therefore, the personal element with which the emperor
infused this process of religious involvement went beyond his being a mere
object of homage. He interacted vigorously with the plebs, an important
constituency. A tangible instance of reciprocity was the money that the populace gave to Augustus as a New Year's present and which he used as a fund
for donating cult images to shrines in the Roman neighborhoods (Suet., *Aug.*
57.2). It included a statue of Apollo Sandaliarius in the *vicus Sandaliarius*, the
locus of the most dynastically oriented of the altars to the Augustan Lares
(Figs. 142a and b). Similarly, on a votive altar of a carpenter guild, Augustus
is shown presenting a statue of Minerva to the *ministri* (Fig. 146) of this
collegial cult of carpenters whose emblems are intermingled with religious
ones on the small side, while the back panel of the altar represents a *magister*
of the cult sacrificing to the new statue. The mutuality of the interaction, as

146. Votive altar of carpenter guild. Augustus presents a statue.

Zanker has suggested,[47] begins with the institution of a new cult by the carpenters' *collegium* in the context of the religious revival. It continues with the donation of a votive statue or cult image by Augustus, which is followed by the carpenters' dedication of a votive altar or perhaps another statue. Augustan religion was not a fixed entity: "The religious exchange made possible direct communication between ruler and *plebs*, one in which aspiring members of the lower classes and even slaves could participate."[48] In this fashion, the plebs was raised to a level of recognition and participation that continued even after Augustus' death, as is shown by a senate decree of A.D. 19 on honors for the deceased Germanicus.[49]

The developing collegial associations of the Augustales provided a similar outlet outside of Rome.[50] There were hundreds of these *collegia*, especially in Italy and the western part of the empire, and they were devoted to the actual cult of Augustus. I will discuss that cult shortly, but it is useful to highlight the social phenomenon at this point.

The Augustales overwhelmingly were wealthy freedmen. This was a large and important segment of the population, which lacked political representa-

tion both in Rome and the *municipia*.[51] Dio's account of their revolt in early
31 B.C. is another chapter in the history of taxation without representation
and a reminder that Octavian's problems in the months before Actium were
not only military or propagandistic:

> Fire also consumed a considerable portion of the Circus itself, along
> with the Temple of Ceres, another shrine dedicated to Spes, and a large
> number of other structures. The freedmen were thought to have caused
> this; for all of them who were in Italy and possessed property worth
> more than 200,000 sesterces or more had been ordered to contribute
> one-eighth of it. This resulted in numerous riots, murders, and the
> burning of many buildings on their part, and they were not brought to
> order until they were subdued by armed force. In consequence of this
> the freedmen who held any land in Italy grew frightened and kept quiet;
> for they also had been ordered to give a quarter of their annual income,
> and though they were on the point of rebelling against this extortion,
> they were not bold enough after what had just happened to make any
> disturbance, but reluctantly brought in their contributions without re-
> sort to arms. (50.10.4–6; Loeb trans.)

More than temporary appeasement was needed. These freedmen had to
be given a part in the construction of social stability. In Rome, they were
enabled to become *vicomagistri* and took care of a cult that was based on an
existing one. Outside of Rome, Augustus could be honored directly as a god
and was. The Augustales became the new functionaries of this cult, but much
more was involved than religious pieties and ceremony. The Augustales
were given official status as a new class between the *decuriones* (i.e., the municipal aristocracy) and the plebs. True to the Augustan pattern, it was not an
institution that came into a fixed existence quickly or by imperial fiat. It
evolved and was diverse. In some towns, the Augustales may at first have
been "genuinely autonomous representatives of the local *plebs* . . . , who
themselves would have selected the Augustales to serve their interests against
those of the town's governing class."[52] The pattern that established itself was
their appointment by the *decuriones*. It was for a renewable one-year term and
it involved substantial contributions to the ongoing needs of the towns, such
as buildings and sponsorhip of festivals and entertainments. These needs were
considerable and it was simply good social policy to broaden the base of
responsible and able contributors beyond the decurions.

With this came social recognition and prestige. In some towns, the Augustales were called *seviri Augustales*, reminiscent of the *seviri* ("six men") of
Roman knights that had the honor of leading the annual equestrian parade
in Rome. Like the *vicomagistri* in Rome, the Augustales were granted the
privilege of wearing the *toga praetexta* of the magistrates and of being accompanied by lictors when they sponsored the games that were connected with

the cult. Wealthy freedmen had been an economic reality for some time. As Augustales, they became a recognized and important social order in both senses of the word.

The whole process again illustrates the workings of Augustus' *auctoritas*. One of its major aspects, as is clear from our initial definition and numerous other examples, was the sanctioning of the initiatives of others. "Sanctioning" includes permitting, approving, and encouraging. In contrast to the reorganization of the *vici* and the Lares cult in Rome, Augustus did not found the Augustus cult of the Augustales. Instead, there was the usual plethora of local initiatives, motivations, and purposes, with very little evidence of any direct intervention on his part. As an *auctor*, however, he cannot have been indifferent to such developments and to the possibility that they might remain incohate or become opprobrious. Auctorial guidance could be invisible and suggestive. Instead of being explicitly stated for each situation, it could be inferred because of the clear sense of overall direction provided by his social and religious policies. Successful institutions find imitators; it was not necessary for any town contemplating the establishment of the cult and its Augustales to ask for directives from Rome, but it could simply—and often competitively—follow the example of other towns. The adoption of Augustus on local coinages throughout the empire is a good parallel.

It is too facile for citizens of twentieth-century liberal democracies, who take more basic rights for granted than most Greeks or Romans could ever hope to possess, to characterize phenomena such as the cult of Lares Augusti and the Augustales as sycophantic. Such developments were integral to the successful restoration of social stability, which in turn rested on wider participation rather than on mere servility or pandering to vanity.

THE ROAD TO DIVINITY

No living man had ever been deified in Rome. Julius Caesar had come closest, erecting a statue in his likeness "To the Unconquered God" (*Deo Invicto*) in the Temple of Quirinus in 45 B.C.[53] There could be no doubt about the identity of that god: within a year he was assassinated and thereupon consigned to divinity for good. The lesson was not lost on his heir who was instrumental in his deification. He had learned from the flop of his first public appearance in Rome after Caesar's death where he had proclaimed that he "aspired to the honors of his father."[54] He preferred both to live long and to come as close to divine status as possible, and he said so outright, and with reference to Caesar, in his "inauguration" speech to the senate on January 13, 27 B.C. (Dio 53.9.4–6). The result was a typically Augustan exercise in carefully nuanced suggestiveness.

As always, Octavian's approach to divinity proceeded in several stages.[55] The first was his identification as *divi filius* within months after Caesar's death. The appearance of the comet was fortuitous and, as Pliny relates (*HN* 2.93–94), Octavian gladly acceded to the opinion of the *vulgus* that it was Caesar's soul. "This," Pliny continues, "was his public statement, but privately he rejoiced because he interpreted the comet as having been born for his own sake and as containing his own birth within it." Pliny, who was no Tacitus, tended to agree: "To confess the truth, it did have a health-giving (*salutare*) influence over the world." The wide extent to which Octavian propagated the notion of Caesar's divinity and of his own descent from the divine Julius is well known.[56] Cicero played right along, proclaiming Rome's salvation by the god-sent *divinus iuvenis* (*Phil.* 5.43) and "his having been born into these times by the good work of the gods" (*deorum beneficio natum ad haec tempora*; *Phil.* 12.9). This gave added poignancy to his double entendre that the same young man, after being praised, needed to be "lifted out of this world," but it was Cicero who lost his head, and not Octavian (cf. chapter 2).

Another notion that developed from early on, therefore, was that of Octavian the savior. Soteriology was a common concept (and business) in Hellenistic Greece, and until his accession as Augustus we find Octavian looking to both Greek and Roman traditions as he was building up his divine aura in Rome. As previously mentioned, he belonged, unlike any Roman leader before him, to all four major priesthoods. The numerous dreams, oracles, and portents linking him with divine parentage and providence also had their genesis in this period. One of them was that upon the assumption of his first consulate on August (still called Sextilis) 19, 43 B.C., twelve vultures appeared to him just as they had to Romulus when he founded Rome.[57] It was what Ennius had called the *augustum augurium* and Octavian eventually opted for taking that epithet as his name, but only after giving some serious attention to Romulus.[58] Vergil's Tityrus hailed Octavian as a savior and *deus* in the first *Eclogue*, and so did many Italian cities after he and Antony seemingly patched up their differences in 40 B.C. (Appian, *BC* 5.314). Episodes like these and Vergil's fourth *Eclogue* demonstrate that after many grim decades, the world of Italy and Rome was rife with soteriological expectations and that even the faintest hope could be greeted with enthusiastic excess.

The next juncture came with the crucial victory over Sextus Pompey at Naulochus in 36 B.C. Octavian was given the *sacrosanctitas* of the tribunes for life and he began building the Temple of Apollo on the Palatine. Cities in Italy honored him by "setting him up with their gods" (Appian, *BC* 5.546). No such attempt, however, was made on Octavian's coinage: "In none of his pre-Actium coinage or known official monuments from this period does Octavian appear like a god or with divine attributes."[59] Those kinds of images were left to Antony, even if he issued them far from Rome. What made up for it was the sacred oath of allegiance that all of Italy and the western provinces swore to Octavian in 32 B.C.[60]

The victory at Actium presented Octavian with far more choices for ele-
vating his status yet further in just about any religious or divine terms he
wished. These considerations were closely linked with the deliberations,
capsulized by the speeches of Agrippa and Maecenas in Dio 52.1–40, about
the future form of his government. He was in full control, *potitus rerum omnium* (RG 34.1), and he explored all the options. They included Greek
autocratic models. Hellenistic kings had been worshiped routinely by their
populations as gods and saviors. It is not surprising, therefore, to find examples now of Octavian's assimilation to divinities. His statue in the Palatine
Library bore the likeness of Apollo "with all of the god's insignia" (Serv. *ad
Ecl.* 4.10; cf. Schol. *ad Horat. epist.* 1.3.17) and some of the coin images
assimilated him to Neptune, the former protector of Sextus Pompey;[61] the
cameo I discussed earlier (Fig. 2) most likely also came from this period. Or
it may have been crafted later: whereas experimentation with divine assimilation ended after 28 B.C. in public art and coinage,[62] poets and private artists
felt no such constraints. For instance, for Vergil Octavian's future apotheosis
was a given, with a preordained place in the sky, and the only question that
remained was exactly what kind of god he would be, of sea or land (*Geo.*
1.24–42). Horace's likening of Augustus to various gods—Mercury, Hercules, Castor and Pollux, and Jupiter—continued unabated.[63] It exhibits the
usual mixture of Hellenistic poetic conventions and Roman reality; often the
former are used to express the latter. *Ode* 3.5 offers a further example.

I have already examined the beginning of *Ode* 3.5 twice from different
perspectives, but the phrase *praesens deus* needs additional comment. One of
the reasons for the ruler cult in the Greek east, which preceded the cult of
Augustus in those provinces, was the realization that the ruler is here and
now (*praesens*), whereas the Olympians tend to be more inaccessible. As the
Athenians put it succinctly in their welcoming chorus for Demetrios Poliorcetes in 290 B.C.: "The other gods are far away, or cannot hear, or are non-
existent, or care nothing for us; but you are here, and visible to us, not carved
in wood or stone, but real, so to you we pray" (Athen. 6.253e). It is interesting to note that on a denarius issued soon after Actium (Fig. 147), the image
of Octavian posing as Neptune may have been modeled on that on some
widely circulated silver tetradrachms of Demetrios (Fig. 148).[64] Exact proof
of such connections is beyond our reach, and the concept of the *praesens deus*,
to which we will return, had found its own articulation in Rome by Augustus' time. As in similar instances, however, the commonalities derive from
the intense discussion at the time of various models and inspirations, and it is
clear that there was more than one discussant. It was also the time when
Octavian, immediately after Actium, spent almost a year and a half in the
Greek east.

His sublimation in Rome continued. The senate showered him with decrees, including the libations in his honor and the establishment of an annual

147. Denarius, ca. 31–28 B.C.
Reverse: Octavian as Neptune.

148. Tetradrachm of Demetrius
Poliorcetes, ca. 305 B.C.
Reverse: Neptune.

festival of thanksgiving to be celebrated on his birthday. His name was incorporated into the prayers of the Roman priests and priestesses in behalf of the senate and the people (Dio 51.19.7) and into the oldest Roman hymn, that of the Salian Priests, "with those of the gods" (Dio 51.20.1). The context in which Augustus mentions this honor in the *Res Gestae* (10.1) deliberately reverberates with sacral language (*sacrosanctus, sanctum*) and leads up to his election as *pontifex maximus*. In 29 B.C., Octavian dedicated the Temple of Divus Julius and, by establishing the cult of Victory in the Curia Julia (Dio 51.22.1), transformed the senate house into a virtual dynastic shrine (cf. Fig. 36).

The final outcome, however, was not a Hellenistic monarchy. In the settlement of 27 B.C., which was carefully considered, negotiated, and orchestrated, Octavian returned the *res publica* to constitutional government and, besides the shield, was honored with the name Augustus. A major aspect of this multivalent appellation was the religious one.

The name, which cannot be translated with a single equivalent, denoted its bearer, in Dio's words (53.16.8), as someone "more than human, for all the most honored and sacred things are called *augusta*."[65] Ovid articulates this more extensively. When he discusses Augustus' name in the *Fasti* (1.587–616), he begins by surveying the honorific names other great leaders of Rome have received, concluding with Magnus (Pompey) and Maximus (the Fabians). Then he continues:

> sed tamen humanis celebrantur honoribus omnes,
>   hic socium summo cum Iove nomen habet.
> sancta vocant "augusta" patres, "augusta" vocantur
>   templa sacerdotum rite dicata manu:
> huius et "augurium" dependet origine verbi

> et quodcumque sua Iuppiter auget ope.
> augeat imperium nostri ducis, augeat annos,
>   protegat et vestras querna corona fores,
> auspicibusque deis tanti cognominis heres
>   omine suscipiat, quo pater, orbis onus!
>
> (607–16)

[But they all are honored with human honors, while he alone has a name kindred to highest Jupiter. "August" call our fathers what is holy, "august" are called the temples that are duly consecrated by the hand of the priests. "Augurium," too, is derived from this origin of the word, and whatever Jupiter increases (*auget*) with his might. May he increase the reign of our leader, may he increase his years, may the oak wreath protect your doors! And under the auspices of the gods, and with the same omen as his father, may the heir of so great a surname take upon himself the burden of (ruling) the world!]

Ovid reflects Roman sensibilities when he places the appellation Augustus clearly in the religious sphere.[66] Cicero may have said that "nobody ever was a great man [*vir magnus*] without some divine adflatus" (*ND* 2.167), but surnames such as Magnus and Maximus simply were not on the same level as Augustus. "August" was used in sacred contexts. It related to *auspices* and *augurium*, and it recalled the *augustum augurium* that sanctioned the first foundation of Rome (Ennius, *Ann.*, fr. 155 [Skutsch]). The etymology is ultimately based on the root *★augos* that connotes the power, bestowed divinely, to foster growth; an Augustus, therefore, is "the holder of that power, one who awakens life and dispenses blessings."[67] Even four centuries later, the suggestiveness of that power was clearly on the mind of the Christian military writer Vegetius. Soldiers need to swear an oath to the Trinity and to "the majesty of the emperor. . . . For when the emperor has taken the name of Augustus, as if it were to a present and bodily god faithful allegiance must be rendered" (2.5: *nam imperator cum Augusti nomen accepit, tamquam praesenti et corporali deo, fidelis est praestanda devotio*). "Augustus" was synonymous with being god present, *praesens deus*.

  That is exactly what he is at the beginning of Horace's *Letter to Augustus*. His survey of the canon of men deified because of their actions—Romulus, Dionysus, Castor and Pollux, Hercules—culminates with Augustus:

> praesenti tibi maturos largimur honores,
> iurandasque tuum per numen ponimus aras.
>
> (*Epist.* 2.1.15–16)

[We bring timely honors to you who are present, and we put up altars on which we must swear by your numen.]

Praesens, the equivalent of the Greek *epiphanēs*—many Hellenistic kings, starting with Alexander, had been such gods—means both "physically present," "alive," and "lending assistance," propitious, "powerful."[68] Horace insists that these honors are timely, if not overdue, because Augustus is still alive. He stresses, in his final official communication to Augustus, that "the living Augustus receives honors customarily reserved for posthumous apotheosis."[69]

It has well been noted that Horace is almost argumentative here.[70] For good reason: the title "Augustus" was devised, aside from its typical richness of associations, to maintain the dignity, taste, and decorum so dear to Augustus and to curb gross kinds of flattery. It is a concern that is evident, for instance, from the kinds of writings he wanted to see about himself (Suet., *Aug.* 89.3) and from his purging the senate in 28 B.C. of toadies.[71] If Tityrus could hail him as a god for helping him out in a situation where no one else could, infinitely more enthusiasts were ready to honor him outright as a god, for a variety of motives, after Actium. Once more Augustus chose to obey Roman sensibilities. There had been two conflicting traditions. One was the attempts, usually propagated by the would-be honorees themselves or later admirers, to create a divine aura, often with a view to Greek practice. Examples are Marcellus, Scipio the Elder, and Sulla.[72] A related notion was the one nurtured by intellectuals, and especially by Stoic philosophers, that some gods, such as those in Horace's canon, were men who had worked tirelessly for mankind (cf. Cic., *Tusc.* 1.28) or, more generally, that all those who make an extraordinary effort for the benefit of the *res publica* would be called after their deaths to their divine abode; the locus classicus for this concept is Cicero's *Dream of Scipio*. The countervailing tendency was that such ideas were not widely accepted and even were resisted.[73] It was an area where Augustus had to step carefully, and he did.

Horace was free from such constraints. He speaks of the emperor as a living god, which derives from the reality of the name Augustus. *Augustus* was equivalent to *sanctus*—a term used by Quintilian for the Doryphoros because such was the aura of the Augustus statues of the Prima Porta type— and Horace was ready to state the consequences openly. His pronouncement illustrates his independence of mind, which is evident throughout the *Letter of Augustus*. He immediately goes on, as we have observed, to castigate the Roman populace for its backwardness, a backwardness that by implication also accounts for Augustus' reluctance to let himself be acknowledged as god present. As for Horace's mention of an oath by Augustus' *numen*, it is otherwise unattested; we know only of Tiberius' dedicating an altar to Numen Augusti much later, sometime between A.D. 5 and 10.[74] If Horace's wording reflects a more widespread attempt to honor Augustus' divinity in this way, the endeavor "came to nothing, probably because of the resistance of

Augustus."[75] Methodologically, it would be imprudent for us to regard any poetic utterance of this kind immediately in terms of real cult institutions; Lucretius' praise of Epicurus as a god (*RN* 5.8) is a good example. But Horace's phrasing is somewhat more specific than the simple exuberance of Tityrus and Lucretius. It was a reminder to Augustus—*Sebastos*, "The Worshipped One," in Greek—that such worship could be effected, if Augustus only approved.

Augustus' circumspection in these matters also is suggested by Horace's references to him and Jupiter. The nuanced phrasing of the beginning of *Ode* 3.5 is one instance, adumbrating Augustus' equality with Jupiter when the Britons and Persians are added to the empire.[76] In *Ode* 1.12.49–60, Horace defines the relationship between Augustus and Jupiter somewhat differently. Even if (or when) Augustus conquers Parthia and India, he will rule the world being subordinate to Jupiter (cf. Ovid, *Met.* 15.858–60), who rules on Olympus, in accordance with the motto: "You rule because you keep yourself lesser than the gods" (*C.* 3.6.5). Stefan Weinstock has suggested that Horace may be engaging here in "some polemics against exaggerated views."[77] The Greeks constantly identified Augustus with Zeus/Jupiter and so did Ovid, even if mostly from exile.[78] Augustus resisted, at least in Rome (Suet., *Aug.* 52; cf. Dio 51.20.8), and for good reason: viewed in the context of the Greek tradition, the association of the ruler and Jupiter all too easily lent itself to being interpreted in terms of a theocratic monarchy that was far more absolutist than the principate.[79] The treatment by the poets and his assimilation to Jupiter on the Gemma Augustea (Fig. 57)[80] show that the very title he had chosen for himself did not preclude further initiatives that were beyond his control. Like *princeps* and *auctoritas*, *Augustus* was an elastic concept that was susceptible to ongoing interpretation.

To give another example of this parallel: in chapters 5 and 6 of the *Res Gestae*, Augustus lists various offices, like the dictatorship, that he was urged to accept but did not. *Non recepi*, "I refused it," becomes a virtual refrain. In particular, he did not want to accept anything that was "counter to the customs of our ancestors," *contra morem maiorum*. He acted in the same way when Agrippa was building the Pantheon (completed in 25 B.C.). Agrippa attempted to name it after Augustus, and placed a statue of Augustus into it, accompanying those of other gods such as Mars and Venus. "But when the emperor would not accept either honor, he (Agrippa) placed in the temple itself a statue of the former Caesar and in the anteroom statues of Augustus and himself."[81] It was a response that undoubtedly came about after extensive discussion with Augustus and, typically, had several purposes. Besides Augustus' refusal of outright deification, it exemplifies his abiding emphasis on Julius Caesar as the divine precursor. This was a constant in Augustus' life. As we have seen, the young Octavian's proclamation that he aspired to the same honors as Caesar was too strident and too direct. Consequently, he chose to gain the same honors through Caesar. As Ovid put it, in order for Augustus to be immortal, Caesar had to be made a god (*Met.* 15.760–61). The young Octavian incessantly pushed the cause of Caesar's deification over the resistance of Antony and others. The Temple of Divus Julius appears on coins (Fig. 1) seven years before its dedication in 29 B.C., with Caesar *in medio* (cf. Vergil, *Geo.* 3.16) as both the *lituus*-bearing *pontifex maximus* and as *divus* because of his star above.[82] Caesar's divinity, as we have seen repeatedly, is a theme that recurs time and again in Augustan art, literature, and architecture as a prototype for Augustus' own divinity. The rejuvenated Julius Caesar reappeared, with the emblematic comet, on the coins heralding the Secular Games (Figs. 40 and 171b). And the arrangement in the Pantheon prefigured that in the Forum of Augustus: Caesar's statue with those of Mars and Venus was inside the temple while Augustus' was in front of it. The grouping with Agrippa also conveyed, at least ostensibly, the end of one-man rule and the sharing of power in the *res publica* after 27 B.C.

A final example that illustrates some of these tendencies is the so-called Belvedere Altar in the Vatican Museum that dates from the period between 12 and 2 B.C.[83] It is not a grand state monument nor is it a simple altar of the *vicomagistri*. It is closer to popular art than the Ara Pacis, but it does not lack in sophistication and the four sides form a coherent conceptual and pictorial program.

The choice of Victoria for the front accentuates, as noted earlier, the significance of victory as a concept and deity for Augustus (Fig. 34).[84] It was the starting point, as we have seen, of his association with Apollo and it was intimately connected, due to the Tarentine cult image in the Curia Julia, with his homage to Caesar; for good reason, that same image was ultimately carried at the head of his funeral cortege (Suet., *Aug.* 100.2). On the Belvedere Altar, Victoria holds the *clupeus virtutis* and is flanked by the two laurel trees. This combination of quintessential Augustan emblems is complemented by narrative representations on the other three sides. On the left (Fig. 149), Augustus is shown in an act of *pietas*. Larger than the other figures on the frieze and attended perhaps by the two consuls, he is shown handing over statuettes of the Lares to three Vestals. The setting, festively adorned with garlands of fruits, may well be his house on the Palatine where Augustus, as *pontifex maximus*, set up an altar and image to Vesta in his own residence.[85] Vesta was worshiped there together with the Lares and Penates of the Julian family; state cult and the household gods of the dynasty intermingled. Priestly symbols—the staff, the bowl, and the pitcher—round out the ensemble in the upper tier.

As on the Ara Pacis, Augustus is associated with his ancestor Aeneas, who appears on the opposite side (Fig. 150). His representation is similar to that

149. Augustus and Vestals. Belvedere Altar.   150. Aeneas' arrival in Latium. Belvedere Altar.

151. Apotheosis of Julius Caesar. Belvedere Altar.

on the Ara Pacis in several details: his attire, the spear, the gnarled oak tree, and the sow, who also is a reminder that pigs were the sacrificial animals of the Lares. The oak tree here has the further function of alluding to Augustus' oaken crown; that is why the latter does not appear among the symbols in front. The figure on the left, who has no discernible breasts or beard, reads from a scroll of prophecy. The identification with Apollo makes good sense as it also links the scene to the Victoria figure. The immediate relevance of the prophecy is to Aeneas' arrival in Latium, where he will encounter "a huge sow beneath the oaks" (Vergil, *Aen.* 3.390: *ingens sub ilicibus sus*), but it also extends to the apotheosis scene on the back of the altar (Fig. 151). Its center is taken up by the quadriga of a more than life-size figure ascending to the sky, indicated as on the Prima Porta cuirass by Caelus, the sky-god, with his billowing mantle. Also familiar from the Prima Porta statue is the chariot of the sun-god, on the upper left, who drives over the sky from the east. A smaller figure stands directly underneath this divine team and behind the god-to-be while a woman with two children waves the latter on.

The most cogent identification, in my view, still is the apotheosis of Julius Caesar. The figure on the left then is Augustus who, despite his deliberately unpretentious size, is typically associated with Caesar's divinity and is linked further to the sun-god Apollo; we may recall the quadriga of that god which stood on the top of the Palatine temple. The dynastic element is enhanced by Venus, the ancestress of both the Julii and their descendants Gaius and Lucius Caesar. The prophecy comes to mind that Venus was given at the beginning of the *Aeneid* (1.286–90).[86] When I discussed that passage earlier, I noted that Vergil intentionally referred to both Caesar and Augustus when he spoke of the Trojan Caesar Iulius who was to be deified. The image on the Belvedere Altar makes the same suggestion: Caesar's deification is inseparable from Augustus'.

Ovid's entry on the day of Augustus' election as *pontifex maximus* (*Fasti* 3.415–28) summarizes the main themes of the Belvedere Altar. Ovid begins with a mention of Phoebus ascending to Olympus and driving across the sky. He links the eternal fire of Vesta with the "*numina* of eternal Caesar" (Augustus). Then he refers to Aeneas and Augustus' descent from him. The final conceit is a prayer that both flame and ruler shall live unextinguished (3.428: *vivite inexstincti, flammaque duxque, precor*).

The divine aura of Augustus, which increased (cf. *augere*) like his *auctoritas*, clearly was unprecedented in its extent, but it was not counter to ancestral customs. Even during the republic, Roman religion had not been immutable nor was it possessed of hidebound conservatism.[87] There had always been room for change—for new cults, for new practices of divination, and for new rites. Gradualism was favored, and it found its perfect exponent in a man whose motto was to make haste slowly.

Others preferred to proceed more quickly. There is considerable evidence from cities in Italy that Augustus was honored as a god during his lifetime.[88] The same, of course, is true of the eastern and western provinces. Before we consider the provinces in some detail, we need to keep in mind that this was a variegated phenomenon. A "god" could mean different things to different people. Official Roman protocol, from the establishment of the terminology *divi filius*, was careful to call a deified Roman emperor a *divus* rather than a *deus*. On a less formal level, however, Servius' comment on *Aeneid* 5.45 shows that there was no clear distinction between *deus* and *divus* at least since Varro, and the Latin inscriptions from Italy and elsewhere that relate to Augustus' divinity bear this out.[89] Still, the suggestion seems largely on the mark that the *deus* or *divus* Augustus generally was not a highly personal deity but rather a sort of "honorary god."[90] That did not mean he lacked reality; after all, he was more immediately present precisely because he was still on earth as a mortal. The cult of Augustus served many different and very real purposes not in the least because of the variety of ways in which its central figure could be regarded.

THE CULT OF AUGUSTUS IN THE GREEK EAST

The "divine" Augustus could be viewed from two principal perspectives.[91] One was simply the equivalent of his secular might in the realm of theology: his was the special capacity to bring blessings to mankind, whether through concrete individual actions or his numinous powers in general. While compatible with the Roman notion of *numen*, the concept had already received a formative expression in the cult of the Hellenistic rulers. They were recognized with divine honors because of their euergetism, the beneficent powers they expended for the citizenry. The other aspect—and the two could intersect easily—was that the ruler was under the protection of special deities. In Augustus' case, this would involve gods like Apollo, Mars, Venus, and Concordia Augusta. Quite appropriately, therefore, the sacrifices at the altars of the Hellenistic kings and Augustus were made not *to* them, but *for* them to the gods.[92] This accords with the emphasis of Augustus, which was cited as exemplary by Tiberius (Tac., *Ann.* 4.37) and followed by Augustus' successors except for the short-lived Caligula: he could be honored, even if in an exceptional manner, as a mortal because of his meritorious achievements though he consistently refused to grant permission, when asked, for his worship as a god by Roman citizens. The precedent was set soon after Actium when the provinces of Asia and of Pontus/Bithynia requested permission to dedicate temples to him. He decided to allow a cult and temple of Divus Julius and the goddess Roma for the citizens of both provinces in Nicaea and Ephesus while the non-Romans—"Hellenes" in his words—could do the same for Roma and himself in Pergamum and Nicomedia.[93] The initiative came from the provincial assemblies, many of whose members were ready to recognize Octavian as a god, and the final decision clearly was preceded by some give-and-take.[94] Octavian's decision stood: nowhere, even in the later documents relating to the cult, is he referred to as a god (*theos*). His decision was all the more remarkable and farsighted as this (30/29 B.C.) was the very period when he was flirting with a more monarchic kind of representation.

This early event illustrates two other characteristics of the imperial cult. Motives were not uniform and there were precedents for such honors. From the 90s B.C., Roman provincial governors had been the recipients of special festivals, games, and even temples.[95] It was an appropriate form to honor the representatives of the Roman government and for that reason alone, Augustus could not recuse himself. The combination of the honoree with the goddess Roma went back to the time of Flamininus (191 B.C.) and obviated any Roman objections to a mere personality cult. Roman officials, of course, changed while the permanence of Augustus, like that of the Hellenistic kings before him, afforded far more satisfying possibilities and a more personal focus for long-term identification and expressions of loyalty. Since the demise of the Greek rulers in the east except for Egypt, the cult of the ruler had been a cult in search of a suitable honoree. Augustus met the need for a continuing flesh-and-blood presence in lieu of the personification of Roman power by a mere abstraction or an ever changing cast of proconsuls. Once more we observe a pattern of leadership that consists of the timely articulation and fulfillment of widespread existing needs.

Another important aspect is that the existing system was polymorphous[96] and continued in that fashion under Augustus, who defined only some of its parameters. As is the case so often in Augustan culture, there were multiple expressions and reasons for the cults. Besides four provincial cults in both east and west, at least thirty-seven municipal cults in his honor are attested during his lifetime. The actual number, of course, was considerably higher; a decree of the province of Asia, for instance, of 9 B.C. suggests their ubiquity.[97] In contrast to the Roman provinces, the individual Greek cities needed no permission from Rome for the way in which they and their leading citizens chose to honor the emperor with a cult. In both instances, there was a variety of motives for this flexibility.

A recent attractive thesis has viewed the genesis of the Hellenistic ruler cult inherited by Augustus as the accommodation of the self-governing Greek cities to an external power on which they became dependent.[98] The cult of the gods furnished an analogue, and the concomitant rituals served to conceptualize the world and define the position of the emperor. This is a welcome alternative to the overstated view that the imperial cult was largely a routine matter of politics and diplomacy. Yet the cult exhausted itself in neither of these concepts nor do we need to begin with the corporate model. To many individual subjects throughout the empire it must have made perfect sense to "construct" the reality of an immensely powerful ruler in terms of divinity or something close to it.[99] Another primary motivation, just as in the cities of Italy, was gratitude pure and simple. If Pergamum could honor a private individual with godlike honors and the attribution of immortality because he succeeded in reducing the city's burdensome obligations to Rome in the 80s B.C. (*IGR* IV.292, 293), there was all the more reason for many eastern cities to be grateful to Octavian because he had delivered them from Antony's depredations (cf. *RG* 24.1) and reduced the immense financial burden, including payments levied ten years in advance, that had been imposed on them for almost two decades. In time, the expression of thanks for specific actions was broadened to a more universal gratefulness for the blessings of peace and liberty. It is in the Greek east that the coins with Pax and the inscription "Libertatis Vindex" (Fig. 23) were issued, and an inscription from Halicarnassus praises Augustus almost in terms of Velleius' (2.89) summary of how conditions improved: "Land and sea are at peace, the cities are flourishing in good order, concord, and prosperity; there is the zenith and bringing forth of everything that is good, there are good hopes for the future and men are full of good hope for the present."[100] The decree of the province of Asia in 9 B.C. expanded on all these points even more extensively, leading up to instituting the beginning of the year on Augustus' birthday.[101] These are equivalents, on a larger scale, to Tityrus' grateful deification of his savior in *Eclogue* 1. For Pliny, the expression of gratitude for benefits received was the raison d'être of the emperor's deification.[102] In other instances, the primary motivation was an expression of loyalty to the victor of Actium on the part of cities and provinces that had sympathized with Antony.

The decree of the province of Asia also is a good example that, as always, there was gradual development when Augustus was involved. Around 29 B.C., the province's assembly offered a crown "for the person who devised the greatest honors for the god" (i.e., Augustus). That award, however, was made not until some twenty years later. There was no coercion: only two of the seven provinces of the Greek east had a provincial cult. In one of the remaining five, Galatia, the failure to institute such a cult during Augustus' lifetime has been attributed to the animosity of one of its leaders,[103] but the more likely reason was Augustus' own reluctance.

As in Italy—witness the Augustales and the *vicomagistri*—the cult became a vehicle for individuals to enhance their social standing. In the Greek cities, that was the philo-Roman local aristocracies. There was less emphasis, however, on personal aggrandizement than on the involvement of the entire community.[104] It is another instance of the lack of a pervasive dichotomy between public and private in the Augustan context. The entire community was involved in the celebrations and festivals, which became an occasion for civic cooperation. The cult, therefore, developed into an agent for unification at the local and the imperial level. While leaving the tremendous diversity, to which we will return, of other institutions, cults, and cultural practices untouched, it provided a unifying force within the cities and provinces, and between them and Rome. Typically enough, this was done in the spirit not of dreary *Gleichschaltung* but of competition that could border on the time-honored practice of divide and rule: there were plenty of intercity rivalries conjoined with the undisguised tendency to show off, as exemplified by Mytilene in 27 B.C., which sent embassies as far as Spain to advertise the exceptional honors it had voted to Augustus.[105] At the same time, the ritual was not simply stiff and remote. For instance, statues of gods were cleaned, anointed, and crowned before being paraded in processions, and we can assume the same for the statues of the imperial god.[106]

What characterizes all these phenomena—and I am not arguing that flattery, the notorious *Graeca adulatio* (Tac., *Ann.* 6.18.2), was absent—is their large degree of spontaneity and autonomy and their evolutionary nature: as Augustan culture in general, the imperial cult was "constantly being invented and revised."[107] This applies both to its actual practices, including the architecture, and to the definitions of Augustus' godhead.

The latter was kept deliberately ambiguous. He received "honors like a god" (*isotheoi timai*), as several inscriptions and some of the literary sources put it. He was not a god to whom one prayed for personal favors such as deliverance from illness, though he was called a god (*theos*) in the municipal cults, and the Greek words for his temples and images were the same as for those of the other gods. When he shared a temple with another deity, however, great care was taken not to represent him, whether by the architectural configuration or the statuary of the cult images, as the traditional gods' equal. In the provincial cults that he was able to sanction, Augustus forbade the appellation *theos* despite the urgings of its proposers.[108] The decree of Asia's provincial assembly refers to the "birthday of the god," but the cult inscriptions speak of him only as *Sebastos* and the son of the *theos*; one semantic problem was the lack of an equivalent of *divus* in Greek. At the same time, a client king like Herod could honor him in the temple at Caesarea with a colossal cult statue modeled on that of Zeus at Olympia, in tandem with a statue of Roma "of the same size as Hera at Argos."[109] Characteristically of the Augustan ambience, however, the situation remained more nuanced in the Greek east. The fine line between homage and worship was constantly being redefined. The Mytilene decree explicitly refers to the ongoing process of "making a god" (*theopoiein*; *OGIS* 456.45; *IGR* IV.39b.15). It also seems to have specified for his cult sacrificial animals that were especially marked and were different both from those used for the cult of previously honored men and from the victims used for sacrifices to the gods. This is a palpable example of the cult of Augustus being *sui generis* and exploring the boundaries of existing norms. Similar experimentation took place in the west—we already have looked at some of Horace's phrasing—where Augustus progressed to being viewed not as possessing a *numen*, but being a *numen* himself.[110] A further parallel is that like the Lares cult in Italy, the eastern imperial cult also developed dynastic overtones and came to include dedications to Livia, the younger Antonia, Gaius and Lucius, and Agrippa.

Overall, the eastern cult of Augustus is a good example of the lack of schematism of Augustan culture, which facilitated the successful integration of the cult into the cultural vernacular of the Greek east. As usual, Greek and Roman elements mixed,[111] particularly in religious architecture and statuary. It is remarkable that the portraiture of Augustus remained unchanged in the process, quite in contrast to that of some later emperors, which was recast especially in the east to suit indigenous notions of how an emperor should look.[112] We may ascribe this not only to Augustus' *auctoritas* per se, but to that of his portrait, which was already sufficiently stylized along the lines of a young god. It corresponded perfectly to his cultic sublimation; in more ways than one, his civic image and his cultic image coalesced.

THE CULT OF AUGUSTUS IN THE WESTERN PROVINCES

The Roman empire was highly diverse. In the west, there were no structures at the provincial level corresponding to those of the east; hence the eastern model was imported in the creation both of provincial assemblies and of a provincial cult of Augustus and Roma centered at Lugdunum (Lyons) in 12 B.C. and at *oppidum Ubiorum* (Cologne) before A.D. 9. The salient points of this action have been well discussed elsewhere[113] and need only to be summarized. The establishment of the cult resulted not from the response to an indigenous request, but from the action of the Roman government. The loyalty issue was important: the two areas were among the most recent and least secure additions to the Roman territory. Hence the prominence given to Victoria, the true Augustan goddess, in the design of the altar at Lugdunum: on two columns, twin Victories, holding crowns, frame the altar that is decorated with the *corona civica* between two laurels and two nude male figures, probably the Lares (Fig. 152). Also typical are the time lag and the receptiveness to adopting initiatives that had originated outside of Rome. The provincial cult of Augustus had been a creation of the east. For all we know, it had not been planned by Octavian even if he may well have outlined some parameters before the two eastern provinces made the formal request; as always, there was dialogue and negotiation. Then the system was given time to prove itself. It was only after almost two decades of observation that it was adapted for the west.

As usual, the municipalities did not wait that long. Soon after 27 B.C., the cities of Arelate (Arles) in the province of Gallia Narbonensis and Tarraco

154. Scabbard medallion with
Augustus.

Two examples from Roman military emplacements in Switzerland and the Rhineland are fairly representative.[118] One (Fig. 154) is a medallion, which decorated a scabbard, of Augustus who is clearly represented as the commander in chief with laurel crown, cuirass, and military cloak (*paludamentum*) held together on the shoulder by a *fibula*. On his left is Victoria with a cornucopia, on his right the *lituus* of the augur: military and religious authority are appropriately joined.

A quite different utensil, a drinking cup with reliefs, shows the busts of Augustus and Livia on the top of columns while the goddesses Venus, Minerva, and, as ever, Victoria appear between various wreaths and sea animals (Fig. 155). It was not a matter of either demonstrating loyalty or following a certain fashion: loyalty was the fashion.

155. Decorated cup from the legionary camp at Xanten, Germany.

THE CULT OF AUGUSTUS IN CONTEXT

In studies centering on Augustus, he often comes to be viewed as the center of all cultural phenomena. In the case of his cult, the evidence is particularly seductive. In city after city of the Greek east, for instance, his altars and temples were placed at important and visible sites, such as the agora (as at Ephesus) or the council house (as at Miletus). The assumption that civic life and religion must have revolved around him is, however, a misleading one. It did not take long, for instance, for a shrine to Augustus and Roma to be set up in Athens.[119] Naturally, the Acropolis was chosen as its site. But no one would argue that it overshadowed all the other cults in Athens.

The real context, therefore, especially in the provincial cities, is that there was a plethora of other deities and cults, both public and private, that also engaged the attention, devotion, and the hearts and minds of the inhabitants.[120] Along with just about any other cultural practice, they were allowed to flourish without impediment. While practicing military imperialism, the Romans, in contrast to many conqueror nations before and after, were not cultural imperialists. The religious panorama of Augustan times was one of immense diversity, ranging from small and isolated cults—the countryside, for instance, was virtually untouched by the imperial cult—to empirewide syncretistic religions such as that of Isis. It was a time of religious toleration like few others in the history of civilization.[121]

The imperial cult was a flexible system of exchange between Rome and the provincial cities and a unifying element amid diversity. It promoted the presence of Rome and Augustus in a language accessible to all. It was a symbol of identification with Rome that was greatly aided by the personal and charismatic dimension in which it cast the emperor. The image that lasts is that of the Pantheon. It was intended, as we saw earlier, to be the Temple of Augustus—the equivalent in Rome of the Kaisareia and Sebasteia that were beginning to spring up in the provinces. Augustus knew better. The result was a cult building named after all the gods with Augustus appearing prominently in the entrance hall.

As so often happened, what had begun as an experiment under Augustus became a virtually binding expectation for his successors. Because the cultic veneration of the emperor proved to be so popular, an emperor's attempt to evade it could only raise questions about his character and motives, an opportunity Tacitus did not pass up when describing Tiberius' refusal of a request from the province of Outer Spain to build a temple for him and Livia (*Ann.* 4.37–38). After Tiberius, citing Augustan precedent and stressing his mortal nature, explained his action to the senate, Tacitus continues:

And thereafter he insisted even in personal communications that he was averse to such a cult for himself. Some considered this modesty, whereas most regarded it as an indication of his lack of self-confidence, and certain people interpreted it as a sign of his degenerate nature. The best of mortals, went the argument, were desirous of the greatest heights; so it came about that Hercules and Dionysus among the Greeks and Quirinus [Romulus] among us had been added to the number of the gods. Augustus had done better because he had set his hopes on it. All other things were immediately available for the *principes*: only for one thing should they prepare insatiably, that their memory should be bountiful, for if they spurned fame, they spurned their accomplishments of virtue [*virtutes*].

Melius Augustum qui speraverit—Augustus had done better because he had set his hopes on it. He had done so almost from the moment of Caesar's assassination and his orchestration was so rich and triumphant because it included variations from many players.[122]

CHAPTER VII

CENTRAL CHARACTERISTICS

GREEK AND ROMAN

Assume you were an educated Greek tourist visiting the new capital of the Mediterranean world around the time of Christ's birth. Public places and buildings would look familiar. Marble temples were built in a style distinctly reminiscent of Greek orders, especially Corinthian. Porticoes framed ample plazas as they did in Hellenistic cities. Together with the temples, they housed an astounding number of Greek statuary from all periods, most of it original, along with some exquisite paintings by Greek masters such as Alexander's favorite court painter Apelles. In one of the rebuilt temples, that of Apollo in the Circus Flaminius, the entire pediment of a fifth-century Greek temple had been installed, to the obvious delight of spectators in the Theater of Marcellus, who could observe the figures at eye level. As for literature, not only was there a large Greek literary colony at Rome, but one of Rome's leading poets had proclaimed himself the new Callimachus, another had prided himself on being the leader in bringing the Aeolic song of early Greece to Roman poetry, while Rome's leading epic poet had consciously written in the tradition of Homer. In public life, not only had the leading men, *principes viri*, of the Roman republic emulated the stature of Hellenistic kings—the curule chair, for instance, of the Roman magistrates was the easily recognizable equivalent of a regal throne—but the current *princeps*, while refraining from the overt use of royal emblems, certainly was the counterpart of a Hellenistic dynast. He adorned the city with buildings, collected art avidly, built a library, patronized poets and artists, and his residence was both public and private, like that of the Pergamene kings. He enjoyed honors equal to a god and was in the process of establishing a dynasty, having virtually designated his favorite grandsons as his successors. The conclusion would be inescapable: Rome was a Greek city.

More than three hundred years earlier, another Greek, Heracleides of Pontus, had already come to that conclusion and put it in precisely those words: Rome was a *polis Hellenis* (Plut., *Cam.* 22.3). And for good reason: the archaeological record bespeaks intensive commercial and even cultural contacts with Greece from the very time of Rome's foundation in the eighth century.[1] Subsequently, the Romans adopted the Greek cults of Castor and

Pollux in 484 B.C. and of Apollo in 431 B.C.; both temples were among the cynosures of Augustus' rebuilding program. There are similarities between the assembly places of Rome and Athens, the Comitium and the Pnyx, that date to the first half of the fifth century,[2] and around 343 B.C. the Romans set up statues of Alcibiades and Pythagoras in the Comitium at the behest of the Delphic oracle (Pliny, *HN* 34.26).

That was only a prelude to what was to come. "Why the Romans," as Arnaldo Momigliano has remarked so aptly, "threw themselves into the difficult business of absorbing the culture of one foreign nation just when they were involved in exhausting wars with another foreign nation [i.e., Carthage], remains one of those puzzles which characterize nations in their most inscrutable and decisive hours. . . . The assimilation of Greek language, manners and beliefs is indistinguishable from the creation of a national literature which, with all the imitation of alien models, was immediately original, self-assured and aggressive."[3] There was aggressiveness in other ways, too. Starting with Marcellus' conquest of Syracuse in 211 B.C., Roman *imperatores* hauled Greek art by the boatload to Rome and set it up both as public testimonials to their own grandeur and as ornaments for the city (cf. Tac., *Ann.* 3.72.1). Corollary building activities ensued. Caecilius Metellus, who celebrated a triumph over the Macedonians in 146 B.C., employed a Greek architect, Hermodorus of Salamis, to build the first marble temple in Rome, that of Jupiter Stator, and surrounded both it and the Temple of Juno Regina (the two cult statues were made by Greek artists) with a portico in which there was a huge display of Greek sculpture, notably twenty-five bronze equestrian statues by Lysippus of Alexander and his companions at the battle of the Granicus.[4] The layout of the whole (Fig. 156), which was rebuilt by Augustus as the Porticus Octaviae, has aptly been considered a forerunner of the Augustus forum;[5] the parallel is enhanced by the representations of Alexander in both instances. Similarly imposing was the building complex, commissioned by Lutatius Catulus in 101 B.C., that incorporated the Porticus Minucia and the Temple of Fortuna Huiusce Diei (Fortune of the day of his battle). The temple was a Greek round temple (tholos) on a Roman podium (cf. the later Augustus/Roma temple on the Athenian Acropolis) and housed, besides a colossal cult statue, an Athena by Phidias (Pliny, *HN* 34.54) along with other Greek sculptures.[6] It is no surprise that Cicero mentions the edifices of Metellus and Catulus as two of the best three places to view Greek art in Rome (*Verr.* 2.4.126). They were only the most outstanding examples of Hellenizing building activity that continued unabated even in the late republic.[7]

These examples (and there were many more) furnish a good visual and architectural background both to Augustus' building activity and to Horace's famous dictum, appropriately expressed in his *Letter to Augustus* (2.156–57), that "captured Greece captured the fierce conqueror and brought arts to

156. Porticus Octaviae and Theater of Marcellus, Rome. From the model of
the city of Rome in the Museo della Civiltà Romana, Rome.

rustic Latium" (*Graecia capta ferum victorem cepit et artis / intulit agresti Latio*).
The applicability of Horace's characterization to Latin literature is clear and
we will return to it. But it is useful to connect it with the presence of Greek
art in Rome also. The question, as the second part of his statement implies,
is whether all this appropriation of Greek art was a matter of civilized accul-
turation rather than purely material acquisition. And if so, did it operate
merely in the realm of aesthetics or did it serve other purposes? These issues
are of obvious relevance to the Augustan context, too.

Not surprisingly, the phenomenon is differentiated, befitting the interaction between Greek and Roman culture in general. The primary intention
behind the utilization of Greek art and architecture by victorious generals
such as Metellus and Catulus was self-promotion rather than education of the
populace.[8] Greek art became the medium for demonstrating to the city population one's claim to power and glory. This is especially evident in the case
of Catulus and others whose military deeds took place in areas quite unconnected with Greece or the Greek east. Command over Greek art expressed
Roman superiority: *Graecia capta* over and over again. Greek art was set up
in religious contexts as a display of divine association with Roman success.
For most of the viewers, the Roman populace, any didacticism may well
have exhausted itself in such functions. For the displayers, it may have carried

the additional meaning of their equivalence and superiority to the Greek dynasts, who were known for their splendid art collections. At the same time, Catulus himself, for instance, had an unusually subtle command of Greek (Cic., *De Or.* 2.28), extending to the writing of epigrams, and was one of the many and well-known Roman nobles in the second and first centuries who had a genuine interest in Hellenism. There was a concurrent trend, therefore, initiated especially by the building programs and literary patronage of individuals such as Fulvius Nobilior and Aemilius Lepidus (both censors in 179 B.C.), of "putting the fruits of war in the service of the advancement of culture."[9] This is part of the more general pattern, which, in Erich Gruen's concise formulation, consisted of "absorbing into the mainstream of Roman culture the traditions, literature, and the art of Hellas" and employing "them to draw out the distinctive features of Roman values."

The use of Greek literary, artistic, and other cultural traditions to express Roman values is another example of the continuity between republican and Augustan culture. Before we examine the specifically Augustan adaptations, it is useful to highlight two instances that illustrate that this interchange between Greek and Roman was an interactive and creative process.

One of the early trends in Hellenistic art was "realism."[10] Realism is an elastic and somewhat subjective term, but the general notion is clear, including such characteristics as emphasis on the variety of experience, detailed attention to nature as it is, and the depiction of the ordinary and the unique. It was an important trend in Hellenistic literature, too.[11] One of the painters working in this tradition was Nicias whose work was prized so highly by Augustus that he exhibited one of his paintings in the Curia Julia (Pliny, *HN* 35.131) while Tiberius placed another, depicting Hyacinthus, in the Temple of Divus Augustus—a salutary reminder, as we will see, that Augustan artistic taste was comprehensive and not rigidly programmatic. Because of its survival, Hellenistic portrait sculpture provides us with most of the evidence for realism and, specifically, the "strident new portrait realism"[12] that begins in the second century and is related to Roman "verism," essentially the portraiture with "warts and all."

The phenomenon, to which I have adverted before,[13] is typical of the cultural Greco-Roman synthesis in that it is difficult to determine where "Greek" leaves off and "Roman" begins. There are, in Hellenistic art, some strikingly realistic portraits of Greeks and of other non-Romans, including the Bactrian king Euthydemos I (Fig. 157), which dates to around 200 B.C. The reason for the surge toward increased realism, documented especially by the statuary of Roman businessmen at Delos (Fig. 158), was the Roman desire for self-representation in terms of an ethos characterized by hard work, candor, seriousness, toughness, earnestness, and responsibility. Hence the sometimes extreme emphasis on furrowed brows, crow's feet, bald heads, sunken cheeks, and bags under the eyes (Fig. 159). The viewer could tell a

157. Hellenistic portrait, ca. 200 B.C., identified with Euthydemus I of Bactria.

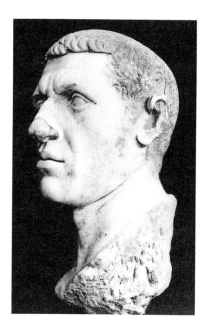

158. Portrait of a Roman, late second   159. Portrait of a Roman, ca. 50 B.C.
century B.C. From Delos.

160. Portrait of a Hellenistic leader
from Pergamum, ca. 70 B.C.,
identified with Diodoros Pasparos.

"Roman" as he could tell a "philosopher"; in both cases, there was etho-
poeia, an attempt at the creation of character. The salient point is that a
Hellenistic art form was utilized, even if it may not have been the sole source
for such Roman portraits, to express Roman values. Along with this, and
again quite relevant to the Augustan context, is a certain degree of stylization. The wrinkles and the like are not necessarily a lifelike depiction, but a
signifier of the general values and character of the leaders of Italy and Rome.
This intent was clearly understood by the philo-Roman aristocracy in the
Greek cities, some of whose members chose to have themselves portrayed,
albeit with some softening of the features, in this manner also (Fig. 160).[14]

While the Romans thus shaped and updated an existing Hellenistic trend,
the taste especially of upper-class art collectors leaned toward older sculpture
either in the original or in the manner of the "master works" of the classical
and archaic periods. Two points need to be stressed here. One is that there
is marked preference for such works and styles decades before Augustus'
reign. We are dealing again with the continuation of an existing phenomenon and will have to determine to what extent it acquired new connotations,
if any, under Augustus. Second, it is important to remember that the convenient periodizing and stylistic terminology with which modern scholars operate was not available to Augustus' contemporaries. The period from Alexander to Actium was not called "Hellenistic" until the work of J. G. Droysen

(1832) while "archaic" art was not rigidly defined as such until Heinrich Brunn did so in 1872.[15] The art (and poetry) of the late republic and the Augustan principate were characterized by an eclectic mix of styles and periods. Moreover, the preference for Greek art was expressed in terms of a much broader category that we already encountered in Horace's complaint at the beginning of his *Letter to Augustus*: "good" was equated with "old." The really valuable works of art were those that were no more recent than Lysippus', who died around 300 B.C. "From then on, art ceased to exist" (*cessavit inde ars*; *HN* 34.52), said Pliny, and not until the middle of the second century B.C. did it come into its own again—because of the interest of Roman patrons.[16] Pliny's statement simply takes notice of late republican taste, which, besides the actual collections, was set forth most impressively in the five volumes of Pasiteles on *Noble Works of Art*. Pasiteles was a Greek sculptor from southern Italy who, in the first half of the first century B.C., founded a classicizing workshop in Rome that continued beyond his death into the time of Augustus.[17] His *Nobilia Opera* was composed between 70 and 50 B.C., but the Roman preference for such works—whether originals, copies, classicizing, or archaizing—is discernible from the second half of the second century.

It was, to be sure, not "anti-Hellenistic"; sometimes such categories tend to confuse rather than clarify. We find the same preference in the collections of the Hellenistic kings, especially at Pergamon. It was bound up with the Attalids' endeavor to make Pergamon the second Athens.[18] Hence they imported not only the statuary of Myron, Praxiteles, and others, but also gave further impetus to creative neoclassicism in Hellenistic art, which had already begun with artists such as Damophon of Messene (first half of second century B.C.). Furthermore, they did something that the Augustans never did: they extensively used Doric architecture, the simplest and most archaic of the architectural orders.

The patronage and taste of upscale Roman republican collectors—some of whom were fond of imitating Hellenistic dynasts—contributed greatly to the rapid development of workshops that specialized almost exclusively in copying classical masterworks, to the related genesis of the neo-Attic tradition, and to the continuation of the archaizing tradition; the latter really had never ceased since the fifth century.[19] The copious documentation for all these phenomena is readily available.[20] The issue is, as outlined before, that Augustan sculpture does not constitute a radical break with the preceding period but, in many ways, a continuation. To what extent can we discern the usual modulation? Specifically, was the preference for works in the classical and archaic Greek styles largely an aesthetic phenomenon in the republic which Augustan public art endowed with a deeper and even moral meaning? And is this also true of Augustan private sculpture? These issues are central to the definition of Augustan "classicism," which needs to be discussed with reference to the utilization of the Greek tradition in Augustan poetry, too.

Concerning the motives for the preference of republican collectors, the only thing that can be said with certainty is that they considered this art valuable, including in the material sense of the word. Classical and archaic sculpture was time-honored and constituted a solid investment. Its original use in temples and other public structures gave it an aura of grandeur and respectability, which now was transferred to the private realm; such collecting now was done for the decor of private houses and extended to marble furniture. Second-century Hellenistic art theory had attributed certain qualities to the works of the grand masters, such as "majesty" and "weight" to Phidias and "idealizing grace" (*decor supra verum*) to Polykleitos.[21] Roman collectors knew such aesthetic distinctions and appreciated the works of the "great masters." Terms like *maiestas* and *pondus* bespoke a certain ethos, but there is no evidence that these valuations were considered to have any moral connotations—certainly not in the sense of Augustus' "moral" legislation, for instance—or that they determined the function of such art in private houses. The principal factor in the acquisition and utilization of such works was the demonstration that the owners could afford a life-style of luxurious leisure with dignity. Cicero's program of *otium cum dignitate* could be realized more easily in the private than the public realm.[22]

Even in the correspondence of Cicero, who was steeped in Greek letters and culture, we find no mention of any ethical or moral dimension of classical art, though plenty about unscrupulous art dealers and inflated prices (e.g., *Fam.* 7.23.1–3), concern for the aesthetic suitability of certain statue types for certain parts of the villa (*Att.* 1.8.3, 1.9.2), preoccupation with proper arrangement (*Att.* 1.10.3), and the understandable desire to buy as many artifacts as possible (*quam plurima*; *Att.* 1.8.2) at the lowest possible price.[23] Or, to offer another example, when a well-to-do Roman trader in Delos juxtaposed a statue of himself modeled on Polykleitos' Diadoumenos (Fig. 161) with an actual—and very good—copy of that work, he may have expressed a certain wishfulness for the elegance of such an athletic body (reality came with the head) besides displaying his affluence, but we are a far cry from the *auctoritas* of the Polycleitan Augustus statue from Prima Porta. Similarly, the continuing preference for statues of gods in private villas in the two hundred years after Augustus is an uncertain indication of any upswing in religiosity but does have to do with the manifestation of wealth, an ennobling aura for the owners, and the creation of a grand ambience.[24] At best, the interest lay in the arrangement of the various pieces, which would lend a collection some individual and original touches. It was a matter of aesthetics, and not of establishing a deeply meaningful program. In the late republic, this kind of art collecting was definitely the prerogative of an aristocratic elite whose appropriation of works based on classical and archaic Greek art could only

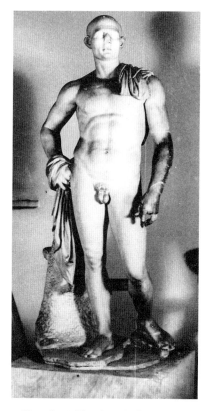

161. "Pseudo-Athlete," early first century B.C.
From Delos.

enhance their social and cultural superiority to the commoners.[25] Representatives of the same elite passed a censorial edict in 92 B.C. against the Latinization—vulgarizing in their eyes—of rhetorical schools and insisted that the traditional, elitist Greek training was the true *mos maiorum*.[26]

It has sometimes been claimed[27] that the change under Augustus was enunciated by Dionysius', then resident at Rome, famous preface (1–3) to his treatise *On the Ancient Orators*. There, using some vivid images and concentrating on the vicissitudes of rhetoric, he praises the "revolution" (*metabolē*) brought about by the current Roman rulers. It is leading to the demise of the degenerate, bordello-like culture, which, after Alexander's death, came from Asia and infested the Greek ancestral home:

> Just as in such households there sits the lawful wife, freeborn and chaste,
> but with no authority over her domain, while an insensate harlot, bent
> on destroying her livelihood, claims control of the whole estate, treating
> the other like dirt and keeping her in a state of terror; so in every city,

and in the highly civilized ones as much as any (which was the final
indignity), the ancient and indigenous Attic Muse, deprived of her possessions, had lost her civic rank, while her antagonist, an upstart that had
arrived only yesterday or the day before from some Asiatic death-hole
. . . claimed the right to rule over Greek cities, expelling her rival from
public life. Thus was wisdom driven out by ignorance, and sanity by
madness.

But this was changing rapidly:

> The ancient, sober Rhetoric has been restored to her former rightful
> place of honor, while the brainless new Rhetoric has been restrained
> from enjoying a fame which it does not deserve and from living in
> luxury on the fruits of another's labors. . . . The cause and origin of this
> great revolution has been the conquest of the world by Rome, who has
> thus made every city focus its entire attention upon her. Her leaders are
> chosen on merit, and administer the state according to the highest prin-
> ciples. They are thoroughly cultured and in the highest degree discern-
> ing, so that under their ordering influence the sensible section of the
> population has increased its power and the foolish have been compelled
> to behave rationally. (Loeb trans.)

A careful historical analysis of the passage leaves no doubt, however, that
Dionysius, a native of Halicarnassus (today's Bodrum) in Asia Minor, is concerned with the problems, cultural and political, of the Greek cities rather
than with the brief controversy between "Asianism" and "Atticism" in
Roman rhetoric or with any reorientation of Roman art under Augustus.[28]
Just as the censors of 92 B.C. had acted on behalf of the Hellenized Roman
aristocracy against the *vulgus*, so Dionysius writes from the perspective of
upholding the power of the philo-Roman oligarchies in the cities of the
Greek east. That power had been severely shaken in the first century B.C. by
waves of discontent among the lower strata of society and by the Mithridatic
War and the civil wars. Athens is a good example of a successful democratic
insurrection against pro-Roman oligarchs (Paus. 1.20.5) and political unrest continued there at various times in Augustus' reign.[29] The Romans, as
Dionysius makes clear in his *Roman Antiquities*, are of Greek descent and
their ruling class in the second half of the first century—by "rulers" Dionysius refers not just to Caesar and Augustus—is reviving the old Greek
ideals of patriotism, justice, responsibility and reverence, and moderation.[30] In so many words, order had been restored with the help of the right
values. In such a cultural and political framework, the local aristocracies in
the Greek cities could reassert themselves. This "classicism"—and I will
shortly define this concept more specifically—is "the best example afforded
to the Greek upper classes for the preservation of unity and identity." Typical
of Augustan culture, another means for unifying these classes and strengthen-

ing their identity was the nonclassical, Hellenistic institution of the imperial cult.

Just as typically, the transition to Augustan sculpture was more nuanced. It was not that a "Hellenistic" orientation was replaced with a "classical" one. Instead, the process had the following basic and interrelated characteristics: (1) Augustan sculpture used the classical/classicizing and archaic/archaizing idiom esteemed by the republican aristocracy. (2) Whereas the aristocracy had increasingly appropriated much of this art for its private realm, the Augustan endeavor was to restore all such art to the public domain, the *res publica*. The endeavor built on the other part of the republican tradition, namely, the use of mostly classical statuary for the cult images in the temples—hence the emphatic use of the classicizing and archaizing styles for the new public monuments. (3) Since the classicizing/archaizing style was used for art that expressed ideas and values, it acquired—or recovered—dimensions beyond the aesthetic and material ones it had in the private villas. A limited number of themes and scenes were chosen for this style, restoring grandeur of meaning to grandeur of form. (4) The sophisticated eclecticism—for example, of a neoclassical statue with a Myronian head, Praxitelean arms, and a Polykleitan chest (*Auct. ad Her.* 9)—that was mostly aesthetic was now complemented with a sophisticated eclecticism of meaningful associations, as in the relief with the Ara Pacis goddess (Fig. 41). (5) Eclecticism and the utilization of *all* Greek traditions (including "Hellenistic") were essential to Augustan classicism. It is "classical" in the sense that it chose the best and most suitable characteristics from a variety of traditions, styles, and genres, recombining them to achieve a surpassing work of art or poetry. Good examples are the Prima Porta Augustus (Fig. 5), and the poetry of Vergil, Horace, and Ovid. (6) Art and poetry become more reflective and self-reflective. Hence the "internalization" of Augustan reliefs into what Zanker has aptly called "contemplative images" (*Andachtsbilder*) and the shift from external to inner dimensions in Vergil's *Aeneid*. (7) Like all genuine classicism, Augustan classicism—in architecture, sculpture, and poetry—was characterized by experimentation and creativity.

Detailing all these strands and the web they constitute could occupy a separate monograph, but some additional comments and examples may suffice. An archaistic relief from the area of Lake Nemi, most likely depicting Orestes' killing of Aegisthus in the presence of Clytemnestra and Electra (Fig. 162), is a good illustration of the fluid boundaries between the late republic and Augustan times: "The question whether the Ariccia relief was produced at the time of Augustus or still in late Republican times cannot be answered with certainty."[31] The archaizing style was popular in both periods (cf. Fig. 122) for its effect of hieratic solemnity. Similarly, the first main type of marble candelabra in the classicizing manner, with the usual eclectic mix of archaic, classical, and Hellenistic elements for its relief decoration (Fig. 163), was well established in late republican times. Its popularity

162. Orestes killing Aegisthus. Marble relief, late republican or early Augustan.

163. Marble candelabra base with the god Dionysus,
last quarter of second century B.C.

continued throughout the Augustan age, and it is only after the end of that period that it was discontinued.[32] The change occurring under Augustus was not simply a break from "Hellenistic" to "classical" or archaizing.

As we have seen, since the second century art in the classical and archaic tradition had become an important means for the Roman nobility to accentuate its prestige. This was done increasingly by using such artifacts for private collections. Even if they served as decor for many of the public areas of their private houses, they were still in the private possession of the owner, *res privata*. The trend accords with the precedence, which we observed earlier (chapter 2), in the late republic, of *res privatae* over the *res publica*. Similarly, their restitution to the public domain is part of the context of Augustus' *res publica restituta* in the political and social realm. In this particular case, the restitution had two aspects. One was that the classical-archaic idiom, which was associated with an elite, now was used for new creations of public art and monuments, as it had been in Greece. The other was the insistence, evident especially from a speech given by Agrippa, that private collections should once more be made available to the public instead of being relegated to "the exile of villas" (Pliny, *HN* 35.26). Again, like the Augustan value system in general, art was returning to proper republican precedent, articulated by such spokesmen as Cato the Elder (*ORF*[2] fr. 98 Malcovati) and Cicero (*Verr.* 2.5.127; cf. *Verr.* 2.4.122). Besides, Asinius Pollio, an erstwhile supporter of Antony's, had shown the way in the early 30s B.C. He built the poignantly named Atrium Libertatis at the foot of the Capitoline along with the first public library of Greek and Roman authors. It featured a large collection of statuary by Praxiteles, Scopas, and mostly neoclassical Hellenistic sculptors.[33] Pollio stated explicitly that such products of the human spirit should be *res publica* (Pliny, *HN* 35.10). This was in contrast with the behavior of Antony, who had kept Caesar's collection, contrary to the slain dictator's wishes, for his private use instead of giving it over to the public domain, a transgression with which Cicero flayed him repeatedly (*Phil.* 2.109, 3.30, 13.11). Augustus practiced what he preached: Suetonius remarks on the fact that his Palatine house and country villas were largely devoid of statuary (*Aug.* 72.3).

In typically Augustan fashion, there are further dimensions to this phenomenon of the *publicatio* of time-honored Greek art. On the one hand, Augustus discouraged its purely private enjoyment by the Roman aristocracy. On the other, his use of the classical/classicizing and archaic/archaizing idiom, which was so highly prized by that class, for the language of the state monuments fits with his general endeavor to communicate and cooperate with this aristocracy, an endeavor that is reflected even by such small matters as his use of Grecisms in his official written communications with its members.[34] Some of the resulting artistic creations, like the Ara Pacis and the Prima Porta statue, were a tribute to the sophistication of this cultivated upper class, though at the same time they were accessible and comprehensible to the commoners. The reliefs on the arch at Susa (around 8 B.C.) in northern Italy show that this was a hard act to follow for artists outside of Rome: the upper-class classical language yields to a simpler native style.[35] Finally, the choice of this art for moral and didactic purposes was a meaningful answer to the recurring denunciations, right into Augustan times, that the large-scale importations of Greek art ushered in laxness and decay at Rome.[36] Quite on the contrary, this art now came to express Roman values more fully than ever before.

The classical and archaic styles became a function of this new purpose: the Ara Pacis reliefs and the Prima Porta statue are primary examples. Signification of Roman values had been the impetus behind the veristic portrait, an idiom that was unsuitable for Octavian/Augustus because of his youth. The principle, however, of having art express such values now appears in the classicizing and archaizing public monuments. The classicizing component of Augustan art was due to the choice of value-oriented themes that called for a different style than did battle narratives. For instance, *pax* and *pietas* were rich, meaningful concepts that demanded introspective, allusive, and dignified treatment. This leads to the sophisticated, multifaceted nature of Augustan public art and the concentration on internalized meaning rather than expansive narrative—witness the reliefs of Aeneas and the polysemous goddess on the Ara Pacis (Figs. 41 and 43). A poetic companion is Vergil's *Aeneid*; while scholars have tended to ignore the importance of Aeneas as a warrior, Richard Heinze's general characterization is still apropos: "When one looks at it from the outside, pretty much the same things happen in the *Aeneid* as in *Odyssey* and the *Iliad*. The deeper difference between the two actions is based on the fact that Vergil, far more decisively than Homer, has shifted the emphasis from external to inner processes, and from the physical to the psychological."[37] In keeping with its serious, "classical" purpose, the *Aeneid* allows of no lighthearted characterization of the deities, such as we frequently find in Homer. A striking counterpart in Augustan sculpture is the recasting of the phallic and randy god Priapus in the archaizing manner (Fig. 127a and b). Solemn in posture and dignified in mien and behavior, he is decently dressed and adorned with small children who climb all over him. They now are testimony to his fatherhood and we have a Priapus who is in tune with the legislation on marriage and morals. In this case, the archaic style is used to create a *Priape moralisé*. More frequently, the choice of style was a function of the inherently serious subject and the values that were conveyed by it. It is typical of Augustan culture, however, that the semantic relationships beween themes, values, and styles in Augustan sculpture were anything but static.[38]

The same is true of Augustan classicism in general. Its true character—in art, architecture, and poetry—was not a stale reproduction of respected forms and idioms, but the endeavor to draw on all previous traditions to create a surpassing whole.[39] The parallel with the Augustan political dispensation is clear: time and again, as we have seen, Augustus drew on a variety of traditions, including those of former opponents, and fused them into a new dynamic construct, thus making them his own. We may recall the many references behind the first sentence of the Res Gestae, his appropriation of Neptune and pietas from Sextus Pompey,[40] or, most broadly, his placing himself in the tradition of Romulus and Numa, the Roman republic, and Alexander all at once. What aided the Augustan poets and artists was the very point in time at which they lived. Greek art, architecture, and literature provided a capacious repertory whose components now could be used synchronically in conjunction with inspirations, especially in architecture and poetry, drawn from the Roman tradition. The result is the sophisticated Greco-Roman synthesis and inclusiveness that is one of the hallmarks of Augustan culture.

The Hellenistic tradition was very much part of it. This is especially evident in Augustan poetry, to which we will turn next, but it is conspicuously represented in Augustan public art, too. Augustus' programmatic Victory goddess in the Curia Julia was an early Hellenistic statue from Tarentum. On the Ara Pacis, the figure of Aeneas (Fig. 43), who is represented in the early classical manner, though the drapery covering his legs recalls late Hellenistic models, stands in a setting familiar from Hellenistic landscape reliefs,[41] a tradition that was used also for the relief panel with Mars and the twins. A frieze with various symbols referring to the battle of Actium (Fig. 164), which was found in the Circus Flaminius area where the triumphal procession departed, is based on similar, Hellenistic trophy friezes, especially those from Pergamon.[42] The Roman admixture in this case is a set of religious symbols that recurs in the relief decoration of some of the altars of the Lares Augusti. In the Actium trophy frieze, a Hellenistic form is adapted for a specific Roman context. The nearby Apollo temple, rebuilt in the 20s B.C. by Gaius Sosius, who had converted to Octavian's cause after Antony's defeat, exhibits a typical mixture of styles: there is a Hellenistic battle frieze, commemorating Octavian's victory over the Illyrians and Pannonians by representing Romans fighting against Gauls (Fig. 165), and another interior frieze with the resulting triumphal and sacrificial procession, executed in "a more matter-of-fact narrative style"[43] (Fig. 166) that recalls, for instance, the census frieze from the republican "Altar of Domitius Ahenobarbus." The pedimental sculptures were transplants, which had been brought to Rome earlier from a fifth-century Temple of Apollo in Eretria.[44] Athena stands in the center, flanked by Herakles and Theseus who are fighting Amazons among fallen and kneeling Greeks (Fig. 167).

Three issues suggest themselves from the consideration of the Apollo temple. The first is the haphazard survival of Augustan public art. It advises caution against applying too limited a definition of classicism. Had we no Ara

164. Fragment from an Augustan frieze with symbols of religion and naval battle, including a ship's prow with the she-wolf.

165. Fragment of frieze with battle scene from the Temple of Apollo Sosianus, ca. 30–20 B.C.

166. Fragment of a processional frieze from the Temple of Apollo Sosianus, ca. 30–20 B.C.

167. Pedimental sculptures from the Temple of Apollo Sosianus.

168. Augustan relief with battle between Romans and Gauls.

Pacis and more material, for instance, from the later Temples of Castor and Pollux (A.D. 6) and of Concord (A.D. 10), our view of the artistic tendencies of the age might be rather different. A battle relief, for instance, again showing a battle of Romans against Gauls (Fig. 168), may have been part of a large frieze in the Temple of the Dioscuri and is definitely done in the Hellenistic manner.[45] It is clear, secondly, that there was no reluctance to use Hellenistic models, whenever appropriate (and we should not forget the many Hellenistic paintings that graced Augustan buildings),[46] although, as can be seen from the sculptural program of the Temple of Palatine Apollo, there was from the beginning a tendency to express not just warlike exploits that almost mandated Hellenistic battle friezes, but the guiding values behind the victorious effort that laid a foundation for the future. For the expression of these values other means of representation were preferred, ranging from concentrated, allusive allegory to the statuary of exemplary men in the Augustan forum: no depiction of an allegorical or historical battle raged inside its precinct. At the same time, the skillful integration of the thematics of the Pergamon Altar into the *Aeneid* suggests that there was no abhorrence of such Hellenistic paradigms.[47]

Third, there is the matter of the reuse of original Greek statuary and the question to what degree it acquired new associations in its new context. As always, such associations were suggested rather than spelled out. They called for the intellectual and imaginative participation of the viewer and the degree of their relevance varied. Amazonomachies had been used symbolically for the victory of Greece over Persia. In Rome, the subject could be easily connected with the victory over the Egyptian east, an equation that could be made all the more readily because of the presence of the Amazon queen Hippolyte. Moreover, the goddess Nike, who appears conspicuously in the pediment of the Sosius temple between Athena and Theseus, fit in perfectly both with the original dedication of the temple to Apollo, the god of victory, and with the prominence of Victory in the Augustan pantheon. Augustus was not simply another Theseus or Herakles, but he was *like* them in some ways.[48] Whereas specific analogues can be found in this instance, an example of a more general connection is the placement of Apelles' painting of Aphrodite rising from the sea (Pliny, *HN* 35.91) in the Temple of Divus Julius. It was apropos because of the Julian claim to descent from Venus, but no more than that. A final category is exemplified by several of the statues and paintings exhibited in Sosius' temple, including a group of the Niobids by either Scopas or Praxiteles. They served primarily as decorative objects since the temple was used, in keeping with Augustus' request that such collections be public, as exhibit space.[49] The same applies, to give but one other example, to a painting by the Hellenistic painter Nicias that Augustus had placed into the inside wall of the Curia Julia. Its subject was the nymph Nemea (Pliny, *HN* 35.131) riding on a lion. Even in some highly programmatic buildings Augustus continued the tradition, established by republican *imperatores*, of exhibiting Greek art because it was an adornment in its own right and because it conferred prestige.[50]

Finally, while much of the sculpture recalled the classical and archaic traditions, much of the architecture that housed it surpassed its Hellenistic predecessors in opulence and magnificence. The Corinthian order was triumphant, with new heights of lavish detail (Figs. 112, 134).[51] Although Vitruvius (1.2.5) considered the Doric order as particularly appropriate for temples of Mars, there was no attempt to return to the solemnity of this style which had shaped the appearance of some of the most imposing archaic and classical Greek buildings. One good reason for not doing so was that there was plenty of architectural venerability around in the form of the older temples, which were rebuilt with the traditional materials of wood and terracotta. Livy's Cato saw in them the essence of Roman religion and contrasted them with Greek *luxuria*.[52] Many decades after Augustus, Pliny emphasized that acroteria made of clay had a greater aura of holiness than gold (*sanctiora auro*) and certainly were "more innocent" (*certe innocentiora*; 35.158). Juvenal (11.116) voiced similar sentiments in connection with the Golden Age. These concerns mirror one of the essential tensions of the Augustan "Golden Age" that we observed earlier.

True classicism—we need to think only of Palladio, Jefferson, Soane, and Schinkel—is a far cry from replication and epigonism. Rather, it involves the attempt to recapture the spirit of the classical model for one's own time. It is, therefore, always experimental, a hallmark of Augustan culture. An outstanding example, in addition to the many we have already cited, is the use of architectural ornament for the Temple of Castor and Pollux in the Roman Forum. The previous temple burned down in 14 or 9 B.C., and a completely new marble temple was dedicated by Tiberius in A.D. 6. Besides the three columns that are a landmark of the Forum today, we have a number of smaller architectural fragments from components such as column capitals and its abaci, the architrave and its palmetto and lotus frieze, soffits, and cymas. Few as they are, they are outstanding especially for their innovative treatment of vegetal forms, prompting Donald Strong and John Ward Perkins to their succinct formulation, which I have cited earlier,[53] of the relation between Augustan classicism and experiment. They also belie the common notion that the later part of Augustus' reign was lacking in vitality and marked by statism, if not decline.

It is a commonplace that the interaction—terms like "influence" are too passive—between Greek and Roman, which had characterized Roman poetry from its inception, reached its apogee in Augustan poetry. The programmatic poem that concludes Horace's first collection of *Odes* (*C.* 3.30) is without equal for the rich succinctness with which it makes this point. The overriding achievement of books 1–3 of the *Odes* was the many-faceted fusion of Greek and Roman in lyric poetry. That claim is triumphantly restated by Horace at the end of this ode: *princeps Aeolium carmen ad Italos / deduxisse modos* (13–14). The ode itself, therefore, is exquisitely crafted as the consummate monument to the Greek and Roman synthesis on which his poetic immortality is based. Greek and Roman elements are interwoven at every turn:[54]

> exegi monumentum aere perennius
> regalique situ pyramidum altius,
> quod non imber edax, non Aquilo impotens
> possit diruere aut innumerabilis
> annorum series et fuga temporum.   5
> non omnis moriar, multaque pars mei
> vitabit Libitinam: usque ego postera
> crescam laude recens, dum Capitolium
> scandet cum tacita virgine pontifex.
> dicar, qua violens obstrepit Aufidus   10
> et qua pauper aquae Daunus agrestium
> regnavit populorum, ex humili potens
> princeps Aeolium carmen ad Italos
> deduxisse modos. sume superbiam
> quaesitam meritis et mihi Delphica   15
> lauro cinge volens, Melpomene, comam.

It will be clear from the following that we would need several translations, if not outright paraphrases, to do justice to the many layers of the poem and its resulting intricacy. It is impossible to translate Horace, but here is a workmanlike approximation:[55]

I have crafted a memorial more lasting through the years than bronze and higher than the royal site of the pyramids, which neither biting rain nor the north wind in its fury can destroy nor the series of years that cannot be numbered (5). Not all of me shall die, and a great part of me shall escape the Goddess of Death: I shall grow, ever renewed, through the praise of posterity, as long as the priest shall climb the Capitol with the silent Vestal virgin. I shall be spoken of, where the violent Aufidus roars (10), and where Daunus, poor in water, has ruled over his rustic peoples, as, mighty from a humble origin, having been the first to bring Aeolian poetry to Italian verse. Take on the pride that has been won by my own merits, Melpomene, and graciously crown my hair with Delphic laurel.

Eduard Fraenkel said about the poem's opening sentence that it "revives thoughts familiar from Greek poetry, especially choral lyrics; in it there is nothing that might not have been said by a Greek poet."[56] That is only one side of it, however. There are multiple echoes of the poetry of Pindar, who wrote that "the treasure house of his songs" was immune to rainstorms and wind (*P*. 6.7–14); as in Horace, there are real buildings behind the metaphor, such as the treasuries at Delphi. Elsewhere, Pindar compared his victory song to a marker (*stēlē*) whiter than Parian marble (*N*. 4.81). Similar is Bacchylides' characterization of his song as "the immortal *agalma* of the Muses" (*Epin*. 10.11); *agalma* connotes statuary. Horace also echoed Simonides' famous epigram on the fallen at Thermopylae (Simon. 26 [Page]) who were immortalized by a grave-altar and by his poetry that will make them survive the effects of time and physical decay. Pindar further emphasized the superiority of his poetry to bronze statues (*N*. 5.1–3); a similar sentiment was expressed by Isocrates who said of one of his speeches that "it will be left behind as a monument that is much more beautiful than bronze offerings" (*Antid*. 7). The list could be continued, but we should take note of two important characteristics at this point. One is that Horace practices the eclectic universalism that is the hallmark of Augustan classicism. He draws on several models for inspiration. The other characteristic is that none of these models is taken over as it is. In each case, Horace adapts and makes changes. Greece comes to Rome, but is creatively transformed. Simonides, for instance, speaks of others; Horace, of himself. With all the echoes, he coins his own phrases: *situs pyramidum*, *annorum series*, and *fuga temporum* have no exact Greek analogues nor do they occur in Latin before this poem.

Another aspect of Horace's blending of Greek and Roman is the tradition of tomb inscriptions and epigrams. That tradition is both Greek and Roman and the relevant parallels to our poem have been well documented.[57] With the similarities come the differences. While to the Roman reader *monumentum* in this context would immediately suggest a tomb, Horace's choice of the word for "to build" has no counterpart in the surviving Roman inscriptions: instead, they use words like *aedificare, locare, facere*, and *absolvere*.[58] *Exigere* also sounds the note of careful craftsmanship in the tradition of Hellenistic poetry.[59] This was more than apropos: for Horace, even less than for the Augustan artists and architects, there was no dichotomy between Hellenistic and archaic art forms. Besides, Hellenistic poets such as Meleager (*AP* 7.417–19) had written fictitious tomb epigrams about themselves, often to punctuate the close of a book. In addition, there had been a proliferation in Hellenistic poetry of imaginary epitaphs for the great poets of the past.[60] Another formal aspect of the poem also is very much in the Alexandrian tradition: it is a *sphragis*, a "seal," by which a poet put a personal imprint on his collection. But immediately, Roman reality makes itself felt, too: besides several tomb *monumenta* of Roman nobles that were built at Horace's time and before, the most conspicuous and familiar example was the mausoleum Octavian constructed for himself and his family between ca. 32 and 23 B.C.[61] Accordingly, Propertius, who understood Horace well, refers to the original Mausoleum in Asia Minor (and to the pyramids) in the elegy with which he wants to set a monument to Cynthia (3.2.21). There is more: Octavian wanted to create a counterexample to Antony's wish to be buried with Cleopatra in Egypt. Hence the fitting reference to the Egyptian pyramids in line 2. The implication of Horace's reference to both monuments is clear: his poetic immortality will be more permanent yet than that of the mightiest wordly rulers. It is typical that *situ* can also connote decay. And it is typical that the extent to which such implications can be pursued is left to the reader.[62]

Aere perennius: the references again do not exhaust themselves in Greek poetry but extend to Roman realities—another, prominent example of an essential symbiosis which Jasper Griffin has illustrated with great care and common sense for Augustan poetry, Horace and the elegists in particular.[63] The range of references here includes bronze plaques on tombs, bronze tablets that had laws engraved on them and were known to melt on occasion (Cic., *Cat.* 3.19), and the long-standing mania for honorific statues in Rome that led Augustus, as we saw earlier, to clear the mass of them from the Capitoline area and relocate them to the Campus Martius.[64] Closer to heaven than all was Octavian's own statue, displayed at the very top of the mausoleum. And, as a by-product of the Augustan building program, there was a veritable explosion of inscriptions, many of them honorific, that became part of the Roman cityscape. Their new, distinctive characteristic was that they were made of large bronze letters, which were either inlaid or affixed to the stone surface.[65] Indeed they would be exposed to the elements. Besides the integration of such Roman *Realien*, Horace strikes another Roman note: a tribute to Ennius, the founding father of Roman poetry, who preceded him in bringing Greek meter, the hexameter, to Roman verse. The homage is paid, as so often in Roman poetry, by allusions to Ennius' poetry, in this case the proem to book 16 of the *Annales*.[66] Another model is Ennius' famous epitaph in which he asserted his immortality (*Varia* 17–18 V.) though it was not an epilogue like Horace's poem. As always, Horace indicates that he is both like and unlike his predecessors.

In the next four lines, the Roman turn continues: the death goddess is called by her Latin name, Libitina (7), and the image at the center of the poem is that of the eternal ritual of the priest and the Vestal on the Capitol, symbol of permanence (cf. Vergil, *Aen.* 9.446–49). The clause, however, into which this Roman reality is imbedded, again echoes the immortality tradition in Greek poetry. "As long as earth and sun exist," said Theognis (252), while Critias (fr. 1.5ff. D.) predicted that Anacreon's songs would survive "as long as wine and water will be mixed."[67] Not unexpectedly, *dum* clauses also occur in Roman tomb inscriptions.[68] We may note in passing that Horace strikes a classical balance between individual and society: he emphatically uses *ego* when he speaks of his future fame, but this fame will exist only in the context of Roman society and cult. This balance continues in the next lines: the geography extends beyond Rome, but is that of Horace's humble origins in southern Italy. Further, while Horace's self-confidence is immense, he does not use the usual trope of saying that his hometown will become famous because of him; he varies the expression.

The mention of the Italian locale again is combined with a Greek grammatical construction, the genitive after *regnare* (12). And there are more associations. As we noted earlier, captured Greece, Horace says in his *Letter to Augustus*, captured her fierce conqueror and brought arts to rustic (*agresti*) Latium. Here, Horace's poetic fame will be spoken of in a part of Italy where Daunus once ruled over rustic (*agrestium*) peoples, but Horace is very much the triumphator who is bringing Greek poetry to his land. We are also reminded of Ennius again, this time through Lucretius' mediation. In language to which Horace is alluding, Lucretius wrote (1.117–21) that Ennius, the maker of eternal verse, was the first Roman poet to bring a crown with lasting (*perenni*) leaves from Mount Helicon, to be gloriously renowned throughout the peoples of Italy. Horace uses the same motifs but again does not simply "imitate." The reference to the Italian river, for instance, takes the place of Mount Helicon, which, like Hippocrene and other waters in Greece, was a common symbol of the seat of the Muses and of poetic inspiration.

Like the poem, the fusion of Greek and Roman reaches its height in the last five lines, centering on Horace's immortal achievement to have brought Greek lyric poetry to Italian verse and on his deserved coronation by the Muse with a laurel wreath. To begin with, Horace reminds us that he was a *homo novus* who rose to the pinnacle from humble origins. Then, as one might expect, the key phrase *princeps Aeolium carmen ad Italos / deduxisse modos* has several meanings and associations. Horace's accomplishment takes place on Italian soil, but the trope of being "the first" puts him in the Greek and, especially, Hellenistic poetic tradition of being an inventor, a *heuretēs*. But by choosing "princeps" instead of "primus" Horace also reinforces the theme of his equivalence, in his realm, to the mightiest worldly ruler, who also rose to his position from relatively humble family origins.[69] Again, Propertius (3.1.1–20) understood Horace perfectly as he followed up, with a triumph rivaling Augustus', on his claim to be the first to spread Callimachus' poetry through Italy. Both Propertian topics are expansions of the connotations of the Horatian *deduxisse*. One is the image of the triumph, which continues the Roman dimension of the poem. The end point of the triumphal procession was the Temple of Jupiter on the Capitoline to which the priest and the Vestal were seen ascending in the poem's center. As for the Greek aspect, *deducere* in the sense of "crafting" or "spinning finely" was a signal characterization of Hellenistic and, especially, Callimachean poetic technique. In addition, the entire phrase *princeps . . . modos* may refer to his achievement of fitting Greek meters to the Latin language and, specifically, to his adaptation of Aeolic meters to Latin by changing the place of the break (caesura) in Sapphic lines.[70] Meter (*modus*) was crucial in ancient poetry and Horace's innovations could rightly be considered part of his claim to fame, just as Ennius' had been. The peculiar phrasing also seems to suggest that Horace has naturalized these alien meters so thoroughly that they are now, in effect, Italian.

It is impossible to catch up all these ramifications in a straightforward English translation. We would have to resort to paraphrase, as David Ross has done:[71] "I, principally, claim for my poetry a descent from the ancient lyric and choral poets, especially Sappho and Alcaeus, in spirit and in my verse form; but I write as well in the spirit of Callimachus and his Roman descendants, and in so doing have naturally transformed my original models; further, I write with a special purpose, to make thoroughly Italian, in manner and matter, this double Greek inheritance." Nor does this exhaust all the connotations of *deduxisse*: the image of founding a colony, of leading a group of people to a new settlement, is also part of the semantic spectrum.

The last example of the Greco-Roman synthesis is the concluding image of the crowning of the poet. It is the Delphic Muse who crowns him, but the poet is also a Roman triumphator who deserves his laurels. For contemporaries of Augustus there was an even more specific connotation. The laurels were his permanent emblem, granted to him in recognition of his achievements: *quo pro* merito *senatus consulto Augustus appellatus sum et* laureis *postes aedium mearum vestiti publice*—"for these merits of mine I was named Augustus by decree of the senate, and the doorposts of my house were publicly adorned with laurel." There are good reasons for this coincidence between the concluding portion of the *Res Gestae* (34.2) and the conclusion of Horace's *Ode* 3.30, which is itself the conclusion to the first collection of

Odes. Both are the proud acknowledgment of the reception of extraordinary honors for extraordinary accomplishments. Horace, of course, did not have to wait for the publication of the *Res Gestae*; the Augustan phrase no doubt mirrors the honorific terminology of 27 B.C. which must have become as common as the emblems of the laurel and the oaken crown (cf. Figs. 17, 142b, 144a and b). Once more, Horace presents himself as equal to Augustus, but the balance is finely spun. With almost tautological hyperbole he announces at the beginning of the poem that his lyric poetry will be even more permanent than the mightiest edifices of rulers. Horace does not need to lessen Augustus to build himself up. On the contrary, his own permanence is bound up with that of Rome and he owes to Roman society and to Augustus his rise to being, in his own way, Augustus' equal. Quite fittingly, therefore, the poem ends with a gift exchange. Once more, the literary precedent is Greek, in the form of epigrams.[72] In contemporary practice, gift exchange was an important model, as we saw earlier, in Augustus' relations with the plebs and its religion, and in the imperial cult.

In sum, the poem thrives on the interaction between learned *imitatio* of Greek poetry and Roman realities. Horace restated it as a general maxim in the *Ars Poetica*:

> respicere exemplar vitae morumque iubebo
> doctum imitatorem et vivas hinc ducere voces.
>
> (317–18)

[I should advise that the learned imitator look to the model of life and customs and bring forth living voices from there.]

This *exemplar* complements the *exemplaria Graeca* with which a Roman poet needs to involve himself day and night (268–69). Another example *in parvo* of the symbiosis of Greek and Roman in Horace's poetry is his penchant for coining programmatic poetic phrases that combine a Greek and a Roman concept, such as *Graia Camena, Romana lyra, Latinus barbitos,* and *lyricus vates*.[73]

There was no doubt about Horace's achievement, which led to the singular honor of being asked to compose the *Carmen Saeculare*; the notion that Augustus might have borne him a grudge because Horace confidently pronounced his equality with the *princeps* is another product of the skewed perspective from which Augustan Rome has been viewed as a precursor of totalitarian regimes in the twentieth century. But Horace was disappointed with the reception of his first collection of *Odes* (books 1–3), and the disappointment may have been shared by Augustus. Brilliant as Horace's achievement was, it was highly aesthetic and too refined to be shared widely—no *publicatio* here, quite in contrast to Greek and Augustan art in Rome. Horace made no bones about not writing lyric poetry for a broader public: "I hate the common folk and keep it away" (*odi profanum vulgus et arceo*; *C.* 3.1.1) is how he pointedly introduces his "Roman Odes." And yet, he had expected a better response; one reason he imitated Alcaeus is that Alcaeus had written on public themes. The reception of *Odes* 1–3 seems to have been meager at best. Further, there was the envy directed at him by less gifted poets (obviously, a considerable number) about whom he complains in *Epistle* 1.19[74] and, to the end, he felt he had to remind Augustus to foster lyric, and not just epic, poetry (*Epist.* 2.1.214ff.).

Vergil, by contrast, did write an epic that appealed not only to connoisseurs but also to the broader populace, as is evident from Pompeian graffiti, tombstones, terracotta lamps, and the like. But the *Aeneid* also exemplifies that the formal models of the Augustan poets did not come from the classical period of Athens. The distinctive poetry of the classical age had been drama. Its state under Augustus was negligible, prompting Horace to lament (see chapter 3), though not to write tragedy himself. Augustan Rome could not replicate fifth-century Athens. What is typical of the *Aeneid*, and of other aspects of Augustan culture too, is that it incorporated a classical model, in this case Greek tragedy, more in spirit than in form. The first seven lines of the epic are an exquisite commingling of the main themes of the *Iliad* and *Odyssey* with a new Roman orientation. Only then comes the invocation to the Muse (1.8–11) and it centers squarely on a cardinal theme from Greek tragedy: the question of divine justice and deserved or undeserved human suffering. This is followed (up to line 296) by a device also adapted from Greek tragedy, an exposition and anticipation of the action by means of a prologue. The further consequence is that, just as in Greek tragedy, the outcome is known and the hearers' attention after the prologue can be focused not on the externals of the plot, but on the real drama: the motivations and psychology of the characters, their emotions, dilemmas, and inner conflicts. That is the underlying reason for Vergil's many "borrowings" from the Greek tragedians.[75] Aristophanes merely expressed the *vox populi* in the *Frogs* when he emphasized the role of the tragic poet as a moral educator of the city; the *Aeneid* and the *Oresteia*, for instance, can certainly be compared in terms of being "both highly public works of literature which seek to validate a social and political order."[76] Homer, however, was also read not merely for aesthetic pleasure but as the educator of all of Greece. Following Ennius, to whom he pays due honors, Vergil used the Homeric form and tradition to express Roman and Augustan values.

As with Horace's *Ode* 3.30, we could demonstrate the constant interaction and layering of Greek and Roman elements in just about any passage of the *Aeneid*. There is no shortage of such studies, however, and it is therefore more profitable to remark on the Augustan poets' fascination with Hellenistic poetry. The main "models" of both Vergil's and Horace's poetry were archaic and Hellenistic. There was no dichotomy between the two; instead, the Hellenistic writers had been preoccupied with both the poetic and the scholarly recovery of the archaic poets. The Latin poets, in turn, "could not know the culture of archaic Greece through any medium other than that provided by the culture of Hellenistic Greece."[77]

The Augustan and the Alexandrian poets faced similar situations. The latter, in Rudolf Pfeiffer's words, "became conscious of a definitive break between the mighty past and a still uncertain present."[78] Hence their attempts both to retrieve and recreate the grand poetry of the past. One result was Alexandrian scholarship. A second result, which is more germane to the Augustans (and we should always keep in mind that they, in contrast to us, had access to the complete works of the archaic and classical writers), was the Alexandrian poets' "desire to come to terms with the cultural heritage of Hellas"[79] in a new and creative way. The Alexandrians were in a foreign land and "felt a deep psychological need for a sense of unity with mainstream Greek culture" in order to shape their own identity. Callimachus pronounced himself to be the new Hesiod (F 2 [Pfeiffer]), but the emphasis was as much on "new" as it was on "Hesiod": he modernized the Hesiodic catalog poem and his verbal and contextual adaptations of Hesiod are characterized by almost constant alterations of the original.[80] The main endeavor of Callimachus, Theocritus, Apollonius, and others was to attune the inherited material to contemporary sensibilities. A result was experimentation including, for instance, the crossing of genres (again Hesiod was invoked as a precursor), which at the time were far from fixed.

It is easy to see how all these characteristics, in varying degrees, apply to Vergil, Horace, Ovid, and the elegists. Their pervasive utilization of Hellenistic material is not merely a bookish exercise; rather, it stems from an existential situation similar to that of the Hellenistic poets. Two brief examples may stand for many others.

Our first example involves the relevance of epic and, specifically, epic heroism. Callimachus, contrary to a view long held by scholars, did not denounce epic, but when Apollonius decided to write his *Argonautica*, he consciously did so at less than Homeric length and with a thoroughly modernized hero.[81] Jason has none of the strong, let alone superhuman qualities of the traditional hero, such as instinctive self-confidence and zest for action. To fulfill a superhuman, heroic task he has available only the resources of an ordinary man—a citizen of Hellenistic Greece, for all practical purposes. The only exception is that he is extremely handsome. The marked absence of machismo and the recourse to restraint and tact may be, from our perspective and that of Apollonius' original audience, a sympathetic consequence of Apollonius' modernization of the hero. The downside is his helplessness, which becomes a leitmotif, and his constant hesitating, stumbling, and improvising. In the end, the arms of the modern hero—skill, improvisation, and persuasion—fail abysmally. Cornered by Medea's pursuing brother

Apsyrtus and his army, Jason is ready to buy his way out by giving up the woman who was his savior. After Medea's outcry, Jason instead lures Apsyrtus into a trap and butchers him right by the Temple of Artemis. "Evil deeds commit us to exploits as evil as the deeds themselves" (4.411–12) is the rationalization.

When we compare this modernization to Vergil's, we can see the difference between a postmodern epic, which lives by the problematic tension between a traditional concept and its new setting, and an attempt to fill the old epic form with some changed, but genuinely substantive meaning. This is not meant to be a value judgment. Vergil knew the challenge that Apollonius had faced; he both owed a great deal to his predecessor and, at the same time, went much beyond him. Aeneas is not a superman either—witness his entrance into the epic which I discussed earlier (pp. 123–24)—and he faces plenty of dilemmas, to the very end of the epic. His actions, however, have a meaningful purpose and he has values to guide him, even if they are constantly tested against the realities of life. And, in contrast to Jason, he remains a dominating warrior on the battlefield, the forerunner of Roman *imperatores* rather than a mere Homeric fighter. In short, Vergil did not simply go back to the archaic Homer, but continued where the Hellenistic Apollonius had left off.

Another example of Vergil's use of a Hellenistic prism is the world of the Homeric simile. Homer likes to juxtapose the mighty exploits of kings and warriors with the rustic world of shepherds and hunters amid the ambience of nature, or with the homely word of humble people. Theocritus, for one, fastened on that aspect of Homer's epics and inverted it:[82] the scenes from the simile now become part of the pastoral world that Theocritus is constructing. Similarly, when Callimachus told the story of Herakles and the Nemean lion, he finished that action off in a few verses while lingering over the domestic activities, reminiscent of Homeric similes, of the farmer Molorchus at whose hut Herakles visited.[83] Vergil followed Theocritus' procedure in the *Georgics*. He set the tone with a programmatic allusion to Homer's famous simile that compared the battle of the river Xanthus against Achilles, and especially his pursuit (*Il.* 21.256–64), to a man who is channeling water from a stream to irrigate his plants. Soon the water flows more quickly than he can guide it. "In this way the flood of the water kept overtaking Achilles, fleet on foot as he was. For the gods are mightier than men." In the *Georgics* (1.104–110), the Homeric details turn into reality as they are being used for the description of the farmer's tasks of irrigation and drainage. In typically Vergilian and Augustan fashion, the adaptation is not simply a matter of aesthetics, but has meaningful and multiple dimensions.[84] While the world of the farmer will be the primary world, the Homeric world of the warrior becomes part of the persistent military metaphor in the *Georgics* for the farmer's unrelenting battle to subdue the land. The Homeric context is also a reminder that nature is difficult to control and the gods need to be reckoned with. Both these themes recur a few lines later in the important "theodicy" passage (see chapter 3). Further, the programmatic allusion to Homer in a non-Homeric way signifies that Vergil is both shaping Homeric epic for the requirements of his own didactic poem and recognizing the didactic function of Homer in the Greek tradition as a shaper of values and exemplars. Lastly, of course, there is the reminder that this kind of adaptation builds on Hellenistic precedent. It underlines the obvious fact that Vergil utilized many Hellenistic works, including Aratus' *Phaenomena*, for the *Georgics*. We are again looking at a fine example, in microcosm, of how the Augustans used *exemplaria Graeca* to express their own distinctive ideas.

Three related considerations are raised by these examples. The first is that the *Georgics*, like the *Aeneid* and the *Metamorphoses*, "drew from the whole range of Greek and Roman literature."[85] As in Augustan art and architecture, it is best to define their "classicism" not simply in terms of "style" but also in terms of the endeavor I have defined before, that is, to create surpassing works that made use of all previous traditions. Second, while any analogy between works of art and works of literature must not be taken to the point of effacing the differences between these media, it is clear that Augustan culture cannot be reduced to the schema of "classicism" (including archaism) versus "Hellenistic." The interactions in poetry alone were much more subtle and complex, and similar considerations apply even to Augustan sculpture. Third, we have seen that the best works of Augustan art ask for a great deal of active participation on the part of the viewer. The same is true, even if in somewhat different ways, of Augustan poetry. The layers of allusion or intertextuality that we have observed engage the reader in a creative dialogue, which explores the many dimensions and nuances of themes adapted from earlier works and integrated into a new poetic context and structure.[86] This is an essential dynamic of Augustan culture. The reason for the Augustan poets' ability to advance this process to unprecedented heights of sophistication, subtlety, and meaning may well be that, despite all the Greco-Roman contact from early on, they still could look upon Greek culture in a more distanced way and thus were removed "from the oedipal mesh of anxiety which necessarily entangled Callimachus and his peers."[87] For the Alexandrian Greeks, Greek culture had been a matter of transfer. For the Romans and the Augustans, it was a matter of reception.[88] This difference may have enabled them to be even more creative than the Hellenistic writers, and certainly more creative than their Greek contemporaries: while Greek literary production during the reign of Augustus was enormous in bulk, "lacking were imagination and genius; creativity—in drama, mime, fiction, elegy, pastoral or epic—was utterly absent."[89] Finally, there was no classical period in Roman literature on which the Augustan poets could fall back or, just as important, by which they could be inhibited. Hence they were free to create it.

Ovid, as we have seen (chapter 5), was very much part of this milieu. Facile labels that have been applied to him, such as "counterclassical" or "un-Augustan," derive from a stereotyped vision of Augustan culture that does little justice to the creativity present in the late Augustan age. As for the fusion between Greek and Roman in his work, it is too simple to say that he told Greek myths in Augustan Rome. His sources may be mostly Greek, but no Greek had created anything remotely similar to the *Metamorphoses*. As Horace did in *Ode* 3.30, Ovid both puts himself in the Callimachean tradition by using the word *deducere* in his proem (1.4) and announces that he will be deviating from it by writing a *carmen perpetuum*, which will be much longer than Callimachus' *Aitia*. The *Metamorphoses* follows, as we have seen, the universalizing framework of Augustan times and appropriately draws on the whole range of Greek and Roman literature with the concomitant crossing of genres.[90] In that sense, it is part of Augustan classicism. Moreover, in terms of presentation, Ovid has a marked preference for the individual episode as opposed to an equilibrated narrative. Augustan public art provides a useful point of reference with its emphasis on individual "contemplative images" rather than narrative friezes. The scenes, of course, are not unconnected—witness the Ara Pacis, the Boscoreale cups, and the figures on the cuirass of the Prima Porta statue. They are tied together by multiple associations, many of which the observer is called upon to make. Ovid appropriates this Augustan mentality for the largely Greek material of the *Metamorphoses*. It is clear that his masterpiece is not "classical" when measured by the criteria of balanced structure and formal perfection, such as we find in Horace's *Odes* and Vergil's *Aeneid* (though we should note that the principle of careful craftsmanship was a hallmark of Alexandrian poetry and is another example that the line between "classical" and "Hellenistic" cannot be drawn rigidly). Overemphasis on limited formal aspects only obscures Ovid's Augustanism and the distinctive contribution he made to one of its central aspects, the synthesis of Greek and Roman.

It is clear from the foregoing that Hellenism in Augustan Rome was much more complex than a mere imitation of classical Athens. The Forum of Augustus is a specific example and we can briefly enlarge our perspective on the phenomenon. Rome had taken Athens' place as the cultural as well as the political capital of the Mediterranean. The Augustan "citations" of Athenian culture, therefore, track those of the Attalid kings, who had claimed the cultural mantle of Athens before. At the same time, these citations continued neo-Attic, classicizing, and archaizing styles from the late republic. Similarly, they include continued importation of original classical works and copies and the incorporation of certain architectural details like the caryatids (which made such an impression that they were copied once more on an Augustan edifice in Mérida).[91] Moreover, the reenactment of the sea battle of Salamis in 2 B.C. seems to have found some resonance in private art.[92] Like much of Augustan art, however, Augustan government and literature did not look to Athens as the dominant model. While Augustus projected himself as *civilis princeps* ruling by virtue of his *auctoritas*, he was not about to be buffeted by a fickle mob like Pericles.[93] Augustus set himself in the tradition of the great figures of Rome, not Greece, with the prominent exception of Alexander, who was anything but a Periclean figure. As for a revival of drama recalling the heyday of Athens, the social and demographic conditions in Augustan Rome were simply too different from those of fifth-century Athens to be conducive to such an attempt. Augustus succeeded, with constant travail, where the senatorial government had failed, that is, in keeping the plebs pacified. The public performance of highly literary plays was hardly an effective means to that end. Different kinds of entertainment were called for including, as we saw earlier (chapter 5), the pantomime, which emptied drama of any spiritual content. What is more, Augustus truly was a man of the people in this regard and avidly attended any type of show; one gets the distinct impression from Suetonius' account (*Aug.* 43–45) that he did not do so under duress. Part of the reason for Horace's inclusion of the sorry state of the contemporary Roman theater in his *querelle* to Augustus (*Epist.* 2.1.161ff.) may have been the realization that this was one area where Augustan Rome lagged conspicuously behind the culture of Athens.

Besides, it was more comfortable to look at Athens as an ideal than to deal with the real Athens at the time. The realities there included a blood-spitting statue of Athena during Augustus' visit in the winter of 22–21 B.C. (Dio 54.7.3), a reflection perhaps of the bad blood between him and the *demos*.[94] It did not help that Augustus reduced income to the Athenian treasury by freeing Eretria and Aegina from their tributary obligations to Athens and by forbidding Athens to sell its citizenship for money. As a result, he spent the winter on a grateful Aegina rather than at Athens. That was not the end of the troubles. The city may also have risen in revolt late in Augustus' reign. In the meantime, the Athenian Agora had been reconstructed to resemble the Porticus Octaviae (Fig. 156), as a temple and Agrippa's Odeion were erected in its midst (Fig. 169).[95] While the temple was native to Attica, having stood previously at a site near Athens, it could be seen, along with the huge Odeion, as a deliberate disruption of civic activities in its new setting. Dedicated to Ares, it was a kind of extension of the Temple of Mars in the Augustan forum whose Athenian borrowings now had produced an annoying case of reciprocity. There is a striking contrast between this forcible restructuring and the Stoa of Attalus, the gift of Pergamon's Athenophile king, which had accommodated itself readily to the Agora's function and layout.

169. Model of the Athenian Agora with Odeion (in center), Temple of Ares, and Stoa of Attalus.

To return to our Greek tourist: the culture of Augustan Rome would have been comprehensible almost completely in terms of Hellenism. There is a difference, however, between this comprehensibility and the degree to which a given Augustan institution, artifact, or work of literature consciously drew on the posited Greek or Hellenistic model. For instance, the *Aeneid* can certainly be read from the perspective of Hellenistic treatises on what makes a good king, but it is not clear that this was one of Vergil's intentions.[96] Similarly, an enumeration of "Hellenistic influences on the structure of the Augustan principate"[97] makes for instructive reading and would have gone over well with an audience of Hellenistic Greeks, but not all resemblances can be attributed to intentional borrowing. At the same time, Greek and Roman could become so thoroughly intermingled as to be indistinguishable. The ongoing controversy about the Terme Ruler (Fig. 76) is a good illustration of that fact, nor is it the only such example.[98]

All this would, no doubt, have utterly delighted Augustus. Before his death, Suetonius tells us (*Aug.* 98.3), the old man sojourned to Capri, which was part of the cultural ambience of Naples, the most Greek city in Italy. There he distributed, for several days, Greek clothing to Romans and Roman clothing to Greeks, and he proposed that Romans and Greeks should use each other's dress and language. It was that ambience, too, to which Vergil paid tribute at the end of the *Georgics* (4.563–64) because "it kept nourishing me as I flourished in the endeavors of inglorious *otium*" (*me . . . alebat Parthenope studiis florentem ignobilis oti*). Vergil's *sphragis* of the *Georgics*, a poem that was as consummate a synthesis of Greek and Roman as Horace's first collection of *Odes*, has often been considered surprising for its lack of emphatic self-proclamation, relative to *Ode* 3.30. Vergil did not use it to announce his poetic immortality. In his own way, however, he said just as much about the Greco-Roman symbiosis, which was so characteristic of the age, as Horace did.

TRADITION AND INNOVATION

No historical period is immune to change: there is always some interplay between tradition and innovation. Yet the phenomenon deserves to be singled out as a characteristic of the Augustan age for two main reasons. First is the extraordinary intensity of the exchange between old and new. Syme well characterized the Augustan principate as the "binding link between the Republic and the Empire."[99] Both the degree of adherence to tradition and the new departures were extraordinary and can be seen in every aspect of Augustan culture. Extraordinary, too, was the creative tension between them. Though intense, such changes, particularly in the areas of Augustan politics and administration, were gradual and evolutionary, but they were all the more thorough for it and led to a stable system of government for the next two hundred years. Second, it is precisely this image of stability and the very identification of the term "Augustan" with the notion in later contexts that led to the Augustan period being regarded as sublimely static and solidly molded by the fixed designs of its prescient maker from beginning to end. To the English, French, and Saxon Augustans the Augustan model represented a high point of established cultural excellence and serenely unshakable royal government. As a result, the formative processes and the dynamic gradualism that were hallmarks of the age were overlooked.

We have seen numerous examples of the mingling of tradition and innovation in Augustan art, literature, architecture, and religion, and it would be easy to add more. The phenomenon is pervasive and in many ways at its most fascinating when it is seen not in the grand design but in the details, such as poetic diction, architectural ornament, or the stupendous increase in the number and function of inscriptions. Instead of expanding on these instances, I will focus on government and administration. The transition that took place in this area is of underlying significance to the world of Augustan arts and letters, too. This is not to say that Vergil, Propertius, and others would otherwise not have been as innovative, but the historical framework in which they lived can be said to have set a certain tone.

Augustan government and administration were an ongoing experiment in pragmatism and the negotiation and renegotiation of precedents with regard to new needs and changing circumstances.[100] There were two parameters that provided continuity. One was Augustus' determination not to relinquish power. He did not want to exercise it illegitimately, let alone continue the massacres of the triumviral period. But he wanted to remain in control, being, in the words of a fourth-century historian, "most desirous of rule, beyond anything we can estimate."[101] As we have seen, it was not a feasible alternative to let the republic revert to its self-destructive ways. The ongoing challenge, in which all parties involved had to feel their way, was the integration of Augustus' special position with the system of republican government. The second parameter, which we also observed earlier, was a clear concept of government on the basis of republican values rather than technicalities. Consonant with this vital concept of the *res publica* was the endeavor to broaden the base of participation, in all kinds of ways, beyond the previous oligarchy while there were continuing attempts to involve the nobility as much as possible and to make its members view the *res publica* in terms of its central values rather than their privileges.

Within these defining boundaries, then, there was a great deal of flux. The term "settlement" that has been used to mark some of the junctures in the process of governmental rearrangement conveys a stronger air of finality than these stages possessed at the time. The overall picture that emerges is neither one of doctrinaire planning nor of sudden ad hoc responses to "crises." Instead it is one of gradual development with considerable flexibility within a guiding framework of ideas. It is instructive to review some specific instances.

That the first "settlement" of 27 B.C. was the product of carefully thought-out negotiations between the senate and Octavian is uncontested. Its provisions and trade-offs had been prepared for by some of his actions in the previous year. Besides, their careful calibration and their complexity attest their deliberate nature. Octavian returned the *res publica* to the *arbitrium* of the senate and the people. The senate reciprocated by giving him command over several provinces while retaining others, including the legions stationed in them, and by granting him special honors, such as the name "Augustus" and the *clupeus virtutis*. He was consul and was able to exert his consular *imperium* even in the senatorial provinces. The entire agreement was a compromise that duly considered the widely shared desire for a return to legitimate government, Octavian's equally strong desire to remain in charge, and the fear that the republic would revert to chaos if the senatorial oligarchy tried to govern without him. What is remarkable is that Augustus could depart within less than half a year on military expeditions in Gaul and Spain and be absent from Rome for three years without the slightest occurrence of civil disorders.

The arrangements made between 23 and 19 B.C. were just as subtle. The number of almost consecutive consulships (eleven) Augustus had held by the year 23 B.C. exceeded republican precedent. Further, in a paradox well described by Syme and Badian, between 27 and 24 B.C. "the *res publica* had not functioned particularly well in the hands of the Senate and the People. Indeed, it had proved impossible to reach serious decisions. An absent consul with such overpowering *auctoritas* that political processes were paralysed without him was, if anything, worse than a present one actively exercising his power."[102] Augustus, therefore, carefully planned to abdicate his consulship and there are indications that his fellow consul, the staunch republican Calpurnius Piso, was in on the plan. Disaster almost struck as Augustus fell seriously ill; on the verge of death, he demonstratively handed his papers to Piso and his ring, to Agrippa; no such transfer was made to Marcellus, his first male heir. After his recovery, he continued his republican gestures: he gave up the consulship in which another senator with unquestioned republican credentials succeeded him. The transactional means by which he could effect control changed: both the *tribunicia potestas* (awarded for life) and the *imperium proconsulare maius* (awarded for a renewable five-year term) were republican powers, but the former was granted to him without the requirement that he actually hold the office of tribune of the people.[103] More republican behavior followed as Augustus returned the provinces of Cyprus and Gallia Narbonensis to the senate in 22 B.C.; two censors were appointed in the same year, and the *tresviri monetales* were reinstated about that time.

The lesson, which may well have been intended, that too much republicanism could be a bad thing was not long in waiting. It includes the disturbance I mentioned earlier, the famine and rioting in 22 B.C. and the politicking by Egnatius Rufus in 19 B.C. The consul Augustus had treated the citizens of Rome to donations of money and grain in 24 B.C. They sorely missed him in 22 B.C. and urged him to accept the dictatorship. This he wisely refused—there were other ways to become a *divus*—though he assumed the care of the grain supply. The important aspect on both occasions, and especially during the disorders of 22 B.C., is that Augustus chose to prolong them by inaction—the bad old days of the Republic (with a capital "R") were there for any takers. The upshot was that after another prolonged absence, which ended with his bringing back, in 19 B.C., the Roman military standards surrendered by the Parthians, Augustus was also given the *imperium consulare* in perpetuity without having to be consul. His special status within the republican tradition was manifest as he would sit in his curule chair between the two consuls. As in the creation of his divine aura, this novelty stretched tradition to the maximum acceptable limit but not beyond it.

We can be sure that none of these details were laid down in a grand master plan soon after Actium. Nor is it surprising that after the relative consolidation of his transactional powers of government Augustus increasingly emphasized the transforming aspects of his leadership; witness the Secular Games in 17 B.C., his ascendance to *pontifex maximus* in 12 B.C., and his proclamation as *pater patriae* in 2 B.C. In the context of this discussion, however, it is important to see how the combination of tradition and innovation, and of programmatic and flexible approaches with clear ends, also informed Augustan administration and foreign policy.

Since the building of the Via Appia in 312 B.C., the building and maintenance of the state roads in Italy had been under the purview of the central
government in Rome rather than the local authorities, for obvious political
and military reasons. For similarly obvious reasons, populist leaders like
Gaius Gracchus, Curio, and Julius Caesar had been engaged in highway
repair programs.[104] The benefit from such projects was both *pro bono publico*
and the enhancement of the sponsor's popularity. All these elements continued under Augustus. His attempted innovation was to get senators interested in such projects. As in the restoration of the temples—and the roads had
suffered from similar neglect—he led by example and had the Via Flaminia
rebuilt at his expense while urging various senators, in particular victorious
generals who had collected war booties, to do likewise with the other roads
(Dio 53.22.2; Suet., *Aug.* 30.1). We know of only two individuals who
heeded his appeal: Calvisius Sabinus, a *novus homo* and staunch Caesarian
who triumphed in Spain in 28 B.C., repaired the Via Latina, and Messalla
Corvinus, who fixed the road to Tusculum and Alba. With those two exceptions, Augustus' initiative was unsuccessful. Highway repair was not a traditional way for senators to achieve honors and recognition and they resisted
new ways that involved tangible concern for the welfare of the *res publica*,
even if such concern was a traditional republican value. This was another
instance of senatorial failure to think creatively in new dimensions, despite
being prodded to do so, and it contributed once again to increasing Augustus' *auctoritas*. For in 20 B.C. Augustus took on the *cura viarum* himself, not
coincidentally after assuming the mantle of tribunician power three years
earlier, an event from which he dated the beginning of his principate. He
now was the heir of republican populist statesmen and the *cura viarum* was a
demonstration of it. He had tried to involve the senate in this essential
matter, but the senate's final involvement was the decree by which this office
was given to Augustus. It is not enough to cite the senate's traditional lack of
administrative capabilities as the reason for this outcome,[105] as there was
ample precedent for administrative officials working under its supervision.
Nor did Augustus himself administer the highway department on a day-to-
day basis. Instead, he appointed *curatores viarum* who had been ex-praetors
to the task and these could be of equestrian or senatorial rank. Each of them
was accompanied by two lictors bearing their *fasces*, which underlined the
status of the office. The institution also is a good example of Augustus' constant attempt to involve more individuals in the life and administration of the
state; Suetonius presents a list of similar, newly created offices, most of which
were formerly handled by the censors, in his *Life of Augustus* (ch. 37). Most
of the appointees came from the senatorial class, which attests Augustus'
continuing effort to enlist its cooperation in the new order.

Similar perspectives apply to the Augustan administration of the grain
supply, which involved both free distributions to the urban plebs and its sale

at a fair market price to the rest of the city's population.[106] Although this had been one of the most vexing problems of the late republic, Augustus at first followed precedent and left the system in the hands of two aediles. The shortage of 23 B.C. forced his more direct involvement. He took over the *cura annonae* and provided twelve rations for each eligible member of the plebs (between 200,000 and 250,000); echoing the first sentence of the *Res Gestae*, he again presents himself as the *privatus* who liberates the populace from great danger (*RG* 5.2 and 15.1; cf. Dio 54.1.3–4). In addition, there was the precedent of Pompey. He soon transferred the actual administration again to ex-praetors. Two of these were in charge each year and Augustus saw to it, by various regulations, that their effective minimum age was thirty-five years. This counteracted the recent lowering of the minimum for aediles by ten years and recalled the republican emphasis on age and experience. Similarly republican was the choice of these *curatores* by lot, their membership in the senatorial class, and their accountability to the senate. Again, however, there are strong indications that such time-consuming work for the common good did not rank high on the senatorial prestige scale. For in 18 B.C., the system was changed to provide for the quadrennial choice, still by lot, of four *curatores*, each of whom would carry out the task for one year (Dio 54.17.1).

The reduction to one official per year and the lack of continuity contributed to the recurrence of severe problems, especially those relating to the actual procurement of the corn supply. In A.D. 5–7 another shortage struck and had to be alleviated by such drastic measures as the eviction of most foreigners from Rome (Dio 55.26.1–3; Suet., *Aug.* 42.3). As always, Augustus helped out with his own financial means, but that did not change the underlying supply deficit. There was an administrative reorganization and two ex-consuls were put in charge by A.D. 7 (Dio 55.31.4). Still, the issue required permanent attention. Augustus finally gave up his obeisance to the principle of republican one-year terms and, some time between A.D. 8 and 14, he appointed an equestrian prefect, who reported to him, to oversee the steady procurement of corn while the ex-praetorian officials were left in place to take care of the actual distribution. This occurred more than thirty years after his assumption of the *cura annonae*.

The whole process illustrates that we are dealing with anything but an Augustan "revolution" in this area and others. There was a great deal of deference on Augustus' part to republican precedent and reorganization proceeded slowly. This is not to say that the pace of change was identical in all areas, but the example of the *cura annonae* was by no means untypical. In the end, tradition was combined with pragmatic innovation. The only "ideological" element was Augustus' abiding effort to alert the senatorial class to larger social values and responsibilities.

Augustus' foreign policy exhibits the same mix of traditional and innovative elements as well as a guiding framework that suited the practical exigencies of Realpolitik.[107] The overall vision again was thoroughly rooted in republican precedent.[108] It was Rome's claim to world *imperium*: "The immortal gods willed that the Roman people rule over all nations" (Cic., *Phil.* 6.19). Like *libertas* or *auctoritas*, *imperium* was an elastic concept that required no dogmatic fixation on a particular plan or strategy. *Imperium* should be differentiated from the strategic thinking in terms of national security that informed many of Augustus' actions.[109] It would be a misnomer to label the resulting policy as "defensive." It plainly aimed at conquest and Augustus added more territory to the Roman domain than did any previous Roman general. After his consulships, his *imperium proconsulare*, which was limited mostly to five-year terms, demanded that he prove himself time and again as Rome's commander in chief, even if he did not lead every military expedition himself. His almost immediate departure for Spain after the "settlement" of 27 B.C. was due more to these expectations than to his indispensability on the Spanish front or to the threat posed by the Cantabrians.

While there can be arguments, therefore, about the cohesiveness of Augustus' military enterprises, the final result was much more than a patchwork of skillful improvisations. The conquest of the Alpine regions in 15 B.C. is a good example. The establishment of a solid land bridge between Illyricum (Yugoslavia) and Gaul and the armies on the Rhine secured the lines of communication to and from Italy. The consideration of this base as a springboard for the conquest of Germanic lands may have been a further, gradual development. The Alpine expedition was also an example of the successful coordination of several army groups which had been rarely achieved during the republic because of personal rivalries between the commanders. In this case, the armies of Drusus, Tiberius, and one of their deputies could blanket the area with connected fan- and pincerlike movements. The timing of the expedition, which was prompted more by the defeat of Marcus Lollius on the Lower Rhine in the previous year rather than by a master schedule, again shows the absence of rigidity and the concern for image, which was enhanced in this case by Horace's odes on the victories of Augustus' stepsons (*C.* 4.4 and 14).

Different parts of the world required different approaches. In the east, Augustus followed Mark Antony's policy of creating a buffer of client kingdoms between the Roman provinces and the kingdom of Parthia. Here as elsewhere, Augustus' policies were both evolutionary and purposeful. There was no Guns of August syndrome determining the response to the Parthians, nor was there any overreaction when Armenia slid into anarchy. The aura and prestige of Roman *imperium* could be stylized rather than paid for by costly wars; witness the representation of Phraates IV as a suppliant and the ensuing imagery of groveling Parthians in art and coinage (Fig. 72a). The strategy in the east was one of consolidation, which did not exclude repeated forays into south Arabia in 25–24 B.C. and in 1 B.C. Further examples of both flexibility and persistence could be provided from the other regions and frontiers, too.

While there was no seamless coherence of planned events—nor had there been such in republican times—the result was a solidified and secure empire of unprecedented proportions: *cuncta inter se conexa*, in Tacitus' phrase (*Ann.* 1.9.5). The parallel with the developments in domestic policy is conspicuous: just as the latter were directed toward the institutionalization of Augustus' power, so was the overriding aim of foreign policy the institutionalization of the *imperium* of Rome. The two coalesced in the *imperator* Augustus, a capacity in which he forcefully presents himself in the *Res Gestae*, and in the refinement of his imitation of Alexander. This imitation again had republican precedents,[110] but Augustus added to the Alexandrian dimension of conquest the equally important one of consolidation and orderly administration.[111] Related was another aspect of consolidation. While remaining an avowed goal, world conquest had also been blamed in the republic as the root of internal decay. The programmatic return to the old *mores* obviated that concern. The marriage legislation, as we have seen, is an illustration of the nexus of such ideas.[112] It is also an outstanding example of Augustus' ability to resort to drastic innovation in his pursuit of traditional values: "By *new* laws passed on my proposal I brought back into use many exemplary practices of our *ancestors* which were disappearing in our time."[113] It included, by transferring the adjudication of adultery cases to a public court, a diminution of the traditional power of the *pater familias*, and, by making remarriage compulsory for widows, a renunciation of the hallowed concept of the *univira*.

A final observation suggests itself. As can be seen, due to their gradualism and their constancy, many of the developments we have surveyed extended into the later part of Augustus' reign. Taken together with the establishment of the *aerarium militare* and the conjoined institution of the inheritance tax, they are another salutary antidote to the conventional view of the period as one of stagnation and gloom, illuminated only by the bright fires in which the books of Titus Labienus and Cassius Severus were burned.[114] There were defeats and setbacks, as in Germany and Pannonia, but we should not forget that they were the result not of Roman inertia, but of Roman initiatives. Nor did they lead to resignation: Augustus' response to Varus' defeat was to mass almost one-third of the Roman army in Germany not for defensive purposes, but to prepare another attack. When it came to Gaul and Germany, he was, as in so many other ways, Caesar's heir.

More generally, it is unreasonable to expect that the mood of revival after the end of the civil wars would continue throughout the forty-five years of Augustus' reign, or that the building activity in Rome would perpetuate itself at the same heady pace after most of the rebuilding had been finished.[115] These phenomena, like others, must be put in their proper perspective and seen from the viewpoint of the evolving character of the period. It was certainly not that activity ceased in the second part of the *aetas Augusta*. That period witnessed the completion of his forum and of the extraordinary temples of Concord and of the Castores. As we have observed, Ovid's chef-d'oeuvre is as Augustan in its way as its Vergilian counterpart and Horace's *Odes*. The marital legislation was renegotiated, as was the administration of the grain supply. Nor was there any standstill in foreign and military affairs. Augustan culture was a constant process.

CONTRADICTIONS

On first observation, the age of Augustus seems rife with contradictions. Octavian's rise to power had been accompanied by a bloodbath and a ruthlessness that appalled even contemporaries calloused by previous civil wars. The rule of the *princeps* was altogether different. It was based on respect for law and precedent. It was patient, fair-minded, and "there is almost no significant evidence that free expression of ideas was seriously curtailed by Augustus."[116] Another principal contradiction was the coexistence of republican and monarchic forms of government. It was accentuated by the claims of a virtual monarch to have saved the republic. Contradictions are also apparent in Augustus' own behavior. He preferred literature, Suetonius relates (*Aug.* 89.2), that offered "precepts and examples that were salubrious for the public or for private individuals" and Augustan public art was singularly sophisticated. Yet, as the same writer points out at far greater length (*Aug.* 43–45), Augustus loved every kind of mindless popular entertainment, gave it his full attention, and reacted with extraordinary concern to the shenanigans of some of its protagonists. Small wonder, as Horace implies, that the Augustan stage was an intellectual wasteland. Nor are contradictions hard to find in Augustan literature. The hero of the *Aeneid* is supposed to be a model of humaneness and self-control. The *Aeneid* ends, however, with Aeneas' killing, in a blaze of fury, an opponent who is on his knees and is begging for mercy. Or, as we have seen, the love poets definitely do not extol the virtues of marriage. At the same time, they describe the relationship with their beloved in terms of marital virtues and values.

Before we proceed with a closer look at some examples, we should be aware that genuine contradictions need to be distinguished from conflicting interpretations. The catalogs offered by Tacitus pro and contra Augustus' achievements (*Ann.* 1.9–10) are a good example. The point that there was *pax*, though one based on bloodshed, encapsulates an inherent contradiction, while most of the other arguments are more in the nature of differing assessments. Further, contradiction is endemic to any period witnessing considerable change while it is also trying to conserve some cherished traditions. Contradiction then is simply part of the multifaceted character of the culture and, as always, becomes a matter of definition and perception. It may result, therefore, from too rigorous a categorization on our part. In those terms Aeneas, for instance, "contradicts" himself by exercising self-restraint on one occasion and acting passionately on another, or the existence of a *princeps* stands in "contradiction" to true republican practice. At the other end of the methodological spectrum is the perceived scholarly task to resolve all contradictions, although they are inseparable from the complexity of human existence. We should not confuse lack of uniformity with contradictoriness.

With these perspectives in mind we can now turn to some major Augustan examples. Augustus as an individual has not been at the focus of this study, but there is no question that some of the major contradictions, perceived or real, center on him. There was, first and foremost, his stunning conversion to a clement, if tough-minded, *pater patriae* after his earlier incarnation as angel, or demon, of death who was possessed of singular bloodthirst, unsparing savagery, and a marked lack of scruples. Events like the Perusine War remained etched in the memories of his contemporaries and their descendants; Propertius is only a particularly conspicuous example. *Moriendum est* ("yours is to die") was Octavian's answer to those pleading for mercy (Suet., *Aug.* 15.1) and the story spread that he sacrificed three hundred knights and senators to the departed spirit of his adoptive father, an occurrence that may have left its imprint even on the *Aeneid*.[117] Even if some details and numbers were exaggerated, this event and others point to a decisive motive besides the elimination of all rivals: the lesson learned from Caesar's clemency. The dictator had recalled and pardoned old enemies, only to be assassinated by them.[118] Octavian was not about to repeat that mistake. Only when, in his own words, he "had gained control of all things" (*potitus rerum omnium*; *RG* 34.1) did he embark on his cooperative venture with the senate and the people of Rome. Many of them could hardly be blamed, therefore, for worrying about the old Octavian lurking behind the new Augustus. It took a generation until they proclaimed him *pater patriae*, the title he considered the true culmination of his efforts.

The contrast is a recurrent theme in the ancient sources. In his treatise *On Clemency* addressed to Nero, Seneca frequently presents Augustus as an example of that virtue to the young emperor. His behavior as Octavian, however, was another matter.[119] Augustus "was moderate and merciful, but that was, to be sure, after having reddened the Actian sea with Roman blood; after, to be sure, smashing his fleets and those of his enemies in Sicily; and after, to be sure, the human sacrifices and proscriptions at Perusia" (1.11.1). True clemency, therefore, Seneca continues, is not simply cruelty that is in remission, but a yet more genuine disposition toward mercy. Sometimes the divergences can be related more generally to the contrast between temperamental youth and later composure, as Seneca states in his prefatory remark. There is little doubt that Octavian sowed some wild oats; Antony made it a special point to appeal, through an emissary during the siege of Alexandria, to the memory of their joint escapades in those happy days (Dio 51.8.1; cf. Suet., *Aug.* 69). Little enough of a moral program was in evidence at the time, and Martial admired the erotic verses that Octavian was capable of writing then:

> Caesaris Augusti lascivos, livide, versus
>   sex lege, qui tristis verba Latina legis:
> 'Quod futuit Glaphyran Antonius, hanc mihi poenam
>   Fulvia constituit, se quoque uti futuam.
> Fulviam ego ut futuam? quid si mi Manius oret
>   pedicem, faciam? non puto, si sapiam.
> "Aut futue, aut pugnemus" ait. Quid quod mihi vita
>   carior est ipsa mentula? Signa canant!'
> Apsolvis lepidos, nimirum, Auguste, libellos,
>   qui scis Romana simplicitate loqui.
>
>   (11.20)

> [These hot six lines, you blue nose, great Augustus wrote,
> Whereas plain, simple Latin is choking in your throat:
> "Antony is screwing Glaphyra, so Fulvia brings suit—
> Now I have to screw her, and for her I don't give a hoot.
> What, I screw Fulvia? Suppose that Manius begged for my tool,
> Would I bugger him? No, never! I don't think I'm quite such a fool.
> 'Screw me or fight,' she demands, but always dearer than breath
> To me is my prick. Ho, trumpets, let's fight to the death!"
> Spicy little books, Augustus, I swear you'd never correct,
> For you too could handle your Latin, however blunt and direct.]
>
>   (trans. J. P. Sullivan)

While Martial puts the contrast between the sonorous title of "Caesar Augustus" and the lewdness of his poetry to good effect, we are clearly dealing with a poem composed by Octavian in 41 B.C. In his closure, however, Martial strikes an even more authentic note by presenting the poem as an example of the kind of graceful and simple Latinity that Augustus prized continually, even if he used it at first in contradistinction to Antony's bombastic, "eastern" style (Suet., *Aug.* 86.2–3; cf. Plut., *Ant.* 2). Nor did Augustus turn into a dour moral zealot.[120] In his letters to Horace we find a penchant for levity and the risqué similar to that in the poem preserved by Martial. Such writings, however, were not meant for public consumption for which a more stylized pose had to be cultivated; the contrast is akin to that between the Prima Porta statue, *gravis et sanctus*, and the charmed fantasy world of the *studiolo*. As for the stories about Augustus' various adulteries, it suffices to quote Balsdon's wise comment: "If the fetid indelicacy of Roman imagination could think of no greater scandals than these with which to tax him, it may be safely assumed that . . . he was a reasonably moral man,"[121] which does not mean that he must have been singularly monogamous.

In his satirical account of his predecessors entitled *Caesars*, the emperor Julian vividly summarized the contradictoriness of Augustus (309B–C). The fictional setting is a banquet. Silenus, Dionysus' helper, is stupefied at Octavian's appearance: "Good Lord, what a changeable monster is this! What awful things will he do to us?" For Octavian had come, "changing colors continually, like a chameleon, turning now pale, now red; one moment his expression was gloomy, somber, and overcast, the next he relaxed and showed all the charms of Aphrodite and the Graces." Apollo alleviates Silenus' concern by handing Octavian over to the Stoic philosopher Zeno who "made him wise and temperate." While this is another variation on the theme of contrasting Octavian and Augustus, Julian's reference to the man's shining gaze, an attribute on which Augustus prided himself and which he utilized effectively (Suet., *Aug.* 79.2), indicates that Julian did not draw much of a dividing line between the characteristics of Octavian and those of Augustus. As for Augustus' chameleon-like diverseness, we can reasonably argue that the underlying cause was not any excessive complexity of his character but the rich variety of both his own activities and those taking place during his reign in general. They resulted in his being many different things to many different people. Their perspectives on him could vary as they have ever since:[122] affable supporter of poets like Horace and harsh exiler of Ovid; vengeful tyrant (including tyranny over his family) or good *Landesvater*; enlightened pardoner or savage butcher; restorer of liberty or book-burner; eager to involve many in the life of the state while highly selective about his dinner company (Suet., *Aug.* 74.1); serious in his pursuit of power, but playful even on his deathbed; and so on. The tendency of historians to exaggerate any perceived act of oppression on Augustus' part may be due to the disbelief that all vestiges of Octavian's behavior could disappear completely.

Similar perspectives apply to the contradiction between the republican and the monarchic aspects of the emerging principate. In Tacitus' mind, the principate and *libertas* were irreconcilable at least until the time of Nerva, whom he praised for melding them (*Agric.* 3.1). It depended, of course, on one's view of *libertas* (see chapter 2). More generally, several generations of scholars viewed "the Augustan Constitution" in terms of the rigid categories "monarchy" and "republic" and were preoccupied with pointing out any minute deviation from the republican system. Such an approach, as we observed earlier, loses the forest for the trees. Augustus' contemporaries were not constitutional scholars; one simple reason is that there was no legal document called the Roman Constitution. An overly legalistic orientation misses the fact that the *res publica* went beyond a mere institutional apparatus; in essence, it was a set of principles and values. It was on those primary aspects that Augustus concentrated in his *res publica restituta*. There was a difference; in one scholar's apt formulation, even if Augustus did not act *as* a republican, at least he acted *like* a republican,[123] not in the least by taking pains to make gradual rather than drastic departures from precedent. For the "Republican Constitution" had never been perceived as unchanging. Even so, Augustus' abidingly preeminent position could be regarded, and not just by Republicans, as standing in contradiction to the republican norm. This brings us back to the concept of leadership whose "cardinal responsibility" it "is to identify the dominant contradiction at each point of the historical process."[124] Much of Augustus' leadership consisted of the management of this very issue and involved both transactional and transforming aspects. This issue also underlies the reception of the Augustan reign in later historiography, historical scholarship, and political writing: we are dealing, in this instance, not so much with contradictory traditions as with the tradition of a contradiction.[125]

To take a final example: the "contradictions" that have been perceived in the period's chef d'oeuvre, Vergil's *Aeneid*, must also be set in a firm historical perspective. On the one hand, the *Aeneid*, like most great literature, "was essentially an exploration of varying and sometimes contrasting aspects of human experience."[126] To this endeavor, as we have seen, the spirit of the times was most congenial, and we should not expect a monolithic work. Yet this—and this is the second point—is precisely the expectation imposed on it, and on its hero in particular, in the course of its receptions over time. For centuries, Aeneas was viewed as a proto-Christian, progressing like a pilgrim from imperfections, such as *furor*, to the blessed state of *pietas*, terms that were used reductively—and, in the case of *pietas*, anachronistically—and with total disregard for their many shades of meaning. Related to this was the consideration of the epic and the hero in a purely Stoic framework despite clear evidence, which has been further confirmed recently, that Vergil studied philosophy with the Epicureans.[127]

Predictably, a reaction formation set in when Vergil's "grander endeavor" (*Aen.* 7.45), the second and more martial half of the *Aeneid*, began to attract increasing attention. There, of course, we do not see a heroic warrior who is consistently meek or stoically immune to great emotions. The previous theses, therefore, were quickly turned into antitheses leading, in the most extreme cases, to the demonization of Aeneas. The underlying premise seems to be the expectation of a schematic, unvarying character portrayal that is the opposite of any literary masterwork. W. B. Yeats gently poked fun at the cliché current at his time: "A plain sailor man took a notion to study Latin and his teacher tried him with Vergil; after many lessons he asked him something about the hero. Said the sailor: 'What hero?' 'Why, Aeneas, the hero.' Said the sailor: 'Ach, a hero, him a hero? Bigob, I thought he was a priest.'"[128] In its own way, the reversal of this portrait of Aeneas is just as reductive; the ferocity with which it has been propounded does not seem to allow, as yet, of gentle anecdotes.

It is again a matter of definition whether we want to consider Aeneas' behavior as contradictory. I prefer to see it in terms of the complex and rich character with whom Vergil chose to present us. The general perspective on innovation in the Augustan age again is applicable; existing traditions were not uprooted, but new departures were made within them. Augustan temples, for instance, are not a break with previous architectural traditions but a highly original synthesis of various Greek and Roman precedents. God, as so often, is in the innovative details. It is the same with Aeneas. We should not be surprised that he, the second most valiant fighter of the Trojans after Hector in the *Iliad*, remains in many ways a Homeric warrior in the *Aeneid*. At the same time, the new departures are highly significant: in addition to his representing, as we saw earlier, an ethic of social responsibility, no other warrior acts on the battlefield as Aeneas does toward Lausus (*Aen.* 10.806–32), and it is unique that Aeneas even hesitates before he kills Turnus (12.940–41). It is certainly a far cry from Achilles' wish to eat Hector raw and throw him to the dogs (*Il.* 22.346–54). Similarly, his anger, which Vergil had to retain as a staple of the epic hero, is more carefully modulated than Achilles', let alone Turnus'. Its delineation includes the influence of Epicurean and Peripatetic philosophy.[129]

As in many other ways, the *Aeneid* is a true reflection of the Augustan age because it is so far from one-dimensional. At the same time, and again reflecting Augustan culture in general, its contradictions, however defined, are not "out of character." It is in its allowance for contradictions, too, that the age of Augustus was exemplary and influential.

CHAPTER VIII

EPILOGUE: *AUCTOR PERPETUUS*

ON THE Ides of February 44 B.C., Julius Caesar proclaimed himself as *dictator perpetuo*, dictator in perpetuity (Fig. 170). That perpetuity lasted all of one month. Twenty-two years later, beset by famine and a host of other woes,

170. Caesar, *dictator perpetuo*. Obverse of denarius, 44 B.C.

the people of Rome clamored for Augustus to accept the dictatorship and, under the threat of burning down the senate house, compelled the senate to vote him this office (Dio 54.1.2–3). He begged off with an emotional display that was commensurate with theirs: "Falling to his knees, he tore his toga from his shoulders and entreated them with bared breast" (Suet., *Aug.* 53.1). He did not need that odious office, adds Dio, because he had enough honor and power (*exousia*). Augustus himself differentiated more carefully between power in the sense of *potestas*, rendered in the Greek version of the *Res Gestae* as *exousia*, and *auctoritas* (*RG* 34.2), a term Dio found untranslatable. And yet, as we saw early on, the concept lay at the very heart of his rule. He was not dictator, consul, let alone king or *dominus* in perpetuity, but his *auctoritas* was perpetual. In short, he was *auctor perpetuus*.

This *auctoritas* was many-faceted and in this epilogue, it is useful to bring together the most important of these aspects. They can be conveniently grouped into those that have a material basis and into those that are more intangible and inspirational. Respectively, therefore, they may seem akin to the transactional and transforming aspects of leadership. But of course the division is not so simple. One of the special characteristics of *auctoritas* is precisely that there is a reciprocity between the two categories. We need to keep this in mind even as we consider the major constituents of Augustus' *auctoritas* individually.

As for the more tangible and manifest components of Augustus' influence or prestige, we can conveniently begin with his wealth, especially as he mentions its utilization prominently in the *Res Gestae* and its preface. The money he amassed was not an end in itself but a means for him to help the *res publica*. A list of expenditures, which is by no means complete, takes up chapters 15–24.[1] They include donatives to the urban plebs, distributions of grain, purchase of land for veterans, building programs, and games and shows. He does not even mention his many largesses to the soldiers and, in particular, the cities of Italy and the provinces. His outlays were monumental and no one else came even remotely close with the exception, while he was alive, of Agrippa, who in turn bequeathed his estate to Augustus. Augustus again followed republican traditions in making such expenditures, but his were wider-reaching: due to his longevity, they went on for a much longer time than those of any republican predecessor and, geographically, they reached far beyond Rome. There were the usual innovations such as direct subsidies to the state treasury and the newly created military treasury; the financing of the corn supply; and interest-free loans to debtors (Dio 55.12.3a; cf. Suet., *Aug.* 41.2). His expenditures dwarfed any precedent in scale. So did his *auctoritas*. He was, quite simply, the richest man and greatest benefactor in the Roman empire.

Wealth alone was not enough for *auctoritas*. Rather, it was its constructive and continuing use for benefactions that made him the unsurpassed *auctor*. Tacitus' acerbic comment on Augustus' largesses (*Ann.* 1.2) ignores that *auctoritas* at its best, as we observed earlier, engenders reciprocity. At the material level, this is illustrated by the New Year's donations from the people to the *princeps*, which he, in turn, dedicated to further philanthropy. Similarly, a significant part of his income came from testamentary bequests by countless individuals. They were both a tangible tribute to his *auctoritas* and kept augmenting it further.

Another aspect of traditional, republican *auctoritas* that Augustus transformed was military leadership and victory. Due to his *imperium proconsulare*, Augustus was Rome's perpetual commander in chief. The military policy he pursued was, as we have observed, flexible and some of his "victories" may have fallen short of that definition in purely military terms. But they were stylized as such because that was essential for his *auctoritas*. His abiding and supreme role in military activity found its reflection in his nomenclature. As Syme pointed out in a fundamental article,[2] Augustus' title "Imperator Caesar Augustus" followed the Roman pattern of *praenomen*, *nomen*, and *cognomen*—in three words, "Imperator Caesar Augustus" became his real name rather than being a mere title.

Just as the *praenomen* "Imperator" preempted that appellation, formerly shared by many individuals, for Augustus and signified his preeminent *auctoritas* in the military realm so too the adoption of "Caesar" as *nomen* reflects another continuing aspect of Augustus' *auctoritas*, his association with Julius Caesar. The *gens Octavia* was undistinguished and of no more than equestrian

171. Augustan denarius, 17 B.C. Obverse: Augustus Divi F(ilius).
Reverse: Deified Caesar with youthful features.

rank. In his early career, therefore, Octavian had no claims to *auctoritas* except for being Caesar's heir. We have noted time and again that he never
dropped that association. Like everything else, it evolved and was modulated, but it remained a constant. After his first public speech in Rome,
which came close to a fiasco, he would never again claim directly that he
aspired to the honors of his father. Yet, in effect, he did so throughout his
life. The *divi filius* became *divus Augustus*. Julius Caesar remained visible
throughout Augustus' reign: in buildings such as the Pantheon and Mars
Ultor temple; on coins that subtly stressed their similarity (Fig. 171); on the
much replicated statue of the Prima Porta Augustus, who is *gravis* and *sanctus*
not in the least because he is wearing, literally, Caesar's mantle; and in the
works of the Augustan poets who fully understood the connection. The
phenomenon resided not only in imagery, but extended to hard-nosed applications: Augustus could invoke Caesarian precedent for instituting new
taxes (Dio 55.25.6). Caesar remained part of Augustus' *auctoritas*. This *auctoritas* assumed a further dimension by virtue of the *cognomen* "Augustus" with
all its paradivine implications, which, in turn, meshed well with the Father's
divinity.

There was another essential aspect. "Active excellence that remains hidden is hardly different from inactivity that has gone to the tomb" (*paulum
sepultae distat inertiae / celata virtus*; *C.* 4.9.29–30), said Horace, pointing to the
importance of poetry in memorializing *virtus*. Similarly, *auctoritas* was not to
be hidden from sight but to be conveyed in stone, marble, and bronze. The
most obvious manifestations were buildings, statues, and inscriptions. They
also provide important perspectives on the latitude of participation given to
others besides Augustus.

As for building activity, the facts speak for themselves. Not only was Augustus the sponsor of a totally unprecedented number of public buildings,

but their geographic range was more unprecedented yet.[3] It encompassed the entire *imperium Romanum* and, in addition to the customary emphasis on the city of Rome, signaled a reorientation of perspective that the traditional sponsors from the senatorial class again found hard to follow. The only precursor again turns out to be Julius Caesar to whom Suetonius ascribes similar designs, some of which, for instance in Antioch and Alexandria, have been verified by archaeological remains.[4]

In Rome, the evidence is clear enough. Caesar had begun to leave his imprint on the Forum Romanum (Fig. 172) by constructing the Basilica Iulia and rebuilding the Curia. Both were completed by Augustus as was the Forum of Caesar. Furthermore, Augustus was involved, to varying degrees, in the building or rebuilding of other major structures on the Roman Forum.[5] There was the Temple of the Deified Julius next to which a grateful senate commissioned a triple arch honoring Augustus' "victory" over the Parthians.[6] The Curia was named after Caesar and its dominant image was that of Augustus' quintessential deity, Victoria. A new Augustan Rostra replaced the old, being on a visual axis with the Rostra of the Temple of Divus Julius. The temple's rostra was decorated with ships' beaks from the Egyptian campaign, recalling the beaks of the old Rostra that had been taken from the Latin fleet at the battle of Antium in 338 B.C. Actium was linked to Antium. And there was the *milliarium aureum*, the golden milestone, the starting and end point for all roads leading to and from Rome. It was erected in the year (20 B.C.) in which Augustus assumed the *cura viarum* and we may safely assume that it bore his name and titles as milestones throughout the empire came to do (Fig. 174).[7] More was to follow: the splendid rebuilding of the Temple of Castor (A.D. 6) and of the Temple of Concord (A.D. 10), which was the Julio-Claudian counterpart to the Temple of the Divine Iulius at the other end of the Forum; in honor of Gaius and Lucius, a monumental arch (called "Portico" in our sources), the counterpart to Augustus', on the other side of the Temple of Divus Iulius for a triumph they never consummated; a Basilica Aemilia rebuilt with Augustus' financial help after 14 B.C.; and, after its destruction by fire, a rebuilding of the Basilica Iulia and re dedication in the names of Gaius and Lucius (A.D. 12).

Before turning briefly to another major site of Augustan (re)building activity in Rome, the Circus Flaminius, we need to assess the meaning of the Augustan involvement in the Roman Forum. On the material level, there was the simple necessity to rebuild after the devastations and the neglect of the civil wars. The question, as in the restoration of the *res publica*, was what the alternatives were. Building in Rome had been a traditional means of self-representation by the nobility. Augustus, therefore, encouraged the participation of the *principes viri*, as Suetonius puts it poignantly (*Aug.* 29.4), as early as in the triumviral period. Suetonius goes on to list several examples

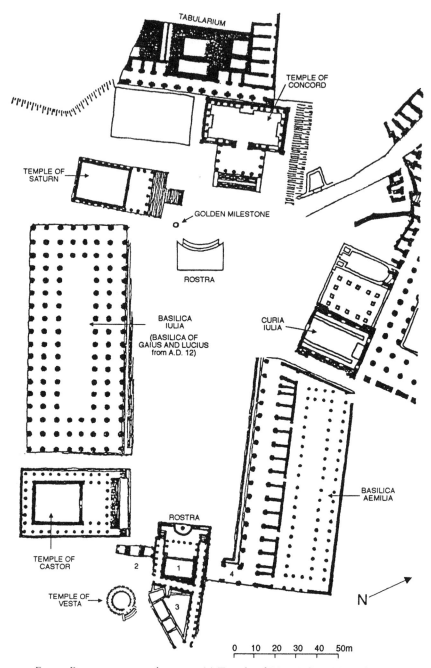

172. Forum Romanum, around A.D. 10. (1) Temple of Divus Iulius; (2) Parthian Arch of Augustus; (3) Regia; (4) Porticus of Gaius and Lucius.

(cf. Tac., *Ann.* 3.72), including Asinius Pollio's Atrium Libertatis,[8] to which we can add the restoration of the Regia in the Forum Romanum by Domitius Calvinus after his Spanish campaign in 36 B.C. and the completion of the rebuilding of the Basilica Aemilia by Aemilius Lepidus Paullus in 34 B.C. A countervailing consideration was that competition in building had also been a manifestation of the *res publica*'s fragmentation into various *res privatae*, and some balance had to be found. An additional circumstance shifting the balance to Augustus was the relative impoverishment of leading senatorial families such as the Aemilii; hence the reconstruction of the Basilica Aemilia, after a fire in 14 B.C., was undertaken "nominally by Aemilius, who was the descendant of the man who had formerly erected it, but really by Augustus and the friends of Paullus."[9]

Even more important, there were two principal factors that shaped the evolution of Augustus' role in this area. He was keen, as we have noted often, to have far more people participate broadly in the Augustan *res publica* than his republican predecessors had been. In particular, he continually sought to enlist the cooperation of the senatorial aristocracy. But he also sought to make them aware that his *res publica* was more inclusive than Rome and the nobility's special interests, and involved new responsibilities, such as helping to rebuild the roads of Italy. Such challenges, as we have seen, met with less than a lukewarm response, forcing Augustus to take over the *cura viarum* himself within a decade. We may view, therefore, Augustus' increasing curtailment of traditional senatorial self-representation in Rome as his response to the senators' failure to transcend their narrow and traditional compass. Besides, as more senators came from the municipal aristocracy outside of Rome, their building activities naturally would be concentrated in their own cities.[10]

A second element was the increasing identification of Augustus with the *res publica*. He was, after all, its chief representative: *quia res est publica Caesar* (Ovid, *Trist.* 4.4.15). His aim was the internal consolidation of the Roman state and the institutionalization of the *imperium Romanum*. Both called for appropriate representations in architecture. Typically, therefore, the line is fluid in such cases between Augustan self-representation and a fitting representation of *res Romana*. It is too one-sided to view the rebuilding of the Roman Forum as mere Augustan glorification. It was also a reaffirmation of the republican past, which was an essential component of Augustus' overall policy. With the exception of the complex of the Arch of Augustus, the Temple of the Deified Julius and the Rostra in front of it, and the Arch of Gaius and Lucius (an architectural group that also screened out the Regia in which Augustus chose not to reside as *pontifex maximus*), the other buildings all dated from republican times. Neither their plan nor their location was altered significantly.[11] They now were clad in marble—Augustus' famous saying (Suet., *Aug.* 28.3; Dio 56.30.3) that he found Rome a city of brick and made it into one of marble is certainly apropos—and their interiors and architectural decoration were revised extensively and innovatively. The process was an apt reflection of the new principate: a continuation of long-standing foundations on which new structures began to be built.[12] Their ever present visual horizon, on the upper side of the Forum, was the imposing repository of republican archives, the Tabularium, built in the early 70s B.C. The evolutionary aspect of the transformation of the Forum Romanum is quite different from that presented by the fora of Caesar and Augustus with their far greater systematization, including, in the latter, the systematization of the Roman past. In both the Augustan and the Roman Forum, there was a mutually enhancing relationship between the *auctoritas* of Rome and the *auctoritas* of its *princeps*.

The same conjuncture is evident from other Augustan restorations of prominent republican buildings. "I rebuilt," Augustus says in the *Res Gestae* (20.1), "the Capitol and the Theater of Pompey, both works at great expense without inscribing my own name on either." The fact of restoring these two landmarks was expressive of his *auctoritas*; his name on them was not needed, although other *principes viri* would not have been so reluctant. The usual practice was to commemorate the restoring patron's name and we may safely assume that it continued, for example, on the Temple of Saturn in the Roman Forum.[13] The process of its rebuilding also is a good illustration of the development of the participation of others besides Augustus, his family members, and Agrippa. The vow to restore the temple was undertaken by Lucius Munatius Plancus, a strong supporter of Caesar's, after his victorious campaign in Raetia (Switzerland) in 44 B.C. Plancus was consul in 42 B.C., the year of Philippi, and then sided with Antony (including the siege at Perugia) with whom he stayed in the east from 40 B.C. on. It is doubtful that the restoration proceeded apace in his absence. Plancus switched allegiances in 32 B.C. and ultimately sponsored the senate decree that bestowed the title "Augustus" on Octavian in 27 B.C.

It is reasonable to infer, therefore, that the restoration of the Saturn temple was not completed until the years immediately following Actium. The allusion to that event in the pediment—Tritons were represented there on shells—alone does not make the temple an "Augustan" building: there was also the restored structure itself, evoking the aura of one of the oldest republican temples at Rome that served as the state treasury; the inscription that proclaimed the *auctoritas* of Plancus; and the Tritons who recalled the event by which Roman traditions had been saved from Egypt—it was Plancus, after all, who had informed Augustus and Rome of the provisions of Antony's will.[14]

The rebuilding of the area of the Circus Flaminius[15] (Fig. 173) exhibits similar tendencies. It had been a key spot for self-display at least since the second century because it was the starting point for the triumphal procession.

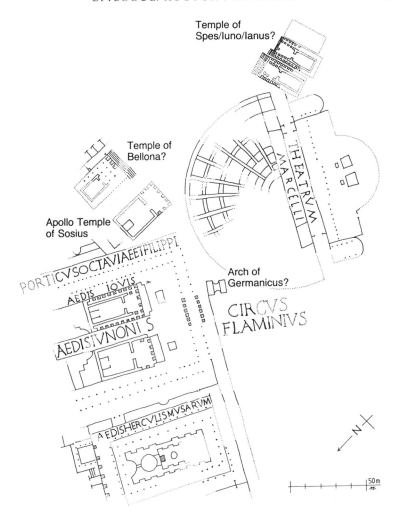

173. Area of the Circus Flaminius, Rome,
based on the Ancient Marble Plan of Rome. Cf. Fig. 156.

The Porticus Metelli (Fig. 156) is a good example of the prevailing ostentation. This sort of competitive self-celebration could not continue. The restoration of the Temple of Apollo set the tone. It was undertaken by Sosius, another convert from Antony. One of its friezes, as we have seen, commemorated Octavian's triple triumph (Fig. 166). As time went on, Augustus as commander in chief would be the supreme victor and actual triumphs were granted only to members of his family. Sosius' temple, then, is another example of an Augustan updating of a republican structure. This Temple of

Apollo had been built because of the god's connection with victory. The new building maintained that association and linked it with the victories of Augustus. The momentous import of these victories and Rome's dependence on the continuing success of Victoria Augusta demanded that traditional rivalries be superseded and that Augustus take the place of competing warlords. Accordingly, the anniversary dates of both the Apollo temple and the Temple of Jupiter Stator in the old Porticus Metelli were changed to September 23; the Porticus Metelli was refurbished splendidly as the Porticus Octaviae in honor of Augustus' sister; the theater of Marcellus, planned by Caesar, was built from the ground up; and the republican Temple of Hercules Musarum was restored sumptuously by Lucius Marcius Philippus, Augustus' stepfather.[16]

At hindsight, which is always kind to scholars, we may see the beginning of this reorientation in Octavian's restoration in 33 B.C. of the Porticus Octavia, built originally by Cn. Octavius after his naval victory over king Perseus in 168 B.C. Less arguably, perhaps, Octavian's action shows that he recognized early on the importance of inserting his name among the victors memorialized in the Circus Flaminius area. The rebuilt portico, a splendid example of *publica magnificentia* (Vell. 2.1.2), served him to display proudly some Roman standards he had recovered during his Illyrian campaign and to link his victory to earlier republican triumphs.[17] And, as he duly points out (*RG* 19.1), he did not even have to change the name of the building.

The transformation of the Circus Flaminius mirrors that of the nobility's self-representation in general.[18] It was, as always, a gradual process. Long-standing manias—and the Roman zeal for self-display can only be so called[19]—could not be simply abolished, and we have evidence of two honorary monuments for private individuals, stunning in their grandioseness, one of which can be dated to around 20 B.C.[20] It was commissioned by two Spanish communities to honor a former Roman governor of Hispania Ulterior, Aelius Lamia. In the course of time, public building in Rome became the prerogative of the *princeps* and his family. As for honorific statues, there were no restrictions as to type—equestrian statues, for instance, were not reserved for Augustus. From the time of Claudius, the senate had to approve the setting up of any such statues, but we do not know whether such a mechanism was already in effect under Augustus. The inflation of this sort of honor—by Augustus' time there was a veritable forest of honorific statues in Rome—"would tend to diminish the probative value of any individual monument."[21] Any curbs on it, therefore, might have been suggested not to enhance the preeminence of the *princeps*, but to save some quarters of the city from clutter. For such reasons, Augustus relocated a bevy of these statues from the *area Capitolina* to the Campus Martius, where they were eventually smashed by Caligula. Suetonius (*Calig.* 34.2) notes on that occasion that no statue or bust of any living person could be erected without Caligula's permission, which is another indication of the absence of any such regulation in Augustus' reign.

Instead, Augustus tried to incorporate such honors and monuments into the *res publica Augusta*. Rather than being put up at random throughout the city, statues honoring the men who had garnered triumphal honors, whether *ornamenta triumphalia* or an *ovatio*, were now given a place of honor in his forum.[22] They were thus linked with the famous Roman leaders of the past and with their *princeps*. Our sources suggest an almost excessive generosity on Augustus' part in awarding triumphal honors,[23] no doubt a kind of over-compensation for granting actual triumphs only to Tiberius after 19 B.C. He did so, however, on only two occasions (in 7 B.C. and A.D. 12) while denying Tiberius a triumph on his first try in 12 B.C. (Dio 54.31.4) and one to Drusus in 11 B.C. (Dio 54.33.5). Agrippa had tactfully declined the honor of a triumph earlier, once in 19 B.C., even though it had been decreed for him at Augustus' behest (Dio 54.11.6), and again in 14 B.C. (Dio 54.24.7). Augustus himself, perhaps following the legendary example of Romulus, did not celebrate another triumph after his triple triumph of 29 B.C. while five other *nobiles* triumphed from 28 to 19 B.C. The aim, therefore, seems to have been a restriction on this signal honor in general rather than an excessive show-casing of triumphs by members of the imperial family. The means by which the aim was accomplished was, as so often, not statutes or decrees, but a subtle process of conveying certain perceptions. If Agrippa declined such an honor, no one else could possibly ask for it.

Other honors were similarly redimensioned. Instead of listing only the title held by the honoree in the year of his honor, honorific inscriptions for the living now came to include the titles of all offices ever held by them,[24] perhaps again as a compensation for the loss of the availability of triumphs and imperatorial acclamations. This new inscription type may well have been used first for the inscriptions of Augustus' victorious contemporaries whose bronze statues were set up in his forum. Another reason for the rapid adoption of this style was its use by Augustus himself, including inscriptions on buildings and milestones.[25] It is again indicative of abiding mentalities that during Augustus' reign the new type was more popular with individuals outside the great republican families.

Not only did the number of statues and portrait busts of Augustus surpass that of any other Roman[26] and proclaim his *auctoritas* throughout the empire, but so did a tidal wave of inscriptions.[27] They had been a traditional medium of communication, but he exploited the medium's capabilities to a hitherto unknown extent. The figures speak for themselves: from the five centuries of the republic, we have 3,000 inscriptions as compared to 300,000 from the five centuries of the empire. Again this creation of an epigraphic culture did not occur by mandate, but by Augustus' providing an impetus that led to autonomous, progressive responses, adaptations, and developments as it did

174. Augustan milestone from Alexandria with name and titles of Augustus.

in art, architecture, and religion. By these, of course, the ultimate success of his *auctoritas* can be measured. More narrowly, inscriptions were an ever present and ubiquitous reminder of his role. They shone forth from buildings in Rome, Italy, and the provinces, and he did build even in the senatorial provinces. Travelers along the roads of Italy and the empire would see his name at every mile (Fig. 174); the terminus of some roads now was called *terminus Augustalis* and there was a *Via Augusta* in Spain. There were the dedicatory inscriptions relating to his cult, and the inscriptions by grateful provinces, communities, and individuals honoring him for his benefactions. Taken altogether they signaled that he was not only *auctor perpetuo*, but *auctor ubique*.

As such, he was the ultimate guarantor (*auctor*) of peace and stability. While enhancing and reflecting his *auctoritas* outwardly, honors like statues and inscriptions did not actually generate it. The root of his *auctoritas* was, quite simply, his deeds. He succeeded where others had failed. He was not the first to recognize the problems of the Roman state in the century before his accession, but he was the first to solve them. For instance, as W. Eder has well observed, "to have turned about three hundred thousand battle-hardened old blades into farmers again—and into farmers who remained farmers—is an achievement of Augustus all too little noticed, one that is surely to be valued more highly than raising an army of five hundred thousand."[28] Issues like these required time to be settled, nor was there any repose after they had been brought to a conclusion. The welfare of the *res publica*, from the feeding of the urban plebs to the prosperity of the provinces, required ongoing hard work and attention, precisely the point of Augustus' implicit comparison between himself and Alexander (Plut., *Mor.* 207D). At the same time, wars of expansion or consolidation continued to be fought and, while there were periods of varying intensity, domestic and foreign initiatives were undertaken to the end of Augustus' rule. In the reciprocity typical of such relationships, all this was both reflected and motivated by the Augustan ethos of seeking challenges rather than placid repose.

It is in this area of motivation, initiative, the generation of ideas, and the effort to promote shared values that the role of Augustus' *auctoritas* was perhaps most significant. An *auctor*, as we saw in the first chapter, can work in various ways. One of them is to set in motion initiatives and ideas that will stand at the center of the discussion and will evoke the responses, from strong agreement to thoughtful dissent, of a large number of participants. This applies to much, though by no means all, of Augustan poetry. As I illustrated in chapter 5, its starting point often is the ideals and values that Augustus helped to bring to the forefront. There are many more examples that could be added of the poets' adaptation, for instance, of themes such as war, peace, and the moral exhortation.[29] Or take Horace's definition of the purpose of poetry amid his discourse of poetry's beginnings:

> fuit haec sapientia quondam,
> publica privatis secernere, sacra profanis,
> concubitu prohibere vago, dare iura maritis,
> oppida moliri, leges incidere ligno.
> sic honor et nomen divinis vatibus atque
> carminibus venit.
>
> (*AP* 396–401)

[It was wisdom in those days to distinguish public from private property, to forbid random sexual intercourse and impose the law of marriage, to toil to build cities, and to inscribe laws on wooden tablets. In
this way honor and renown came to the divinely inspired bards and
their songs.]

The "echo of cherished ideas and laws of the Emperor"[30] is readily apparent:
the difference between private and public property (with the *res publica* being
once more the guarantor of private property), the prohibition of adultery,
and the "moral" legislation about marriage. The phrase *oppida moliri* recalls
the central theme of the *Aeneid*: *tantae molis erat Romanam condere gentem*
(1.33).

At the same time, some of the basic ideas of the age were not created by
Augustus, which in turn, illustrates another aspect of his *auctoritas*, namely the
"sanctioning" of the initiatives of authors. We also saw this process at work
in the area of religion, as shown by the cult of the Lares Compitales, the cults
of some guilds, and the imperial cult. One of their hallmarks, which again is
basic to *auctoritas*, is constant reciprocity that found one of its expressions in
gift exchange. Similar considerations apply to the adaptation in private art of
many motifs from Augustan public art. It was marked by an even more
autonomous development and was more complex, too, as some of the preferred styles and motifs already occurred in the late republic. They were
"sanctioned," if we want to formulate a schema, by their reappropriation for
Augustan public art and thus acquired additional *auctoritas*, which in turn
increased their stature and desirability in the private realm. The ubiquity of
these images neither expressed a servile mentality nor should it be overinter-
preted as creating new identities.[31] Without a doubt, however, the images
enhanced Augustus' *auctoritas*.

Just as Augustan culture was not simply the product of Augustus so his
auctoritas was not, to any major extent, the result of his personality. His personality was interesting and complex, of course, but we would be looking in
vain for anything truly fascinating, flamboyant, or charismatic. Suetonius
offers the usual details.[32] Augustus certainly was not ugly or deformed, which
saved him from possible overcompensations and us from psychohistorical
scholarship. His physique was not imposing, but he struck a handsome and
graceful appearance, although one he did not always keep up as well as he
might have. He had that bright gaze on which I remarked earlier.[33] Overall,
we are looking at a man whose appearance, both by nature and comportment, was perfectly suited for the role of *princeps*. He was not, like Shake-
speare's Julius Caesar, a colossus who bestrode the world and thus stood out
among and above his peers, but like his favorite stylized statue, his authority
would be unmistakable because he was *gravis et sanctus*. At the same time, he
was unpretentious and had a marked sense of humor and lightheartedness.

His consummate behavior as *civilis princeps* certainly was part of his *auctoritas*, which cannot be simply reduced to a dynamic personality type.

The Roman people, from the capital to the provinces, would view him as the hardworking, fair, and resourceful *auctor* of peace, stability, security, and orderly government. He was able to usher in the new by appealing to the past and he laid the foundations of a system, whose normative exemplar he remained, that endured for almost two hundred years. As I pointed out in the introduction, no historian can afford to neglect these tangible and material qualities of Augustus' reign that were the true basis for its acceptance and continuity. For the cultural or intellectual historian, the significance of his *auctoritas* is even more extensive. It essentially lies in the power of identifying the cardinal issues and contradictions of his time, and in the ability to stimulate creativity and shape its new directions. Ever the *auctor*, Augustus did so both by initiatives of his own and by encouraging those of others, leading to the dynamic development of various kinds of mutuality, reciprocity, and autonomy. The result was a singularly rich culture, characterized by experimentation and change, that significantly transcended its own time to claim an indelible *auctoritas* in the annals of Western culture.

ABBREVIATIONS
FOR FREQUENTLY
CITED WORKS

The abbreviations for archaeological journals follow mostly those used in the *American Journal of Archaeology*; for a complete list see *AJA* 95 (1991) 4–16. For philological and other journals I have drawn generally on the abbreviations listed in J. Marouzeau, *L'Année Philologique*. An exception, for instance, is *RM* for *Römische Mitteilungen*.

ANRW   H. Temporini and W. Haase, eds., *Aufstieg und Niedergang der römischen Welt* (Berlin 1972–).

CAH   *Cambridge Ancient History.*

CHCL   *Cambridge History of Classical Literature.*

EJ   V. Ehrenberg and A. H. M. Jones, eds., *Documents Illustrating the Reigns of Augustus and Tiberius*, 2nd ed. (Oxford 1955).

Giard   J.-B. Giard, *Catalogue des monnaies de l'Empire Romain* I. *Auguste*, Bibliothèque Nationale (Paris 1976).

KA   *Kaiser Augustus und die verlorene Republik.* Catalog of the exhibit (June 7–August 14, 1988) in the Martin-Gropius-Bau, Berlin (Mainz 1988).

Kienast   D. Kienast, *Kaiser Augustus. Prinzeps und Monarch* (Darmstadt 1982).

LIMC   *Lexicon Iconographicum Mythologiae Classicae* (1981–).

RE   Pauly-Wissowa, *Real-Encyclopädie der classischen Altertumswissenschaft.*

RIC I²   C. H. V. Sutherland and R. A. G. Carson, *The Roman Imperial Coinage*, vol. 1, 2nd ed. (London 1984).

RRC   M. H. Crawford, *Roman Republican Coinage* (Cambridge 1974).

Syme, *AA*   R. Syme, *The Augustan Aristocracy* (Oxford 1986).

Syme, *RR*   R. Syme, *The Roman Revolution* (Oxford 1939).

Zanker,   P. Zanker, *Augustus und die Macht der Bilder* (Munich 1987); Engl. transl.
   AMB   by A. Shapiro: *The Power of Images in the Age of Augustus* (Ann Arbor 1988).

NOTES

PREFACE

1. Wallace-Hadrill (1985) 245.

INTRODUCTION

1. Syme, *RR* viii; the citations that follow are from pp. ix and viii. Important assessments of Syme include Momigliano (1966); Bowersock (1980); Millar (1981); Alföldy (1983) and (1993); Galsterer (1990); and Yavetz (1990).

2. See Weinbrot (1978) and Stahlmann (1988).

3. Momigliano (1940) 77.

4. Fergus Millar in *JRS* 63 (1973) xi.

5. See, e.g., Parry (1963) and Lyne (1987) and, for a more sophisticated assessment of the various viewpoints operative in Vergilian epic, Conte (1986). Great poetry is inherently polyphonal.

6. Putnam (1965) 201.

7. Cf. G. Williams' just strictures (1978, p. 92 n. 72) of my interpretation (1967b) of the Cipus episode in Ovid's *Metamorphoses*.

8. For a further articulation of this perspective see, e.g., Raaflaub and Toher (1990) and Alföldy (1991) 290–91.

9. An excellent recent synopsis is that of Brunt (1988) 2ff. For the evolutionary view of Roman institutions see, e.g., Livy 4.4; Cic., *Manil.* 60; cf. Cic., *Rep.* 2.2–3 (citing Cato), 30, 37; Polyb. 6.10.13.

10. Kunkel (1962) 76. For similar perspectives, besides the sources I have cited in chapter 2, see especially Earl (1967) 11ff. and Brunt (1988) 2ff.

11. An aspect emphasized especially by Cicero; see Wood (1988) 105ff. and Nicolet (1984).

12. Suet., *Aug.* 28; cf. the occurrence of the same phrase at Cic., *Rep.* 2.30.

13. Nicolet (1984) 111. As S. Treggiari (*CAH* 10^2 ch. 18) points out, the relative size of the propertied classes within the citizen body increased under Augustus.

14. Raaflaub and Samons (1990) 452; cf. Brunt (1988) 56ff.

15. Eder (1990) 118–19.

16. Cf. Momigliano (1940) 80.

17. Feeney (1992) 9.

18. Recent discussions include Millar (1981) 148; Brunt (1988) 2ff.; Galsterer (1990) 12ff.; Yavetz (1990) 24ff.

19. Syme's phrase (*RR* vii), which he applies more narrowly to "the composition of the oligarchy of government." Eder (1990) interprets it more widely in his excellent analysis of the transitional nature of the Augustan reign.

20. *De ant. orat.* 1.1–3. See Gabba (1991) 23ff.

21. Raaflaub and Samons (1990) 452 n. 138.

22. *RR* 521.

1. Ode 4.15.4. On the connection between the Horatian poem and Augustan art, see most recently Putnam (1986) 327–39; cf. Wickert (1949 [1969]) 121.

2. For details see Ramage (1987) and the bibliography cited there; also, Kienast 174ff. Yavetz (1984) 22 rightly stresses the importance of the *Res Gestae* as "a prime source" rather than "only as an auxiliary illustration." This is all the more important as our main narrative source for the Augustan period, Cassius Dio (third century A.D.), "is itself dependent upon an unknown and lost source as to whose credentials no judgment can be made" (J. Crook in *CAH* 10² ch. 2).

3. For a discussion of *RG* 34.1 see chapter 2. For the *Res Gestae*, I follow the translation of Brunt and Moore (1967) with a few exceptions.

4. For a different view, see Girardet (1990) who argues that Octavian had legitimate consular powers in 32 B.C. In that case, he would hardly have needed the oath of allegiance sworn by Italy and the western provinces (*RG* 25.2). Cf. Pelling in *CAH* 10² ch. 1, appendix 1.

5. Our main sources are Dio 53.1–13, 53.32.5, 54.3.3. Important modern discussions are Adcock (1951); Salmon (1956) 462ff.; Millar (1973) 61ff.; Kienast 72ff.; Eder (1990) 91ff.; Bleicken (1990). Contrary to custom, Augustus still controlled the legions in his provinces as part of his *imperium consulare* from 27 to 23 B.C. The other solution, command by virtue of a special *imperium proconsulare* while he was consul, would be even more anomalous; cf. Badian (1986) 81ff.

6. Studied in detail by Béranger (1953) and (1973).

7. Syme, *RR* 524.

8. Weber (1936) 221: "Er liebt die Verhüllung und überläßt anderen ihre Deutung."

9. Neuhauser (1972). For a discussion of modern notions of ambiguity, see Bahti (1986).

10. The quotations are from Hellegouarc'h (1972) 312 and Béranger (1953) 115.

11. The best discussion of the meaning of *auctoritas* is still that of Heinze (1925 [1960]); cf. Syme's remarks in *CR* 52 (1938) 194–95. Extensive collection of material by Fürst (1934) and Hellegouarc'h (1972) 295–314; cf. Béranger (1953) 114–31; Wickert (1954) 2287ff.; and Pollitt (1974) 311–18 (in connection with the visual arts). The attempts of von Premerstein (1937) 176ff., Grant (1946), and Magdelain (1947) to construe *auctoritas* in terms of statutory authority are misplaced for the time of Augustus. See also chapter 8.

12. Heinze (1925 [1960]) 46.

13. E.g., Plautus, *Poen.* 145–48; *Merc.* 312; *Trin.* 107, 217. Given the weight of the emperor's *auctoritas*, Tiberius once remarked that he would rather be a *suasor* (giver of counsel) than *auctor* (Suet., *Tib.* 27) because his *auctoritas* inhibited the ability of others to decide freely.

14. Syme, *RR* 459–75, but cf. Salmon (1956) 461: "*Auctoritas* enabled a man to propose a policy, it did not enable him to implement it."

15. Woodman and West (1984) 195; cf. White (1993), and chapter 5.

16. Hellegouarc'h (1972) 302.

17. Detailed documentation in Fürst (1934) 37–74; cf. Bonnefond-Coudry (1989) 683ff.

18. For full discussion, see Bleicken (1955).

19. For some further discussion, see chapter 2. Cf. Brunt (1988) 61ff.

20. See chapter 3.

21. Cf. Bonnefond-Coudry (1989) 683ff., especially 709, and Fürst (1934) 46.

22. For detail, see Raaflaub (1974) and Brunt (1988) 55ff.

23. Our main source again is Cicero: *Inv.* 1.109; *De Or.* 2.2.30, 2.154; *Brut.* 109; *Verr.* 2.3.70, 2.5.54; *Rosc.* 7; *Balb.* 49; *Att.* 1.14.5; *Fam.* 3.10.1; *ad Brut.* 1.9.2. Cf. Cic., *Tusc.* 5.34, and Pliny, *Ep.*2.7.4; 9.23.1.

24. *Dom.* 130, but cf. the discussion of *libertas* in chapter 2.

25. But a Roman *pater* also had *potestas.* A further reference in *RG* 35.1 is the repetition of the principle of universal consent (*senatus et sequester ordo populusque Romanus universus*, recalling the *consensus universorum* of 34.1); *RG* 35.1, too, is an example of multiple associations. For the several connotations of *pater patriae* alone, see Alföldi (1971).

26. Documentation in Fürst (1934) 47–50; the interpretations of subsequent scholars have been more doctrinaire without being convincing.

27. Connections with *augurium* and *augere*: Ovid, *Fasti* 1.608ff. and Suet., *Aug.* 7.2; for more detail, see chapter 6.

28. E.g., Livy 2.56.4; 4.48.7; Cic., *Sest.* 105; *De Or.* 1.211; *Att.* 8.2.2; cf. Cic., *Rep.* 1.69; 2.57.

29. Vergil, *Ecl.* 9.47–49 with Servius' commentary; cf. Pliny, *HN* 2.93–94; Suet., *Iul.* 88; Dio 45.7.1. See Weinstock (1971) 370ff. for full discussion and Zanker, *AMB* 42–46, for Octavian's subsequent self-representation as *divi filius.*

30. Vergil, *Aen.* 9.642; Prop. 4.1.46–48; Ovid, *Met.* 15.746–50; Manilius 1.925–26. White (1988) offers a balanced assessment of Julius Caesar's role in Augustan poetry.

31. For a discussion of the archaeological evidence, see E. Nedergaard in *KA* 224ff.

32. As is well brought out by Ramage (1987) 38–54.

33. And membership in the college of the *XVviri sacris faciundis* in whose power it was to consult the Sibylline Books.

34. For further discussion, see chapter 3.

35. Burns (1978).

36. Dio 53.2.3; cf. Nicolet (1984) 102.

37. Burns (1978) 20 and 40. With Augustus' emphasis on *auctoritas*, compare Franklin Roosevelt's view of the moral authority of the American presidency and, in particular, his use of the presidency as a "bully pulpit."

38. Peters and Waterman (1982) 82–83, with references to further studies of leadership.

39. On the definition of propaganda, see my subsequent discussion. For the relational nature of power, see Foucault (1976) 123, and Bachrach and Bahratz (1970).

40. For a good characterization, see already Heinze (1915) 475; cf. Brunt (1988) 56ff.

41. On its programmatic function, see Pöschl (1977) 19ff.

42. I have used Fitzgerald's version for this line.

43. Serv. *ad Aen.* 1.151 (*quia illi auctoritas ob pietatem est gravis*). Cf. Austin's translation: "A man of authoritative virtue and service" (Austin [1971] 69).

44. For eloquence as an ingredient of *auctoritas*, cf. Cic., *Brut.* 222 (with reference to one of Augustus' ancestors). Augustus took it very seriously: Suet., *Aug.* 84.1.

45. Plut., *Cato Minor* 44; Cic., *Mil.* 58; *Brut.* 56.

46. Constans (1938) 51.

47. Zanker, *AMB* 102–3; Vollenweider (1966) 51; Gagé (1936) 85–86.

48. Vollenweider (1966) 51–52. The image also recasts the one at the end of the first book of the *Georgics* (512–14), where Vergil amid the turmoil of the 30s expresses his fear

that Octavian, the charioteer, may not be able to control the chariot and the team of horses.

49. Cf. Cairns (1989) 95 n. 38. Cairns, who does not refer to the cameo, concludes that "Poseidon's help for Trojans in *Aen.* 1 indicates both their moral rectitude and the support for their mission of the fates and Jupiter," another example of multiple dimensions.

50. *BMCRR* II.515 no. 151; Pollini (1990) 344 with fig. 11.

51. Details in Pollini (1990) 346–47; Zanker, *AMB* 48–50; W. Murray and Petsas (1990); cf. Suet., *Aug.* 18.2. We will see repeatedly that Augustus not only appropriated symbols and slogans from opponents but also successfully recruited former adversaries.

52. For an extensive analysis, to which I will return several times, see Hölscher (1980) 271ff.; cf. Hölscher (1982) and the interpretations of the so-called Altar of Ahenobarbus, for which see, most recently, Gruen (1992) 145ff.

53. See especially J. Griffin (1985) 194–95; cf. chapter 5.

54. Useful discussions: Kähler (1959); Gross (1959); Brilliant (1963) 66ff.; Simon (1957b), (1986) 53ff., and (1991); D. Kleiner (1992) 63–67; Hölscher in *KA* 386–87 and, with reference to *auctoritas*, 361. For further details, especially the iconography of the armor, see chapter 4.

55. See, most recently, Colonna (1991).

56. Brilliant (1963) 67 with extensive discussion of various restorations, to which add Pollini (1978) 9ff. and Simon (1986) 56–57.

57. The same terms are used by Velleius (2.59.2) for Octavian's father.

58. As is evidenced by its absence from the list in Pollitt (1974); cf. his discussion of *semnos* on pp. 233–36.

59. Cf. Jucker (1950) 167; Zanker, *AMB* 104; Hölscher (1987) 55ff. Octavian invoked Achilles as an exemplar when he came to Rome after Caesar's assassination (Appian, *BC* 3.47).

60. For the following discussion I am much indebted to Wallace-Hadrill (1986), even while coming to some different conclusions, and to Levick (1982), Belloni (1974) and (1976), and Crawford (1983).

61. For the organization of the monetary system, see Sutherland in *RIC* I².24ff.; cf. Burnett (1977) and Sutherland (1976) 11ff.

62. The first comprehensive publication is that by Burnett, Amandry, and Ripollès (1992).

63. Wallace-Hadrill (1986) 73. He argues that this applies to all Roman coins and not just to local issues.

64. Arrian, *Discourses of Epictetus* 3.3.3–4 and 4.5.15–18.

65. Cf. Crawford, *RRC* 725ff.; Hölscher (1980) 271ff. and (1982); Classen (1986).

66. See chapter 2.

67. Grant (1950) 8; cf. Hannestad (1986) 9–14.

68. Levick (1982) 107; critiqued by Sutherland (1986).

69. Zanker, *AMB* especially 264ff.; cf. Crawford (1983) 54ff.

70. See, e.g., Salmon (1956); Eck (1986); Burnett (1977) 61–62; and my comments in chapter 7. Cf. Crawford (1983) 59.

71. See Hollstein's (1991) discussion of an important period of republican coinage under this aspect.; cf. Sutherland's remarks (1976) on topicality (p. 101).

72. Dio (51.2.5) mentions two Aquillii Flori, father and son, who were partisans of Antony and died after his defeat; their exact relation to the moneyer is not clear.

73. Giard nos. 111–12, *RIC* I².64 no. 316; Trillmich in *KA* no. 348; on Durmius, see Wiseman (1971) 229.

74. Fullerton (1985), despite some circular arguments; cf. Schneider (1986) 31 and 36, and Wallace-Hadrill (1986) 77–79.

75. For the prestige it regained, see Wiseman (1971) 150; for the general development, Kienast 324ff.

76. Syme, *AA* 368; for the general argument, see Wallace-Hadrill (1986) 82. The controversy about the significance of the symbols SC is summarized by Kienast 326–28; I basically follow the views of Kraft (1962).

77. *RIC* I².71 nos. 390–93, with Sutherland's comment; Giard 103; Burnett (1977) 48ff., whose views on the authenticity of some specimens I follow; Evans (1992) 141ff.; cf. Wallace-Hadrill (1986) 82–83.

78. Cf. the remarks of Gros (1976) 27–28, with reference to Livy 1.19–21.

79. *RRC* 446/1 with Crawford's remarks on p. 738; *RRC* 334 and 346, on which see the comments of Fabbricotti (1968). Cf. Evans (1992) 136ff.

80. In the context of *RG* 1.1; see chapter 2.

81. See Gagé (1955) 297ff., 479ff., and the discussion of the Palatine Apollo temple in chapter 5.

82. Burnett (1977) 44 lists several examples, including *RRC* 403 from Pompey's first consulate in 70 B.C.

83. Cf. Lummel (1991) 35ff.

84. Zanker, *AMB* 132–35.

85. Alföldi (1973), especially 2–17; Lummel (1991) 36.

86. Cf. the denarius issued by L. Aquillius Florus in 19 B.C. with the sun-god and his crown of rays on the obverse, and a quadriga and the legends CAESAR AUGUSTUS and SC on the reverse (*RIC* I².63 no. 303, Giard nos. 169–72). The range of associations includes achievements by Aquillius' ancestors, and allusions to Augustus as Alexander and Apollo (with many different nuances) and to Sol, the Latin ancestor; see Cogrossi (1978).

87. See Chastagnol (1980) for more extensive discussion; cf. Kienast 135.

88. Nicolet (1984) 92–93, 103–4; cf. Maecenas' arguments in Dio 52.19.2. Augustus instituted it not to encourage materialism, but because, if properly acquired, it was a reflection of *industria* and *virtus*.

89. Dio 54.26.5; see Chastagnol (1980) 469.

90. See Wiseman (1971) 147–53.

91. For a different view, see Wallace-Hadrill (1986) 79, citing the change in senatorial self-representation (Eck [1984]). That, however, is another relative phenomenon (see chapter 8), which cannot be simply equated with downgrading as it involved the innovation of listing a man's honors during his lifetime. The former moneyer L. Aquillius Florus is the earliest securely attested example of such an honoree; see *CIL* III.551 = *ILS* 928.

92. Sutherland (1976) 108.

93. See Sutherland (1945) and Kienast 313ff.

94. Cf. Mannsperger (1974) 941. On the *cura* and *tutela* of Augustus, see von Premerstein (1937) 120ff. and Béranger (1953) 201ff.

95. See especially the writings of Levick, Belloni, and Crawford cited in n. 60. Wallace-Hadrill (1981) 307–8 aptly observes that "not only was propaganda itself very much a live issue [in the 1930s], but the numismatic material was for the first time properly catalogued, indexed, and discussed with particular awareness of its 'ideological' content."

Cf. Consigliere (1978) and the careful assessments by Mannsperger (1991) 351–52; Bengtson (1981) 305–8; Crook in *CAH* 10² ch. 3.

96. *RIC* I².55–56 nos. 205–15; Giard nos. 1648–66; cf. Levick (1982) 107.

97. A recent exception, with limited results, is Evans (1992); cf. Wyke (1992), especially 100 and 118ff. Nor have historical surveys been more than superficial, such as Ferguson (1979).

98. Martin (1958) 10ff.

99. Fraser (1957) 1.

100. Martin (1958) 199.

101. Fraser (1957) 195ff.

102. See especially the work of Foulkes (1983), drawing on Morris (1971) and Ellul (1973). Cf. Kennedy (1984).

103. Foulkes (1983) 3.

104. Crawford (1983) 57. For a different view, see Sutherland (1986) who argues that the legionaries were the main intended audience. Crawford does not quite explain what he means by "official."

105. Ellul (1973) 73.

106. As for the appeal of the coin to the user, cf. Morris (1971) 105 and 401–2 and Foulkes (1983) 23 on what they call the "interpretant," that is, the "disposition to respond in certain ways to a certain kind of object under certain circumstances." As so often in modern theory, terms like these are elastic enough to be widely applicable, with a resulting lack of precision.

CHAPTER II

1. Some of these, however, may have been covered in his actual autobiography; for its remains, see Malcovati (1969) xlii–xlvi and 84–98. Similarly, Nicolaus of Damascus devotes a long section of his biography of Augustus to his devotion to Julius Caesar: chs. 6–15 (Hall [1923]); *FGH* 90 F 127.

2. For some good comments on this, see Weber (1936) 102ff.; Brunt and Moore (1967); and Lacey (1974) 184.

3. Our primary ancient sources for the events detailed in this section are Appian, *BC* 3 and Dio, books 45 and 46 (cf. Gowing [1992] 57ff.), along with several of Cicero's letters. Important modern treatments are Syme, *RR* 123–86; Walser (1955); Alföldi (1976) 76ff.; Bellen (1985); Ortmann (1988); Eder (1990) 88ff.; cf. Kienast 25–32.

4. For further details, see Appian 3.175ff.; Walser (1955) 359–60.

5. Antony, of course, is not even mentioned in *RG* 1.1: a classic example of *damnatio memoriae*. Another reason, however, is to extend the frame of reference beyond Antony; see my subsequent comments. Cf. Vell. 2.61.1 with Woodman's (1983) notes.

6. That was Cicero's delusion as late as July 43 B.C. as is clear from *ad Brut.* 23.6: *Caesarem hunc adulescentem . . . fluxisse ex fonte meorum consiliorum.* Brutus could rightly say that Cicero helped Octavian ascend not in the least because he lent him his unparalleled *auctoritas* (*Ad Brut.* 12.2).

7. See pp. 73–74.

8. Cf. Syme, *RR* 163 and Levi (1933) 1.139: "The speech, in substance, is grounded in one of the most audacious legal argumentations recorded in the history of Roman eloquence."

9. An indication that Octavian's campaign to be the son of the deified Caesar was beginning to take hold; cf. *Phil.* 5.43.

10. For various discussions see Weber (1936) 136ff.; Béranger (1973) 128ff.; Schäfer (1957) 323–24; Walser (1955) 355–56; Bellen (1985) 163; Ramage (1987) 67–68; cf. Cic., *Fam.* 11.7.2.

11. Extensive citation and discussion of the relevant sources in Weber (1936) 143*–145* (n. 569).

12. *RG* 24.2; cf. Suet., *Aug.* 52; Dio 53.22.3. Cf. Zanker, *AMB* 46–49, and Mannsperger (1982).

13. *Fam.* 11.20.1; Octavian's response was that he was in no hurry to get there. Extensive discussion of the sources and events in Bellen (1985) 180ff. and Ortmann (1988) 395ff.

14. Appian 3.337–39; Dio 46.42.2–3; cf. Plut., *Cic.* 53.4.

15. Suet., *Aug.* 26.1; Dio 46.43.4–5; cf. Bengtson (1972) 973–77.

16. Hölscher (1967) 97 and (1980) 269ff. Cf. Wickert (1949 [1969]) 125 (on the *Res Gestae*, without reference to the arts); and Wesenberg's (1985) characterization of the innovative aspect of the third style in Roman wall painting, which was bitterly attacked by the more literal-minded Vitruvius (7.5.1–8): "The picture is now freed from its link to a fictive reality, and this increases its capacity to take on conceptual contents" (p. 488).

17. Cf. Eder (1990) 119.

18. See Michel (1967) and Weippert (1972).

19. Gross (1985) 36; Zanker, *AMB* 50–52; Massner (1982) 10ff., 32ff.

20. Pliny, *HN* 37.10; Suet., *Aug.* 50; see Instinsky (1962).

21. Vergil, *Aen.* 6.791–807 with Austin (1977) especially on 6.796; cf. Prop. 4.3.7–10, 35–36, 63–64. For additional documentation and Augustus' Alexander emulation in general, see Gruen (1985) 68–72.

22. A point made by Cic., *Phil.* 5.48, including a reference to Alexander.

23. Vell. 2.61.3; cf. Lahusen (1983) 59. No mention is made of Lepidus' receiving the same honor (Cic., *Phil.* 5.41; 13.8), probably because his statue was removed before very long. The hypothesis that *RG* 1.1 is identical with the inscription on the base of Octavian's statue is suggestive but unproved.

24. Valuable collection of sources in Weber (1936) 135* (note 550) and discussion by Béranger (1973) 243ff.; cf. C. Ehrhardt (1986).

25. I.e., OB CIVIS SERVATOS; see the indexes in Giard 253 and *RIC* I² p. 291.

26. *Manil.* 62 and the repeated references to Pompey and Crassus in *Sest.* 40–41, 43, 47, 69, 89; cf. *Planc.* 66, 88.

27. For fuller discussion see Weber (1936) 140–41; Skard (1955); Walser (1955) 357–64; Béranger (1973) 245 n. 8.

28. Cic., *Phil.* 3.3, 5; 5.3; cf. *Fam.* 11.7.2. Cf. his similar arguments in behalf of Decimus Brutus (*Phil.* 3.12, 14; 5.3, 28; 10.23) and Caecilius Bassus (*Phil.* 11.32).

29. The fashionable dichotomy, posited especially by recent American interpreters of Augustan poetry, between "public" and "private"—usually with reference to "voices" (cf. introduction)—ignores the essential Roman context.

30. See chapter 3. The most concise formulation is Horace, *C.* 3.24.35–36: *quid leges sine moribus vanae proficiunt?*

31. E.g., Spurius Maelius: Livy 4.13.1; Cic., *Rep.* 2.49; Appius Claudius: Livy 9.34.1–2; cf. Cic., *Manil.* 61–62; *Fam.* 8.10.2.

32. Documentation in Hellegouarc'h (1972) 562–65.

33. Complete compilation by Weber (1936) 137*–140* (note 557) on which all subsequent discussions have been drawing with varying degrees of acknowledgment; cf. Wirszubski (1950)103 and Hellegouarc'h (1972) 550 n. 13.

34. . . . *ut tribunum plebis iniuria ex civitate expulsum in suam dignitatem restitueret et se et populum Romanum factione paucorum oppressum in libertatem vindicaret* (*BC* 1.22.5).

35. Ps.-Caes., *BA* 22.2.

36. Douglas (1966) 154.

37. Good discussion by Raaflaub (1974) 155ff.

38. *Rep.* 3.44 (Scipio speaking): *vides igitur ne illam quidem, quae tota sit in factionis potestate, posse vere dici rem publicam.* This perspective on *res publica* and *potestas* is another link between the first and final chapters of the *Res Gestae*.

39. For detailed discussion of the first two, see chapter 4. For the Gemma Augustea (Fig. 57), see Kähler (1991) and Simon (1986) 156–60.

40. *RIC* I².79 no. 476; Giard nos. 908–10; Sutherland (1970) 40–44, 88–90. It is also worth noting that one of the temples Augustus specifically singles out in the summary of his restoration program in Rome (*RG* 19.1) is that of Jupiter Libertas; its dedication date was changed to September 1, the anniversary of Actium.

41. Brunt (1988) 283; his discussion of "*Libertas* in the Republic" (pp. 281–350) is authoritative. Other important studies are Kloesel (1935); Wirszubski (1950); Wickert (1949); Bleicken (1962); the important collection of essays edited by Klein (1969), including his preface (pp. 1–22); Kunkel (1969).

42. See Büchner (1984) 220 on *Rep.* 2.46. Brutus in that context is called *auctor* and *princeps*.

43. See especially his discussion in *Rep.* 2.53–57, 59; *Leg.* 3.23–25, 28; Brunt (1988) 324–26.

44. *tribuniciam potestatem, munimentum libertatis* (Livy 3.37.5); cf. Livy 3.45.8; Cic., *Agr.* 2.15; *Sest.* 30; *De Or.* 2.199.

45. Especially *Leg.* 3.38–39; cf. Kunkel (1969) 85–86.

46. Brunt (1988) 326 n. 112. Cf. Cic. *Rep.* 2.43; Tac., *Ann.* 6.42.

47. See Robinson (1940) and Momigliano (1942a).

48. Momigliano (1940) 80. The next citation is also taken from there.

49. Momigliano (1940) 80; cf. Nicolet (1984) 107ff. and Brunt's (1988) discussion of the economic implications of *libertas* (346ff.), to which should be added that a great deal of Rome's spending power was concentrated in the hands of Augustus; see Sutherland, *RIC* I².23–24.

50. Brunt (1988) 350. Cf. the judicious assessment of Raaflaub and Samons (1990) 450–54.

51. Brunt (1988) 326.

52. See, e.g., Weinbrot (1978).

53. DuQuesnay (1984) 29–32; for what follows I am indebted to his argument on p. 30 in particular. Cf. Reckford (1991) 216–17 and D. Kennedy (1992) 31ff.

54. DuQuesnay (1984) 30.

55. Cf. Kienast's (1989) comments (p. 179) on the change of the connotations of republican concepts in the *Res Gestae*.

56. As is argued by Braunert (1974) 351–52. The Greek translation, however, is *kyrieia* ("supreme authority") rather than *politeia*.

57. See pp. 64–65. Cf. Lacey (1974) 184: "*Res Gestae* 34–35 is not a political or constitutional statement at all, but the capstone of Augustus' achievement," and Brunt and Moore (1967) 9–10, 77. [Augustus] *rem publicam p. R.* restituit: *Fasti Praen.* for January 13, 27 B.C. (*EJ* p. 45). *De reddenda re publica bis cogitavit:* Suet., *Aug.* 28.1.

58. Excellent overview in Pöschl (1956b).

59. *Ben.* 2.20.2: (Brutus) *existimavit civitatem in priorem formam posse revocari amissis pristinis moribus.*

60. For full documentation see Meier (1980a) 1–3; cf. Bellen (1987) 324ff. It withstands even the reservations of Gruen (1974), especially 498–99.

61. Pref. 9. Cf. Vergil's use of the same key terms in his famous articulation of the Roman national character (*Aen.* 6.851–52): *imperio, artes, morem.*

62. Thomas Jefferson, not untypically, viewed it as one of the causes of the republic's fall (Letter to John Adams, May 10, 1819).

63. Büchner (1984) 392.

64. Cf. Sattler's (1960) apt remarks on "the cult of the Republic" (p. 6); Gruen (1974) 503.

65. Galinsky (1992b) 69.

66. Meier (1980a) 3. Cf. Heinze (1915) 475.

67. Hölscher (1980) 269–81; cf. Crawford, *RRC* 745–50 and Belloni (1985).

68. Livy 2.49.1. On the painting, see B. Andreae in Helbig II⁴ no. 1600; Coarelli in *Roma medio repubblicana* (1973) 200ff.; Hölscher (1980) 270–71; Evans (1992) 9–10; for a different interpretation, see La Rocca (1984).

69. Details in Heinze (1929); Hellegouarc'h (1972) 23ff.; and Noerr (1989); cf. Pöschl (1956b) 195.

70. Hölscher (1980) 271–73; Crawford, *RRC* 728ff.; Classen (1986); cf. Meier (1980a).

71. Hölscher (1967) 138–56; cf. Alföldi (1956) 72ff.

72. For details, see Hölscher (1982) and (1980) 271ff.

73. See the chapter by Zehnacker (1973) 764ff. on "Polyvalence et diversité des effigies divines."

74. *RIC* I². 59 no. 253; *BMCRE* I.100 nos. 611–14; Giard nos. 6–11; *KA* no. 330. Cf. Wlosok (1967) 120 n. 67; Kraft (1969) 6–11; and Trillmich in *KA* 509–10 with further bibliography.

75. G. Binder (1971) 94.

76. Cf. Wirszubski (1950) 121. For the many meanings of *res publica*, see Stark (1967) especially 80 n. 97; cf. my introduction and Kienast's discussion (pp. 16–18) of the correspondence between Cicero and the Caesarian C. Matius (*Fam.* 11.29 and 30).

77. Cf. Wallace-Hadrill in *TLS* January 25 (1991) 24.

78. Kunkel (1962) 76.

79. Detailed documentation in Millar (1973) 61ff.; cf. Sattler (1960) 36ff.; Adcock (1951); Lacey (1974); Eder (1990) 104ff.; Bleicken (1990) 82ff.

80. *CIL* I² p. 315 (Feriale Cumanum); *CIL* XI.1421; cf. Ennius' invocation of Romulus as *custos patriae* (1.107 Skutsch).

81. See the documentation in the *ThLL*. The nuance proved untranslatable in the Greek version of the *Res Gestae*. On the latitude of its meaning in *RG* 34.1 compare Millar (1973) 65: "The word 'arbitrium,' again, can refer to a historical fact if it alludes to Octavian's offer and the subsequent vote of the Senate and the People in January 27 B.C.;

but if it carries an implication of a continued political freedom lasting beyond that point, that is another matter."

82. Manuwald (1979) 89 argues convincingly that Dio's version of the speech is not simply fictional.

83. Caesar, *BC* 1.9.5–6; cf. Cic., *Fam.* 16.12.3 and Raaflaub (1974) 267ff. In his speech in Dio, Augustus refers to Caesar twice (53.6.4, 8.1).

84. The most comprehensive discussion is that of Kuttner (1995); she plausibly argues that the prototype was a public monument. For the general interpretation I follow Hölscher (1980) 281ff.; for the date, Simon (1986) 143; cf. Ryberg (1955) 141ff.; Brilliant (1963) 73ff.; Koeppel (1982) 521–22; Zanker, *AMB* 229–32. The Augustus cup in particular has been heavily damaged—hence our reliance on the original publication by Héron de Villefosse in *MonPiot* 5 (1899) 133ff. for photographs (pls. 31ff.).

85. Hölscher (1980) 290.

86. Not that such memories were lost: "May you be luckier than Augustus, better than Trajan" (*sis felicior Augusto, melior Traiano*) was the formula spoken at the inauguration of late Roman emperors (Eutropius 8.5.3).

87. Nicolet (1984); cf. chapter 3.

88. See, e.g., the important studies by Price (1984) and MacCormack (1981).

89. Eder (1990) 104ff.; Bleicken (1990) 82ff.; Sattler (1960) 36ff.; Kienast 71ff.; cf. Adcock (1951) and Lacey (1974). Cf. chapter 7.

90. Eck (1984) especially 150ff.; Alföldy (1991) 319ff.; and chapter 8.

91. Brunt (1984) 444. Besides Brunt's article, the books of Sattler (1960) and Talbert (1984) are especially useful; cf. Kienast 126ff., and Crook and Talbert in *CAH* 10², chs. 3 and 9.

92. Chapter 1.

93. See, e.g., Dio 53.21.3, 55.25.4–6, and 56.28.4–6 (a particularly instructive example from late in his reign); cf., for an example of freedom of speech in general, Sen., *Contr.* 2.4.12–13 and the discussions by Toher (1990), especially 142 ("there is almost no significant evidence that free expression of ideas was seriously curtailed by Augustus"), and by Raaflaub and Samons (1990), especially 439ff. on the book burnings.

94. Brunt (1984) 442; cf. Sattler (1960) 31–34. For the use of the same criterion in 18 B.C. see Dio 54.13.1 and chapter 1.

95. Cf. Kienast 149–51; Talbert (1984) 136–37 and *CAH* 10² ch. 9. One year before Augustus' death, the *consilium* was reconstituted and its decisions preempted those of the senate. Apparently, the reason was Augustus' ill health; the arrangement was promptly cancelled by Tiberius.

96. Talbert (1984) 222ff.

97. E.g., Vergil, *Ecl.* 4; *Geo.* 1.463ff.; Hor., *Epode* 16; *Ode* 1.2. Quite properly, their fears did not subside promptly after Actium; see Powell (1992) 162ff.

98. Vell. 2.91.3; 92.2–4; cf. Syme, *RR* 371, and chapter 7.

99. Raaflaub and Samons (1990) 453.

100. Wallace-Hadrill (1985) 250.

101. Galinsky (1986) 24; cf. chapter 3.

102. Chapter 1.

103. Raaflaub and Samons (1990) 452.

104. The split is mirrored by Tacitus. In *Hist.* 1.1.1, he summarily states that writers of great talent (specifically, historians) ceased to exist after Actium (*ingenia magna cessere*). In

the corresponding section of the *Annales* (1.1.2), however, he allows that there were talented writers (*non defuere decora ingenia*) at Augustus' time until they were inhibited by the growth of flattery (rather than by repression). Cf. Velleius (2.36), who characterizes both the late republic and Augustus' reign as a time of outstanding *ingenia* (such as Cicero, Lucretius, Catullus, Vergil, Ovid, and Livy).

105. Brunt (1984) 444; cf. Dio 53.21.3–6.

106. See Wirszubski (1950) 164ff.; cf. Jens (1956). Perceptive treatments of such reciprocal interactions in areas of literature and art are Woodman and West (1984) especially 189ff.; J. Griffin (1984); White (1993); Zanker. *AMB* 264ff.; Massner (1982).

107. See chapter 7.

108. Eder (1990) 104.

109. An apt characterization used by White (1993) 96.

110. Cf. the concise remarks of Wallace-Hadrill (1985) 246.

111. See, e.g., von Premerstein (1939) 3ff.; Walser (1955) 354f.; Schäfer (1957); Béranger (1959); Bellen (1985) 187ff.; more balanced: Lepore (1954) and Wickert (1974) 19–24.

112. Or, to use another figure of speech, he preferred to sit in two chairs at once (Sen., *Contr.* 7.3.9; Macrob., *Sat.* 2.3.10). For a more favorable assessment, see Habicht (1990) 97–99. Cf. Syme, *RR* 135–48 and Meier (1980b) 103ff. Augustus graciously called Cicero "an eloquent man and one who loved his country" (Plut., *Cic.* 49).

113. Cf. Brunt (1988) 56–68.

114. Full documentation in Lepore (1954) 21ff., 292ff.

115. E.g., *Rep.* 2.67; *De Or.* 1.211; 3.63; cf. the list in Wickert (1954) 2014–29 (ninety-three names) with additional comments by Wickert (1974) 11–12, and, for the general argument, Brunt (1988) 506–8.

116. E.g., *Rep.* 1.3; 1.13; 5.11; *Att.* 8.11.1.

117. Ovid and the *RG*: G. Binder (1971) 94; Propertius and the *RG*: Hallett (1985). For the general perspective: Schäfer (1957) 323–24, who cites Carl Koch (Augustan "Allgemeinbildung," i.e., common intellectual property). Cf. Helmbold's (1958) elegant and mercifully brief solution to the "problem" of the relationship between Vergil's fourth *Eclogue* and Horace's sixteenth *Epode*: mutual, ongoing discussion.

118. Cf. Salmon (1956); Eck (1986); Eder (1990); also, Augustus' famous motto to "make haste slowly" and Dio 52.41.1–2.

119. The classic treatment is still that of Scott (1933), but see now the detailed study of Wallmann (1989). For the contest of images, see Zanker, *AMB* 42ff.

120. See chapter 3.

121. See, e.g., Elton (1967) 10–11.

122. Compilation of sources in Hellegouarc'h (1972): *regnum* (pp. 560–61); *tyrannus* (pp. 561–62); *dominatio* and *dominatus* (pp. 562–65).

123. Cf. Meier (1990) whose interpretation, however, is somewhat different and who therefore concludes that "Augustus could only defeat the Republic thoroughly and definitely by restoring it" (pp. 69–70). I find the conclusions in his earlier work (1980a, pp. 301–6) more applicable: the republican institutions could not be sufficiently altered, hence the only way out of the republic's malaise was a betterment of general morals. That was precisely the cornerstone of Augustus' program.

124. A current illustration is the events in the former Soviet Union.

125. Eder (1990) 118–19.

126. Heinze (1925 [1960]) 58.

127. Some points of contact have been noted by Urban (1979) and by Goodyear (1972) 104 on *Ann.* 1.2.1; on Tacitus' knowledge of Augustus' writings, see Schmitt (1983).

128. *Ann.* 1.2.1. *Dux* again has frequent pejorative connotations. At best, it is differentiated from *auctor* or *princeps* by denoting not the initiator (with the intellectual equipment that requires) but the mere executor of an action. As such *dux* is near the lower end of purely transactional leadership; see Hellegouarc'h (1972) 324–26.

129. Suetonius (*Aug.* 28.2) holds the middle position between Augustus' claim and Tacitus' debunking of it by characterizing the Augustan government as *novus status*. That is not enough for Tacitus who proceeds to use the far more negative phrase *res novae*. For Tacitus' consistently downplaying the role of the *princeps' auctoritas*, see Syme (1958b) 413.

130. See n. 90.

131. Cf. Gabba's (1984) assessment of Tacitus (pp. 77ff.) and Weinbrot's (1993) comments on Tacitus' rediscovery and use for partisan controversies in eighteenth-century England.

CHAPTER III

1. If one uses the definitions, e.g., of Arendt (1961) and Minogue (1985). Cf. Burns (1978) 248–51; Eagleton (1991); and Geertz (1973) 193: "It is one of the minor ironies of modern intellectual history that the term 'ideology' has itself become thoroughly ideologized." Christ (1992) 168 distinguishes between *Ideologeme* and an Augustan ideology.

2. For some earlier bibliography not listed here, see Ramage (1987) 74–76 and Korpanty (1991). I have drawn in particular on the discussions of Wallace-Hadrill (1981a); Weinstock (1971) 228–59; Classen (1986); Fears (1981c); Wickert (1954) 2231ff.; Ramage (1987) 74–100; Charlesworth (1937); Hölscher (1967) 102–12; Hellegouarc'h (1972).

3. *RG* 34; see chapter 1.

4. Details in Classen (1986) especially 282–83; cf. Fears (1981c) 884.

5. Plato: *Rep.* 4.428a, *Protag.* 349d, *Lach.* 199d; Cato (the Younger): Cic., *Att.* 7.2.7 (50 B.C.).

6. Full documentation in Hölscher (1967) 103ff. Vatican altar: Inv. 1115; Helbig I⁴ no. 255 (E. Simon); Ryberg (1955) 56ff. Augustan denarius: *RIC* I².44 nos. 47a, b.; Giard 1325–26.

7. Scholia on Lucan, *Pharsalia* 1.11: *duae sunt praecipuae Romanae virtutes, virtus militaris et pietas.*

8. Pompey: Appian, *BC* 2.104; *RRC* 477. Sextus Pompey: Cic., *Phil.* 5.39; *RRC* 477; cf. Powell (1992) 153–55. The Antonii: Dio 48.5.4; *RRC* 516/4–5; *BMCRR* II.400–402 nos. 65–72. Cf. the coinage of Caesar (*BMCRR* I.505–8 nos. 3953–61; *RRC* 450/2) and of the triumvirs in 42 B.C. (*RRC* 494/19).

9. Liegle (1941) 101 with fig. 7c.; Giard nos. 51–56.

10. Detailed documentation in Weinstock (1971) 233–43.

11. For details see Wallace-Hadrill (1981a) 306–7.

12. Cf. chapter 7.

13. See Hellegouarc'h (1972) 244ff.; cf. Wickert (1954) 2231 and Earl (1967) 20.

14. See note 2; cf. Prop. 3.22.21–22. The general distinction between "competitive"

and "cooperative" virtues (made by Adkins [1960] 6–7 with reference to Homer) is useful but does not imply my acceptance of all of Adkins' theses.

15. Earl (1967) 21. Besides Earl, useful discussions of *virtus* in general are Hellegouarc'h (1972) 244ff. and 478ff.; Weinstock (1971) 230–33 (with special reference to Caesar); Ramage (1987) 76–86 (with special reference to the *Res Gestae*).

16. Cf. *RG* 34.1: *postquam bella civilia exstinxeram.*

17. See pp. 132–35.

18. Cf. Wiseman (1971) 107ff.

19. I am much indebted to the discussion of Weinstock (1971) 233–43; cf. Hellegouarc'h (1972) 261–63; Bux (1948); T. Adams (1970), especially 86–88; Alföldi (1985) 173ff.

20. See especially Bux (1948) 205.

21. E.g., 5.1., 5.3, 6.1, 10.2; see Ramage (1987) 86ff. Cf. Maecenas in Dio 52.18.3.

22. *Fasti Praen. CIL* I² p. 231, 306; K. Latte in *RE* X.1339.

23. Cf. Liegle (1967); Hellegouarc'h (1972) 276–79; Traina (1988).

24. See Gros (1976) 21–22 and below, chapter 6.

25. Vell. 2.71.1 with the comments of Woodman; on Messalla and his descendants, see Syme, *AA* 200–43.

26. Details in Weinstock (1971) 256–59.

27. Aeneas does not lack this quality as is indicated, e.g., by *Aen.* 10.825–30 and 11.105–7. Cf., generally, G. Binder (1971) 278–81 and 53–55.

28. Santirocco (1986) 116 with references (pp. 110–25) to the compendious earlier bibliography on the "Roman Odes." Cf. La Penna (1963) 104ff.

29. Documentation in Hölscher (1967) 102–12; Giard, pp. 46–48, 166–67, 170–73, 188, 190–93; cf. Ramage (1987) 74.

30. Liegle (1932 [1967]) 237–41.

31. Cf. Tac., *Dial.* 12.3; cf. Sen., *Contr.* 2.7.7, Quint. 8.6.24, and the comments of Gatz (1967) 142–43.

32. The bibliography on *Ecl.* 4 is massive (see W. Briggs in *ANRW* II.31.2 [1981] 1311–25); it is larger than the entire bibliography to Syme's *Roman Revolution*, and that does not necessarily mean progress. The best up-to-date treatments, summarizing much of the earlier discussion, are Gatz (1967) 87–103; DuQuesnay (1977); and Benko (1980).

33. See the detailed and useful discussion of Nisbet (1978).

34. For the evidence (Censorinus 17) see Weinstock (1971) 192; cf. the article "saeculum" in the *Enc. Virg.* 4.637–41.

35. Cf. Brenk (1980) 83.

36. G. Miles in *Vergilius* 27 (1981) 79, summarizing Vernant (1969), Engl. trans. (1983) 3–72.

37. The concept of the "Golden Age," it should be noted, is already a modification of the Greek concept of a "golden race"; such a transition made it possible to experiment with the whole concept yet further. Important discussions of the Golden Age concept, its tradition, and development are Baldry (1952); Gatz (1967); Johnston (1977) and (1980); and the article "aurea aetas" in *Enc. Virg.* 1.412–18. Cf. Wallace-Hadrill (1982a).

38. For further context, see pp. 121–23.

39. Cf. Sallust, *Cat.* 2.7: agriculture, seafaring, and building are indications of *virtus*.

40. See especially Johnston (1977) and (1980) 62ff.; also, the article "Saturno" in *Enc. Virg.* 4.685–88. Cf. W. Anderson (1958).

41. For the general phenomenon—Vergil's presentation of different versions of a myth—see the perceptive remarks of Horsfall (1981).

42. See especially Seneca's *Letter* 90 based on Posidonius; cf. Hor., *C.* 3.24.35–36.

43. I have followed Fitzgerald's translation for line 323.

44. In E. Montanari's apt phrase (with reference to Diomedes' appellation of the Latins as *fortunatae gentes, Saturnia regna* in *Aen.* 11.252): "uno stato di pace laboriosa" (*Enc. Virg.* 4.686).

45. Austin (1977) 243–44.

46. For the documentation, see Baldry (1952) 86ff. Cf. Pliny, *HN* 35.157–58.

47. See Zanker, *AMB*, especially 110ff., 141ff. (on the Porticus Liviae, among others).

48. J. Griffin (1985) 1–31.

49. *RG* 22–23; Suet. *Aug.* 45; see now Will (1991) 140–46.

50. For a more extensive discussion, see Galinsky (1983). On *simplicitas*, see Ferrero (1979).

51. Details in Bömer's commentary (1969) 48ff.; Gatz (1967) 70–79.

52. *Clem.* 2.1.4 with the remarks of Jal (1957) 261–62. For a complete catalog of poetic references, see Gatz (1967) 138–39; cf. Mattingly (1934) 163–64 and (1947).

53. On the *ludi saeculares* see M. Nilsson in *RE* IA (1920) 1696ff.; Pighi (1965); Kienast 185–88; Moretti (1982–84); Price in *CAH* 10².

54. Details in *Enc. Virg.* 4.639–40.

55. See *Enc. Virg.* 4.638; cf. Alföldi (1930) and Weinstock (1971) 192–93. On Sulla, see Cic., *Cat.* 3.9, and on Pompey, Cic., *Manil.* 41–42; cf. Cic., *Cat.* 3.26 (regarding Pompey and Cicero himself).

56. A point not understood by Suetonius (*Aug.* 27.5) and Dio (54.10.5), who present him as *curator legum et morum* anyway and are followed by von Premerstein (1937); see his extensive discussion on pp. 149ff. The same offer was made to Augustus in 11 B.C., with the same result. Cf. Bellen (1987) 311–15.

57. Brunt and Moore (1967) 47 with reference to *RG* 6.2; cf. the continuing modification of the electoral process as evidenced by the Tabula Hebana (*EJ* 94a), referring to such a change in A.D. 5. For the various laws, see Kienast 97–99; Kunkel in *RE* XXIV (1963) 769ff.; and already Heinze in his commentary on the *Carmen Saeculare*.

58. *C.* 3.24.35–36: *quid leges sine moribus / vanae proficiunt?* Cf. Cic., *Leg.* 2.23.

59. See Ovid, *Trist.* 1.2.103–4 with Luck's commentary and the dedicatory inscription by the people of Narbo to the *numen Augusti* (*EJ* 100); cf. Suet., *Aug.* 58.2; Vell. 2.89.2.; Erkell (1952) 108ff.

60. Mattingly (1934) 162; Wissowa (1912) 236ff., 296.

61. I have discussed his relevance in this regard to the *Carmen Saeculare* in (1967a).

62. See Heinze's commentary *ad loc.*

63. All of the pertinent attestations, however, are post-Augustan, and possibly influenced by Horace's use of the word here.

64. Heinze, *ad loc.*

65. Detailed documentation in *ThLL* 1.1164–70.

66. Esp. *Aen.* 1.283, where a form of *lustrum* is used for the only time in the *Aeneid*, followed by the mention of *aetas*, echoed by Horace's *aevum*.

67. Suetonius at one point remarks on Tiberius' ushering in the Iron Age after the Golden Age of Saturn. (*Tib.* 59.1; cf. *Aug.* 100.3).

68. Giard nos. 273–77; *RIC* I².66 nos. 339–40; *KA* no. 357.

69. A. Boyce (1965); cf. Grant's interpretation in terms of the Genius Augusti (1954) 279 n. 58.

70. Serv. Dan. *ad Ecl.* 9.46; cf. Weinstock (1971) 195, 370–71.

71. See pp. 251–52.

72. For a detailed discussion of the Ara Pacis and its context see chapter 4, where the relevant bibliography is listed also. For the perspective followed here, cf. Gruen (1985) 51ff. and especially 61–63.

73. The most comprehensive discussion is that of Fittschen (1976a); cf. Simon (1986) 223 and Zanker, *AMB* 224–26.

74. P. Zanker (1968) 19 with n. 99 and figs. 48 and 49; *LMIC* II.1 (1984) 515 no. 24 (E. Simon).

75. Berczelly (1985) 131–2.

76. See Heinze's commentary and Kilpatrick (1986) 88.

77. *RRC* 58. Overall, there are over thirty republican coin types with a cornucopia or cornucopiae. Cf. the application of "golden" and "iron" ages to republican periods by the historian Florus (1.19.2–3). For the nonnumismatic evidence see Sieveking (1895) and, for double cornucopiae, Ducati (1908) especially 142ff.

78. *RRC* 397 and 403.

79. *RRC* 409 and 376.

80. *RRC* 464/3a and 516/1; cf. note 8.

81. *RRC* 525/1.

82. See Lehmann-Hartleben (1927) 164ff.; cf. Alföldi (1930) 371ff.

83. Furtwängler 3 (1900) 315; Megow (1987) 185.

84. Cleopatra: *BMC Ptol. Kings*, pl. VIII.2; Antony: *RRC* 520.

85. Altar in Bologna (Museo Civico Archeologico), published by Lehmann-Hartleben (1927).

86. Giard nos. 1264–78; *RIC* I².50 nos. 125–30. On the Capricorn as Augustus' astral sign, see Schütz (1991).

87. Hölscher (1967) 163.

88. Walters (1914) no. 1372 with fig. 316; Hölscher (1967) 109.

89. Giard nos. 616–20; *RIC* I².75 nos. 426 and 426A.

90. British Museum, Walters (1926) no. 1977; Vollenweider (1966) pl. 91.4–6.

91. For the following examples (with the exception of the detail from the Ara Pacis), see Zanker, *AMB* 181–84, 288 (with figs 138, 139, 226). The Grimani reliefs are dated to the time of Tiberius by Bianchi Bandinelli in *DArch* 1 (1967) 126–29 and the time of Vespasian by Strocka (1965) 90.

92. Murray (1965) 169 with reference to Philodemus' treatise col. IX, 14ff. For a list of other sources, see Woodman (1983) 255 on Vell. 2.89.4. Velleius includes among his praises of Augustus the return of cultivation to the fields (*rediit cultus agris*).

93. Cf. Nicolet (1984) 113–14.

94. Potter (1979) 133.

95. Carter and Costantini (1994); cf. Brunt (1971) 345ff., especially 375.

96. See Kienast 328–36; cf. Pliny, *HN* 7.149.

97. The most recent discussions are those of Simon (1986) 156–61 and Hölscher in *KA* 371–73.

98. Fuhrmann (1983) 249. In this section I have drawn on my earlier article (Galinsky [1984], with extensive references to earlier bibliography) with consideration of additional discussions, such as Fuhrmann's.

99. *ThLL* 7.693, 46ff.

100. Cf. especially 5.1430: *ergo hominum genus incassum frustraque laborat* ("therefore the human race toils in vain and to no purpose"); the mention of *labor* occurs at the end of the accounts of both Lucretius and Vergil. With *Geo.* 1.123 (*curis acuens mortalia corda*) compare Lucr. 5.1431: *et in curis consumit inanibus aevum*.

101. For some further aspects of these passages see pp. 246–47.

102. *RN* 3.18: *apparet divum numen sedesque quietae*. For the characterization of Aeneas in this episode in *Aeneid* 3, see R. Grimm (1967).

103. Otis (1938) especially 206.

104. See Leach (1964).

105. *Vita Horati* in *De poetis*, ed. Rostagni (1944) 116–17; for the views of Pope and others, see Weinbrot (1978) 182ff. Cf. Becker (1963) 194–237 and Brink (1982) 193ff.

106. As is evidenced, e.g., by his speaking and writing style (Suet., *Aug.* 86.2) and his modernization of archaic religion (Tac., *Ann.* 4.16, cited in chapter 6).

107. Graves (1962), especially 13: "Whenever a Golden Age of stable government, full churches, and expanding wealth dawns among western nations, Virgil always returns to supreme favor. His reputation flourished in . . . Paris under Louis XIV, London under Queen Anne and Queen Victoria, Baltimore in the first half of the nineteenth century, Boston in the second half, and Potsdam under Kaiser Wilhelm II." One wonders about possible candidates in the late twentieth century.

108. Ortega y Gasset (1932) 30.

109. For earlier bibliography on the topic, see Galinsky (1981b). Since then, the following important discussions have appeared: Raditsa (1980); Wallace-Hadrill (1981b); des Bouvrie (1984); Nicolet (1984) 96ff.; Badian (1985); Mette-Dittmann (1991); Edwards (1993) 34–62; Bauman (1993); cf. Treggiari (1991) 287–90 and in *CAH* 10², and Kienast 137ff.

110. See especially Sen., *Epist.* 90 and Posidonius fr. 60 (Edelstein-Kidd) with the comments of K. Reinhardt in *RE* XXII (1953) 632–33 and Gatz (1967) 157–59.

111. Burns (1978) 237.

112. Cf. Bellen (1987) 308–11.

113. See, e.g., Last in *CAH* 10 (1934) 442–43 and 452–53 with reference to Dio 56.7.3.

114. See especially Badian (1985) whose solution that Propertius refers to a triumviral edict begs many questions; cf. G. Williams (1990) 267.

115. Peters and Waterman (1982) 82–83.

116. Suet., *Aug.* 89.2; cf. Livy, *Per.* 59. For surviving citations from the speech, see Gell., *NA* 1.6.2; Malcovati, *ORF* ² 107–8. The speech was satirized by Lucilius; see Gruen (1992) 285–87.

117. *FGH* 90 fr. 125.

118. Wells (1972) 3. References to conquest permeate the *Res Gestae*: see, e.g., 3.1, 3.4, 4.2, 26, 27, 29.1, 30; cf. Nicolet (1991) 15ff.

119. P. Zanker (1968) 12; for the Forum Augustum, see chapter 4.

120. *RG* 35.1. Cf. the allusion in *RG* 1.2 to his early equestrian statue. This is another example of the relation, noted in chapters 1 and 2, between *RG* 1 and *RG* 34–35. The *Res Gestae* has come full circle, but there has also been an evolution.

121. Even that is arguable; see Ober (1982).

122. For detailed documentation, see Galinsky (1981b) 134–42; cf. Capelle (1932) 98–104; Desideri (1972); and Brunt (1978) 186, with the reservations of Gruen (1984) 351–55.

123. E.g., Cic., *ad Q. Fr.* 1.1.34; *Rep.* 3.37; Augustine, *CD* 19.21.

124. Detailed documentation in Wiseman (1971) 107ff.; Earl (1967) 44ff.

125. Wiseman (1971) 116; Cic., *Att.* 6.3.1.

126. See G. Williams (1962) 29–35; cf. G. Williams (1968) 604–16. Badian's (1985, 92–94) critique of Williams downplays essential passages of the poems; see Galinsky (1985) 24 n. 16. Putnam (1986) 277–78 well emphasizes Horace's strong exhortation to Augustus especially in *C.* 3.24.25–32.

127. See chapter 4. As Luce (1990) illustrates, Augustus and Livy went their own ways about such exemplars.

128. Details in Wallace-Hadrill (1981b). The inheritance tax (*vicesima*), instituted in A.D. 6, had a similar aim; see Nicolet (1984) 110.

129. Detailed discussion by H. Last in *CAH* 10 (1934) 429ff.; Biondi (1939) 232ff.

130. D. Kleiner (1978) 776.

131. For detailed documentation, see H. Fuchs (1958) and for additional perspectives, Döpp (1989).

132. See Gabba (1991) 41ff.

133. Gell. *NA* 6.3.14 (= Peter, *HRR* ^{2} 1.85, fr. 95a; Malcovati, *ORF*^{2} 62, fr. 163).

134. Appian, *Pun.* 65; Plut., *Cato* 27.

135. Even if at various points: *Cat.* 2.3; 10.1–2; 11.6; 12.1; *Iug.* 41.1–3; see H. Fuchs (1958) 381–82 and Klingner (1928) 165ff. and 184ff.

136. Sen., *Contr.* 1, praef. 6ff.; Pliny, *HN* 2.117–18 and 14.2–7; cf. "Longinus," *On the Sublime,* ch. 44, and Gabba (1991) 42–45 who argues for a first-century A.D. date for *On the Sublime.* Florus 2.34.65 offers a variation of the theme: Augustus' moral legislation prevented Rome from succumbing to *luxuria* brought about by *magnitudo imperii.*

CHAPTER IV

1. Major discussions, where much of the extensive bibliography can be found, are Moretti (1948); Simon (1967); Galinsky (1969) 191ff.; Borbein (1975a); Torelli (1982) 27ff. and in *CAH* 10^2 ch. 20; La Rocca (1983); Simon (1986) 30ff.; S. Settis in *KA* 400ff.; Koeppel (1987) and (1988); Galinsky (1992c); D. Kleiner (1992) 90ff.; Spaeth (1994).

2. For the general concept, see Gruen (1985).

3. All reported by Dio 54.25.

4. Torelli (1982) 55 with reference to earlier scholarship; cf. Borbein (1975a) 245–46 and 260; Settis in *KA* 421. Similarly, Koeppel (1988) suggests that the processional friezes represent, in a general way, a *supplicatio* upon Augustus' return. For a different view, see Bowersock (1990) 390ff. ("procession of the imperial family on the day that Augustus became *pontifex maximus*").

5. Cf. Hölscher (1980) 314 and in *KA* 360.

6. Torelli (1982) 28ff.

7. Full discussion in Buchner (1982); cf. Buchner in *KA* 240–45. His calculations have been challenged by Schütz (1990).

8. Suet., *Aug.* 94.12; see Bowersock (1990) 385–87 and Schütz (1991).

9. See Koeppel (1985) and Borbein (1975a) 249ff.

10. Pallottino (1938); Hölscher (1987) 45–49.

11. The so-called Forbes type; see below, pp. 175–76.

12. See Kraus (1953) and Börker (1973).

13. Cf. Pliny's remark (though in connection with Cicero): "How much greater is it to have extended the boundaries of the Roman way of life and mentality than the boundaries of the empire" (*HN* 7.117).

14. Weinstock (1960), answered by Toynbee (1961).

15. Trillmich in *KA* 510 and 483–85; cf. Kraft (1969) and Zanker, *AMB* 61–63.

16. For concise summary, see B. Andreae in *KA* 275–76.

17. Mommsen in *CIL* I², pp. 322–23; cf. E. Simon in Helbig II⁴.828.

18. An apt term ("Andachtsbild") used by Zanker, *AMB* 178.

19. Momigliano (1942b) 229; cf. D. Kleiner (1978) 772ff. and Galinsky (1981b) 126ff., especially 142 with n. 76.

20. See Zanker, *AMB* 209–10; Hölscher in *KA* 359.

21. For a good summary with illustrations and complete bibliography, see Hölscher in *KA* 384–86; also Hölscher (1984a) 17–18.

22. Bibliography in Spaeth (1994); see also Hölscher (1984a) 31.

23. D. Kleiner (1978) 767ff. and (1985) 108–12.

24. Stier (1975) 49 has some good remarks on this.

25. See D. Kleiner (1978) and Galinsky (1981b).

26. See Büsing (1977) 248 and Sauron (1977) 209. For an expanded characterization of the floral frieze, from various viewpoints, cf. Galinsky (1992c) 463ff.; Pollini (1993); Kellum (1994) 31ff.; and Castriota (1995).

27. E. Simon in Helbig II⁴.827–28 no. 2057; cf. Hölscher in *KA* 373–74 no. 206; Kraus (1953) 41–42.

28. Zanker, *AMB* 180. Cf. Andreae (1973) 115 on the connection between the Ara Pacis and Augustus' *auctoritas*.

29. See Galinsky (1969) ch. 5; Hanell (1960) 118ff.; Putnam (1986) 327ff.

30. See Förtsch (1989) and, for the *Aeneid*, Pöschl (1977) 13–23.

31. In addition to the works cited in chapter 1, see especially Fittschen (1976a) 201ff., Pollini (1978) 9ff., and Simon (1991) on the imagery of the cuirass. For the date, see Brommer (1980).

32. Documentation in H. D. Meyer (1961), with the essential review of Brunt (1963) to which my discussion is much indebted. Cf. Gruen (1985) 63–67.

33. *Redacta in potestatem populi Romani*; Vell. 2.94.

34. *RIC* I².62 nos. 287–89; Giard nos. 118–39, 173–76, 199–206 (Parthians); *RIC* I².62 nos. 290–92; Giard nos. 140–46, 177–78; cf. Sutherland (1976) 104–5 and Schneider (1986).

35. Simon (1991) 207ff. gives specific iconographic reasons for the identification of the figure with Mars rather than Tiberius, which has led some scholars to date the sculptural program of the armor to Tiberian times.

36. *KA* 364–66 no. 200; Helbig II⁴ nos. 1382 and 1664.

37. See Matz (1952).

38. For its range, see most recently Strazzulla (1990).

39. *C.* 4.6.38, cited by Zanker, *AMB* 195, but see Ovid, *Met.* 2.116–17, where Au-

rora's advent leads to the evanescence of the moon. Further iconographic arguments for Aurora and Venus in Simon (1991) 214.

40. Varro as quoted by Servius (*ad Aen.* 1.382).

41. Cf. Horace's contemporary *Epist.* 1.12.

42. Zanker, *AMB* 79 with fig. 56; cf. the modeling of the boukrania on the exterior frieze of the Apollo Sosianus Temple (La Rocca in *KA* 22).

43. See chapter 1; cf. Price (1984) 185–86.

44. On the *Hüftmantel* type, see Maggi (1990) and, for the poets, White (1988).

45. See the judicious discussion of Fraenkel (1957) 376–77.

46. Austin (1977) 243–44. on *Aen.* 6.792ff.

47. Without, of course, disappearing altogether; see chapter 7 where the whole subject is discussed more fully.

48. For an attempt at a hermeneutic approach, see Hölscher (1987), especially 33–37; cf. the thoughtful comments of Wallace-Hadrill (1989) 160–62.

49. See the summary in Pollini (1978) 9–10.

50. Kroll (1924) 202–24; cf. Rossi (1971) and for a more sophisticated approach, Conte (1986).

51. The "Terme Ruler" represents a Greek rather than a Roman; see Smith (1988) cat. no. 44; for the opposite view, Zanker, *AMB* 14–15. Cf. Hölscher (1990) 83.

52. Bibliography in Balty (1978) 670; important discussion in Arnold (1969) 231–32.

53. For details see especially Kienast (1969) 448ff.

54. For a good illustration see Vierneisel and Zanker (1979) 76. The deified Augustus could be so represented (p. 65).

55. Details in Galinsky (1967a).

56. Alföldi (1959).

57. Important recent discussions are Simon (1986) 57–67; P. Zanker (1973); Zanker, *AMB* 103–6; Vierneisel and Zanker (1979); Fittschen and Zanker (1985) nos. 1–9, 20; Massner (1982) 6–41; Hausmann (1981); Smith (1988) 125ff.; M. Hofter in *KA* 291ff.; Fittschen (1991); D. Kleiner (1992) 61–69; cf., on the immediate republican background, Giuliani (1986). A complete collection of all the Augustus portraits has been published by Boschung (1993), with a somewhat different view of their typology and development.

58. I am concentrating on freestanding sculpture, probably the most influential and important genre; for the portraits on reliefs, coins, cameos, metalwork, and the like, see Fittschen (1991) 153–54 with notes 12–19, and for a detailed comparison of numismatic and sculptural portraits, Mannsperger (1991) 354ff.

59. Schmaltz (1986).

60. See, in terms of Augustan art in general, Zanker, *AMB* and the concise characterization by Kienast (1988) 139.

61. See chapter 5.

62. I am referring to the declarative qualities of the portrait and not to stylistic variations due to different provincial cultures, for which see P. Zanker (1983a) and Boschung (1993) 83ff.

63. Cf. Hofter in *KA* 291–92; Vessberg (1941) 110ff.

64. Restio: *RRC* 455/1; Vollenweider (1972) pl. 16.1–6; 24.10–11; 89.3. Cf. Smith (1988) 130 who posits a contrast with the softer portraits of contemporary Greek rulers, such as Mithridates VI.

65. Smith (1988) 129; cf. Giuliani (1986) 190ff.

66. Crawford, *RRC* 740–41; Massner (1982) 13–16; cf. Vollenweider (1972) pls. 140–44.

67. Those who accept Type "B" (so designated by Brendel [1931]) as a portrait of Octavian include Massner (1982) 10ff. (albeit with some overinterpretations of other portraits); Smith (1988) 137 with n. 20; Simon (1986) 57–62; and G. Grimm (1989) 357; for counterarguments, see especially Fittschen and Zanker (1985) 1.21–25; Pollini (1987) 63–64; and Fittschen (1991) 163–64, 182ff. For the images on gems, see Vollenweider (1972) pls. 157–59.

68. Simon (1986) 58–60.

69. The resulting incongruity is discussed with much insight by Giuliani (1986) especially 97–100.; cf. D. Kleiner (1992) 42.

70. Cf. Giuliani (1986) 200–201.

71. E.g., P. Zanker (1973) especially 36ff; *contra*, Massner (1982) 33ff.; Smith (1988) 138; G. Grimm (1989) 355. Cf. Fittschen and Zanker (1985) 1.1–3 with pls. 1–4.

72. Kienast (1969) especially 453; cf. Instinsky (1962) 30ff.

73. Cf. Smith (1988) 138.

74. *RRC* 535/1; *KA* no. 303.

75. *RRC* 534/2; *KA* no. 306.

76. Fronto, *M. Caes.* 4.12.6; see now Pfanner (1989) on the mechanics and massive scope of the copying industry. He estimates, conservatively, that 25,000 to 50,000 portrait heads of Augustus were made during his rule; the 250 that have survived constitute 0.5 to 1 percent.

77. See Toulopa (1986) and in *KA* 311–12 (no. 149).

78. Smith (1988) 138–39.

79. There are more than 170 known sculptural copies versus approximately 20 for the "Actium" type. I am omitting reflections of these types on the coinage, which in many ways is a separate problem.

80. See especially P. Zanker (1973) 45–46; cf. Jucker (1950) 167–68 and Massner (1982) 37–38.

81. Massner (1982) 38; Schmaltz (1986) 242.

82. Massner (1982) 38.

83. Massner (1982) 38; cf. Price (1984) 185–86.

84. Details in Schmaltz (1986).

85. See Fittschen and Zanker (1985) 4.

86. Fittschen and Zanker (1985) 7–10; Simon (1986) 65–66; *KA* no. 169. Pfanner (1989) 208–9 points out that the dimensions of the profile are the same in the Actium and Forbes types: Augustus did not sit for a new portrait.

87. Cf. Wallace-Hadrill (1982b). Smith (1988) 139 regards this characterization as more appropriate for the Prima Porta type; we are dealing with nuances.

88. See *KA* no. 151 and Johansen (1987).

89. Zanker, *AMB* 292–93; cf. Alföldy (1991) for parallels in epigraphy, and my previous discussion of the Ara Pacis for similar trends set by that monument.

90. Hölscher in *KA* 363 with reference to the popularization of themes from historical reliefs.

91. Chiaramonti Museum, Vatican, inv. 1977. Helbig I⁴ no. 373; *KA* no. 153. The identification with Marcellus is hypothetical.

92. See Johansen (1971) 30–32. Cf. Hofter in *KA* 313–14.

93. Holtzman and Salviat (1981) 285–87.

94. See Wallace-Hadrill (1988) and (1994). Important discussions of Roman painting, and especially its transition in the Augustan period, are Barbet (1985); W. Ehrhardt (1987) and (1991); Charles-Picard (1970); Mielsch (1981); Wesenberg (1985); Andreae in *KA* 273–87; Simon (1986) 182–205; Carettoni (1983); Bastet and de Vos (1979); Zanker, *AMB* 279–84; Leach (1982) and (1988); Beyen (1938) and (1960); von Blanckenhagen (1990); Andreae and Kyrieleis (1975); Mau (1882); Schefold (1952) and (1962); Ling (1991); Clarke (1991); Torelli in *CAH* 10² ch. 20.

95. For good reason, therefore, Hölscher (1987) omits wall painting completely from his attempted hermeneutic of Roman art, which he basically limits to sculpture. Cf. Zanker's rather brief treatment (previous note); Augustan wall painting defies tidy categorization.

96. Barbet (1985) 273.

97. For the debate on whether they represent Greek or Roman buildings, see Lehmann (1953) and (1979); Fittschen (1976b); Leach (1982) 146ff.

98. Borbein (1975b); cf. Andreae in *KA* 279–80.

99. Rizzo (1936b) 17. For the relation between this kind of compositional structure and that of Ovid's *Metamorphoses*, see Galinsky (1975) 83–84.

100. For a comprehensive discussion of the Villa and its context, see Bragantini and de Vos (1982); cf. Leach (1982) 164 who reminds us that the question of its ownership is unresolved.

101. On the Boscotrecase painter and his previous work in the Villa under the Farnesina, see von Blanckenhagen and Alexander (1990).

102. See J. Griffin (1985) 1–31 and Friedländer 2 (1922) 325ff.; cf. Drerup (1981) on architecture in general. On the indebtedness of the pictorial decorations of the Villa Imperiale at Pompeii and the Boscotrecase Villa to intaglio and gold and silver work, see W. Ehrhardt (1987) 150.

103. More details in Zanker, *AMB* 141–44.

104. See Cain (1985) who interprets the phenomenon differently. On the candelabra style as such, see now W. Ehrhardt (1987) 28ff.

105. Rightly emphasized by Barbet (1985).

106. Carettoni (1983) 23–27; cf. Simon (1986) 217–21.

107. Suet., *Aug.* 99.1 (trans. Graves); cf. Dio 56.30.4. There is no need to assume, with Flach (1972) 284–85, that the vignette is the product of a tradition hostile to Augustus. On the pantomime, see chapter 5.

108. Carettoni in *KA* 288; full description in Carettoni (1983) 67ff.; cf. Iacopi and Tedone (1990). Much of the decoration, of course, was not preserved on the actual walls but splintered into a plethora of fragments. Their totality, however, provides a virtually complete picture of the decorative scheme and its details.

109. Full discussion by de Vos (1980).

110. J. M. Carter (1982) 194. It is important to note that the house of Augustus was destroyed, at least in part, by fire around A.D. 2 (Dio 55.12.4–5; Suet., *Aug.* 57.2) and rebuilt handsomely (cf. Ovid, *Trist.* 3.1.33–38). I would allow, therefore, for the possibility (advocated by Professor Eleanor W. Leach in discussion) of the study's decoration dating to that time.

111. Recent discussions are W. Ehrhardt (1987) 152–62 and Leach (1982) 139ff.

414

112. Cf. chapter 3; also Raaflaub and Samons (1990).

113. See Frischer (1991) 74–85.

114. Leach (1982) 166.

115. Cf. Wesenberg (1985) 488.

116. See Green (1982) 363ff.; for the variety of the functions of myth in the *Metamorphoses*, see Galinsky (1975). Even in Roman funerary art the range of meanings of the Daedalus/Icarus myth was extensive; see Calderone (1982).

117. Rizzo (1936b) 39–40.

118. Cf. Zanker, *AMB* 284.

119. For recent scholarship on Studius, see Ling (1977) and Leach (1988) 263ff.

120. For an extended characterization of that episode, see Galinsky (1975) 197–203; cf. chapter 5.

121. Suet., *Aug.*, 53.2, 71.3, 75, 85.2, 98.3–4; the next two quotations are from Suetonius, *De Poetis* (Rostagni), *Vita Horatii* 35–36, and *Vita Vergilii* 120–24. Further examples in Yavetz (1990) 36–38.

122. J. Griffin (1984) 203.

123. In a (never published) lecture on "Die Humanitätsidee in der Antike" at the Boehringer Foundation in Ingelheim, Germany, 1960.

124. Important modern literature: P. Zanker (1968); Sauron (1981) 294ff.; *KA* 149–200 (J. Ganzert and V. Kockel); Simon (1986) 46–51; J. Anderson (1984) 65–100; Kockel (1983); Wesenberg (1984); Ganzert (1985); Evans (1992) 109–18; D. Kleiner (1992) 99–102. The ancient literary sources in Lugli (1965). The forum was excavated only partially in the 1930s; a detailed publication of the Temple of Mars Ultor (by Ganzert and Kockel) is in progress. Additional perspectives on Mars Ultor are found in Herbert-Brown (1994) 95–108.

125. Cf. also Sallust, *Cat.* 52.19–22: the younger Cato states that "our forebears did not make the *res publica* great from its small beginnings by arms" but by *industria* at home, *iustum imperium* abroad, and absence of *libido*.

126. Cf. the Porticus Metelli (renamed Porticus Octaviae under Augustus): Fig. 156.

127. Further details in Heilmeyer (1970) 29–31. More speculative is Ganzert's (1990) argument for a strong oriental aspect of the temple.

128. Cf. Ganzert in *KA* 166–67 with color plate 3.

129. Cf. Kockel in *KA* 153.

130. See Hölscher (1984b); cf. Frischer (1982–83) 76.

131. See Spinazzola (1953) 151ff.; for the widespread copying of the Trojan group, Galinsky (1969) 7–35.

132. J. Anderson (1984) 82 has an updated list. In addition, there was the growing number of (bronze) statues of those who earned triumphal honors; they may have been erected in the intercolumniations. See Lahusen (1983) 24 and 70ff.

133. Suet., *Aug.* 40.5; Augustus made the wearing of a toga mandatory for those who remained for any length of time "in the forum or circus."

134. J. Anderson (1984) 84.

135. See Degrassi (1937); further recent discussions by Frisch (1980) and Luce (1990).

136. Degrassi (1945) is still fundamental.

137. For a discussion of the evidence see Menichetti (1986).

138. Several of our other sources, however, including Ovid (*Fasti* 5.545–98), name May 12 as the dedication date; see the discussion in J. Anderson (1984) 68–69.

139. For similar such representations of Augustus, including the famous relief in Ravenna, see Hommel (1954) 88 n. 220.

140. E.g., 4.8.12–15; Putnam (1986) 329–39.

141. Cf. Evans (1992) 42ff. on the emphasis, in other Augustan monuments and artifacts, on Aeneas' *pietas* in relation to Augustus' *pietas* in avenging Julius Caesar.

142. Eder (1990) 118–19.

143. Strong and Ward Perkins (1962) 28 (referring to the rebuilding of the Temple of Castor).

144. Ganzert (1985) 215–16.

145. E.g., Vell. 2.81.3 ("singulari munificentia"); Josephus, *BJ* 2.6.81. The literary sources about the Palatine buildings and sites referred to in this section can be conveniently found in Lugli (1960). Important modern discussions are: Carettoni (1983) and in *KA* 263–72; F. Castagnoli in *Enc. Virg.* 1.222–24; Coarelli (1994) 158ff.; Gurval (1995); Jucker (1982); Kellum (1985); Lefèvre (1989); Simon (1986) 19–25; Strazzulla (1990); P. Zanker (1983b); D. Kleiner (1992) 82–84.

146. Syme, *RR* 230ff.

147. Good discussion by Wiseman (1981), updated here with reference to Pensabene (1988); cf. Wiseman (1984) 123–28. Sources in Lugli (1960) 103–5.

148. *Fasti Praen.*; see *EJ* p. 49 (cf. *NSc* 1896 [1897] 421–22), and Lugli (1960) 104, no. 305.

149. For documentation, including the statue of Victory in the Curia Iulia that was dedicated in 29 B.C., see Hölscher (1985) 89–97; cf. Hölscher (1967) 6–17.

150. Dio 49.15.5 with the important note by Woodman (1983) 208 on Vell. 2.81.3.

151. See the detailed study of Gagé (1955); cf. Simon (1978) and (1990) 27–34; Liebeschuetz (1979) 82ff.; Gurval (1995). For the Sosius temple, see chapter 7.

152. See Gosling (1986) and Pollini (1990). Another example is the Sphinx, which Octavian used for his seal at the time (Pliny, *HN* 37.10) and which recurs in the sculptural decoration of the temple complex (see Strazzulla [1990] 81–84).

153. Details in W. Murray and Petsas (1989).

154. See Hölscher in *KA* 377 with Fig. 173 and Strazzulla (1990) 115ff. with Fig. 43, both with references to the Sorrento base. As Zagdoun (1989) 105–8 points out, we are dealing with a specifically Augustan adaptation of an existing type.

155. See Alföldi (1973); Mannsperger (1973) 396; and Bömer on Ovid, *Met.* 1.559–60.

156. Sources in Lugli (1960) 109–13.

157. See the discussion by F. Kleiner (1988).

158. Cf. P. Zanker (1983b) 24. For various reconstructions of the Palatine *area Apollinis*, see Lefèvre (1989), figs. 6, 7, and 9.

159. Discussed by Knell (1990); cf. Castriota (1992). For the problems concerning the configuration of the Danaid monument and its interpretation, see especially Lefèvre (1989); Sauron (1981) 286–94; P. Zanker (1983b) 27–31; Simon (1986) 20–24; Kellum (1985) 173–75. For the myth in literature and art, cf. *LIMC* 3.1 (1986) 336–41 (E. Keuls).

160. Giard nos. 362–64; *RIC* I².69 nos. 366–67; *KA* 522–23 no. 364 (W. Trillmich). The coin image does not fit the memorial at Nicopolis; see W. Murray and Petsas (1989) 87–90, nor is it certain that it actually reproduces the Palatine statue in all its details, such as the statue's platform.

161. Horace's version of the myth in *Ode* 3.11, for instance, which dates before 29 B.C., exalts Hypermestra who spared her husband.

162. Harrison (1991) 198, summarizing the view of G. B. Conte in the context of surveying various other interpretations.

163. Keuls (1974) 116.

164. Another relevant example is Vergil's use, in the proem to the third *Georgic* (16–39), of the building of a temple as a metaphor for his planned epic. The inspiration, as all commentators have noted, came from the building of the Temple of Apollo. The inspirational commonality extends yet further: the *Aeneid* followed the sculptural program of the Temple complex in being, on its face, mythological rather than historical; cf. chapter 5. With Vergil's statement that his future epic will be a temple with Caesar in its midst (*Geo.* 3.16) compare the contemporaneous coins with Julius Caesar in the center of the Temple of Divus Julius (Fig. 1).

165. *KA* 269 no. 121 (G. Carettoni). Cf. Borbein (1968), especially 176–78, and Strazzulla (1990) 17–22. According to Parke and Boardman (1957), the struggle over the tripod was used for political symbolism in Greece. It arose because Hercules, too, wanted to be purified from blood guilt.

166. Cf. Kroll (1924) 202–24; Galinsky (1989) 71–73; and Conte (1992) 104–23.

167. See, e.g., Alföldi (1973) 55 with pls. V.2–3 and XXI.1; cf. Kellum (1990) 282–83 and Pollini (1993) 193ff. (with reference to the Ara Pacis). The head of Dionysus/Liber appears prominently on the coinage of Turpilianus in 19 B.C. (Giard, pp. 74–77).

CHAPTER V

1. Bowra (1945) 34. The bibliography on Augustan literature is immense. Recent surveys and treatments include *CHCL* 2 (1982) 297–494; *ANRW* II.30.1–3 and 31.1–4 (1980–83); *Saeculum Augustum* 2 (1988); Woodman and West (1984); von Albrecht (1992) 509–704.

2. Cf. Veyne (1988) with the review by Wyke (1989).

3. The anachronism of this view is well documented by White (1993), especially 95ff.

4. See the basic article by Salmon (1956) on "The Evolution of Augustus' Principate" and Kienast 67–125; cf. Badian (1982) and chapter 7.

5. I follow the discussion of Lefèvre (1988).

6. G. Williams (1968) 578; on the Horatian passage, cf. *Epist.* 2.1.128ff. and J. Griffin (1984) 204.

7. For the events at Perusia (modern-day Perugia), see Syme *RR* 207ff.; for an extensive discussion of Prop. 1.22, Stahl (1985) 99–129, Nethercut (1971), and Putnam (1976); cf. Lefèvre (1988) 185–86. I have decided to let this short poem speak for itself: it is both "personal" and "political."

8. Luck in *CHCL* 2 (1982) 414; for the death theme, see Michels (1955), Boucher (1965) ch. 3, and Papanghelis (1987).

9. See pp. 99–100, with further quotations from the same passage in the *Art of Love*, including the reference to *cultus* (3.128).

10. Extended discussion in Galinsky (1989) 73–77. Knox (1986) considers the *Metamorphoses* as Augustan purely from the viewpoint of literary history. Cf. the revisionary view of Millar (1993).

11. Quinn (1982) attempts a rare systematic discussion of the actual audience of the poets; cf. Woodman and Powell (1992).

12. Otis (1963) 62ff.

13. I am following Jauss' distinction between three kinds of readings that comprise the total interpretation; see Jauss (1981) and for an application to the end of the *Aeneid*, Galinsky (1992a) 8–11.

14. See Cairns (1989) 129ff.; Monti (1981); La Penna in *Enc. Virg.* 2.48–57; Pease (1935) 11ff.; Heinze (1915) 115ff.; Clausen (1987) 40ff.; Knauer (1964) 208–18; Wlosok (1976); Pöschl (1977) 84ff.; cf. Suerbaum (1980) 148–51.

15. By Valerius Probus; see Gellius 9.9.12 and, for the argument, Cairns (1989) 129ff.

16. *Arg.* 1.307–11; cf. 1.536–39; 2.676–79; Conrardy (1904) 31–32.

17. Detailed documentation in Fenik (1960); Wlosok (1976); Clausen (1987) 53ff.

18. Hercules and Dido: Pease (1935) 22; Hercules and Aeneas: Galinsky (1990) 277–94.

19. Cairns (1989) 136.

20. Horsfall (1990).

21. *Aen.* 4.173ff.; see La Penna in *Enc. Virg.* 2.54. There are also several striking parallels between Dido and Horace's portrayal of Cleopatra in *C.* 1.37.

22. Clausen (1987) 58.

23. Good discussion by G. Williams (1968) 374ff.

24. Cf. J. Griffin (1985) 195–96 with reference to the characters of the *Aeneid* in general.

25. Principal discussions include A.H.F. Griffin (1991); Gamel (1984); Galinsky (1975) 197ff.; Beller (1967); Guillemin (1958), along with the commentaries by Bömer (1977) and Hollis (1970).

26. A.H.F. Griffin (1991) 71; cf. Bömer's commentary (1977) 191. For a combination of parallel motifs in Genesis and the Ovidian story, see Griffin 68–70 and Beller (1967) 21–27.

27. That Callimachus took pains to reduce the religious and cultic elements even more is clear from a comparison of the summary of his story with Plutarch's account, based on an ancient Attic chronicle, of the same events that led to the Hecalesian festival (Plut., *Thes.* 14, compared with the *Diegesis* of the *Hecale*). Both texts, translated into English and juxtaposed, are conveniently found in C. A. Trypanis' Loeb Library edition of Callimachus (1958) 176–77.

28. For a listing of the passages, see Bömer's commentary on the *Fasti* (1958) 321.

29. Ovid's Nicandrian manner: A.H.F. Griffin (1991) 65–68; his humor: Galinsky (1975) 199–203.

30. Genette (1980), especially 227ff., and Genette (1988) 114ff.; cf. Winkler (1985) 73–76; Gamel (1984) (without reference to Genette); and Barchiesi (1989) for other examples of narrative differentiation.

31. Genette (1980) 203, citing Leo Spitzer and Marcel Muller. This aspect does not get in the way of the meaning that is reinforced by *sed pia Baucis* in the next line: piety resides in the houses of the humble rather than the rich.

32. Details in Galinsky (1975) 61ff.

33. Gamel (1984) 130.

34. Excellent summary in Ross (1975) 4–8.

35. Good discussion by Armstrong (1989) 55ff.; N. Rudd in *CHCL* 2.375–76; and Lefèvre (1993) 61ff.

36. See Nauta (1990).

37. See, respectively, Du Quesnay (1977); Knox (1986) 10ff.; Conte (1986) 100ff.

38. Conte (1992) 117.

39. For detailed discussions of Propertius' style, see Boucher (1965); Sullivan (1976); La Penna (1977) 101ff.; Benediktson (1989) 18ff.; Tränkle (1960); Uhlmann (1909). On 3.20.25, cf. Brink (1972) 31–33.

40. See Luck (1974), especially 27ff.; cf. Burck (1952).

41. Görler (1979) 186ff. discusses more of the latter and sensibly concludes that this kind of "deviation" from classical models is, in fact, an essential aspect of Augustan classicism.

42. See pp. 270–79. For *foedus* and *fides*, cf. already Cat. 76.3 and 87.3 with the comments of Lyne (1980) 33ff.

43. See Nethercut (1983) 1849–50 with reference to the alternation of elegies about Cynthia with poems about Rome in 3.8–11 and Macleod (1977) 144, who aptly compares 3.9.49–52 with 4.1.57–60.

44. See Macleod (1977) 143–45. The relationship of the two parts of 4.1 has caused endless discussion; see the summary of earlier views by Stahl (1985) 266–69. The view expressed here is an elaboration of Conte (1992) 118–19; cf. Nethercut (1983) 1850–51; Miller (1982) 382; Pillinger (1969) 175ff.

45. Chapter 3. According to Ross (1975) 130, Propertius found his earlier love elegies too constricting and returned to the spirit and manner of the elegies of Cornelius Gallus; as so many hypotheses pertaining to Gallus' role, this one is unprovable but is another example of the increasingly held view that book 4 was written for poetic reasons rather than as a contribution forced by Augustus. Cf. von Albrecht (1982) and White (1993) 189–90.

46. See chapter 7.

47. See already Heinze (1915) 281.

48. Otis (1963), especially 41ff.

49. The passage is quoted on pp. 123–24; cf. Stahl (1981).

50. More detail in Kraggerud (1968) 31ff.

51. The fundamental discussion is still that of Pöschl (1977) 13–23.

52. For a short survey, see Ludwig (1965) 78–80; the writers include Diodorus and Augustus' Greek biographer, Nicolaus of Damascus.

53. Otis (1963) 354; cf. Wlosok (1990) 365, 379.

54. Details in chapter 7. Good recent discussions of essential aspects of Horace's lyric poetry are Armstrong (1989) 68ff.; von Albrecht (1992) 572ff.; N. Rudd in *CHCL* 2.370ff.; Connor (1981); Lefèvre (1993) 141ff.

55. In "Was ich den Alten verdanke" in *Götzendämmerung* (1888).

56. Connor (1981) 1615. Cf. Lefèvre (1993) 34: *Leichte Geistigkeit*.

57. To the bibliography listed in the commentary by Nisbet and Hubbard (1978) 252 should be added Porter (1987) 136–39; Santirocco (1986) 101–3; and Lefèvre (1993) 203–7.

58. I have followed the translation by Margaret Hubbard (1973) 2, with some modifications.

59. See André (1966) for a comprehensive discussion; cf. Latte (1935).

60. Pöschl (1956a) 88.

61. Porter (1987) 137–38.

62. Cf. Anderson (1963) 27.

63. Solodow (1988) 156.

64. Hor., *Epist.* 2.1.232–34; *AP* 357–58.

65. Zetzel (1982) 101. For various perspectives on patronage, see Gold (1982) with the review of Badian in *CP* 80 (1985) 341–57, and G. Williams (1990) 258–75. The most significant treatment of the issue is White (1993); cf. Saller (1982), especially ch. 2.

66. Dalzell (1956); Lefèvre (1981); White (1993), especially 134ff.

67. E.g., by Sforza (1935).

68. Graff (1987) 206.

69. Galinsky (1992a) 1–40 and (1992b) 74–92.

70. See chapter 3. For balanced characterizations of the *Aeneid* and recent scholarship on it see R. D. Williams (1967 [1990]); Wlosok (1973); Galinsky (1981a); J. Griffin (1986); and S. Harrison (1990) 1–20. For its relation to earlier Roman epic, see Goldberg (1995).

71. Crook in *CAH* 10² ch. 2.

72. Bowra (1945) 37.

73. Feeney (1983).

74. I have followed the translation of C. Day Lewis with some modifications in the last three lines.

75. Thornton (1976) appendix A; on the Augustans' appreciation of martial epic, see S. Harrison (1991) xxivff. For good reason, the *Aeneid* begins on the note of *arma*.

76. R. D. Williams (1967 [1990]) 28.

77. Clausen (1987) 99. More detail in Galinsky (1988) and (1994); cf. Erler (1992).

78. Cf. the perspectives taken by Hardie (1986) and Cairns (1989).

79. See Dobbin (1995) for the most recent detailed discussion and references to earlier bibliography.

80. White (1988) 355.

81. White (1988) 355. On Augustus' name: Syme (1958a). In addition, Caesar's statue was displayed not only in the Temple of Divus Julius, but also in that of Mars Ultor and in the Pantheon.

82. Klingner (1967) 399.

83. G. Williams (1969) 10.

84. Detailed discussion in Mayer (1986).

85. E.g., Sestius (*C.* 1.4); Munatius Plancus (1.7); Dellius (2.3); Messalla Corvinus (3.21); Pompeius (Varus?) (2.7); Cato (1.12.35–36; 2.1.24); Antony's partisan Asinius Pollio (2.1). Murena (2.10) was subsequently involved in a conspiracy against Augustus. For Horace's economic status, see Armstrong (1986).

86. G. Williams (1968) 298.

87. Santirocco (1986) 161. On *C.* 3.29, cf. Pöschl (1961).

88. Collinge (1961).

89. See Salmon (1946) 11–12.

90. I have benefited especially from the discussions of G. Williams (1969); Connor (1972); Jameson (1984); and Porter (1987).

91. *C.* 2.7.11–12; 3.5.29–30; 3.29.54–55; cf. Porter (1987) 230ff.

92. *Aitia* fr. 1 (Pfeiffer) with the comments of Hinds (1989) 270–71 and Cameron (1992). For a comprehensive study of *recusationes* in Augustan poetry, see Wimmel (1960).

93. The evidence has been well collected and discussed by Neuhauser (1972). For Horatian examples, including those discussed here, see in detail Wimmel (1962).

94. By the emperor Julian (*Caesars* 309B–C).

95. By far the best study is that of Putnam (1986) to which I am indebted for several

points; cf. Becker (1963) 113–93. Suetonius' *vita* of Horace (Rostagni [1944] 116) simply says that Augustus "forced" Horace to add *Odes* 4 to the previous collection.

96. Putnam (1986) 320.

97. *Ad Aen.* 1.1: *cano polysemus sermo est*; cf. Patterson (1987) 30: "It was of course Servius who introduced into European critical discourse the crucial word *polysemous*."

98. See especially Putnam (1986) 327–39 and Benario (1960).

99. In addition to the works cited earlier, Due (1974) and Schmidt (1991) are important studies of the poem; cf. Barchiesi (1994).

100. Documentation in F. Williams (1978) 87–89, 98–99.

101. Cairns (1989) 150.

102. Cf. Zanker, *AMB* 242ff.; Galinsky (1989) 71ff.

103. P. Zanker (1968) 11; Kraus (1953); see chapter 4.

104. Strong and Ward Perkins (1962); cf. their emphasis on the "very great variety and extraordinary amount of detailed experiment that took place within the framework of conventional practice" (p. 28). Cf. *KA* 213–24.

105. The most recent, balanced discussion is Döpp (1991).

106. Kirk (1970) 252–61. Cf. Galinsky (1975) 16ff.

107. Bieber (1961) 165. On the pantomime in general, see E. Wüst in *RE* 18 (1949) 834–69 and Wagenvoort (1920).

108. Cf. Zinn (1960) and Klingner (1961) 690ff. For more extensive discussions of Ovid's humor see Frécaut (1972) and Galinsky (1975) 158–209. Ovid characterized his Muse as *iocosa* (*Trist.* 2.354).

109. Cf. Bernbeck (1967) 4–29.

110. In Rome, *regia* was the house of the *pontifex maximus*, an office held by Augustus from 12 B.C. on, and Augustus used the term in jest when he invited Horace to become his private secretary; the next time Ovid refers to Hades' house, Hades is called *tyrannus* (4.444). Here as elsewhere, the very ease with which "anti-Augustan" connotations can be construed is the strongest argument against their existence.

111. Bernbeck (1967) 30.

112. "Ovid" in *OCD*, 2nd ed. (1970) 765.

113. Zanker, *AMB* 188.

114. As Raaflaub and Samons (1990) 445–46 well point out, silence about Ovid's exile also applies to ancient sources other than Ovid; "it gained significance only in modern times as evidence of Augustus' attempt to control Roman authors." Cf. White (1993) 152–54.

115. Comprehensive bibliography in Glatt (1991) and von Albrecht (1992). For the following discussion, I have drawn in particular on Burck (1952), Steidle (1962), Cairns (1979), Lyne (1980), and Gaisser (1983), in addition to Glatt and von Albrecht.

116. This includes, as in Augustan poetry in general, the sophisticated and complex use of literary antecedents on which ample discussion can be found in the relevant scholarly literature.

117. Cairns (1979) 20. The Latin text used for Tibullus is that of Lenz and Galinsky (1971).

118. *Geo.* 2.485ff. Detailed parallels in Glatt 117–18.

119. See pp. 241–43. Cf., most clearly, *contentus vivere parvo* (25) with *vivitur parvo bene* (*C.* 2.16.13).

120. In contrast, e.g., to Sappho's influential model of the "transvaluation of values": she simply opposes her own preferences to those of her society (16 Lobel and Page).

121. For its most extensive elaboration, see Ovid, *Am.* 1.9; for its most succinct summary, Prop. 4.1.135.

122. E.g., Prop. 2.26B.27; 1.12.7; 2.20.34; 3.20; 3.25.3–4; detailed discussion in Burck (1952), especially 170ff. and Luck (1974) 25ff.

123. Prop. 3.1.9ff.; Ovid, *Am.* 1.2; cf. 2.9 and 2.18. See Galinsky (1969) 88ff.

124. I am indebted to the discussions of Zanker, *AMB* 264–79 (I am using "privatization" for his term *Verinnerlichung*); Hölscher (1985) and *KA* 374–75; and Alföldi (1973) 46–50 and 56–57; cf. Evans (1992) 51–52 and P. Zanker (1988).

125. It includes various aspects of the *labor* of love: 1.1.9, 1.6.23, 2.23.7, 2.24B.29, 4.1.139; also, Tib. 1.4.47.

126. See chapter 4 with n. 164. Some of my observations on Prop. 3.1 have benefited from an unpublished paper by John F. Miller.

127. Lyne (1980) 17–18.

128. In 2.22A, for instance, Propertius flatly negates the notion of perpetual *fides*; cf. 2.34.3–6 (followed by a reference to the Trojan War). Cf. Lee's (1974) elegant summary of Tibullan contradictions (p. 110) and my discussion of Augustan contradictions in chapter 7.

129. Cf. Neumeister (1986) 55–56.

130. Details in Glatt (1991) 31–32.

131. Gaisser (1977) 131.

132. Important studies of Livy include von Albrecht (1992) 659–86 (with extensive bibliography); Ogilvie (1965) and in *CHCL* 2 (1982) 458–66; Walsh (1961), (1974), and (1982); Luce (1977); Woodman (1988) 128ff.; Moore (1989); Mazza (1966); Syme (1959).

133. Syme, *RR* 513; Momigliano (1940) 78. Cf. Livy's appreciation of the *pax* and *concordia* brought on by Augustus (9.19.17).

134. Balanced discussion in Deininger (1985).

135. Burns (1978) 20.

136. See Luce (1965) and Woodman (1988) 128–35; cf. Syme (1959) 42–50.

137. Cf. 1.19.4; 2.54.1; 3.9.1; 6.21.2; 30.44.8; 34.9.4; 39.1.2. Cf. Luce (1977) 271 and Woodman (1988) 153 n. 77.

138. Cf. Burck (1982) and Earl (1967) 17–19.

139. Moore (1989) 5–14 and 151–52.

140. A key passage is 2.1.3–6; see the discussion by Luce (1977) 243ff.

141. Moore (1989) 154.

142. See Luce (1977) 248–49.

143. Cf. Prop. 2.34.53–54, only a few lines before Propertius' reference to the *Aeneid* (61–66).

144. Von Albrecht (1992) 669: "Er hat die römische Geschichte nicht nur nacherzählt, sondern durchempfunden."

145. Balanced discussion in Aili (1982); cf. J. Adams (1974); von Albrecht (1992) 670–71; Walsh (1974) 29.

146. Strebel (1934) 28.

147. Ogilvie in *CHCL* 2 (1982) 466.

148. Syme (1959) 53.

149. Walsh (1955).

150. See especially Burck (1982) 1185ff. and Woodman (1988) 137–39.

151. Florus, *Praef.* 8; Tac., *Hist.* 1.1.4 and *Agr.* 3.1; Amm. Marc. 31.5.14; Rut. Nam. 1.140.

152. Luce (1990). On the other hand, Scipio's prayer (29.27) seems to have been inspired by one of the prayers of the Augustan Secular Games; see L. Moretti (1982–84) 378–79.

153. Not surprisingly, the moralistic emphasis in historiography was traditional and restated by Cicero; for details, see Mazza (1966) and Walsh (1982) 1065–69.

154. See, e.g., Hor., *C.* 3.30.8–9; Vergil, *Aen.* 1.278–79; Tib. 2.5.23–24; Ovid, *Fasti* 3.72. The concept is discussed by Koch (1952).

155. S. Treggiari in *CAH* 10² ch. 18.

156. See Luce (1977) 276ff. Livy's contemporary Pompeius Trogus deliberately cast his *Historiae Philippicae* (forty-four books) as a complement to Livy's *History* by chronicling the history of non-Roman empires, such as Assyria, Persia, and, in particular, Macedonia.

CHAPTER VI

1. For previous general treatments of Augustan religion, often with emphases quite different from mine, see Nock in *CAH* 10 (1934) 465–505; Latte (1960) 294–311; Liebeschuetz (1979) 56–108; Ogilvie (1969); Kienast 185–214. Cf. Price in *CAH* 10².

2. Geertz (1973) 98ff.

3. See chapter 2.

4. Nock in *CAH* 10 (1934) 469.

5. Cf. Ovid's plea to Augustus in *Trist.* 3.1.49–52 to save one more citizen—Ovid—because Augustus is a god. For religiosity as the basis of Roman greatness, cf. Cic., *ND* 2.3.8; *Har. Resp.* 19; Sallust, *Cat.* 12.3; Polybius 6.6.8.

6. *Leg.* 2.33; *ND* 2.7, 2.9; *Div.* 1.25, 1.27–28, 2.71; cf. *Att.* 7.7.3; Dion. Halic., *AR* 2.62; Pliny, *HN* 10.20. Laments about the decay or abuse of sacred buildings: Cic., *ND* 1.82; Livy 4.20.7; Prop. 2.6.35–36, 3.13.47. Cf. Gros (1976) 21ff.

7. For this aspect, see especially the careful discussion of Liebeschuetz (1979) 39ff.

8. Cf., once more, Horace's famous observation that laws are ineffective without mores (*C.* 3.24.35–36).

9. For detailed discussions, see Rawson (1985) 298–316; Momigliano (1984); and Cardauns (1978); cf. Latte (1960) 291–93.

10. See Gros (1976) 22.

11. Esp. by Weinstock (1971).

12. Cf., for the general sentiment, Cic., *ND* 1.3.

13. "Le prince a été conduit en grande partie autant qu'il a conduit" (Boyancé [1972] 42, citing the views of F. Altheim); cf. Scheid (1990) 680–86 for a useful survey of opinions on the meaning of "restoration."

14. Extensively studied by Scheid (1990), whose conclusions I share, and Scheid (1975); cf. Wissowa in *RE* 2 (1896) 1463–86, the collection of materials by Henzen (1874), and Paladino (1988).

15. Jerome, *Chron. Rom.* 18. See Syme, *AA* 211–12 and Raaflaub and Samons (1990) 434.

16. The connection of the origins of the Arval brotherhood with Romulus probably was also created in the Augustan age.

17. See the classic treatment by Taylor (1964) 76–97.

18. In marked contrast to his triumviral period when he eagerly sought any favorable prodigies; see Kienast 180–81.

19. Kienast 190.

20. On the importance, which has often been ignored, of this office to Augustus, see Bowersock (1990).

21. Detailed discussion in Gros (1976); cf. H. G. Martin in *KA* 251–63.

22. Cf. G. Sauron and P. Gros in *KA* 60–61 for further details.

23. Gros (1976) 51.

24. Zanker, *AMB* 110ff.

25. Ch. 3; cf. Drerup (1981) 6–8.

26. Sources in Richardson (1992) 226–27.

27. See Martin in *KA* 255, 263.

28. Extensive documentation in Alföldi (1973); cf. my subsequent discussion of the altars to the Lares and the Belvedere Altar.

29. For the most recent discussion of the temple and its program see Kellum (1990).

30. Iustitia Augusta: *Fasti Praen.* in *CIL* I² p. 306, and Ovid, *Ex Pont.* 3.6.23, with Latte (1960) 300 n. 4; Victoria Augusta: Dio 51.22.1, cf. Suet., *Aug.* 100.1; Pax Augusta: *RG* 12.2, Ovid, *Fasti* 1.709, Dio 54.25.3, cf. chapter 4; Ops Augusta: *EJ* p. 50; Fortuna Redux: *RG* 11, *EJ* pp. 53 and 55, Dio 54.10.3, *CIL* I² p. 330, Richardson (1992) 157. The annual celebrations at the Altar of Fortuna Redux were called Augustalia; for the coin, see Giard nos. 1345–48; *RIC* I². 45 no. 54a; *KA* no. 353.

31. For further details, see Gros (1976) 32–36 and Herz (1978) 1147–51.

32. Important discussions are Taylor (1931) 184ff.; Accame (1942); Ryberg (1955) 49ff.; Niebling (1956); Alföldi (1973) 18ff.; Hölscher (1984a) 27–30 and *KA* 390–98; Zanker, *AMB* 135ff. and (1975); Simon (1986) 97ff.; Hano (1986), a survey article; Fröhlich (1991); cf. Kienast 164–66.

33. For the most recent documentation, see Fröhlich (1991) 28ff.

34. *CIL* I². 753 (= *CIL* V.4087); cf. *CIL* V.4865. See Erkell (1952) 16 and Alföldi (1973) 24 n. 101.

35. Ryberg (1955) 53; cf. Kolbe (1966–67).

36. See A. Mau, *RM* 5 (1890) 244–45 and G. K. Boyce (1937) 93 no. 466. Cf. further Ovid, *Fasti* 2.635–38 and Taylor (1931) 151; Ryberg (1955) 54; Alföldi (1973) 24ff.

37. Kunckel (1974), especially 10 and 22ff.

38. A. Degrassi, *Inscr. Ital.* XIII, 1 (1947) 279.

39. Catalog raisonné in Hano (1986), to be supplemented by the subsequent discussions of Hölscher, Zanker, and Simon that are listed in note 32.

40. Hano (1986) 2338 no. 1; Hölscher (1984a) 27–28.

41. Hano (1986) 2339–40 no. 3; Hölscher *KA* 390–91; Simon (1986) 102.

42. Alföldy (1991); *compitum Acili*: Hano (1986) 2340 no. 5; H. von Hesberg in *KA* 398–400.

43. Hano (1986) 2345 no. 12; Hölscher in *KA* 391–92.

44. Hano (1986) 2338–39 no. 2; Hölscher (1984a) 27–28; Simon (1986) 70–71. The specific identity of the female figure has been suggested to me by Professor Brian Rose.

45. Hano (1986) 2340–41 no. 6; Hölscher in *KA* 392.

46. Hano (1986) 2347–48 no. 15b; Hölscher in *KA* 392–93.

47. Zanker, *AMB* 139–40.

48. Zanker, *AMB* 140. The exchange model also is relevant to the imperial cult in the east; see Price (1984) 65ff.

49. The Tabula Siarensis, publ. by González (1984). See Lebek (1993), especially 115.

50. I follow the interpretation of Ostrow (1990) where the earlier bibliography can be found, especially the important survey article by Duthoy (1978). Cf. Kienast 209–10.

51. The standard work is Treggiari (1969).

52. Ostrow (1990) 365 n. 2, summarizing Kneissl (1980). The evidence for the institution of the Augustales is a paradigm of the limitations of the literary evidence: there are some 2,500 inscriptions from imperial times pertaining to it, as opposed to only one mention in our literary sources (Petronius' *Satyricon*). It is a useful reminder, if one were needed, to keep senatorial literary sources, such as Tacitus, in a healthy perspective.

53. Dio 43.45.3; Cic., *Att.* 12.45.3, 13.28.3. See Weinstock's discussion (1971) 186ff.

54. Cic., *Att.* 16.15.3. Cf. chapter 2.

55. Good collection of material in Kienast 178ff.; Taeger 2 (1960) 96ff.; Taylor (1931) 149ff.

56. See, most recently, Zanker, *AMB* 44–46. Cf. Ovid, *Met.* 15.760–61, cited later.

57. Suet., *Aug.* 95; Appian, *BC* 3.388; Dio 46.46.2.

58. Suet., *Aug.* 7; Dio, 53.16.5–7; see Scott (1925); Gagé (1930); and Kienast 79–80 with extensive bibliographical references.

59. Pollini (1990) 345.

60. *RG* 25.2; cf. Dio 50.6.6. See Syme, *RR* ch. 20.

61. Pollini (1990) 346–47.

62. Liegle (1941) 117 aptly characterized the coinage between 31 and 28 B.C. as "die einzige monarchische Prägung Octavians." It fittingly coincided with the building of his mausoleum, for which see von Hesberg and Panciera (1994) and with his choice of Alexander's head for his seal (Instinsky [1962] 31ff.).

63. E.g., *C.* 1.2.41ff., 1.12.49ff., 3.3.9ff., 4.4.35–36; *Ep.* 2.1.5ff.; cf. Doblhofer (1966).

64. Octavian's denarius: *RIC* I². 59 no. 256; Giard nos. 13–18. Demetrios' tetradrachms: Newell (1927) nos. 115–24 and 134–61; Kraay (1966) 349, 351, no. 573. See the discussion by Pollini (1990) 346–48; cf. Liegle (1941) 106 who stresses the multiplicity of the image and interprets it as Octavian as Genius with the symbols of a naval victory. Another aspect of that multiplicity is that the denarius deliberately usurps a coin type of Sextus Pompey (*RRC* no. 511/3); see Zanker, *AMB* 48–50 and Trillmich in *KA* 509, no. 328.

65. Cf. Pliny, *HN* preface 11, addressing Vespasian: *te quidem excelsissimo generis humani fastigio positum* ("you who have been placed on the loftiest pinnacle of mankind").

66. More material in Bömer's commentary on Ovid, *Fasti* 1.609; Kienast 79–80; Scheid (1990) 703–4; Speyer (1986) 1797; cf. Erkell (1952) 13ff.

67. See Walde-Hofmann (1965) 82–83 and von Premerstein in *Berl. Phil. Wochenschrift* 49 (1929) 846–50; Bömer 2 (1958) 69. Cf. the relation of *augere* and *auctoritas* and Giovannini (1985), who argues that the *auctoritas patrum* was based on their power to take the auspices and thus become *auctores*.

68. See C. O. Brink's (1982) commentary on the Horatian passage (pp. 49ff.) with extensive citation of previous scholarship.

69. Brink (1982) 52; cf. Fishwick (1970) 191: "For to pray to the *numen Augusti* was to ascribe to the human emperor the quintessential property of a god."

70. Brink (1982).

71. See chapter 2. It should be noted also that the Athenians' worship of Demetrios Poliorcetes was considered by all the ancient sources (e.g., Plut., *Dem.* 12) as a paragon of abject flattery. It was a good reason to give up on such a model.

72. See Classen (1963); cf. Taylor (1931) 35–37.

73. Documentation in Classen (1963) 321ff.; cf. Tac., *Ann.* 15.74 and Weinstock (1971) 287ff.

74. *Fasti Praen.*, *CIL* I² p. 231.

75. Weinstock (1971) 213. The cult of his Genius with the Lares may have been a compromise.

76. With *praesens divus* compare *praesens deus* in Cic., *Tusc.* 1.28.

77. Weinstock (1971) 304.

78. E.g., *Trist.* 1.1.81; 2.143, 179; 3.1.33–38 (which can be usefully compared with the humorous version of his assimilation of Jupiter's abode to Augustus' in *Met.* 1.168–76); 5.2.46; *Fasti* 1.650; *Pont.* 3.1.117; 3.6.17. For the complete evidence, see Scott (1930) 52ff. and Bömer *ad Met.* 15.858–60; cf. Feeney (1991) 214ff.

79. Full discussion in Fears (1981a), especially 69.

80. Cf. his representation in the dedication of the freedman Varenus at Tibur: Zanker, *AMB* 313–14; Maderna (1988) 173–74. Both Zanker, *AMB* 232–39, and Maderna (1988) 18ff., discuss the Jupiter-Augustus assimilation in art more extensively.

81. Dio 53.27.3. Dio's wording cannot be attenuated to mean that Caesar's statue and the statue initially contemplated for Augustus were mere honorary statues in the republican tradition. A pertinent context is the mausoleum and Octavian's "monarchic" coinage, on which see n. 62.

82. *RRC* 540; see Prayon (1982) 322 and Trillmich in *KA* 501–2 no. 308.

83. See Hölscher in *KA* 394–96 with further bibliography; Simon (1986) 99–100; P. Zanker (1969); Niebling (1956) 312–19; Ryberg (1955) 56–58; D. Kleiner (1992) 102–3.

84. On the "theology" of Victoria, see Fears (1981b); cf. Hölscher (1967) 157ff.

85. See Kolbe (1966–67) and Bömer *ad Met.* 15.864; cf. the various discussions of the Sorrento base, such as Ryberg (1955) 49–53; Hölscher in *KA* 375–78; D. Kleiner (1992) 88.

86. See pp. 251–52 for citation; cf. Ryberg (1955) 58.

87. For a concise discussion, see North (1976).

88. See Taeger 2 (1960) 142–45 and Hänlein-Schäfer (1985) 16ff., 128ff. Cf. Alföldy (1991) 303–4.

89. To the evidence cited by Taeger and Hänlein-Schäfer (previous note) add, e.g., *Année Epigr.* 1939, 113: *deo Caesari Augusto* (Stobi); *ILS* 9495: *Augusto deo* (Africa). Ovid constantly calls Augustus *deus*: e.g., *AA* 1.203–4; *Trist.* 2.54, 3.1.34, 4.4.20; *Pont.* 1.2.97; see Scott (1930) 58ff.

90. Mann (1991) 176.

91. Taeger 2 (1960) 131–32; cf. Fishwick (1969) 365–66, incorporating the views of A. D. Nock. Important scholarly treatments of the Augustus cult in the east include Taylor (1931) 205ff.; Bowersock (1965) 112–21; Habicht (1973); Price (1984); Hänlein-Schäfer (1985); cf. Deininger (1965).

92. Price (1980).

93. Dio 51.20.6–9 who, here as elsewhere, mentions only Augustus. We know from the epigraphic sources that in this case and most others, the joint cult of Augustus and Roma was involved. Cf. Mellor (1975).

94. See Habicht (1973) 81–85.

95. For the relevant documentation, see Bowersock (1965) 112ff. and Habicht (1973) 60ff.

96. Bowersock (1965) 115.

97. OGIS 458 (=EJ 98), lines 65ff.; see Laffi (1967) 49ff. Cf. Philo, Legatio 149–50.

98. Price (1984); cf. the reviews by Liebeschuetz in JRS 75 (1985) 262ff.; Fishwick in Phoenix 40 (1986) 225ff.; and Mellor in AJP 107 (1986) 296ff.

99. Cf. Mann (1991) 176–77.

100. GIBM 894, lines. 9ff.; cf. Habicht (1973) 87.

101. OGIS 458 (= EJ 98). See the discussion by Price (1984) 54ff. and Laffi (1967).

102. Paneg. 11.1, 35.4, 52.1; cf. Pliny, HN 2.18: deus est mortali iuvare mortalem.

103. Hänlein in AA 1981, 511–13.

104. See Price (1984) 101ff. for details.

105. OGIS 456 = IGR IV.39; Price (1984) 126ff. As always, some degree of standardization (cf. Zanker, AMB 299ff.) was to come only after Augustus' death; cf. the provisions of honors for Germanicus in the Tabula Siarensis of A.D. 19 (see note 49), though considerable latitude remained; see Lebek (1993).

106. See Pekáry (1985) 117ff.; cf. Price (1984) 188ff.

107. Price (1984) 61; cf. his useful discussion on pp. 65–72 of the cult as "a system of exchange" that is also relevant, e.g., to Augustus' interaction with the cults sponsored by guilds in Rome.

108. See Tac., Ann. 4.37; Philo, Legatio 154, and the thorough discussion of Habicht (1972) 76ff.

109. Josephus, BJ 1.414; AJ 15.339. The colossal statue of Augustus as Zeus in the Metroon at Olympia (Paus. 5.20.9) is of a later date. The plan of Herod and others to complete the Temple of Olympian Zeus in Athens and dedicate it to the Genius of Augustus (Suet., Aug. 60) was not carried out, possibly because of Augustus' objections. Later emperors had no such scruples; see Price (1984) 187.

110. See Fishwick (1969).

111. See Price (1984) 168 and chapter 7.

112. See the detailed study of P. Zanker (1983a). Nor is there much evidence for the cost-effective renaming of existing statues (on the practice, see Pekáry [1985] 101ff.); the only reported exception is the transformation of a former Orestes in the Argive Heraion into Augustus (Paus. 2.17.3).

113. Especially by Habicht (1973) 65ff.; Hänlein-Schäfer (1985); and Fishwick (1978), (1987), and (1992).

114. Detailed discussion in Étienne (1958) 355ff. and Fishwick (1982). The provincial cult is post-Augustan; see Hänlein-Schäfer (1985) 232ff.

115. Val. Max 2.6.11; cf. Caesar, BG 3.22; Étienne (1958) 357–62.

116. Étienne (1958) 379ff.; Fishwick I (1987) 141ff.

117. On the Roman army religion, see the recent articles and surveys by J. Helgeland, E. Birley, and M. P. Speidel and A. Dimitrova-Wilceva in ANRW II.16.2 (1978) 1470ff., with considerable discussion of the important earlier work of A. von Domaszewski. For Augustus' army reforms, see Raaflaub (1987).

118. Vierneisel and Zanker (1979) pp. 23 and 25.

119. Hänlein-Schäfer (1985) 156–59, following W. Binder (1969).

120. For recent discussions of some of the evidence see *ANRW* II.17.3 (1981) and II.17.4 (1984).

121. Agrippa's "prohibition" of the Isis cult in Rome in 28 B.C. is sometimes regarded as the proverbial exception. The treatment of the cult, however, was highly nuanced (see Becher [1988] 149ff.). There were to be no new shrines for the goddess inside the *pomerium*; the existing shrines were kept and the building of Isis temples was encouraged in harbor districts (Vitr. 1.7.1). The extension of the prohibited zone to 7.5 stades (less than one mile) in 21 B.C. resulted from the unrest and riots in the city at the time; like the *compitalia*, the Egyptian cult centers had often been seedbeds for agitation. It was an additional reason to create a positive outlet by restructuring the Lares cult in Rome's neighborhoods. Outside of Rome, there was not even such minor interference. Cf., in Rome, the marble Ara Augusta of the freedman L. Lucretius Zethus where Isis appears among the patron deities of Augustus and the Roman state, such as Apollo, Jupiter, Diana, Fortuna, and Pietas (*CIL* VI. 30975).

122. Cf. D. Boschung's observation in the course of his review of Hänlein-Schäfer's book in *Gnomon* 59 (1987) 382 that the monuments of the cult are characterized by their variegated character rather than by uniform tendencies.

CHAPTER VII

1. For a survey of the evidence, see La Rocca (1977); cf. Galinsky (1992) 97–98.

2. Sjöqvist (1951).

3. Momigliano (1975) 17.

4. Vell. 11.3–5; Pliny, *HN* 34.64, cf. 36.24; H.G. Martin (1987) 153; Gruen (1992) 116–17.

5. Kyrieleis (1976) 435–36.

6. H. G. Martin (1987) 104–6, 158.

7. The bibliography on Greco-Roman cultural relations in the republic and the Augustan reign is vast. Important recent discussions of some of its aspects are Gruen (1990a) and (1992), with extensive earlier bibliography; Froning (1981); H. G. Martin (1987); Neudecker (1988); Pape (1975); Pollitt (1978); Rawson (1975) and (1985); Hölscher (1990); cf. Jucker (1950); Becatti (1951); Bowersock (1965); Flashar (1979); Torelli in *CAH* 10² ch. 20.

8. Good details in H. G. Martin (1987) 157ff.; cf. Gruen (1992) 116–17 and Eck (1984) 139–40.

9. Gruen (1992) 109; the following quotations are from p. 318. Cf. H. G. Martin (1987) 151–52 and Gruen 108ff. on Lepidus and Catulus.

10. Documentation in Pollitt (1986) 63ff., 141ff.; Hafner (1954); cf. Himmelmann (1981) and Bonacasa (1990).

11. G. Zanker (1987).

12. Smith (1991) 255. For varying discussions of the problems of verism, see Gruen (1992) 152ff.; D. Kleiner (1992) 31ff.; P. Zanker (1976) 581–619; Smith (1981), (1988) 125ff., and (1991) 255ff.; cf. Lahusen (1989) 75ff.

13. Chapter 4 with Fig. 77.

14. Cf. Smith (1991) 257, and Smith (1988) 125ff.

15. Cf. Most (1989).

16. See Hafner (1990), especially 32; cf. Smith (1991) 7–8. Preisshofen (1979) 265 dates the turn of Hellenistic art theory to classicism to the same period.

17. Detailed documentation in Borda (1953); cf. D. Kleiner (1992) 29–31 and Smith (1991) 259ff.

18. See Pollitt (1986) 166ff.

19. Harrison (1965); cf. Fullerton (1990) 1–12 and Stewart (1979) 34ff.

20. See especially Pollitt (1986) ch. 8; Smith (1991) 258ff.; D. Kleiner (1992) 27ff.; Borda (1953); Dentzer (1981); Zagdoun (1989); Fullerton (1990); for marble furniture, Moss (1989); for marble candelabra, Cain (1985); for marble craters, Grassinger (1991) 17ff. Also relevant is the evidence from the shipwrecks of Mahdia (W. Fuchs [1963]) and Antikythera (Svoronos [1908]). Cf. the incisive discussion of Torelli in *CAH* 10² ch. 20.

21. For a collection of the various passages see Jucker (1950) 118ff.; cf. Hölscher (1987) 54ff. Jucker's suggestion, going back to Schweitzer's (1932) hypotheses, that these were expressions of moral values rather than quality judgments is developed by Zanker, *AMB* 248ff., into a keystone of his interpretation of Augustan art, but see the careful assessment of Preisshofen (1979).

22. On the setting of aristocratic houses, cf. Wiseman (1987) 393–99.

23. See the detailed discussion of Neudecker (1988) 8ff.; cf. Froning (1981) 8ff.; Becatti (1951) 92–93. For Cicero's artistic judgments in his literary treatises (e.g., *Brut.* 70 and *Orator* 8–9), see the commentaries by Douglas (1966) and Sandys (1973) lxxi ff.

24. Neudecker (1988) 39. Cf. chapter 5 on the appropriation of motifs from public art into Augustan private art. The extent to which more than an aesthetic dimension was involved cannot be determined. On the arrangement of private sculptural collections, cf. Bartman (1991).

25. See, e.g., Coarelli (1970–71) who, however, draws much of his evidence from the building activity in the Circus Flaminius that was undertaken by plebeian consuls. Cf. Hölscher (1990) 79ff.

26. Suet., *Rhet.* 1.1; Gellius 15.11.2. Detailed discussion in Gruen (1990a) 179ff.

27. E.g., by Zanker, *AMB* 240, followed by Galinsky (1992b) 108.

28. Gabba (1991) ch. 2.

29. The Athenian resistance to Rome in the late republic and under Augustus has been surveyed well by Bowersock (1965) 101ff. and Hoff (1989).

30. Gabba (1991) especially 31–32. The following quotation is from p. 34.

31. Froning (1981) 93. She discusses the relief in detail on pp. 81–100.

32. Cain (1985) 26–38, 71; cf. Grassinger (1991) 17ff.

33. See the list in Pollitt (1978) 170. Again, the contrast that Zanker, *AMB* 77, is postulating between the supposed "Hellenistic" gaudiness of this collection (it did contain the Farnese Bull) and Octavian's "programmatic commitment to archaic and classical art" is overstated. So is Pollio's "opposition" to Augustus; see Raaflaub and Samons (1990) 438–39.

34. Gelsomino (1958) has collected the evidence.

35. D. Kleiner (1992) 110–11; cf. the reduction of the complexity of the Ara Pacis goddess on the relief in Carthage (Fig. 67).

36. For the evidence see Pollitt (1978) 158–59.

37. Heinze (1915) 281.

38. See Hölscher's (1987) incisive discussion, especially 54ff.

39. Well explained by Gelzer (1979); cf. Quint. 10.2.25.

40. Neptune: Fig. 147. Pietas: see Powell (1992) 152ff.

41. See Hölscher (1987) 17 for specific parallels. Cf. Torelli in *CAH* 10^2 ch. 20.

42. Hölscher (1984b) 204ff. and *KA* no. 200; cf. H. Meyer (1991–92).

43. D. Kleiner (1992) 86. The Gallic theme was another link to republican traditions; see Hölscher (1990) 80–82.

44. Excellent discussion by La Rocca (1985) and in *KA* 121ff.; cf. Simon (1986) 104ff.; D. Kleiner (1992) 84–86.

45. D. Kleiner (1992) 86.

46. Another possible example is the frieze in the Basilica Aemilia. I accept, however, its dating to the late republican period; see H. Bauer in *KA* 200ff. (55 B.C. rather than 78 B.C., as is suggested by Kränzle [1991], with earlier bibliography); cf. Hölscher (1993) 79. The interest in depicting scenes from early Rome even with didactic intent should not be considered an exclusive prerogative of Augustan art. Again, there is continuity from republican to Augustan art.

47. Hardie (1986).

48. An essential distinction made by Maderna (1988) 122–23 in connection with representations of Augustus in the manner of Jupiter.

49. See A. Viscogliosi in *KA* 139.

50. Besides the homoerotic relief with Pan and Olympos in the Saepta Iulia (Zanker, *AMB* 147 with fig. 115), cf. the paintings chosen by Caesar for exhibit in the Temple of Venus Genetrix: their subjects were Medea and Ajax (Pliny, *HN* 35.136). The contemporary relevance of the other painting in the Curia, by Philochares, is clearer. It showed the father-and-son pair of Glaukion and Aristippos, "persons otherwise quite obscure," but the son had a marked resemblance to the father, and an eagle gripping a snake flew above (Pliny, *HN* 35.27–28); see Hölscher (1989) 327–29.

51. Cf. Zanker's (*AMB* 258) comments on the resulting mixture of styles.

52. Livy 34.4.4 with the comments of Luce (1977) 252; cf. 39.6.3–9 and Pliny, *HN* 34.34.

53. Pp. 212–13; besides their article, see also S. Sande and J. Zahle in *KA* 213–24.

54. Besides the various commentaries, I am indebted especially to the following in my discussion of this aspect of *C.* 3.30: Doblhofer (1992) 111–15; Woodman (1974); Korzeniewski (1972) and (1974); Suerbaum (1968) 165–67, 324–29; Koster (1983) 36–43; Ross (1975) 133–37; Syndikus (1973) 273–82; Feeney (1993) 57–58; Pöschl (1991) 246–62.

55. My starting point has been the translation provided by Gordon Williams (1969) 150, in which I have made several changes.

56. Fraenkel (1957) 302.

57. Especially by Korzeniewski (1972).

58. E.g., *CLE* (Buecheler) 89, 137, 139, 140, 369.

59. See Prop. 3.1.8 with Fedeli's note.

60. Listed and discussed by Bing (1988) 58ff.

61. See von Hesberg and Panciera (1994).

62. Cf. Chapter 5.

63. J. Griffin (1985) 1–31, 48–64.

64. Chapter 6. The statues of the *viri triumphales* that were to be set up in the Augustan forum in addition to the *summi viri* were to be made of bronze; see Lahusen (1983) 25.

65. Alföldy (1991) 293—99.

66. For details see Suerbaum (1968) 165–67.

67. Cf. the socalled Midas epigram in T. Preger, *Inscr. Graecae Metricae* (1891) no. 233.

68. Examples in Korzeniewski (1974) 385–86.

69. Suet., *Aug.* 2.3–4.2, who records the sneers of Mark Antony at Octavian's lack of noble parentage.

70. For details see Ross (1975) 135; cf. Woodman 126 (1974) with notes 50 and 51.

71. Ross (1975) 136.

72. Korzeniewski (1974).

73. McDermott (1981) 1662–63 (with a somewhat different interpretation).

74. Excellent discussion by Lefèvre (1993) 247–51.

75. A useful compilation is König (1970); cf. the bibliography listed by Suerbaum (1980) 267–68.

76. Hardie (1991) 29.

77. Feeney (1993) 44. Cf. Clausen (1964) 196 on Callimachus' mediation of Hesiod.

78. Pfeiffer (1968) 87.

79. G. Zanker (1987) 229. The quotation in the next sentence is from p. 19.

80. The relevant passages have been collected by Reinsch-Werner (1976); for comment, see Cameron (1992) 310 and Bing (1988) 83ff.

81. For detailed discussions see, e.g., G. Zanker (1987) 201ff.; Galinsky (1972) 108ff.; Clauss (1993).

82. See, e.g., Halperin (1983) 228 and Farrell (1991) 213.

83. *SH* 2454–69; cf. Bing (1988) 47.

84. I am indebted to the discussion of Farrell (1991) 212–13, to which I have added some observations of my own.

85. Thomas 1 (1988) 5.

86. See the excellent expositions by Farrell (1991) and Conte (1986). More reductive is what I would call the "subversiveness fallacy"; see, e.g., Lyne (1994).

87. Feeney (1993) 55.

88. I am employing the useful distinction made by Hölscher (1990) 73–74 in the context of Hellenistic art.

89. Bowersock (1965) 139.

90. The following remarks are a summary of my discussion in *ICS* 14 (1989) 71–76; some of these aspects also apply to the *Fasti* and even the *Heroides*. For other views of Ovid as an Augustan, see Knox (1986) and Millar (1993).

91. Mierse (1990) 323–24 with fig. 10.

92. Details in Hölscher (1984b).

93. I am indebted to R. Talbert for some observations on Augustus' refusal to use Pericles as a model.

94. Plut., *Mor.* 207F; see the discussion by Bowersock (1965) 106. On the later Athenian uprising, see Bowersock 106–7 and Hoff (1989).

95. For the Odeion, see Thompson (1959); for the Temple of Ares, McAllister (1959); cf. Zanker, *AMB* 261–62, and Shear (1981). The Athenians dedicated a statue to the "new Ares," Gaius Caesar, with whom Augustus had dedicated the Temple of Mars Ultor in Rome; cf. Bowersock (1984) 171ff.

96. See G. B. Conte's review of Cairns (1989) in *Gnomon* 63 (1991) 487–97. On the other hand, Vergil was a student of Philodemus' and is mentioned among the dedicatees of one of Philodemus' treatises; see Gigante and Capasso (1989).

97. Hammond (1940). Cf. Gabba (1991) on the tenor of Dionysius' *Roman Antiquities*.

98. See, most recently, Hölscher (1990) 83.

99. Syme, *RR* vii.

100. Some good discussions of this subject are Salmon (1956); Eck (1986); Eder (1990); Christ (1992) 83ff.

101. Aur. Victor, *Epit.* 1.21: (Augustus) *autem dominandi supra quam aestimari potest, cupidissimus.* Cf. Fadinger (1969) 334 on Dio's presentation of Augustus.

102. Badian (1982) 31; I am indebted to his discussion and Eder's (1990) 107ff.

103. On the powers this gave him see Brunt and Moore (1967) 10ff. As compensation for the loss of the annual consulship, he was awarded the permanent right (not inherent in the tribunate) to bring any business of his own choosing before the senate (Dio 53.32.5).

104. See, most recently, Culham (1988); also, Eck (1986) 109ff.

105. Talbert (1984) 374–75.

106. See Eck (1986) 114–15; Brunt and Moore (1967) 44–45; and Rickman (1980), especially 61ff.

107. Recent overviews include Kienast 264–310; Gruen (1990b), expanded version in *CAH* 10² ch. 4; Christ (1992) 120–33. Cf. Wells (1972) with the review by H. von Petrikovits in *GGA* 228 (1976) 163–73, and Brunt (1963).

108. Cf. Brunt (1978); Harris (1979), especially 105ff.; Yavetz (1984) 9–10 (with the literary sources); Nicolet (1991); and chapter 3.

109. Cf. Bringmann (1977) 47–48.

110. Weippert (1972); cf. Michel (1967).

111. Plut., *Mor.* 207D. On Augustus' unification (another example of his following Caesar's policies) of the empire rather than treating it as a conglomeration of provinces, see the excellent analysis of Kienast 366ff.

112. See chapter 3. Cf. Bringmann (1977).

113. *RG* 8.5. See chapter 3 for discussion and the Latin text.

114. Sen., *Contr.* 10, pr. 5.4, 7.1, 7.3; Tac., *Ann.* 1.72; cf. Suet., *Calig.* 16. Augustus' involvement is far from certain; see Raaflaub and Samons (1990) 439ff. In *CAH* 10² ch. 2, J. Crook sensibly attributes the "imbalance of emphasis upon the first part of his [Augustus'] reign" to the loss of a significant portion of the manuscript of Dio's history.

115. For the data, see Shipley (1931).

116. Toher (1990) 142.

117. *Aen.* 10.517–20; cf. the commentary by S. Harrison (1991) 203, and Mackie (1988) 187. What matters is not the story's truth or lack of it (on which see Syme, *RR* 212) but its circulation.

118. Cf. Alföldi (1985) 336. Velleius (2.100.4) makes the same point about Augustus' behavior toward Iullus Antonius.

119. Detailed discussion by Jal (1957).

120. Cf. J. Griffin (1985) 22–23.

121. Balsdon (1962) 68–69.

122. See, e.g., Weinbrot (1978) for eighteenth-century views, and Stahlmann (1988) for the fluctuating assessment of Augustus in German classical scholarship.

123. Eder (1990) 86.

124. Burns (1978) 237.

125. Stahlmann (1988) 192.

126. R. D. Williams (1967 [1990]) 36. For scholarship on the *Aeneid*, see chapter 5, notes 70–78.

127. One of Philodemus' works includes Vergil's name among the dedicatees; see Gigante and Capasso (1989).

128. Quoted by Ezra Pound, *ABC of Reading* (New Haven 1934) 31.

129. See Galinsky (1988) and (1994), and Erler (1992).

CHAPTER VIII

1. Good discussion by Brunt and Moore (1967) 57–66; for the extent and sources of Augustus' wealth, see Shatzman (1975) 357ff. Cf. Sutherland (1945) 151–57.

2. Syme (1958a). On imperatorial acclamations, cf. Schumacher (1985).

3. Detailed survey in Kienast 336ff. Cf. Mierse (1990).

4. Suet., *Caes.* 28; specific examples in Kienast 344 n. 137 and Shear (1981) 356ff.

5. P. Zanker (1972) with the important review by R. Brilliant in *Gnomon* 46 (1974) 523–25; Coarelli (1985).

6. See E. Nedergaard in *KA* 224ff. for a discussion of this arch and its relation to the earlier Actian arch.

7. See Alföldy (1991) 299–302.

8. Bosworth (1972) has convincingly demonstrated that Pollio was an *amicus* of Augustus rather than being oppositional; cf. Raaflaub and Samons (1990) 438–39.

9. Dio 54.24.3; cf. Tac., *Ann.* 3.72; Nicolet (1984) 94–95.

10. Cf. Eck (1984) 141–42.

11. Quite in contrast, e.g., to the Augustan modification of the Athenian Agora, which was "as clear a statement of the new order in the world as can be made through the medium of architecture" (Shear [1981] 361).

12. Cf. S. Sande and J. Zahle in *KA* 213.

13. As suggested by the find of such an inscription (*CIL* VI. 1316) in the vicinity; cf. *CIL* X. 6087. For Munatius' restoration of the temple, see Fittschen (1976a) 208ff. and Pensabene (1984).

14. Cf. Vell. 2.83, a remarkably unflattering presentation of Plancus by one of Augustus' most enthusiastic admirers.

15. Cf. La Rocca (1987) with perspectives that are somewhat different from mine.

16. Richardson (1977) 359–60.

17. Cf. Gruen (1990b) 402; on the building itself, Richardson (1992) 317.

18. On this subject, Eck's article (1984) is fundamental.

19. Abundant documentation in Lahusen (1983).

20. Eck (1984) 146–47; cf. Alföldy (1992) 113ff. The other monument, for a certain proconsul Rufus, cannot be dated exactly, but seems to belong to the Augustan period.

21. Eck (1984) 145.

22. Dio 55.10.3; cf. Eck (1984) 142–43 and Lahusen (1983) 25.

23. Suet., *Aug.* 38.1; Dio 54.12.1; Vell. 2.104.2. For a list of individuals so honored, see Gordon (1952) 305ff.; the total number reported by Suetonius is more than thirty.

24. Eck (1984) 149ff.

25. For which see Alföldy (1991) 296, 300.

26. Cf. Pfanner's (1989) estimate (p. 178) of 25,000–50,000 portrait busts, based on the existence of over 1,000 cities in the Augustan empire; cf. chapter 4.

27. See Alföldy (1991).

28. Eder (1990) 78; cf. the assessments by Raaflaub and Samons (1990) 452ff. and Kienast 424ff.

29. J. Griffin (1984) 204–5. Victory celebrations: Vergil, *Geo.* 3.8ff (cf. chapter 4 n. 164); Hor., *C.* 3.14 (cf. chapter 5) and 4.2.33ff.; Ovid, *AA* 1.205ff. Peace: Vergil, *Geo.* 1.500ff.; Prop. 3.5 (cf. chapter 5); Hor., *C.* 4.5. Exhortations against *luxuria* and *avaritia*: Vergil, *Geo.* 2.167–69; Hor., *C.* 1.8, 3.2 (cf. chapter 5) and 3.6 (cf. chapter 3); Prop. 2.16; cf. Tib. 1.1, 1.10, and 2.3 as discussed in chapter 5.

30. J. Griffin (1984) 204. Cf. Hor., *Epist.* 2.1.118ff., on the moral foundation of poetry, but see *Sat.* 1.2.121ff. for quite a different attitude.

31. As posited by Zanker; see Eder's (1990) judicious critique (p. 84).

32. *Aug.* 72–80; 90–92. For a more extensive assessment, see Yavetz (1990) 30ff.; cf. Boschung (1993) 93ff.

33. Pp. 174, 373; cf. Aurel. Victor, *Epit.* 1.20; Pliny, *HN* 11.143; Tac., *Ann.* 1.42.3.

BIBLIOGRAPHY

Accame, S. (1942). "La legislazione romana intorno ai collegi nel I secolo a.C.," *BMIR* 13.13–48.

Adams, J. N. (1974). "The Vocabulary of the Later Decades of Livy," *Antichthon* 8.54–62.

Adams, T. (1970). *Clementia Principis* (Stuttgart).

Adcock, F. (1951). "The Interpretation of *Res Gestae Divi Augusti* 34.1," *CQ* 45.130–35.

Adkins, A.W.H. (1960). *Merit and Responsibility: A Study in Greek Values* (Oxford).

Aili, H. (1982). "Livy's Language. A Critical Survey of Research," *ANRW* II.30.2.1122–47.

Albrecht, M. von (1982). "Properz als augusteischer Dichter," *WS* 95.220–36; repr. in G. Binder 2 (1988) 360–77.

———. (1992). *Geschichte der Römischen Literatur* 1 (Berne).

Alföldi, A. (1930). "Der neue Weltenherrscher der IV. Ekloge Vergils," *Hermes* 65.369–85.

———. (1956). "The Main Aspects of Propaganda on the Coinage of the Roman Republic," in R.A.G. Carson and C.H.V. Sutherland, eds., *Essays in Roman Coinage Presented to Harold Mattingly* (Oxford) 63–94.

———. (1959). "*Hasta Summa Imperii*. The Spear as an Embodiment of Sovereignty in Rome," *AJA* 63.1–27.

———. (1971). *Der Vater des Vaterlandes im römischen Denken* (Darmstadt).

———. (1973). *Die zwei Lorbeerbäume des Augustus* (Bonn).

———. (1976). *Oktavians Aufstieg zur Macht* (Bonn).

———. (1985). *Caesar in 44 v. Chr.* (Bonn).

Alföldy, G. (1983). *Sir Ronald Syme, "Die römische Revolution" und die deutsche Althistorie.* Sitzungsber. Heidelberg. Akad., phil.-hist. Kl., no.1.

———. (1991). "Augustus und die Inschriften: Tradition und Innovation," *Gymn.* 98.289–324.

———. (1992). *Studi sull' epigrafia augustea e tiberiana di Roma* (Rome).

———. (1993). "Two Principes: Augustus and Sir Ronald Syme," *Athenaeum* 81.101–22.

Anderson, J. C. (1984). *The Historical Topography of the Imperial Fora.* Coll. Latomus 182 (Brussels).

Anderson, W. S. (1958). "Juno and Saturn in the *Aeneid*," *SPh* 55.519–32.

———. (1963). "Multiple Change in the *Metamorphoses*," *TAPA* 93.1–27.

André, J. M. (1966). *L'otium dans la vie morale et intellectuelle romaine* (Paris).

Andreae, B. (1973). *L'art de l'ancienne Rome* (Paris).

———. (1989). *Die Kunst des alten Roms* (Freiburg).

———, and Kyrieleis, H., eds. (1975). *Neue Forschungen in Pompeji* (Recklinghausen).

Arendt, H. (1961). *The Origins of Totalitarianism* (London).

Armstrong, D. (1986). "*Horatius Eques et Scriba*: Satires 1.6 and 2.7," *TAPA* 116.255–88.

———. (1989). *Horace* (New Haven).

Arnold, D. (1969). *Die Polykletnachfolge. JdI* Suppl. 25 (Heidelberg).

Austin, R. G. (1971). *P. Vergili Maronis Aeneidos Liber Primus* (Oxford).

————. (1977). *P. Vergili Maronis Aeneidos Liber Sextus* (Oxford).

Bachrach, P., and Baratz, M. S. (1970). *Power and Poverty; Theory and Practice* (New York).

Badian, E. (1982). "'Crisis Theories' and the Beginning of the Principate," in G. Wirth, ed., *Romanitas-Christianitas. Festschrift für Johannes Straub* (Berlin and New York) 18–40.

————. (1985). "A Phantom Marriage Law," *Philologus* 129.82–98.

————. (1986). "The Young Betti and the Practice of History," in G. Crifò, ed., *Costituzione romana e crisi della repubblica* (Perugia) 73–96.

Bahti, T. (1986). "Ambiguity and Indeterminacy: The Juncture," *Comp. Lit.* 38.9–23.

Baldry, J. (1952). "Who Invented the Golden Age?," *CQ* n.s. 2.83–92.

Balsdon, J.P.V.D. (1962). *Roman Women* (London).

Balty, J. C. (1978). "La statue de bronze de T. Quinctius Flamininus *ad Apollinis in Circo,*" *MEFR* 90.669–78.

Barbet, A. (1985). *La peinture murale romaine: les styles décoratifs pompéiens* (Paris).

Barchiesi, A. (1989). "Voci e istanze narrative nelle *Metamorfosi* di Ovidio," *MD* 23.55–97.

————. (1994). *Il poeta e il principe. Ovidio e il discorso augusteo* (Rome and Bari).

Barnabei, F. (1901). *La villa pompeiana di P. Fannio Sinistore* (Rome).

Bartman, E. (1991). "Sculptural Collecting and Display in the Private Realm," in E. Gazda, ed., *Roman Art in the Private Sphere* (Ann Arbor) 71–88.

Bastet, F. L., and de Vos, M. (1979). *Proposta per una classificazione del terzo stile pompeiano* (The Hague).

Bauman, R. (1993). "The Rape of Lucretia, *quod metus causa* and the Criminal Law," *Latomus* 52.550–66.

Becatti, G. (1951). *Arte e gusto negli scrittori latini* (Florence).

Becher, I. (1988). "Augustus und seine Religionspolitik gegenüber orientalischen Kulten," in G. Binder 2 (1988) 143–70.

Becker, C. (1963). *Das Spätwerk des Horaz* (Göttingen).

Bellen, H. (1985). "Cicero und der Aufstieg Oktavians," *Gymn.* 92.161–89.

————. (1987). "*Novus status—novae leges*. Kaiser Augustus als Gesetzgeber," in G. Binder 1 (1987) 308–48.

Beller, M. (1967). *Philemon und Baucis in der europäischen Literatur* (Heidelberg).

Belloni, G. (1974). "Significati storico-politici delle figurazioni e delle scritte delle monete da Augusto a Traiano," in *ANRW* II.1.997–1144.

————. (1976). "Monete romane e propaganda," in M. Sordi, ed., *I canali della propaganda nel mondo antico* (Milan) 131–59.

————. (1985). "Monete romane (repubblica e impero) in quanto opera d'artigianato e arte," in *ANRW* II.12.3.89–115.

Benario, J. (1960). "Book 4 of Horace's *Odes*: Augustan Propaganda," *TAPA* 91.339–52.

Benediktson, D. T. (1989). *Propertius. Modernist Poet of Antiquity* (Carbondale).

Bengtson, H. (1972). "Die letzten Monate der römischen Senatsherrschaft," in ANRW I.1.967–80.

————. (1981). *Kaiser Augustus. Sein Leben und seine Zeit* (Munich).

Benko, S. (1980). "Virgil's Fourth Eclogue in Christian Interpretation," *ANRW* II.31.1. 646–705.

Béranger, J. (1953). *Recherches sur l'aspect idéologique du principat* (Basel).

———. (1959). "Cicéron précurseur politique," *Hermes* 87.103–17; repr. in Béranger (1973) 117–34.

———. (1973). *Principatus* (Geneva).

Berczelly, L. (1985). "Ilia and the Divine Twins. A Reconsideration of Two Relief Panels from the Ara Pacis Augustae," *Acta AArtHist* 5.89–149.

Bernbeck, E. J. (1967). *Beobachtungen zur Darstellungsart in Ovids Metamorphosen* (Munich).

Beyen, H. G. (1938, 1960). *Die Pompejanische Wanddekoration vom zweiten zum vierten Stil.* Vols. 1 and 2 (The Hague).

Bieber, M. (1961). *The History of the Greek and Roman Theater*, 2nd ed. (Princeton).

Binder, G. (1971). *Aeneas und Augustus. Interpretationen zum 8. Buch der Aeneis* (Meisenheim).

———, ed., *Saeculum Augustum.* Vol. 1 (1987); vol. 2 (1988); vol. 3 (1991) (Darmstadt).

Binder, W. (1969). *Der Roma-Augustus Monopteros auf der Akropolis in Athen und sein typologischer Ort* (Stuttgart).

Bing, P. (1988). *The Well-Read Muse. Present and Past in Callimachus and the Hellenistic Poets* (Göttingen).

Biondi, B. (1939). "La legislazione di Augusto," in R. Paribeni, ed., *Conferenze Augustee* (Milan) 198–232.

Blanckenhagen, P. H. von, and Alexander, C. (1990). *The Augustan Villa at Boscotrecase* (Mainz).

Bleicken, J. (1955). *Das Volkstribunat in der klassischen Republik* (Munich).

———. (1962). "Der Begriff der Freiheit in der letzten Phase der römischen Republik," *HZ* 221.1–20.

———. (1990). *Zwischen Republik und Prinzipat.* Abh. Göttingen, phil.-hist. Kl., ser. 3 no. 185.

Bömer, F. (1957–58). *P. Ovidius Naso. Die Fasten.* 2 vols. (Heidelberg).

———. (1969–86). *P. Ovidius Naso. Metamorphosen. Kommentar.* 7 vols. (Heidelberg).

Börker, C. (1973). "Neuattisches und Pergamenisches an den Ara Pacis Ranken," *JdI* 88.283–317.

Bonacasa, N. (1990). "Realismo, naturalismo e verismo nella scultura alessandrina. Una revisione," *Acts of the 13th Intern. Congress of Class. Archaeology* (Berne) 137–43.

Bonnefond-Coudry, M. (1989). *Le Sénat de la république romaine de la guerre d'Hannibal à Auguste. BEFR* 273 (Rome).

Borbein, A. (1968). *Campanareliefs. Typologische und stilkritische Untersuchungen. RM* Suppl. 14 (Heidelberg).

———. (1975a). "Die Ara Pacis Augustae. Geschichtliche Wirkung und Programm," *JdI* 90.242–66.

———. (1975b). "Zur Bedeutung von Scherwand und Durchblick auf den Wandgemälden des 2. Pompejanischen Stils," in Andreae and Kyrieleis (1975) 61–71.

Borda, M. (1953). *La scuola di Pasiteles* (Bari).

Boschung, D. (1993). *Die Bildnisse des Augustus* (Berlin).

Bosworth, A. B. (1972). "Asinius Pollio and Augustus," *Historia* 21.441–73.

Boucher, J. P. (1965). *Étude sur Properce. Problèmes d'inspiration et d'art* (Paris).

Bowersock, G. W. (1965). *Augustus and the Greek World* (Oxford).

———. (1979). "Historical Problems in Late Republican and Augustan Classicism," in Flashar (1979) 57–78.

Bowersock, G. W. (1980). "The Emperor of Roman History," *NY Review of Books* (March 6) 8–13.

———. (1984). "Augustus and the East: The Problem of Succession," in Millar and Segal (1984) 169–88.

———. (1990). "The Pontificate of Augustus," in Raaflaub and Toher (1990) 380–94.

Bowra, M. (1945). *From Virgil to Milton* (London).

Boyancé, P. (1972). *Étude sur la religion romaine. CEFR* 11 (Paris).

Boyce, A. A. (1965). *Festal and Dated Coins of the Roman Empire.* Num. Notes and Monogr. 153 (New York).

Boyce, G. K. (1937). *Corpus of the Lararia of Pompeii. MAAR* 14 (Rome).

Bragantini, I., and de Vos, M. (1982). *Museo Nazionale Romano. Le pitture II.1. La decorazione della villa romana della Farnesina* (Rome).

Braunert, H. (1974). "Zum Eingangssatz der *res gestae Divi Augusti*," *Chiron* 4.343–58.

Brendel, O. (1931). *Ikonographie des Kaisers Augustus* (Nuremberg).

Brenk, F. (1980). "The Twofold Gleam: Vergil's Golden Age and the Beginnings of Empire," *Thought* 55.81–97.

Brilliant, R. (1963). *Gesture and Rank in Roman Art* (New Haven).

Bringmann, K. (1977). "Weltherrschaft und innere Krise Roms im Spiegel der Geschichtsschreibung des zweiten und ersten Jahrhunderts vor Christus," *A&A* 23.28–49.

Brink, C. O. (1971). *Horace on Poetry 2: The Ars Poetica* (Cambridge).

———. (1972). "Limaturae," *RhM* 115.28–42.

———. (1982). *Horace on Poetry 3: Epistles Book II: The Letters to Augustus and Florus* (Cambridge).

Brommer, F. (1980). "Zur Datierung des Augustus von Prima Porta," in *Eikones. Festschrift für H. Jucker* (Berne) 78–81.

Brunt, P. A. (1963). Review of H. D. Meyer (1961) in *JRS* 53.170–76.

———. (1971). *Italian Manpower* (Oxford).

———. (1978). "Laus imperii," in P. Garnsey and C. Whitaker, eds., *Imperialism in the Ancient World* (Cambridge) 159–91.

———. (1984). "The Role of the Senate in the Augustan Regime," *CQ* 34.423–44.

———. (1988). *The Fall of the Roman Republic and Related Essays* (Oxford).

Brunt, P. A., and Moore, J. M., eds. (1967). *Res Gestae Divi Augusti* (Oxford).

Buchner, E. (1982). *Die Sonnenuhr des Augustus* (Mainz).

Büchner, K. (1984). *Cicero. De re publica* (Heidelberg).

Büsing, H. (1977). "Ranke und Fries an der Ara Pacis Augustae," *AA* 92.247–57.

Burck, E. (1952). "Römische Wesenszüge in der augusteischen Liebeselegie," *Hermes* 80.163–200.

———. (1982). "Die römische Expansion im Urteil des Livius," *ANRW* II.30.2.1148–89.

Burnett, A. (1977). "The Authority to Coin in the Late Republic and the Early Empire," *NC* 137.37–63.

Burnett, A., Amandry, M., and Ripollès, P. P. (1992). *Roman Provincial Coinage* (London and Paris).

Burns, J. M. (1978). *Leadership* (New York).

Bux, E. (1948). "Clementia Romana. Ihr Wesen und ihre Bedeutung für die Politik des römischen Reiches," *WJA* 3.201–30.

Cain, H.-U. (1985). *Römische Marmorkandelaber* (Mainz).

Cairns, F. (1979). *Tibullus: A Hellenistic Poet at Rome* (Cambridge).

––––––. (1989). *Virgil's Augustan Epic* (Cambridge).

Calderone, S. (1982). "Il mito di Dedalo-Icaro nel simbolismo funerario romano," in G. Wirth, ed., *Romanitas—Christianitas. Festschrift für Johannes Straub* (Berlin and New York) 749–67.

Cameron, A. (1992). "Genre and Style in Callimachus," *TAPA* 122.305–12.

Capelle, W. (1932). "Griechische Ethik und Römischer Imperialismus," *Klio* 25.86–113.

Cardauns, B. (1978). "Varro und die römische Religion. Zur Theologie, Wirkungsgeschichte und Leistung der *Antiquitates Rerum Divinarum*," *ANRW* II.16.1. 80–103.

Carettoni, G. (1983). *Das Haus des Augustus auf dem Palatin* (Mainz).

Carter, J. C., and Costantini, L. (1994). "Settlement Density, Agriculture, and the Extent of Productive Land Cleared from Forest in the Time of the Roman Empire in Magna Graecia," in B. Frenzel, ed., *Evaluation of Land Surfaces Cleared from Forests in the Mediterranean Region during the Times of the Roman Empire*. Special Issue: European Science Foundation Project European Palaeoclimate and Man 5 (Stuttgart) 101–18.

Carter, J. M., ed. (1982). *Suetonius. Divus Augustus* (Bristol).

Castriota, D. (1992). *Myth, Ethos, and Actuality. Official Art in Fifth-Century Athens* (Madison).

––––––. (1995), *The Ara Pacis Augustae and the Imagery of Abundance in Later Greek and Roman Imperial Art* (Princeton).

Charbonneaux, J. (1948). *L'art au siècle d'Auguste* (Lausanne).

Charles-Picard, G. (1970). *Roman Painting* (London).

––––––. (1981). "Les grotesques: un système décoratif typique de l'art césarien et néronien," *CEFR* 55.143–49.

Charlesworth, M. P. (1937). "The Virtues of a Roman Emperor: Propaganda and the Creation of Belief," *PBA* 23.105–33.

––––––. (1943). "Pietas and Victoria: The Emperor and the Citizen," *JRS* 33.1–10.

Chastagnol, A. (1980). "La crise du recrutement sénatorial des années 16–11 av. J. C.," in M. S. Fontana et al., eds., *Miscellanea di studi classici in onore di E. Manni* 2 (Rome) 465–76.

Christ, K. (1992). *Geschichte der römischen Kaiserzeit*, 2nd ed. (Munich).

Clarke, J. R. (1991). *The Houses of Roman Italy, 100 B.C.–A.D. 250. Ritual, Space, and Decoration* (Berkeley).

Classen, C. J. (1963). "Gottmenschentum in der römischen Republik," *Gymn.* 70.312–38.

––––––. (1986). "*Virtutes Romanorum* nach dem Zeugnis der Münzen republikanischer Zeit," *RM* 93.257–79.

Clausen, W. (1964). "Callimachus and Latin Poetry," *GRBS* 5 (1964) 181–96.

––––––. (1987). *Virgil's Aeneid and the Tradition of Hellenistic Poetry* (Berkeley).

Clauss, J. (1993). *The Best of the Argonauts* (Berkeley).

Coarelli, F. (1970–71). "Classe dirigente romana e arti figurative," *DialArch* 4/5.241–65.

––––––. (1985). *Il Foro Romano*. Vol. 2: *Periodo repubblicano e augusteo* (Rome).

––––––. (1994). *Roma. Guide Archeologiche Mondadori* (Milan).

Cogrossi, C. (1978). "L'apollinismo augusteo e un denario con il Sole radiato di L. Aquilio Floro," in M. Sordi, ed., *Aspetti dell' opinione pubblica nel mondo antico* (Milan) 138–58.

Collinge, N. (1961). *The Structure of Horace's Odes* (Oxford).

Colonna, G. (1991). "Il posto dell'Arringatore nell'arte etrusca di età ellenistica," *SE* 56.99–119.

Connor, P. J. (1972). "The Balance Sheet: Consideration of the Second Roman Ode," *Hermes* 100.241–48.

———. (1981). "The Actual Quality of Experience: An Appraisal of the Nature of Horace's 'Odes,'" *ANRW* II.31.3.1612–39.

Conrardy, C. (1904). *De Vergilio Apollonii Rhodii imitatore* (Freiburg).

Consigliere, L. (1978). *'Slogans' monetarii e poesia augustea* (Genoa).

Constans, L. A. (1938). *L'Éneide de Virgile, étude et analyse* (Paris).

Conte, G. B. (1984). *Il genere e i suoi confini* (Milan).

———. (1986). *The Rhetoric of Imitation. Genre and Poetic Memory in Virgil and Other Latin Poets* (Ithaca).

———. (1992). "Empirical and Theoretical Approaches to Literary Genre," in Galinsky (1992a) 104–23.

Crawford, M. (1983). "Roman Imperial Coin Types and the Formation of Public Opinion," in C. Brooke, ed.,*Studies in Numismatic Method Presented to Philip Grierson* (Cambridge) 47–64.

Culham, P. (1988). "Programmatic or Pragmatic Augustus? The Case of the Italian Highways," *Aug. Age* 8.5–21.

Dalzell, A. (1956). "Maecenas and the Poets," *Phoenix* 10.151–62.

Degrassi, A. (1937). *Inscriptiones Italiae* 13.3 (Rome).

———. (1945). "Virgilio e il foro di Augusto," *Epigraphica* 7.88–103.

Deininger, J. (1965). *Die Provinziallandtage der römischen Kaiserzeit von Augustus bis zum Ende des 3. Jahrh. n. Chr.* (Bonn).

———. (1985). "Livius und der Principat," *Klio* 67.265–72.

Dentzer, J. M. (1981). "Reliefs grecs au banquet d'Italie: importation, copies, pastiches," *CEFR* 55.1–18.

Des Bouvrie, S. (1984). "Augustus' Legislation on Morals—Which Moral and What Aims?" *SO* 59.93–113.

Desideri, P. (1972). "L'interpretazione dell'impero romano in Posidonio," *RIL* 106.481–93.

de Vos, M. (1980). *L'egittomania in pitture e mosaici romano-campani della prima età imperiale* (Leiden).

Dobbin, R. (1995). "Julius Caesar in Jupiter's Prophecy, *Aeneid* Book I," *Class. Ant.* 14.5–41.

Doblhofer, E. (1966). *Die Augustuspanegyrik des Horaz in formalhistorischer Sicht* (Heidelberg).

———. (1992). *Horaz in der Forschung nach 1957* (Darmstadt).

Döpp, S. (1989). "*Nec omnia apud priores meliora*: Autoren des frühen Principats über die eigene Zeit," *RhM* 132.73–101.

———. (1991). "Vergilrezeption in der ovidischen 'Aeneis,'" *RhM* 134.327–45.

Douglas, A. E., ed. (1966). *Cicero. Brutus* (Oxford).

———. (1968). *Cicero* (Oxford).

Drerup, H. (1981). *Zum Ausstattungsluxus in der römischen Architektur*, 2nd ed. (Münster).

Ducati, P. (1908). "Ara di Bagnacavallo," *RM* 23.130–44.

Due, O. S. (1974). *Changing Forms. Studies in the Metamorphoses of Ovid* (Copenhagen).

DuQuesnay, I. (1977). "Vergil's Fourth *Eclogue*," in F. Cairns, ed., *PLLS* 1976.25–99.

———. (1984). "Horace and Maecenas: The propaganda value of *Sermones* I," in Woodman and West (1984) 19–58.

Duthoy, R. (1974). "La fonction sociale de l'Augustalité," *Epigraphica* 36.134–54.

———. (1978). "Les *Augustales," *ANRW* II.16.2.1254–1309.

Eagleton, T. (1991). *Ideology: An Introduction* (London).

Earl, D. (1967). *The Moral and Political Tradition of Rome* (London).

———. (1968). *The Age of Augustus* (New York).

Eck, W. (1984). "Senatorial Self-Representation: Developments in the Augustan Period," in Millar and Segal (1984) 129–68.

———. (1986). "Augustus' Administrative Reformen: Pragmatismus oder Systematisches Planen?," *Acta Class.* 29.105–120.

Eck, W., Fittschen, K., and Naumann, F. (1986). *Kaisersaal. Porträts aus den Kapitolinischen Museen in Rome* (Cologne).

Eder, W. (1990). "Augustus and the Power of Tradition: The Augustan Principate as Binding Link between Republic and Empire," in Raaflaub and Toher (1990) 71–122.

Edwards, C. (1993). *The Politics of Immorality in Ancient Rome* (Cambridge).

Ehrhardt, C. (1986). "Two Quotations by Augustus Caesar," *LCM* 11.8.132–33.

Ehrhardt, W. (1987). *Stilgeschichtliche Untersuchungen an römischen Wandmalereien von der späten Republik bis zur Zeit Neros* (Mainz).

———. (1991). "Bild und Ausblick in der Wandmalerei 2. Stils," *AK* 34.28–65.

Ellul, J. (1973). *Propaganda: The Formation of Men's Attitudes* (New York).

Elton, G. R. (1967). *The Practice of History* (New York).

Erkell, H. (1952). *Augustus, Felicitas, Fortuna* (Goteborg).

Erler, M. (1992). "Der Zorn des Helden. Philodems 'De Ira' und Vergils Konzept des Zorns in der 'Aeneis,'" *GB* 18.103–26.

Étienne, R. (1958). *Le culte impérial dans la péninsule ibérique d'Auguste à Dioclétien* (Paris).

Evans, J. D. (1992). *The Art of Persuasion. Political Propaganda from Aeneas to Brutus* (Ann Arbor).

Fabbricotti, E. (1968). "Numa Pompilio e tre monetieri di età repubblicana," *AIIN* 15.31–78.

Fadinger, V. (1969). *Die Begründung des Prinzipats* (Berlin).

Farrell, J. (1991). *Vergil's Georgics and the Tradition of Ancient Epic* (New York).

Fears, R. (1981a). "The Cult of Jupiter and Roman Imperial Ideology," *ANRW* II.17.1.3–141.

———. (1981b). "The Theology of Victory in Rome: Approaches and Problems," *ANRW* II.17.2.736–826.

———. (1981c). "The Cult of Virtues and Roman Imperial Ideology," *ANRW* II.17.2.827–948.

Fedeli, P. (1985). *Properzio. Il libro terzo delle elegie* (Bari).

Feeney, D. (1983). "The Taciturnity of Aeneas," *CQ* 33.204–19; repr. in S. Harrison (1990) 267–90.

———. (1991). *The Gods in Epic* (Oxford).

———. (1992). "*Si licet et fas est:* Ovid's *Fasti* and the Problem of Free Speech under the Principate," in Powell (1992) 1–25.

Feeney, D. (1993). "Horace and the Greek Lyric Poets," in N. Rudd, ed., *Horace 2000: A Celebration* (Oxford) 41–63.

Fenik, B. (1960). *The Influence of Euripides on Vergil's Aeneid* (Diss. Princeton).

Ferguson, J. (1979). "Classical Civilization," in H. D. Casswell et al., eds., *Propaganda and Communication in World History* (Honolulu) 257–98.

Ferrerro, A. M. (1979). "Il concetto di *simplicitas* negli autori augustei," *Boll. di Studi Latini* 9.52–59.

Fishwick, D. (1969). "Genius and Numen," *HThR* 62.356–67.

———. (1970). "Numina Augustorum," *CQ* 64.191–97.

———. (1978). "The Development of Provincial Ruler Worship in the Western Roman Empire," *ANRW* II.16.2.1201–53.

———. (1982). "The Altar of Augustus and the Municipal Cult of Tarraco," *Madr. Mitt.* 23.222–33.

———. (1987 and 1992). *The Imperial Cult in the Latin West. Studies in the Ruler Cult of the Western Provinces of the Roman Empire*. Vols. 1 and 2 (Leiden).

Fittschen, K. (1976a). "Zur Panzerstatue in Cherchel," *JdI* 91.175–210.

———. (1976b). "Zur Herkunft und Entstehung des 2. Stils," in P. Zanker (1976) 539–57.

———. (1991). "Die Bildnisse des Augustus," in G. Binder 3 (1991) 149–86.

———. Fittschen, K. and Zanker, P. (1985) *Katalog der römischen Porträts in den Capitolinischen und den anderen Kommunalen Sammlungen der Stadt Rom* 1 (Mainz).

Flach, D. (1972). "Zum Quellenwert der Kaiserbiographien Suetons," *Gymn.* 99.273–89.

Flashar, H., ed. (1979). *Le classicisme à Rome aux Iers siècles avant et après J. C.* Entret. Fond. Hardt 25 (Geneva).

Förtsch, R. (1989). "Ein Aurea-aetas Schema," *RM* 96.333–45.

Foucault, M. (1976). *La volonté de savoir* (Paris).

Foulkes, A. (1983). *Literature and Propaganda* (London).

Fraenkel, E. (1957). *Horace* (Oxford).

Fraser, L. (1957). *Propaganda* (Oxford).

Frécaut, J.-M. (1972). *L'esprit et l'humour chez Ovide* (Grenoble).

Friedländer, L. (1922). *Darstellungen aus der Sittengeschichte Roms*, 10th ed. Vols. 1–4 (Leipzig).

Frisch, P. (1980). "Zu den Elogien des Augustusforums," *ZPE* 39.91–98.

Frischer, B. (1982–83). "*Monumenta et Ara Honoris Virtutisque Causa:* Evidence of Memorials for Roman Civic Heroes," *BCAR* 88.51–86.

———. (1991). *Shifting Paradigms. New Approaches to Horace's Ars Poetica* (Atlanta).

Fröhlich, T. (1991). *Lararien und Fassadenbilder in den Vesuvstädten. RM* Suppl. 32 (Mainz).

Froning, H. (1981). *Marmorschmuckreliefs mit griechischen Mythen im 1. Jahrhundert v. Chr.* (Mainz).

Fuchs, H. (1958). "Der Friede als Gefahr," *HSCP* 63.363–85.

Fuchs, W. (1963). *Der Schiffsfund von Mahdia* (Tübingen).

Fürst, F. (1934). *Die Bedeutung der auctoritas im privaten und öffentlichen Leben der römischen Republik* (Diss. Marburg).

Fuhrmann, M. (1983). "Fluch und Segen der Arbeit," *Gymn.* 90.240–57.

Fullerton, M. (1985). "The *Domus Augusti* in Imperial Iconography of 13–12 B.C.," *AJA* 89.473–83.

————. (1990). *The Archaistic Style in Roman Statuary* (Leiden).

Furtwängler, A. (1900). *Die Antiken Gemmen.* Vols. 1–3 (Leipzig).

Gabba, E. (1984). "The Historians and Augustus," in Millar and Segal (1984) 61–88.

————. (1991). *Dionysius of Halicarnassus and the History of Archaic Rome* (Berkeley).

Gagé, J. (1930). "Romulus—Augustus," *MEFR* 47.138–81.

————. (1936). "Actiaca," *MEFR* 53.37–100.

————. (1955). *Apollon romain* (Paris).

————. (1977). *Res Gestae Divi Augusti,* 3rd ed. (Paris).

Gaisser, J. (1977). "Tibullus 2.3 and Vergil's *Tenth Eclogue,*" *TAPA* 107.131–46.

————. (1983). "*Amor, rura,* and *militia* in Three Elegies of Tibullus: 1.1, 1.5, and 1.10," *Latomus* 42.58–72.

Galinsky, K. (1967a). "Sol and the *Carmen Saeculare,*" *Latomus* 26.619–33.

————. (1967b). "The Cipus Episode in Ovid's *Metamorphoses* (15.565–621)," *TAPA* 98.181–92.

————. (1969). *Aeneas, Sicily, and Rome* (Princeton).

————. (1972). *The Herakles Theme* (Oxford).

————. (1975). *Ovid's Metamorphoses* (Oxford and Berkeley).

————. (1981a). "Vergil's *Romanitas* and His Adaptation of Greek Heroes," *ANRW* II.31.2.985–1010.

————. (1981b). "Augustus' Legislation on Morals and Marrriage," *Philologus* 125.126–44.

————. (1983). "Some Aspects of Ovid's Golden Age," *GB* 10.193–205.

————. (1984). "Vergil and the Formation of the Augustan Ethos," *Atti del Convegno mondiale scientifico di studi su Virgilio* 1 (Milan) 240–54.

————. (1986). "Recent Trends in the Interpretation of the Augustan Age," *Aug. Age* 5.22–36.

————. (1988). "The Anger of Aeneas," *AJP* 109.321–48.

————. (1989). "Was Ovid a Silver Latin Poet?," *ICS* 14.69–89.

————. (1990). "Hercules in the *Aeneid,*" in S. J. Harrison (1990) 277–94.

————. (1992). "Aeneas at Rome and Lavinium," in R. Wilhelm and H. Jones, eds., *The Two Worlds of the Poet* (Detroit) 93–108.

————, ed. (1992a). *The Interpretation of Roman Poetry: Empiricism or Hermeneutics?* (Frankfurt and New York).

————. (1992b). *Classical and Modern Interactions* (Austin).

————. (1992c). "Venus, Polysemy, and the Ara Pacis Augustae," *AJA* 96.457–75.

————. (1994). "How to be Philosophical about the End of the *Aeneid,*" *Studies in Honor of M. Marcovich. ICS* 19.191–201.

Galsterer, H. (1990). "A Man, a Book, and a Method: Sir Ronald Syme's *Roman Revolution* after Fifty Years," in Raaflaub and Toher (1990) 1–20.

Gamel, M. K. (1984). "Baucis and Philemon: Paradigm or Paradox?," *Helios* 11.117–31.

Ganzert, J. (1985). "Der Mars Ultor Tempel auf dem Augustusforum in Rom," *RM* 92.201–19.

————. (1990). "Der Mars Ultor Tempel. Fusion von Orient und Okzident," *Acts of the 13th Int. Congress of Class. Archaeology* (Berne) 538–41.

Gardthausen, V. (1891–1906). *Augustus und seine Zeit.* Vols. 1 and 2 (Leipzig).

Gatz, B. (1967). *Weltalter, goldene Zeit und sinnverwandte Vorstellungen* (Hildesheim).

Geertz, C. (1973). *The Interpretation of Cultures* (New York).

Gelsomino, R. (1958). "I grecismi di Augusto," *Maia* 10.148–56.

Gelzer, T. (1979). "Klassizismus, Attizismus und Asianismus," in Flashar (1979) 1–41.

Genette, G. (1980). *Narrative Discourse* (Ithaca).

————. (1988). *Narrative Discourse Revisited* (Ithaca).

Gigante, M., and Capasso, M. (1989). "Il ritorno di Virgilio a Ercolano," *SIFC* 3rd ser. 7.3–6.

Giovannini, A. (1985). "Auctoritas patrum," *MH* 42.28–36.

Girardet, K. (1990). "Der Rechtsstatus Oktavians im Jahre 32 v. Chr.," *RhM* 133.322–50.

Giuliani, L. (1986). *Bildnis und Botschaft* (Frankfurt).

Glatt, M. (1991). *Die 'andere Welt' der römischen Elegiker* (Frankfurt and New York).

Görler, W. (1979). "'Ex verbis communibus *kakozelia*.' Die augusteischen 'Klassiker' und die griechischen Theoretiker des Klassizismus," in Flashar (1979) 175–202.

Gold, B. K., ed. (1982). *Literary and Artistic Patronage in Ancient Rome* (Austin).

Goldberg. S. (1995). *Epic in Republican Rome* (New York and Oxford).

González, J. (1984). "Tabula Siarensis, Fortunales Siarenses et Municipia Civium Romanorum," *ZPE* 55.55–100.

Goodyear, F.R.D., ed. (1972). *The Annals of Tacitus. Books 1–6*. Vol. 1 (Cambridge).

Gordon, A. E. (1952). *Quinctus Veranius Consul A.D. 49*. Univ. Cal. Public. in Class. Archaeology 2.5 (Berkeley).

Gosling, A. (1986). "Octavian, Brutus, and Apollo: A Note on Opportunist Propaganda," *AJP* 107.586–89.

Gowing, A. (1992). *The Triumviral Narratives of Appian and Cassius Dio* (Ann Arbor).

Graff, G. (1987). *Professing Literature. An Institutional History* (Chicago).

Grant, M. (1946). *From Imperium to Auctoritas* (Cambridge).

————. (1950). *Roman Anniversary Issues* (Cambridge).

————. (1954). *Roman Imperial Money* (New York).

Grassinger, D. (1991). *Römische Marmorkratere* (Mainz).

Graves, R. (1962). "The Virgil Cult," *Virg. Quart. Rev.* 38.13–35.

Green, P. (1982). *Ovid. The Erotic Poems* (Harmondsworth).

Griffin, A.H.F. (1991). "Philemon and Baucis in *Ovid's Metamorphoses*," *G&R* 38.62–74.

Griffin, J. (1984). "Augustus and the Poets: 'Caesar qui cogere posset,'" in Millar and Segal (1984) 189–218.

————. (1985). *Latin Poets and Roman Life* (London).

————. (1986) *Virgil* (Oxford).

Grimm, G. (1989). "Die Porträts der Triumvirn C. Octavius, M. Antonius und M. Aemilius Lepidus. Überlegungen zur Entstehung und Abfolge der Bildnisse des Kaisers Augustus," *RM* 96.347–64.

Grimm, R. (1967). "Aeneas and Andromache in *Aeneid* III," *AJP* 88.151–62.

Gros, P. (1976). *Aurea Templa. Recherches sur l'architecture religieuse de Rome à l'époque d'Auguste* (Rome).

Gross, W. H. (1959). "Zur Augustusstatue von Prima Porta," *Nachr. Akad. Göttingen* 8.143–68.

————. (1985). "Ways and Roundabout Ways in the Propaganda of an Unpopular Ideology," in Winkes (1985) 29–50.

Gruen, E. (1974). *The Last Generation of the Roman Republic* (Berkeley).

————. (1984). *The Hellenistic World and the Coming of Rome* (Berkeley).

_____. (1985). "Augustus and the Ideology of War and Peace," in Winkes (1985) 51–72.

_____. (1990a). *Studies in Greek Culture and Roman Policy* (Leiden).

_____. (1990b). "The Imperial Policy of Augustus," in Raaflaub and Toher (1990) 395–416.

_____. (1992). *Culture and National Identity in Republican Rome* (Ithaca).

Guillemin, A. (1958). "Ovide et la vie paysanne (*Mét.*, 8, 626–724)," in N. I. Herescu, ed., *Ovidiana. Recherches sur Ovide* (Paris) 317–23.

Gurval, R. (1995). *Actium and Augustus. The Politics and Emotions of Civil War* (Ann Arbor).

Habicht, C. (1973). "Die augusteische Zeit," in W. den Boer, ed., *Le culte des souverains dans l'empire romain*. Entr. Fond. Hardt 19 (Geneva) 41–88.

_____. (1990). *Cicero the Politician* (Baltimore).

Hänlein-Schäfer, H. (1985). *Veneratio Augusti. Eine Studie zu den Tempeln der ersten römischen Kaiser* (Rome).

Hafner, G. (1954). *Späthellenistische Bildnisplastik* (Berlin).

_____. (1990). "'Cessavit inde ars,'" *RdA* 14.29–34.

Hall, C. M. (1923). *Nicolaus of Damascus' Life of Augustus* (Northampton).

Hallett, J. (1985). "Queens, *Princeps* and Women of the Augustan Elite: Propertius' Cornelia-elegy and the *Res Gestae Divi Augusti*," in Winkes (1985) 73–88.

Halperin, D. (1983). *Before Pastoral. Theocritus and the Tradition of Ancient Bucolic Poetry* (New Haven).

Hammond, M. (1940). "Hellenistic Influences on the Structure of the Augustan Principate," *MAAR* 17.1–25.

Hanell, K. (1960). "Das Opfer des Augustus an der Ara Pacis," *OpRom* 2.31–123.

Hannestad, N. (1986). *Roman Art and Imperial Policy* (Aarhus).

Hano, M. (1986). "A l'origine du culte impérial: les autels des Lares Augusti," *ANRW* II.16.3.2333–81.

Hardie, P. (1986). *Virgil's Aeneid: Cosmos and Imperium* (Oxford).

_____. (1991). "The *Aeneid* and the *Oresteia*," *PVS* 20.29–45.

Harris, W. V. (1979). *War and Imperialism in Republican Rome, 327–70 B.C.* (Oxford).

Harrison, E. B. (1965). *Archaic and Archaistic Sculpture*. The Athenian Agora. Vol. 11 (Princeton).

Harrison, S. J., ed. (1990). *Oxford Readings in Vergil's Aeneid* (Oxford).

_____. (1991). *Vergil. Aeneid 10* (Oxford).

Hausmann, U. (1981). "Zur Typologie und Ideologie des Augustusporträts," *ANRW* II.12.2.513–98.

Heilmeyer, W.-D. (1970). *Korinthische Normalkapitelle. RM* Suppl. 17 (Heidelberg).

Heinze, R. (1915). *Virgils epische Technik*, 3rd ed. (Leipzig and Berlin), repr. Stuttgart (1965). Engl. trans. by H. Harvey et al. (Berkeley 1993).

_____. (1925). "Auctoritas," *Hermes* 60.348–66; here cited by its reprint in *Vom Geist des Römertums*, 3rd ed. (Stuttgart 1960) 43–58.

_____. (1929). "Fides," *Hermes* 64.140–66; repr. in *Vom Geist des Römertums* (1960) 59–81.

_____. (1930). *Die Augusteische Kultur* (Leipzig), repr. Darmstadt (1960).

Helbig, W. (1963–72). *Führer durch die öffentlichen Sammlungen klassischer Altertümer in Rom*, 4th ed., ed. H. Speier. Vols 1–4 (Tübingen).

Hellegouarc'h, J. (1972). *Le vocabulaire latin des relations et des partis politiques sous la République*, 2nd ed. (Paris).

Helmbold, W. C. (1958). "*Eclogue* 4 and *Epode* 16," *CP* 53.178.

Henzen, W. (1874). *Acta Fratrum Arvalium* (Berlin).

Herbert-Brown, G. (1994). *Ovid and the Fasti: A Historical Study* (Oxford).

Herz, P. (1978). "Kaiserfeste der Prinzipatszeit," *ANRW* II.16.2.1135–1200.

Hesberg, H. von (1978). "Archäologische Denkmäler zum römischen Kaiserkult," *ANRW* II.16.2.911–55.

Hesberg, H., and Panciera, S. (1994). *Das Mausoleum des Augustus. ABAW*, phil.-hist. Kl., n. f. 108 (Munich).

Himmelmann, N. (1981). "Realistic Art in Alexandria," *PBA* 57.193–207.

Hinds, S. (1989). Review of Knox (1986), *CP* 84.267–71.

Hölscher, T. (1967). *Victoria Romana* (Mainz).

———. (1980). "Die Geschichtsauffassung in der römischen Repräsentationskunst," *JdI* 95.265–321.

———. (1982). "Die Bedeutung der Münzen zum Verständnis der Repräsentationskunst der römischen Republik," *Proceedings of the 9th Int. Congress of Numismatics* (Louvain).

———. (1984a). *Staatsdenkmal und Publikum* (Konstanz).

———. (1984b). "Actium und Salamis," *JdI* 99.187–214.

———. (1985). "Denkmäler zur Schlacht von Actium. Propaganda und Resonanz," *Klio* 67.81–102.

———. (1987). *Römische Bildsprache als semantisches System* (Heidelberg).

———. (1989). "Griechische Bilder für den römischen Senat," in H.-U. Cain et al., eds., *Festschrift für Nikolaus Himmelmann* (Mainz) 327–33.

———. (1990). "Römische Nobiles und hellenistische Herrscher," *Acts of the 13th Int. Congress of Class. Archaeology* (Berne) 73–84.

———. (1993). "Mythen als Exempel der Geschichte," in F. Graf, ed., *Mythos in mythenloser Gesellschaft. Das Paradigma Roms* (Stuttgart and Leipzig) 67–87.

Hoff, M. (1989). "Civil Disobedience and Unrest in Augustan Athens," *Hesperia* 58.267–76.

Hollis, A. (1970). *Ovid. Metamorphoses, Book VIII* (Oxford).

Hollstein, W. (1991). *Die stadtrömische Münzprägung der Jahre 78–50 v. Chr. zwischen politischer Aktualität und Familienthematik* (Diss. Marburg).

Holtzman, B., and Salviat, F. (1981). "Les portraits sculptés de Marc-Antoine," *BCH* 105.265–88.

Hommel, P. (1954). *Studien zu den römischen Figurengiebeln der Kaiserzeit* (Berlin).

Horsfall, N. (1981). "Vergil and the Conquest of Chaos," *Antichthon* 15.141–50; repr. in S. J. Harrison (1990) 466–77.

———. (1990). "Dido in the Light of History," in S. J. Harrison (1990) 127–44.

Hubbard, M. (1973). "The Odes," in C.D.N. Costa, ed., *Horace* (London) 1–28.

———. (1974). *Propertius* (New York).

Iacopi, I., and Tedone, G. (1990). "Lo 'studiolo' di Augusto," *Bull. Archeol.* 1.1–2. 143–48.

Instinsky, H. U. (1962). *Die Siegel des Kaisers Augustus* (Baden-Baden).

Jal, P. (1957). "Images d'Auguste chez Sénèque," *REL* 35.242–64.

———. (1961). "Pax civilis—Concordia," *REL* 39.210–31.

Jameson, V. (1984). "Virtus Re-formed: An 'Aesthetic Response' Reading of Horace, Odes III 2," *TAPA* 114.219–40.

Jauss, H. R. (1981). "Zur Abgrenzung und Bestimmung einer literarischen Hermeneutik," in M. Fuhrmann et al., eds., *Text und Applikation* (Munich) 459–81.

Jens, W. (1956). "Libertas bei Tacitus," *Hermes* 84.331–52.

Johansen, F. J. (1971). "Ritratti marmorei e bronzi di Marco Vipsanio Agrippa," *Anal Rom* 6.17–48.

———. (1987). "The Portraits in Marble of Gaius Julius Caesar. A Review," *Ancient Portraits in the J. Paul Getty Museum* 1 (Malibu) 17–40.

Johnston, P. A. (1977). "Vergil's Conception of Saturnus," *CSCA* 10.57–70.

———. (1980). *Vergil's Agricultural Golden Age: A Study of the Georgics* (Leiden).

Jucker, H. (1950). *Vom Verhältnis der Römer zur bildenden Kunst der Griechen* (Frankfurt).

———. (1982). "Apollo Palatinus und Apollo Actius auf augusteischen Münzen," *MH* 39.82–100.

Kähler, H. (1959). *Die Augustus Statue von Prima Porta* (Cologne).

———. (1960). *Rom und seine Welt* (Baden-Baden); Engl. transl. *Rome and Her Empire* (London 1963).

———. (1991). "Die Gemma Augustea," in G. Binder 3 (1991) 303–307, repr. from (1960) 186–88.

Kellum, B. (1985). "Sculptural Programs and Propaganda in Augustan Rome: The Temple of Apollo on the Palatine," in Winkes (1985) 169–76.

———. (1990). "The City Adorned: Programmatic Display at the Aedes Concordiae Augustae," in Raaflaub and Toher (1990) 276–307.

———. (1994). "What We See and Don't See: Narrative Structures and the Ara Pacis Augustae," *Art History* 17.26–45.

Kennedy, D. (1984). Review of Woodman and West (1984) in *LCM* 9.10.158–60.

———. (1992). "'Augustan' and 'Anti-Augustan': Reflections on Terms of Reference," in Powell (1992) 26–58.

Keuls, E. (1974). *The Water Carriers in Hades* (Amsterdam).

Kienast, D. (1969). "Augustus und Alexander," *Gymn.* 76.430–56.

———. (1988). Review of Simon (1986) in *HZ* 247.137–39.

———. (1989). Review of Ramage (1987) in *AJP* 110.177–80.

Kiessling, A., and Heinze, R., eds. (1961). *Q. Horatius Flaccus: Satiren*, 8th ed. (Zurich and Berlin).

———. (1961). *Q. Horatius Flaccus: Briefe*, 7th ed. (Zurich and Berlin).

———. (1964). *Q. Horatius Flaccus: Oden und Epoden*, 11th ed. (Zurich and Berlin).

Kilpatrick, R. (1986). *The Poetry of Friendship: Horace's Epistles Book 1* (Edmonton).

Kirk, G. S. (1970). *Myth. Its Meaning and Function in Ancient and Other Cultures* (Berkeley).

Klein, R., ed. (1969). *Prinzipat und Freiheit* (Darmstadt).

Kleiner, D.E.E. (1978). "The Great Friezes of the Ara Pacis Augustae: Greek Sources, Roman Derivatives, and Augustan Social Policy," *MEFR* 90.753–85.

———. (1985). "Private Portraiture in the Age of Augustus," in Winkes (1985) 107–36.

———. (1992). *Roman Sculpture* (New Haven).

Kleiner, F. S. (1988). "The Arch in Honor of C. Octavius and the Fathers of Augustus," *Historia* 37.347–57.

Klingner, F. (1928). "Über die Einleitung der Historien Sallusts," *Hermes* 63.165–93.

———. (1961). *Römische Geisteswelt*, 4th ed. (Munich).

Klingner, F. (1967). *Virgil. Bucolica, Georgica, Aeneis* (Zurich).

Kloesel, H. (1935). *Libertas* (Diss. Breslau).

Kloft, H., ed. (1979). *Ideologie und Herrschaft in der Antike* (Darmstadt).

Knauer, G. N. (1964). *Die Aeneis und Homer* (Göttingen).

Kneissl, P. (1980). "Entstehung und Bedeutung der Augustalität: zur Inschrift der ara Narbonensis (CIL XII 4333)," *Chiron* 10.291–326.

Knell, H. (1990). *Mythos und Polis. Bildprogramme Griechischer Bauskulptur* (Darmstadt).

Knox, P. E. (1986). *Ovid's "Metamorphoses" and the Tradition of Augustan Poetry* (Cambridge).

Koch, C. (1952). "Roma aeterna," *Gymn.* 59.128–43, 196–209.

Kockel, V. (1983). "Beobachtungen zum Tempel des Mars Ultor und zum Forum des Augustus," *RM* 90.421–55.

König, A. (1970). *Die Aeneis und die griechische Tragödie* (Diss. Berlin).

Koeppel, G. (1982). "The Grand Pictorial Tradition in Roman Historical Representation during the Early Empire," *ANRW* II.12.507–35.

———. (1985). "The Role of Pictorial Models in the Creation of the Historical Relief during the Age of Augustus," in Winkes (1985) 89–106.

———. (1987 and 1988). "Die historischen Reliefs der römischen Kaiserzeit: Ara Pacis Augustae," *BonnJbb* 187.101–57, 188.97–106.

Kolbe, H. G. (1966–67). "Noch einmal Vesta auf dem Palatin," *RM* 73/74.94–104.

Korpanty, J. (1991). "Römische Ideale und Werte im augusteischen Prinzipat," *Klio* 73.432–47.

Korzeniewski, D. (1972). "Exegi monumentum. Hor. carm. III, 30 und die Topik der Grabgedichte," *Gymn.* 79.380–88.

———. (1974). "Sume superbiam. Eine Bemerkung zu Hor. carm. III, 30," *Gymn.* 81.200–209.

Koster, S. (1983). *Tessera. Sechs Beiträge zur Poesie und poetischen Theorie der Antike* (Erlangen).

Kraay, C. M. (1966). *Greek Coins* (New York).

Kränzle, P. (1991). *Die zeitliche und ikonographische Stellung des Frieses der Basilica Aemilia* (Hamburg).

Kraft, K. (1962). "S(enatus) C(onsulto)," *JNG* 12.7–49; repr. in Schmitthenner (1969) 336–403.

———. (1969). *Zur Münzprägung des Augustus*. Sitzungsber. Frankfurt 1968, vol. 7.5 (Wiesbaden).

Kraggerud, E. (1968). *Aeneisstudien* (Oslo).

Kraus, T. (1953). *Die Ranken der Ara Pacis* (Berlin).

Kroll, W. (1924). *Studien zum Verständnis der römischen Literatur* (Stuttgart).

Kunckel, H. (1974). *Der römische Genius. RM* Suppl. 22 (Heidelberg).

Kunkel, W. (1962). *Untersuchungen zur Entwicklung des römischen Kriminalverfahrens in vorsullanischer Zeit* (Munich).

———. (1969). "Zum Freiheitsbegriff der späten Republik und des Prinzipats," in Klein (1969) 68–93.

Kuttner, A. (1995). *Dynasty and Empire in the Age of Augustus: The Case of the Boscoreale Cups* (Berkeley).

Kyrieleis, H. (1976). "Bemerkungen zur Vorgeschichte der Kaiserfora," in P. Zanker (1976) 431–38.

Lacey, W. K. (1974). "Octavian in the Senate, January 27 B.C.," *JRS* 64.176–84.

Laffi, U. (1967). "Le iscrizioni relative all'introduzione nel 9 A.C. del nuovo calendario della provincia d'Asia," *SCO* 16.5–98.

Lahusen, G. (1983). *Untersuchungen zur römischen Ehrenstatue in Rom* (Rome).

———. (1984). *Schriftstellen zum römischen Bildnis* I (Bremen).

———. (1989). *Die Bildnismünzen der römischen Republik* (Munich).

La Penna, A. (1963). *Orazio e l'ideologia del principato* (Turin).

———. (1977). *L'integrazione difficile. Un profilo di Properzio* (Turin).

La Rocca, E. (1977). "Note sulle importazioni greche in territorio laziale nell' VIII secolo a. C.," *PP* 32.375–97.

———. (1983). *Ara Pacis Augustae* (Rome).

———. (1984). "Fabio o Fannio," *DialArch* n.s. 3.2.31–53.

———. (1985). *Amazzonomachia. Le sculture frontali del Tempio di Apollo Sosiano* (Rome).

———. (1987). "L'adesione senatoriale al 'consensus': i modi della propaganda augustea e tiberiana nei monumenti 'in Circo Flaminio,'" *CEFR* 98.347–72.

Latte, K. (1935). "Eine Ode des Horaz (II, 16)," *Philologus* 79.294–304.

———. (1960). *Römische Religionsgeschichte* (Munich).

Leach, E. W. (1964). "Georgic Imagery in the *Ars amatoria*," *TAPA* 95.142–54.

———. (1982). "Patrons, Painters, and Patterns: The Anonymity of Romano-Campanian Painting and the Transition from the Second to the Third Style," in Gold (1982) 135–73.

———. (1988). *The Rhetoric of Space* (Princeton).

Lebek, W. D. (1993). "Roms Ritter und Roms Pleps in den Senatsbeschlüssen für Germanicus Caesar und Drusus Caesar," *ZPE* 95.81–120.

Lee, A. G. (1974). "Otium cum indignitate: Tibullus 1.1," in Woodman and West (1974) 94–114.

Lefèvre, E. (1981). "Horaz und Maecenas," *ANRW* II.31.3.1987–2029.

———. (1988). "Die unaugusteischen Züge der augusteischen Literatur," in G. Binder I (1987) 173–96.

———. (1989). *Das Bildprogramm des Apollo-Tempels auf dem Palatin* (Konstanz).

———. (1993). *Horaz. Dichter im augusteischen Rom* (Munich).

Lehmann, P. (1953). *Roman Wall Paintings from Boscoreale in the Metropolitan Museum of Art* (Cambridge, Mass.).

———. (1979). "Lefkadia and the Second Style," in G. Kopcke and M. B. Moore, eds., *Studies in Classical Art and Archeology. A Tribute to Peter Heinrich von Blanckenhagen* (Locust Valley, N.Y.) 225–29.

Lehmann-Hartleben, K. (1927). "Ein Altar in Bologna," *RM* 42.162–76.

Lepore, E. (1954). *Il princeps ciceroniano e gli ideali della tarda repubblica* (Naples).

Levi, M. A. (1933). *Ottaviano capoparte*. Vols. 1 and 2 (Florence).

Levick, B. (1982). "Propaganda and Imperial Coinage," *Antichthon* 16.104–16.

Liebeschuetz, J. (1979). *Continuity and Change in Roman Religion* (Oxford).

Liegle, J. (1932). "Pietas," *ZfN* 42.59–100; repr. in Oppermann (1967) 229–73.

———. (1941). "Die Münzprägung Octavians nach dem Siege bei Aktium und die augusteische Kunst," *JdI* 56.91–119.

Ling, R. (1977). "Studius and the Beginnings of Roman Landscape Painting," *JRS* 67.1–16.

Ling, R. (1991). *Roman Painting* (Cambridge).

Luce, T. J. (1965). "The Dating of Livy's First Decade," *TAPA* 96.209–40.

———. (1977). *Livy. The Composition of his History* (Princeton).

———. (1990). "Livy, Augustus, and the Forum Augustum," in Raaflaub and Toher (1990) 123–38.

Luck, G. (1974). "The Woman's Role in Latin Love Poetry," in K. Galinsky, ed., *Perspectives of Roman Poetry* (Austin) 15–31.

Ludwig, W. (1965). *Struktur und Einheit der Metamorphosen Ovids* (Berlin).

Lugli, G. (1960 and 1965). *Fontes ad topographiam veteris urbis Romae pertinentes*. Vols. 8, book 19, and 6.1, book 16 (Rome).

Lummel, P. (1991). *"Zielgruppen" römischer Staatskunst. Die Münzen der Kaiser Augustus bis Trajan und die trajanischen Staatsreliefs* (Munich).

Lyne, R. O. (1980). *The Latin Love Poets. From Catullus to Horace* (Oxford).

———. (1987). *Further Voices in Vergil's Aeneid* (Oxford).

———. (1994). "Vergil's *Aeneid*: Subversion by Intertextuality," *G&R* 41.187–204.

MacCormack, S. (1981). *Art and Ceremony in Late Antiquity* (Berkeley).

Mackie, C. J. (1988). *The Characterisation of Aeneas* (Edinburgh).

Macleod, C. W. (1977). "Propertius 4.1," in F. Cairns, ed., *PLLS* 1976. 141–53; repr. in *Collected Papers*, ed. J. Bramble (Oxford 1983) 202–14.

Maderna, C. (1988). *Iuppiter, Diomedes und Merkur als Vorbilder für römische Bildnisstatuen* (Heidelberg).

Magdelain, A. (1947). *Auctoritas Principis* (Paris).

Maggi, S. (1990). "Augusto e la politica delle immagini: lo *Hüftmanteltypus*," *RdA* 14.63–73.

Malcovati, E. (1955). *Oratorum Romanorum Fragmenta*, 2nd ed. (Turin).

———. (1969). *Caesaris Augusti Operum Fragmenta*, 5th ed. (Turin).

Mann, J. C. (1991). "Numinibus Augustis," *Britannica* 22.173–77.

Mannsperger, D. (1973). "Apollon gegen Dionysus. Numismatische Beiträge zu Octavians Rolle als Vindex Libertatis," *Gymn.* 80.381–404.

———. (1974). "ROM. ET AUG. Die Selbstdarstellung des Kaisertums in der römischen Münzprägung," *ANRW* II.1.919–96.

———. (1982). "Annos undeviginti natus. Das Münzsymbol für Octavians Eintritt in die Politik," in B. Freytag, ed., *Praestant interna. Festschrift für Ulrich Hausmann* (Tübingen) 331–37.

———. (1991). "Die Münzprägung des Augustus," in G. Binder 3 (1991) 348–99.

Manuwald, B. (1979). *Cassius Dio und Augustus* (Wiesbaden).

Martin, H. G. (1987). *Römische Tempelkultbilder* (Rome).

Martin, L. J. (1958). *International Propaganda. Its Legal and Diplomatic Control* (Minneapolis).

Massner, A. K. (1982). *Bildnisangleichung. Untersuchungen zur Entstehungs- und Wirkungsgeschichte des Augustusporträts* (Berlin).

Mattingly, H. (1934). "Virgil's Golden Age: Sixth *Aeneid* and Fourth *Eclogue*," *CR* 48.161–65.

———. (1947). "Virgil's Fourth *Eclogue*," *JWI* 10.14–19.

Matz, F. (1952). *Der Gott auf dem Elephantenwagen* (Wiesbaden 1952).

Mau, A. (1882). *Geschichte der dekorativen Wandmalerei in Pompeji* (Berlin).

Mayer, R. (1986). "Horace's *Epistles* I and Philosophy," *AJP* 107.55–73.

Mazza, M. (1966). *Storia e ideologia in Tito Livio* (Catania).

McAllister, M. H. (1959). "The Temple of Ares at Athens," *Hesperia* 28.1–64.

McDermott, E. (1981). "Greek and Latin Elements in Horace's Lyric Program," *ANRW* II.31.3.1640–72.

Megow, W.-R. (1987). *Kameen von Augustus bis Alexander Severus* (Berlin).

Meier, C. (1980a). *Res publica amissa*, 2nd ed. (Frankfurt).

———. (1980b). *Die Ohnmacht des allmächtigen Diktators Caesar* (Frankfurt).

———. (1990). "C. Caesar Divi filius and the Formation of the Alternative in Rome," in Raaflaub and Toher (1990) 54–70.

Mellor, R. (1975). *ΘΕΑ ΡΩΜΗ. The Worship of the Goddess Roma in the Greek World* (Göttingen).

Menichetti, M. (1986). "La testa colossale della Pigna, il Colossus Divi Augusti e 'l'imitatio Alexandri' in età giulio-claudia," *MEFR* 98.565–93.

Mette-Dittmann, A. (1991). *Die Ehegesetze des Augustus* (Stuttgart).

Meyer, H. (1991–92). "Rome, Pergamum und Antiochus III. Zu den Siegesreliefs von Sant' Omobono," *BCAR* 94.17–32.

Meyer, H. D. (1961). *Die Aussenpolitik des Augustus und die augusteische Dichtung* (Cologne).

Michel, D. (1967). *Alexander als Vorbild für Pompeius, Caesar und Marcus Antonius* (Brussels).

Michels, A. K. (1955). "Death and Two Poets," *TAPA* 86.160–79.

Mielsch, H. (1981). "Funde und Forschungen zur Wandmalerei der Prinzipatszeit von 1945 bis 1975, mit einem Nachtrag 1980," *ANRW* II.12.2.157–264.

Mierse, W. (1990). "Augustan Building Programs in the Provinces," in Raaflaub und Toher (1990) 308–33.

Millar, F. (1973). "Triumvirate and Principate," *JRS* 63.50–67.

———. (1977). *The Emperor in the Roman World* (London).

———. (1981). "Style Abides," *JRS* 71.144–52.

———. (1993). "Ovid and the *Domus Augusta*: Rome Seen from Tomoi," *JRS* 83.1–17.

Millar, F., and Segal, E., eds. (1984). *Caesar Augustus. Seven Aspects* (Oxford).

Miller, J. F. (1982). "Callimachus and the Augustan Aetiological Elegy," *ANRW* II.30.1.371–417.

Minogue, K. (1985). *Alien Powers: The Pure Theory of Ideology* (New York).

Momigliano, A. (1940). Review of Syme, *The Roman Revolution, JRS* 30.75–80.

———. (1942a). Review of Robinson (1940), *JRS* 32.120–24.

———. (1942b). "The Peace of the Ara Pacis," *JWI* 5.228–31.

———. (1966). "Introduzione a Ronald Syme, *The Roman Revolution*," *Terzo Contributo alla storia degli studi classici e del mondo antico* (Rome) 729–37.

———. (1975). *Alien Wisdom: The Limits of Hellenization* (Cambridge).

———. (1984). "The Theological Efforts of the Roman Upper Classes in the First Century B.C.," *CP* 79.199–211.

Monti, R. (1981). *The Dido Episode and the Aeneid* (Leiden).

Moore, T. J. (1989). *Artistry and Ideology: Livy's Vocabulary of Virtue* (Frankfurt).

Moretti, G. (1948). *Ara Pacis Augustae* (Rome).

Moretti, L. (1982–84). "Frammenti vecchi e nuovi del commentario dei Ludi Secolari del 17 A.C.," *RPAA* 55–56.361–79.

Morris, C. W. (1971). *Writings on the General Theory of Signs* (The Hague).

Moss, C. F. (1989). *Roman Marble Tables* (UMI, Ann Arbor).

Most, G. (1989). "Zur Archäologie der Archaik," *A&A* 35.1–23.

Murray, O. (1965). "Philodemus and the Good King according to Homer," *JRS* 55.161–82.

Murray, W., and Petsas, P. (1989). *Octavian's Campsite Memorial for the Actian War.* Transact. Amer. Philosoph. Soc. 79.4 (Philadelphia).

Nauta, R. (1990). "Gattungsgeschichte als Rezeptionsgeschichte am Beispiel der Bukolik," *A&A* 36.116–37.

Nethercut, W. (1971). "The *sphragis* of the *Monobiblos,*" *AJP* 92.464–72.

———. (1983). "Recent Scholarship on Propertius," *ANRW* II.30.3.1813–57.

Neudecker, R. (1988). *Die Skulpturenausstattung römischer Villen in Italien* (Mainz).

Neuhauser, W. (1972). "*Ambiguitas* als Wesenszug der lateinischen Sprache," *Innsbrucker Beiträge zur Kulturwissenschaft* 17.237–58.

Neumeister, C. (1986). *Tibull. Einführung in sein Leben und Werk* (Heidelberg).

Newbie, J. (1938). *A Numismatic Commentary on the Res Gestae of Augustus* (Iowa City).

Newell, E. T. (1927). *The Coinages of Demetrius Poliorcetes* (London).

Nicolet, C. (1984). "Augustus, Government, and the Propertied Classes," in Millar and Segal (1984) 89–128.

———. (1991). *Space, Geography, and Politics in the Early Roman Empire* (Ann Arbor).

Niebling, G. (1956). "Laribus Augustis Magistri Primi," *Historia* 5.303–31.

Nisbet, R. (1978). "Virgil's Fourth Eclogue: Easterners and Westerners," *BICS* 25.59–78.

Nisbet, R., and Hubbard, M., eds. (1970 and 1978). *A Commentary on Horace: Odes, Book I and Book II* (Oxford).

Nörr, D. (1989). *Aspekte des römischen Völkerrechts. Die Bronzetafel von Alcántara. ABAW,* phil.-hist. Kl., n. f. 101 (Munich).

North, J. (1976). "Conservatism and Change in Roman Religion," *PBSR* 44.1–12.

Ober, J. (1982). "Tiberius and the Political Testament of Augustus," *Historia* 31.306–28.

Ogilvie, R. M. (1965). *A Commentary on Livy Books 1–5* (Oxford).

———. (1969). *The Romans and their Gods in the Age of Augustus* (London).

Oppermann, H., ed. (1967). *Römische Wertbegriffe* (Darmstadt).

Ortega y Gasset, J. (1932). *The Revolt of the Masses* (New York).

Ortmann, U. (1988). *Cicero, Brutus und Octavian—Republikaner und Cäsarianer. Ihr gegenseitiges Verhältnis im Krisenjahr 44/43 B.C.* (Bonn).

Ostrow, S. E. (1985). "*Augustales* along the Bay of Naples: A Case for Their Early Growth," *Historia* 34.64–101.

———. (1990). "The *Augustales* in the Augustan Scheme," in Raaflaub and Toher (1990) 364–79.

Otis, B. (1938). "Ovid and the Augustans," *TAPA* 69.188–229.

———. (1963). *Virgil. A Study in Civilized Poetry* (Oxford).

———. (1970). *Ovid as an Epic Poet,* 2nd ed. (Cambridge).

Paladino, I. (1988). *Fratres Arvales. Storia di un collegio sacerdotale romano* (Rome).

Pallottino, M. (1938). "L'Ara Pacis e i suoi problemi artistici," *BdA* 32.162–78.

Papanghelis, T. (1987). *Propertius: A Hellenistic Poet on Love and Death* (Cambridge).

Pape, M. (1975). *Griechische Kunstwerke aus Kriegsbeute und ihre Aufstellung in Rom* (Hamburg).

Parke, H. W., and Boardman, J. (1957). "The Struggle for the Tripod and the First Sacred War," *JHS* 77.276–82.

Parry, A. (1963). "The Two Voices of Virgil's *Aeneid*," *Arion* 2.66–80; repr. in S. Commager, ed., *Virgil: A Collection of Critical Essays* (Englewood Cliffs, N.J., 1966) 107–23.

Parsi-Magdelain, B. (1964). "La cura legum et morum," *RHD* 42.373–412.

Patterson, A. (1987). *Pastoral and Ideology: From Vergil to Valéry* (Berkeley).

Pease, A. S. (1935). *P. Vergili Maronis Aeneidos Liber Quartus* (Cambridge, Mass.).

Pekáry, T. (1985). *Das römische Kaiserbildnis in Staat, Kult und Gesellschaft* (Berlin).

Pensabene, P. (1984). *Tempio di Saturno* (Rome).

―――. (1988). "Scavi nell'area del Tempio della Vittoria e del santuario della Magna Mater sul Palatino," *Archeol. Laziale* 9 (=QArchEtr 16) 54–67.

Peters, T., and Waterman, R. (1982). *In Search of Excellence* (New York).

Pfanner, M. (1989). "Über das Herstellen von Porträts. Ein Beitrag zu Rationalisierungsmaßnahmen und Produktionsmechanismen von Massenware im späten Hellenismus und in der römischen Kaiserzeit," *JdI* 104.157–257.

Pfeiffer, R. (1968). *A History of Classical Scholarship* (Oxford).

Pighi, I. B. (1965). *De ludis saecularibus populi Romani Quiritium*, 2nd ed. (Amsterdam).

Pillinger, H. (1969). "Some Callimachean Influences on Propertius," *HSCP* 73.171–99.

Pöschl, V. (1956a). "Die Curastrophe in der Otiumode des Horaz (c. 2, 16, 21–24)," *Hermes* 84.74–90, repr. in Pöschl (1991) 118–42.

―――. (1956b). "Die römische Auffassung der Geschichte," *Gymn.* 63.190–206.

―――. (1961). *Die große Maecenasode des Horaz (c. 3,29)*. Sitzungsber. Heidelberg, phil.-hist. Kl. no. 1; repr. in Pöschl (1991) 198–245.

―――. (1977). *Die Dichtkunst Virgils*, 3rd ed. (Berlin and New York).

―――. (1981). "Virgil und Augustus," *ANRW* II.31.2.710–27.

―――. (1991). *Horazische Lyrik*, 2nd ed. (Heidelberg).

Pollini, J. (1978). *Studies in Augustan "Historical" Reliefs* (Diss. Berkeley).

―――. (1987). *The Portraiture of Gaius and Lucius Caesar* (New York).

―――. (1990). "Man or God: Divine Assimilation and Imitation in the Late Republic and the Early Principate," in Raaflaub and Toher (1990) 334–63.

―――. (1993). "The Acanthus of the Ara Pacis as an Apolline and Dionysiac Symbol of *Anamorphosis*, *Anakyklosis*, and *Numen Mixtum*," in M. Kubelik and E. Schwartz, eds., *Von der Bauforschung zur Denkmalpflege. Festschrift für Alois Machatschek* (Vienna) 182–217.

Pollitt, J. J. (1974). *The Ancient View of Greek Art: Criticism, History, and Terminology* (New Haven).

―――. (1978). "The Impact of Greek Art on Rome," *TAPA* 108.155–74.

―――. (1986). *Art in the Hellenistic Age* (Cambridge).

Porter, D. (1987). *Horace's Poetic Journey. A Reading of Odes 1–3* (Princeton).

Potter, T. (1979). *The Changing Landscape of South Etruria* (New York).

Powell, A., ed. (1992). *Roman Poetry and Propaganda in the Age of Augustus* (London).

Prayon, F. (1982). "Projektierte Bauten auf römischen Münzen," in B. Freytag, ed., *Praestant Interna. Festschrift für Ulrich Hausmann* (Tübingen) 319–30.

Preisshofen, F. (1979). "Kunsttheorie und Kunstbetrachtung," in Flashar (1979) 263–77.

Premerstein, A. von (1937). *Vom Wesen und Werden des Prinzipats. ABAW*, phil.- hist. Abt., n. f. 15. (Munich).

Price, S.R.F. (1980). "Between Man and God: Sacrifice in the Roman Imperial Cult," *JRS* 70.28–45.

———. (1984). *Rituals and Power. The Roman Imperial Cult in Asia Minor* (Cambridge).

Putnam, M. (1965). *The Poetry of the Aeneid* (Cambridge, Mass.).

———. (1976). "Propertius I.22: A Poet's Self-Definition," *QUCC* 23.93–123.

———. (1986). *Artifices of Eternity. Horace's Fourth Book of Odes* (Ithaca).

Quinn, K. (1982). "The Poet and his Audience in the Augustan Age," *ANRW* II.30.1.75–180.

Raaflaub, K. (1974). *Dignitatis Contentio* (Munich).

———. (1987). "Die Militärreformen des Augustus und die politische Problematik des frühen Prinzipats," in G. Binder 1 (1987) 246–307.

Raaflaub, K., and Samons, L. J. (1990). "Opposition to Augustus," in Raaflaub and Toher (1990) 417–54.

Raaflaub, K., and Toher, M., eds. (1990). *Between Republic and Empire. Interpretations of Augustus and His Principate* (Berkeley).

Raditsa, L. F. (1980). "Augustus' Legislation concerning Marriage, Procreation, Love Affairs and Adultery," *ANRW* II.13.278–339.

Ramage, E. (1987). *The Nature and Purpose of Augustus' "Res Gestae"* (Wiesbaden).

Rawson, E. (1975). "Caesar's Heritage: Hellenistic Kings and their Roman Equals," *JRS* 65.148–59.

———. (1985). *Intellectual Life in the Late Roman Republic* (Baltimore).

Reckford, K. (1991). "Horace Revisited," *Arion* 3rd ser. 1.3.209–222.

Reinhold, M. (1988). *From Republic to Principate. An Historical Commentary on Cassius Dio's Roman History Books 49–52 (36–29 B.C.)* (Atlanta).

Reinsch-Werner, H. (1976). *Callimachus Hesiodicus* (Berlin).

Richardson, L. (1977). "Hercules Musarum and Porticus Philippi," *AJA* 81.355–61.

———. (1992). *A New Topographical Dictionary of Ancient Rome* (Baltimore).

Rickman, G. (1980). *The Corn Supply of Ancient Rome* (Oxford).

Rizzo, G. E. (1936a). *Le pitture dell'Aula Isiaca di Caligola. Monumenti della pittura antica scoperti in Italia. Sez. 3, vol. 2* (Rome).

———. (1936b). *Le pitture della Casa di Livia. Monumenti della pittura antica scoperti in Italia. Sez. 3, vol. 3* (Rome).

Robinson, L. (1940). *Freedom of Speech in the Roman Republic* (Baltimore).

Ross, D. O. (1975). *Backgrounds to Augustan Poetry: Gallus, Elegy and Rome* (Cambridge).

———. (1987). *Virgil's Elements: Physics and Poetry in the Georgics* (Princeton).

Rossi, L. E. (1971). "I generi letterari e le loro leggi scritte e non scritte nelle letterature classiche," *BICS* 18.69–94.

Rostagni, A., ed. (1944). *Suetonio De poetis e biografi minori* (Turin); repr. New York (1979).

Ryberg, I. S. (1955). *Rites of the State Religion in Roman Art. MAAR* 22 (Rome).

———. (1966). "Clupeus Virtutis," in L. Wallach, ed., *The Classical Tradition. Literary and Historical Studies in Honor of Harry Caplan* (Ithaca) 232–38.

Saller, R. (1982). *Personal Patronage under the Early Empire* (Cambridge).

Salmon, E. T. (1946). "The Political Views of Horace," *Phoenix* 1.2.7–14.

———. (1956). "The Evolution of Augustus' Principate," *Historia* 5.456–78.

Sandys, J. E., ed. (1973). *Cicero, Orator* (repr. Hildesheim).

Santirocco, M. (1986). *Unity and Design in Horace's Odes* (Chapel Hill).

Sattler, P. (1960). *Augustus und der Senat* (Göttingen).

Sauron, G. (1977). "Les modèles funéraires classiques dans l'art décoratif néo-attique," *MEFR* 91.183–236.

———. (1981). "Aspects du Néo-Atticisme à la fin du Ier siècle av. J. C.: formes et symboles," *CEFR* 55.285–319.

Schäfer, M. (1957). "Cicero und der Prinzipat des Augustus," *Gymn.* 64.310–35.

Schefold, K. (1952). *Pompejanische Malerei: Sinn und Ideengeschichte* (Basel).

———. (1962). *Vergessenes Pompeji* (Berne and Munich).

Scheid, J. (1975). *Les frères Arvales* (Paris).

———. (1990). *Romulus et ses frères. BEFR* 275 (Rome).

Schmaltz, B. (1986). "Zum Augustus–Bildnis Typus Primaporta," *RM* 93.211–43.

Schmidt, E. A. (1991). *Ovids poetische Menschenwelt. Die Metamorphosen als Metapher und Symphonie.* Sitzungsber. Heidelberg, phil.-hist. Kl. No. 2.

Schmitt, H. H. (1983). "Tacitus und die nachgelassenen Schriften des Augustus," in H. Heine, ed., *Althistorische Studien. Festschrift für H. Bengtson* (Wiesbaden) 178–86.

Schmitthenner, W., ed. (1969). *Augustus* (Darmstadt).

Schneider, R. (1986). *Bunte Barbaren* (Worms).

Schütz, M. (1990). "Zur Sonnenuhr des Augustus auf dem Marsfeld," *Gymn.* 97.432–58.

———. (1991). "Der Capricorn als Sternzeichen des Augustus," *A&A* 37.55–67.

Schumacher, L. (1985). "Die imperatorischen Akklamationen der Triumvirn und die Auspicia des Augustus," *Historia* 34.191–222.

Schweitzer, B. (1932). *Xenokrates von Athen. Schriften der Königsberger Gelehrten Gesellschaft.* Geisteswiss. Kl. 9.1 (Halle).

Scott, K. (1925). "The Identification of Augustus with Romulus-Quirinus," *TAPA* 56.82–105.

———. (1930). "Emperor Worship in Ovid," *TAPA* 61.43–69.

———. (1933). "The Political Propaganda of 44–30 B.C.," *MAAR* 11.7–49.

Sforza, F. (1935). "The Problem of Virgil," *CR* 49.97–108.

Shatzman, I. (1975). *Senatorial Wealth and Roman Politics* (Brussels).

Shear, T. L. (1981). "Athens: From City-State to Provincial Town," *Hesperia* 50.356–77.

Shipley, F. W. (1931). "Chronology of Building Operations in Rome from the Death of Caesar to the Death of Augustus," *MAAR* 9.7–60.

Sieveking, J. (1895). *Das Füllhorn bei den Römern* (Munich).

Simon, E. (1957a). *Die Portland Vase* (Mainz).

———. (1957b). "Zur Augustusstatue von Prima Porta," *RM* 64.46–88.

———. (1967). *Ara Pacis Augustae* (Tübingen).

———. (1978). "Apollo in Rom," *JdI* 93.202–27.

———. (1986). *Augustus. Kunst und Leben in Rom um die Zeitenwende* (Munich).

———. (1990). *Die Götter der Römer* (Munich).

———. (1991). "Altes und Neues zur Statue des Augustus von Primaporta," in G. Binder 3 (1991) 204–33.

Sjöqvist, E. (1951). "Pnyx and Comitium," in G. Mylonas, ed., *Studies presented to David M. Robinson on his seventieth birthday* 1 (St. Louis) 400–411.

Skard, E. (1955). "Zu Monumentum Ancyranum," *SO* 31.119–21.

Smith, R.R.R. (1981). "Greeks, Foreigners, and Roman Republican Portraits," *JRS* 71.24–38.

———. (1988). *Hellenistic Ruler Portraits* (Oxford).

Smith, R.R.R. (1991). *Hellenistic Sculpture* (London).

Solodow, J. (1988). *The World of Ovid's Metamorphoses* (Chapel Hill).

Spaeth, B. (1994). "The Goddess Ceres in the Ara Pacis Augustae and the Carthage Relief," *AJA* 98.65–100.

Speyer, W. (1986). "Das Verhältnis des Augustus zur Religion," *ANRW* II.16.2.1777–1805.

Spinazzola, V. (1953). *Pompei alla luce degli scavi nuovi di Via dell'Abbondanza* (Rome).

Stahl, H.-P. (1981). "Aeneas—An 'Unheroic' Hero?" *Arethusa* 14.157–77.

———. (1985). *Propertius: "Love" and "War": Individual and State under Augustus* (Berkeley).

Stahlmann, I. (1988). *Imperator Caesar Augustus. Studien zur Geschichte des Principatsverständnisses in der deutschen Altertumswissenschaft bis 1945* (Darmstadt).

Stark, R. (1967). "Res Publica," in Oppermann (1967) 42–110.

Steidle, W. (1962). "Das Motiv der Lebenswahl bei Tibull und Properz," *WS* 75.100–140.

Stewart, A. (1979). *Attika. Studies in Athenian Sculpture of the Hellenistic Age* (London).

Stier, H. E. (1975). "Augustusfriede und römische Klassik," *ANRW* II.2.3–54.

Strasburger, H. (1983). "Vergil und Augustus," *Gymn.* 90.41–76.

Strazzulla, M. J. (1990). *Il principato di Apollo* (Rome).

Strebel, H. G. (1934). *Wertung und Wirkung des thukydideischen Geschichtswerks in der griechisch-römischen Literatur* (Munich).

Strocka, V. (1965). "Die Brunnenreliefs Grimani," *Antike Plastik* 4.87–102.

Strong, D., and Ward Perkins, J. (1962). "The Temple of Castor in the Forum Romanum," *PBSR* 30.1–32.

Suerbaum, W. (1968). *Untersuchungen zur Selbstdarstellung der römischen Dichter* (Hildesheim).

———. (1980). "Hundert Jahre Vergil-Forschung: Eine systematische Arbeitsbibliographie mit besonderer Berücksichtigung der Aeneis," *ANRW* II.31.1.3–358.

Sullivan, J. P. (1976). *Propertius: A Critical Introduction* (Cambridge).

Sutherland, C.H.V. (1945). "*Aerarium* and *Fiscus* during the Early Empire," *AJP* 66.151–70.

———. (1970). *The Cistophori of Augustus* (London).

———. (1976). *The Emperor and the Coinage* (London).

———. (1986). "Compliment or Complement? Dr. Levick on Imperial Coin Types," *NC* 146.85–93.

Svoronos, J. N. (1908). *Das Athener National Museum* (Athens).

Syme, R. (1958a). "Imperator Caesar Augustus. A Study in Nomenclature," *Historia* 7.172–88; repr. in *Roman Papers* (Oxford 1979) 1.361–77.

———. (1958b). *Tacitus* (Oxford).

———. (1959). "Livy and Augustus," *HSCP* 64.27–87; repr. in *Roman Papers* (Oxford 1979) 1.400–454.

Syndikus, H.-P. (1973). *Die Lyrik des Horaz: Eine Interpretation der Oden.* Vol. 2 (Darmstadt).

Taeger, F. (1957 and 1960). *Charisma.* Vols. 1 and 2 (Stuttgart).

Talbert, R. (1984). *The Senate of Imperial Rome* (Princeton).

Taylor, L. R. (1931). *The Divinity of the Roman Emperor* (Middletown).

———. (1964). *Party Politics in the Age of Caesar* (Berkeley).

Thomas, R., ed. (1988). *Virgil: Georgics* (Cambridge).

Thompson, H. A. (1959). "The Odeion in the Athenian Agora," *Hesperia* 19.31–141.

Thornton, A. (1976). *The Living Universe. Gods and Men in Vergil's Aeneid* (Leiden).

Toher, M. (1990). "Augustus and the Evolution of Roman Historiography," in Raaflaub and Toher (1990) 139–54.

Torelli, M. (1982). *Typology and Structure of Roman Historical Reliefs* (Ann Arbor).

Toulopa, E. (1986). "Das bronzene Reiterstandbild des Augustus aus dem nordägäischen Meer," *AM* 101.185–205.

Toynbee, J.M.C. (1961). "The Ara Pacis Augustae," *JRS* 51.153–56.

Tränkle, H. (1960). *Die Sprachkunst des Properz und die Tradition der lateinischen Dichtersprache* (Wiesbaden).

Traina, A. (1988). "Pietas," *Enc. Virg.* 4.93–101.

Treggiari, S. (1969). *Roman Freedmen during the Republic* (Oxford).

———. (1991). *Roman Marriage* (Oxford).

Uhlmann, W. (1909). *De Sexti Properti genere dicendi* (Diss. Münster).

Urban, R. (1979). "Tacitus und die *Res gestae divi Augusti.* Die Auseinandersetzung des Historikers mit der offiziellen Darstellung," *Gymn.* 86.59–74.

Vernant, J. P. (1969). *Mythe et pensée chez les Grecs* (Paris); trans. as *Myth and Thought among the Greeks* (London 1983).

Vessberg, O. (1941). *Studien zur Kunstgeschichte der römischen Republik* (Lund).

Veyne, P. (1988). *Roman Erotic Elegy: Love, Poetry, and the West* (Chicago).

Vierneisel, K., and Zanker, P., eds. (1979). *Die Bildnisse des Augustus* (Munich).

Volkmann, H., ed. (1969). *Res Gestae Divi Augusti*, 3rd ed. (Berlin).

Vollenweider, M. (1966). *Die Steinschneidekunst und ihre Künstler in spätrepublikanischer und augusteischer Zeit* (Baden-Baden).

———. (1972). *Die Porträtgemmen der römischen Republik* (Mainz).

Wagenvoort, H. (1920). "Pantomimus und Tragödie im augusteischen Zeitalter," *NJA* 45.101–13.

Walde A., and Hofmann, J. B. (1965). *Lateinisches etymologisches Wörterbuch*, 4th ed. (Heidelberg).

Wallace-Hadrill, A. (1981a). "The Emperor and His Virtues," *Historia* 30.298–323.

———. (1981b). "Family and Inheritance in the Augustan Marriage Laws," *PCPS* 27.58–80.

———. (1982a). "The Golden Age and Sin in Augustan Ideology," *Past and Present* 95.19–36.

———. (1982b). "Civilis Princeps. Between Citizen and King," *JRS* 72.32–48.

———. (1985). Review of Kienast, Buchner (1982), Carettoni (1983), and Millar and Segal (1984), *JRS* 75.245–50.

———. (1986). "Image and Authority in the Coinage of Augustus," *JRS* 76.66–87.

———. (1988). "The Social Structure of the Roman House," *PBSR* 56.43–97.

———. (1989). "Rome's Cultural Revolution," *JRS* 79.157–64 (review of Zanker, *AMB*).

———. (1993). *Augustan Rome* (London).

———. (1994). *Houses and Society in Pompeii and Herculaneum* (Princeton).

Wallmann, P. (1989). *Triumviri rei publicae constituendae. Untersuchungen zur politischen Propaganda im zweiten Triumvirat* (Frankfurt).

Walser, G. (1955). "Der Kaiser als Vindex Libertatis," *Historia* 4.353–67.

Walsh, P. G. (1955). "Livy's Preface and the Distortion of History," *AJP* 76.369–83.

———. (1961). *Livy. His Historical Aims and Methods* (Cambridge).

———. (1974). *Livy. Greece & Rome* Surveys in the Classics 8 (Oxford).

———. (1982). "Livy and the Aims of *historia*. An Analysis of the Third Decade," *ANRW* II.30.2.1058–74.

Walters, H. B. (1914). *Catalogue of the Greek and Roman Lamps in the British Museum* (London).

———. (1926). *Catalogue of the Engraved Gems and Cameos, Greek, Etruscan, and Roman, in the British Museum* (London).

Weber, W. (1936). *Princeps. Studien zur Geschichte des Augustus* 1 (Stuttgart).

Weinbrot, H. (1978). *Augustus Caesar in "Augustan" England* (Princeton).

———. (1993). "Politics, Taste, and National Identity: Some Uses of Tacitism in Eighteenth-Century Britain," in A. J. Woodman and T. J. Luce, eds., *Tacitus and the Tacitean Tradition* (Princeton) 168–84.

Weinstock, S. (1960). "Pax and the Ara Pacis," *JRS* 50.44–58.

———. (1971). *Divus Julius* (Oxford).

Weippert, O. (1972). *Alexander-Imitatio und die römische Politik in republikanischer Zeit* (Augsburg).

Wells, C. (1972). *The German Policy of Augustus. An Examination of the Archaeological Evidence* (Oxford).

Wesenberg, B. (1984). "Augustusforum und Akropolis," *JdI* 99.161–85.

———. (1985). "Römische Wandmalerei am Ausgang der Republik: Der zweite pompejanische Stil," *Gymn.* 92.470–88.

White, P. (1988). "Julius Caesar in Augustan Rome," *Phoenix* 42.334–56.

———. (1993). *Promised Verse. Poets in the Society of Augustan Rome* (Cambridge, Mass.).

Wickert, L. (1949). "Der Prinzipat und die Freiheit," in *Symbola Coloniensia I. Kroll oblata* (Cologne) 111–41; repr. in Klein (1969) 94–135.

———. (1954). "Princeps civitatis," in *RE* 22.1998–2296.

———. (1974). "Neue Forschungen zum römischen Prinzipat," *ANRW* II.1.3–76.

Will, W. (1991). *Der römische Mob* (Darmstadt).

Williams, F. (1978). *Callimachus' Hymn to Apollo: A Commentary* (Oxford).

Williams, G. (1962). "Poetry in the Moral Climate of Augustan Rome," *JRS* 52.28–46.

———. (1968). *Tradition and Originality in Roman Poetry* (Oxford).

———. (1969). *The Third Book of Horace's Odes* (Oxford).

———. (1978). *Change and Decline. Roman Literature in the Early Empire* (Berkeley).

———. (1990). "Did Maecenas Fall from Favor? Augustan Literary Patronage," in Raaflaub and Toher (1990) 258–275.

Williams, R. D. (1967). "The Purpose of the *Aeneid*," *Antichthon* 1.29–41; repr. in S. Harrison (1990) 21–36.

Wimmel, W. (1960). *Kallimachos in Rom* (Wiesbaden).

———. (1962). "Doppelsinnige Formulierung bei Horaz?," *Glotta* 40.119–43.

Winkes, R., ed. (1985). *The Age of Augustus: An Interdisciplinary Conference Held at Brown University April 30–May 2, 1982* (Louvain).

Winkler, J. (1985). *Auctor et Actor. A Narratological Reading of Apuleius' Golden Ass* (Berkeley).

Wirszubski, C. (1950). *Libertas as a Political Idea at Rome during the Late Republic and the Early Empire* (Oxford).

Wiseman, T. P. (1971). *New Men in the Roman Senate* (Oxford).

———. (1981). "The Temple of Victory on the Palatine,"*Antiquaries Journ.* 61.35–52.

———. (1984). "Cybele, Virgil, and Augustus," in Woodman and West (1984) 117–28.

———. (1987). "*Conspicui postes tectaque digna deo*: The Public Image of Aristocratic and Imperial Houses in the Late Republic and the Early Empire," *CEFR* 98.393–413.

Wissowa, G. (1912). *Religion und Kultus der Römer*, 2nd ed. (Munich).

Wlosok, A. (1967). *Die Göttin Venus in Vergils Aeneis* (Heidelberg).

———. (1973). "Vergil in der neueren Forschung," *Gymn.* 80.129–51.

———. (1976). "Vergils Didotragödie: ein Beitrag zum Problem des Tragischen in der Aeneis," in H. Görgemanns und E. A. Schmidt, eds., *Studien zum antiken Epos* (Meisenheim); repr. in (1990) 320–43.

———. (1990). *Res humanae—res divinae. Kleine Schriften*, ed. by E. Heck and E. A. Schmidt (Heidelberg).

Wood, N. (1988). *The Social and Political Thought of Cicero* (Berkeley).

Woodman, T. (1974). "*Exegi monumentum*: Horace, *Odes* 3.30," in Woodman and West (1974) 115–28.

———. ed. (1983). *Velleius Paterculus. The Caesarian and Augustan Narrative (2.41–93)* (Cambridge).

———. (1988). *Rhetoric in Classical Historiography* (London and Sydney).

Woodman, T., and Powell, J., eds. (1992). *Author and Audience in Latin Literature* (Cambridge).

Woodman, T., and West, D., eds. (1974). *Quality and Pleasure in Latin Poetry* (Cambridge).

———. (1984). *Poetry and Politics in the Age of Augustus* (Cambridge).

Wyke, M. (1989). "In Pursuit of Love, the Poetic Self, and a Process of Reading: Augustan Elegy in the 1980's," *JRS* 79.165–73.

———. (1992). "Augustan Cleopatras: Female Power and Poetic Authority," in Powell (1992) 98–140.

Yavetz, Z. (1969). *Plebs and Princeps* (Oxford).

———. (1984). "The *Res Gestae* and Augustus' Public Image," in Millar and Segal (1984) 1–36.

———. (1990). "The Personality of Augustus: Reflections on Syme's *Roman Revolution*," in Raaflaub and Toher (1990) 21–40.

Zagdoun, M.-A. (1989). *La sculpture archaisante dans l'art hellénistique et dans l'art romain de l'Haut Empire. BEFR* 269 (Rome).

Zanker, G. (1987). *Realism in Alexandrian Poetry: A Literature and Its Audience* (London).

Zanker, P. (1968). *Forum Augustum. Das Bildprogramm* (Tübingen).

———. (1969). "Der Larenaltar im Belvedere des Vatikans," *RM* 76.205–18.

———. (1972). *Forum Romanum. Die Neugestaltung unter Augustus* (Tübingen).

———. (1973). *Studien zu den Augustus-Porträts I. Der Actium-Typus* (Göttingen).

———. (1974). *Klassizistische Statuen* (Mainz).

———, ed. (1976). *Hellenismus in Mittelitalien* (Göttingen).

———. (1975). "Über die Werkstätten augusteischer Larenaltäre und die damit zusammenhängenden Probleme der Interpretation," *BCAR* 82 (1970–71) 147–55.

———. (1979). "Zur Funktion und Bedeutung griechischer Skulptur in der Römerzeit," in Flashar (1979) 283–306.

———. (1983a). *Provinzielle Kaiserporträts. ABAW* phil.-hist. Kl., n. f. 90 (Munich).

Zanker, P. (1983b). "Der Apollotempel auf dem Palatin. Ausstattung und politische
    Sinnbezüge nach der Schlacht von Actium," *Anal. Rom.* Suppl. 10 (Rome) 21–40.
———. (1988). "Bilderzwang: Augustan Political Symbolism in the Private Sphere," in
    Image and Mystery in the Roman World (Gloucester) 1–13.
Zehnacker, H. (1973). *Moneta. Recherches sur l'organisation des émissions monétaires de la
    République romaine. BEFR* 222 (Rome).
Zetzel, J. (1982). "The Poetics of Patronage in the Late First Century B.C.," in Gold
    (1982) 87–102.
Zinn, E. (1960). "Elemente des Humors in der augusteischen Dichtung," *Gymn.* 67.41–
    56.

PROVENIENCE OF
ILLUSTRATIONS

ABBREVIATIONS

ANS   American Numismatic Society.
BM   British Museum, London.
BN   Bibliothèque Nationale de France,
      Cabinet des Médailles, Paris.

DAI   German Archaeological Institute.
DAIR German Archaeological Institute,
      Rome.

PLATES

1. Naples, Museo Nazionale Archeologico,
   inv. 147501. Photograph by L. von Matt.
2. Rome, Antiquario del Palatino. Photograph by H. N. Loose.
3a. Photograph by H. N. Loose.
3b. After *KA* pl. 3.1.
4. DAIR   F82.426,   F82.436,   F82.427,
   F82.423.

5a. Photograph by H. N. Loose.
5b. Rome, Antiquario del Palatino. Photo-
    graph by H. N. Loose
6. Photograph by A. Foglia. By courtesy of
   F. Rutzen.

FIGURES

1. Naples, Museo Nazionale Archeologico,
   Medagliere. Fiorelli 3358; cf. *RRC* 540/2.
   Photograph by Soprintendenza Archeologica delle Province di Napoli e Caserta.
2. Boston, Museum of Fine Arts, inv. 27.733,
   Francis Bartlett Donation. Museum photograph.
3. *RRC* 507/2. BM photograph.
4. After A. Banti and L. Simonetti, *Corpus
   Nummorum Romanorum*, (Florence 1973)
   II.105.24.
5. Rome, Vatican Museums, Braccio
   Nuovo, inv. 2290. Alinari/Art Resource,
   NY; Anderson 1318.
6. Florence, Museo Archeologico, inv. 3.
   DAIR 63.599.
7. *RIC* I².59 no. 253. BM photograph.
8. Naples, Museo Nazionale Archeologico.
   DAIR 66.1831.
9a. Alinari/Art Resource, NY; Anderson
    6513.
9b. DAIR 64.1804.

10. After Kähler (1960) p. 32.
11. *RPC* no. 977. BM photograph.
12. Hirmer Archive 2001.857. Cf. Giard no.
    183.
13a. *RIC* I².63 no. 310. BM photograph.
13b. *RRC* 401/1. BM photograph.
14. Giard no. 112. BN photograph.
15. *RRC* 505/3. BM photograph.
16. Photograph by Leu Numismatik (Auk-
    tion 54 [1992] no. 216).
17. Giard no. 415. BN photograph.
18. Staatl. Museen zu Berlin. Preußischer
    Kulturbesitz, Münzkabinett. Museum
    photograph.
19. Rome, Museo Nazionale delle Terme,
    inv. 56230. DAIR 65.1111.
20. Numismatik Lanz (Auktion 54 [1990]).
    Cf. Giard nos. 883–86. Photograph by
    courtesy of Hubert Lanz.
21. Rome, Palazzo dei Conservatori, Meda-
    gliere, inv. 1900. Photograph by courtesy
    of J. Bergemann.

22. Private collection in La Alcudia, Mallorca. Photo DAI Madrid R 1–71–11.
23. ANS photograph. Cf. *RIC* I².79 no. 476.
24. *RIC* I².68 no. 358. BM photograph.
25. Rome, Capitoline Museums, Braccio Nuovo, inv. 1025. DAIR 34.1929.
26. *RRC* 281. BM photograph.
27. *RRC* 480/5. BM photograph.
28. *RIC* I².59 no. 253. BM photograph.
29. *RRC* 392/1b. BM photograph.
30. Hirmer Archive 2000.068R. Cf. *RRC* 508/3.
31. Naples, Museo Nazionale Archeologico, Medagliere. Fiorelli 456; cf. *RRC* 480/6. Photo by Soprintendenza Archeologica delle Province di Napoli e Caserta.
32a. From *Mon. Piot* 5 (1899), pl. 31.1.
32b. From *Mon. Piot* 5 (1899), pl. 31.2.
33a. From *Mon. Piot* 5 (1899), pl. 36.2.
33b. From *Mon. Piot* 5 (1899), pl. 35.1.
34. Rome, Vatican Museums, inv. 1115. DAIR 75.1285.
35. *RIC* I².44 no. 47a. BM photograph.
36. Fototeca 2979. Cf. Giard nos. 52–56.
37 Musée de l'Arles Antique. Photograph by M. Lacanaud.
38. Tunis, Bardo Museum. From Galinsky (1969) fig. 7.
39. Musée de Carthage. After Hölscher (1967) pl. 13.2.
40. Fotoarchiv am Seminar für Griech. und Röm. Geschichte, Universität Frankfurt a. M.; Collection W. Niggeler II.1039. Cf. Giard nos. 273–76.
41. DAIR 86.1448.
42. Photographic Archive of the Capitoline Museums, Rome. Photograph by H. Serra.
43. Alinari/Art Resource, NY; Anderson 2021.
44. DAIR 55.6.
45. Cherchel, Algeria, Musée Archéologique. Photograph by Gisela Fittschen-Badura.
46. Rome, Capitoline Museums. DAIR 75.2253.
47. Rome, Villa Medici. DAIR 77.1741.
48. Cleveland Museum of Art, inv. 25.947. Gift from J. H. Wade. Museum photograph.
49. *RRC* 516/1. BM photograph.
50. *RRC* 525/1. BM photograph.

51. Vienna, Kunsthistorisches Museum, inv. 22507. Museum photograph.
52. Bologna, Museo Civico Archeologico, inv. B 87. Photograph by CNB Studio, Bologna.
53. Hirmer Archive 2001.613R. Cf. Giard nos. 1264–78.
54. BM inv. 1372. After Hölscher (1967) 109.
55. Hirmer Archive 2001.020a. Cf. Giard nos. 684–86.
56. BM inv. 1977. Museum photograph.
57. Vienna, Kunsthistorisches Museum. Museum photograph.
58. DAIR 72.2400.
59. DAIR 72.2403.
60. Fototeca 1049.
61. Drawing by Chris Williams.
62. DAIR 57.883.
63. Alinari/Art Resource, NY; Anderson 41087.
64. From Buchner (1982) fig. 14.
65. Fototeca 1042.
66. *RIC* I².59 no. 252. BM photograph.
67. Paris, Louvre, inv. MA 1838. Photo by Service Photographique de la Réunion des Musées Nationaux.
68. Rome, Villa Doria Pamphili. DAIR 62.641.
69. Photograph by Diane Conlin.
70. Photograph by Diane Conlin.
71. DAIR 63.1233.
72a. Hirmer Archive 2001.004R. Cf. Giard no. 173.
72b. *RIC* I².62 no. 290. BM photograph .
73. Alinari/Art Resource, NY, 47101.
74. DAIR 37.744.
75. DAIR 37.743.
76. Rome, Museo Nazionale delle Terme, inv. 1049. Hirmer Archive 561.1074.
77. *RRC* 455/1. BM photograph.
78. *BMCRR* Gaul 80. BM photograph.
79. Florence, Uffizi, inv. 1914.83. DAIR 78.2138.
80. Verona, Museo Archeologico. Photograph by U. Tomba.
81. Arles, Musée de l'Arles Antique, inv. 51.1.22. Photograph by M. Lacanaud.
82. DAIR 58.1448.
83. Copenhagen, Ny Carlsberg Glyptothek, inv. 597. Museum photograph.
84. Florence, Uffizi, inv. 1914.76. DAIR 72.156.

85. Rome, Capitoline Museums. Photograph by Gisela Fittschen-Badura.
86. Venice, Museo Archeologico, inv. 200. Photograph by Gisela Fittschen-Badura.
87. Hirmer Archive 2000.65. Cf. *RRC* 535/1.
88. *RRC* 534/2. BM photograph.
89. Athens, National Archaeol. Museum. DAI Athen 80/975.
90. BM, inv. GR 1911.9–1.1. BM photograph.
91. DAIR 57.1180.
92. Rome, Capitoline Museums, Rome, inv. 495. Photograph by Gisela Fittschen-Badura.
93. Rome, Vatican Museums, Sala dei Busti, inv. 713. Museum neg. VII.37.3.
94. Rome, Vatican Museums, Museo Chiaramonti, inv. 1977. Museum neg. XXXIV.33.3/3.
95. Venice, Museo Archeologico, inv. 1723. Photograph by Soprintendenza Archeologica per il Veneto.
96. DAIR 56.937.
97. DAIR 56.1235.
98. DAIR 71.1175.
99. After Rizzo (1936a) pl. II.2.
100. Rome, Museo Nazionale delle Terme. DAIR 56.318.
101. Rome, Museo Nazionale delle Terme. Alinari/Art Resource, NY; Anderson 2937.
102. DAIR 77.1370.
103. DAIR 59.1978.
104. Rome, Antiquario del Palatino. Photograph by Soprintendenza Archeologica di Roma.
105. After Rizzo (1936b) fig. 8.
106. After Carettoni (1983) fig. 16.
107. After Rizzo (1936b) fig. 27.
108. DAIR 4387.
109. DAIR 59.1992
110. After Rizzo (1936b) fig. 30.
111. After G. Gatti (in Degrassi [1937]) and P. Zanker (1968).
112. Fototeca. After P. Zanker (1968) fig. 20.
113. Rome, Antiquarium of the Forum of Augustus. Photograph by Gisela Fittschen-Badura.
114. Fototeca 3562.
115. After Spinazzola (1953) fig. 183.
116. After Spinazzola (1953) fig. 184.

117. Fototeca 12598. Cf. *BMCRE* Ant. Pius no. 2065.
118. After Degrassi (1937) p. 4.
119. After H. Kähler, *Der römische Tempel* (Berlin: Gebr. Mann Verlag, 1970) fig. 6.
120. Alinari/Art Resource, NY, 47176.
121. Adapted from Wiseman (1981) fig. 1.
122. Rome, Villa Albani 1014. Alinari/Art Resource; Anderson 5100.
123. Sorrento, Museo Correale. DAIR 65.1255.
124. Staatl. Münzsammlung Munich. Hirmer Archive 2001.541R. Cf. Giard no. 362.
125. Rome, Antiquario del Palatino. Photograph by Soprintendenza Archeologica di Roma.
126. Berlin, Staatl. Mus. inv. 3779.62. Museum photograph.
127a. Rome, Capitoline Museums, Museo Nuovo, inv. 1873. Alinari/Art Resource, NY; Anderson 17894.
127b. Rome, Capitoline Museums, Palazzo dei Conservatori, inv. 980. Alinari/Art Resource, NY, 27203.
128. Rome, Galleria Doria. DAIR 71.1463.
129. Naples, Museo Nazionale Archeologico, inv. 72982. Alinari /Art Resource, NY; Anderson 25866.
130. Naples, Museo Nazionale Archeologico. DAIR 83.1993.
131. Fototeca 2976. Cf. Giard nos. 1098–1103.
132. Museum of Fine Arts, Boston, inv. 00.316. H. L. Pierce Fund. Museum photograph.
133. Photograph by courtesy of Classics Slide Library, Univ. of Texas at Austin.
134. Rome, Tabularium. Alinari/Art Resource, NY, 27223.
135. *RIC* I².45 no. 54a. BM photograph.
136a-c. Rome, Vatican Museums. Museum negs. XXI.25.13–14; XII.23.1.
137. Rome, Capitoline Museums, Palazzo dei Conservatori, inv. 855. DAIR 60.1472.
138. DAIR 60.1247.
139. Rome, Garden of the Antiquarium on the Caelian. Fototeca 6086.
140. Rome, Capitoline Museums, Palazzo dei Conservatori, inv. 3352. DAIR 30.660
141. DAIR 30.661.
142. Florence, Uffizi. DAIR 65.2155; 59.68.

143. DAIR 75.291; 75.294

144. Rome, Capitoline Museums, Palazzo dei Conservatori, inv. 2144. DAIR 35.211; 35.210.

145. Rome, Museo Nazionale delle Terme, inv. 49481. DAIR 76.1784; 76.1783; 76.1785.

146. Rome, Capitoline Museums, inv. 1909. DAIR 50.45.

147. Fotoarchiv am Seminar für Griech. und Röm. Geschichte, Universität Frankfurt a. M.; Collection W. Niggeler II.1010. Cf. Giard no. 13.

148. Hirmer Archive 13.0573R.

149. Rome, Vatican Museums, inv. 1115. DAIR 75.1290.

150. DAIR 75.1286.

151. DAIR 75.1289.

152. Hirmer Archive 2001.019. Cf. Giard no. 1739.

153. RPC 221. BM photograph.

154. Vindonissa Museum, Brugg, Switzerland. Photograph by T. Hartmann.

155. Rheinisches Landesmuseum, Bonn, inv. 22534a. Museum neg. 7693.

156. From the Model of the City of Rome, Museo della Civiltà Romana. Photograph by Barbara Malter.

157. Rome, Villa Albani. DAIR 33.23.

158. After École Française d'Athènes, Exploration Archéologique de Délos 13 (1932) pl. XXVII.

159. Rome, Museo Torlonia. DAIR 1933.58.

160. Bergama Museum inv. 3438. DAI Istanbul 75.559.

161. Athens, Nat. Archaeol. Museum, inv. 1828. Museum photograph.

162. Copenhagen, Ny Carlsberg Glyptothek, inv. 30. Museum photograph.

163. Palestrina, Museo Archeologico, inv. 140. Museum für Abgüsse Klass. Bildwerke, Universität München. Photograph by courtesy of H.-U. Cain.

164. Rome, Capitoline Museums, Stanza dei Filosofi. DAIR 31.657.

165. Rome, Capitoline Museums, Palazzo dei Conservatori. DAIR 60.1252.

166. Rome, Capitoline Museums, Palazzo dei Conservatori. DAIR 71.45.

167. Photographic Archive of the Capitoline Museums, Rome. Photograph by H. Serra.

168. Mantua, Palazzo Ducale. Alinari/Art Resource, NY, 18805.

169. Photograph by American School of Classical Studies, Athens: Agora Excavations. Neg. 86–586.

170. Photograph by Leu Numismatik (Auktion 57 [1993] no. 180). Cf. RRC 480/13.

171. Photograph by Leu Numismatik (Auktion 57 [1993] no. 221). Cf. Giard no. 279.

172. Drawing by Chris Williams.

173. After P. Zanker, AMB (English trans. 1988) fig. 118, based on E. Rodriguez Almeida, Forma urbis marmorea: Aggiornamento generale 1980 (Rome 1981), pl. XXIII.

174. IGR I/II 1056. Alexandria Museum; photograph by courtesy of G. Alföldy.

INDEX OF
PASSAGES

The following register lists the passages that are cited in the text.

KARL GALINSKY is the Floyd Cailloux Centennial Professor of Classics at the University of Texas at Austin. He is the author of many books, including *Classical and Modern Interactions: Postmodern Architecture, Multiculturalism, Decline, and Other Issues*, and *Aeneas, Sicily, and Rome* (Princeton).